Fundamentals of Investments
for Financial Planning

Huebner School Series   *H. King McGlaughon, Jr., Editor*

Huebner School Series

Fundamentals of Investments for Financial Planning

Fourth Edition

Walt J. Woerheide
David M. Cordell

The American College/*Bryn Mawr, Pennsylvania*

This publication is designed to provide accurate and authoritative information about the subject covered. While every precaution has been taken in the preparation of this material, the authors, the editor, and The American College assume no liability for damages resulting from the use of the information contained in this publication. The American College is not engaged in rendering legal, accounting, or other professional advice. If legal or other expert advice is required, the services of an appropriate professional should be sought.

© 2004 The American College
270 Bryn Mawr Avenue
Bryn Mawr, PA 19010
(888) AMERCOL (263-7265)
www.theamericancollege.edu

Library of Congress Control Number 2004103994
ISBN 1932819029

Printed in the United States of America

Contents

v

Preface

This edition of *Fundamentals of Investments for Financial Planning* is substantially different from the previous three editions. The previous editions were written primarily as undergraduate textbooks in investments. The target audience was investors, portfolio managers, brokers, and financial planners. The target audience of this book is only financial planners. The emphasis is on investment planning, not investments *per se*. Thus, although the book presents the principles and concepts of investment theory and practice, the focus is always on how a financial planner can use this information to serve his or her client.

We are mindful that many people are taking this course in preparation to sit for the CFP® exam. The student syllabus that accompanies this book contains two lists of all the investment-related study points covered in this course. One list indicates the study points and identifies the chapter in which they are covered. A second list indicates by chapter which study points are covered in that chapter. The student must remember that the study points are not intended as an exhaustive or comprehensive listing of material that will be on the CFP® exam. Hence, all of the chapters provide additional coverage relevant to these topics so that the student is more fully prepared to sit for that exam if he or she opts to do so.

This book includes numerous pedagogical features designed to help students focus their study of investments. Among the features found in every chapter of the book are

- *Learning objectives:* Statements at the beginning of each chapter are designed to provide direction to students studying the subject matter in the chapter.
- *An outline:* Following the learning objectives, the subject matter is organized and listed in the order in which it appears in the chapter.
- *Key terms:* In the margins where the terms first appear, as well as grouped together at the end of each chapter, certain terms or phrases are singled out because of their importance to the specific subject matter.

- *Examples:* Problem sets interspersed throughout the chapter are designed to help students see how difficult concepts are applied in specific situations.
- *Review questions:* Essay-style questions and computational problems at the end of each chapter are designed to test the student's knowledge of the learning objectives.
- *Self-test questions:* True-false statements following the review questions at the end of each chapter are designed to provide students with a quick assessment of their grasp of the subject matter.

Features located in the back of the book are

- *A glossary:* Key terms found in each chapter are defined and included in the back of the book.
- *An answer section:* Answers to all the review questions and self-test questions are located in this part of the book.
- *An index:* The book has a comprehensive index to help identify pages on which various topics are found.

Walt J. Woerheide
David M. Cordell

Acknowledgments

We would like to especially thank Ben Branch, professor of finance in the school of management, the University of Massachusetts at Amherst, for his contributions to this book. Its foundation and starting point was the second edition of *Investments: Principles and Practices* by Ben Branch, which was published in 1989 by Longman Financial Services Publishing. In addition, Ben made several contributions to the first edition of The American College's version of this textbook.

We would like to thank the following professors at The American College for their contributions to previous editions: Roger C. Bird, professor of economics and holder of the Frank M. Engle Distinguished Chair in Economic Security Research; the late Thomas A. Dziadosz, associate professor of economics; Paul Hoffman, former assistant professor of finance; Barbara S. Poole, former associate professor of finance and insurance; Robert S. Graber, former assistant professor of finance; and C. Bruce Worsham, associate vice president and director of educational development.

In addition, we wish to thank Don Taylor, assistant professor of finance; Mary Elizabeth Pfeil, adjunct faculty member; and Elliott Server, a member of The College's board of trustees, for reading this book and offering some excellent suggestions. Don Taylor and Chris Coyne, St. Joseph's University, also provided substantial help in preparing questions for The College's national exam.

We gratefully thank the members of The American College's editorial and production departments, especially Keith de Pinho, editor; Lynn Hayes, editorial director; and Evelyn M. Rice, production assistant.

All of these individuals made this a better book. In spite of their help, however, some errors have undoubtedly been successful in eluding our eyes. For these we are solely responsible. At the same time, however, we accept full credit for giving those readers who find these errors the exhilarating intellectual experience produced by such discovery. Nevertheless, each of the authors acknowledges that any errors discovered are the fault of one of the other authors.

Walt J. Woerheide
David M. Cordell

About the Authors

Walt J. Woerheide, PhD, is the vice president and director of the Irwin Graduate School at The American College. His bachelor's degree is from Brown University, and his MBA and PhD are from Washington University in St. Louis. He previously served on the faculties at the Rochester Institute of Technology for 11 years, University of Michigan-Flint for 6 years, and University of Illinois at Chicago for 10 years. He is a past president of both the Academy of Financial Services and the Midwest Finance Association. He has authored two other books, the most recent a college textbook, *Introducing Personal Finance,* and has published about 24 articles, mostly in refereed academic publications.

David M. Cordell, PhD, CFA, CFP®, CLU, is associate professor of personal financial planning at Texas Tech University and was formerly professor of finance at The American College. Cordell is a member of the Certified Financial Planner™ Board of Examiners and has written numerous articles on finance and investments for both academic and practitioner publications. He is author, editor, or contributing author of the following books: *Financial Decision Making at Retirement, The Financial Services Professional's Guide to the State of the Art, Financial Planning Applications, Tax Companion 1995, Solutions Handbook for Financial Planning,* and *Fundamentals in Financial Planning.* Cordell earned MBA and PhD degrees in finance from The University of Texas at Austin.

Fundamentals of Investments for Financial Planning

Survey of Investment Instruments

Learning Objectives

An understanding of the material in this chapter should enable the student to

1-1. Describe nonmarketable and marketable short-term debt investments.

1-2. Describe the various types of bonds.

1-3. Describe the various types of equity securities.

1-4. Describe the equity-related instruments.

1-5. Describe some of the other investment opportunities.

Chapter Outline

INTRODUCTION TO INVESTMENT PLANNING

A central element of financial planning involves advising on or even managing a client's financial assets. Therefore, a financial planner needs to be knowledgeable with regard to asset or investment choices, the expected rates of return and risk exposures associated with each asset choice, and the suitability of each asset category for a client. Each investment opportunity has advantages and disadvantages. Each investor has a unique set of needs, goals, attitudes, and resources that influence the relative attractiveness and suitability of particular investments for that investor. The goal of this book is to provide this requisite knowledge of what a financial planner needs to know to advise clients effectively.

In this first chapter, we will review the variety of investment choices, focusing on the major advantages and disadvantages of each. Because entire chapters in this book are devoted to some of these investments, the discussion will be more extensive on assets that are not covered later. The second chapter will then look at issues associated with the mechanics of investing, including such topics as types of accounts, types of orders, buying on margin, and selling short. Chapter 3 provides a discussion of how to measure return and risk, and what is meant by expected return. Chapters 4 and 5 will examine issues associated with the theory of managing a portfolio and evaluating portfolio performance. Chapter 6 will then look at the issue of market efficiency. Chapters 7 through 12 focus on comprehensive discussions of the major asset categories: stocks (7 and 8), bonds (9), investment companies (10), options (11), and futures contracts (12). Chapter 13 examines the tax implications of the various investments. Finally, chapter 14 looks at the practical issues of managing a portfolio.

DEBT INSTRUMENTS

Many of us are introduced to the concept of investing when a savings account is opened in our name. Such an account is a debt instrument—

basically an IOU. The bank (or other type of financial institution) holding the account is in debt to the depositor for the balance in the account.

Most loans are accompanied by provisions that constitute a legally enforceable contract. The lender agrees to provide the borrower with a sum of money for a period of time. The borrower agrees to pay interest at a specified rate and repay principal (amount borrowed) according to the terms of the debt contract. Failure of the borrower to fulfill any of the contract's provisions (such as missing a scheduled interest or principal payment) constitutes a default. If the default itself is not cured, the lender may take appropriate legal action. This action may eventually result in a seizure of assets (collateral), bankruptcy, and/or liquidation of the borrower's assets.

Debt instruments are classified in several different ways. The most common is according to the length of time until the creditor must be paid back (time until maturity). Securities that mature in 1 year or less are classified as short-term, and those with longer maturities are referred to as either intermediate-term or long-term. Debt instruments are also commonly classified according to who issues them. Finally, they may be classified as nonmarketable or marketable securities, depending on whether or not they can be traded.

Nonmarketable Debt Securities

depository institution

The most commonly owned financial assets are nonmarketable debt securities offered by the various depository institutions. A *depository institution* is one that accepts deposits. These institutions include banks, mutual savings banks, savings and loan institutions, and credit unions.[1] These nonmarketable debt securities include savings accounts and nonmarketable certificates of deposit (CD). Funds can normally be deposited into or withdrawn from a savings account at any time, and the Federal Deposit Insurance Corporation (FDIC) insures most accounts up to a maximum of $100,000. Accordingly, depositors need not spend any time shopping around for a "safe" bank. Instead, they should focus on convenience, service, and interest rate. Savings institutions have generally paid similar rates, although credit unions sometimes offer slightly higher rates.

Certificates of Deposit

CDs are typically offered with maturities varying from 30 days to 10 years. The interest is usually accrued in the CD, and at maturity, the depositor receives all of the accrued interest and the original deposit. Although most investors have traditionally purchased CDs through local banks, many brokerage firms now offer CDs. These brokerage firms—known as "deposit brokers"—can sometimes negotiate a higher rate of interest for a

CD by promising to bring a certain amount of deposits to the institution. The deposit broker can then offer these "brokered CDs" to their customers. Traditionally, CDs paid a fixed rate of interest, and that rate usually increased as the time until maturity increased. CD providers today offer CDs with many special features, such as variable-rate CDs, CDs with extremely long terms to maturity, bump-up CDs, FDIC-insured CDs denominated in foreign currencies, and callable CDs.[2]

When the depositor is acquiring a variable-rate CD, it is critical to understand the frequency with which the interest rate might change, and how the new interest rate will be determined. Some variable-rate CDs have a predetermined schedule of changes, and others fluctuate according to some specified market rate.

A bump-up CD allows the owner the one-time right to have the bank raise the interest rate on the CD for the remainder of the term, if the bank has raised interest rates on new CDs of comparable maturity.

A callable CD allows the issuer to close out the CD at any time during the call period. A callable CD would be terminated at such time as market interest rates have fallen, and thus the depositor would be forced to redeposit his or her funds a lower interest rate. Sometimes, depositors confuse the noncallable period with the maturity period.

Example: The First National Bank of Everytown offers your client a 10-year CD paying 5 percent that is federally insured and noncallable for 1 year. As the best alternative security being considered pays only 4 percent, this CD looks attractive. What are the risks?

If interest rates fall, the bank will almost certainly call in the CD after 1 year. The client may then be looking at alternative investments that pay less than 5 or maybe even 4 percent. If interest rates rise, the bank will assuredly NOT call in the CD. The client could be locked in for 10 years to what is later considered an unusually low interest rate. For the first year, this is unquestionably an attractive rate; however, the possible long-term drawbacks make purchasing this CD a difficult decision.

The penalty for early withdrawal is the biggest drawback to any non-marketable CD. Although there is a maximum penalty that may be imposed, the actual penalty may vary among providers. It is not uncommon to see advertisements for brokered CDs as not having a penalty for early withdrawal. This is not quite true. What should be made clear by the broker and is required to appear in the fine print of the ad is an explanation of the ability of the purchaser to sell the CD at the then-current rates, which may be higher or lower than the original purchase price.

When CDs are directly purchased from a depository institution, there is an alternative to premature withdrawals. The CD owners may borrow up to the amount of the CD's principal using the CD as collateral. The drawback, of course, is that the rate of interest charged on this loan will exceed the interest rate paid on the CD. However, if the excess interest exceeds the early withdrawal penalty, such a strategy may be beneficial. This strategy should particularly be considered when the CD principal is large and the term of maturity is short.

Money Market Deposit Accounts

An alternative to CDs that is offered by most depository institutions are money market deposit accounts (MMDAs). (These are more typically referred to as money market accounts, or MMAs, in contrast to money market mutual funds, which will be discussed later.) These accounts are federally insured up to $100,000 but are limited to a specified number of withdrawals per month and a nontrivial minimum balance requirement. The rates paid on these accounts fluctuate with market rates, such as the yields on Treasury bills (which will be discussed shortly). One drawback to MMDAs is that the interest on these accounts is subject to state and local income taxes, whereas the interest on T-bills is exempt from these taxes.

Savings Bonds

The other significant nonmarketable investments are U.S. government savings bonds. The savings bonds currently issued include the EE, HH, and I bonds. The rates on these bonds tend to be below but close to the market rates on other short-term instruments. The EE savings bond, the most popular of the three, accumulates in value over time rather than paying periodic interest. There is a redemption schedule for these bonds that allows the owners to cash out early. HH bonds pay a steady amount of interest income, and the interest rate on I bonds is adjusted regularly to reflect the recent rate of inflation.

Early redemption results in a yield reduction. The EE savings bonds allow investors to defer federal income taxes on their returns until maturity. In addition, no state and local income taxes are assessed on interest earned on savings bonds. Series I and Series EE bonds now have a minimum holding period of 1 year. The Savings Bonds for Education program can make the earnings tax free when savings bonds are used for eligible college expenses.

Nonmarketable Debt Securities

- Savings accounts
- Nonmarketable CDs
- Money market deposit accounts
- U.S. savings bonds (EE, HH, and I)

Liquidity and Money Market Securities

The major marketable short-term debt securities are collectively known as money market instruments. These securities share the following characteristics: their maturity is 1 year or less, they have negligible risk of default, and there is an active market for buying and selling them. The principal money market instruments are Treasury bills (T-bills), commercial paper, marketable CDs, bankers' acceptances, and Eurodollar deposits. An alternative to directly purchasing these securities is to acquire money market mutual funds and short-term unit investment trusts that invest in money market securities.

Liquidity

liquidity

As we discuss money market instruments, as well as other securities, it is important to understand the degree of liquidity (or marketability) of each. *Liquidity* is defined as

> The ability to convert securities to cash at a price similar to the price of the previous trade in the security, assuming no significant new information has arrived since the previous trade. Equivalently, the ability to sell an asset quickly without having to make a substantial price concession.[3]

It should be noted that the New York Stock Exchange (to be discussed in chapter 2) has earned its reputation by providing one of the most liquid markets in the world.

Treasury Bills and Other Short-Term Government Securities

Short-term U.S. government securities (governments) are the largest segment of the money market, and they consist of securities that mature within a year. Treasury bills (T-bills) are issued at a discount and mature at par (face value), whereas other governments are sold initially at or near par and pay a semiannual coupon. T-bills are issued in $10,000 minimum denominations, and are traded in book-entry form only.[4] A person might buy a T-bill for $9,500 and receive $10,000 back at maturity. The $500 difference between purchase price and maturity payoff is the investor's interest income.

New issues of T-bills can be bought through a broker or bank for a commission. In this case the order is placed in what is called the Commercial Book-Entry System. T-bills also can be purchased directly from the nearest Federal Reserve Bank at a weekly auction. They can even be bought online by opening an account at www.treasurydirect.gov. Bills with maturities of 13 weeks and 26 weeks are offered each week. The Treasury used to offer 52-week bills every fourth week, but now do so only occasionally. The Treasury also sells cash management bills (CM bills) around tax collection dates (such as the quarterly installment dates), when it anticipates a short-term cash need that will be quickly reversed with cash inflows. CM bills may have maturities of only a few days, but otherwise they function the same as Treasury bills.[5]

Bids may be entered on either a competitive or a noncompetitive basis. The Treasury accepts all noncompetitive bids, and buyers who enter these bids agree to pay the price that corresponds to the lowest price of all the competitive bids that are accepted. Buyers entering competitive bids state a price they are willing to pay and the Treasury accepts these bids, taking the highest prices first until the issue is sold out. However, the price that all buyers with winning competitive bids actually pay is the same as the price that noncompetitive buyers pay. In other words, once the lowest price that the Treasury is willing to accept is determined, then all buyers (both competitive and noncompetitive) pay that price.

Example: Suppose the Fed wants to sell $8 billion of 13-week T-bills. It receives $14 billion in bids, $5 billion of which are noncompetitive. The $5 billion of noncompetitive bids are accepted. The remaining $9 billion in bids are put in order, from the highest price (lowest yield) to the lowest price (highest yield). The Fed then accepts $3 billion worth of these competitive bids (to round out its goal of $8 billion), taking the highest prices first. It is the last bid in this group, which is the lowest price bid accepted, that determines the price paid by all. All bids are provisional until this final step of the auction when the price is determined.

Dealers in government securities maintain an active secondary market in T-bills. The terms offered by these dealers are reported daily in the financial section of most major newspapers as well as online at the Federal Reserve's website. Rather than quote prices in dollars and cents, T-bill prices are quoted in an archaic formula known as the bank discount yield. The yield is defined as

$$BDY = [(10,000 - Price)/10,000] \times (360/DTM)$$

where BDY = bank discount yield
Price = actual T-bill price
DTM = days to maturity[6]

T-bills are quoted with a bid price and an ask price. The bid price represents the price a dealer will pay an investor who wants to sell his holdings. The ask price is the price the dealer wants from an investor looking to buy the T-bills. The difference between bid and ask prices is called the dealer's *spread*, or bid-ask spread. It is through this spread that a dealer earns his or her living.

A typical T-bill quotation will be presented as follows:

Maturity	Days to Mat.	Bid	Ask	Chg.	Ask Yld.
Jun 01 '04	29	2.64	2.60	−0.04	2.64

The maturity date is the day on which the Treasury bill will be paid off. It is the clearest number in the quotation. The number of days to maturity is always off because there is a 2-day settlement period for T-bill trades. This means that if I buy a T-bill today, I will not legally take ownership until 2 days from now and will not start accruing interest until then. Hence, the fact that the above quotation shows 29 days to maturity means that the quote is for 31 days prior to maturity. Because May has 31 days, this quote is for the close of trading on May 1, and would have appeared in the financial press on May 2.

bid price   The *bid price* is the price (as a discount percentage) that a dealer is willing to pay for the T-bill (as of mid-afternoon of the previous trading day). If we plug this number into the above formula,

$$.0264 = [(\$10,000 - Price)/\$10,000] \times (360/DTM)$$

we can solve for the price as follows:

$$\$10,000 - [(.0264 \times \$10,000)/(360/29)] = \$9,978.73$$

ask price   The *ask price* is the price (as a discount percentage) that a dealer is willing to sell the T-bill for (as of mid-afternoon of the previous trading day). Again, if we plug this number into the above formula,

$$.0260 = [(\$10,000 - \text{Price})/\$10,000] \times (360/\text{DTM})$$

we can solve for the price as follows:

$$\$10,000 - [(.0260 \times \$10,000)/(360/29)] = \$9,979.05$$

bond equivalent yield (BEY)

"Chg." is the change between the bid price as listed in the bid column and the bid price from the previous trading day. The figure of –0.04 indicates a decrease of 4/100. "Ask Yld." is the *bond equivalent yield (BEY)* for the T-bill based on its ask price. This involves a different formula for converting a yield number to a price. In this case, the formula is:[7]

$$\text{BEY} = [(10,000 - \text{Price})/\text{Price}] \times (365/\text{DTM})$$

In this case we can verify the BEY by plugging the asked price into the above formula to obtain

$$.0264 = [(\$10,000 - \$9,979.05)/\$9,979.05] \times (365/29)$$

The purpose of the BEY is to make the asked yield into a more realistic measure of the rate of return available to an investor if he or she were to buy the security at that particular price. The major distinctions between the BDY and BEY is that the BDY is based on a 360-day year and the BEY is based on a 365-day year. Because both formulas are tied to the price of a T-bill, one can derive a third formula that ties these two together. A little algebraic manipulation of the above two formulas produces the following:

$$\text{BEY} = (365 \times \text{BDY})/[360 - (\text{DTM} \times \text{BDY})]$$

Example: In the above quotation, the BDY is 2.60 percent. What should the BEY be?

      If we plug in the values of .0260 for BDY and 29 for DTM, we obtain

$$\text{BEY} = (365 \times .0260)/[(360 - (29 \times .0260)] = .0264$$

Commercial Paper

Corporations that seek to raise short-term debt capital in the public markets often sell what is called commercial paper. This is a short-term IOU issued by large corporations with solid credit ratings. The maximum maturity is 270 days, but most commercial paper is issued with a shorter maturity. The paper is secured only by the issuer's good name. The issuer usually has a backup line of credit at a bank. This credit line is available to repay the commercial paper issue when due if sale of new paper is not possible in the existing market environment and the cash is not available. Corporations issue commercial paper because they find they can obtain a lower interest rate on such financing than if they borrow the same money directly from their bank, and the interest savings is enough to also pay their banks the fees on their backup credit lines. From the investor perspective, the rates of return on commercial paper are higher than comparable term CDs.

Commercial paper is rated, but as a practical matter, only high-grade issues are marketable. It is marketed in round lots of $250,000, and it is seldom available in smaller than $100,000 denominations. Commercial paper always has a maturity of less than 9 months; usually it is 6 months or less.

Negotiable CDs

Earlier we discussed the nonmarketable CDs sold by banks. Banks also sell negotiable CDs. Banks will sell negotiable CDs with a minimum denomination of $100,000. However, trades in negotiable CDs have a minimum denomination of $1,000,000. Several New York–based CD dealers handle most secondary market trading. The first $100,000 in principal of a negotiable CD is covered by FDIC insurance. Unfortunately, this means that most of the principal of high-denomination CDs ($1 million or more) is uninsured. Despite the lack of FDIC insurance guarantee, negotiable CDs are considered essentially as safe as commercial paper. Hence, the yields on these two instruments are nearly identical. Troubled banks generally have difficulty selling uninsured CDs even at high interest rates. Moody's Investors Service rates the quality of some CDs. Most CDs have short-term maturities. Trading activity in negotiable CDs ceases when there are 14 or fewer days to maturity. Negotiable CDs are the only interest-bearing money market security.[8]

Bankers' Acceptances

A banker's acceptance involves an obligation to pay a certain amount at a prespecified time. This type of instrument is usually created as a result of international trade. This obligation becomes a bankers' acceptance once it is accepted (guaranteed) by a bank. The acceptance is a liability of the bank. As such, the bank is required to redeem it whether or not the issuer funds the redemption. With this possibility in mind, banks are inclined to carefully check the credit standing of the issuers of these obligations.

Example: An American firm wishes to finance the importation of sombreros using a banker's acceptance. After negotiating with the foreign exporter of these hats, the American importer arranges with its U.S. bank for the issuance of an irrevocable letter of credit (L/C) in favor of the foreign exporter.

The L/C specifies the details of the shipment and states that the exporter may draw a time draft for a certain amount on the U.S. bank. In conformity with the terms of the L/C, the foreign exporter draws a draft on its local bank, receiving immediate payment. The foreign bank forwards the draft and the shipping documents conveying title to the sombreros to the U.S. bank that issued the L/C. The U.S. bank stamps the draft as being accepted (accepts an obligation to pay the draft at maturity), and an acceptance is created.

The new acceptance is either returned to the foreign bank or sold to a dealer, with the proceeds credited to the foreign bank's account. The acceptance can then be traded on the secondary market. The shipping documents conveying title to the sombreros are released to the American importer so that it can take delivery of the goods for resale to customers. The proceeds of the sales are deposited by the American importer at the accepting U.S. bank in time to honor the acceptance. At maturity, the owner of the acceptance (the foreign bank or someone else who purchased it from a dealer) presents it for payment, and the transaction is completed.

The purpose of an acceptance is to substitute the creditworthiness of a bank, which is known and respected both nationally and internationally, for that of a local merchant, who may be relatively unknown, especially in the international market.

Once an acceptance is created, it trades like other money market securities. Acceptances are available in a wide variety of denominations and maturity dates. A small number of dealers buy and sell acceptances, quoting bid-ask spreads of about 1/4 of 1 percent. Acceptances are also known as **two-name paper** *two-name paper* because both the importer and the bank guarantee the payoff at maturity.

Eurodollar Deposits

Eurodollar deposits are dollar-denominated liabilities of banks located outside the United States (usually in Europe). Eurodollar yields are usually slightly higher than other money market rates. Eurodollar deposits of U.S.

investors may occasionally be difficult to repatriate. Moreover, disputes between borrower and lender must be settled without reliance on the protections of the U.S. legal system. In addition, the issuing bank's depositors are rarely as protected by insurance and government regulation as those of U.S. banks. In fact, one reason that many foreign banks can afford to pay a higher interest rate than U.S. banks is that they do not have the reserve requirements and other costs of complying with government regulations that U.S. banks face. Many issuers are subsidiaries of U.S. banks, and others are large institutions with long histories of sound operations. Thus, risks in the Eurodollar market should be considered but not overrated. Defaults have been rare.

Money Market Securities

Type	Issuer
Treasury bill	U.S. Treasury
Commercial paper	Large corporations
Negotiable CD	Depository institutions
Banker's acceptance	Export/import companies; bank-guaranteed
Eurodollar deposit	Foreign-based banks

Securities and Interest Rates Related to Money Market Securities

Although it is the money market securities that the individual investor buys, there are other interest rates and securities with which a financial planner should be familiar. This is because some of these yields provide upper or lower limits to the yields on money market securities. Thus, movements in some of these other rates may signal imminent movement in the yields on the money market securities.

Prime Rate

The prime rate used to be known as the rate that banks charged their largest, safest borrowers. However, in the competition for business, some banks were found to be offering their best customers loan rates that were below prime. This created legal problems for the banking community. These problems were resolved by redefining a bank's prime rate as an index rate the bank uses to price its loans. Thus, a loan applicant approaching a bank might be told that he would be charged prime rate plus 1 percent. This would mean that whatever the prime rate was at the time the loan was closed, the interest rate would be that rate plus 1 percent.

Each bank usually has a committee that sets its own prime rate. As with any business entity, banks are free to set their own prices, and the prime rate is the "price" a bank charges for loans. Nonetheless, banks constantly watch each other's prime rates. Any bank charging a lower rate than necessary will attract substantial business with less than appropriate profitability. Any bank charging a higher rate than necessary will find its customers going elsewhere. Certain banks have gained a reputation for being a leader in initiating a change in the prime rate. When one of these banks announces such a change, most other banks quickly follow. When one looks at changes in the prime rate over time, it follows along with all of the other money market–related yields. Citibank has been a traditional leader in changes in the prime rate. The *Wall Street Journal* also publishes a prime rate that some people look to as defining the current value. The *Journal*'s definition of the prime rate is whatever rate is posted by at least 75 percent of the country's 30 largest banks.

Unless a client happens to own and operate a large, secure business, he or she will not be able to borrow at the prime rate. However, the interest rate he or she will pay is linked to the prime rate. Changes in the prime rate affect the rate at which businesses can borrow from a bank. Similarly, the interest rates that banks pay on its deposits, including savings accounts, CDs, money market deposits, and negotiable CDs, is limited by the prime rate. Banks cannot pay more for deposits than what they are able to earn in loaning out those deposits. Plus, there must be enough of a spread between the deposit rate and the prime rate to cover the bank's operating expenses and earn a profit.

Federal Funds, Discount Loans, and Repurchase Agreements

Banks and other types of financial institutions also participate in several active short-term debt markets. By law, banks must have at any point in time a certain amount of reserves. The required reserves are based on each bank's level of deposits. Cash on hand is the primary reserve. However, a significant component of reserves is money a bank has on deposit at a Federal Reserve Bank. At times, some banks find that they have more reserves than they need. At other times, they have fewer reserves than are required. The problem of excess and deficit reserves is solved by banks with excess reserves lending some of the funds on deposit at a Federal Reserve Bank to a bank with a shortage in reserves. The funds on deposit are known as federal funds. The exchanging of these deposits is known as the *federal funds market*. The loan of these deposits is an overnight loan, although some banks make it a practice to borrow such funds on a daily basis, and others make it a practice to be a continuous lender. Like the prime rate, the federal funds rate is an indicator of how much a bank has to pay for some of its money. Changes in federal funds rates is a leading indicator of changes in other rates that banks charge on loans and pay on deposits.

federal funds market

**discount rate
(monetary policy)**

A key rate that affects the federal funds rate is the *discount rate,* which is the rate the Federal Reserve Bank charges its members for loans. Simply put, when a bank is short of reserves, an alternative to borrowing federal funds is to borrow cash directly from the Federal Reserve Bank itself. Sometimes the discount rate is above the federal funds rate, and sometimes it is lower. When the discount rate is the higher of the two, banks borrow more federal funds. When the discount rate is lower than the federal funds rate, banks tend to borrow more from the Federal Reserve. Banks always have a slight preference for borrowing federal funds because excessive borrowing from the Federal Reserve may invite additional auditing by the Fed.

The Federal Reserve uses changes in the discount rate to make dramatic statements about changes in the direction of monetary policy. That is, the Fed tries to keep the discount rate and the federal funds rate in close proximity of one another; therefore, a change in the discount rate that opens the gap between the two rates signals the Fed's intention to conduct open-market operations so that the federal funds rate will gravitate toward the discount rate.

Repurchase agreements (repos) are sales of securities with guaranteed repurchase at a prespecified price and date (often 1 day later). The relationship between the purchase and sales prices establishes the instrument's rate of return. For example, a guaranteed resale in 6 months at 5 percent above the purchase price would generate a 10 percent annual rate of return (actually 10.25 percent if compounding is considered). This is an indirect way for banks to borrow from other banks, using the security as collateral. Payment is generally required to be in immediately available reserve-free funds transferred between financial institutions. These arrangements are extremely safe. It should also be noted that the Fed uses repurchase agreements in its open-market operations on almost a daily basis to manage the federal funds rate.

LIBOR

LIBOR stands for the London Interbank Offered Rate. It is the rate at which London banks are willing to lend money to each other. Thus, it is somewhat analogous to the federal funds rate in this country. It is the rate that is frequently quoted on dollar-denominated loans in Europe, and it is the premier short-term interest rate quoted in the European money market. It is frequently used as a reference rate on a worldwide basis. For example, on a floating-rate loan, a bank might agree to charge a borrower an interest rate of LIBOR plus 2 percent.

Money Market Mutual Funds

Money market mutual funds and short-term unit investment trusts (discussed next) were developed several years ago in response to interest rate ceilings on many bank savings instruments (known as Regulation Q) coupled with generally higher money market rates. These funds invest resources from many small investors in a large portfolio of money market securities. While some funds have no minimum account size, many set a $1,000 or larger minimum. Still other funds have implemented a rate structure that pays higher rates for larger balances. The net income of the portfolio is distributed to the fund's owners and may be paid monthly or reinvested.

Money market funds can be redeemed in whole or in part on short notice without a redemption charge. Most funds permit several types of redemption: the fund holder can write, e-mail, or call toll free for an immediate check-mailing or wire transfer into the fund holder's bank account. Most funds also permit checks to be written on the shareholder's account. Use of this feature allows the investor's funds to earn interest until the check clears.

The returns paid on money market funds are slightly below the prevailing rates in the money market because of the expenses of the fund. Yields among money market funds differ because of differences in portfolio allocation among money market instruments and differences in maturities. Some money market funds invest only in Treasury bills, whereas other portfolios contain slightly riskier money market investments (for example, Eurodollars or commercial paper). Some funds hold only short-term instruments. Others are willing to incur the somewhat reduced liquidity of slightly longer maturities, although all have average maturities of less than 90 days. Still others vary their average maturity on the basis of their interest rate expectations. Some short-term municipal funds offer (lower) tax-free yields. Thus, different types of money market funds appeal to various types of investors.

Most money market funds of a given class (general, governments only, or municipal) offer similar risks and returns, but they do differ slightly. There are organizations that rate the safety and performance of these funds, such as Moody's Investors Service and Standard and Poor's.

Short-Term Unit Investment Trusts

Short-term unit investment trusts (UITs) offer many of the same advantages as money market funds: low-risk, low-denomination investment and money market yields. The key difference is that money market funds are managed and perpetual investments, whereas UITs are unmanaged and have a maturity date. Although UITs are less convenient than money market funds, their yields are higher. Units must be held until maturity (generally 6 months) or sold in a relatively inactive secondary market.

Unlike money market funds, UIT yields are established when they are purchased. Yields on existing units do not change when market interest rates change. For example, if market rates move up, the trust holder continues to earn the rate originally promised. He or she must wait until the units mature to reinvest at the higher rate available in the market. However, if interest rates decline, the holder will receive an above-market rate until the trust matures.

Because of the large minimum denominations and the transaction fees associated with the direct purchase of the various money market securities, most investors cannot afford direct purchase. Nonetheless, when the financial planner deems that it is appropriate for a client to have liquidity in his or her asset holdings, money market securities make the most sense. The easiest way to reconcile these two facts is to advise the client to own a money market mutual fund or a short-term UIT.

Money Market Rates

As mentioned earlier, the yields on the various money market securities all move together. In addition, there is a certain rank order they maintain due to the basic features of the instruments and certain built-in relationships. These relationships are shown below.

> T-bill yield < federal funds rate < CD rates
> bankers' acceptances yield < commercial paper rate < prime rate
> CD rates < prime rate

Sample Money Market Rates: November 6, 2003

Prime rate	4.00%
Federal Reserve Board discount rate	2.00
Federal funds rate	1.00
Treasury bills (secondary market, 3 months)	.94
Commercial paper (nonfinancial, 3 months)	1.06
Eurodollar deposits (3 months)	1.10
Certificates of deposit (3 months)	1.12
Bankers' acceptances (3 months)	1.05

Sources: http://www.federalreserve.gov/releases/h15update/, and http://www.bondheads.com/fixed_income.htm

Treasury bills always offer the lowest yield because as a direct obligation of the U.S. Treasury they are considered the safest security in the world. Federal funds are extremely safe, but they are not an investment available to the individual. The yields on CDs are greater than those on T-bills and federal funds because there is a lack of liquidity to CDs. The yield on bankers' acceptances is less than that on commercial paper because the former is "two-name" paper; that is, it has the guarantee of a corporation and a bank. Commercial paper yields are always less than the prime rate because commercial paper is sold only by those companies who believe they can get better deals in the marketplace than from a bank. The yields on CDs are less than the prime rate because banks acquire money from depositors at the CD rate and make a profit only by lending it out at higher rates.

Long-Term Debt Instruments

Long-term debt securities are generally categorized as government bonds (including agencies), municipals (state and local), and traditional corporate bonds. Other categories include mortgage loans and mortgage-related securities, bank CDs, bond funds, income bonds, floating-rate securities, zero-coupon bonds, Eurobonds, and private placements. Preferred stock also competes for the same income-oriented investor dollars that might otherwise go into long-term debt securities.

Before reading on, it may be helpful to remember that for all its complex language and provisions, a bond or other debt instrument is still basically an IOU. The contract for a bond can be rather complex. Nonetheless, all debt obligations involve the same basic features: the amount of the loan, when the loan must be repaid (maturity date), the rate of interest, the frequency with which interest payments are to be made, the nature of collateral (if any), what is to happen in case of default, and the priority of repayment obligations of a borrower with multiple debts (subordination). Other features that may come into play include whether the borrower has the option of repaying the debt before it is due (call provision), whether the lender has the option of exchanging the financial obligation for an ownership interest (conversion), and whether the lender has the option of demanding repayment prior to maturity (put provision).

Treasury Notes and Bonds

In addition to the Treasury bills discussed earlier in this chapter, the U.S. Treasury also auctions debt instruments that have intermediate-term and long-term maturities (notes and bonds). Notes are issued with maturities from 1 to 10 years; bonds have maturities greater than 10 years at the time of issuance. Both notes and bonds are issued in denominations of $1,000 or more, and both are traded in an active secondary market consisting of dealers in U.S. government securities. Price quotations for notes and bonds in the over-the-counter market are published daily in various publications. Current quotes for a few key bonds may be found at various locations on the Internet. An example of a typical Treasury bond quotation is as follows:

**Treasury Note and Bond Quotations
(Sample Quotes from the OTC Market)**

Rate	Maturity Mo./Yr.	Bid	Ask	Chg.	Ask Yld.
6 1/2	May 07n	112:05	112:09	–5	4.16
7	June 08	110:02	110:05	....	4.20
9 1/8	May 09-14	113:20	113:24	–3	6.79

The "Rate" column represents the coupon rate at which interest is paid as a percentage of par value. For the first bond listed above, if the par value is $1,000, then the investor will receive $65.00 ($1,000 x .065) per year in interest payments. This number is obtained by multiplying the coupon rate times the par value. As a matter of convention, interest payments on bonds are paid on a semiannual basis. Thus, the owner of this bond would actually receive interest payments of $32.50 twice per year.

The "Maturity Mo./Yr." column indicates the month and year in which the note or bond will be paid off. A small n after the maturity date identifies the security as a note, while a range of years given as the maturity date identifies the security as a callable bond. The third bond listed above is callable at par beginning in 2009.

The "Bid" column shows the price that a dealer is willing to pay for the note or bond (as of mid-afternoon of the previous trading day). Unlike T-bills, Treasury bond prices are quoted in 32nds and as a percentage of par. The above quote of 112:05 means that the bid price is 112 5/32 percent of par. If par were $1,000, the actual price would be $1,121.56 ($1,000 x 112 5/32%). It is obtained by multiplying the bid price times par value. The Ask column gives the price a dealer is willing to sell the note/bond for (as of mid-afternoon of the previous trading day).

The "Chg." column is the change (in 32nds) between the bid price as listed in the bid column and the bid price from the previous trading day. For the first bond shown, the number –5 means that the bid price is 5/32nds of 1 percent lower than on the previous day. On a $1,000 par value bond, this translates into a price decline of $1.56, which is computed by multiplying the price change by the par value.

The "Ask Yld." column provides an approximation of the yield to maturity for the note or bond based on its ask price. The concept of yield to maturity will be discussed in chapter 9. Suffice it to say that this is the single most important number in the quotation.

Since mid-1983, all newly issued Treasury notes and bonds are in registered form (payable only to the registered owner). Prior to mid-1983, some notes and bonds were issued in bearer form (payable to bearer). All notes that were issued in bearer form have long since matured, but some bearer bonds still remain outstanding. An advantage to having securities issued in the registered form is that if they are lost or stolen, the issuer will replace them.

Treasury notes and bonds make coupon payments semiannually, with the par or face value paid at maturity. The distinction between a note and a bond is nothing more than the maturity dates at the time the security is issued. Also, some bonds have call provisions that allow them to be called during a specified period prior to maturity (although no callable Treasury bonds have been issued since 1984). This period usually begins 5 years before maturity and ends at the maturity date. This means that at any scheduled coupon payment date during the callable period, the Treasury can require the bondholders to sell the bonds back to the government at par.

The yield to maturity for Treasury securities is calculated using the ask price. However, if the ask price for a callable bond is greater than par, then the yield to call is calculated on the assumption that the bond will be called at the earliest allowable date.

Treasury notes and bonds are generally traded in an over-the-counter market composed of about two dozen dealers. Most of these dealers are New York investment or commercial bankers. Treasury notes and bonds are also traded on the NYSE. Finally, the Treasury conducts an active original-issue auction for notes and bonds. Banks and others may bid for newly issued notes and bonds at this auction.

All Treasury securities (that is, bills, notes, and bonds) will continue to be considered the most secure in the world as long as the government is willing and able to raise sufficient tax revenues to finance the debt.

Treasury Strips

In 1985, the Treasury introduced a program call STRIPS (Separate Trading of Registered Interest and Principal Securities). Under this program, the Treasury prestrips certain interest-bearing Treasury securities so that investors who purchase a strip bond can keep whatever cash payments they want and sell the rest. For example, a 20-year coupon bond could be stripped of its 40 semiannual coupons, and each of these coupons would then be treated as a stand-alone zero-coupon bond. The maturities of these 40 bonds would range from 6 months to 20 years. The final payment of principal would also be treated as a stand-alone zero-coupon bond.

Treasury Inflation-Protected Securities

In 1997, the U.S. Treasury added Treasury Inflation-Protected Securities (TIPS) to its menu of offerings. The goal of TIPS has been to provide inflation protection to investors. Naturally, when a feature like inflation protection is

Sample U.S. Treasury STRIPS Quotations

Mat.	Type	Bid	Ask	Chg.	Ask Yld.
May 06	ci	68:15	68:19	– 10	6.29
May 02	np	98:14	98:15	– 1	2.34
May 11	bp	71:19	71:23	– 2	3.50

- Mat.: the month and year in which the principal will be paid off
- Type: ci—indicates stripped coupon interest; np—indicates Treasury note, stripped principal; bp—indicates Treasury bond, stripped principal
- Bid: the price (in 32nds) that a dealer is willing to pay for the security (as of 3 p.m. Eastern Time of the previous trading day)
- Ask: the price (in 32nds) that a dealer is willing to sell the security for (as of 3 p.m. Eastern Time of the previous trading day)
- Chg.: the change (in 32^{nd}s) between the bid price as listed in the bid column and the bid price from the previous trading day (which is really 2 trading days previous); for instance, a –10 indicates a decrease of 10/32
- Ask Yld.: the yield to maturity for the security based on its ask price

added to a security, something is taken away. In this case, the coupon rate is set lower than what it would be on bonds without the inflation protection. To compensate for the lower coupon rate, the par value of the bond is adjusted on a semiannual basis by the amount of the inflation rate, as reported by the Bureau of Labor Statistics in its Consumer Price Index (CPI). The coupon rate is then applied to the par value to determine the interest payment that is due.

Whether or not this is a good deal depends on how the reported inflation rates compare to what people were expecting. Lower-than-expected inflation rates would make the regular bonds a better deal, and higher-than-expected inflation rates would make TIPS the better deal. The worst-case scenario would be a period of deflation, in which case the CPI declines. An unexpected bout of disinflation (a slowing of the inflation rate) would also make this a poor investment. One attribute of TIPS is that the principal will not be reduced below the original value. So during a period of disinflation, although the coupon payments shrink, the par value is guaranteed as a floor at maturity.

Let's look at an example of how this would work. Suppose a TIPS is offered with a 1 percent coupon rate. If the inflation rate averages 3 percent during the investment period (1.5 percent per 6-month period), then the coupon payments and principal would rise at that rate. For the first semiannual payment, a client with a $100,000 investment would receive interest on the TIPS of $507.50 ($101,500 principal x 1 percent coupon rate x 1/2 semiannual factor). However, his total income during this period is

$2,007.50, because he receives both the interest ($507.50) and the increase in principal ($1,500), although he will not actually receive the cash associated with the increased principal until the bond matures. If the inflation rate continues to average 1.5 percent per 6-month period, then the interest payment and principal will both increase at this rate.

Example:	You have a 70 year-old client who has a morbid fear of the impact of inflation. The client indicates he would like to invest $100,000 in a new issue of TIPS. The coupon rate on the TIPS is 1.0 percent, and the coupon rate on regular Treasuries of comparable maturity is 3.0 percent. Is this a good deal?
	The quickest way to get a read on TIPS is simply to look at the difference between the coupon rates on regular Treasuries of comparable maturities and those of the TIPS. In this case, the differential is 2 percent. Hence, if the actual inflation rate turns out to be less than 2 percent, the regular bonds are a better deal. If the inflation rate turns out to be more than 2 percent, the TIPS are a better deal (at least for this investment). TIPS provide an inflation hedge, but at the risk of current income. They make sense as a component of a portfolio, especially where the client has a high degree of anxiety about the inflation rate, but it is unlikely they should be an unduly large percentage of the portfolio.

Agency Issues

In addition to the Treasury department, several federal agencies, as well as federally sponsored agencies, issue debt obligations. The federally sponsored agencies are privately owned agencies that issue securities and use the proceeds to support the granting of certain types of loans to farmers, homeowners, and others. Most federal agency securities are not guaranteed by the U.S. Government but are nevertheless quite safe. Moreover, it is generally presumed that federal assistance would be forthcoming if there were any danger of default on these securities. For the sake of analysis, all federal and federally sponsored agencies are lumped together and simply referred to as federal agencies. Like Treasury bonds, the interest from most federal agency issues is not subject to state or local income taxes. The most significant exceptions include the bonds of the Federal National Mortgage

Association (Fannie Mae) and the Government National Mortgage Association (Ginnie Mae).

Agency securities provide slightly higher returns than Treasury securities of comparable maturity. This is due to two reasons. One is the lack of an absolute full faith and credit guarantee, and the other is their somewhat lower marketability. Because the trading volume for most agency issues is less than that for Treasury securities, the bid-ask spreads are wider. This results in greater trading costs for agency issues and forces investors to demand a higher return.

Mortgage Loans and Mortgage-Backed Securities

Many agency and some types of nonagency securities are either backed by or represent ownership in a pool (portfolio) of mortgage loans. The vast majority of outstanding mortgage debt is collateralized by a first claim (first mortgage) on developed real estate, such as single-family homes, apartments, or commercial property. Most such mortgage loans require a minimum initial down payment of 10 to 20 percent. These mortgages are generally amortized with level monthly payments over an extended period (typically 20 to 30 years). Thus, the amount owed usually declines over time. Moreover, the property securing the mortgage loan usually (but not always) appreciates as time passes. As a result, the ratio of collateral value to mortgage debt tends to rise over time. Accordingly, first mortgages are usually declining-risk investments. Even in a default and distress sale of the property, the mortgage holder is likely to recover a high percentage of the outstanding debt.

Financial intermediaries, such as banks, savings and loan associations (S&Ls), and insurance companies, write the vast majority of mortgages. The federal government backs some mortgages through the Veterans Administration (VA) guarantee program or the Federal Housing Administration (FHA) insurance program, which add further protection. Several federal agencies and some other groups promote mortgage lending by purchasing mortgage loans from the originator.

Federal agencies and a handful of large banks issue virtually all actively traded mortgage-backed or mortgage-related securities. The oldest and largest of these agencies is the Federal National Mortgage Association (FNMA). It purchases mortgages from original mortgage lenders (mortgage bankers, commercial banks, S&Ls, and savings banks) with the proceeds of its own debt security sales. Its bonds have fixed coupons and maturities and trade in a secondary market much like other bonds.

The Government National Mortgage Association (GNMA) bundles together packages of similar mortgages. These mortgage packages are created by private institutions (mortgage bankers, commercial banks, S&Ls, and savings banks) and contain only individual mortgages insured by the FHA or guaranteed by the VA. Once a package is bundled together, an application is made to GNMA for a guarantee on these "pass-through" securities. Once guaranteed, GNMA pass-through securities are backed by the full faith and credit of the U.S. government and therefore are nearly riskless debt instruments. They are the only pass-through securities with this guarantee.

The principal drawbacks of GNMA pass-throughs are a relatively high minimum denomination ($25,000, but they may be bought in $5,000 units thereafter) and an uncertain amortization rate. Pass-through owners literally own a part of a mortgage pool. They receive monthly interest and amortization payments (minus a small service fee to GNMA and the financial institution that administers the mortgage).

Mortgages are often prepaid either because the mortgage is refinanced or the house is sold. The prepayment rate cannot be predicted with certainty. As a result, a typical GNMA pass-through security with a stated life of 30 years may actually have a much shorter life. This can cause a loss for an investor who buys an existing GNMA pass-through that is selling at a premium. If, for whatever reason, homeowners decide to prepay their mortgages, the investor receives par value on the security, thereby incurring a loss. In spite of this drawback, GNMA's relatively secure high yields make GNMA pass-throughs quite attractive to income-oriented investors.

The Federal Home Loan Mortgage Association (Freddie Mac) also sells mortgage-related securities. Freddie Mac purchases conventional (not government-backed) mortgages, pools them, and sells participations that have much in common with GNMA pass-throughs. Freddie Mac participations trade in $100,000 minimum denominations. Substantial collateral generally underlies the mortgages, and Freddie Mac guarantees them; therefore, these participations are also quite safe.

Because of the success of FNMA, GNMA, and Freddie Mac, several large banks started packaging and marketing their own mortgage pools. These pools offer somewhat higher yields and are a bit more risky than the agency securities. Although they are not government backed, these private pass-throughs are backed by the underlying mortgage collateral, and most have a partial guarantee from a private insurer.

Some depository institutions also sell mortgage-backed bonds. These securities are, however, just another type of corporate bond that happens to have mortgages as collateral. Finally, some mutual funds invest only in mortgage-backed security portfolios, thereby allowing small investors relatively easy access to the mortgage market.

Personal Mortgages

Sellers of homes will sometimes accept first or second mortgages as part of the proceeds. Some entrepreneurs make a lucrative living by buying these mortgages from the seller, usually at a substantive discount from their face value. Such mortgages are risky because of the potential legal expenses associated with any defaults. In addition, there is no secondary market.

Securitization

The various categories of mortgage-related securities are an example of a broader phenomenon called securitization. Securitization involves taking assets that heretofore were not easily traded in a secondary market and structuring a marketable security or group of securities from them. The goal of the process is to convert assets with poor marketability into assets with much greater market acceptance. If the effort is successful, the institution doing the converting will be able to sell the marketable assets for appreciably more than the less-marketable assets could be sold for. The difference between the book value of those assets and their market value, minus the cost of the conversion, represents the profit earned by the converting institution.

Looked at from another perspective, securitization allows an institution to turn over its assets much more frequently than is possible with the more traditional buy-and-hold approach to the intermediation process. Thus, a bank that is only able to make and service loans equal to a percentage of its deposit base can securitize, earn an origination fee, and earn a service fee on a multiple (several hundred percent) of its deposit base.

One major benefit of securitization, from the standpoint of the investor, is that it effectively creates a diversified pool of loans, thus reducing the overall risk to the investor. (Risk reduction through diversification is discussed in greater detail in chapter 4.) While the risk of default would deter most investors from providing a large loan to an unknown individual, investing in a diversified pool of such loans is relatively safe.

Most of the activity in securitization has been based on first-mortgage real estate loans. More recently, however, other types of assets have been securitized. For example, auto loans, credit card loans, second mortgages, sovereign loans to Third World countries, student loans, and a variety of other types of loans are (or are suggested as) the basis for securitization. Moreover, real estate mortgages themselves are coming in for further securitization, as discussed in the following section.

Collateralized Mortgage Obligation (CMO)

As mentioned before, a basic feature of mortgages and traditional mortgage pass-throughs is their uncertain rate of repayment. The average 25- or 30-year mortgage is paid off in 5 to 7 years. The rate of prepayments, however, will vary with a number of factors, including market interest rates compared to the stated rate on the mortgage, the amount of labor mobility (and the divorce rate) in the community, inflation, the stage of the business cycle, economic conditions (for example, the bankruptcy rate) in the area originating the mortgages, and so on. Many investors prefer a more certain time frame of payments than is provided by the typical mortgage. The collateralized mortgage obligation (CMO) was devised to deal with this problem. CMOs are multiclass pass-through securities. They offer a potentially improved way of securitizing mortgage loans.

Owners of the various classes (known as tranche*s*) of CMO securities are paid out at different but defined rates. Thus, one class might receive payments equivalent to a 1-year zero-coupon bond, a second class might receive payments equivalent to a 5-year zero-coupon bond, and a third class might receive payments equivalent to a 10-year zero-coupon bond. The CMO issuer would be left with the residual cash flow, which might itself be sold as another security. In this way, the uncertain cash flows of a pool of mortgages are restructured into a series of bond-like predictable cash flows and a residual. Virtually all of the uncertainty of the payment timing is impounded into the residual security. Because of the market's general preference for predictable payments, the total value of a mortgage pool subdivided into CMOs can be higher than as a single-class pass-through.

State and Local Government Debt Obligations

revenue bonds

general obligation bonds

A large number of state and local government securities are also part of the debt security market. These securities are called municipals or municipal bonds. Municipals may be *revenue bonds* (which are backed by revenues from a designated project, authority, or agency, or by the proceeds from a specific tax) or *general obligation bonds* (which are backed by the taxing power of the issuing government). The issuing government or authority may be as well known as the State of New York or the New York Port Authority or as obscure as a small rural water district. The adequacy of the tax or revenue bases of these units varies enormously. A major determinant of municipal bond quality is the unit's ability to pay, as measured by its tax or revenue base.

Even well-known, long-established issuers of municipals can default. Issuers of municipals can purchase insurance for the benefit of investors, with the municipalities benefiting from lower interest costs due to lower default risks. A lower default risk on a bond would cause an increase in its rating as well as its marketability. In addition, traders, bond dealers, and institutional investors can purchase insurance for municipal bonds traded in the secondary market.

Corporate Bonds

A major vehicle used by corporations for financing growth is a bond. Corporate bonds have all the basic features that Treasuries have: a coupon rate, a maturity date, and a maturity or par value. However, corporate bonds can be more complex because they have default risk, a greater variety of collateral, and sometimes some interesting features, such as convertibility.

Corporate bonds are almost always issued with $1,000 face values and are usually issued to new investors at the face value. This is accomplished by the underwriter of the issue setting a coupon rate for the bond that reflects current market interest rates for bonds with the same level of risk as the bond being issued. Bond prices are generally quoted as a percentage of par. Therefore, a bond selling at 90 is priced at $900.

Relatively few bonds default, and those that have were almost always rated as speculative prior to their default. Thus, an investor can largely avoid default risk by investing only in nonspeculative bonds, known as *investment-grade bonds*. (The schemes for categorizing bonds is discussed in chapter 9.) If a client is going to hold only a few bonds, then investment-grade bonds are highly appropriate. If a client has a large bond portfolio and can spread this investment across a large number of bond issues, then he or she might well consider more speculative bond holdings. The reason for this is the simple fact that the speculative bonds provide higher rates of return. As long as the incremental return is enough to offset the losses associated with any particular bond issue, the client may well come out ahead.

investment-grade bonds

Example 1:	Your client has $10,000,000 invested in Treasuries that provide an annual return of 4 percent, and is complaining she would like to increase her annual interest income. How might she utilize speculative bonds that provide an annual return of 7 percent?
	Let's suppose that the $10,000,000 portfolio is used to buy 100 different speculative issues. This provides an investment of $100,000 per issue. The annual income would increase from $400,000 to $700,000 per year, less any losses associated with defaults. As long as no more than three companies default per year, the client is no worse off, and may be better off.
Example 2:	Let's now consider that fact that even when there are bond defaults, there is frequently some sort of payoff at a later date. It is truly rare for a bond to end up being totally worthless. Suppose that in the above example, as many as six of the bond holdings end up in default each year, but that the average payoff on these bonds is 50 cents on the dollar. Again, the client might be better off.

In summary, corporate bonds are riskier and provide higher rates of return than most short-term debt securities. However, they tend to have less liquidity than short-term debt securities. Relatively little time or effort is required to manage most investment-grade bond portfolios.

Promissory Notes

Any two people can enter into a loan agreement. If the amount of money loaned is significant, then a more formal promissory note rather than a simple IOU should be utilized. Forms for such promissory notes are readily available on the Internet. Promissory notes are also used in business relationships. A business will sometimes borrow money from an investor and issue a promissory note. Conversely, businesses sometimes lend money to individuals, such as officers and key employees. These loans may be for the personal convenience of the individual, or they may be a form of compensation in which particularly attractive loan terms are agreed to. The SEC has warned that some popular scams involve marketing these notes directly to individuals.[9] Promissory notes typically have no specific property pledged as collateral, but their maturity may be short-term or long-term. Each promissory note is a truly unique document.

Long-Term Debt Securities: Primary Types

- Treasury notes and bonds: lowest risk category
- Agency issues: slightly higher risks and yields than Treasuries—prepayment risk
- Mortgage-related securities
  - FNMA: mortgage-backed (VA and FHA)
  - GNMA: mortgage pass-throughs (VA and FHA)
  - Freddie Mac: conventional mortgages, with Freddie Mac guarantee
  - Bank-issued: conventional mortgages, often with a private guarantee
- Direct mortgage, seller financing: risk varies; second mortgages usually quite risky
- Municipals: tax-free; risk varies
- Corporates: vary greatly in risks and yields
- Promissory note

Insurance-Based Investments

An insurance-based investment is one that is issued by an insurance company. It may or may not involve the application of the mortality table. There are two broad categories of this type of investment: guaranteed investment contracts and annuities.

Guaranteed Investment Contracts. A guaranteed investment contract (GIC), also known as a stable value contract, is usually an investment option available in a 401(k) retirement plan. More recently, it is available in some profit-sharing plans, and even some IRAs and mutual funds. It is an investment choice provided by the plan sponsor, but it also is a contract between an insurance company and the employee. GICs offer a specified maturity date or dates and a rate of return that is guaranteed through maturity by the insurance company. Neither the FDIC nor any other governmental agency insures these contracts. Employees may make withdrawals against these accounts for a variety of reasons, including: death, disability, attainment of age 59 1/2, financial hardship, bona fide termination of employment, in-service plan withdrawals, plan loans, and participant-directed transfers to noncompeting funds offered through the 401(k) plan.

GICs come in many forms. The simplest GICs are "bullet" contracts under which the funds are returned in a lump sum. Other contracts allow for payouts over time. GICs may be denoted as floating-rate. In this case, the interest rate paid would be tied to some benchmark rate, such as a specific maturity Treasury yield. GICs may also be characterized as participating, in which case the interest rate paid is tied to the performance of the portfolio in which the GIC deposit is invested.

GICs also may differ according to deposit methods (lump sum or "window" periods) and maturity (ranging from 1 to 10 years). In recent years, companies have offered indexed or floating-rate GICs in addition to the fixed-rate instruments. The primary noninsurance competition for GICs is the bank investment contract (BIC), which is particularly popular for maturities of less than 3 years. As the BIC is not a deposit, it does not receive FDIC insurance coverage. However, BICs provide higher rates of return than that promised by comparable insured deposits.

The rate of return provided on GICs has historically been about the same as intermediate-investment-grade corporate bonds. To date, the risk has been less due to the fact that few insurance companies have completely collapsed.

qualified annuity
nonqualified annuity

Annuities. Annuities are particularly well-designed investments for retirees. An annuity may be designated as qualified or nonqualified. A *qualified annuity* is one that is purchased through a tax-sheltered program, such as a 401(k), a 403(b), or an IRA; a *nonqualified annuity* is one purchased outside of any tax-sheltering program. Regardless of the qualification status, the major advantage of a deferred annuity is that the money in a person's account grows on a tax-deferred basis. If the annuitant dies before starting the withdrawals from the annuity, there is usually a guaranteed death benefit.

Annuities can be grouped into four categories, depending on when the premium is paid, when the benefits start, and how long the benefits last:

single-premium deferred annuities (SPDAs)

flexible-premium deferred annuities (FPDAs)

CD-type annuities

single-premium immediate annuities (SPIAs)

1) *Single-premium deferred annuities (SPDAs).* A nonqualified SPDA is appropriate for when a client has suddenly come into a lot of money that he or she would like to apply toward retirement. The windfall cash might be from such events as the sale of a home or an inheritance. A qualified SPDA would be ideal for an individual taking money from a pension plan, IRA, 401(k), or other tax-deferred savings program.

2) *Flexible-premium deferred annuities (FPDAs).* A nonqualified FPDA would be a form of savings program for retirement. Qualified FPDAs are used for IRAs, 401(k)s, and Teacher's Retirement Plans. FPDAs allow one to contribute on a monthly basis.

3) *CD-type annuities.* These are similar to SPDAs, but they have guaranteed rates over selected periods of time and a predetermined number of payments.

4) *Single-premium immediate annuities (SPIAs).* They are similar to SPDAs, but the benefit payments begin upon receipt of the single premium. They are also referred to as income annuities.

Note that with SPDAs and SPIAs, an investor might elect to do his or her primary saving for retirement in other forms, and then as the investor approaches or reaches retirement, move the money into an annuity program. The alternative is to place the contributions directly into the annuity over the working career (i.e., buy an FPDA). With a deferred annuity, two periods are associated with the policy, the accumulation period and the distribution phase or payout period.

An annuity may be either fixed or variable. In the case of a CD-type annuity where the number of payments is certain, the rate of return is explicit. Such an annuity is usually quoted by its yield. For any other fixed annuity, the dollar payments are certain, but the number of payments is not because of the uncertainty as to how long the annuitant will live. In a variable annuity, the premiums are essentially placed in equity investments (to be discussed next), and thus there is uncertainty as to both the number and amount of payments.

With a deferred annuity, the investor may choose one type of policy during the accumulation period, then switch during the payout period. People typically choose a variable annuity during the former and switch to a fixed annuity during the latter. In addition, the premiums do not have to be placed into only one policy; investors are usually allowed to split their contract between two policies. Thus, one might put half of one's premium into a fixed-rate policy and half into a variable-rate policy.

The distribution phase begins with the payment of the first benefit amount from the annuity to the annuitant. There are a variety of payout options for distributing the principal and earnings in an annuity. These annuity payout options include the following:

- *straight life annuity*—provides income to the annuitant regardless of how long the annuitant lives. Thus, if the owner dies 2 months after purchasing a straight life annuity, the insurance company keeps the remainder of the premium used to purchase it.
- *life income with period certain annuity*—provides lifetime income as well as a guaranteed minimum number of payments for a certain amount of time, such as 5, 10, 15, or 20 years. If the annuitant dies during the guarantee period, the remaining guaranteed payments go to the beneficiary. Most clients select this option.
- *life with cash or installment refund annuity*—provides lifetime income as well as a guarantee that the total dollar value of the payments will not be less than the total premiums paid into the contract.
- *joint and survivor life annuity*—the benefits are paid as long as at least one of the couple is living. The couple may choose that at the death of the first annuitant, the survivor would receive a reduced payment. The joint and survivor life annuity option can be combined with either the period certain option or the cash or installment refund option.
- *fixed-period annuity*—provides a fixed payment of principal and interest over a predetermined period of time, such as 10 years, on a monthly, quarterly, semiannually, or annual basis. If the annuitant dies before all payments are made, the remaining payments go to a beneficiary.
- *fixed-amount annuity*—provides that a specified amount is paid each period until all principal and interest are exhausted. If the annuitant dies before the funds in the annuity have been paid, the remainder is generally paid to the annuitant's beneficiary.

Annuities are not insured or otherwise guaranteed by a federal agency; if the insurance company paying the annuity fails, the annuitant could sustain a substantial loss. Such failures do happen, albeit rarely. Thus the solvency of the insurance company matters in the selection of a policy. Insurance companies are rated as to financial solvency. The ratings are provided by A.M. Best, Weiss, and Moody's.

Some annuity contract holders are protected against loss of deposit due to the failure of the issuing insurance company by state insurance guarantee funds. This raises the question of why all annuity contracts are not similarly covered. In fact, many large companies with solid A.M. Best ratings choose to do business in various states on a "nonadmitted" basis. Nonadmitted companies are not required to seek approval of their rates or coverage forms from the state Department of Insurance. The underwriting, claims, and financial sections of the Department of Insurance do not routinely audit nonadmitted companies. Finally, should a nonadmitted company fail or go out of business, its policies are not guaranteed by the various state insurance guarantee funds. On the other hand, admitted companies are required to have all rates and forms approved by the Department of Insurance, they are routinely audited by various sections of the state insurance departments, and their policies are backed by the state insurance guarantee funds. The implication here is that if the best annuity contract is offered by an admitted company, then that is the best deal. However, if the best annuity is offered by a nonadmitted company, then the investor has to trade off its risk of default with the extra benefits.

The major criticisms of annuities are the fees associated with the products. There may be as many as three types of fees associated with an annuity policy. The first are sales fees and surrender charges. As of March 31, 2003, only about 2 percent of variable annuity contracts charge front-end loads. Nearly all of the others have back-end loads, also known as surrender charges or contingent deferred sales charges. These charges are assessed at the time of a withdrawal from a variable annuity as a percentage of the amount withdrawn according to a contractually defined schedule. The terminology for the annuity value before any surrender charges is usually the *accumulation value,* and *surrender value* refers to the account value after surrender charges have been deducted. The surrender value is the actual amount the owner would receive upon a complete and total surrender of the policy.

accumulation value
surrender value

The second type of fee includes an annual contract charge that is used to offset some of the insurance company's administrative costs for servicing these contracts. These charges range from $10 to $50, with an average of about $30 per year, and they may be waived when fund values exceed some minimum amount, such as $10,000 or $20,000. Insurance expenses, often referred to as M & E (mortality and expense) charges, are asset-based charges against the investment subaccounts in a variable annuity. The insurance company assesses these charges to cover its costs for the guarantees it provides (such as a minimum guaranteed interest rate in the general account) and for the guaranteed annuity factors for annuitization calculations. These charges also cover the guarantee that, in the event of death, the beneficiary will receive the greater of the deposits made into the contract or the account value—a protection against adverse investment results.

The third type of fee is the fund expense fee. This is analogous to the management expense fee that mutual funds have. It is the asset-based fee for actually managing the portfolio. When analyzing an annuity, a financial advisor should focus primarily on the total expense ratio, which combines both the M & E and the fund expenses. It is commonly used to compare expenses inside annuities to regular mutual funds. The average total annual expense ratio in the 19,386 variable deferred annuity subaccounts as tracked in Morningstar's Principia™ for VA/L subaccounts as of March 31, 2003, was 2.26 percent, ranging from 0.33 percent to 8.99 percent.

EQUITY INSTRUMENTS

Equity securities represent ownership shares. The owners have a residual claim (which comes after a creditor's claim) on the corporation's assets and earnings. Equity-related assets include publicly traded common stock, preferred stock, options, convertibles, and mutual funds as well as ownership positions in small firms and venture capital investments. Each of these investments represents direct or indirect ownership in a profit-seeking enterprise. Equity holders' claims are subordinate to those of all debtors but include all residual value and income in excess of the claims of the senior securities.

Common Stock

Common stock is by far the most important type of equity-related security. One out of every seven Americans is a stockholder, and half of these people live in households that earn less than $20,000 per year.[10] As the residual owners, shareholders are paid dividends out of their firm's profits. The portion of profits not paid out (earnings retained) is reinvested in the company, thereby helping it grow. The expectation of growth in sales, assets, and particularly profits increases the value of the firm. The benefit of any appreciation in the firm's value accrues to its owners, the stockholders. A company's stockholders theoretically control it by electing its board of directors. The board, in turn, selects upper-level management and makes major policy decisions. Most stock ownership groups are, however, widely dispersed and unorganized. Existing management usually fills the resulting power vacuum by nominating and electing friendly slates of directors. In general, stock returns compare favorably with those of all the investments discussed so far (see table 1-1). However,

---

TABLE 1-1
Basic Series: Summary Statistics of Annual Total Returns (1926–2002)

Series	Geometric Mean	Arithmetic Mean	Standard Deviation
Large company stocks	10.2%	12.2%	20.49%
Small company stocks	12.15	16.95	33.19
Long-term corporate bonds	5.9	6.23	8.67
Long-term government bonds	5.45	5.84	9.40
Intermediate-term government notes	5.44	5.59	5.77
U.S. Treasury bills	3.79	3.83	3.15
Inflation	3.05	3.14	4.37

Source: Calculated using information and data presented in Ibbotson Analysis Software, © 2003 Ibbotson Associates, Inc. All rights reserved. Used with permission.

their variability of returns, as measured by the standard deviation of their returns, is also greater than that of the other investments. (Standard deviations are discussed in chapter 3.)

Dividend payments on stocks are not assured or contractually guaranteed, and common stock never matures. Investors who own stocks that reduce or eliminate their dividends are likely to see a dramatic decline in the values of their shares. Bond prices generally fluctuate much less than stock prices. Moreover, firms are legally obligated to pay interest on bonds, whether they have a profitable year or not. For these reasons, as well as others, stockholders have a greater risk exposure than do bondholders within the same firm.

Preferred Stock[11]

Preferred stocks have more price variability than bonds do, and generally less than common stock does. Although preferred stock is technically a form of ownership, preferred shareholders usually have no real control of the company. All "preferreds" carry promised annual dividend payments. Virtually all preferred stock is *cumulative,* which means that any missed dividends must be made good before common shareholders can receive dividends. Preferred shareholders, as a group, can elect directors only if a certain number of dividend payments have been missed. Moreover, in any reorganization of the company, the preferred shareholders must be paid the liquidation value of their stock before common stockholders receive anything.

cumulative

The returns on preferred stock have always been substantially less than those on common stock. As fixed-income securities, preferreds are subject to the same type of interest rate risk as bonds. The preferred stock of a weak company may be riskier and have a higher expected yield than the common stock of a strong company.

Corporations own most preferred stock. This is because dividend income to a corporation is 70 percent tax exempt. Preferred stock is usually priced to reflect this tax treatment. Historically, the returns on preferred stock have been lower than the returns on long-term corporate bonds.

Example: The Crunch Auto Insurance Company has an extra $100,000 to invest. High Roller Realty has asked Crunch if it would like to buy $100,000 worth of a new issue of preferred stock. (This is referred to as a private placement.) This preferred stock has a dividend yield of 8 percent. What will Crunch's after-tax return on this investment be? Assume a 25 percent corporate tax rate.

The 8 percent dividend yield means Crunch will receive $8,000 per year in dividends. Of this, $5,600 (70% x $8,000) is tax exempt. The taxes owed on the remaining $2,400 are $600 ($2,400 x 25%). Therefore, Crunch's after-tax income is $7,400 ($8,000 − $600); its after-tax return is 7.4 percent ($7,400/$100,000).

In summary, preferred stocks may be inappropriate for most individual investors for several reasons. First, it is overpriced to individual investors for whom dividends are fully taxable as ordinary income.[12] In addition, individuals would incur most of the interest rate risk associated with bonds, none of the upsides associated with common stock, and none of the security of an investment that eventually matures.

Limited Partnerships and Master Limited Partnerships

Most businesses are organized as corporations. The corporate form of organization provides limited liability for owners (shareholders), but its income is taxed at the corporate level, and its shareholders are taxed again on their dividends and then on any capital gains when the stock is sold.[13]

Some businesses are organized as partnerships. The income of a partnership is taxed only once. Partnership profits, whether distributed or retained by the partnership, are treated for tax purposes as the imputed income of the partners, where the allocation of income is based on the partnership agreement.

The limited partnership is an alternative way of organizing a business enterprise. These partnerships combine the benefits of a corporation's limited liability with the single-taxation advantage of a partnership. A single general partner, who is usually the organizer and may be a corporation, *does* have unlimited liability. The limited partners, however, are not generally liable for the partnership's debts and obligations beyond their initial capital contribution. Most limited partnerships have one major drawback: Because they are relatively small, their ownership units trade in very thin markets. In addition, there may be legal or contractual restrictions on the sale of a limited partnership interest.

The master limited partnership (MLP) is designed to overcome this drawback. Most MLPs are relatively large (compared to limited partnerships). Their ownership units are designed to trade actively in the same types of markets as stock.

MLPs have generally been organized around oil and gas holdings. Others are designed for real estate. Investing in MLPs involves many of the same advantages and disadvantages as investing in common stock.

Private Placement/Venture Capital

Venture capitalists provide risk capital to otherwise undercapitalized companies that they believe have attractive growth prospects. In exchange, venture capitalists receive ground-floor equity positions in what may turn out to be highly lucrative ventures.

Venture capital may be used to help fund both start-up firms and undercapitalized going concerns. Most types of direct venture capital investing are available only to institutions and wealthy individuals because the new ventures being funded generally require substantial capital. Investors of more modest means can participate indirectly through public venture-capital funds, venture-capital limited partnerships, venture-capital clubs, and small business investment companies (SBICs) geared toward venture-capital investing. Regardless of how investors participate, they will find venture capital to be a risky business.

Equity Securities: Direct Ownership of a Company

- Common stock: provides residual ownership of a corporation
- Preferred stock: receives preference over common stock for dividends and liquidation of assets
- Limited partnership: has limited liability and tax benefits but poor secondary market
- Master limited partnership (MLP): combines the tax advantage of a partnership with the limited liability and ease of trading of a corporation
- Private placement/venture capital: has high risk, but a high potential return

---

EQUITY-RELATED INSTRUMENTS AND DERIVATIVES

Warrants and Rights

Warrants permit their owners to purchase a specified amount of stock at a specified price prior to a specified date. Warrants, which are issued by the company whose stock underlies the warrant, are generally exercisable for relatively long periods, such as several years. Some warrants have no expiration date. When exercised, warrants result in newly created shares and provide new cash investment for the issuer. The issuing company usually creates warrants so that they can be attached to a bond issue. The attachment normally allows a company to pay a lower interest rate on the bond than would otherwise be the case. Companies who attach warrants to a bond offering are usually attempting to balance their financing by selling bonds today and hoping to sell stock in the future at such time as the warrants are exercised.

Rights, like warrants, are company-issued options to buy stock. Rights differ from warrants in two ways. First, rights always have short lives. They usually expire within a few weeks of the time of their issue. Second, the exercise price on a right is usually set substantially below the market price of the stock when the rights are issued. Some companies have a rights offering because it is mandated in their corporate charter that new issues of common stock be sold through a rights offering. The benefit of a rights offering, as opposed to simply selling a block of new shares of common stock, is that it allows current investors to maintain their pro rata ownership of a company. Thus, if an investor owns 5 percent of the outstanding stock of a company, he or she can maintain his or her 5 percent ownership by exercising all of the rights awarded to him or her. Stockholders normally receive one right for each share they own. There are three key features to a right:

- the expiration date
- the number of rights required to buy a new share of stock (may be as many as 10 or 20 rights per new share)
- the price per share the investor pays for the new share

Convertible Bonds and Convertible Preferred Stocks

exchange ratio

Convertible bonds (convertibles) are debt securities that can be exchanged for the issuing company's stock at a specified exchange ratio. The number of shares of stock received upon conversion is known as the *exchange ratio*. Although convertibles are technically debt instruments, their conversion feature gives them an equity-related component. Their value tends to increase with increases in the underlying stock's price. As a result, they offer a combination of the relatively ensured income of bonds and the

conversion value

upside potential of stock. Convertibles sell for more than their *conversion value*. Conversion value is the product of the exchange ratio and the current price of the company's common stock. Consequently, with a set amount of money, the investor can always buy more shares of the underlying stock directly than by purchasing convertibles. Accordingly, direct stock ownership is normally more profitable in a rising market.

straight bonds

The conversion feature allows convertibles to be sold with lower interest rates than equally risky *straight bonds*. Straight bonds are any bonds that have no conversion feature. Straights are generally more attractive in declining stock markets. Convertibles offer a compromise between investing in a company's stock and its nonconvertible (straight) bonds. Convertible bonds are almost always sold as subordinated debt, which means there is less chance of any recovery in the event of the issuer entering bankruptcy than if the bonds were not subordinated to another issue.

Convertible preferred stock works mostly the same way as convertible bonds. The major difference is that the bonds have a maturity date. Hence, if the price of the stock is very low as the maturity date approaches, the investor knows he or she should receive back par at maturity, even though the conversion value may be essentially worthless. Because preferred stocks have no maturity date, there is nothing to force the price of the preferred stock back up to par.

Derivative Securities

Derivative securities (derivatives) are securities whose values are derived from other securities or assets. Options are a derivative security. The special feature of options is that they give the owner (holder) the choice of whether or not to engage in a particular transaction in the future. The owner of a call option has an option to buy a specified number of shares of stock at a specified price (strike price or exercise price) prior to a specified date (expiration date). A *put* option is an option to sell a specified number of shares of stock at a specified price prior to a specified date. Exercising an option is solely at the owner's (not the seller's) discretion. Anyone buying a call option expects the price of the underlying asset to rise. People who buy put options expect the price of the underlying asset to fall.

Example: Suppose an investor pays $200 for a call option to buy 100 shares of stock at a strike price of $20 per share, and that the stock coincidently trades for $20 per share. If the stock's price subsequently rises to $30 per share, the investor can exercise the option, buy the stock at $20, and then immediately sell that same stock at $30. That trade would produce a gain of $1,000 ($3,000 – $2,000). After deducting the cost of the option, the set of transactions would yield a net profit of $800 ($1,000 – $200) before commissions, compared with an initial cost of $200 for the call. (Note: You don't have to exercise to realize the gain—you can just sell the option, since its current selling price will reflect the gain in the stock price.)

The same $200 could, in contrast, have purchased 10 shares at $20. This would have produced a $100 gain when the stock rose to $30 per share.

Standardized option trading began with the 1973 opening of the Chicago Board Option Exchange (CBOE) and soon spread to other exchanges. Listed options now exist for a large number of different stocks. Other options are written on stock indexes and commodities futures contracts. Most options have relatively short lives (9 months or less).

Investment Companies

Many investors would just as soon have professional management of some or all of their investments. The easiest way to do this is through an investment company. There are quite a few different types of investment companies, but they all share the same basic characteristics: They pool investors' money to purchase various investments, and they have professional portfolio managers. The largest single type of investment company is a *mutual fund* (also known as an open-end investment company). The next biggest category is the closed-end investment company. The difference between these two is that when the closed-end company is created, an initial block of shares is sold to investors, and that block remains fixed. The shares in the closed-end company are then traded among investors at whatever price they can agree upon. The shares of a mutual fund are not traded; rather, new investors are required to buy their shares from the fund, and investors wanting to cash out must sell their shares back to the fund.

Because investors can only buy shares from or sell their shares to the mutual fund, the price must be predetermined. It is referred to as the *net asset value* and is basically the market value of the fund's portfolio divided by the number of shares of the fund outstanding. This number is recomputed at the close of business each day to determine the price that new investors will pay and the price that current investors will receive if they want to sell.[14]

The most important feature of each investment company is its stated investment objective. Many investment companies specialize in one particular type of investment. Thus, for each of the other investment vehicles described in this chapter, there are investments companies that specialize in holding only these. Examples include money market mutual funds, municipal bond mutual funds, Treasury bond mutual funds, aggressive growth stock funds, and so on. There are also investment companies that are dedicated to particular strategies, such as "dogs of the Dow."[15] Finally, although a major attribute of investment companies is diversification, some companies provide concentration. Examples include companies that invest in stock from only one country (The Mexico Fund) and companies that invest in stock from only one industry (for example, a fund that buys only companies involved in mining for gold).

A critically important feature about investment companies is their fee structure. All investment companies have management fees, which are

mutual fund

net asset value (NAV)

load funds

no-load funds

charged to the portfolio to compensate the portfolio manager and to cover the expenses of operating the company. When investors buy or sell closed-end funds, they pay the same commission schedule they normally would if they traded shares of common stock of any other type of company. Some mutual funds—*load funds*—are sold by agents who receive a fee (up to 8.5 percent of the purchase price). *No-load funds*, in contrast, deal directly with their investors, thereby eliminating the need for a sales force and load fees. No-load fund portfolios usually achieve the same average risk-adjusted returns on their portfolios as those of load funds.

unit investment trusts

A popular form of investment company is the unit investment trust. *Unit investment trusts* hold unmanaged portfolios. Most of these trusts hold bonds. They raise money for the purpose of buying a specific portfolio of bonds, buy that portfolio, and then eventually self-liquidate as the bonds mature. Occasionally a unit investment trust buys a portfolio of stocks. In this case, there is a date on which the portfolio is liquidated and the proceeds distributed to the investors.

exchange-traded fund (ETF)

Some relatively recent innovations in the genre of investment companies have been the emergence of *exchange-traded funds (ETFs)* and index securities. An ETF is a closed-end investment company that duplicates the portfolio of a particular stock market index, such as the Dow Jones Industrial Average or the Standard & Poor's 500 Average.[16]

OTHER INVESTMENTS

Futures Contracts

Futures contracts, like options, are derivatives. Their values are derived from the values of the underlying assets on which the contracts are based. Futures speculators and hedgers buy (go "long") and sell (go "short") contracts for future delivery of a specified amount of some asset, such as so many bushels of corn, ounces of silver, or thousands of dollars worth of Treasury bills.

To execute a trade, market participants are required only to deposit a small percentage of the contract's value. As a result, any given percentage price fluctuation is magnified many times in terms of profit or loss.

Example: Buying a 6-month contract valued at $100,000 might require a 10 percent deposit ($10,000 in earnest money). A 20 percent increase in the contract's value (to $120,000) would produce a profit of $20,000 (minus commissions), or 200 percent of the original $10,000 deposit. A 10 percent fall in the contract's price would, however, wipe out the original $10,000 deposit.

Most brokerage firms require individuals seeking to open a commodity trading account to establish a relatively large beginning balance (initial deposit of funds) and to have a substantial net worth. Commissions on commodity trades are only a tiny fraction of the potential gains or losses.

Collectibles

Although a relatively minor investment medium, collectibles have grown substantially in popularity in recent years. Coins, stamps, art, and antiques have long been of interest to collectors. As an indication of their importance, both *Barron's* and *Forbes* report the Sotheby Index of prices on a variety of types of art, ceramic, silver, and furniture collectibles.

A wide assortment of items is now considered collectible. Collectibles are usually extremely speculative and illiquid. They are generally sold at a high markup, subject to a substantial fraud risk, and involve all of the uncertainties present in the more traditional types of investments. Selling is one of the most difficult aspects of investing in collectibles. Investors may, of course, use the same outlets to sell as they used to buy, but this approach may not always be best. Transaction costs are usually quite high.

Noncollectibles

Noncollectibles would include such things as Broadway shows, movies, California vineyards, racehorses, baseball clubs, and freight cars—that is, unique and expensive items. All of these can be quite legitimate. Well-to-do clients with a large, well-diversified portfolio may consider such an investment as an added element of diversification, or even if they would like an interesting investment that they can mention at cocktail parties! Some people have made fortunes from investments such as these, and others have lost their total investment. It is clearly prudent that the financial planner be highly knowledgeable in the field of this particular investment, or at least that the client is receiving advice from someone who is appropriately informed.

Natural Resources

Yet another investment opportunity is natural resources. Two obvious examples in this category include timber and oil. In the case of timber, a person would buy land with trees or would plant trees, and then at such time as the tree sizes seem optimal, have the trees cut and start the process again. One drawback to timber is there are usually some carrying costs in the form of property taxes. In addition, there are risks from such natural disasters as infestations, fires, and windstorms, and even from poachers.

Some people acquire the mineral rights on land (or land with the potential for oil). They then lease to developers the rights to drill for oil, with the benefit of a royalty on each barrel extracted. There is even a special tax benefit here in that an investor may take a deduction of 15 percent of the income as a *depletion allowance*. As with timber, one of the drawbacks to such an investment is the property tax owed each year.

depletion allowance

Many people opt to invest in natural resources either by investing in companies whose line of business involves the development of natural resources, or an investment company that specializes in investing in companies in the field of natural resources.

Investments Other Than Debt or Equity Securities

- Futures: contracts calling for deferred delivery of some physical commodity
- Collectibles: diverse array of tangible assets
- Noncollectibles: pricey and unique investments
- Natural resources
- Real estate: land and property that is permanently attached to it

---

Real Estate

About two-thirds of all households in the United States own their own homes. Thus, a financial planner will find that the vast majority of his or her clients will already have an investment in real estate. In fact, for younger clients, the investment in their home may dominate their assets.[17] In cases where the client's personal residence dominates the assets, investor-owned real estate is not a good investment due to the lack of diversification. However, where a client's residence is a relatively small part of his or her portfolio, investor-owned real estate might make sense. If the client is a renter, real estate may be a particularly attractive investment.

There are two significant drawbacks to investor-owned real estate. First, it is highly illiquid, meaning that it can take a long time to sell, substantial expenses can be associated with selling it, and a good deal of uncertainty exists as to the price for which it can be sold. Second, it requires a personal commitment of time and money to manage, which the owner either provides directly or hires someone else to do.

Some people promote real estate investment with such clichés as, "Buy land, they aren't making any more of it." The problem with this observation is that it overlooks the fact that the relative desirability of a piece of property may change substantially. A particular section of town may be the "in place"

market approach

cost approach

income approach

to live now, but in a few years various changes in the community may render that section much less desirable.

There are three different ways of estimating real estate values: the market approach, the cost approach, and the income approach. The *market approach* involves looking at the sale prices of comparable real estate. No two properties are precisely equivalent, but many are similar to others. The *cost approach* involves a consideration of what it would cost to buy similar land and build a comparable structure. There are times when it is cheaper to buy and build rather than to buy existing property. The *income approach* involves a consideration of the future cash flows that a property will provide to its owner. Whereas the first two approaches would apply either to the purchase of a personal residence or to rental or commercial real estate, the income approach clearly applies only to the purchase of real estate to be used in a business activity, such as rentals or commercial property.

Three Approaches to Valuing Real Estate

- Market approach: bases value on asking and sale prices of comparable properties
- Cost approach: bases value on cost of constructing equivalent property
- Income approach: bases value on future net cash flow produced by the property

---

Alternative Real Estate Investments

real estate investment trust (REIT)

Because of the time, effort, and risk associated with direct real estate investments, many people prefer to do their real estate investing indirectly. The easiest way to do this is through a *real estate investment trust (REIT),* which is a closed-end investment company that specializes in the real estate area. There are essentially three types of REITS:

- Equity REITs invest in office buildings, apartments, shopping malls, and hotels.
- Mortgage REITs make both construction and mortgage loans.[18]
- Hybrid REITs hold both equity and loan holdings.

Equity REITS are typically the most popular type with investors who want to participate in the growth of real estate values. Dividends should rise if rents increase more than expenses, and share prices generally reflect changes in property values. Mortgage REITs are similar to bonds. REITs traditionally have higher dividend yields than most common stocks.

REITs are subject to the same law as any investment company in that they must pay out 95 percent or more of their income as dividends. In addition, REITs must hold at least 75 percent of their assets in real estate, and no less than 75 percent of their income must be derived from real estate.

An alternative to direct investment in REITs is to buy mutual funds that restrict their investments to REITs. A middle ground between direct investment and REITs is the real estate limited partnership (RELP), an example of the limited partnerships discussed earlier. Each RELP has a specific set of properties associated with it. A number of brokerage firms have sponsored the issuance of RELPs through public offerings. All limited partnerships must have a general partner who assumes general liability. Usually the sponsor takes on this role. The principal drawback to RELPs is their relatively limited secondary markets and their relatively high overhead structure of fees and expenses. Such investments are generally difficult to sell prior to their scheduled liquidation.

A final way to invest in real estate is to invest in companies that have substantial real estate holdings. This could include paper and forest products companies, railroads, ranch and farm companies, and oil and mining companies, among others.

SUMMARY AND CONCLUSIONS

A financial planner needs to have a good understanding of the variety of investment alternatives available to an investor. The easiest investments to understand are debt obligations, in which money is loaned and there is a promise to repay principal at maturity, along with a promise to pay interest. Debt obligations can be classified by maturity as short-term (1 year or less) or intermediate- or long-term. They may also be classified as nonmarketable or marketable. Nonmarketable ones include nonnegotiable CDs, money market deposit accounts, and savings bonds (EE, HH, and I).

Money market securities are instruments that have a high degree of liquidity and safety and mature in less than 1 year. These include Treasury bills, commercial paper, negotiable CDs, bankers' acceptances, and Eurodollar deposits. The yield on money market instruments is affected by changes in the prime rate and the discount rate and by yields on federal funds. Many investors can access money market investments through money market mutual funds and short-term unit investment trusts.

Long-term debt instruments fall into three categories: government bonds, municipal bonds, and traditional corporate bonds. A relatively recent addition to the bond menu has been Treasury-Inflation Protected Securities (TIPS), which incorporates the inflation rate into its returns. Securitization is the process whereby assets that are not normally marketable are bundled together and claims based on these assets are sold as liquid assets.

Investors also have access to insurance-based investments. These include guaranteed investment contracts and annuities. Both GICs and annuities can come with a wide variation in terms.

The most basic form of equity investments is common stock. However, other forms include preferred stock, limited partnerships, and master limited partnerships. There are several instruments whose value is based on or derived from the value of other securities, including warrants and rights, convertible bonds, preferred stocks, and put and call options.

Investment companies are a particularly important investment vehicle for many investors. These include mutual funds, closed-end companies, unit investment trusts, variable annuities, and private placement/venture capital firms. Other investment opportunities are provided by futures contracts, collectibles, noncollectibles, natural resources, and real estate.

CHAPTER REVIEW

Answers to the review questions and the self-test questions start on page 733.

Key Terms

depository institution
money market deposit accounts
   (MMDAs)
savings bonds
liquidity
Treasury bills (T-bills)
bid price
ask price
bond equivalent yield (BEY)
commercial paper
negotiable CDs
bankers' acceptances
two-name paper
Eurodollar deposits
prime rate
federal funds market
discount rate (monetary policy)
Treasury notes
Treasury bonds
revenue bonds
general obligation bonds

corporate bonds
investment-grade bonds
qualified annuity
nonqualified annuity
single-premium deferred annuities
   (SPDAs)
flexible-premium deferred annuities
   (FPDAs)
CD-type annuities
single-premium immediate annuities
   (SPIAs)
accumulation value
surrender value
common stock
preferred stock
cumulative
limited partnerships
master limited partnerships
venture capital
warrants
rights

convertible bonds

convertible preferred stocks

exchange ratio

conversion value

straight bonds

derivative securities

mutual fund

net asset value (NAV)

load funds

no-load funds

unit investment trusts

exchange-traded fund (ETF)

collectibles

noncollectibles

depletion allowance

market approach

cost approach

income approach

real estate investment trust
   (REIT)

Review Questions

1-1.   What is meant by liquidity?

1-2.   a.   Compute the bank discount yield for a T-bill priced at $9,732 that has 130 days to maturity.

   b.   Compute the price for a T-bill with a bank discount yield of .0484 that has 88 days to maturity.

   c.   Compute the bond equivalent yield for a T-bill with a price of $9,855 and 120 days to maturity.

   d.   For the bond described in part b, compute the bond equivalent yield.

1-3.   Name and describe the five money market instruments.

1-4.   For each of the following pairs of rates and securities, indicate which one would normally be lower in rate or yield and indicate why:

   a.   T-bill and commercial paper

   b.   Prime rate and commercial paper

   c.   Banker's acceptance and negotiable CD

   d.   Eurodollar deposit and negotiable CD

   e.   Prime rate and negotiable CD

1-5.   What is securitization, and why is it good for borrowers?

1-6.   Name and describe the four types of annuities.

1-7.   Why are few straight life annuities sold?

1-8.   Why would preferred stock be thought of more as a debt instrument than as an equity?

1-9.   Compare and contrast call options, warrants, and rights.

1-10.   Tremendous fortunes are made with noncollectibles. Why wouldn't more investors purchase such items?

Self-Test Questions

T   F   1-1.   Most money market securities have relatively high minimum denominations ($100,000 or more).

T   F   1-2.   T-bills are sold initially at or near par value and pay a semiannual coupon.

T   F   1-3.   Commercial paper is usually issued by large corporations to finance their short-term needs.

T   F   1-4.   The entire principal of negotiable CDs issued by bank and thrift institutions is protected by government deposit insurance.

T   F   1-5.   Once a banker's acceptance is created, it trades like other money market securities.

T   F   1-6.   The federal funds rate is the interest rate that banks charge other banks for overnight loans.

T   F   1-7.   Discount loans are extended by the Federal Reserve to member banks for the purpose of covering a short-term reserve deficiency.

T   F   1-8.   Short-term unit investment trusts (UITs) are managed and perpetual.

T   F   1-9.   U.S. Treasury bonds are issued with maturities from 1 to 10 years.

T   F   1-10.   Treasury note and bond price quotations are expressed in hundredths.

T   F   1-11.   Treasury securities are subject to state and local taxes.

T   F   1-12.   Agency issues generally bear a slightly higher interest rate than Treasury securities of comparable maturity.

T   F   1-13.   The principal drawbacks of Government National Mortgage Association (GNMA) pass-through securities are their relatively high minimum denomination and an uncertain amortization rate.

T   F   1-14.   The goal of the securitization process is to convert assets with poor marketability into assets with much greater market acceptance.

T   F   1-15.   The category of municipal bonds known as revenue bonds is backed by the taxing power of the issuing government.

T   F   1-16.   The payment of preferred stock dividends is required before common stock dividends can be paid.

T   F   1-17.   Preferred stockholders' claims to corporate assets receive the lowest priority.

T   F   1-18.   Dividend payments on common stock are as secure as interest payments on bonds.

T   F   1-19.   Small company stocks, over time, have outperformed large company stocks.

T   F   1-20.   Partnership profits, whether distributed or retained by the partnership, are treated for tax purposes as the imputed income of the partners, where the allocation of income is based on the partnership agreement.

T   F   1-21.   Mutual funds are classified as closed-end investment companies, which neither issue new shares nor redeem outstanding shares.

T   F   1-22.   Some warrants have no expiration date.

T   F   1-23.   Rights usually have longer lives than warrants.

T   F   1-24.   The conversion value of a convertible bond equals par divided by the conversion price.

T   F   1-25.   The price of a mutual fund share is its net asset value.

T   F   1-26.   Futures contracts are derivatives whose values are derived from the values of the underlying assets on which the contracts are based.

T   F   1-27.   Commissions on commodity trades are a large portion of the potential gains or losses.

T   F   1-28.   The income approach is the best method to value owner-occupied, domestic residences.

T   F   1-29.   The Sotheby Index provides an indication of price changes on a variety of types of art, ceramic, silver, and furniture collectibles.

T   F   1-30.   REITS only take equity positions in commercial real estate.

NOTES

1. For simplification, this discussion will henceforth use the term "banks" in lieu of the more comprehensive term "depository institutions." The rules that apply to banks also apply to all of the competing institutions.
2. The FDIC website offers a nice piece on brokered CDs, "Certificates of Deposit: Tips for Savers" at www.fdic.gov/deposit/deposits/certificate/index.html.
3. *Investments: Third Canadian Edition,* by William F. Sharpe, Gordon J. Alexander, Jeffery V. Bailey, David J. Fowler, and Dale L. Domian, Prentice-Hall Canada, Scarborough, Ontario, 2000, p. 47.
4. Book-entry form means that there are no paper certificates denoting the security. Ownership is tracked only by computer records.
5. For additional information on CM bills, see www.pfm.com/articles/CashBill.pdf.
6. See www.sba.muohio.edu/wyattjg/webpage/401/tech-Tbill.html.
7. See www.sba.muohio.edu/wyattjg/webpage/401/tech-Tbill.html.
8. See http://www.ameritrade.com/education/html/encyclopedia/tutorial3/t3_s10.html #certificates.
9. See http://www.sec.gov/investor/pubs/promise.htm.
10. See http://www.thesolutionsite.com/lpnew/lesson/1121/org.htm.

11. The following discussion pertains to nonconvertible preferred stock. Convertible preferred stock is discussed later along with convertible bonds.
12. Tax issues are discussed more fully in chapter 13.
13. The details of taxation are provided in chapter 13.
14. One of the recent scandals in the mutual fund industry is that some funds were letting a few investors place orders to buy or sell shares after the cut-off time. That gave the lucky few the opportunity to trade at what was effectively yesterday's prices knowing today's news.
15. This concept is discussed in chapter 6.
16. Stock market indices are discussed in chapter 2.
17. On personal balance sheets, homes should be listed at market value on the asset side, and the mortgage listed as a separate liability, rather than listing the home at net equity value (which is market value minus the mortgage outstanding).
18. A construction loan is for the purpose of constructing a building. Once the building is completed, the construction loan is paid off with the funds obtained from a mortgage loan. Thus, construction loans can range from a few months to a few years, and mortgage loans can be as much as 30 years.

Appendix 1A

The Financial Planning Context

While mutual fund portfolio managers select investments that are appropriate to the portfolio objective of the fund, financial planners must recommend investments that are appropriate for clients, each of whom has different characteristics. Among these characteristics are goals, financial strength, family situation, and risk tolerance. In other words, financial planners approach the topic of investments within the financial planning context.

Financial planning is a *process* that requires a disciplined methodology. This process includes proscribed steps and practices that are efficient and professional. The Certified Financial Planner™ Board of Standards, Inc., has taken a lead role in promoting professionalism in financial planning. Standards promoted by the CFP® Board are the de facto standards for the industry. Even financial planners who are not CFP® designees should be conscious of the fact that they are likely to be held to these standards, both professionally and legally.

STEPS IN THE FINANCIAL PLANNING PROCESS

The Certified Financial Planner™ Board of Standards has promulgated a six-step financial planning process that is appropriate for professional financial planners. Individuals who intend to take the Certified Financial Planner™ comprehensive examination should be aware that any reference to the financial planning process on that examination will relate to the CFP® Board's model.

Step 1: Establishing Client-Planner Relationships

The CFP® Board asserts that the first step in financial planning involves establishing the working relationship with the client. Planners should explain issues and concepts related to the overall financial planning process as appropriate to the client's situation and needs. They should also explain services provided, the process of planning, and the documentation required. Also included in this step is a clarification of the client's and planner's responsibilities.

Step 2: Gathering Client Data and Determining Goals and Expectations

The data-gathering aspect of this step includes obtaining information about the client's financial resources and obligations via interview and questionnaire and collecting applicable client records and documents. The planner must also determine the client's time horizons and risk tolerance level. Planners must determine the client's personal and financial goals, needs, and priorities and assess the client's values, attitudes, and expectations.

Step 3: Analyzing and Evaluating the Client's Financial Status

Several categories are involved in analyzing the client's financial status. The general category includes the client's current financial status (such as assets, liabilities, cash flow, and debt management), capital needs, attitudes and expectations, risk tolerance, risk management, and risk exposure. In the special needs category are divorce/remarriage considerations; charitable planning; adult dependent, disabled child, and education needs; terminal illness planning; and closely held business planning. The risk management category includes needs and current coverage for life; disability, health, and long-term care coverage; homeowners, auto, and other liability coverage (for example, umbrella, professional, errors and omissions, and directors and officers coverage); and commercial insurance. The investments category covers analysis and evaluation of current investments and current investment strategies and policies. Evaluation of the tax category involves tax returns, current tax strategies, tax compliance status (such as estimated tax), and current tax liabilities.

In the retirement category, planners should evaluate and analyze current retirement plan tax exposures (for example, excise tax and premature distribution tax), current retirement plans, Social Security benefits, and current retirement strategies. Planners should evaluate the client's employee benefits, including the benefits available and the client's current participation in those benefits. Finally, the planner should analyze the client's current estate plan, which includes an evaluation of estate planning documents and strategies as well as estate tax exposure.

Step 4: Developing and Presenting the Financial Plan

The planner should develop and prepare a client-specific financial plan tailored to meet the client's goals and objectives, commensurate with client's values, temperament, and risk tolerance. In addition to the client's current financial position, the plan should include the client's projected financial statements under the status quo as well as projected statements if the planner's recommendations are followed. Similarly, the planner should include the current status, projections under the status quo, and projections if recommendations are followed for the following categories: cash flow, estate tax, capital needs at retirement, capital needs at death, capital needs at disability, special capital needs, income taxes, and employee benefits. The planner should also provide a current asset allocation statement along with strategy recommendations and a statement that assumes that the recommendations will be followed. Investments should be summarized, and the planner should propose an investment policy statement and additional policy recommendations. The plan should also include an assessment of risk exposures along with recommendations for insurance and other risk management techniques. Finally, the plan should include a list of prioritized action items.

After developing and preparing the plan, the planner should present the plan to the client and review it with him or her. The planner should collaborate with the client to ensure that the plan meets the goals and objectives of the client and should revise it as appropriate.

Step 5: Implementing the Financial Plan

The planner should assist the client in implementing the recommendations. Often this requires coordinating with other professionals, such as accountants, attorneys, real estate agents, investment advisers, stockbrokers, and insurance agents.

Step 6: Monitoring the Financial Plan

After the plan is implemented, the planner should periodically monitor and evaluate the soundness of recommendations, and review the progress of the plan with the client. The planner should discuss and evaluate changes in the client's personal circumstances such as family births or deaths, illness, divorce, job status, or retirement. Any relevant changes in tax laws and the economic environment should be reviewed and evaluated before the planner makes recommendations to accommodate new or changing circumstances.

Six Steps of Financial Planning: The CFP® Board Model

1. Establish client-planner relationships
2. Gather client data and determine goals and expectations
3. Analyze and evaluate the client's financial status
4. Develop and present the financial plan
5. Implement the financial plan
6. Monitor the financial plan

FINANCIAL PLANNING PRACTICE STANDARDS[*]

Through its certification process, the CFP® Board established fundamental criteria necessary for competency in the personal financial planning profession and, through its *Code of Ethics and Professional Responsibility,* the Board

---

[*] This section is derived with permission from the CFP® Board's website and preserves the original language as much as possible.

TABLE 1A-1
Steps in the Financial Planning Process

Note: Students preparing for the CFP® Board's comprehensive Certification
      Examination should give special attention to the following list of steps in the
      financial planning process, which is also referred to as the Financial Planning
      Task List.

Step 1: Establish Client-Planner Relationship
- Explore with the prospective client his/her financial planning needs and expectations, as well as the CFP® professional's suitability and desire to meet those needs and expectations.
- Discuss with the prospective client issues and concepts related to the overall financial planning process.
- Explain to the prospective client the scope of financial services offered by the CFP® professional and his/her firm.
- Explain the sources and methods of compensation for the services provided.
- Provide to the prospective client disclosures as required by the CFP® Board's Code of Ethics and Professional Responsibility.
- Clarify the prospective client's responsibilities and those of the CFP® professional.
- Mutually define the scope of the engagement.
- Document the scope of the engagement.

Step 2: Gather Client Data and Determine Goals and Expectations
- Obtain information necessary to formulate the financial plan (e.g., through client interviews and questionnaires).
- Collect applicable client records and documents.
- Determine the client's personal and financial goals, needs, and priorities with active client participation.
- Determine the client's time horizon for each identified goal.
- Identify the client's values, attitudes, and expectations that may affect the financial. Determine the client's level of knowledge about financial matters.
- Determine the client's risk tolerance level.

Step 3: Determine the Client's Financial Status Through Analysis and Evaluation
- Analyze and evaluate the client's current financial situation, preparing projections when appropriate:
  - Statement of financial position/balance sheet
  - Cash flow statement/budget
  - Debt (e.g., consumer, mortgage, investment, and contingent liabilities)
  - Estate documents, strategies, and estate tax liabilities
  - Education funding
  - Employee benefits
  - Retirement plans and strategies
  - Special circumstances (e.g., divorce, disabilities, and nontraditional families)
  - Income tax
  - Investments
  - Asset allocation

TABLE 1A-1 (continued)
Steps in the Financial Planning Process

> ➢ Insurance coverage
> ➢ Closely held business
> ➢ Asset protection
> ➢ Capital needs analysis

Step 4: Develop and Present Financial Planning Recommendations and/or
   Alternatives
- Prepare appropriate alternative recommendations to meet the client's goals and objectives.
- Conduct quantitative sensitivity analysis (e.g., changing assumptions, such as inflation rate, rates of return, and time horizon).
- Provide documentation for recommendations where appropriate (e.g., prospectus and financial reports).
- Present alternatives and recommendations, and review assumptions with the client.
- Obtain feedback from the client and revise the recommendations, as appropriate.
- Prioritize action items.
- Obtain client's agreement.

Step 5: Implement the Financial Plan
- Create an implementation plan with an appropriate timeline.
- Implement the recommendations.
- Coordinate as necessary with the client and/or other professionals.

Step 6: Monitor the Financial Plan
- Monitor and evaluate effectiveness of recommendations.
- Review the performance and progress of the plan with the client.
- Discuss and evaluate changes in the client's personal circumstances.
- Review and evaluate changes in the legal, tax, and economic environments.
- Make recommendations to accommodate changed circumstances.

---

identified the ethics standards to which personal financial planning professionals should adhere. Consistent with its objective to promote professional standards and continuing competency among CFP® designees, the CFP® Board subsequently addressed standards of practice for personal financial planning and established the Board of Practice Standards, a subsidiary board consisting exclusively of CFP® practitioners. The Board of Practice Standards developed 10 practice standards, which the Board of Governors adopted with a few revisions and technical corrections.

Practice standards establish the level of professional practice that is expected of CFP® designees engaged in personal financial planning. The services provided depend on the facts and circumstances of a particular situation. Practice standards (1) ensure that the practice of financial planning by CFP® designees is based on agreed-upon norms of practice, (2) advance professionalism in financial planning, and (3) enhance the value of the personal financial planning process.

Practice standards apply to CFP® designees in performing the tasks of personal financial planning regardless of the person's title, job position, type of employment, or method of compensation. Practice standards should be considered by all personal financial planning professionals when performing the financial planning task or activity addressed by the standard, but they are enforceable by the CFP® Board only against CFP® designees. Conduct inconsistent with a standard in and of itself is not intended to give rise to a cause of action or to create any presumption that a legal duty has been breached. The standards are designed to provide CFP® designees a structure for identifying and implementing expectations regarding the professional practice of personal financial planning. They are not designed to be a basis for legal liability.

Practice standards are not intended to prescribe step-by-step procedures for providing any particular service. Such procedures may be provided in practice aids developed by various financial planning organizations and other sources. The practice of financial planning consistent with these standards is required for CFP® designees and will be enforced by the CFP® Board.

Practice Standard 100-1: Defining the Scope of the Engagement

The financial planning practitioner and the client shall mutually define the scope of the engagement before any financial planning service is provided.

Prior to providing any financial planning service, a financial planning practitioner and the client shall mutually define the scope of the engagement. The process of "mutually defining" is essential in determining what activities may be necessary to proceed with the client engagement. This is accomplished by

- identifying the service(s) to be provided
- disclosing financial planning practitioner's compensation arrangement(s)
- determining the client's and the financial planning practitioner's responsibilities
- establishing the duration of the engagement
- providing any additional information necessary to define or limit the scope

The scope of the engagement may include one or more financial planning subject areas. It is acceptable to mutually define engagements in which the scope is limited to specific activities. This serves to establish realistic expectations both for the client and the practitioner.

This practice standard does not require the scope of the engagement to be in writing. However, Rule 402 in the *Code of Ethics and Professional Respon-*

sibility requires a financial planning practitioner to make "timely written disclosure of all material information relative to the professional relationship. In all circumstances such disclosure shall include sources of compensation."

Practice Standard 200-1: Determining a Client's Personal and Financial Goals, Needs, and Priorities

The financial planning practitioner and the client shall mutually define the client's personal and financial goals, needs, and priorities that are relevant to the scope of the engagement before any recommendation is made and/or implemented.

Prior to making recommendations to a client, a financial planning practitioner and the client shall mutually define the client's personal and financial goals, needs, and priorities. In order to arrive at such a definition, the practitioner will need to explore the client's values, attitudes, expectations, and time horizons as they affect the client's goals, needs, and priorities. The process of "mutually defining" is essential in determining what activities may be necessary to proceed with the client engagement. Personal values and attitudes shape a client's goals and objectives and the priority placed on them. Accordingly, these goals and objectives must be consistent with the client's values and attitudes in order for the client to make the commitment necessary to accomplish them.

Goals and objectives provide focus, purpose, vision, and direction for the financial planning process. It is essential that objectives relative to the scope of the engagement are determined and that they are clear, precise, consistent, and measurable. The role of the practitioner is to facilitate the goal-setting process in order to clarify, with the client, goals and objectives, and, when appropriate, the practitioner must try to assist clients in recognizing the implications of unrealistic goals and objectives.

This practice standard addresses only the tasks of determining a client's personal and financial goals, needs, and priorities; assessing a client's values, attitudes, and expectations; and determining a client's time horizons. These areas are subjective, and the practitioner's interpretation is limited by what the client reveals. A practitioner performing the activity of "gathering client data" should consider together the various practice standards applicable to such activity.

Practice Standard 200-2: Obtaining Quantitative Information and Documents

The financial planning practitioner shall obtain sufficient quantitative information and documents about a client relevant to the scope of the engagement before any recommendation is made and/or implemented.

Prior to making recommendations to a client and depending upon the type of client engagement and its scope, a financial planning practitioner shall determine what quantitative information and documents are sufficient and relevant.

A practitioner shall obtain sufficient and relevant quantitative information and documents pertaining to the client's financial resources, obligations, and personal situation. This information may be obtained directly from the client or other sources through interview, questionnaire, client records, and documents.

A practitioner shall communicate to the client a reliance on the completeness and accuracy of the information provided and that incomplete or inaccurate information will affect conclusions and recommendations.

If a practitioner is unable to obtain sufficient and relevant quantitative information and documents to form a basis for recommendations, the practitioner shall either: (a) restrict the scope of the engagement to those matters for which sufficient and relevant information is available; or (b) terminate the engagement.

A practitioner shall communicate to the client any limitations on the scope of the engagement, as well as the fact that this limitation could affect the conclusions and recommendations.

Practice Standard 300-1: Analyzing and Evaluating the Client's Information

The financial planning practitioner shall analyze the information to gain an understanding of the client's financial situation and then evaluate to what extent the client's goals, needs, and priorities can be met by the client's resources and current course of action.

Prior to making recommendations to a client, it is necessary for the financial planning practitioner to assess the client's financial situation and to determine the likelihood of reaching the stated objectives by continuing present activities.

The practitioner will utilize client specified, mutually agreed upon, and/or other reasonable assumptions. Both personal and economic assumptions must be considered in this step of the process. These assumptions may include but are not limited to the following: personal assumptions, such as retirement age(s), life expectancy(ies), income needs, risk factors, time horizon, and special needs; and economic assumptions, such as inflation rates, tax rates, and investment returns.

Analysis and evaluation are critical to the financial planning process. These activities form the foundation for determining strengths and weaknesses of the client's financial situation and current course of action. These activities may also identify other issues that should be addressed. As a result, it may be appropriate to amend the scope of the engagement and/or to obtain additional information.

Practice Standard 400-1: Identifying and Evaluating Financial Planning Alternative(s)

The financial planning practitioner shall consider sufficient and relevant alternatives to the client's current course of action in an effort to reasonably meet the client's goals, needs, and priorities.

After analyzing the client's current situation (Practice Standard 300-1), and prior to developing and presenting the recommendation(s) (Practice Standards 400-2 and 400-3), the financial planning practitioner shall identify alternative actions. The practitioner shall evaluate the effectiveness of such actions in reasonably achieving the client's goals, needs, and priorities.

This evaluation may involve, but is not limited to, considering multiple assumptions, conducting research, or consulting with other professionals. This process may result in a single alternative, multiple alternatives, or no alternative to the client's current course of action.

In considering alternative actions, the practitioner also must recognize and, as appropriate, take into account his or her legal and/or regulatory limitations and level of competency in properly addressing each of the client's financial planning issues.

More than one alternative may reasonably achieve the client's goals, needs, and priorities. Alternatives identified by the practitioner may differ from those of other practitioners or advisers, illustrating the subjective nature of exercising professional judgment.

Practice Standard 400-2: Developing the Financial Planning Recommendation(s)

The financial planning practitioner shall develop the recommendation(s) based on the selected alternative(s) and the current course of action in an effort to reasonably meet the client's goals, needs, and priorities.

After identifying and evaluating the alternative(s) and the client's current course of action, the practitioner shall develop the recommendation(s) expected to reasonably achieve the client's goals, needs, and priorities. A recommendation may be an independent action or a combination of actions that may need to be implemented collectively.

The recommendation(s) shall be consistent with, and will be directly affected by, the following:

- a mutually defined scope of the engagement
- mutually defined client goals, needs, and priorities
- quantitative data provided by the client
- personal and economic assumptions

- the practitioner's analysis and evaluation of client's current situation
- alternative(s) selected by the practitioner

A recommendation may be to continue the current course of action. If a change is recommended, it may be specific and/or detailed or provide a general direction. In some instances, it may be necessary for the practitioner to recommend that the client modify a goal.

The recommendations developed by the practitioner may differ from those of other practitioners or advisers, yet each may reasonably achieve the client's goals, needs, and priorities.

Practice Standard 400-3: Presenting the Financial Planning Recommendation(s)

The financial planning practitioner shall communicate the recommendation(s) in a manner and to an extent reasonably necessary to assist the client in making an informed decision.

When presenting a recommendation, the practitioner shall make a reasonable effort to assist the client in understanding the client's current situation, the recommendation itself, and its effect on the ability to achieve the client's goals, needs, and priorities. In doing so, the practitioner shall avoid presenting the practitioner's opinion as fact.

The practitioner shall communicate the factors critical to the client's understanding of the recommendations. These factors may include but are not limited to the following material:

- personal and economic assumptions
- interdependence of recommendations
- advantages and disadvantages
- risks
- time sensitivity

The practitioner should indicate that even though the recommendations may achieve the client's goals, needs, and priorities, changes in personal and economic conditions could alter the intended outcome. Changes may include (but are not limited to) legislative, family status, career, investment performance, and/or health.

If there are conflicts of interest that have not been previously disclosed, such conflicts and how they may affect the recommendations should be addressed at this time.

Presenting recommendations provides the practitioner an opportunity to further assess whether the recommendations meet client expectations, whether the client is willing to act on the recommendations, and whether modifications are necessary.

Practice Standard 500-1: Agreeing on Implementation Responsibilities

The financial planning practitioner and the client shall mutually agree on the implementation responsibilities consistent with the scope of the engagement.

The client is responsible for accepting or rejecting recommendations and for retaining and/or delegating implementation responsibilities. The financial planning practitioner and the client shall mutually agree on the services, if any, to be provided by the practitioner. The scope of the engagement, as originally defined, may need to be modified.

The practitioner's responsibilities may include, but are not limited to, the following:

- identifying activities necessary for implementation
- determining division of activities between the practitioner and the client
- referring to other professionals
- coordinating with other professionals
- sharing of information as authorized
- selecting and securing products and/or services

If there are conflicts of interest, sources of compensation, or material relationships with other professionals or advisers that have not been previously disclosed, such conflicts, sources, or relationships must be disclosed at this time.

When referring the client to other professionals or advisers, the financial planning practitioner shall indicate the basis for the referral.

If the practitioner is engaged by the client to provide only implementation activities, the scope of the engagement shall be mutually defined, orally or in writing, in accordance with Practice Standard 100-1. This scope may include such matters as the extent to which the practitioner will rely on information, analysis, or recommendations provided by others.

Practice Standard 500-2: Selecting Products and Services for Implementation

The financial planning practitioner shall select appropriate products and services that are consistent with the client's goals, needs, and priorities.

The financial planning practitioner will use professional judgement in selecting the products and services that are in the client's interest. Professional judgement incorporates both qualitative and quantitative information. A financial planning practitioner shall reasonably investigate and evaluate products or services that address the client's needs. The practitioner shall have a reasonable basis for believing that the products or services selected are suitable for the client.

Products and services selected by the practitioner may differ from those selected by other practitioners or advisers. Alternative products or services may be suitable for the client and could reasonably achieve the client's goals, needs, and priorities, illustrating the subjective nature of exercising professional judgement.

The practitioner must make all disclosures required to comply with applicable regulations.

Practice Standard 600-1: Defining Monitoring Responsibilities

The financial planning practitioner and client shall mutually define monitoring responsibilities.

The purpose of this standard is to clarify the extent of the practitioner's role in the monitoring process. The practitioner and the client may have different perceptions about monitoring responsibilities.

When monitoring is included in the scope of the engagement, the financial planning practitioner shall identify which monitoring activities may be appropriate. The practitioner shall make a reasonable effort to define and communicate which monitoring activities the practitioner is able and willing to provide.

The practitioner and client shall mutually agree on the extent, frequency, and duration of the monitoring activities, if any, to be provided by the practitioner. The scope of the engagement, as originally defined, may need to be modified.

Monitoring responsibilities may include but are not limited to:

- identifying changes in conditions that would affect existing recommendations
- obtaining information from the client to determine changes in personal circumstances
- reviewing work done by other professionals or providers
- reviewing the client's progress toward financial goals

The monitoring process may reveal the need to reinitiate any or all of the steps of the financial planning process.

Advisory Opinions

Another way that the CFP® Board provides guidance to CFP® designees is through the issuance of Advisory Opinions. The CFP® Board's Board of Professional Review has published two Advisory Opinions, which help clarify the Board's interpretation of its Code of Ethics and Professional Responsibility.

The two Advisory Opinions in effect are as follows:

- *Advisory Opinion 2001-1:* Loans between CFP® Board designees and their clients should be avoided in the client-planner relationship.
- *Advisory Opinion 2003-1:* CFP® Board designees must avoid possible misrepresentation when using the term "fee only."

Additional information about these advisory opinions is available at the CFP® Board's website, www.cfp.net.

CONTENT OF A COMPREHENSIVE FINANCIAL PLAN

For those cases in which the planner is called upon to prepare a comprehensive financial plan for a client, whether entirely in one engagement or incrementally over a period of years, what should the plan contain? Clearly, comprehensive financial planning is such an ambitious and complex undertaking that it must cover numerous elements. For quality of service and protection from lawsuits, financial planning practitioners need guidelines to make certain that their plans are truly comprehensive. Likewise, consumers need assurance that a planner will be able to provide a well-rounded, comprehensive plan that spans all aspects of his or her financial situation. Each group benefits from the existence of a set of standards by which a comprehensive financial plan can be judged.

Elements of a Comprehensive Financial Plan: General Guidelines

Over a decade ago, the Registry of Financial Planning Professionals developed the following guidelines for comprehensive financial plans. They represent the first formal, written presentation of a set of standards for practitioners to follow. Although the Registry no longer exists, the guidelines are still valid.

Overview of Plan Elements

A comprehensive financial plan should contain an analysis of all pertinent factors relating to the client. While order and style of presentation may vary, the plan should include, but not necessarily be limited to, the following elements:

1. Personal data
2. Client goals and objectives
3. Identification of issues and problems

4. Assumptions
5. Balance sheet/net worth
6. Cash-flow management
7. Income tax
8. Risk management/insurance
9. Investments
10. Financial independence, retirement planning, education, and other special needs
11. Estate planning
12. Recommendations
13. Implementation

When developing a comprehensive financial plan, the planner is responsible for all of the elements of the plan, from data gathering through analysis and presentation to the client. Those elements of the plan that the planner does not personally perform remain the responsibility of the planner to coordinate.

When technical areas (such as legal and insurance services) are not personally performed by the planner, the financial plan or supplement should include supporting documentation that these areas have been or will be coordinated by the planner.

Analysis of each element of the plan should consist of a review of pertinent facts, a consideration of the advantages and/or disadvantages of the current situation, and a determination of what, if any, further action is required. The plan should include a summary statement providing the planner's comments on the analysis and his or her recommendations, where appropriate, for each element of the plan.

Guidelines for A Comprehensive Financial Plan

1. **Personal Data**

     Should include relevant personal and family data for parties covered under the plan.

    - Should include, but not be limited to, name, address, social security number, birth date, and other relevant data.

2. **Client Goals and Objectives**

     A reiteration of the client's stated goals and objectives, indicating their priority and including a time frame where applicable.

    - The statement of goals and objectives will form the basic framework for the development of the financial plan.
    - The client's goals and objectives should be expressed in as specific and precise language as possible. For example, a

statement of a goal should read "Retire at age 62 in present home and maintain a current standard of living" rather than "A comfortable retirement."

3. Identification of Issues and Problems

A plan must address relevant issues and problems identified by the client, the planner, and/or other advisers.

- List personal and financial issues and problems that affect the client, such as major illness, education costs, taxes, etc. While the client may be aware of many, if not all, of the issues, the planner may discover other areas that are or could develop into problems.
- These issues and problems, when combined with the client's goals and objectives, will complete the framework and direction for the financial plan. Since style and order are not the primary consideration, the analysis of recommendation section(s) of the plan may be more appropriate for identifying issues and problems.

4. Assumptions

Identify and state material assumptions used in the plan's preparation.

- Assumptions should include, but not be limited to, inflation, investment growth rate, mortality, etc.

5. Balance Sheet/Net Worth

A presentation and analysis to include, but not be limited to, a schedule listing assets and liabilities with a calculation of net worth and itemized schedules of liabilities and assets to be included as appropriate.

- In addition to the schedules, footnotes should be included as appropriate.

6. Cash-Flow Management

Statements and analysis to include, but not be limited to, a statement of the client's sources and uses of funds for the current year and for all relevant years, indicating net cash flow, as well as a separate income statement, where appropriate.

- Sources—earned income, investment income, sale proceeds, gifts, etc.
- Uses—living expenses, debt service, acquisition of assets, taxes paid, etc.
- Net cash flow—both positive and negative.

7. Income Tax

An income tax statement and analysis to include, but not be limited to, the income taxes for the current year and for all relevant years covered in the plan.

- Projections should show the nature of the income and deductions in sufficient detail to permit calculation of the tax liability. The analysis should identify the marginal tax rate for each year and any special situations, such as alternative minimum tax, passive loss limitations, etc., that affect the client's tax liability.
- The financial plan should include footnotes to let the client know which taxes (i.e., state or city) have not been addressed.

8. Risk Management/Insurance

A. Analysis of a client's financial exposure relative to mortality, morbidity, liability, and property, including business as appropriate.

- Mortality—survivor income and capital needs analysis.
- Morbidity—effect of loss of health.
- Liability—legal exposure.
- Property—loss of value.
- Business—loss due to business involvement.

B. Listing and analysis of current policies and problems to include, but not be limited to, life, disability, medical, business, property/casualty, and liability.

- Analysis of existing coverage and/or risk exposure in relationship to the client's needs, goals, and objectives.
- If any area of insurance is not within the competency range of the financial planner, the planner has the responsibility to coordinate with other professionals and document such coordination in the financial plan. Documentation of the above areas can include the insurance professional's summary, if completed, or the professional's name and time frame when such review will be completed.

9. Investments

A listing of the current investment portfolio and an analysis or discussion of the liquidity, diversification, and investment risk exposure of the portfolio. In addition, the suitability of the investments in relationship to the client's needs, goals, and objectives should be addressed to include, but not be limited to, risk tolerance, risk management of investments, suitability, liquidity, diversification, and personal management efforts.

- Risk tolerance—addresses the client's willingness to accept investment risk.
- Risk management—analysis of client's exposure relative to loss of invested capital.
- Suitability—appropriateness of the investment for the client.
- Liquidity—the availability of assets that can be converted into cash at acceptable costs.
- Diversification—appropriate mix of assets to meet the client's needs, goals, and objectives.
- Personal management efforts—the degree to which the client wants to manage and is capable of managing his or her assets.

10. **Financial Independence, Retirement Planning, Education, and Other Special Needs**

   An analysis of the capital needed at some future time to provide for financial independence, retirement, education, or other special needs. The analysis should include a projection of resources expected to be available to meet these needs at that time.

- In achieving the above, inflation, growth of assets and company benefits should be considered where applicable.
- Special sections of the above topics may require a separate heading in the financial plan. For example, company benefits may require an analysis of types available, pre- and post-tax contributions needed, tax treatment of plans, and investment of benefit plan assets.

11. **Estate Planning**

   Identification of assets that can be included in the client's estate and an analysis of the control, disposition, and taxation of those assets.

- Control—authority to manage or direct the use of assets by means of title, trusteeship, power of attorney, etc.
- Disposition—transfer of ownership by will, trust, beneficiary designation, or operation of the law.
- Taxation—taxation of the client's estate and the income tax and estate tax consequences to the beneficiaries.

12. **Recommendations**

   Written recommendations that relate to goals and objectives as well as financial issues and problems.

- Written recommendations should specifically address the client's goals and objectives and all issues and problems identified in the plan, as well as a determination of the actions necessary to compensate for any shortfalls. Recommendations should be clearly identified and stated. They should not be conveyed by implication or inference.

13. Implementation

A prioritized list of actions required to implement the recommendations, indicating responsible parties, action required, and timing.

- Implementation should include a schedule reflecting actions to be taken as well as priority, dates, and responsible parties.

Elements of a Comprehensive Financial Plan: CFP® Board Guidelines

The CFP® Board of Standards addressed elements of a comprehensive financial plan in its 1996 *Job Knowledge Requirements*. (This document has been superseded by the *Topic List for CFP® Certification Examinations*.) The *Job Knowledge Requirements* specified that a comprehensive plan should be tailored to meet the goals and objectives of the client, commensurate with the client's values, temperament, and risk tolerance, and that it should address the following items:

1. Financial position
2. Cash flow
3. Estate tax
4. Capital needs: retirement
5. Capital needs: projections at death
6. Capital needs: disability
7. Capital needs: special needs
8. Income tax
9. Employee benefits
10. Asset allocation
11. Investments
12. Risk exposures
13. List of prioritized items

Securities Markets and Market Mechanics

Learning Objectives

An understanding of the material in this chapter should enable the student to

---

2-1.   Explain the difference between the primary and the secondary markets.

2-2.   Describe the institutions and the people associated with the secondary market.

2-3.   Describe the various trading costs, types of orders, and the process of short selling.

2-4.   Describe the critical laws that affect trading today.

2-5.   Discuss the pros and cons of owning in street name, the different types of accounts, and how one can measure the volume of trading activity in an account.

Chapter Outline

This chapter explores the structure of U.S. securities markets, the mechanics and regulation of these markets, and the mechanics of trading. We will consider first the primary market, which is where companies issue securities to raise cash. Then we will look at the players, the institutions, and the transactions of the secondary market. We will then consider some of the more critical laws affecting markets.

THE PRIMARY MARKET

When corporations want to acquire cash, they issue new securities. Corporations' sales of newly created securities to investors are referred to as the primary market. Investment bankers are the people who handle the sale of new securities, and the process is referred to as underwriting the offering.

Investment Bankers

Most large brokerage firms have investment banking divisions. An investment bank works with companies to facilitate the issuance of new securities, and with holders of large blocks of shares to facilitate the resale of these securities. Think of an investment banker or underwriter as a wholesaler of securities.

Once an issue has been sold in the primary market, all subsequent trades take place in the secondary market. Some shares of a primary distribution may already be actively traded in the secondary market. Alternatively, the

go public

**initial public
offering (IPO)**

stock of the issuing firm may have heretofore been privately held (owned by one person or a small number of people). A private firm that sells a substantial block of additional shares and thereby creates a more active and diverse ownership is said to *go public,* and this sale of shares is known as an *initial public offering (IPO)*. When the issue is large, the investment banker assembles a syndicate to underwrite the issue.

To initiate a public offering, the issuing firm and its investment banker compose a registration statement. This is submitted to the Securities and Exchange Commission (SEC) for review. During the review period, the investment banker may distribute this registration statement. Because the front page of this statement contains a paragraph in red ink indicating that the company is not attempting to sell its shares before the SEC approves the registration, it is known as a *red herring*. Red herrings are sometimes revised several times before the issue is ready for sale to the public.

red herring

Once the SEC gives its approval, the investment banker may proceed with the offering. A final offering price is set, along with the size of the issue. The investment banker must give to each prospective buyer a prospectus. The main difference between a red herring and a prospectus is that the former omits the selling price and the size of the issue.

The investment banker's underwriting fees are deducted from the proceeds. Most offerings are done on a *firm-commitment basis*, which means that the investment banker buys the offering from the firm and resells it to the market. The investment banker bears the risk if the offering is less than fully successful, and occasionally absorbs huge losses in this process.

**firm-commitment
basis**

best-effort basis

Sometimes the underwriting is taken on a *best-effort basis*, in which case the investment banker acts as an agent for the issuing firm. Best efforts are used when the investment banker feels there is significant risk that the issue may not completely sell.

Financial Planning Issue

There are three nice features to having a client subscribe to a primary offering. First, the investor directly pays no commission. Second, one of the banker's obligations is to attempt to maintain a floor price for the securities offered, thus reducing the risk of an immediate loss. Third, research shows that, on average, primary offerings are usually slightly underpriced, thus producing a slight windfall gain in the first few days of trading. As a result, there is usually more demand to subscribe to a new offering than there are shares available.

Sometimes the market goes through a period in which IPOs become a "hot" commodity. Some IPOs will double in value during the first day or first few days of trading. Hot markets are particularly good times to be a participant in an IPO if one can get shares.

Shelf Registration

While most primary sales are marketed quickly after their registration, the SEC's Rule 415 permits shelf registration. Under this rule, a firm can file one registration statement for a relatively large block of stock and then sell parts of it over a 2-year period. The shelf registration option tends to reduce red tape and expenses, and because the stock can be sold directly to institutional investors, it sometimes eliminates the underwriting fee.

Private Placements

New issues are sometimes sold in large lots to a small group of buyers in what is called a private placement. These placements allow start-up firms to demonstrate viability by successfully raising some capital on their own. Additional shares may subsequently be marketed to the public through an underwriter. The private placements are usually sold below the public offering price. In exchange for a favorable price, the initial investors may agree to accept lettered stock. Under SEC Rule 144, *lettered stock* can be resold only after a holding period of at least 2 years and in a gradual manner that does not disrupt trading markets. Many debt issues are placed privately, usually to large buyers, such as insurance companies.

lettered stock

THE SECONDARY MARKET: THE PLAYERS

It is the secondary market that most people think about when the stock market is mentioned. It takes a variety of people and institutions to make the secondary market work. In this section, we will consider the key people in this market. In the next two sections, we will look at the institutions and the mechanics of trading.

Brokers, Dealers, and Brokerage Firms

The term broker/dealer is a term used to describe an individual or a company that is licensed to buy investment products for or sell them to clients. Companies that sell securities that they own are referred to as dealers. Firms that only buy and sell securities on behalf of investors are known as brokers. Brokers implement their customers' trading instructions and act as the customer's agent. A dealer, in contrast, trades for his or her own accounts and makes markets by advertising a willingness to buy and sell. To be in the securities business, an individual or a company must be a broker/dealer or an individual must be affiliated with a broker/dealer as a *registered representative*. Although some people refer to both the individual who handles their accounts and to the firm employing said individual as their

registered representative

broker, technically the term broker means the employee, and the term brokerage firm (or brokerage house) means the employer.

Brokers must be licensed to sell securities. They typically hold one of two licenses issued by the National Association of Securities Dealers (NASD) upon successful completion of the appropriate exam. The most common is known as *Series 7*, or general securities registered representative license. This license qualifies the broker to solicit, purchase, and/or sell all securities products, including corporate securities, municipal securities, options, direct participation programs, investment company products, and variable contracts. The other is the *Series 6* license, which qualifies the broker to sell open-end mutual funds, initial offerings of closed-end investment companies, and such variable products as variable annuities provided the individual also holds the appropriate insurance license.

Series 7

Series 6

As the financial services industry has become more product integrated in recent years, many brokerage firms have added such product lines as CDs, life insurance, portfolio management plans, and financial planning. As brokerage firms have expanded into these new areas, other types of financial service firms have expanded into their areas. Although the lines between brokerage firms and other financial services firms, particularly commercial banks and insurance companies, have been eroding for years, the erosion accelerated with the passage of the *Gramm-Leach-Bliley Act* in 1999 that repealed the Glass-Steagall Act (the Bank Act of 1933). The *Glass-Steagall Act* prohibited investment banks from operating commercial banks and vice versa. Indeed, some nonfinancial firms have entered the field, mainly through acquisitions.

Gramm-Leach-Bliley Act

Glass-Steagall Act

What Should Investors Expect of a Broker?

The brokerage industry can be dichotomized as full-service firms and discount firms. Although not every firm can be perfectly classified in this scheme, the general distinction is that in full-service brokerage firms, a specific individual handles each account. The emphasis is on personalized service, including such things as investment research advice. Full-service brokers will contact their customers to suggest trades. Most full-service firms allow the establishment of discretionary accounts (which are discussed in the next section). Historically, the income of most stockbrokers who work at full-service brokerage firms is based solely on the commissions they generate. The commission the investor pays on trades is split between the firm and the broker. Generally, the higher the total commissions a broker produces in a year, the higher the percentage of those commissions the broker keeps.

In a discount brokerage firm, accounts are with the firm, not a specific broker. Customers simply place an order with the firm rather than with a specific broker. A discount broker never calls a customer to initiate a trade.

Accounts at discount brokerage firms are for investors who want to manage their own accounts and seek to minimize the cost of maintaining their accounts.

Until a few years ago, it was easy to distinguish the level of service between a full-service broker and a discount broker. More recently, the distinction has blurred. Many of the traditional full-service brokerage firms are moving to implement discount service operations for those customers who want substantially discounted commissions. In addition, many of the discount brokerage firms are seeking ways to provide higher levels of service for those customers who want more personalized contact. It should be noted that having more personalized service at a discount brokerage firm typically requires the customer to have in the account a significant amount of assets. Some firms require a minimum of $500,000 or $1 million in assets for personalized service.

Discretionary and Other Accounts

In a discretionary account, the investor appoints his or her financial advisor a "true, sufficient, and lawful agent and attorney-in-fact to act on my behalf and in my name."[1] These accounts may also be known as controlled accounts or managed accounts. There are generally two rationales for opening a discretionary account. One is that, although the investor continues to be the primary decision maker, he or she does not want to miss an attractive trading opportunity if the broker cannot reach the investor in a timely manner. The other rationale for a discretionary account is that the investor wants his or her broker to act as the portfolio manager and to make the trades that he or she deems appropriate for the account. An alternative to a discretionary account is the *limited discretionary account*, in which the investor gives the broker the authority to make only certain types of trades without prior consent. Discretionary accounts can be of any size.

limited discretionary account

wrap account

Similar to a discretionary account is the *wrap account*. Some firms also refer to this as a separate account or managed account, although this latter term could simply mean a discretionary account. In wrap accounts, a single annual fee known as a *wrap fee* is paid. This covers all commissions as well as any other expenses incidental to the account. In discretionary accounts, the only income to the broker is the commission from each trade. Wrap accounts can be solicited whereas discretionary accounts are opened as a matter of convenience to clients. There is always a minimum size to open a wrap account; many firms require assets of at least $100,000.

wrap fee

Discretionary accounts create an obvious potential for conflict of interest on the part of the broker in that he or she may make some trades for the primary purpose of enhancing his or her commission income rather than for the benefit of the client, a practice known as *churning*. In a managed account,

churning

churning would be counterproductive because the fee for the account is fixed and independent of the amount of trading activity.

It is tempting to compare wrap or separate accounts to mutual funds. The wrap fee usually appears to be much larger than the management fees paid on a mutual fund. Nonetheless, there may be some advantages to a wrap account. These include:

- customization. The portfolio can be tailored to an individual's specific needs. Clients may choose not to hold a particular company or industry for personal, ethical, or economic reasons.
- tax efficiency. Optimal tax treatment can be achieved.
- simple fee structure. The single wrap fee makes the cost of the account clear, unlike the complex and sometimes hidden nature of fees in a mutual fund.

The Specialist

The stock exchanges (described in the next section) base their trading on specialists. The specialist is charged with making a market in a particular security. This means the specialist stands ready to trade with anyone in that particular stock. It is the existence of the specialist that guarantees the marketability of stocks. The specialist is also charged with maintaining a smooth continuity to the trading of a particular stock. He or she does this by providing bid and asked quotations and by maintaining an inventory of their assigned stocks. (See figure 2-1.) A given specialist may make markets in a dozen or so securities.

The specialist is expected to fill any temporary gaps by offering to buy or sell as necessary. Specialists are supposed to be net buyers when the public wishes to be net sellers. Under normal circumstances, specialists' firms may be managing a few stocks that are under selling pressure while others have more public buyers than sellers. During the October 1987 crash, however, almost all of the public orders were on the sell side. Most of the specialists' capital was quickly committed. Some firms were unable to provide an orderly market as they were hit with more and more sell orders at lower and lower prices.

Registered Competitive Market Makers (RCMMs)

floor traders

Individuals called registered competitive market makers (RCMMs) or *floor traders* serve a role as a back-up specialist.[2] RCMMs own exchange seats and trade for their own account. However, they also have "a specific Exchange-imposed obligation to enhance the quality of NYSE markets by injecting their own or their firms' capital into difficult market-making

---

FIGURE 2-1
Four Roles of Specialists

Specialist as Auctioneer
The specialist continually shows the best bids and offers throughout the trading day. These quotes are disseminated electronically through the NYSE quote and other market data systems that transmit the information instantly worldwide. The specialist maintains order in the crowd and interacts with agents representing customers.

Specialist as Agent
A specialist is the agent for all SuperDot (electronically routed) orders. A floor broker may also choose to leave an order with a specialist to represent it until it can be executed at a specified price. This frees brokers up to concentrate on other orders that require their immediate attention. As agent, a specialist assumes the same fiduciary responsibility as a broker.

Specialist as Catalyst
Unique to the agency-auction is the specialist as a conduit of order flow. The specialist knows who has been interested in a stock, and keeps track of all known interest. As all buyers and sellers aren't always represented in the crowd at the same time, the specialist can call in all interested parties to let them know what has become available in the market. By giving updates to a previously interested party, a specialist helps trades occur where they otherwise might not happen.

Specialist as Principal
Specialists, in order to fulfill their role, agree to several obligations. The first is to place and execute all customer orders ahead of their own. At the NYSE, three out of four transactions take place between customers, without the capital participation of the specialist.

Reproduced from the "Specialist" entry in the glossary of the New York Stock Exchange's web site, http://www.nyse.com. Used with the permission of NYSE.

---

situations. At the request of an Exchange official, an RCMM must make a bid or offer that narrows an existing quote spread or improves its depth. An RCMM may also be asked to assist a commission broker or floor broker in executing a customer's otherwise nonexecutable order."[3] The failure of an RCMM to enter into trading upon request can result in a financial penalty, suspension, or even loss of the use of one's membership.

Floor Brokers

Floor brokers can either be commission or independent brokers. A commission broker is associated with a specific firm, e.g., Merrill Lynch. An independent broker will accept orders from any of the firms. When an investor places an order with his or her stockbroker or brokerage firm, it is transmitted to a floor broker—either their firms' commission brokers or independent brokers—for execution on the trading floor.

THE SECONDARY MARKET: THE INSTITUTIONS

Any two people can get together and trade a stock or any other investment, just as they can trade used cars. The one catch with regard to trading securities directly is that the issuer of the security must be notified of the change in ownership. One of the major pillars of any economy is the strength of its financial markets in terms of the quantity of trading of securities that occurs. The United States has the strongest and deepest set of trading institutions of any country in the world.

The Stock Exchanges

New York Stock Exchange

In terms of the market value of trades, and the market value of companies listed on an exchange, the dominant trading institution is the New York Stock Exchange (NYSE). Only members can transact business on the exchange, and only listed securities may be traded. A membership is referred to as a *seat,* and there are 1,366 seats. There is actually a market in seats on the NYSE. The price of a seat may be quite volatile. For example, a seat traded for $1,850,000 on September 18, 2003. The next trade was on October 23, when two seats exchanged hands for $1,350,000.

seat

Seats on the NYSE did not always trade as a marketable asset. Originally, the number of NYSE memberships simply waxed or waned as people acquired seats or died or resigned from their membership. It was in 1868 that the exchange fixed the number of seats and revised its rules to allow members to sell their seats. At that time, seats traded for as little as $4,000 (although that was certainly a great deal of money back then). By 1900, prices had soared to $80,000. The highest price ever paid for a seat, which was on August 23, 1999, was $2.65 million. The major determinant of the price of a seat has been the trading volume on the NYSE, although the general level of stock prices played a role when brokerage commissions were based on a percentage of the stock price. Rules regarding seats have now been relaxed enough that an owner may actually lease out his or her seat.[4]

In June 2004, the NYSE had about 2,800 listed companies with a market value of nearly $18 trillion. Of these, 470 were non-U.S.-based companies, whose market value was about $6 trillion.[5] The number of securities listed on the NYSE is well over 3,000, because many companies list not only their common stock on the exchange but their preferred stock, warrants, and rights as well. To be listed on the exchange, a company must apply, pay initial and any annual listing fees, and meet certain initial and continuing listing market value and accounting value requirements. Some of these requirements are shown in table 2-1. Most companies on the NYSE exceed these minimum requirements by a wide margin.

TABLE 2-1
U.S. Company Listing Requirements

	NYSE	NASDAQ/NMI	Amex[6]
Pretax income (most recent year)	$2.5 million[7]	$1 million	$.75 million
Stockholders' equity	Not specified	$15 million	$4 million
Shares publicly held	1.1 million	1.1 million	.5 million[8]
Market value of public shares	$100 million	$8 million	$3 million
Number of round-lot holders	2,000[9]	400	Not specified
Minimum share price	$1	$5	$3

The initial listing fee ranges from $150,000 to $250,000, and the continuing listing fee is up to $35,000. Companies are delisted from the NYSE if their share price drops below $1, their market capitalization drops below $15 million, or both their market capitalization and their shareholders' equity drops below $50 million.

American Stock Exchange

For many years, the next-largest exchange had been the American Stock Exchange (Amex). In 1998, the NASD acquired the Amex. On November 3, 2003, the Amex announced it had reached an agreement with the NASD to once again become an independent organization. The Amex started out as a group of traders who met on a particular street to trade securities. After World War II, the group opted to become more formal and move indoors. Because of its early trading location, the Amex carries the nickname the *curb exchange*, which refers to a street curb.

curb exchange

Traditionally, the Amex has been the exchange for firms too small to be listed on the NYSE. Currently there are about 1,000 stocks listed on the Amex. The Amex is also one of the largest exchanges for the trading of options, and it also provides bond trading. The requirements to be listed on the Amex are shown in table 2-1. Although the minimum requirements are clearly lower than those for the NYSE, not every firm immediately moves from the Amex to the NYSE at the earliest opportunity.

The Regional Exchanges

The NYSE and Amex are national exchanges in that their listings are national, and even international, in nature. There are five other exchanges around the country that are known as regional exchanges. A regional exchange has substantially lower listing requirements than the Amex, and it specializes primarily in companies located in that region. In addition, some

dual listing

of the regionals accept NYSE-listed companies for *dual listing,* meaning that the company is traded on both exchanges.

One of the largest regional exchanges is the Chicago Stock Exchange (CSE). It currently lists over 3,500 stocks, which includes stocks dually listed with the NYSE, the Amex, or the NASDAQ as well as its own exclusive listings. Another major regional is the Pacific Exchange (PCX). Although this exchange traces its roots back to 1882, its modern form was established in 1957. The Pacific exchange trades options on more than 1,200 firms. The PCX is also the regulator of the Archipelago Exchange (ArcaEx), a fully electronic market for securities listed on the NYSE, the Amex, the Pacific Exchange, and the NASDAQ Market. The remaining regionals include the Boston Stock Exchange (BSE), which lists approximately 2,000 stocks; the Philadelphia Stock Exchange (PSE), which lists approximately 2,200 stocks and provides option trading for over 900 stocks; and the Cincinnati Stock Exchange.

NASDAQ and the Over-the-Counter Market

The over-the-counter (OTC) market is any trading done by a dealer. Almost any dealer can decide to make a market in any stock in which he or she thinks there is a profit to be made from such trading. Dealers profit from the bid-ask spread. There are over 35,000 securities in this market. The main problem with this system is the lack of public information.

The National Association of Security Dealers Automated Quotation System (NASDAQ) was formally organized in 1971 as the world's first electronic market in order to provide price quotations from this market. There are currently about 3,600 companies listed on the NASDAQ Market. Unlike the more formal exchanges, there is no trading floor; the market is strictly people connected electronically. The NASDAQ currently generates more trading volume than any other trading market.

The NASDAQ Market is reported in financial publications as three markets: the National Market issues (NMI), the National Market Small Cap issues, and the Small Cap issues. The NMI has higher listing requirements than the Small Cap markets. Newspaper quotations for the NMI use the same format as NYSE and Amex securities. The two Small Cap markets use a more abbreviated format.

Level 3

Level 2

Level 1

There are three levels of subscription to NASDAQ quotations. A *Level 3* subscription entitles users to enter their own bid and ask prices and to update them at any time. This level is clearly for dealers who are making a market in one or more of these stocks. *Level 2* subscribers can receive all prices, but cannot enter any quotes of their own. This level is for brokers who need to have current quotes. *Level 1* subscribers receive only the highest bid and lowest ask prices on a security. This lowest level is for institutional investors who want current information but will not be initiating any trades.

The OTC market continues today for securities that are not listed with the NASDAQ Market. The NASD regulates it. The OTC market remains the primary one for bond trading. Many bank and insurance companies are also traded in the OTC market. Commercial paper, large CDs, municipal bonds, and other money market instruments trade primarily in similar OTC markets. Unlike the exchanges with specialists, the OTC market is a dealer market. More than one dealer may make a market in a particular security. Thus, when a broker is executing a trade in the OTC market, he or she is obligated to find the best price among the various dealers. The broker may attempt to negotiate a better price with a dealer, or a broker may end up acting as a dealer for the trade. In this last situation, the broker is obligated to provide as good or better a price as he or she could have obtained externally for the customer.

pink sheets

The National Daily Quotation Service reports the bid and ask prices for all actively traded OTC issues (about 6,000 NASDAQ and 22,000 other issues). These price quotations appear each day in the *pink sheets*, copies of which are available at most brokerage firms.

The Third and Fourth Markets

Most trading and virtually all trades involving individual investors take place on an exchange or in the traditional OTC market for unlisted issues. Institutional investors, on the other hand, make significant use of two other markets. OTC trading of listed stocks constitutes what is called the third market. The fourth market is an informal arrangement for direct trading between institutions. Both third and fourth markets involve off-exchange trading of what are usually large blocks of exchange-traded stock.

The third market grew up back when the exchanges had fixed commission schedules. Exchange-set commissions did not bind third-market dealers. Thus, they tended to charge high-volume institutional traders much less than the commissions charged on the exchanges. By the time the exchanges stopped setting commissions, the third market was already established. Third-market dealers may well offer a more attractive overall price (stock price and commission) than is available on the exchanges.

electronic communications network (ECN)

The fourth market provides its institutional participants with an even less costly way of trading. Because the institutions trade directly with each other, no commission is incurred. Organizations that provide this market are known as *electronic communications networks* (ECNs). The two best-known ECNs are Instinet (www.instinet.com) and POSIT.

Consolidated Tape

Congress has mandated that all of the exchanges and other securities markets (third and fourth) be fully linked. If and when that mandate is

How POSIT Works

Buy and sell orders, including both individual stocks and portfolios, are entered into the system from many sources. Fifteen times daily...POSIT compares and matches all orders confidentially. POSIT intraday matches take place within a 1-minute window after the match times. . .

POSIT intraday trades are priced at the midpoint of the bid/offer spread (the difference between the best seller's asking price and the best buyer's bid) in the stock's primary market . . . at the moment the match is run.

Source: http://www.itginc.com/products/posit/index.html

realized, buyers and sellers in all submarkets will be able to trade directly with each other. The more numerous alternatives should move buying and selling prices closer together (narrower bid-ask spreads), and the greater diversity of reachable markets should allow larger blocks to be more easily absorbed. Not surprisingly, this vision requires a number of difficult changes.

Until the mid-1970s, securities trading was highly segmented. To obtain the best available price, each market had to be checked separately, and NYSE members could not trade in the third market. Most NYSE brokers simply funneled their orders to the market with the greatest volume. In 1974, consolidated trades began to be reported on a common ticker tape. The financial press initiated consolidated quotation reporting in 1976.

Consolidated reporting without fully consolidated trading is confusing, however. The various submarkets cannot be linked without exposing the participants to additional competition. Not surprisingly, though, NYSE specialists, regional specialists, and third-market dealers are each interested in preserving their existing advantages. These conflicts, coupled with the SEC's unwillingness to impose a solution, have slowed the pace of reform.

The consolidated tape one sees today is a high-speed, electronic system that constantly reports the latest price and volume data on sales of exchange-listed stocks. The data reflected on the consolidated tape derives from various market centers, including all securities exchanges, ECNs, and third-market broker-dealers. The NASDAQ Stock Market runs a similar tape for its securities.

If you tune into financial news television programs or log on to Internet sites that provide updated market information, you may have seen trade reports from the consolidated tape running across your screen. If you consult the consolidated tape for NASDAQ securities any time after 4:00 p.m., you may see the letter T next to some of the prices. The T designates those trades that occurred in after-hours trading. Prices on trades tagged with a T do not affect the regular session closing price (or the regular session high and low prices) for the stock. The consolidated tape for exchange-listed securities is implementing a similar feature.

THE SECONDARY MARKET: THE TRANSACTIONS

Transaction Fee Components

There are three components to the transaction fees an investor pays when trading. One is explicit, and the other two are implicit. They are:

- commissions (explicit)
- bid-ask spread (implicit)
- price concession (implicit)

Commissions

When a group of brokers got together in New York City in 1792 to formalize the origin of the NYSE with the so-called Buttonwood Agreement,[10] they included a rate-fixing clause. Later, the NYSE prohibited exchange-member firms from trading listed securities off the exchange. This restriction stayed in place until the late 1960s. At this time, institutional traders made up a large and growing percentage of stock market volume, and they began to find various ways around the fixed commissions. The NYSE began to make special exceptions to the fixed-rate schedule. Finally, the SEC mandated the fixed-commission schedule be abolished on May 1, 1975 (known in the industry as *May Day*), and that each brokerage firm would be free to set its own schedule. The full-service firms have the higher commission rates, but they will gladly negotiate with their largest customers. The discount brokerage firms can have some incredibly inexpensive rates, especially those that emphasize Internet service.

May Day

Bid-Ask Spreads

As we have discussed before, everyone making a market in securities, which includes OTC dealers and stock exchange specialists, quote both a bid price at which they will buy and an ask price at which they will sell. In the OTC market, one has the option of finding alternative dealers who might offer better prices. On the exchanges, there is only one specialist per stock. However, there are frequently other brokers who are looking to trade. Thus, to the extent that brokers can find each other, it is in their mutual interest to agree upon a trading price that is inside the bid-ask spread. Thus, if a specialist were quoting 22 bid, 22.10 ask, it would make sense for two brokers to trade at, say, 22.05. Unfortunately, investors have no way of knowing if their brokers paid the ask price or received the bid price, or had negotiated a better price. To the extent an ask price is paid, the investor is implicitly paying a bid-ask spread. Spreads tend to represent a smaller percentage of the price for higher-priced and more actively traded stocks. Listed stocks generally have lower bid-ask spreads than those traded over-the-counter.

paying for order flow

One particular concern in the industry has been the practice of *paying for order flow,* which occurs when a dealer pays a firm or a particular broker for the number of orders that are sent to him or her. The problem here is that this dealer may not have the best bid-ask spread from the customer's perspective. The dealer is happy because he makes more money on his trades, the broker is happy because he gets the supplemental income in addition to the commission. The customer is usually unaware that he or she has paid a higher price than necessary for the stock.

Price Concessions

Price concessions may occur on large trades. Although dealers and specialists stand ready to provide a bid-ask quote to anyone at anytime, this quote is only for a limited number of shares. Thus, suppose an investor wants to sell 10,000 shares, and the specialist's quote is good only for the first 1,000 shares. When a specialist is asked for his quotes, he or she does not know which way the broker wants to trade (i.e., buy or sell). However, when the broker sells 1,000 shares the first time, then the specialist knows the broker is likely looking to sell a large amount of additional shares. Sooner or later, the specialist will start lowering his bid-ask prices as his inventory grows beyond the desire number of shares. This adjustment in the bid-ask spread as larger orders are processed is the price concession.

Types of Orders

Market and Limit Orders

There are only two types of orders that almost all investors use: the market order and the limit order. A market order means an immediate execution at the best available price. If a specialist is quoting a stock at 23 bid and 23.25 ask, a market order to buy would generally result in a purchase at 23.25 and a market order to sell in a sale at 23. Naturally, one always hopes that a matching order arrives on the trading floor at the same time and the brokers can make the trade at a price within the bid-ask range.

A limit order to buy sets the maximum price the investor is willing to pay, and a limit order to sell sets the lowest price an investor will accept. A good way to remember this is to think of a limit order as an order that sets a limit on how much the customer is willing to pay. A market order ensures a transaction, but the price is uncertain. A limit order ensures a good price, but only if the trade takes place.

> ***Example:*** A particular limit order to buy 100 shares at 23 may be preceded by another limit buy order at 23 for 500 shares, and another limit buy order for 300 shares at 23 may follow the 100-share buy order. Once the 500 shares at 23 are purchased, the 100-share order will be crossed with any incoming market sell order or limit order with a minimum sale price of $23 or less. However, if any offer to pay more than 23 should arrive prior to the 100-share order's being executed, it would immediately supersede the 100-share order.

trading stations (posts)

When an order is received, the brokerage firm representatives take this order to the section of the exchange where this stock is traded (*trading stations,* or *posts*) and attempt to execute it. In the case of a limit order, if the order cannot be quickly executed, the representative will leave it with the specialist for that stock. The order will then be put on the specialist's book for later execution, if possible.

Financial Planning Issue

Suppose a stock is trading at 23.40 bid and 23.65 ask. An investor notes that the stock has traded as high as 24.00 in recent days, and so places a limit order to sell at 24. If in fact the stock rises to 24 in the next few days, the investor will make an additional $60 profit for each 100 shares owned. However, if the stock were to drop to $20 over the next few days, the investor would receive $340 less per hundred shares than he or she would have received with a market order.

Everyone feels like a market genius as long as his or her limit orders are eventually executed and they save a little something on the purchase price or make some extra profit on the sale price. However, the first time the limit order causes the investor to miss a bigger profit or take a bigger loss, that will probably be the last limit order the person uses.

Stop-Loss and Stop-Limit Orders

Occasionally, people will use stop orders (both stop-loss and stop-limit) to limit exposure to an adverse price move. Most stop orders are designed to sell a position before the stock goes any lower. A stop-loss order to sell implements a sale at market (which means the best immediately available price) if the price falls to the prespecified level. These orders seek to protect the investor from a further fall. Because the stock must be traded immediately after the stop price is reached, the realized price is usually relatively close (but not necessarily identical) to the stop-loss price.

Therefore, a stop-loss order at 20 might result in a sale at 20, but it could result in a sale at a lower price if the stock is dropping rapidly.

A stop-limit order, in contrast, activates a limit order when the market reaches the stop level. Thus, when the stop level is reached, a stop-limit order may not liquidate the position. The vast majority of stop orders are set to sell a position if the price drops. Buy stop orders, in contrast, are triggered by a price rise. Such an order might be used to protect a short position. (Short positions are discussed later.) A stop-loss buy order at 30, therefore, might be placed on a stock trading at 25. As long as the price stays below 30, nothing is done. Once it touches 30, the stock is bought.

Principal Types of Orders

- Market order: requires an immediate execution at the best available price
- Limit order: stipulates the minimum (sell) or maximum (buy) price acceptable for a trade to take place
- Stop-loss order: requires an immediate trade if the specified price is reached
- Stop-limit order: activates a limit order if a specified price is reached

---

Good-'Til-Canceled, Day, Fill-or-Kill, and All-or-Nothing Orders

Because market orders require immediate execution, specifying how long to keep trying to fill the order is not necessary. Limit, stop-loss, and stop-limit orders, in contrast, may be entered either as good 'til canceled (GTC) orders or as executable for a specified period. An order can be placed to remain on the books for a day, a week, or for some other period. Day orders are canceled automatically at the close of the day's trading, whereas the broker must remember to cancel other orders on the prespecified day. Fill-or-kill orders must be either executed immediately or canceled.

Period for Which an Order Is Executable

- GTC order: executable until filled or canceled
- Day order: executable only during the day the order is placed
- Fill-or-kill order: canceled if not immediately executed

Commission charges are based on trades of the same security that take place during the same day. If an order to purchase 500 shares is executed in several pieces throughout the same day, the commission will (or should) be computed for a single 500-share trade. If that same trade takes several days to be executed, however, the commissions would be computed separately on each day's trade. The total commission on a stretched-out trade would appreciably exceed that on a single 500-share transaction. A customer who wishes to trade more than one round lot may either allow the order to be filled a bit at a time or stipulate an all-or-nothing order. All-or-nothing orders must trade as a unit incurring a single commission (with any volume discount applying) but can be executed only when sufficient volume is available. A regular order might be filled in pieces when insufficient volume exists for a single fill. Moreover, all-or-nothing orders are automatically superseded by any other limit orders placed by other customers at the same price. Thus, those who would use all-or-nothing orders need to realize that the potentially lower commission is accompanied by a reduced likelihood of execution.

Versus Purchase Orders

Investors sometimes sell only a portion of their holdings of a particular issue. For example, an investor might sell 200 shares from a 1,000-share position. The holdings may themselves have been accumulated at different prices over an extended period. The tax implication of the trade will depend heavily on the price applied to the purchase side of the trade. (Tax issues are discussed in chapter 13.) The higher the cost basis, the lower the gain or the higher the loss that is reported to the IRS. Normally, the shares purchased earliest are recorded as the ones sold (first in, first, or FIFO). The seller may, however, prefer to utilize a trade with a different purchase price. Identifying securities that were purchased at a later date as the ones that were sold may produce a higher basis (reducing the profit or increasing the loss for tax purposes). Making the order versus purchase allows the seller to specify which block of shares is to be sold.

SuperDot[11] and PERS

SuperDot stands for the Super Designated Order Turnaround System used at the NYSE. It is this system that transmits member firms' market and day limit orders, up to specified sizes in virtually all listed stocks, through the common message switch to the proper trading floor workstation. The largest market order that can be handled is 30,099 shares. Specialists receiving orders through SuperDot execute them in the trading crowd at their posts as quickly as market interest and activity permit, and return reports to the originating firm's offices via the same electronic circuit that brought them to the floor. SuperDot can handle daily volume exceeding 2 billion shares. It is **program trading** particularly used for program trading. *Program trading* is anytime an investor wants to arrange for the simultaneous execution of multiple orders.

This is particularly critical in hedging and arbitraging strategies, which are discussed in later chapters. The comparable system on the Amex is the Post-Execution Routing System, or PERs.

Short Selling

Most of the time, investing involves buying a security, hoping that the price goes up, and then selling it. This is referred to as taking a long position, or going long. Being long XYZ stock means one owns XYZ stock. It is possible to reverse this sequence of events, that is, sell a security one does not own, hope the price goes down, and then buy the security back at a lower price. This is known as short selling or selling short, and it is a perfectly legal practice. The short seller borrows the shares from his or her broker and sells them at the current market price. The short seller's broker borrows the shares from someone else's account. The short seller then owes the brokerage firm (actually, the lender) the shorted shares. Being short XYZ stock means one has borrowed and sold the stock, and has an obligation to return it in the future.

The customer whose stock is borrowed is as secure as a bank depositor whose funds are loaned out by the bank. If the lender wishes to sell the loaned stock, the brokerage firm simply borrows replacement shares from another customer or brokerage firm. If a loan of additional shares cannot be made to return to the original lender, then the short seller must buy the shares in the open market and return those shares.

The short seller hopes the price will fall far enough so that when the stock is repurchased, he or she will make a profit after covering trading costs. This gain would be reduced somewhat by commissions on the short sale and the covering (repurchase) transaction. Furthermore, the short seller must pay any dividends accruing on the borrowed stock. Moreover, the short sale proceeds and an additional percentage (margin)[12] of the sale price must be left in a non-interest-bearing account at the brokerage house. If the price of the shorted stock starts going up, the short seller is usually asked to deposit additional cash as proof of his or her ability to return the stock later.[13] If the short seller cannot come up with the cash, he or she is forced to buy the stock and return it to the lender's account.

Example: Shorting 100 shares at 50 and then repurchasing them (covering the short position) at 35 produces a gross profit of $1,500 (100 x [$50 – $35]) minus commissions and accrued dividends. However, should the stock price increase to 65, the seller would show a loss of $1,500 ($100 x [$50 – 65]) plus commissions and accrued dividends.

A short seller may remain in a short position indefinitely. The dividend payment and margin deposit requirements, however, could make such a position costly to maintain.

One limit to short selling is the brokerage firm's ability to borrow stock to facilitate the short sale. For widely held stocks, this need to find shares to short sell is generally not much of a problem. Sometimes, however, the interest in selling a less widely held stock short is so great relative to the shares available to short that brokerage firms run out of available shares. This situation is particularly likely for small companies in which only a few people hold the shares and/or none of the brokerage firm's other customers hold these shares in their accounts. Simply put, it may not be physically possible to short certain stocks. Similarly, an investor who shorts a stock may be required by his or her brokerage firm to close the position if the firm finds that it can no longer borrow the shares needed to maintain the short position.

bear raid

downtick

uptick

In the past, unscrupulous investors have used a rapid series of large short sales to attempt to force a rapid decline in a stock's price, which was known as a *bear raid*. Bear raids are now an illegal attempt to manipulate the market. To forestall such attempts, the SEC does not allow traders to sell short after a negative price change (*downtick*) in a stock. If the last price change was a decline, a would-be short seller must wait until an *uptick* (positive price change) and then can place the short sale only at that price or a higher price.

Example: A stock just sold at $23.50, down $.05 from the previous trade. No short sales can be made at this price. Either the stock must trade at a price higher than $23.50, or it must move back up from any new, lower price. Hence, a short sale could be made at $23.40, but only if the stock first traded at a price even lower than that.

Financial Planning Issue

If a client goes long a particular stock, the most he or she can lose is 100 percent of his or her investment. If a client shorts a particular stock, he or she may lose many times that amount. Suppose a client shorts 1,000 shares of Obscure Research Labs at $50 per share, and overnight the company announces it has found a cure for cancer. The price of the stock could easily open at $500 or more per share. The client might well be forced into bankruptcy to cover the repurchase and return of these shares!

Large Secondary Market Trades

The specialists on the exchange or the dealers in the OTC market who earn their living positioning the stock can handle the vast majority of secondary market trades comfortably. Other institutional arrangements are, however, used to handle trades that would strain the specialist's or market maker's capital resources. Really large amounts of stock usually require a secondary distribution (sale) or tender offer (buy); intermediate-sized trades may go through a block trader or be handled as a special offering.

Block Trades

Attempting to buy or sell 10,000 shares or more in the ordinary channels might result in an unfavorable price for the trader. For example, an attempt to purchase 10,000 shares of a less actively traded stock could temporarily raise its market price appreciably while the buying is under way. This is the price concession discussed earlier. Therefore, a professional who specializes in handling large quantities in ways designed to minimize the market **block trader** disruptions often implements these trades—the *block trader.*

For a large sell order, the block trader first obtains buyer commitments for part or all of the shares. He or she then offers to buy and resell the lot slightly below the current price, charging commissions to both sides of the trade. The block trader may purchase some of the lot to facilitate the transaction. This facilitating purchase may ultimately have to be sold at a loss. While block traders are usually given the task of selling large quantities of stock, they sometimes are asked to assemble large blocks for single buyers.

Special Offerings

Special offerings or spot secondaries are also sometimes used to sell relatively large blocks of stock. Brokers who buy the securities for their clients receive a special incentive fee. The exchange must approve the offering, which is then announced on the ticker. It must remain open for at least 15 minutes. The offering price must generally equal or exceed the current bid but not exceed either the last sale price or the current ask.

Secondary Distributions

Unusually large holdings are generally sold in secondary distributions through an investment banker, and they are handled in much the same way as a primary offering. In a secondary offering, the selling price is set and the buyer pays no direct commissions.

Tender Offers

A tender offer is used when someone wants to acquire all or a large block of a company's shares. If the buyer is an outside party, then the purpose is usually to acquire control of the company. If the buyers consist primarily of management, then the purpose is usually to take the company private. If the buyer is the company itself, then either the board of directors believes the stock is significantly undervalued, the company has substantial cash holdings that cannot be profitably invested, or the company is attempting to increase its financial leverage. (See chapter 8 for a discussion of financial leverage.) In a tender offer, the buyer offers to purchase a substantial block of stock for a limited period, normally at a premium price. The bidder pays an additional fee to brokers who handle their customers' trades. Tender offers sometimes contain limits on the number of shares to be bought. If there is such a limit and the offer is oversubscribed, then if the buyer does not want the excess, stock may be bought on a pro rata basis. If too little is tendered, the buyer may reject all bids or purchase what is offered.

SECURITIES MARKETS REGULATION

Because they are "clothed with the public interest," the securities markets are regulated. It is important that investors understand the nature and direction of this regulation. There are seven laws that are considered significant with regard to regulation today.

The Securities Act of 1933

The first significant modern legislation to protect investors was the Securities Act of 1933. This is often referred to as the "truth in securities" law. This legislation focused on the primary market. As part of this act, a prospectus that fully discloses all material information must accompany public security offerings. Essentially, it is this act that prohibits deceit, misrepresentations, and other fraud in the sale of securities.

The Securities Exchange Act of 1934

The next major legislation quickly followed the first. It was the Securities Exchange Act of 1934. This law created the SEC and charged it to oversee the provisions of the 1933 Act. It also empowered the SEC with broad authority over all aspects of the securities industry. This includes the power to register, regulate, and oversee brokerage firms, transfer agents, and clearing agencies as well as the nation's securities self-regulatory organizations. The various stock exchanges, such as the New York Stock Exchange and American Stock Exchange, are *self-regulatory organizations,* as is the NASD. The 1934 Act

self-regulatory organizations

also requires publicly traded firms to file periodic financial statements with the SEC (Forms 10K and 10Q)[14], the exchanges where they are traded, and their stockholders (annual reports). Trading by insiders must be reported to the SEC.

One of the weaknesses of the 1934 Act is that although it prohibits insider trading, it does not define an insider. Various court cases over the years have slowly expanded the definition of who is an insider, to the point that a person receiving advanced information from a newspaper columnist about a future column has been considered an insider. Even Martha Stewart has been identified as an insider, with the SEC arguing that she traded on information her broker provided her regarding the trades of another company's president.

Trust Indenture Act of 1939

This act applies to debt securities, such as bonds, debentures, and notes, that are offered for sale to the public. Even though such securities may be registered under the Securities Act, they may not be offered for sale to the public unless a formal agreement between the issuer of the bonds and the bondholder, known as the trust indenture, conforms to the standards of this act.

Investment Company Act of 1940

This act requires that investment companies disclose their financial condition and investment policies to investors when stock is initially sold and, subsequently, on a regular basis. It is because of this act that anyone buying a mutual fund must receive a prospectus at the time of purchase and on a regular basis thereafter.

Investment Advisers Act of 1940

This act requires that firms or sole practitioners compensated for advising others about securities investments must register with the SEC and conform to regulations designed to protect investors. Currently, only advisors who have at least $25 million of assets under management or advise a registered investment company must register with the Commission.

Securities Investor Protection Act of 1970

Securities Investor Protection Corporation (SIPC)

As part of the Securities Investor Protection Act of 1970, Congress set up the *Securities Investor Protection Corporation (SIPC)*. It is patterned after the Federal Deposit Insurance Corporation (FDIC), with the objective of protecting customer property. The SIPC is a nonprofit, nongovernment, membership corporation funded by member broker/dealers. Virtually all broker/dealers registered with the SEC are SIPC members; those few that are not must disclose this fact to their customers. SIPC's power to protect customers of former SIPC members ends 180 days after the member loses SEC registration. The SEC normally does not terminate a broker/dealer's registration if the SEC knows that the broker/dealer owes securities or cash to customers. Customers can therefore better protect themselves and assist the SEC by reporting a broker's failure to return cash and/or securities promptly.

SIPC protection technically is for when a clearing firm became insolvent. In the securities industry, two separate broker/dealers typically work together to service a customer account. These firms are known as the introducing firm and the clearing firm. The *introducing firm* employs the individual broker, who takes the customer's order and sees that the order gets executed. The *clearing firm* holds the customer's cash and securities and sends out statements describing the assets it holds "on deposit" for the customer. Assets on deposit are referred to as being in "street name." If the clearing firm becomes insolvent or otherwise cannot return the customer's property, it is the SIPC's responsibility, not the introducing firm's, to make sure the customer's cash and securities are returned.

introducing firm

clearing firm

SIPC coverage also includes protection against unauthorized trading in a customer's account. This coverage can include unauthorized trading by persons associated with the introducing firm and may be available even if the clearing firm is still solvent.[15] Because there would be a great temptation for an investor who took a large loss on a trade to later try to claim such trade was unauthorized, there is a high hurdle that must be jumped for such claims. Customers must clearly establish that the trades were unauthorized and file a complaint in writing as soon as they become aware of the unauthorized trade.

The SIPC liquidates troubled firms at the SEC's request. Customers are insured up to $500,000, not more than $100,000 of which may be in cash. Any claims above those sums are applied against the firm's available assets during liquidation. Most brokerage firms, however, have purchased additional insurance coverage for their customers. Coverage of $2,000,000 or more may not be unusual. For clients with large holdings of financial assets, a financial advisor should make sure the assets are with a brokerage firm with adequate insurance coverage. The SIPC does not protect customer funds placed with a broker/dealer just to earn interest.

Sarbanes-Oxley Act of 2002

This act mandates a number of reforms to enhance corporate responsibility and financial disclosures and to combat corporate and accounting fraud; it also created the Public Company Accounting Oversight Board (PCAOB) to oversee the activities of the auditing profession.

FDIC Act of 1933

Although it does not directly involve the securities market, an equally important piece of legislation involved the creation of the FDIC under the

Banking Act of 1933. The initial amount of deposit coverage was quite low, but the coverage has been raised steadily over the years to where it now stands at $100,000, a sum that vastly exceeds what most people have on deposit. The rules of coverage are not well understood. The $100,000 coverage is based on the name on the account, and not the account. Thus, a person who has multiple accounts at the same bank is limited to the $100,000 deposit insurance on the combined accounts, not on each account separately. For anyone with substantial bank deposits (i.e., more than $100,000), there are several strategies to avoid the aggregate limitation. The first is to put the different accounts at different banks. The second is to use different legal titles on the accounts.

Example: A couple has $250,000 in their checking account, savings account, and some CDs, all at the XYZ National Bank, and all of the accounts are joint accounts.[16] They are extremely risk averse. What alternatives might a planner suggest to this couple?

There are two simple choices. First, they could transfer some of their holdings to at least two other banks, so that each bank has less than $100,000 in total deposits under this joint name. The second is that they could use multiple titles. Thus, one account could be in the husband's name, a second in the wife's name, and the third in the joint title. As long as the sum of accounts under each title is less than $100,000, they would be completely covered.

OTHER ISSUES

Street Name

Most investors leave their holdings in their account with their broker (that is, the broker's clearing firm). These securities are referred to as being in street name. This is because the name of the brokerage firm is the only name of which the company issuing them is aware. Thus, if a client owns 10,000 shares of Citibank and the stock is in street name, then Citibank is completely unaware that the client owns this stock. Despite the use of street name, it is the investor who legally retains beneficial ownership. Street-name registration offers secure storage. Remember, accounts at most firms are covered by the SIPC. In addition, most brokerage firms supplement this coverage with additional increased protection that they purchase to protect the customer.

Street name also allows securities to be traded without new certificates having to be issued. Furthermore, an investor who holds a diversified portfolio of securities and who changes addresses needs to file only one change of address notice with the brokerage firm, rather than notifying all the companies separately. In addition, investors receive only one Form 1099 from their brokerage firm, rather than separate ones for each stock owned. This can be a tremendous convenience when it is time to file one's tax returns.

Advantages of Street-Name Registration

- Secure storage
- Lets securities be traded without new certificates being issued
- Allows customers who move to file only one change of address
- Single Form 1099

Street-name registration has a number of disadvantages. Assets held in street name may be tied up during a bankrupt brokerage firm's reorganization. Moreover, dividends and interest on street-name securities are sometimes credited to an improper account. The customer must discover and report the error before it is likely to be corrected. The broker in a non-interest-bearing account may retain even a properly credited dividend for a few days before sending to the shareholder. Furthermore, all company reports (annual reports, quarterly reports, proxy materials, class-action suit notices, and so on) for street-name securities are sent initially to the brokerage firm. Thus, street-name holders receive their company reports only after the brokerage firm has forwarded them. Also, some companies send discount coupons and sample products to investors who own the shares directly, but not to street-name accounts.

Disadvantages of Street-Name Registration

- Assets may be tied up during the reorganization of a bankrupt brokerage firm.
- Dividends and interest may be credited to an improper account.
- The broker in a non-interest-bearing account may retain properly credited dividends for a few days before sending them to the shareholder.
- The shareholder receives forwarded copies of corporate correspondence.
- Discount coupons and sample products are not sent to street-name accounts.

Stock Certificates

In this day of computerized accounting and electronic transfers, using stock certificates to prove ownership is similar to a cash-only payment system. Stock certificates must be issued whenever a stock is ordered out or otherwise registered in an individual's name. Virtually all financial institutions and most individuals leave their holdings in street name (even through there are some disadvantages to doing so). As such, appropriately safeguarded bookkeeping entries have largely eliminated the need for stock certificates. The National Securities Clearing Corporation (NSCC) minimizes stock certificate reissues. It records all members' transactions, verifies the consistency of their accounts, and reports net positions daily. NSCC members settle within the clearinghouse rather than between individual brokerage firms. Moreover, the Depository Trust Company (DTC) immobilizes many certificates by holding member firms' securities. Securities traded between members can be handled internally by simply debiting one account and crediting another.

Types of Accounts

When one opens an account, an account number is assigned. The account is also classified as to what activities the investor is allowed to do. The most basic account is the *cash account*. This is sometimes referred to as a Type 1 account. To buy stock in a cash account, an investor must have sufficient cash already in the account to complete the purchase.

cash account

The next classification is a *margin account* (also known as a Type 2 account). In a margin account, an investor can borrow money from the brokerage firm to purchase stocks. The borrowing process is discussed in more detail in chapter 3. Anyone with a margin account must also have a cash account. The distinction between the accounts is transparent to the investor, as both accounts have the same account number, and thus are grouped together on the same monthly statement. Short sales can only occur in a margin account. Also, because any securities bought in a margin account serve as collateral for any money borrowed to buy the securities, all securities in a margin account must be left in street name. In fact, when one opens a margin account, the investor must sign a statement allowing the broker to borrow any of the securities and lend them out for short sales. Another benefit of margin accounts is that one can also borrow money from the broker for other purposes, pledging the securities in the account as collateral.

margin account

The third category of accounts is the *option account*. It is in this account where trades in puts and calls occur. An investor opening an option account must sign a statement indicating he or she fully understands the risks inherent in option trading.

option account

SUMMARY AND CONCLUSIONS

This chapter provides the institutional framework in which market trading occurs. The market can be divided into the primary market, which is where new securities are sold, and the secondary market, which is where investors trade securities among themselves. The key player in the primary market is the investment banker, and in the secondary market the key players are the brokers, dealers, brokerage firms, specialists, RCMMs, and floor traders. The secondary market involves seven exchanges (two national and five regional), the NASDAQ Stock Market, and the OTC market. The third and fourth markets involve OTC trading of exchange-listed issues and direct trading among institutional investors.

There are three costs associated with trading: commissions, bid-ask spreads, and price concessions. Investors usually use only market or limit orders, although they may also use stop-loss orders and stop-limit orders. Buying a stock and selling it later is called going long. Going short means borrowing a security and selling it. Sooner or later the short seller must buy that security and return it to the lender. When someone wants to sell an unusually large number of shares, they may use a block trade, a special offering, or a secondary distribution. Unusually large purchases may be done via block trades or a tender offer.

The major laws affecting security markets today are the Securities Act of 1933, the Securities Exchange Act of 1934, the Trust Indenture Act of 1939, the Investment Company Act of 1940, the Investment Advisers Act of 1940, the Securities Investor Protection Act of 1970, and the Sarbanes-Oxley Act of 2002.

There are advantages and disadvantages to leaving a security in street name, but almost all investors do so. A brokerage account may be classified as a cash account, a margin account, or an option account. An investor may have all three types of accounts; they will appear as a single account on the monthly statement.

CHAPTER REVIEW

Answers to the review questions and the self-test questions start on page 733.

Key Terms

primary market	lettered stock
go public	registered representative
initial public offering (IPO)	Series 7
red herring	Series 6
firm-commitment basis	Gramm-Leach-Bliley Act
best-effort basis	Glass-Steagall Act

discretionary account

limited discretionary account

wrap account

wrap fee

churning

registered competitive market
    makers (RCMMs)

floor traders

seat

curb exchange

dual listing

over-the-counter (OTC) market

Level 3, 2, or 1

pink sheets

electronic communications
    network (ECN)

May Day

paying for order flow

market order

limit order

trading stations (posts)

stop-loss order

stop-limit order

program trading

short selling

bear raid

downtick

uptick

block trader

self-regulatory organizations

Securities Investor Protection
    Corporation (SIPC)

introducing firm

clearing firm

stock certificates

cash account

margin account

option account

Review Questions

2-1.   The primary and secondary markets are both critical to economic growth and development, but each in a different way. Explain why each is important.

2-2.   Investment bankers facilitate new-issue sales of debt and equity securities. Describe the two underwriting approaches they use to accomplish this objective.

2-3.   What are the two major categories of stock brokers, and how do their services tend to differ?

2-4.   Explain the roles of the third and fourth markets.

2-5.   What are the four roles of a specialist?

2-6.   What are some of the differences in listing requirements between the NYSE, the Amex, and the NASDAQ National Market Issues?

2-7.   Explain the four principal types of orders.

2-8.   a.   You are thinking about placing an order to buy 100 share of Lubricant Oil. The stock currently trades at $15.25. The following sequence of prices is observed: $15.20, $15.15, $15.10, $15.15, $15.10, $15.07, $15.02, $14.99, $15.05. What would have been your likely purchase price if you had placed a market buy order at the start of this process?

   b.   What would have been your likely purchase price if you had placed a limit buy order at $15 at the start of the above price sequence?

c. Suppose that you placed a market order for a short sale at the start of the above price sequence. What would your trade price have been?

2-9. What guarantees does the lender of shares for a short sale have that his or her stock will be returned?

2-10. Explain the purpose of the SIPC.

Self-Test Questions

T   F   2-1. Investment bankers generally agree to sell a new issue on a best-effort basis where they act as agents for the issuing firm.

T   F   2-2. The most basic function that brokers and their firms perform is to link investors to the securities markets.

T   F   2-3. The lines between brokerage and other types of financial service firms, particularly commercial banks, are quickly eroding, and the erosion is likely to accelerate.

T   F   2-4. A specialist is charged with making a market in a security.

T   F   2-5. Churning is the practice of reducing commissions for special customers.

T   F   2-6. Although corporate bonds may be listed on exchanges, most are traded OTC.

T   F   2-7. The two major costs of executing a trade are commissions (broker fees) and spreads (markups).

T   F   2-8. Specialists maintain an inventory of their assigned stocks and buy for and sell from that inventory.

T   F   2-9. Floor traders or RCMMs own exchange seats and trade for their own account.

T   F   2-10. The third market involves informal arrangements for direct trading between institutions.

T   F   2-11. High-volume stocks can trade simultaneously on the NYSE, several regional exchanges, and OTC.

T   F   2-12. Off-exchange member trading of listed securities is strictly prohibited.

T   F   2-13. Security market commission rates are fixed by agreement among the brokerage firms.

T   F   2-14. Bid-ask spreads tend to represent a larger percentage of the price for higher-priced and more actively traded stocks.

T   F   2-15. A limit order ensures a transaction because it requires an immediate execution at the best available price.

T   F   2-16.   A stop-limit order activates a limit order when the market reaches the stop level.

T   F   2-17.   The total commission on a trade that takes several days to be executed would be far less than that on a single transaction involving the same number of shares.

T   F   2-18.   An all-or-nothing order must be either executed immediately or canceled.

T   F   2-19.   Between 75 percent and 85 percent of all stock exchange transactions utilize stop-loss orders.

T   F   2-20.   A limit order might not result in a trade and therefore might not generate a commission for the broker.

T   F   2-21.   Short sales may occur in either a cash account or a margin account.

T   F   2-22.   Traders typically use short sales to drive a stock's price down.

T   F   2-23.   Margined securities must be left on deposit with the shareholder's brokerage house.

T   F   2-24.   The SIPC protects brokerage customers against losses due to market fluctuations.

T   F   2-25.   The Securities Act of 1933 focuses on the secondary market.

T   F   2-26.   A client has $75,000 in a checking account and $30,000 in a savings account at the same bank. Both accounts are in his name only. Both deposits are fully insured because each account is under $100,000.

T   F   2-27.   The Securities Exchange Act of 1934 fails to clearly define who is an insider.

T   F   2-28.   It is the clearing firm who tracks the ownership of shares in an account.

T   F   2-29.   SIPC insurance coverage does not apply to cash left on deposit in a brokerage account for the primary purpose of earning interest income.

T   F   2-30.   Stock certificates must be issued whenever a stock is registered in an individual's name.

NOTES

1. See http://www.leggmason.com/privateclient/pdf/discretionary_account_agreement.pdf.
2. The RCCM title is used at the NYSE. The Amex uses the title of *registered trader* or *market maker* for essentially the same function.
3. See the Glossary at www.nyse.com.
4. See www.nyse.com/glossary/1042235995786.html.
5. See "Listed Companies" at www.nyse.com.
6. The Amex has four different standards a U.S. company could meet. The requirements listed here are for Standard 1.

7. There is an additional requirement of pretax earnings of $2 million for the previous 2 years. Alternatively, a company may have $4.5 million in pre-tax income for the current year and not have lost money in the previous 2 years.
8. This assumes there are at least 800 shareholders. Other combinations of shareholders and publicly held shares can satisfy this requirement.
9. Alternatively, a company may have 2,200 or more shareholders with an average monthly trading volume of 100,000 shares, or 500 or more shareholders with an average monthly trading volume of 1,000,000 shares.
10. The agreement was named for the buttonwood tree where the brokers met.
11. Some of this material is quoted from the Glossary at www.nyse.com.
12. The topic of margin is discussed in chapter 3.
13. There are precise rules about when additional cash should be deposited and how much should be deposited, but those are beyond the scope of this material.
14. Form 10K is filed annually. As it contains basically the same information as the annual report, some firms take their annual report to the shareholders, attach a few pages with additional required information, and make that their 10K report. The 10Q report is the quarterly report. It provides unaudited financial results for each of the firm's first three fiscal quarters.
15. www.nasd.com/stellent/idcplg?IdcService=SS_GET_PAGE&nodeId=475, November 10, 2004.
16. Technically, the accounts are joint tenancies with right of survivorship. For more discussion of joint ownership, see *Fundamentals of Estate Planning* by Constance Fontaine, published by The American College.

3

Measuring Returns and Risk

Learning Objectives

An understanding of the material in this chapter should enable the student to

3-1. Compute a holding period return, a holding period return relative, a per-period return, a portfolio's holding period return, a geometric mean return, and an effective annual rate.

3-2. Describe what is meant by risk in an investments context.

3-3. Name and describe the sources of risk.

3-4. Compute semivariance, variance, and standard deviation.

3-5. Distinguish among computing variance from a probability distribution, from an equally weighted distribution, and from historical returns.

3-6. Describe the process of buying on margin and the relationship between ROA and ROE when buying on margin.

3-7. Compute the buying power of a margin account, its equity value, the price at which a margin call will be made, the amount of cash that must be added when a margin call is made, and the amount of additional cash that can be withdrawn from a margin account.

Chapter Outline

People invest because they hope to earn a satisfactory return on their investment. The expected return on an investment is a key factor in determining its relative attractiveness. Returns generally take two forms: current income and price changes. Many investments are structured to provide periodic and relatively dependable income payments (such as interest, rents, royalties, or dividends). Other investments (such as common stock) are structured to provide returns primarily in the form of price appreciation, although there is usually the risk of price decline. Some investments offer both current income and expected price appreciation.

Determining an Investment's Overall Return

- Periodic payments: interest, rents, royalties, or dividends
- Changes in market value: price appreciation or decline

Although investments are expected to yield a positive return, their actual return may be different from the expected level. Indeed, many investments produce negative returns. The potential difference between expected and actual returns is a function of risk. In this chapter, we will look first at the various definitions and concepts of investment returns. Then we will focus on the definitions of risk and the common measures of risk. First, however, we need to explore the definition and computation of returns.[1]

MEASURES OF INVESTMENT RETURN

The Holding Period Return

The most basic measure of overall profitability is the holding period return (HPR). The HPR relates the profit on an investment directly to its beginning value. The HPR is the sum of the income received from an investment and the change in market value, divided by the initial value (or cost) of the investment. This is expressed as

$$HPR = \frac{\text{Income received} + \text{Change in value}}{\text{Beginning value}} \qquad \text{(Equation 3-1)}$$

holding period return relative (HPRR)

A closely related measure of return is the *holding period return relative (HPRR),* which is the sum of the income received from an investment and the ending market value, divided by the initial value (or cost) of the investment:

$$HPRR = \frac{\text{Income received} + \text{Ending value}}{\text{Beginning value}} \qquad \text{(Equation 3-2)}$$

Although these two formulas look similar, the key difference is that the HPR uses the change in market value, whereas the HPRR uses the ending market value. Because the change in market value is defined as ending value minus beginning value, we can plug this definition into the HPR formula to see the relationship between the two measures. Simply put:

$$HPR = \frac{\text{Income received} + \left(\text{Ending value} - \text{Beginning value}\right)}{\text{Beginning value}}$$

$$= \frac{\text{Income received} + \text{Ending value}}{\text{Beginning value}} - \frac{\text{Beginning value}}{\text{Beginning value}}$$

$$= HPRR - 1$$

One way to think about the above formula is that subtracting 1 from the HPRR represents the return of principal on the investment. Sometimes the relationship is also expressed as follows:

$$HPRR = HPR + 1$$

Example 1:   Suppose an investment cost $1,000, provided a payment of $100 during the holding period, and was sold for $1,500. The HPR and HPRR can then be computed as follows:

$$\text{Change in value} = \$1,500 - \$1,000 = \$500$$
$$\text{HPR} = (\$100 + \$500)/\$1,000 = .60 \text{ or } 60\%$$
$$\text{HPRR} = (\$100 + \$1,500)/\$1,000 = 1.60$$

Note that we could have just as easily computed the HPRR as:

$$\text{HPRR} = \text{HPR} + 1 = .60 + 1 = 1.60$$

Example 2:   If an investment was purchased for $10, has paid $1 in dividends, and is now worth $8, what are its HPR and HPRR?

The HPRR is now computed as:

$$\text{HPRR} = (\$1 + \$8)/\$10 = .9$$

and the HPR as:

$$\text{HPR} = \text{HPRR} - 1 = -.1 \text{ or } -10\%$$

This investment has resulted in a loss. When there is a loss, the HPR is negative, and the HPRR is less than 1.

expected HPR

When the HPR is measured using expected values, it is referred to as an *expected HPR* or expected return. When it is measured using actual (historical) values, it is referred to as an actual HPR. An HPR computation must always state the period of the computation. To say an investment had an HPR of 3 percent would be outstanding if the holding period were 2 days, but it would be poor if the holding period were 10 years.

Per-Period Return

A better way to measure returns is to compute the per-period return (PPR), where a period represents a standard-length holding period. The universal unit for measuring returns is the year. Thus, it is highly unprofessional to quote a rate of return on any basis other than an annual basis. An asset's PPR is defined as the sum of that period's income and change in value divided by its beginning-of-period market value:

$$PPR = \frac{\text{Period's income} + \text{Change in value}}{\text{Beginning-of-period value}} \qquad \text{(Equation 3-3)}$$

This formula is obviously quite similar to the formula for the HPR. The three differences are that in the PPR formula (1) the income is for a single period only, (2) the price change is the price change for the single period, and (3) the denominator is the value of the investment at the start of the period. Note that one can also construct a per-period return relative (PPRR) by using the ending value rather than change in value in the numerator.

Example: Cindy Field bought a stock on July 1 for $25. It pays a total of $1 in dividends during the first year, and at the end of the first year (that is, on June 30), the stock trades for $30. During the second year, it pays a total of $2 in dividends, and at the end of the second year, the stock trades for $26. What is Cindy's HPR and her two PPRs?

HPR = ($1 + $2 + [$26 – $25])/$25 = .16 or 16%
PPR$_1$ = ($1 + [$30 – $25])/$25 = .24 or 24%
PPR$_2$ = ($2 + [$26 – $30])/$30 = –.0667 or –6.67%

Note that there is no clear and obvious relationship between the HPR for the 2-year period and the two annual PPRs.

Impact of Compounding

Returns are compounded when an investment earns a return for more than one period and the return from each period is added to the initial investment. The investment earns a return on both the initial sum invested and on the returns that accumulate from earlier periods. In other words, compounding reflects the impact of earning a return on both the amount initially invested and the returns that have been earned on the initial investment in prior periods. When an investment is made for multiple periods, returns are compounded, and the annual return is fixed, then the ending value of the investment is computed as:

Ending Value = Beginning value x $(1 + \text{rate of return})^t$ (Equation 3-4)

where t = the number of time periods

Example:	Your client is offered an investment that promises to pay 10 percent per year for 2 years, but your client must leave the money untouched for the 2-year period. If the initial investment is $10,000, how much will the investment pay off in 2 years?
	It would be tempting to say $12,000, based on a quick calculation:

Ending value = Beginning value x No. of years x Rate

It would also be wrong. At the end of the first year, the investment will be worth $11,000. However, for the second year, the full $11,000 is being invested, so the ending value will be the $11,000 times the HPRR of 1.10, or $12,100. The extra $100 comes from the fact that the $1,000 return from the first year was left in the account. Had it been removed from the account and held as idle cash, then the ending value of the account combined with the idle cash would have been $12,000. The quick formula solution for this problem would be:

$$\text{Ending value} = \$10,000 \times 1.10^2 = \$12,100$$

Expected Return

ex post

ex ante

In many problems, returns are measured strictly on a historical basis. These are referred to as ex post returns. *Ex post* means after the fact. Although there are many occasions for measuring past rates of returns, there are many other occasions for estimating future or expected returns. An expected return number is referred to as an ex ante calculation. *Ex ante* means before the fact. If cash payments and prices are noted by specific figures, then the same formulas (that is, HPR, HPRR, and PPR) can be used.

Example:	You receive a report on a stock in which a security analyst predicts that during the coming year, the stock will pay $2 in dividends and will trade at a price of $60 at the end of the year. If the current price is $55, what is the expected holding period return?

Change in value = $60 – $55 = $5

HPR = ($2 + $5)/$55 = .127 or 12.7%

Sometimes, expected return is expressed in terms of a probability distribution. That is, a combination of different returns might be indicated, along with the probability for each return being the actual return. When this happens, multiply each return by the associated probability, and add the products together. The sum is then defined as the expected return. In mathematical notation, this is expressed as:

Expected return $= (P_1 \times R_1) + (P_2 \times R_2) + \ldots + (P_n \times R_n)$ (Equation 3-5)

This equation can be expressed more compactly by using the summation notation (capital sigma).[2] The summation notation would read as follows:

$$E(R) = \sum_{t=1}^{n} P_t \times R_t \qquad \text{(Equation 3-6)}$$

where P_t = the probability of each rate of return being the actual one
   R_t = each potential rate of return
   n = the number of possible rates of return
   $P_1 + \ldots P_n = 1$

$\sum_{t=1}^{n}$ followed by a formula, such as $P_t \times R_t$, means "the sum of" that formula

for each value of t from 1 through n; $\sum_{t=1}^{n} P_t \times R_t$ means $(P_1 \times R_1) + (P_2 \times R_2)$

$+ \ldots + (P_n \times R_n)$.

Example: The press has mentioned rumors regarding a potential buyout of Blue Goose Airlines. After reading the report, you believe there is a good chance the buyout will occur, but not a perfect certainty. You can summarize your feelings as follows:

1. There is a 40 percent probability the buyout offer will bring in another bidder, in which case the stock's rate of return would be 35 percent.

2. There is a 30 percent probability the buyout offer will occur as planned, in which case the rate of return would be 20 percent.

3. There is a 30 percent probability the buyout offer will fizzle, and people will end up dumping the stock, in which case the rate of return would be –10 percent.

What is the expected rate of return?

$E(R) = (.40 \times .35) + (.30 \times .20) + (.30 \times [-.10]) = .17$

A Portfolio's HPR

The rate of return on a portfolio can be measured in the same way as the return on a single investment. That is, if one knows the beginning value of the portfolio, the income received on the portfolio, and the ending value, then one can use equation 3-1 to compute the portfolio's HPR.

Example 1:   You are reviewing the monthly statement of Joan Gimar. At the beginning of the month, the portfolio was worth $158,212. Joan received $1,524 in interest and dividends during the month (which were paid directly to her). The ending value of the portfolio was $161,918. What was her HPR for the month?

HPR = ($1,524 + [$161,918 – $158,212])/$158,212
= .033 or 3.3%

Example 2:   Assume the same facts as in the previous example, except that Joan leaves the dividends and interest in the account. In this case, the ending value of the portfolio represents all of the investments, plus any cash that has accrued in the account; that is, the ending value INCLUDES the dividend and interest income. Thus, counting it separately would be double counting. Hence, the HPR can now be computed based only on changes in the account's value, as follows:

HPR = ($161,918 – $158,212)/$158,212 = .023 or 2.3%

In some cases, one might want to compute a portfolio's rate of return based on the performance of the individual securities in the portfolio. In this case, you first figure out the percentage of portfolio value represented by each security in the portfolio. This is obtained by dividing the beginning value of each holding by the value of the entire portfolio, which are frequently referred to as the *weights* of the portfolio. Next, you multiple each weight by the rate of return for that particular security, and then these products are added together. The sum is sometimes referred to as the weighted average rate of return. In mathematical notation:

weights

Weighted average = $(W_1 \times R_1) + (W_2 \times R_2) + \ldots + (W_n \times R_n)$ (Equation 3-7)
    rate of return

where W_i =   percentage of portfolio invested in security i
       R_i =   the per-period return on security i
       $W_1 + \ldots + W_n = 1$

Example 1:   You have identified for your clients a recommended portfolio. This portfolio has three securities.[3] The first security's recommended weight is 50 percent, and the suggested weights for the second and third are 25 percent each. If these three securities had PPRs of 10 percent, 6 percent, and 9 percent, the portfolio's per-period return would be:

$$(.5 \times .1) + (.25 \times .06) + (.25 \times .09) = .0875 \text{ or } 8.75\%$$

Note that equation 3-7 is nearly identical to equation 3-5. Equation 3-5 involves multiplying rates of return with probabilities (where the probabilities add up to 1), and equation 3-7 involves multiplying rates of return with weights (where the weights add up to 1). It is basically the same equation, but a different interpretation is placed on the coefficients.

It should also be noted that if a portfolio is invested equally among different securities, then equation 3-7 reduces to the formula for the arithmetic mean. Thus, in that special situation, one could simply compute the arithmetic average.

Example 2:   Suppose we have a portfolio of five investments that individually had annual returns of 3 percent, 7 percent, 9 percent, 11 percent, and 15 percent. Assume that there is $20,000 invested in each of these five securities.

To compute the PPR of this five-investment portfolio, we can add the five separate returns and divide by 5:

$$(.03 + .07 + .09 + .11 + .15)/5 = .45/5 = .09 \text{ or } 9\%$$

The above example is often referred to as an unweighted or equally weighted rate of return.

Annualized Return

It was noted earlier that rates of return should be quoted on an annualized basis. Let's now look at the mechanics of how one computes an annualized rate of return when an investment is held for several years.

Many people would approach such a problem by computing the arithmetic average. The arithmetic average has the advantage that it is simple to compute, and reasonably accurate when the returns are almost the same from year to year. The disadvantage is that it is wrong!

Example: An investment that earned successive returns of 12
percent, 10 percent, and 8 percent would grow to a
compound value equal to 1.3306 times its initial level.
The arithmetic average of these three returns is 10
percent. Had the investment actually earned 10
percent per period for 3 years, its compound value
would be 1.3310. Thus, the actual compound value
and the value derived from using the arithmetic mean
are very similar.

When the individual returns are dissimilar, the arithmetic average of
returns will always overstate the true return, and the more dissimilar the
PPRs, the greater the overstatement.

Example: To see just how misleading the use of this arithmetic
mean can be, consider an investment of $1,000 that
doubles in value (to $2,000) in the first period (a
return of 100 percent) and then falls to half of its
value (to $1,000) during the next period (a return of
–50 percent). This investment would have the same
value at the end of the second period ($1,000) as it
had at the start of the first ($1,000). All would agree
that an investment with the same beginning and
ending values has an HPR of 0 percent over the two
periods. Yet if we average 100 percent and –50
percent, we obtain 25 percent!

**geometric mean
return (GMR)**

Conceptually, the number reported for the overall return should be one
that, if earned every period, would produce the same end-of-period value
which has resulted from the separate PPRs actually earned. The number that
has this characteristic is known as the *geometric mean return (GMR)*. The
GMR for n periods is obtained by first computing the PPRRs for each of the
n periods. These n values of PPRRs are all multiplied together and the nth
root is calculated. Remember, taking the nth root of a number is the same as
taking that number to the 1/n power. This result minus 1 is the GMR. Stated
as equations:

$$HPRR = PPRR_1 \times PPRR_2 \times \ldots \times PPRR_n$$

where $PPRR_i$ = per-period return relative for period i
$HPRR$ = holding period return relative for the entire n periods
$GMR = HPRR^{1/n} - 1$

In the previous example where n = 2:

$$PPR_1 = 1.00 \text{ and } PPR_2 = -.50$$
$$PPRR_1 = 2.00 \text{ and } PPPR_2 = .50$$
$$HPRR = 2.00 \times .50 = 1.00$$
$$GMR = 1.00^{\frac{1}{2}} - 1 = 0.00 \text{ or } 0\%$$

This is exactly the result that we would expect for an investment whose ending value is identical to its beginning value (that is, $1,000). Note once again that the subtraction of 1 from the equation could be thought of as investor's principal.

Example:

Now let us consider a more complicated example. Suppose we want to determine the GMR for an investment that generated annual returns of –13 percent, 17 percent, –2 percent, 8 percent, and 18 percent. We could start the search by computing its HPRR based on its PPRRs:

HPRR = .87 x 1.17 x .98 x 1.08 x 1.18 = 1.2713

To find the GMR we must take the nth root of the HPRR. In this instance n is 5, so the exponent (measured as 1/n) is .2.

$$GMR = 1.2713^{.2} - 1.00$$
$$= 1.0492 - 1.00 = .0492 \text{ or } 4.92\%$$

The arithmetic mean is:

$$(-13\% + 17\% - 2\% + 8\% + 18\%)/5 = 5.6\%.$$

There are three points to remember about the relationship between the GMR and the arithmetic mean return. First, only when all the PPRs are identical will the GMR and arithmetic mean be equal. Second, if the PPRs are not identical, then the GMR will always be less than the arithmetic mean return. Third, this difference increases as the variability among the PPRs increases.

Geometric Mean Using an HP-10BII

Calculating a geometric mean return is easy with a calculator that has an exponent key, such as the Hewlett-Packard HP-10BII calculator. Before entering the data, though, familiarize yourself with the calculator. To turn it on, press the ON key. To turn it off, you must use the gold SHIFT key. Note that, after the gold SHIFT key is pressed, the subsequent key pressed will have the function marked in gold, not the function more prominently marked in white. Although there is also a purple SHIFT key, we will not be using its related functions; when we refer to the SHIFT key, we mean the gold SHIFT key. To turn off the calculator, hit:

SHIFT, OFF   (display turns off)

Now after turning your calculator on again, you should also adjust the number of decimal places displayed. For four decimal places, the following keystrokes are necessary:

SHIFT, DISP, 4

Whenever you are working on a problem that involves the use of decimal notation, you should set the display to four decimal places. Whenever you are working on a problem using percentages or dollars, you should set the display to two decimal places.

It is also highly recommended that you adjust the number of periods per year to one from the factory setting of twelve, as follows:

1, SHIFT, P/YR

For geometric mean calculations, we use the exponent key (y^x). As an example, we could calculate 1.05^4 by multiplying 1.05 x 1.05 x 1.05 x 1.05 for a total of 1.2155, or we could use the exponent key as follows:

SHIFT, C ALL   (clears memory)
1.05, SHIFT, y^x, 4, =   (display: 1.2155)

Note that the exponent in this problem is 4, but the exponent in a geometric mean problem will be a decimal between 0 and 1.0 because it must equal $1/n$. For example, if there are 25 periods, $1/n = 1/25 = .04$, so the exponent would be .04.

To help in the calculation of the geometric mean, let's look at two more keys on the HP-10BII. The M+ key allows us to store a number in the calculator's memory. If we enter another number and press the M+ key, that number will be added to the value in the memory. Any subsequent calculations will not affect the value in the memory unless the M+ key is pressed or the SHIFT, C ALL sequence is pressed. The following example shows this capability, and it includes some arbitrary calculations for demonstration.

SHIFT, C ALL
4, +, 6, =, M+   (10 is stored)
RM   (10 is in memory)
8, M+   (8 is added to memory)
RM   (18 is in memory)
7, x, 9, =   (arbitrary calculation)
4, SHIFT, y^x, 3, =   (arbitrary calculation)
RM   (18 is still in memory)
SHIFT, C ALL   (clears memory)
RM   (memory is empty)

We can use the memory and exponent functions in the geometric mean calculation. Returning to the example with consecutive returns of –13 percent, 17 percent, –2 percent, 8 percent, and 18 percent, the keystrokes are as follows:

SHIFT, C ALL
1, ÷, 5, =, M+   (stores exponent: 1/n = 0.2)
.87, x, 1.17, x, .98, x,
  1.08, x, 1.18, =   (display: 1.2713)
SHIFT, y^x, RM, =   (display: 1.0492)
–, 1, =   (display: 0.0492)

To Predict Future Performance

Past performance is sometimes computed to provide a best guess for future performance. However, when one is forecasting future rates of return, it is not immediately obvious whether such forecasts should be based on the arithmetic average rate of return or the geometric mean rate of return. For example, suppose a financial planner is reviewing a client's portfolio and notes that over the past 10 years, the arithmetic average rate of return is 10 percent, and the geometric mean rate of return is 8 percent. Which rate of return would make most sense to use in projecting the future value of the portfolio?

The traditional rule-of-thumb is that if one is forecasting for a single year, then the arithmetic average is the best forecast of future return. However, if one is forecasting for a large number of years, then the geometric mean is the best forecast of future return. Using the above example, this means that if the planner were making a 1-year forecast of the portfolio's value, he or she could use a 10 percent rate of return. If the planner were forecasting 10 years into the future, an 8 percent annual rate of return would be more appropriate. This rule-of-thumb obviously leaves open the question of which rate of return one should use if forecasting a limited number of years, say 2 or 3 years.

Recent research by Jacquier, Kane, and Marcus[4] suggests that a weighted average of the two historical rates of returns provides the best forecast, where the weights depend on the number of time periods used to compute the historical rates of return and the number of time periods over which one is forecasting. The formula is:

Forecast   =   (Arithmetic mean x [1 – H/T]) + (Geometric mean x [H/T])

    where T   =   number of time periods used in the historical computation
              H   =   number of time periods being forecasted (that is, horizon)

Note that in the above formula, if the forecast is for a single period (that is, H = 1), and the number of periods used in the historical computation is relatively large, then the forecasted rate of return should be primarily based on the arithmetic mean. Note also that if the number of historical periods used equals the number of periods being forecasted (that is, H = T), then the best rate of return for forecasting is strictly the geometric mean rate of return. Conceptually, it would be highly inappropriate to forecast over a longer time horizon than one has used to compute the historical rate of return. That is, it would be unprofessional to use this model in a situation where H > T.

Example: In analyzing a client's portfolio, you look at the performance over the last 5 years and compute that the arithmetic average annual rate of return has been 12 percent, and the geometric mean rate of return has been 10 percent. You want to forecast the rate of return for the next 2 years. What is the most appropriate rate of return assumption to use if you want to base the future rate of return on past performance?

Optimal forecast   =   (12% x [1 – 2/5]) + (10% x [2/5])
                            =   7.2% + 4% = 11.2%

UNDERSTANDING INVESTMENT RISK

Making investment decisions would be incredibly easy if all that was required was to compare the expected returns on the investment choices. The difficulty in investing arises from the presence of risk. There are two steps necessary to better understand risk. The first is to understand the sources of risk or reasons that risk exists. The second is to understand the common techniques for analyzing risk. In this section, we will go through these two steps in order.

What Is Investment Risk?

pure risk

In insurance, risk typically is viewed as the potential for loss. In this context, a *pure risk* involves only the chance of loss or no loss. For example, auto theft insurance is based on the fact that during the term of the policy, either one's car will be stolen (loss) or it will not be stolen (no loss). Thus, the purchase of such insurance will result in compensation for the value of the car if it is stolen, or nothing if the car is not stolen. There is no chance for a profit through the purchase of such a policy.

speculative risk

In investments, assets are acquired with the expectation of receiving some type of gain; thus potential for loss is inadequate in explaining investment risk. Since gain can result from owning investment assets, a more useful definition of investment risk must include positive, zero, and negative returns; this is called *speculative risk*. The magnitude of positive and negative returns can vary considerably. When both elements (positive-negative returns and variation in magnitude) are considered, investment risk can be defined as the variability in the investment's expected return. The greater the expected potential variation in the return, the greater is the risk of the investment.

A multitude of factors are responsible for the variability in an investment's returns. Some of these factors affect returns on an almost daily basis, while others do so only infrequently or never. Some have minor impacts, and others have major ones. Let us consider these different sources of risk.

Sources of Investment Risk

Inflation Risk

Inflation risk, sometimes called purchasing-power risk, includes the variation in real returns that can be caused by changes in the general level of prices. In theory, the general level of prices may rise (inflation), be stable, or fall (deflation). Sometimes the economy will be in a period of disinflation, which is where prices are rising at a lower rate than was previously the case. Disinflation is something of a misnomer, as inflation is still occurring, just at a lower rate than what had been the case. Because one of the major economic problems in the twentieth century was inflation, discussions of purchasing-power risk focus almost exclusively on inflation scenarios, hence most people use the term inflation risk.

Inflation can affect investments in two ways. First, to the extent one owns stock, inflation may affect the profitability of the companies in which one is invested. There has been extensive debate over whether corporations are net gainers or losers during inflationary periods. The results seem to be that it depends on the nature of the company; some businesses benefit from inflation, and some lose.

The second way is that the purchasing power of one's returns from investments will be affected. It is correct to say that regardless of the returns on one's investments, inflation reduces the purchasing power of those returns. However, some investors may benefit from inflation if they own stocks in companies that benefit from inflation. So, even though the returns of these investors have less purchasing power, they may have higher returns than would otherwise be the case. (This topic is discussed in detail in chapter 7.)

It should also be pointed out that investors are not stupid with regard to inflation. During inflationary periods, investors will not make new investments unless they believe there is compensation built into the investment for the expected level of inflation. In the case of bonds, this would mean a higher coupon rate. If the rate of inflation turns out to be lower than what was expected, then investors have actually benefited from the inflationary expectation.

Where investors truly suffer from inflation is when the actual inflation rate turns out to be higher than the expected inflation rate. The investments that are most susceptible to this risk are fixed-income investments, such as savings accounts, certificates of deposit, bonds, bond funds, other debt instruments, life insurance cash values, and fixed annuities. During deflationary periods (2 of the last 60 years),[5] fixed-income investments should provide windfall gains since the income (such as the interest on a bond) typically does not vary with economic conditions; thus the purchasing power of that income stream rises.

The common technique for analyzing the impact of inflation is to argue that investors start with an expectation of a desired real rate of return, and this is adjusted for inflation to determine the nominal rate of return they need. Nominal rates are the rates we see and work with every day. In equation form, this is noted as follows:[6]

$$(1 + \text{real rate}) \times (1 + \text{inflation rate}) = (1 + \text{nominal rate})$$

or $(1 + \text{real rate}) \times (1 + \text{inflation rate}) - 1 = \text{nominal rate}$ (Equation 3-8)

Again, subtracting 1 reflects a return of principal.

Example: Jeff Robins tells his financial planner that he wants to earn a 10 percent rate of return because he wants a 4 percent real rate of return and he expects a 6 percent inflation rate. The financial planner should advise Jeff that he is mistaken. If we plug Jeff's numbers into equation 3-8, we obtain the following:

$$(1 + .04) \times (1 + .06) - 1 = .1024 \text{ or } 10.24\%$$

Thus, Jeff actually needs a 10.24 percent nominal rate of return based on his goal and his inflation expectation.

Most of the time, people approach the relationship between the real and nominal rates in the opposite direction. That is, given their nominal rates of return and the inflation rate, what are their real rates of return? To answer this question, we can simply solve equation 3-8 for the real rate, as shown in the following equation:

$$\text{Real rate} = \frac{1 + \text{nominal rate}}{1 + \text{inflation rate}} - 1 \qquad \text{(Equation 3-9)}$$

Example: A financial planner is meeting with her client to discuss the portfolio's performance over the last year. The client is particularly concerned about inflation. The client earned 7 percent on her portfolio and the inflation rate was 3 percent during the same period. Her real rate of return was as follows:

$$\text{Real rate} = \frac{1.07}{1.03} - 1$$

$$= .0388 \text{ or } 3.88\%$$

As a quick and dirty approximation, the nominal rate can be approximated as follows:

$$\text{Real rate} \approx \text{nominal rate} - \text{inflation rate}$$
$$\approx .07 - .03$$
$$\approx .04$$

Financial Planning Issue

Some clients, particularly older ones, will obsess over the impact of taxes and inflation. The concern about inflation is not inappropriate as such clients have little or no working years to adjust their investments and investment income to compensate for unexpected rates of inflation. The only way to help clients deal with this issue is to incorporate assets that either benefit from inflation or are at least neutral with regard to inflation. This would suggest TIPS, Series I savings bonds, and common stock as critical elements of a portfolio. The drawbacks are that if inflation is lower than expected, TIPS and the Series I bonds will provide lower returns than non-inflation-related bonds, and stocks add investment risk to the portfolio.

Interest Rate Risk

Market interest rates are subject to many forces at work in the economy. Among these forces are actions of the Federal Reserve System to control the money supply (Federal Reserve activity is discussed in chapter 8), changes in the demand for borrowed funds for consumption or investment, geopolitical conditions, and exchange rate variability. The result of any of these forces is a change in the value of securities, the income earned on securities, or both. Interest rate risk refers to the degree to which an investment is subject to these forces.

Interest rate risk has two components: price risk and reinvestment rate risk. *Price risk* refers to the fact that any change in market interest rates typically leads to an opposite change in the value of investments—when interest rates rise (fall), the value of an investment declines (increases). This inverse relationship is most pronounced for financial instruments that have a contractually specified rate of interest and a specified maturity, such as bonds; the longer the term to maturity, the greater the resulting change in market price.

price risk

This potential change in the market price of debt securities takes on importance if a sale of the security is anticipated prior to its stated maturity date. If no sale is planned, changes in the market price are of little consequence to the investor unless an unexpected event creates the need to sell. This does not mean to say such an investor sustains no real loss. It just means that their losses have taken the form of an opportunity loss. For example, suppose an investor buys a 5-year CD that pays 4 percent, and then the following week the bank starts offering 5 percent on these same CDs. The investor sustains no loss as he or she will receive the promised interest and the principal back at maturity, but there has been a substantial opportunity loss.

For other instruments, such as common stock or real estate, the relationship is not as pronounced. In fact, as with inflation, some companies actually benefit from higher interest rates. (Banks are often more profitable during periods of high interest rates.)

Financial Planning Issue

For active management of interest-sensitive investments, decision rules for anticipated changes in interest rates are clear. If interest rates are expected to increase, the investor should sell the debt instruments in his or her portfolio. If interest rates do rise, securities similar to those that were sold can be repurchased at lower prices. If interest rates are expected to decrease, the investor should purchase debt securities that can be sold at a gain after the rates decrease. (Typically, longer-term bonds will appreciate most.) Note, however, that these actions are speculative, and there may be tax or other reasons that make them imprudent.

reinvestment rate risk

The second element of interest rate risk is *reinvestment rate risk,* which is the risk related to what the interest rate will be when income and/or principal from investments are reinvested. If interest rates have fallen, then investors will be worse off at the time of reinvestment. Conversely, if interest rates have risen, they would be better off when reinvestment occurs. The concept of reinvestment rate risk can also be applied to the principal of bonds when they mature.

Financial Planning Issue

Reinvestment rate risk can be dealt with in several ways. First, if the client lives off of the income and principal returned from investments, then there is no reinvestment and no built in assumptions about future rates of return. Second, clients can focus on "zero-coupon" types of investments, although they still have to worry about reinvestment of principal at maturity. Third, an investment technique known as immunization (discussed in chapter 9) simultaneously minimizes price risk and reinvestment rate risk. Fourth, another investment technique known as a laddered portfolio distributes bond holdings equally across a range of maturities, and the investor simply ignores fluctuations in interest rates.

Market Risk

Market risk is risk from any events that affect all investments. Inflation risk and interest rate risk are components of market risk. Market risk can also derive from political, economic, demographic, or social events and trends. Market risk is sometimes referred to as systematic risk (a topic discussed in chapter 4). About the only way to escape market risk is to simply hide one's cash, but even here one is still subject to inflation risk. Some assets are much more affected by market-risk types of events than others. The degree to which assets are affected by market-risk types of events is measured by a statistic known as beta. How beta is computed and interpreted is also discussed in chapter 4.

Financial Planning Issue

A classic example of a specific market risk event is the terrorist attack of September 11, 2001. The attack led people to rethink the risk–expected return relationship, leading to a significant drop in stock prices. Since not all investment sectors are affected by these factors to the same degree at the same time, diversifying an investor's assets over numerous types of investments can lessen the effect of market-wide events and thus market risk.

Business Risk and Default Risk

Enterprises can experience financial difficulties and fail for numerous reasons, such as a change in consumer preference away from a particular good or service, ineffective management, changes in the law, or foreign competition. The degree to which an enterprise's performance is subject to relatively unique events is its business risk. Since every enterprise has its own set of factors and degree of exposure, business risk is unique for each enterprise. Business risk is also referred to as unsystematic risk, a topic elaborated upon in chapter 4.

Closely related to business risk is default risk, which is the risk that contractual payments, primarily on debt securities, will not be honored. If debt principal or interest payments are not made on a timely basis, the borrower goes into default. In addition to loss of current and future interest payments, investors in these bonds often lose some or all of the entire initial sum invested. This result can occur with investments in both profit-seeking businesses and nonprofit institutions, such as municipalities. Because all debts must be paid in full before any funds can flow to the stockholders, rarely is anything left to the owners of profit-seeking firms that have failed.

Financial Planning Issue

Investment tactics to minimize default risk include the purchase of investments only issued by organizations having a high credit rating. Moody's, Standard & Poor's, Fitch, Duff & Phelps, and others provide assessments of the issuing organization for such securities as bonds (see chapter 9), but obtaining the information for other forms of investments, such as limited partnerships, can be difficult. Both business risk and default risk can be reduced through judicious diversification.[7]

Liquidity Risk

We have already defined liquidity as the ability to quickly convert an asset to cash with little or no loss of principal. Thus, liquidity risk refers either to the inability to sell an asset quickly, or the inability to have near certainty as to selling price. Since funds can be withdrawn from a savings account any time at no loss of principal, a savings account has no liquidity risk. The requirement of a 30-day wait to withdraw from a savings account would make the account less liquid.

There are several measures of liquidity risk. One is the magnitude of commission. One reason commissions on real estate are so large relative to any other commission structure is the time and effort typically involved in selling property. Another measure of liquidity risk is the bid-ask spread in the market for a particular asset. The less active the trading activity, the larger the bid-ask spread.

Financial Planning Issue

Liquidity is an especially critical concept when evaluating the appropriateness of investment assets for a client's emergency reserves. Only highly safe, highly liquid assets—such as savings accounts, short-term CDs, life insurance cash values, Treasury bills, and similar investments—are recommended for emergency reserves.

Political (Sovereign) Risk

Investments in foreign-based companies or U.S. companies with significant revenue or assets overseas are subject to additional risks in those countries. This political or sovereign risk includes the effects of trade disputes, wars, political unrest, tariffs, corruption, and expropriation, any of which can cause the value of these investments to drop precipitously.

Financial Planning Issue

There is basically only one way to deal with political risk, and that is diversification. In this case, one should not have an undue portion of one's wealth invested in companies in any one country (with the one partial exception being one's own country) or in companies doing business in any one country.

Exchange Rate Risk

Movements in currency exchange rates can be a significant source of risk, called exchange rate risk. This risk is relevant for individuals investing in foreign companies since the value of their investment in dollars can decline even if the company does well, if the value of the dollar rises relative to the value of the currency in the country where the investment is located. Even investment in U.S. companies is subject to exchange rate risk since virtually all large corporations (and even most middle and many smaller ones) generate considerable revenue overseas, manufacture overseas, or obtain raw materials from overseas.

Financial Planning Issue

As with political risk, the primary tool for managing exchange rate risk is diversification. However, to the extent a client has extensive holdings in a foreign country (for example, a family's business has its manufacturing plant located in a foreign country), the advisor should consider different techniques for hedging that risk, including the use of foreign currency futures and forward contracts, and possibly foreign currency options.

Tax Risk

Most investments have some tax consequences. The extent to which an investment is exposed to changes in tax laws is its tax risk. Income and appreciation in value will at some time be subject to income taxation, and investment assets may be subject to estate and inheritance taxation and gift taxation when ownership is transferred.

The government can also eliminate tax advantages. When the tax laws remove some favorable, or add some unfavorable, tax consequences, the intrinsic value of the affected investment assets falls. New laws could also penalize certain investments by imposing special tax consequences on income or appreciation.

To cope with the effects of this type of investment risk, financial planners and investors must monitor events occurring in the national tax arena and make investment decisions accordingly. (Tax issues are covered in chapter 13.) Just as important, investments should be based primarily on their economic value and contribution to the investor's goals and should not be based solely on their tax advantages.

Additional Commitment Risk

When an investment requires the buyer to put additional money into the investment in the future, it is said to have additional commitment risk. This additional funding requirement may arise at an inopportune time for the investor. If funds are not available, the investor might be forced to sell the assets at an unfavorable market price. Investments, such as certain limited partnerships that can require additional contributions, are viewed as being more risky than those that require no further investment.

MEASURES OF INVESTMENT RISK

As mentioned earlier, most people think of risk in the insurance framework as the chance of a loss. This is not apt in investments because of the presence of opportunity loss and the concept that people require an expectation of incremental return for agreeing to take risk. Simply put:

- Almost all investments contain risk.
- No one will hold these investments unless there is a reward of an expected return sufficient to compute for this exposure to risk.
- Therefore, earning anything less than the expected return is a form of loss.

So in the investments world, a loss is not just losing money, it is earning less than what you should fairly expect to earn. If you could have earned the same amount or more on an investment that was less risky, you have lost.

Example:	You are reviewing the portfolio of Ashok Lessard, a prospective client. Last year, the broad-based market indices were all up about 10 percent. Ashok holds an aggressive portfolio of mostly common stocks in small- to medium-sized firms. Ashok should have had at least a 10 percent rate of return. Ashok's portfolio increased in value by 5 percent. Regardless of Ashok's own feelings about the portfolio's performance, in truth, he lost at least 5 percent from what he should have had, based on his risk exposure.

Risk–Expected Return Trade-Off

There are some people who thrive on speculative risk. They love to gamble even when they know the odds are heavily against them. The vast majority of people (and nearly all investors) prefer to limit their exposure to unpleasant surprises. The profitability and success of the insurance industry illustrates the demand for the reduction of pure risk.

As stated above, investors accept risk in exchange for incremental expected return. Modern financial theory is based on the simple premise that this risk–expected return trade-off is linear, as shown in figure 3-1. Another way to

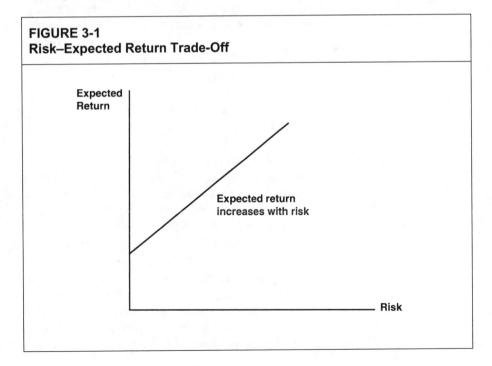

FIGURE 3-1
Risk–Expected Return Trade-Off

look at this relationship is that most investors are also willing to sacrifice some potential return if they can thereby obtain a sufficiently large reduction in risk. Thus, corporate bonds, having some risk of default, yield a higher expected return than otherwise similar U.S. government bonds. Likewise, higher-risk corporate bonds provide a higher expected return than otherwise similar low-risk corporate bonds. When an investment offers too low an expected return to justify its risk, the asset's price will fall until the market views its risk to be in line with its expected return.

Simple Example of Investment Risk

Consider the following investment alternatives. Suppose investment A guarantees a return of precisely 5 percent. Now consider investment B with a 5 percent chance of a 0 percent return, a 90 percent chance of a 5 percent return, and a 5 percent chance of a 10 percent return. B's expected return is 5 percent ([.05 x .00] + [.90 + .05] + [.05 x .10] = .00 + .045 + .005 = .05), which is the same as A's. B's actual (or realized) return is less likely to equal its expected return than A's is, because 10 percent of the time investment B will not earn 5 percent. Investment A offers an equivalent expected return and lower risk than investment B does. Thus, risk-averse investors would prefer A to B. To be *risk averse* simply means that, for a given expected return, an individual chooses the least risky alternative. Comparing A to B is very straightforward.

risk averse

Now consider asset C with a 5 percent chance of a 3 percent return, a 90 percent chance of a 5 percent return, and a 5 percent chance of a 7 percent return. Like A and B, C offers an expected return of 5 percent [(.05 x .03) + (.90 x .05) + (.05 x .07) = .05]. Because C's actual return is uncertain, risk averters would prefer A. On the other hand, because C's return variation (or range of possible returns) is less than B's, C is less risky than B. That is, the possible returns for B are 0 percent, 5 percent, and 10 percent; for C, they are 3 percent, 5 percent, and 7 percent. B's actual return could be 5 percent above or below its expected value, whereas C's can differ only 2 percent from its expected return in either direction.

Return possibilities like these are often illustrated graphically, as shown in figure 3-2, as a histogram of investment return possibilities. The vertical axes in figure 3-2 report the probability of each event; the horizontal axes identify the event (the realized return).

Although determining the expected return is rather straightforward, measuring its risk is more complex. Because B's range of possible returns is greater, everyone would rate B as riskier than C. This comparison suggests that a measure of risk could be based on the difference between the maximum and minimum possible returns. However, this approach ignores possible differences in the shape of the distribution of the returns. Imagine an investment D with a 50 percent chance of a 10 percent return and a 50 percent chance of a

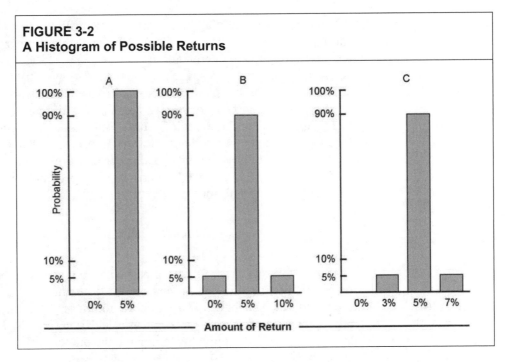

FIGURE 3-2
A Histogram of Possible Returns

0 percent return. It has the same range as investment B, yet it is clearly a riskier investment.

Rather than use the range of possible returns, a risk measure could be based on the dispersion or deviation from the expected return. The simplest technique, known as the sum of the deviations, involves taking the difference between each return and the expected mean, and multiplying each difference by the associated probability. The only drawback to this approach is that the answer is always 0. An example of this is shown below.

Example: An investment offers a 30 percent probability of a –2 percent return, a 40 percent probability of an 8 percent return, and a 30 percent probability of an 18 percent return. The expected return is 8 percent (.30 x –2%) + (.40 x 8%) + (.30 x 18%). The deviations from the mean are –10 percent (–2% – 8%), 0 percent (8% – 8%), and 10% (18% – 8%). The sum of the products of the three probabilities and the three deviations is 0 ([–10% x .30] + [0% x .40] + [10% x .30]).

An obvious alternative to the above approach is to compute the absolute values of the deviations, multiply these by the associated probabilities, and then compute the sum of these products. Although the answer obtained by this method is nontrivial, it is statistically difficult to work with, limits subsequent mathematical modeling of the investment process, and does not lend itself to intuitive interpretations.

semivariance

A more commonly suggested method for measuring variability is a statistic known as the *semivariance,* and financial analysts occasionally use it. The argument in favor of semivariance is that all that investors care about is earning less than the expected return. Potential returns equal to or greater than the expected return are not relevant. Hence, risk should be measured by looking only at returns less than the expected return. Potential returns greater than or equal to the expected return are simply ignored in the calculation. The mathematical definition of semivariance is

$$\text{SEMIVAR} = \sum P_t \times [\min(R_t - E(R), 0]^2 \qquad \text{(Equation 3-10)}$$

What this formula says is that if a particular return is less than the expected return (that is, negative), then square that difference and multiply it by the probability of that return. If a particular return is greater than the expected return, then ignore it in the subsequent calculation. Finally, add up all of the squared terms. Let's apply this formula to the previous example:

Example: An investment offers a 30 percent probability of a –2 percent return, a 40 percent probability of an 8 percent return, and a 30 percent probability of an 18 percent return. The expected return is 8 percent, and the deviations from the mean are –10 percent, 0 percent, and 10 percent. If only the negative terms are squared, then only the first differential is used, and the square of –10 percent is 100 percent-squared.[8] When this is multiplied by the associated probability of .30, the semivariance turns out to be 30 percent-squared.

Once again, the primary defect with the semivariance computation is that it is mathematically difficult to work with, and it limits subsequent applications.

variance

The measure of variability that turns out to be computationally reasonable AND mathematically tractable for other applications is called the *variance.* For this reason, the common method used by analysts to measure variation is to compute the weighted average of the squared deviations. The mathematical symbol most commonly used to represent variance is sigma-squared. The formula for the variance is:

$$\sigma^2 = \sum_{t=1}^{n} P_t \times \left[R_t - E(R_t) \right]^2 \qquad \text{(Equation 3-11)}$$

What this says is to first compute the difference between each term and the expected return; then to square these differences; next, to multiply each squared term by its associated probability; and finally, to sum up these products. Let us apply this formula to the previous example.

Example: An investment offers a 30 percent probability of a –2 percent return, a 40 percent probability of an 8 percent return, and a 30 percent probability of an 18 percent return. The expected return is 8 percent, and the deviations from the mean are –10 percent, 0 percent, and 10 percent. The squares of these three differences are 100 percent-squared, 0, and 100 percent squared. When these squared terms are multiplied by the associated probabilities and added up, the sum is 60 percent-squared, computed as follows:

$$.30 \times 100\%^2 + .40 \times 0 + .30 \times 100\%^2 =$$
$$30\%^2 + 0\%^2 + 30\%^2 = 60\%^2$$

Because the units of the variance term are meaningless, and the magnitude of the variance is difficult for many to grasp, the actual measure of risk used is the standard deviation, which is nothing more than the square root of the variance as follows:

$$\sigma = \sqrt{\sigma^2} = \text{standard deviation} \qquad \text{(Equation 3-12)}$$

In the above example, the standard deviation is 7.746 percent. It turns out that the standard deviation statistic has many nice features, which we will describe in the next section. It should also be noted that for symmetrical distributions, the semivariances are always proportional to the variances. Thus, if one were looking at several different return distributions, such as A, B, C, and D described earlier, and if one ranked them by both semivariance and variance, then the rank orders would be identical. To fully understand the benefits of the standard deviation measure, let us digress for a moment to a discussion about probability distributions.

Probability Distributions

Histograms like those in figure 3-2 relate possible discrete events to their likelihoods or frequencies. Probability distributions are used for continuous phenomena, which are phenomena with infinite possible outcomes. Figure 3-3, a symmetrical probability distribution, illustrates the relation between expected returns and their probabilities. The probabilities rise to a peak at return $\overline{R}$ (the mean, or expected return) and decline symmetrically thereafter. With a symmetrical distribution, the probabilities for returns equidistant from $\overline{R}$ are equal. The simple average of these paired returns is $\overline{R}$.

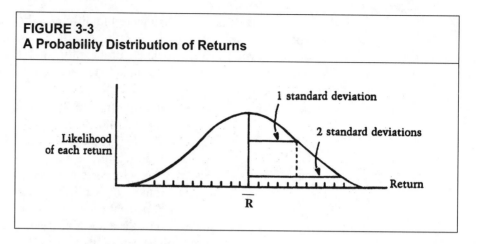

FIGURE 3-3
A Probability Distribution of Returns

Figure 3-3 also illustrates returns one and two standard deviations from the average. For most commonly encountered distributions (the most prevalent example is the normal distribution), the actual observation will be within one standard deviation of the mean approximately two-thirds of the time; about 95 percent of the time it will be within two standard deviations. Thus, the standard deviation of the return distribution is a useful measure of a distribution's spread. It may be used as an index of the degree of confidence (or risk) in the expected return.

Simple Example: Equal Probabilities

In many cases, a financial planner will encounter scenarios in which all of the potential rates of return are equally likely. When this type of problem occurs, then the computations can be greatly simplified. The expected return becomes nothing more than the arithmetic average, as shown in equation 3-13, and the variance becomes the sum of the squared differences between each return and the expected return, divided by the number of observations, as shown in equation 3-14.

$$E(R) = \overline{R} = \sum_{t=1}^{n} R_t/n = \frac{1}{n} \sum_{t=1}^{n} R_t \qquad \text{(Equation 3-13)}$$

$$\sigma^2 = \sum_{t=1}^{n} \frac{\left[R_t - E(R)\right]^2}{n} = \frac{1}{n} \sum \left[R_t - E(R)\right]^2 \qquad \text{(Equation 3-14)}$$

The reason for the simplification of these two equations over equations 3-5 and 3-11 is that for n equally weighted returns, the probability of any return t is simply $1/n$, so P_t can be expressed as $1/n$. If one makes this substitution into equations 3-5 and 3-11, one gets equations 3-13 and 3-14.

Example: Assume equal probabilities of returns of −2 percent, 4 percent, 10 percent, and 16 percent:

$$P(R_1) = P(R_2) = P(R_3) = P(R_4) = .25$$

R_1	R_2	R_3	R_4
−.02	.04	.10	.16

The expected return is then computed as:

$$E(R) = \left(\frac{-.02 + .04 + .10 + .16}{4} \right) = \frac{.28}{4} = .07$$

Next, we compute the deviation of each possible return from these expected value:

$$X_t = R_t - E(R)$$

X_1	X_2	X_3	X_4
(−.02 − .07)	(.04 − .07)	(.10 − .07)	(.16 − .07)
(−.09)	(−.03)	(.03)	(.09)

These values are then squared:

$$(X_t)^2 = [R_t - E(R)]^2$$

X_1^2	X_2^2	X_3^2	X_4^2
$(-.09)^2$	$(-.03)^2$	$(.03)^2$	$(.09)^2$
.0081	.0009	.0009	.0081

The results are then totaled and averaged. The result of this computation is the variance (σ^2):

$$\text{Sum} = .0081 + .0009 + .0009 + .0081 = .0180$$

$$\sigma^2 = \frac{.0180}{4} = .0045$$

Finally, the standard deviation is the square root of the variance:

$$\sigma = \sqrt{.0045} = .0671 \text{ or } 6.71\%$$

Thus, this investment has an expected return of 7 percent and a standard deviation of 6.71 percent. This means that the best guess for this investment's rate of return is 7 percent. If its returns are normally distributed, about two-thirds of the time the yield should be between .29 percent (7% − 6.71%) and 13.71 percent (7% + 6.71%).

Computations Using Historical Data

So far in our discussion of risk, our examples have dealt with ex ante (before the fact) data; that is, we defined all the possible future returns and the probabilities of each of those returns. In practice, expected return and variances are frequently calculated from ex post (after the fact) or historical data. The reason is simple: Defining future possible returns is a task that may be almost undoable. Thus, if one is willing to make the assumption that the future is likely to be similar to the past, then one can take some historical observations and use these as reasonable estimates of future observations.

When statistics are calculated with historical data, there are some adjustments to the formulas. The use of historical data normally implies that the observations are equally weighted in importance. This means that the mechanics for computing the expected return with historical data are identical to those for computing the expected return with ex ante data where all the probabilities are equal. Thus, one can also use equation 3-13 for computing expected return.

However, the formula for computing variance from historical data has one slight difference from equation 3-14. The one difference is that the sum of the squared differences is divided by (n – 1) rather than by n. This is shown in equation 3-15:

$$\sigma^2 = \frac{1}{n-1} \sum_{t=1}^{n} \left[R_t - E(R) \right]^2$$

(Equation 3-15)

Thus, the standard deviation is computed as:

$$\sigma = \sqrt{\sum \frac{\left(R_t - E(R) \right)^2}{n-1}}$$

(Equation 3-15a)

The variance and standard deviation calculations shown above are called the sample variance and sample standard deviation because they are based on a sample of data, rather than on the universe of possible data points. In other words, the set of future returns is the universe, and the set of past returns we use for our calculation is the sample.[9] Note that equation 3-15a is one of the formulas provided by the CFP® Board for the CFP® exam.

Example: You are looking at a stock and note that the returns for the last 5 years are –15 percent, 5 percent, 10 percent, –3 percent, and 28 percent. You believe these returns are representative of future returns, and you are willing to base your estimate of expected return and standard deviation on these historical data. What would the expected return and standard deviation be? The expected return is:

$$E(R) = \frac{-15\% + 5\% + 10\% - 3\% + 28\%}{5} = 5\%$$

The standard deviation is derived from the variance as follows:

$$\sigma^2 = \frac{1}{5-1} \times \left[(-15-5)^2 + (5-5)^2 + (10-5)^2 + (-3-5)^2 + (28-5)^2 \right]$$

$$= \frac{1}{4} \times (400 + 0 + 25 + 64 + 529)$$

$$= 254.5$$

$$\sigma = \sqrt{254.5} = 15.95\%$$

HP-10BII keystrokes
> SHIFT, C ALL
> .15, +/−, Σ+
> .05, Σ+
> .10, Σ+
> .03, +/−, Σ+
> .28, Σ+
> SHIFT, s_x, s_y (display: 0.1595)

We use the s_x, s_y key (the 8 key) rather than the σ_x, σ_y key (the 9 key) because the set of returns is considered to be a sample. Calculating a standard deviation for an entire population requires use of the σ_x, σ_y key.

Coefficient of Variation

One measure of risk can at times be quite effective in providing useful information to the financial planner: the coefficient of variation (CV). It is computed as the standard deviation divided by the expected return or mean return.

$$CV = \sigma/E(R) \qquad \text{(Equation 3-16)}$$

The CV provides a measure of risk per unit of return. Thus, if one were looking at two investments, A and B, and A had a standard deviation of 1 percent and an expected return of 5 percent, and B had a standard deviation of 3 percent and an expected return of 10 percent, then the CV tells us that investment B has substantially more risk per unit of return than investment A.

Now this does not mean that one would always choose investment A. If one owned investment B, any return that was no worse than one standard deviation *below* the expected return (that is, any return greater than 7 percent) would still be better than any return on investment A that is no better than two standard deviations *above* the expected return (that is, any return no more than 7 percent). This argument makes B a much more tempting investment choice than A, but one has to remember that there is more risk exposure per unit of return in B.

BUYING ON MARGIN

initial margin rate

In addition to all of the other sources of risk discussed above, there is a self-induced form of risk: financial leverage, also known as buying on margin. Marketable securities provide excellent collateral for lenders. The Federal Reserve Board (the Fed) allows most stocks to be bought using borrowed funds for part of the purchase price. This is referred to as buying on margin. The Fed also decides which stocks are marginable. However, each brokerage firm can add to the list of stocks that it will not trade on margin.

An *initial margin rate* of x percent permits marginable stock to be purchased with x percent cash (called the initial margin) and (100 − x) percent borrowed funds. Thus, a 60 percent margin requirement would allow the purchase of $10,000 worth of stock with as little as $6,000 in cash. In the past, the Fed lowered and raised the margin requirement on stocks as part of its economic policy. Since 1974, the margin requirement on stocks has remained at 50 percent. Although the actual margin rate is 50 percent, in this discussion we will use a different number, usually 60 percent, so that in numerical examples it will be clear to the reader when we are using the margin rate and when we are using the complement of the margin rate, which is 40 percent.

buying power

A margin account is said to have buying power based on the net equity in the account and the amount of margin borrowing already outstanding. A margin account, as opposed to a cash account, is one in which the investor is allowed to buy on margin. *Buying power* is the amount of additional stock an investor could buy without having to come up with additional cash.

The buying power of a portfolio of marginable stocks is equal to the net equity of the portfolio divided by the initial margin rate, minus the current account value. In equation form:

$$BP = \frac{E}{IMR} - MV \qquad \text{(Equation 3-17)}$$

where BP = buying power
E = equity (marginable stocks)
IMR = initial margin requirement
MV = market value of the assets in the account

equity value

The *equity value* of an account is the market value of all the securities in an account, minus the loan balance. In equation form:

$$E = MV - LOAN \qquad \text{(Equation 3-18)}$$

where LOAN = current loan balance

There is a potential difference between the true equity value of an account and the equity value based on marginable securities. In our discussions, we will assume all holdings are marginable. Nonetheless, if there are non-marginable securities in the account, then the equity value in equations 3-17 and 3-18 are based on only the marginable securities. The "true" equity value of the account would, of course, include all securities.

Example 1:   An investor with $120,000 worth of marginable stocks and no margin debt outstanding could, with a 60 percent margin rate, buy another $80,000 worth of marginable stocks with the account's buying power.

$$BP = \frac{120,000}{.60} - 120,000$$

$$= 80,000$$

Example 2:   An investor with $80,000 in marginable stocks, a 60 percent margin rate, and an outstanding loan balance of $20,000 would be able to purchase another $20,000 worth of marginable stock with the account's buying power.

$$E = 80,000 - 20,000$$

$$= 60,000$$

and

$$BP = \frac{60,000}{.60} - 80,000$$

$$= 20,000$$

Margin Calls

Margin loans may remain outstanding as long as the borrower's equity position does not fall below the maintenance margin percentage. The

maintenance margin
percentage

maintenance margin percentage is the minimum amount of equity an investor can have, as a percentage of the portfolio, without having to repay part of the loan. Maintenance margin rates (which are also set by the Fed) are applied to the portfolio, not the individual security. However, individual brokerage firms may set higher rates. Remember, when an investor is buying securities on margin, he or she is borrowing money from the broker and pledging the securities as collateral. Lenders always have the right to set their own loan terms. Maintenance margin rates are always less restrictive than initial margin rates.

Although interest is charged every month on the loan balance, margin borrowers are not required or expected to make payments according to any particular schedule. The only time that the borrower may be required to make a payment is when the equity in the account falls below the maintenance margin rate. In theory, a margin loan has no maturity.

The only time an actual cash payment would be due in a margin account is if the equity in the account fails satisfy the following relationship:

$$MV \times (1 - MMR) \geq LOAN \qquad \text{(Equation 3-19)}$$

where MMR = maintenance margin rate

The concept here is that as long as the value of the collateral comfortably exceeds the amount of the loan, the outstanding loan is considered to be secure.

house call
Fed call

The current maintenance margin rate set by the Federal Reserve Board is 25 percent. Some brokerage firms set their rates at 35 percent. An investor whose market value fails to satisfy equation 3-19 (counting only marginable securities) will receive a margin call. A margin call can be either a *house call* (if the brokerage firm has a higher maintenance margin rate) or a *Fed call.* The brokerage firm has the option of enforcing or waiving the enforcement of a house margin call. However, a Fed call must be enforced. In either instance, the brokerage house may give the customer a modest amount of time to restore the account to the compliance level.

A margin call may be settled in any of several ways. One way is to deposit sufficient cash into the account to pay down enough of the loan so that the maintenance margin requirement specified in equation 3-19 is met. A second way to settle up is to deposit other marginable securities into the account, thus increasing the equity value of the account. A third way is to sell

---

Ways to Satisfy a Margin Call

- Add more money to the account.
- Add more collateral (marginable securities) to the account.
- Sell stock from the account and use the proceeds to reduce the margin debt.

In each case, the result must raise the equity percentage above the margin maintenance minimum to satisfy the margin call.

a sufficient number of shares from the portfolio and use the sale proceeds to pay down the loan until the maintenance margin requirement is met.

If the investor opts to add cash to the account, then the amount of cash needed is the amount necessary to meet the maintenance margin requirement. In mathematical terms:

$$\text{Cash added} = \text{LOAN} - [\text{MV} \times (1 - \text{MMR})] \qquad \text{(Equation 3-20)}$$

Example:	An investor buys $10,000 worth of stock using $6,000 in cash and a $4,000 loan. The stock falls to a market value of $5,000. If there have been no deposits to offset the loan, what is the amount of the margin call if the maintenance margin rate is 25 percent?
	Cash added = $4,000 – [$5,000 x (1 – .25)]
	= $4,000 – $3,750 = $250

Concentrated Positions

Investors with margin accounts should have relatively well-diversified portfolios of marginable stocks. These accounts are vulnerable to a general market decline, but they tend to be rather well protected against price declines limited to a few individual stocks. If one or two stocks in a diversified portfolio decline sharply, the overall account value will generally be able to withstand the pressure and thereby avoid a margin call.

Example:	If a single stock position representing 10 percent of a portfolio's value falls to half its previous value, that fall would cause the portfolio's overall value to fall by 5 percent. If the account had met the initial margin requirement (50 percent) prior to the stock's decline, it should still be considerably above any maintenance rate.

If, however, a large percentage of the account's value is concentrated in one or a very few stocks, the risk to the margin borrower (and the margin lender) goes up. If the one or few stocks on which most of the account value is derived suffer a serious decline, the danger of a margin call becomes much greater than with a well-diversified portfolio.

Example:	Suppose a stock representing 50 percent of the portfolio's value falls to half its previous value. The portfolio's value would fall by 25 percent (.5 x .5 = .25), which could easily trigger a margin call.

So far, we have talked only about margin calls when a stock declines. If an investor is short a particular stock, and that stock's price rises, he or she could also face a margin call, or be forced to buy back the shorted security.

Incremental Borrowing

In the previous section, we considered the situation in which the value of the portfolio declines and the investor must meet a margin call. Now, let's consider a more pleasant scenario, the removal of cash from a portfolio. In this case, we are not saying that there is actually cash in the portfolio. We are saying that cash is removed as a result of taking out a margin loan, or of increasing one's loan. All that is required to remove cash from a margin account is that the investor's loan balance be lower than what would be required under the initial margin rate. The investor could then remove an amount of cash equal to the difference between the maximum loan allowable using the initial margin rate and the current loan balance. In equation form:

Maximum cash withdrawal = MV x (1 – IMR) – LOAN   (Equation 3-21)

Example: Your client, Ted Kurzy, contacts you to indicate he needs $50,000 in about a week and asks you about the easiest way to acquire the cash. You note that the stocks in his portfolio have a market value of $250,000, the initial margin rate is 60 percent, and his current loan balance in the account is $50,000. You compute his maximum cash withdrawal as follows:

$250,000 x (1 – .60) – $50,000 = $50,000

This is just enough to meet his needs. You would need to point out that should the value of his holdings decline before this loan is repaid, he is at an increased risk of a margin call.

The Leverage of Margin Borrowing

Buying on margin has two effects. The first is that it magnifies any gain or loss to the investor. The second and related effect is that it increases the variability of the returns on the portfolio. To demonstrate these effects, consider the concepts of return on assets (ROA) and return on equity (ROE). In this context, ROA is the equivalent of a holding period return (HPR) for an investment without regard to leverage. ROE is the holding period return actually earned by the investor based on the money invested and the interest expense incurred.

We can present ROA without leverage as follows:

$$ROA = \frac{\text{Ending value} - \text{Beginning value}}{\text{Beginning value}}$$

Ending value is assumed to include reinvested dividends.

ROE differs from ROA in that it incorporates the interest payments, and uses the out-of-pocket cash invested as the base for measuring the return. The formula is:

$$ROE = \frac{\left(\text{Ending value} - \text{Beginning value}\right) - \text{Interest charges}}{\text{Initial investment}}$$

(Equation 3-22)

The return to the investor in the numerator is the change in the total value of the investment (that is, ending value minus beginning value), where dividend payments are included in the ending value and consideration is given to the interest charges. Thus, ROE focuses on the change in the total value of the investment relative to what the investor actually paid for it.

Example: An investor buys 1,000 shares at $50 per share. One year later the shares are worth $55 per share. The ROA (and HPR) would be:

$$ROA = \frac{\$55,000 - \$50,000}{\$50,000}$$

$$= .10 \text{ or } 10\%$$

If the investor had margined the investment at 60 percent with an interest rate of 7 percent, then the ROE would be:

$$ROE = \frac{\$55,000 - \$50,000 - \left(.07 \text{ x} \left[1 - .60\right] \text{ x } \$50,000\right)}{\$50,000 \text{ x } .60}$$

$$= \frac{\$3,600}{\$30,000}$$

$$= .12 \text{ or } 12\%$$

Thus, one can say that the security provided a 10 percent rate of return (that is, ROA), but the investor received a 12 percent rate of return (that is, ROE).

Of course, leverage entails risk. If the price had risen by only 1 dollar to $51 during the year, the ROA would have been:

$$ROA = \frac{\text{Ending value} - \text{Beginning value}}{\text{Beginning value}}$$

$$= \frac{\$51,000 - 50,000}{\$50,000}$$

$$= .02 \text{ or } 2\%$$

The ROE would have been:

$$ROE = \frac{\$51,000 - \$50,000 - \left(.07 \times [1 - .60] \times \$50,000\right)}{\$50,000 \times 0.6}$$

$$= \frac{-\$400}{\$30,000}$$

$$= -.0133 \text{ or } 1.33\%$$

In the above example, the interest rate was applied to the beginning loan balance to compute the annual interest expense. As will be discussed in the next section, the interest rate is actually a variable rate, and if the investor accrues interest charges, the loan balance and interest expense would actually grow over time. Hence, the above loan charges are a simplification.

Table 3-1 provides a comparison of ROA and ROE for cash and margin purchases with price movements in 5-dollar increments.

TABLE 3-1
Margin Example: Purchase 100 Shares at $50 Per Share, No Dividends, 7% Borrowing Rate, Holding Period of 1 Year

	Cash Purchase	60% Margin Purchase
Ending Price	ROA	ROE
$35	−30%	−54.67%
$40	−20%	−38.00%
$45	−10%	−21.33%
$50	0%	−4.67%
$55	10%	12.00%
$60	20%	28.67%
$65	30%	45.33%

The two key points the reader should note in table 3-1 are the same as noted earlier. Buying on margin has two effects: magnifying the percentage gain or loss that is achieved, and increasing the variability of the investor's returns. When the investment does well, the investor benefits from buying on margin; when it does badly, he or she suffers even more.

Financial Planning Issue

There are two ways to think about using margin. One is that with a purchase on margin, the investor can buy the same amount of stock he or she would have bought and just have to pay less out-of-pocket cash. The second is that the investor could pay the same amount of cash as he or she would have paid without the margin purchase, but now buy substantially more shares. The latter approach will result in a larger loan in absolute terms and a bigger commitment to this risky investment. Although only aggressive investors should even consider buying on margin, the latter approach should be considered only by the more aggressive in this group.

The Mechanics of Buying on Margin

credit balance
debit balance
broker call-loan rate

Brokerage firms finance some of their margin lending from other customers' credit balances, such as those generated through short sales. A positive balance in a customer's account is called a *credit balance*; a negative one (a margin loan) is referred to as a *debit balance*. Brokerage firms obtain additional funds to loan from commercial banks at the *broker call-loan rate*.

Interest charges on margin loans are based on the exact time and amount of the loan. If, for example, $10,000 is borrowed and then $750 is repaid a week later, interest will be calculated on $10,000 for one week and then on $9,250 thereafter. Margin loan interest rates are usually determined by a sliding scale added to the broker call-loan rate. Table 3-2 is representative.

TABLE 3-2
Typical Margin Loan Rates

Net Debit Balance	Call Rate Plus
$ 0 – 9,999	2.25%
$10,000 – 29,999	1.75%
$30,000 – 49,999	1.25%
$50,000 and over	.75%

Banks generally set their broker call-loan rate equal to or below their prime rate. Margin loan rates are normally no more than 2 percent above the prime business rate. Relatively favorable interest rates and flexible payment schedules make margin loans an attractive credit source.

Preferreds, warrants, and convertibles are subject to the same margin requirements as common stocks. Margin restrictions also apply to corporate bond purchases, although their proportional collateral value is typically higher. (Only 25 percent margin rate is required on most nonconvertible bonds.) A 10 percent margin requirement applies to government bonds with a 10-year or greater maturity; the margin requirement is lower for shorter-term governments.

While brokerage houses specialize in margin loans, banks and other financial intermediaries also accept securities as collateral. If these loans finance other security purchases, the Fed's margin restrictions apply. Otherwise, the lender can determine the maximum loan value on such collateral.

SUMMARY AND CONCLUSIONS

The two key parameters to evaluating investments are return and risk. Return includes periodic payments, such as dividends, interest, rents, and royalties, as well as changes in market value. The most basic measure of return is the HPR, which is defined as the sum of the income received and the change in value, divided by the beginning value. A closely related term is the HPRR, which substitutes ending value for the change in value. The HPRR equals the HPR plus 1. More sophisticated analysis requires computation of PPRs, which have the same formula as HPRs, except the terms are adjusted for each period.

An expected return can be calculated with the HPR if one wants to guess specific future values. More commonly a probability distribution is specified, and the expected return is then the sum of the products of the possible returns and the associated probabilities. A portfolio's HPR can be computed either by treating the portfolio as a single security and using the HPR formula, or by taking the sum of the products of the market weights of each holding and the HPR of that holding.

When converting a series of PPRs to an average annual return, it is tempting to use the arithmetic average, but it is also wrong. Although this answer may be approximately correct, the correct answer is defined by the geometric mean, which is the nth root of the product of n terms, minus 1.

In investments, risk is conceived of as variability of return, not just the chance of losing money. There are a wide variety of sources of investment risk. These include:

- Inflation risk—the risk of loss of purchasing power
- Interest rate risk—includes both price risk and reinvestment rate risk
- Market risk—the risk from events that affect the entire market
- Business (default) risk—the risk of a specific company doing poorly or going bankrupt

- Liquidity risk—the risk that the investor will not be able to sell an asset quickly at or near the current market price
- Political (sovereign) risk—the risk of expropriation or other calamities that could result from owning assets in foreign countries
- Exchange rate risk—the risk of loss in value of business operations located in foreign countries due to an adverse move in exchange rates
- Tax risk—the risk of future changes in the tax code that may adversely affect one's holdings
- Additional commitment risk—the risk that an investment may require the owner to invest additional monies

Although such measures as semivariance would seem intuitive for measuring riskiness, the most common measures are variance and its square root, the standard deviation. Three different formulas are used to compute variance, depending on the nature of the numbers being analyzed. One is for when one works with an ex ante probability distribution; the second is for when all of the possible returns have equal probabilities; and the third is for when one is using historical data. A related measure of risk is the coefficient of variation, which is the standard deviation divided by the expected return or the mean.

Buying on margin increases the risk of any investment. Buying on margin means paying for only part of the purchase price out-of-pocket (that is, the margin), and then borrowing the rest of the proceeds from the broker. When buying on margin, one's primary concern is receiving a margin call, which happens whenever the equity balance as a percentage of the market value of the investment falls below the maintenance margin rate. When this happens, the investor must either deposit additional cash, add securities to the account, or sell some holdings and use the proceeds to pay down the loan. Buying on margin can be extremely risky when one has a significant concentration of holdings.

CHAPTER REVIEW

Answers to the review questions and the self-test questions start on page 733.

Key Terms

holding period return (HPR)
holding period return relative
    (HPRR)
expected HPR
per period return (PPR)

compounding
ex post
ex ante
weights
geometric mean return (GMR)

pure risk	semivariance
speculative risk	variance
inflation risk	coefficient of variation
interest rate risk	buying on margin
price risk	initial margin rate
reinvestment rate risk	buying power
market risk	equity value
business risk	margin call
default risk	maintenance margin percentage
liquidity risk	house call
political risk	Fed call
exchange rate risk	credit balance
tax risk	debit balance
additional commitment risk	broker call-loan rate
risk averse	

Review Questions

3-1. Compute the HPRR and the HPR for each of the following:

    a. an investment in land purchased for $5,000 and sold for $7,000

    b. a $3,000 non-interest-bearing note purchased for $1,800 and held until maturity, at which time it is paid off at its face value

    c. a building that is held for 9 months, during which time it generates $3,500 in rental income (in excess of costs), and then is sold for a $30,000 profit. Its original purchase price was $195,000

3-2. Compute the annual return (that is, the HPR) for each of the following investments:

    a. an investment in 100 shares of stock that cost $10 per share, sold 1 year later for $11 per share, during which time a 30-cent-per-share dividend is received (ignore commissions in your computations)

    b. a bond that is bought for $950, pays $70 interest during the year, and is sold at the end of the year for $940

3-3. a. Compute the PPR of a portfolio that consists of equal amounts invested in assets yielding returns of 7.8 percent, 9.3 percent, 4.5 percent, and 11.5 percent.

    b. Now suppose the amounts invested (in a. above) are in the proportions of .2, .3, .4, and .1. What would this portfolio's PPR be?

3-4. Compute the GMR for an investment with the following PPRs: −8.9 percent, 5.6 percent, 10 percent, 7.7 percent, and 13.0 percent.

3-5. Compute the expected return and standard deviation for an investment with the following probabilities of return:

    a.   equally probable returns of –5 percent, 0 percent, 5 percent, 10 percent

    b.   10 percent chance of a 0 percent return, 15 percent chance of a 5 percent return, 25 percent chance of a 10 percent return, 25 percent chance of a 15 percent return, 15 percent chance of a 20 percent return, 10 percent chance of a 25 percent return

    c.   100 percent chance of a 10 percent return

3-6.   Assume equal amounts are invested in venture capital opportunities with the following 5-year HPRs: 80 percent, –25 percent, –15 percent, 12 percent, 10.5 percent, –80 percent, 350 percent, –100 percent, and 0 percent.

    a.   What would the overall HPR be?

    b.   Based on your answer in part a., what would the per-period (annual) GMR be for this 5-year holding period?

3-7.   You have looked up the rates of return on the Crazy Go-Go Mutual Fund for the last 10 years, and computed that its arithmetic mean return is 15 percent, but its GMR is only 10 percent. You want the optimal forecasted rate of return for next year for this fund. What would be the single best guess?

3-8.   a.   If an investor wants a 5 percent real rate of return, and the inflation rate is 4 percent, what nominal rate must he or she obtain?

    b.   If an investor is receiving a nominal rate of return of 15 percent, and the inflation rate is 10 percent, what is his or her real rate of return?

3-9.   XYZ stock has the following rates of return for the last 3 years: –15 percent, 10 percent, and 35 percent. Determine XYZ's expected return, variance, standard deviation, and coefficient of variation based on this historical data.

3-10. David Gordon buys 100 shares of Uhoh Corp. at $50 per share. The initial margin rate is 60 percent and the maintenance margin rate is 25 percent, and he buys it with minimum margin.

    a.   How much does he initially borrow?

    b.   If the stock rises to $80 per share shortly thereafter (ignore interest charges), how much cash could he withdraw from his account?

    c.   If the stock rises to $80 per share shortly thereafter (ignore interest charges), how many additional shares could he buy?

    d.   If the stock falls, rather than rises, what is the lowest price it can fall to before he receives a margin call?

    e.   Suppose the stock falls to $20 per share. What is the size of the margin call?

3-11. Assume the broker call-loan rate is 8 1/2 percent and that the margin loan rates of table 3-2 apply. Compute the cost of margin for each of the following, using monthly compounding:

    a. $53,000 borrowed for 6 months

    b. $27,000 borrowed for 3 months

Self-Test Questions

T   F   3-1.   The holding period return (HPR) relates the profit on an investment directly to its beginning value.

T   F   3-2.   An asset's per-period return (PPR) is defined as the sum of that period's income payments and price appreciation minus its beginning-of-period price.

T   F   3-3.   Accumulating returns over time and earning a return on the return of previous periods is called compounding.

T   F   3-4.   If an investor deposits $10,000 in an account that yields 5 percent annually and has no withdrawals for 2 years, then he or she will end up with $11,000.

T   F   3-5.   Unless the PPRs are all identical, the geometric mean return will always be less than the arithmetic mean.

T   F   3-6.   In finance and economics, the term risk refers to the dispersion of possible returns.

T   F   3-7.   Risk is defined as the chance that the actual outcome from an investment will be less than the expected outcome.

T   F   3-8.   Inflation risk is the risk that the general level of prices will grow at a slower rate.

T   F   3-9.   Additional commitment risk is the risk that one might have to put additional monies into an investment.

T   F   3-10. Interest rate risk is the risk that the interest rate on a margin loan will exceed the rate of return on the investment.

T   F   3-11. Market risk is the risk that a security cannot be sold quickly at the current market value.

T   F   3-12. Business risk is the risk from events that affect a particular company.

T   F   3-13. Political risk is the risk of loss in value due to fluctuations in the exchange rate.

T   F   3-14. Tax risk is the risk that one might have to pay taxes on one's income.

T   F   3-15. The standard deviation is a measure of an asset's riskiness.

T   F   3-16. If two investments, A and B, have equal expected returns, but A has a larger standard deviation than B, then all risk-averse investors would choose A.

T   F   3-17. Calculating the semivariance involves using only the prospective returns that are above the expected return.

T   F   3-18. To compute the variance, one has to calculate the standard deviation and then square the result.

T   F   3-19. The calculation of the expected return when all returns are equally weighted is the same procedure as calculating expected return when using historical data.

T   F   3-20. The calculation of the variance when all returns are equally weighted is the same procedure as calculating the variance when using historical data.

T   F   3-21. The initial margin rate is the amount of money one can borrow to buy a security.

T   F   3-22. The Federal Reserve Board has set the initial margin requirement on stocks at 25 percent.

T   F   3-23. Buying on margin reduces the variability of an investor's returns.

T   F   3-24. All margin loans are at the call-loan rate.

T   F   3-25. Margin loans may remain outstanding as long as the borrower's equity position does not fall below the maintenance margin percentage.

T   F   3-26. Preferreds, warrants, and convertibles are subject to the same margin requirements as common stock.

T   F   3-27. The maintenance margin rate is lower than the initial margin rate.

T   F   3-28. The three ways to satisfy a margin call are to add cash to the account, add marginable securities, or to sell holdings and use the proceeds to pay down the loan balance.

T   F   3-29. Buying on margin is even riskier when a significant portion of the portfolio is concentrated in one holding.

T   F   3-30. As long as an account has borrowing power, one can withdraw cash by increasing the loan balance.

NOTES

1. Return and risk are two of the most critical topics tested on the CFP® exam.
2. The summation symbol is used whenever a series of identical terms are added together. The summation always has beginning and ending sequence numbers, which are specified below and above the summation symbol. The beginning number is then substituted into each term, augmented by one each time. As a simple example, consider the following:

$$\sum_{i=1}^{i=3} i = 1 + 2 + 3 = 6$$

When symbols are used, then

$$\sum_{i=1}^{i=3} X_i = X_1 + X_2 + X_3$$

3. A three-security portfolio would normally be a terrible recommendation because of the lack of diversification. However, we will limit ourselves to three securities to keep this example simple.

4. "Geometric or Arithmetic Mean: A Reconsideration," by Eric Jacquier, Alex Kane, and Alan Marcus, *Financial Analysts Journal,* November/December 2003, pp. 46–53.

5. The only 2 years of deflation were 1949 and 1955, and the inflation rates were −1.2 percent and −.4 percent. See http://www.halfhill.com/inflation.html.

6. Actually, long-term nominal rates have three unobserved components: the real rate, the inflation compensation, and a premium for inflation uncertainty. However, since this third component is so small compared to the other two, it is essentially ignored. See *Monetary Trends*, Federal Reserve Bank of St. Louis, February 2004, p. 1.

7. The magnitude of diversification that is necessary, and how one measures that diversification, is discussed in chapter 4.

8. The units of this term, percent-squared, have no relevancy, and should be ignored for practical purposes.

9. In statistical terms, we lose one degree of freedom by using a sample to describe the entire distribution. The adjustment for this loss of a degree of freedom is to use $(n − 1)$ instead of n in the denominator.

Appendix 3A

Monte Carlo Simulation

Heretofore expected returns have been described with a single number. For example, one can say the annual expected return on a stock or a portfolio is 10 percent. We have also shown how these expected returns are the result of a distribution of returns. For example, we can project a 20 percent probability that a stock will earn 15 percent over the next 12 months, a 60 percent probability that it will earn 6 percent, and a 20 percent probability that it will lose 5 percent. Based on this distribution, the expected return is 5.6 percent. We have also looked at the issue of measuring annual average returns over multiple years, and the importance of arithmetic versus geometric mean returns. Another way to talk about returns with a client is Monte Carlo simulation.

Simple Monte Carlo simulation is the process whereby one uses a technique of repeated samplings from a probability distribution to ascertain a final distribution.[1] Let's consider a simple example. A planner is presenting a proposed stock portfolio to a client. The planner tells the client that the annual expected rate of return on the portfolio is 8 percent, and that the standard deviation of return is 15 percent. The client is 45 years old and plans to retire in 20 years. Naturally, the client wants to know not what the expected annual rate of return is or what the standard deviation of return is, but what the dollar value of the portfolio will be at the time of retirement. Suppose the current value of the client's portfolio is $200,000. If the portfolio achieved exactly an 8 percent rate of return each and every year for 20 years, its value in 20 years would be $932,191 (C ALL, 200,000, PV, 8, I/YR, 20, N, FV [display: –932,191.43]).

However, a good planner knows that it is incredibly unlikely that the portfolio will exactly equal this amount because it is unlikely that an 8 percent rate of return will be earned each year. Thus, it would be more appropriate for the planner to present to the client some sense of the range of possible terminal portfolio values. This range of possible values is where Monte Carlo simulation comes into play.

The key to Monte Carlo simulation is looking upon a return as being generated by a random distribution process. In the above example, let's simulate the first year's rate of return by randomly selecting a number from a standard deviation distribution table of random numbers. These are numbers that are randomly generated for a normal distribution whose mean is 0 and whose standard deviation is 1. Suppose the number drawn from such a table is .625. Multiply .625 by the estimated standard deviation of 15 percent to obtain a return that is 9.375 percent above the mean. Add this to the projected mean of 8 percent to obtain a simulated first year's return of 17.375 percent. Thus, after 1 year, the portfolio would be worth $234,750 ($200,000 x [1 + .17375]).

To simulate the second year's return, draw another number from the normal distribution random number table. Suppose the second number so drawn is −1.86. Again, multiply the −1.86 by the 15 percent standard deviation of return to find a return that is 27.90 percent below the mean. Subtract this from the mean of 8 percent, to find that the second year's simulated return is −19.90 percent. Thus, after two years, the portfolio would be worth $188,035 ($234,750 x [1 − .1990]).

This process is repeated 18 more times to obtain annual rates of return for the projected 20-year period and the value of the portfolio after 20 years. Let's suppose that when this exercise is completed, the ending value of the portfolio turns out to be $910,000. This represents one example of an ending portfolio value. Next, assume that this exercise is repeated a large number of times, say 999 more times. Each of these 999 additional exercises will produce an ending portfolio value. What we are interested in is the summary statistics of these 1,000 different portfolio values.

The most obvious statistic will be the arithmetic mean, but we already know that this number will be approximately $932,191. Of more interest are the statistics on the range of outcomes. Again, an obvious statistic to compute is the standard deviation of ending portfolio values. Some clients may be able to make sense of this number. For others, a more meaningful representation might be portfolio values representing different likelihoods of outcome. Think about it as if all 1,000 ending values were rank ordered, with the 1st portfolio representing the largest value and the 1,000th portfolio representing the smallest value. For example, this exercise might produce an outcome in which the 50th portfolio (i.e., the lowest portfolio representing the top 5 percent) has a value of $945,000. The 333rd portfolio (i.e., the lowest portfolio representing the top one-third) has a value of $937,250, the 667th portfolio has a value of $926,880, and the 951st portfolio has a value of $928,725. These numbers would now give the client a better sense of the risk exposure he or she faces in terms of achieving a desired portfolio value.

The key to this simulation, of course, is whether or not the mean and standard deviation of the hypothesized distribution is correct. Unfortunately, we have no way of knowing what the appropriate numbers are for the future. Thus, for applications most people will look at the historical mean and standard deviations of stocks or similar portfolios to see what would be reasonable numbers.

NOTE

1. For a good discussion on Monte Carlo simulation and similar tools, see "Decision Making Under Conditions of Uncertainty: A Wakeup Call for the Financial Planning Profession," by Lynn Hopewell, CFP®, *Journal of Financial Planning,* April 2004, pp. 76–86.

Managing Portfolios: Theory

Learning Objectives

An understanding of the material in this chapter should enable the student to

---

4-1. Explain why portfolio risk is different from individual security risk.

4-2. Explain why the combination of two risky securities can produce a portfolio with less risk and why covariance and the correlation coefficient affects the final level of risk.

4-3. Describe how the optimal portfolio for an investor is the tangency between the efficient frontier and the highest possible indifference curve.

4-4. Distinguish between the "old" efficient frontier produced by n risky assets and the "new" efficient frontier as defined by the capital market line (CML).

4-5. Explain the roles of beta and the coefficient of determination in defining the risk of a particular security as part of the capital asset pricing model (CAPM).

4-6. Describe the multifactor asset pricing model.

4-7. Describe why an understanding of modern portfolio theory is so important for today's practitioner, and what its legal implications are.

Chapter Outline

This chapter is about theory! Nobody says that the theory that will be presented herein is a realistic description of how securities are priced. Nonetheless, the theory that follows is critical to understanding how many people think about assets and the issues associated with constructing a portfolio. This theory, known as modern portfolio theory, is about the concepts of assembling and managing a portfolio of stocks. It provides a basis for the common techniques that are used to evaluate the performance of portfolio managers. It is the only commonly accepted theory about stock market returns that currently exists. If someone comes along with a better theoretical model that also seems to be a better description of reality, then we would abandon modern portfolio theory and move to the new theory. However, such an alternative theory has not yet been developed, and there is no indication that one will appear anytime soon. Modern portfolio theory started with the research of Harry M. Markowitz in the 1950s and by the mid-'60s was pretty well developed. So it has provided the basic building blocks of financial research for well over 40 years. In the chapters that follow, we will look at the various issues associated with applications of modern portfolio theory.

INDIVIDUAL VERSUS PORTFOLIO RISK

As discussed in chapter 3, risk in investments is defined in terms of speculative risk. Thus, simply earning less than one expects to earn, even though the actual return is positive, is considered an undesirable outcome. As long as the possible returns are symmetrical about the expected return (for example, as long as earning 5 percent more than expected is as equally likely as earning 5 percent less than expected), the standard deviation is a useful measure of an individual investment's risk. The standard deviation of an individual asset's expected return is an inadequate risk measure, however, if the asset is part of a larger portfolio. The reason is that if poor performance by some parts of the portfolio tends to be offset by more favorable performance in the rest of the portfolio, the investor's overall wealth position may not suffer. The investor is unlikely to know ahead of time those investments that will do well and those that will not, but he or she will know that some investments will do better than others. The more diversified the portfolio, the more likely individual losses in the portfolio are offset by other investments that are doing well because of the same set of events. Accordingly, investors should concern themselves primarily with portfolio risk, rather than the risks of each of the portfolio's individual components. If the values of two investments fluctuate by offsetting amounts, the owner is no worse off than if neither had varied. This following example shows the benefits of diversification.

Example: Imagine a sunscreen business and an umbrella business at the beach. Let's say there is a 50 percent chance that it will rain and a 50 percent chance that it will be sunny. The sunscreen business will have a 20 percent return if it is sunny but a 0 percent return if it rains. The umbrella business will have a 20 percent return if it rains but a 0 percent return if it is sunny. Each business will have an expected return of 10 percent (.5 x 20%) and a standard deviation of 10 percent. Now imagine a diversified portfolio consisting of equal weights of the sunscreen and umbrella businesses. It will still have an expected return of 10 percent, but the standard deviation is now zero (that is, the portfolio is risk-free) since there will be a 10 percent return whether it is sunny or rainy.

As the simplified example above shows, diversification has been used to create a risk-free portfolio out of two risky investments. Note that risk has been eliminated without any reduction in the expected return.

TWO-ASSET PORTFOLIO RISK

The simplest type of portfolio contains a single asset, such as stock in one company. This portfolio is, by definition, totally undiversified. The next simplest portfolio contains two assets, such as stock in two different companies. A two-asset portfolio might be able to take advantage of the risk-reduction potential of diversification. The expected return of the two-asset portfolio is

$$E\left(R_p\right) = W_i\left[E\left(R_i\right)\right] + W_j\left[E\left(R_j\right)\right] \qquad \text{(Equation 4-1)}$$

where W_i = portfolio weight of asset i
       W_j = portfolio weight of asset j

Recall that expected return was presented in chapter 3 as being based on the sum of the products of the different possible returns and the probability associated with each return. This expected return formula is based on the product of the weight for each asset and the expected return for each asset. The expected return on each asset (that is, $E(R_i)$ and $E(R_j)$) could easily be computed using the expected return formula in chapter 3.

The one requirement for the weights is that they add up to 1 (100 percent):

$$W_i + W_j = 1 \qquad \text{(Equation 4-1a)}$$

The fact that they total 1 simply means the portfolio is fully invested in those two assets. Normally, we think about each separate weight as being bounded by 0 and 100 percent. However, this is not a requirement. Obviously, if one weight were less than 0, the other would have to be greater than 100 percent. A weight less than 0 would imply the person has taken a short position in that asset and used the proceeds from the sale to buy more of the other asset.

Example: Your client has two stocks, Xylog and PT&A. The expected return on Xylog is 8 percent, and on PT&A it is 12 percent. The client has 30 percent of the portfolio's value invested in Xylog and the remaining 70 percent invested in PT&A. What is the portfolio's expected return?

$$E(R_p) = (30\% \times .08) + (70\% \times .12) = .1080 \text{ or } 10.8\%$$

The risk of the portfolio depends on both the individual risk of its two components and the degree to which the two components' returns are related. The portfolio variance for a two-asset portfolio is shown in equation 4-2:

$$\sigma_p^2 = W_i^2\sigma_i^2 + 2W_iW_j COV_{ij} + W_j^2\sigma_j^2 \qquad \text{(Equation 4-2)}$$

where σ_i^2 = variance of asset i
       σ_j^2 = variance of asset j
       COV_{ij} = covariance of asset i with j

As with expected return, variance was defined in chapter 3 for a single asset. The chapter 3 definition would be used to compute σ_i^2 and σ_j^2 as they appear in equation 4-2. The terms $W_i^2\sigma_i^2$ and $W_j^2\sigma_j^2$ are the squares of each component's weight multiplied by its respective variance.

The remaining term, $2W_iW_j\,COV_{ij}$, requires further explanation. The first part of the term, $2W_iW_j$, is two times the product of the weights W_i and W_j. The key—indeed, a central aspect of portfolio risk in general—is the covariance term COV_{ij} (the symbol σ_{ij} is also sometimes used), which is defined in the next section. The covariance quantifies the effect of portfolio diversification.

Covariance

The covariance, like the mean and standard deviation, is a statistic that is almost always estimated from ex post (historical) values of the relevant variables. It measures the comovement or covariability of two variables. Thus, the covariance of two assets' returns is an index of how they tend to move relative to each other. For example, the market prices of stocks of two similar companies that operate in the same industry would probably tend to move together. On the other hand, stock prices of two different types of companies operating in different industries would probably tend to move largely independently of each other. There sometimes exist companies whose stock prices tend to move opposite to each other (like the sunscreen/umbrella example earlier). The first pair of stocks (same industry) would have a relatively high positive covariance with each other, the second pair (different industries) would have a covariance closer to 0, and the last pair (sunscreen/ umbrella) would have a negative covariance. Stocks with negative covariances are the best bet for diversification, but stocks with covariances near 0 are almost as good. Stocks with high positive covariances are poor vehicles for diversification and should not be held in tandem.

To understand how the covariance statistic is defined, recall that when we computed the variance of a security's returns, we multiplied the probability of each return by the square of the difference between that return and the expected return (see equation 3-11). Because of the squaring process, all of the terms in the summation are positive. Had the squaring process not been used, some of the terms would have been positive and some negative. Now consider the product of the differences between each expected return and its respective mean for assets i and j, namely $[(R_{it} - E(R_i))][R_{jt} - E(R_j)]$. When the returns of the two assets are either both above or both below their means, the product is positive. The product of two positive numbers is positive, and the product of two negative numbers is also positive. The product of these two differences is negative when one is above its mean and the other below. The covariance is defined as the average of the products $[R_{it} - E(R_i)][R_{jt} - E(R_j)]$.

When ex ante data are used (that is, projected rates of return and the associated probability distribution), the formula for covariance is:

$$\text{COV}_{ij} = \sum_{t=1}^{n} P_t \times \left[R_{it} - E(R_i) \right]\left[R_{jt} - E(R_j) \right] \quad \text{(Equation 4-3)}$$

where COV_{ij} = covariance of the returns on securities i and j
P_t = probability of R_{it} and R_{jt} occurring

Example: Consider again two businesses at the beach, selling sunscreen lotion and umbrellas. The rate of return on each business depends on the weather. Suppose that after listening to the weather forecast, you believe the following probabilities and rates of return would apply to these businesses:

P_t Probability	R_{it} (sunscreen)	R_{jt} (umbrella)	$R_{it} \times P_t$	$R_{jt} \times P_t$
30% (rain)	–30%	40%	–9%	12%
50% (cloudy)	10%	2%	5%	1%
20% (sunny)	30%	–30%	6%	–6%
		Total	2%	7%

The expected returns for each business are 2 and 7 percent. The covariance of returns between these two business would be computed using equation 4-3 as follows:

$$\begin{aligned}
\text{COV}_{ij} &= .30 \times (-30\% - 2\%) \times (40\% - 7\%) \\
&\quad + .50 \times (10\% - 2\%) \times (2\% - 7\%) \\
&\quad + .20 \times (30\% - 2\%) \times (-30\% - 7\%) \\
&= -316.8\%^2 - 20\%^2 - 207.2\%^2 = -544\%^2
\end{aligned}$$

Notice that all three cross products are negative, which is why the sum is a large negative number.

(Note in the above example that the units for the covariance term is "percent-squared," the same units obtained when calculating variances. Again, because no one really knows what a "percent-squared" is, people tend to express covariance numerically without units attached.)

When dealing with ex post data, the covariance of a two-asset portfolio is defined as follows:

$$COV_{ij} = \sum_{t=1}^{n} \left[R_{it} - E(R_i) \right]\left[R_{jt} - E(R_j) \right] / (n - 1)$$

$$= \frac{1}{(n-1)} \sum_{t=1}^{n} [R_{it} - E(R_i)][R_{jt} - E(R_j)] \qquad \text{(Equation 4-4)}$$

Example: Suppose that for the last 5 years we have the following five annual rates of return for securities i and j (expressed in percentages):

$$(R_{i1}, \ R_{j1}) \ = \ (5, 4)$$
$$(R_{i2}, \ R_{j2}) \ = \ (10, 15)$$
$$(R_{i3}, \ R_{j3}) \ = \ (-7, -12)$$
$$(R_{i4}, \ R_{j4}) \ = \ (-2, 2)$$
$$(R_{i5}, \ R_{j5}) \ = \ (19, 16)$$

To compute the covariance between these two securities, we must first compute their average returns.

$$\overline{R}_i = E(R_i) = \left(\frac{5+10-7-2+19}{5} \right) = \frac{25}{5} = 5$$

$$\overline{R}_j = E(R_j) = \left(\frac{4+15-12+2+16}{5} \right) = \frac{25}{5} = 5$$

Note that in computing the average return (that is, arithmetic mean) for each security, we use the number of observations in the denominator. Next, we must compute the values of the differences $(R_{it} - \overline{R}_j)$ and $(R_{jt} - \overline{R}_j)$, and their product for each year t:

$R_{it} - \overline{R}_i$	$R_{jt} - \overline{R}_j$	$(R_{it} - \overline{R}_i)(R_{jt} - \overline{R}_j)$
5 – 5 = 0	4 – 5 = –1	0 x –1 = 0
10 – 5 = 5	15 – 5 = 10	5 x 10 = 50
–7 – 5 = –12	–12 – 5 = –17	–12 x –17 = 204
–2 – 5 = –7	2 – 5 = –3	–7 x –3 = 21
19 – 5 = 14	16 – 5 = 11	14 x 11 = 154

Finally, we can determine the covariance by adding the values in the right hand column, then dividing by (n–1), because the data represent a sample:

$$COV_{ij} = \frac{0 + 50 + 204 + 21 + 154}{5 - 1} = 107.25$$

In this case, the covariance is positive, telling us that these two rates of return tend to move together.

Correlation Coefficient

As indicated above, the covariance statistic is usually difficult to interpret because of the ambiguity of its units. A second problem involves interpretation of its magnitude. In the last example (using ex post data), we computed the covariance as 107.25 (percent-squared). The real question facing a user of this statistic is whether this is a "large" number. The answer is that it depends on the magnitudes of the variances of the two securities. If the variances were each 1,000 or more, than this covariance is "small." If the variances were about 150, then this is a "huge" number.

The most common way to deal with the deficiencies of the covariance as a measure of comovement or covariability is to use instead the statistic known as the correlation coefficient. The correlation coefficient of two securities, i and j, is usually denoted as ρ_{ij}. It is defined as the covariance divided by the product of the standard deviations, as shown in equation 4-5.

$$\rho_{ij} = COV_{ij}/\left(\sigma_i \times \sigma_j\right)$$ (Equation 4-5)

Sometimes the covariance is defined as a function of the correlation coefficient. In this case, the formula is written as follows:

$$COV_{ij} = \sigma_i \times \sigma_j \times \rho_{ij}$$ (Equation 4-5a)

It is this version of the equation that is shown on the CFP® Board's formula sheet.

Note that although the units of the numerator are percent-squared, the unit for the standard deviation is percent, so the unit of the product of two standard deviations is also percent-squared. Because the numerator and denominator have the same units, a correlation coefficient has no units—it is simply a unitless numerical statistic.

It can be mathematically proven that correlation coefficients will always fall between a maximum of 1 and a minimum of −1. Thus, it is sufficient by itself to indicate the degree of relationship between the returns on any two securities. If the prices of two securities change at the same time, in the same direction, and are always perfectly proportional, then $\rho_{ij} = 1$. If the prices change at the same time and are perfectly proportional but change in opposite directions, then $\rho_{ij} = -1$. If there is absolutely no relationship between the two returns, then $\rho_{ij} = 0$. Again, the range of possible values for ρ_{ij} is $-1 \le \rho_{ij} \le 1$.

Examples of correlation coefficients are shown in figure 4-1. The axes of the graphs are R_i on the horizontal axis and R_j on the vertical axis. Each point on the graph represents one time period's rates of return for these two securities. Whenever investments i and j are above their averages together, the point is plotted in the upper right-hand quadrant. When they are simultaneously below their means, the point is plotted in the lower left-hand quadrant. Investments that tend to vary together in this way will largely plot in an area concentrated in those two quadrants. Most asset pairs exhibit this positive covariance.

Graph A shows a fairly tight positive relationship between two returns, meaning that there is a strong tendency to move together. The correlation coefficient might be something like .7. Graph B shows a negative and weak relationship between the two sets of returns. Its correlation coefficient might be something like −.2. Graphs C and D both show examples of correlation coefficients of 0. Graph C clearly indicates there is no relationship between the two returns. Graph D shows a clear relationship, but also that this relationship is not linear. Correlation coefficients only measure how closely two returns are to a linear relationship. Finally, graphs E and F show perfect linear relationships, one positive (E) and one negative (F). Note that proportionality does not imply that returns are necessarily equal, only that they exhibit a constant relationship. If, for example, an asset i always has returns equal to two times those of asset j, the returns are exactly proportional and their correlation coefficient would be 1. In this example, the points on the graph would form a line whose slope is 2. The following example illustrates the effects of a correlation coefficient on two-asset portfolios.

Example of a Two-Asset Portfolio's Risk

Returning to equations 4-1 and 4-2, consider a simple example. Suppose i and j have standard deviations of 10 and 15 percent respectively, and a covariance of 100. We could form a portfolio composed half of i and half of j. If the expected returns of i and j were 9 and 11 percent, the portfolio's expected return would be 10 percent. This is calculated as follows:

$$E\left(R_p\right) = .5\left(9\%\right) + .5\left(11\%\right) = 4.5\% + 5.5\% = 10\%$$

If we insert the value of the covariance as stated in equation 4-5a into equation 4-2, we obtain the following equation:

$$\sigma_p^{\,2} = W_i^{\,2}\sigma_i^{\,2} + 2W_i W_j \sigma_i \sigma_j \rho_{ij} + W_j^{\,2}\sigma_j^{\,2}$$

Suppose we are considering a portfolio of two securities with standard deviations of 10 and 15 percent, and the portfolio is split evenly between these two securities (that is, 50 percent in each). It would be tempting to think that the standard deviation of the portfolio is 12.5 percent, but this is incorrect. That is, if we assume the following values ($\sigma_i = .10$, $\sigma_j = .15$, $W_i = .5$,

FIGURE 4-1
Examples of Correlation Coefficients

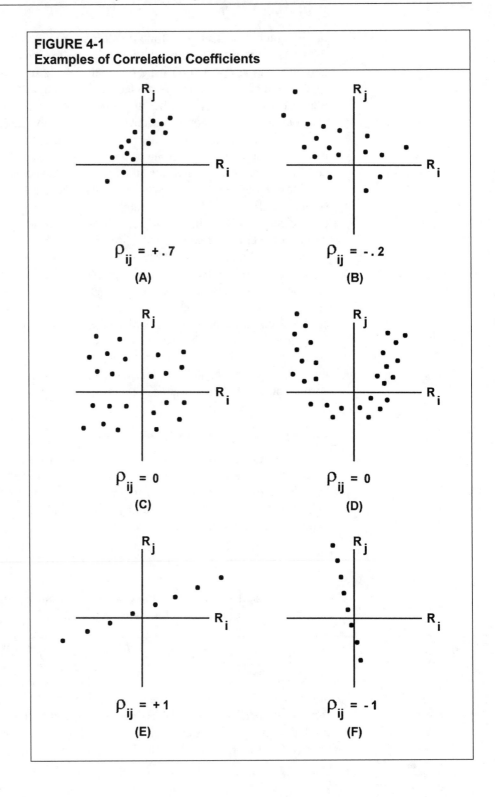

$W_j = .5$, and $\rho_{ij} = .6667$) and insert these values into the above equation, we can compute the variance as follows:

$$\sigma_p^2 = (.5)^2 \times (.10)^2 + 2(.5)(.5)(.10)(.15)(.6667) + (.5)^2 \times (.15)^2$$

$$\sigma_p^2 = .0025 + .0050 + .005625 = .013125$$

Since the standard deviation is the square root of the variance,

$$\sigma_p = \sqrt{.013125} = .1146 \text{ or } 11.46\%$$

In this case, diversifying the portfolio has clearly reduced the risk below the average of the two components' risks. The average risk of the two components is 12.5 percent, compared with the portfolio's overall risk of 11.46 percent. The next section will consider the issue in greater detail.

Three Special Cases

To really understand the impact that the correlation coefficient has on a portfolio's standard deviation, let us consider three special cases. We will first consider the case of what the combination of all possible portfolios would look like if one combines two assets whose correlation coefficient is 1. Then we will proceed to the more interesting case of what the possible combinations of two securities would look like if their correlation coefficient were –1. Finally, we will consider the case where the correlation coefficient is 0.

Before doing so, it is important to remember that regardless of the value of the correlation coefficient, the expected return on the combination of any two assets is simply the weighted average of their expected returns, as defined in equation 4-1.

Correlation Coefficient Equals 1

When the correlation is at its maximum value of 1, the standard deviation formula reduces to the following:

$$\sigma_p = W_i\sigma_i + W_j\sigma_j \qquad \text{(Equation 4-6)}$$

Equation 4-6 says that under this scenario, the standard deviation of the portfolio is a weighted average of the individual standard deviations of securities i and j.

Let's look at a graph of all possible portfolio combinations of these two assets. In figure 4-2, the horizontal axis measures the standard deviation of the portfolios, and the vertical axis measures the expected return. The point

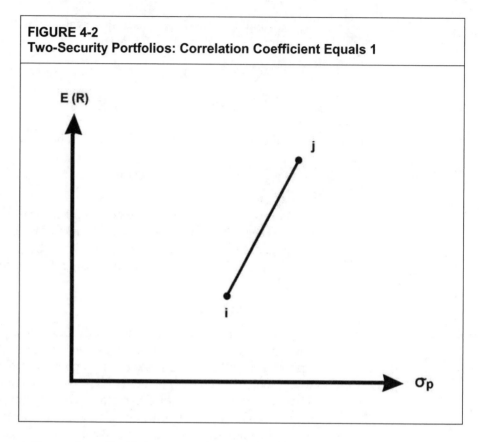

FIGURE 4-2
Two-Security Portfolios: Correlation Coefficient Equals 1

on the graph marked i represents the portfolio that has 100 percent in security i and 0 percent in security j, and the point on the graph marked j represents the portfolio that has 100 percent in security j and 0 percent in security i. To keep the graph simple, we will consider only those combinations of holdings represented by nonnegative weights. One way to think of the graph is that we are plotting 101 different portfolios. The first is invested 100 percent in i and 0 percent in j, the second is invested 99 percent in i and 1 percent in j, and so on. The last portfolio is invested 0 percent in i and 100 percent in j.

Because all of the portfolios' expected returns and standard deviations are linear functions of the two expected returns and standard deviations, the locus of points formed on our graph will be a straight line. That is, the graph of this function is a straight line connecting the points corresponding to assets i and j.

Correlation Coefficient Equals –1

When the correlation is at its minimum value of –1, the standard deviation formula has two solutions:[1]

$$\sigma_p = \begin{cases} -W_i\sigma_i + W_j\sigma_j \text{ or} \\ W_i\sigma_i - W_j\sigma_j \end{cases} \qquad \text{(Equation 4-7)}$$

In figure 4-3, this shows up as two lines. The first line starts at the portfolio that consists of only security i, and moves upward and to the left until in intersects with the vertical axis. The second line then continues moving upward but to the right, until it ends with the portfolio that consists only of security j.

There are two extremely important things about this graph. The first is that when the correlation coefficient is –1, it is possible to choose weights W_i and W_j so that $\sigma_p = 0$. That is, there exists one unique combination of the two securities that is risk-free.[2] On the graph, the point at which the two lines intersect the vertical axis represents this. This one special portfolio is marked with the letter f (which stands for risk-free).

The second important point is that no rational person would choose to hold a portfolio on the lower line segment. The reason is that for any portfolio on the lower line segment, there exists another portfolio on the upper line segment that has the same amount of risk (as measured by the portfolio's standard deviation), but a higher expected return.

FIGURE 4-3
Security Portfolios: Correlation Coefficient Equals –1

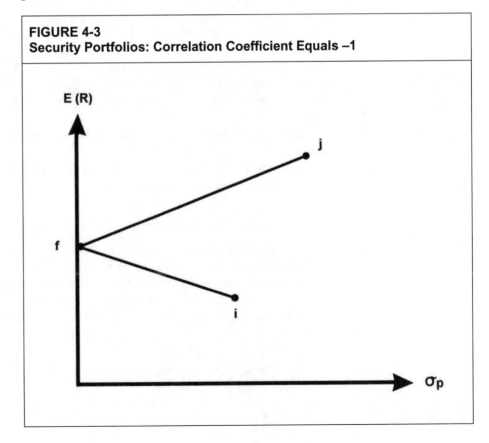

This observation even holds true for the portfolio that consists of holding only security i. If one draws a vertical line through security i, this line will intersect the other line, and provide a portfolio that has the same amount of risk as security i (as measured by its standard deviation) but more expected return. Thus, no rational person would invest only in security i, if he or she could hold a combination of i and j.

Another way to look at the inferiority of the lower line segment is to note that the risk-free portfolio has a higher expected return and less risk than any of the portfolios shown on the lower line segment. Thus, the risk-free asset can be described as dominating every portfolio on the lower line. One portfolio is said to dominate another whenever one of the following three observations holds true:

1. Portfolio X dominates portfolio Y if the two have equal expected returns and portfolio X has less risk (that is, a lower standard deviation).
2. Portfolio X dominates portfolio Y if the two have equal standard deviations and portfolio Y has a lower expected return.
3. Portfolio X dominates portfolio Y if portfolio X has both a higher expected return and a lower standard deviation than portfolio Y.

It is important to remember that in these graphs we are only describing what the possible portfolios that could be held by combining securities i and j look like in terms of the two fundamental characteristics of expected return and risk. We are not making any judgments as to which of these portfolios an investor should hold, other than we have identified some that are dominated by others and should not be held. We will return shortly to the topic of which portfolio an investor should hold.

Because rational investors would only want to choose among portfolios on the upper line segment, and would not want to hold any of the portfolios on the lower line segment, we give a special name to the upper line segment—the *efficient frontier*.

efficient frontier

Correlation Coefficient Equals 0

The third special case occurs when the correlation coefficient equals 0. Although this may sound like an intriguing case, it actually is not. The locus of points formed by these portfolios is shown in figure 4-4. To better understand the relationship among these three cases, the portfolios formed in the first two cases (when $\rho = 1$ and $\rho = -1$) are reproduced in figure 4-4. Note that unlike the first two cases, we are dealing with a curved line with its end points at securities i and j.

The formula for the standard deviation of any of the portfolios that can be created when ρ_{ij} equals zero is

$$\sigma_p = \sqrt{W_i^2\, \sigma_i^2 + W_j^2\, \sigma_j^2} \qquad\qquad \text{(Equation 4-8)}$$

It is not a particularly easy formula with which to work.

The two important features in the previous case (that is, when the correlation coefficient equals −1) still apply. That is, there is one portfolio that has less risk than all of the other combinations. The only difference here is that this portfolio still has some risk to it; it is not a risk-free portfolio. For this reason, we give this portfolio the name MVP, which stands for minimum variance portfolio.

The other important feature is that the curved line can be divided into two segments. The upper segment, which starts at the MVP and moves upward to the portfolio that contains only asset j, is the efficient frontier. Investors would only be interested in portfolios on this segment. The lower segment, which starts just below the MVP and proceeds downward to the portfolio that contains only asset i, represents portfolios that no rational person would want to hold.

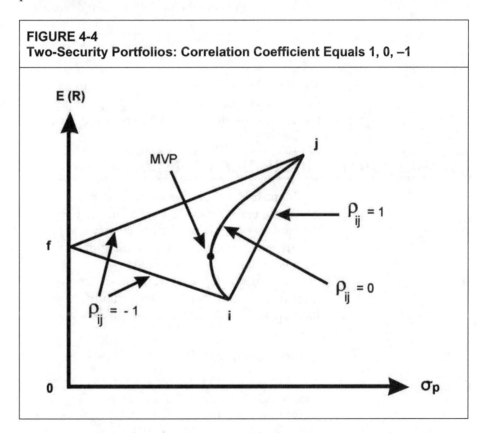

FIGURE 4-4
Two-Security Portfolios: Correlation Coefficient Equals 1, 0, −1

All Other Cases

Having dealt with three special cases of two-asset portfolios (when the correlation coefficient is 1, –1, and 0), let us now consider all of the other potential values for the correlation coefficient. All correlations between the extreme values of –1 and 1 result in portfolios in the interior of the triangle shown in figure 4-4 that is bounded by asset i, asset j, and the risk-free combination of i and j that is marked as portfolio f.

As the correlation coefficient starts to fall from 1, the locus of possible portfolios moves away from the straight line connecting i and j, bowing out slightly to the left of this line. As the correlation coefficient continues to fall, the locus of combinations continues to move to the left. We have already identified the case for when the correlation coefficient equals 0. As the correlation coefficient drops below 0, the line of possible combinations continues to move to the left, until eventually the correlation coefficient hits the minimum value of –1, and the locus of combinations is the two lines forming two sides of the triangle.

The general formula for the standard deviation of a two-asset portfolio is:

$$\sigma_p = \sqrt{W_i^2 \sigma_i^2 + 2 W_i W_j \rho_{ij} \sigma_i \sigma_j + W_j^2 \sigma_j^2} \qquad \text{(Equation 4-9)}$$

The formula for the standard deviations given for the three cases discussed in the previous section were derived by plugging the values of 1, –1, and 0 into this formula for the value of the correlation coefficient.

WHICH PORTFOLIO SHOULD BE HELD?

In the previous section we looked at the issue of what portfolios *could* be held when only two assets were available to choose from. The line describing the choices depends on the correlation coefficient for the rates of return of the two securities. Let us now look at the other side of the question—which portfolio should an investor hold?

The answer depends on what are known as indifference curves. Each investor has his or her own set of indifference curves. The derivation of an indifference curve starts with what are known as utility functions of wealth.

Utility Functions

A utility function for wealth reflects the value (or utility) of incremental wealth. Although one of the basic principles of economics is that everyone derives pleasure from incremental wealth (that is, everyone is greedy), the value (or utility or pleasure) of incremental wealth is not equal among all of us. The real question facing investors is NOT "Would you like an additional

$1,000?" The real question facing investors is "Would you prefer $1,000 with perfect certainty, or a 50 percent chance of receiving $2,000 combined with a 50 percent change of receiving nothing?" When faced with this choice, most rational people would choose the $1,000 with perfect certainty. Note that in this simple example, the expected value of the gamble is $1,000 ([.50 x $2,000] + .[50 x $0] = $1,000).

A person's utility for money is defined by what the probabilities of the gamble would have to be for him or her to prefer the gamble over the perfect certainty. For example, someone with a high tolerance for risk might be willing to take the gamble if the probability of receiving $2,000 were 55 percent versus a 45 percent chance of receiving nothing. A person with a low tolerance for risk might not take the gamble with anything less than a 90 percent chance of winning $2,000.

In the above example, some people might opt for the gamble even with probabilities at 50-50 because the excitement of the gamble may more than offset what they see as a relatively small bet. In such a case, utility for wealth could be better explored by changing the above example to $100,000 with perfect certainty versus a gamble of $200,000 or nothing, or even changing it to $1,000,000 with perfect certainty versus a gamble of $2,000,000 or nothing.

Indifference Curves

Indifference curves evolve from utility curves. An indifference curve is a locus of portfolios among which an investor is indifferent. For example, an investor might be indifferent between the following three portfolios:

Portfolio	Expected Return	Standard Deviation
A	5%	0%
B	6%	2%
C	7%	3.5%

Each investor has an infinite number of indifference curves. Thus, a figure showing all possible indifference curves would be a totally darkened figure. Therefore, let us simplify by presenting three indifference curves in figure 4-5. Each point on an indifference curve represents the same level of utility, hence the indifference between points on the curve. Each indifference curve represents a different level of utility, and since more utility is preferred to less, the investor will choose the highest level of utility available to him but will be indifferent to different approaches to reaching that level of utility.

Indifference curves are traditionally thought of as curved lines that slope up as they move to the right. An investor's objective is to find and hold a portfolio on the highest possible indifference curve. The investor depicted in figure 4-5 is, by definition, indifferent between holding portfolios A and B.

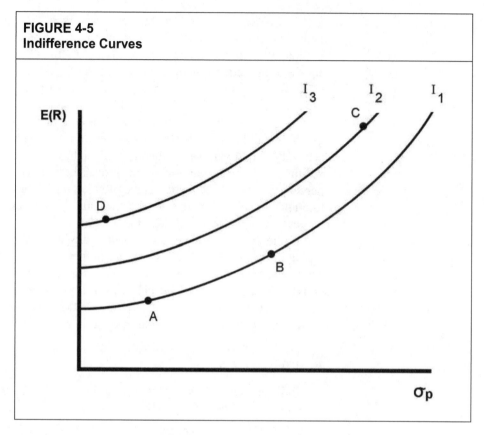

FIGURE 4-5
Indifference Curves

Portfolio C would be preferable to either A or B, and D would be the most preferred of the four portfolios. Notice that among the four portfolios, D has the lowest risk. Although portfolio C has a greater expected return than portfolio D, it has too much incremental risk for this investor, and thus lies on a lower indifference curve.

Deriving an investor's indifference curves is obviously one of the most critical components of financial planning. Unfortunately, there is no known technique for mapping these curves for an individual. Nonetheless, in chapter 14 we will look at the issues of how a financial planner should consider indifference curves in practice.

Combining What Is Possible with What Is Desirable

We are now ready to look at the critical question of financial planning, which portfolio should an investor hold? The answer to this question requires no more than combining the prior two figures. To illustrate this point, let's combine the indifference curves of figure 4-5 with the locus of possible portfolios in figure 4-3 when the correlation coefficient is –1. This is shown in figure 4-6.

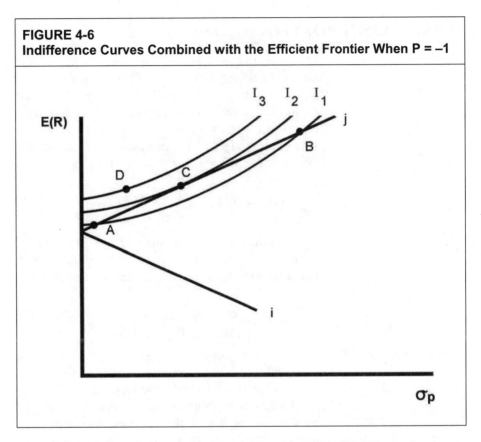

FIGURE 4-6
Indifference Curves Combined with the Efficient Frontier When P = –1

An investor could choose portfolio A or B and be indifferent between these, but would prefer to hold portfolio C because it lies on a higher indifference curve. The investor would love to hold portfolio D, or any other portfolio on I_3, but none of these portfolios are obtainable. So in this case, the investor should hold portfolio C, because it is the one portfolio that lies on the highest possible indifference curve.

Why Low Correlation Coefficients are Desirable

By now, the reader should appreciate that if a financial planner could control the correlation coefficient between any two assets, he or she would set it equal to –1. Most people think that the reason he or she would do so is that it allows the existence of a risk-free portfolio (see portfolio f in figure 4-3). However, the real reason is that the lower a correlation coefficient is, the more it allows an investor to hold a portfolio on a higher indifference curve. Note that in figure 4-6, even though the risk-free portfolio could be held, it is not the portfolio of choice. The desired portfolio, C, has almost as much risk as if the investor held only investment i, although it has substantially more expected return than that provided just by investment i.

THREE-ASSET PORTFOLIO RISK

Interesting things begin to happen when a third risky asset is added to our two existing risky assets. Let us look at the combination of possible portfolios that can be created when we combine securities i, j, and k. There is no additional value in looking at the special extreme cases of the correlation coefficient, so let's consider only the case where the correlation coefficient is between 1 and −1. The expected return on this portfolio is the weighted average of the three expected returns, as shown in equation 4-10.

$$E(R_p) = W_i[E(R_i)] + W_j[E(R_j)] + W_k[E(R_k)]$$ (Equation 4-10)

The formula for the variance of any portfolio created from these three securities becomes much more complex than that for the two-security case. For simplicity, let us use the covariance notation again. The formula is

$$\sigma_p^2 = W_i^2\sigma_i^2 + W_j^2\sigma_j^2 + W_k^2\sigma_k^2 + 2W_iW_jCOV_{ij}$$
$$+ 2W_iW_kCOV_{ik} + 2W_jW_kCOV_{jk}$$ (Equation 4-11)

Note that by adding one more security to the portfolio, we have added three terms to the computation of the variance.

To derive the graphical representation of the possible portfolios, we start by considering all of the possible portfolios that could be created on a pairwise basis. That is, we could identify all of the combinations of i and j, i and k, and j and k. These three sets of combinations are shown in part A of figure 4-7; the resulting figure is scalloped on the right and has a long smooth curve on the left.

The second step in identifying all of the possible portfolios that could be held is to consider combinations of all of the portfolios that could be created by combining any two of the two-security portfolios identified in step one. There would, of course, be an infinite number of combinations that could be so created, and these are shown in part B of figure 4-7. However, there are two key features to this infinite number of combinations. First, the curve that lies furthest to the left will most likely consist of various combinations of all three securities, even though in the graph it appears that this line is made up of combinations of just i and k. This point is emphasized by noting that the left line in figure 4-7A shows the locus of portfolios that can be created with only combinations of i and k. The only way to move to the left of this line in figure 4-7A is to add some of security j to the mix. Hence, the left side of the opportunity set in figure 4-7B lies further to the left than the left side of figure 4-7A.

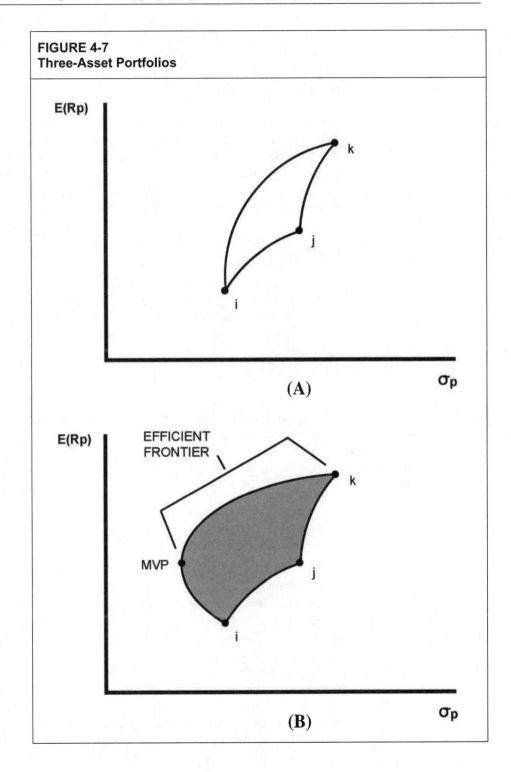

FIGURE 4-7
Three-Asset Portfolios

The second key feature is that the locus of all possible portfolios now becomes a solid entity, as shown by the blackened figure. Any portfolio on the outer perimeter or in the interior of this figure can be held. Most of these portfolios consist of combinations of all three securities, and a few of them consist of combinations of just two.

What is important to the financial planner in this situation is that there still exists a minimum variance portfolio (shown as the MVP in figure 4-7B) and an efficient frontier. In this case, the efficient frontier starts with the minimum variance portfolio and runs along the perimeter up to the portfolio that consists of holding only security k. A financial planner should only consider holding portfolios that lie on this efficient frontier.

N-ASSET PORTFOLIO RISK

Now that we have thoroughly considered two-asset and three-asset portfolios, let us expand the discussion to consider what happens when n assets are combined into a portfolio. The expected return on an n-asset portfolio is simply the weighted average of the expected returns on the individual assets, shown as follows:

$$E\left(R_p\right) = \sum W_i \ x \ E\left(R_j\right)$$

The variance and standard deviation for an n-asset portfolio are shown in equations 4-12 and 4-12a.

$$\sigma_p^{\ 2} = \sum_{i=1}^{n} W_i^2 \sigma_i^2 + \sum_{i=1}^{n}\sum_{\substack{j=1 \\ i \neq j}}^{n} W_i W_j COV_{ij} \qquad \text{(Equation 4-12)}$$

$$\sigma_p = \sqrt{\sum_{i=1}^{n} W_i^2 \sigma_i^2 + \sum_{i=1}^{n}\sum_{\substack{j=1 \\ i \neq j}}^{n} W_i W_j COV_{ij}} \qquad \text{(Equation 4-12a)}$$

Equation 4-12a is provided on the formula sheet for the CFP® certification exam. The first summation in equation 4-12 gives the variances and their weights. The double summation gives every covariance with the appropriate weights. Note that there are n x (n − 1)/2 covariance terms, and they incorporate the covariance of every asset with every other asset.

The n-asset risk formula demonstrates that the number of covariance terms increases substantially faster than the number of variance terms. This is because each time a new security is added to the portfolio, the variance formula must incorporate a covariance term between that security and each security already in the portfolio. The implication is that diversification benefits quickly increase due to the direct link between covariance and diversification.

Let us now consider the graphical representation of the locus of the various portfolios that could be held when there are n risky assets from which to choose, and n is a fairly large number. As with the 3-asset portfolio, we would start by considering all of the portfolios that could be held if one looked at all possible combinations of two securities. Figure 4-8A shows this scenario for n = 10. There are a lot of lines, and not all of them have been drawn! Next, let's consider all of the combinations of combinations of pairs. This will give us a solid figure. However, looking at pairs of pairs means we are considering only portfolios that hold any four of the ten securities. We must continue this process by looking at all of the combinations that could be held, all the way up to all the combinations of all ten securities. The resultant figure, shown in figure 4-8B, looks similar to that in figure 4-7B, except that there are more scallops to the right, and the figure is larger. Once again, the two most important features of figure 4-8B are that it has a minimum variance portfolio (shown as MVP in the figure) and that it has an efficient frontier.

Financial planners would only consider portfolios that lie on the efficient frontier. The actual portfolio that a client should hold would be represented by the intersection of the efficient frontier with the highest possible indifference curve. Hence different clients would hold different portfolios. Clients with a high degree of risk aversion (that is, clients whose indifference curves are quite steep) would hold portfolios with a lower expected return, but lower risk. Such portfolios would presumably consist of stocks considered relatively safe, such as utilities and large, stable companies. An example of an optimal portfolio is identified as portfolio P in figure 4-9A. Clients with a low degree of risk aversion (that is, clients whose indifference curves are relatively flat) would hold portfolios with a higher expected return, and higher risk. Such portfolios would presumably consist of stocks considered aggressive. An example of an optimal portfolio is identified as portfolio P in figure 4-9B.

Estimating Variances and Covariances

Covariance and variance statistics can be estimated from past (historical) data. When possible, however, these estimates should also utilize future-oriented information. For example, the stock of a firm whose future environment is expected to be similar to its past is likely to behave much as its historically estimated variance and covariance statistics imply. On the other hand, some firms may have recently experienced a major change, such as a merger, new product introduction, different regulatory environment, or large capital infusion. These firms are more likely to behave differently than they had prior to the changes. If the change has a tendency to increase risk, historical risk estimates should be adjusted upward. Similarly, a change that decreases risk should lead to a downward adjustment in the historically based measure of risk.

FIGURE 4-8
N-Asset Portfolios

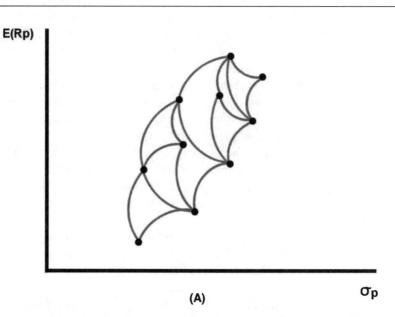

(A)

NOTE: As with the three-asset portfolio, we would start by considering all of the portfolios that could be held if one looked at all possible combinations of two securities, although all such combinations are not shown above. Figure 4-8A shows this scenario for n = 10.

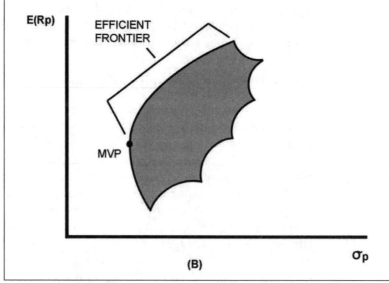

(B)

FIGURE 4-9
Identification of the Optimal Portfolio for a Risk-Averse Investor in a World of N Risky Assets

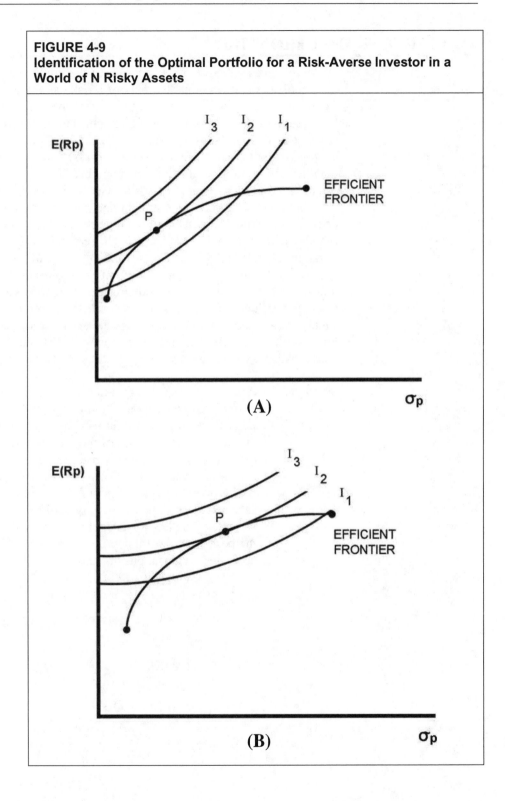

BETTER EFFICIENT FRONTIER

In the preceding section, we considered the implications of portfolio management if our choices consisted only of n risky assets. In 1958, James Tobin extended the analysis by considering the effects of adding a risk-free asset that has a return of R_f, the risk-free rate. In practical terms, most people think of the risk-free asset as a 90-day Treasury bill. Let us consider first the simple case of a two-asset portfolio, where one of the two assets is the risk-free asset and the other asset is a risky asset ("i"). The combination of all of the portfolios that can be created by combining these two assets is shown in figure 4-10A.

The locus of portfolios is a straight line, running from the risk-free asset located on the vertical axis (by definition the standard deviation of returns for the risk-free asset is 0) to the risky asset i. The reason it is a straight line is that the covariance between any asset's return and the return of the risk-free asset is 0.

By itself, this is not a particularly interesting result, but it has significant implications. Let's start by considering negative weights. When one of the assets from which one can choose is the risk-free asset, then a negative weight simply means one is borrowing money at the risk-free rate rather than investing it at the risk-free rate. The money that is borrowed is used to buy more of the risky asset, because those are the only two assets in the portfolio.

Example: Assume the risk-free rate of return is 5 percent, and the rate of return and standard deviation of return on a risky asset i is 10 percent and 8 percent. Let us consider two portfolios. One is a "saving" or "lending" portfolio, in which a person puts 50 percent of his portfolio in the risk-free asset and the other 50 percent in the risky asset. The other is a "borrowing" portfolio in which one borrows an amount equal to 50 percent of one's assets and uses the loan to buy more of the risky asset. The weights of the lending portfolio are .50 and .50. The weights for the borrowing portfolio are −.50 and 1.50. The expected returns and standard deviations of the two portfolios are as follows:

Saving Portfolio

$E(R_p) = (.50 \times 5\%) + (.50 \times 10\%) = 7.5\%$

$\sigma_p^2 = (.50^2 \times .00^2) + (2 \times .50 \times .50 \times .00^2) + (.50^2 \times .08^2) = .0016$

$\sigma_p = \sqrt{.0016} = .04$ or 4%

Borrowing Portfolio

$E(R_p) = (-.50 \times 5\%) + (1.50 \times 10\%) = 12.5\%$

$\sigma_p^2 = (-.50^2 \times .00^2) + (2 \times [-.50] \times 1.50 \times .00^2) + (1.50^2 \times .08^2)$

$= .0144$

$\sigma_p = \sqrt{.0144} = .12$ or 12%

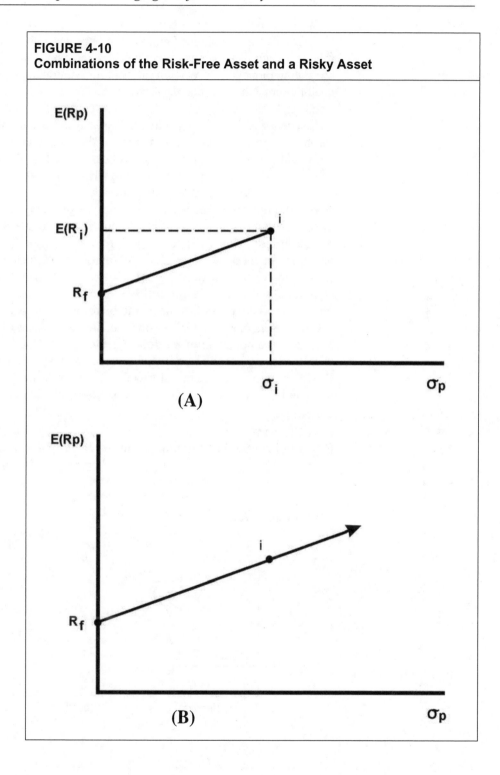

FIGURE 4-10
Combinations of the Risk-Free Asset and a Risky Asset

Note that in the above example, the expected return on the lending port-folio is greater than the rate of return on just the risky asset. This is the benefit of borrowing money at a 5 percent rate and investing it at an expected 10 percent rate of return. Note also that the standard deviation is substantially larger than the standard deviation of just the risky asset. Regarding a graphical representation, the existence of lending portfolios means that the line shown in figure 4-10A can be extended past asset i. In theory, if there were no limits on the amount one could borrow, the extension would be unlimited, as shown in figure 4-10B.

Let's now consider what happens when a risk-free asset is added to a world of n risky assets. We have already seen that in a world of n risky assets, the only relevant portfolios are those on the efficient frontier. When the opportunity is available to divide one's assets between any one portfolio on the efficient frontier and the risk-free asset, then the locus of possible portfolios of these two assets is a straight line connecting those two assets. For example, in figure 4-11, the risk-free asset (denoted by R_f) could be combined with the risky portfolio H. The line connecting these two points represents all the portfolios that could be formed by this combination.

However, one could also combine the risk-free asset with portfolio A. Again, the combination of portfolios created fall on the line R_fA. Note, how-ever, that every portfolio on R_fH is dominated by at least one portfolio on line R_fA. Hence, no rational investor would hold portfolio H or any combination of R_f and H if he or she could hold A or any combination of R_f and A.

FIGURE 4-11
Efficient Frontier With Lending and Borrowing at the Risk-Free Rate

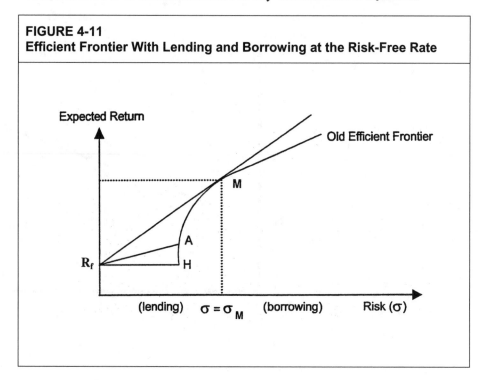

Note that the combination of R_f and M will dominate all portfolios to the left of M. The line R_fM can be extended beyond M if borrowing at the risk-free rate is allowed and the borrowed funds are then invested in further shares of portfolio M. Portfolios on this extension of the R_fM line will also clearly dominate any of the portfolios on the efficient frontier past the portfolio M. In other words, the addition of a risk-free asset results in a new efficient frontier that consists of a straight line beginning at R_f and passing through portfolio M.

If we now impose an investor's indifference curves on this new efficient frontier, as shown in figure 4-12, we see that a conservative investor (represented by indifference curves I_1 to I_3) will hold portfolio P_1, a combination of portfolio M and the risk-free asset, and an aggressive investor (represented by indifference curves I_4 to I_6) would hold portfolio P_2, also a combination of the risk-free asset and portfolio M.

This is an incredible result. It means that M will now be the only risky asset that rational investors will hold. Investors with varying degrees of risk tolerance will attain their desired risk levels by adjusting the relative proportions of R_f and M.

FIGURE 4-12
Indifference Curves with Extended Efficient Frontier

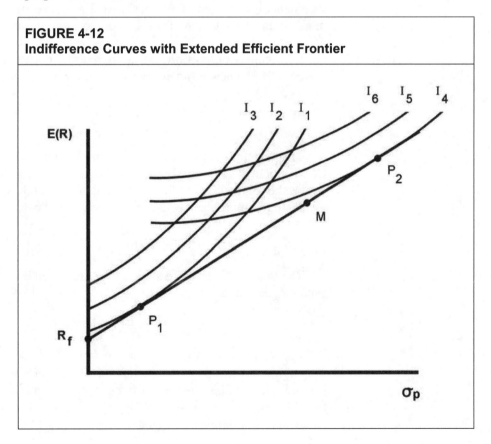

Tobin's insight simplified portfolio choice to selecting the relative proportions of the risk-free asset and a single risky portfolio. This is the essence of the *separation theorem*—that an investor's risk preferences do not affect his or her choice of risky assets, because M is the only rational choice. This was a valuable theoretical innovation, but practical problems remained. The primary one was that the optimum risky portfolio, M, was not specified.

The Capital Market Line

As people thought about the nature of portfolio M, it became clear that it could represent only one portfolio, the market portfolio. The *market portfolio* is the portfolio of all assets, with the weight of each based on its market value. As a practical matter, the market portfolio is an unfathomable entity, but it has interesting implications for managing portfolios. The reason that portfolio M must be the market portfolio is that, as noted before, in this model everyone would hold some combination of M and the risk-free asset—nothing more, nothing less. Furthermore, as all assets are owned by someone (there are no ownerless assets), the only way to reconcile these two statements is if M represents the market portfolio. In practice, most people think of the Standard & Poor's 500 Index as a surrogate for the market portfolio.

By recognizing portfolio M as the market portfolio, we can specify the equation for the new efficient frontier as follows:

$$E(R_p) = R_f + \sigma_p \left(\frac{E(R_M) - R_f}{\sigma_M} \right) \qquad \text{(Equation 4-13)}$$

This equation is called the capital market line (CML). It is on the CFP® Certification Exam formula sheet, although on that sheet the lowercase r is used rather than the more formal expectation notation shown above. In other words, the formula sheet equation is stated as follows:

$$R_p = r_f + \sigma_p(r_m - r_f)/\sigma_m \qquad \text{(Equation 4-13a)}$$

The bracketed term in equation 4-13 (repeated below) is the slope of the capital market line:

$$\text{Slope}_{CML} = \left(\frac{E(R_M) - R_f}{\sigma_M} \right)$$

This slope represents the market price of risk in our financial markets. It signifies the equilibrium trade-off between risk and return at any point in time. Keep in mind that this slope changes any time any of the three parameters that define it change.

Figure 4-13 illustrates the capital market line. The CML tells us one thing only—the expected return on a fully diversified portfolio. Remember, the old efficient frontier (made up of n risky assets) constituted the most efficient portfolios that could be constructed. This means they offered the maximum possible expected return for any given level of risk. The new efficient frontier dominates the old efficient frontier. Thus, a portfolio that is fully and effectively diversified should fall somewhere along the CML. Individual securities and inefficient portfolios (that is, those lacking adequate diversification) would fall underneath the CML.

Put another way, one cannot use the CML to evaluate the performance of a single stock. Nor can one use the CML to evaluate the performance of a portfolio that lacks full diversification.

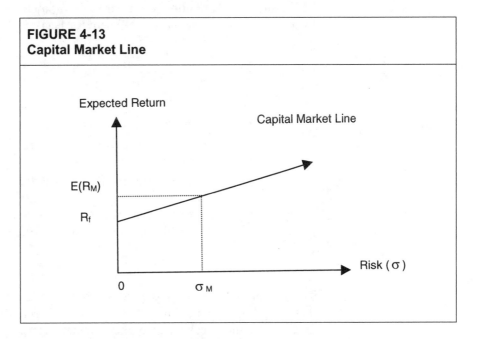

FIGURE 4-13
Capital Market Line

The Capital Asset Pricing Model

William F. Sharpe approached the unknown risky portfolio problem by postulating that returns are related through a common relationship with a basic underlying factor. The foundation of his capital asset pricing model (CAPM) begins with six assumptions. These range from everyone's possessing the same expectations about the risk and return of assets, to a market consisting of all assets, to the assumption that all investments consist of only publicly traded securities (for example, there are no private corporations). Many of these assumptions have been relaxed by subsequent research without unduly altering the implications of Sharpe's conclusions.

Proceeding from these assumptions, Sharpe's model enters familiar territory by constructing an efficient frontier for risky assets. Introduction of a risk-free asset leads to a new efficient frontier (a straight line) made up of varying proportions of the risk-free asset and the market portfolio.

Sharpe then posed the question of what would determine the expected return on an individual asset. Remember, the CML defines the expected return only on effectively diversified portfolios. Portfolios that are not effectively diversified, which would include single securities, would plot somewhere below the capital market line.

Sharpe proved that the expected return was a function of how the individual asset affected the variability of a portfolio's returns. The greater the contribution to a portfolio's variability, the greater the expected return should be. An asset's contribution to a portfolio's variability could then be measured **beta** by a term known as the *beta* coefficient (or beta statistic). It can be computed as follows:

$$\beta_i = \frac{COV_{iM}}{\sigma_M^{\,2}} \qquad \text{(Equation 4-14)}$$

where β_i = market risk of asset i

COV_{iM} = covariance between the returns of asset i and the returns of the market portfolio

$\sigma_M^{\,2}$ = variance of the market portfolio

Note the similarity between the formulas for beta and for the correlation coefficient. The full model is formally stated as follows:

$$E(R_i) = R_f + \beta_i \left[E(R_M) - R_f \right] \qquad \text{(Equation 4-15)}$$

This equation is also on the CFP® Certification Examination formula sheet, and as with the CML, it uses a lowercase r to represent expected return and does not use the Greek letter to represent beta. Hence, it is stated as follows:

$$r_i = r_f + (r_m - r_f)B \qquad \text{(Equation 4-15a)}$$

security market line (SLM) The graph of the CAPM, known as the *security market line (SML),* is shown in figure 4-14.

The SML crosses the $E(R_i)$ axis at R_f and has a slope of $[E(R_M) - R_f]$. There is one readily identifiable portfolio on the SML—the market portfolio. The market portfolio has a beta coefficient equal to 1, and an expected return equal to $E(R_M)$. Note that there is a major difference between this graph and all of the previous graphs that involved an analysis of risk. It is that we are now measuring risk in terms of the beta coefficient, NOT standard deviation. Standard deviation is the relevant measure of risk for an entire portfolio. The

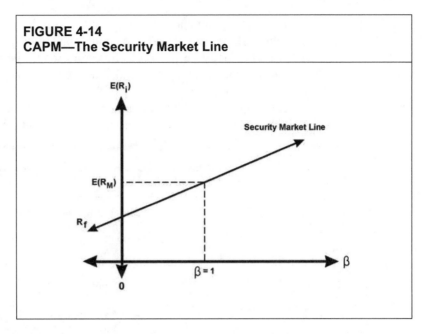

FIGURE 4-14
CAPM—The Security Market Line

CAPM considers how an individual security affects the overall risk of a portfolio. Hence, the current measure of risk for a single security is the impact of that security's returns on the overall volatility of a portfolio.

Beta and Expected Return

For a specified beta, risk-free rate, and projected market return, the CAPM shows the required rate of return of an asset in equilibrium.

Example: If beta $\beta_i = 1.3$, $R_f = 5.0\%$, and $E(R_M) = 10.0$ percent, applying equation 4-15 yields the following:

$$
\begin{aligned}
E(R_i) &= 5.0\% + 1.3(10.0\% - 5.0\%) \\
&= 5.0\% + 1.3(5.0\%) \\
&= 5.0\% + 6.5\% \\
&= 11.5\%
\end{aligned}
$$

Thus, a stock with a beta of 1.3 would be expected to return 11.5 percent when the risk-free rate is 5 percent and the market portfolio's return is expected to be 10 percent.

Note that the SML extends to the left of the $E(R_i)$ axis. Since betas are based on the covariance between the asset and market portfolio, they can, in theory, have negative values. Simply put, any asset whose beta is negative would have an expected return lower than the risk-free rate of return. If the beta has a large enough negative value, then the expected return would actually be negative! Investors would be willing to hold such assets because the negative betas indicate that these assets would do very well when the rest of the market was collapsing. Think of a negative-beta asset as analogous to term life insurance. If you live, the payment of the premiums was a waste of money; if you die, the policy is incredibly valuable.

Expected Asset Returns for Different Betas and Market Returns

Range	Expected Asset Return for Positive Market Return	Expected Asset Return for Negative Market Return
$\beta > 1$	Above market	Below market
$\beta = 1$	Market	Market
$0 < \beta < 1$	Below market	Above market
$\beta = 0$	Risk-free rate	Risk-free rate
$\beta < 0$	Less than risk-free rate, or even negative	Positive

---

As can be seen in figure 4-14 and equation 4-15, return is a linear function of risk (constant returns to risk). Investors who desire greater expected return must accept greater risk as measured by beta. Correspondingly, investors who desire less risk must accept lower expected returns. In short, an investor's risk preferences determine his or her preferred beta, which in turn determines the expected returns.

The CAPM equation has very important implications. First, expected returns for all assets can be estimated once we know their respective betas. Second, an asset's expected return is related only to its market risk, represented by beta. In other words, *nonmarket risk* (individual and all other types of risk) is not rewarded with higher expected returns because it can be diversified away.

By definition, the beta coefficient for the market portfolio is 1. This is easy to see if in equation 4-14 we substitute M for i. The numerator of the beta coefficient then becomes the covariance of the market portfolio with itself. The covariance of any security's return with itself is simply its variance. Hence, equation 4-14 reduces to the variance of M divided by the variance of M, or 1.

An important mathematical property of the beta coefficient is that the beta coefficient of a portfolio is simply the weighted average of the beta coefficients of the securities in the portfolio. In equation form:

$$\beta_p = \sum W_i \times \beta_i \qquad \text{(Equation 4-16)}$$

Example: A portfolio has three securities in it, with the following market values and betas. What is the portfolio beta?

Security	Market Value	Beta
X	$20 million	1.2
Y	$30 million	1.8
Z	$50 million	−.3

The total market value of the portfolio is $100 million. Hence, the market weights are .20, .30, and .50. The portfolio beta is:

$$\beta_p = (.20 \times 1.2) + (.30 \times 1.8) + (.50 \times [-.3]) = .63$$

The CAPM is much more broadly used than the CML. The reason is that it defines the expected return on any security, and any portfolio, regardless of whether said portfolio is fully diversified.

The Market Model

Since its unveiling in the 1960s, the applicability of the CAPM has been extended by finding ways to relax Sharpe's original assumptions. The model has thereby gained enough versatility that it can be applied in a great variety of situations. Its utility has garnered it wide acceptance among academics and within the financial industry.

Any uses of the CAPM require knowledge of beta. Unfortunately, there is nothing in the theory that would indicate how beta should be calculated. In fact, implicit in the CAPM is the assumption that the beta of a security is either stable (thus allowing one to calculate it from historical returns) or predictable. Alas, these assumption are weak at best. There is no question that the beta of any asset changes over time as the nature of the company represented by the stock changes, and as the nature of our economy changes. The real issue is, how fast do betas change? There are no answers to this question. Similarly, betas are not predictable other than by extrapolating historical data. We will return to this topic in the next chapter.

index model
characteristic line

Betas are calculated by using the statistical tool of regressing an asset's returns against the market's returns. This is called the market model, or *index model,* and the regression line is called the *characteristic line.*

$$R_i = \alpha_i + \beta_i R_M + \varepsilon_i \qquad \text{(Equation 4-17)}$$

where R_i = return to asset i
   R_M = return to the market in the same period
   α_i = y-intercept value
   β_i = slope of the line
   ε_i = random error term

As mentioned earlier, a proxy (such as the S&P 500) is used in place of the theoretical market portfolio. The process begins by pairing returns by time (R_{Mt}, R_{it}) where t is the time period. (See figure 4-15.)

The regression calculations attempt to find a regression line that passes through the point that represents the mean market return and the mean asset return $\left(\overline{R}_M, \overline{R}_i\right)$ while minimizing the sum of the squared, vertical distances from data points to the line. By minimizing the sum of these squared error terms, the process finds the best-fitting line. Beta is the slope of the regression line and alpha (α_i) its intercept with the vertical axis.

The market model can be used to estimate asset returns as a function of the market return.

coefficient of determination (R^2)

A statistic that is sometimes mentioned in conjunction with beta is the *coefficient of determination (R^2)*. R^2 is a measure of how well the regression line fits the data. R^2 is a percentage and therefore ranges from 0 to 1 (that is, 0 to 100 percent). In relation to betas, R^2 can be interpreted as the percentage of a stock's variability in return that can be attributed to the variability in the market's return. It is therefore a measure of "relatedness."

In simple regressions, such as the characteristic line, it turns out that the R^2 equals the square of the correlation coefficient between the dependent variable (in this case, the returns on the particular stock) and the independent variable (in this case, the returns on the market). When the R^2 is close to 1, then the beta is a highly reliable estimate of how a particular stock will perform relative to the market. When the R^2 is close to 0, then regardless of the value of the beta, the particular security tends to move relatively independent of the market.

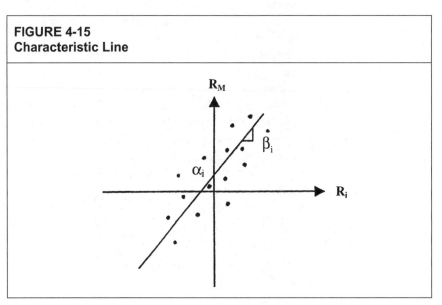

FIGURE 4-15
Characteristic Line

Market Risk and Nonmarket Risk

The market model provides a convenient vehicle to demonstrate one additional aspect of market risk. If we were to compute the variance of both sides of equation 4-17, as shown in equation 4-18, then we see that the total risk of a security (σ_i^2) can be broken down into two components:

$$\sigma_i^2 = \left(\beta_i^2\right) \times \sigma_M^2 + \sigma_\varepsilon^2 \qquad \text{(Equation 4-18)}$$

The first component is the product of the square of the beta and the variance of the market portfolio. This product is referred to as market risk. The second term measures nonmarket risk, and is unique for each security.

No matter how many securities a person holds, there is exposure to market risk. Beta is sometimes referred to as an index of market risk. The larger the value of beta, the greater the contribution of market risk to the total risk of a security. Remember, the variance of the market portfolio is the same for all securities when one breaks down total risk into its two components.

Nonmarket risk can be nearly eliminated if one holds a large enough portfolio. Market risk can never be eliminated no matter how large of a portfolio one owns. (We will return to this point in chapter 14.) The impact of market risk can be augmented or downplayed by adjustments in the portfolio beta. In theory, if the portfolio beta were 0, then market risk could be eliminated. As a practical matter, nearly all betas are between 0 and 2, and the largest percentage are between 1.5 and 2.5. So assembling a zero-beta portfolio is virtually impossible in practice.

Multifactor Asset Pricing Models

The advent of the CAPM revolutionized financial theory, but many researchers were not convinced that this single-index model sufficiently explained the variability of asset returns. Various multi-index models have been proposed, including the multifactor asset pricing model. This model is derived from the economic principle that perfect substitutes must have the same price, or arbitrage profits will be available to traders. Through the action of arbitrage, all prices of financial assets remain in equilibrium.

Multi-index models are based upon the belief that an asset's risk is a linear function of its correlation with a variety of factors. These models postulate that asset returns are affected by various basic economic forces, which might include industrial production, interest rates, inflation rates, and so on. The *arbitrage pricing model (APM)* is as follows:

arbitrage pricing model (APM)

$$E\left(R_i\right) = \alpha_i + \beta_{i1}F_1 + \beta_{i2}F_2 + \ldots + \beta_{iM}F_M \qquad \text{(Equation 4-19)}$$

In this equation, F_1 to F_M are the relevant economic factors influencing R_i. Note that these factors are not the actual values of the factors, but the difference between the expected value of these factors and the actual values. This equation is also on the CFP® Certification Exam formula sheet, but in that format, the expected return is represented with a lowercase r, and the subscript i is omitted from the beta coefficients. The omission of the subscripts is actually a notational error on the exam's formula sheet.

In the APM, alpha (α) represents the expected return when all of the independent variables (F_1, F_2, ... F_M) are equal to their expected values. The beta coefficients represent the sensitivity of a stock's price to that particular factor. For example, if F_2 represents the price of oil, then for an oil exploration company, β_{i2} might be quite large. However, for a bakery, β_{i2} might be virtually 0.

Example: The XYZ company has an alpha of 8 percent, a gross domestic product (GDP) beta of .9, and a 90-day Treasury-bill interest rate beta of 1.2. Assume that GDP had been expected to increase at the rate of 3 percent, and the interest rate is currently 4 percent. In the morning news, an announcement is made that GDP is now expected to grow at a 2 percent rate, and that the Treasury bill rate has risen to 5 percent. The expected rate of return on this company's stock is:

$$E(R_{XYZ}) = 8\% + (.9 \times [-1\%]) + (1.2 \times 1\%) = 8.3\%$$

A significant problem with the APM is that the theory specifies no specific factors. The theory only hypothesizes that such factors exist and are relevant. Moreover, empirical investigation for relevant factors has been inconclusive. Also, as with the CAPM, the theory provides no statement as to how one would know the true value of the betas. The APM has offsetting positive attributes, such as not requiring the use of a market portfolio, allowing for different expectations of market participants, and pricing that may exceed the CAPM in accuracy.

Note that the CAPM could be viewed as a special case of multi-index models. If a multi-index model were based on only one factor, then alpha would be the risk-free rate and the single factor would be the excess return on the market (that is, the return on the market minus the risk-free rate). A graph of this equation would be conceptually similar to that of the CAPM. If two or more factors are specified, then the first factor could be the excess returns on the market, and the other factor some relevant economic variable. If there are two factors, the graph is a plane in three dimensions; models with more than two factors cannot be visualized.

The important question in comparing the two approaches: Does the greater complexity of the APM add appreciably to our understanding of markets and our ability to explain real-world prices? The initial tests on the APM failed to demonstrate clear superiority over the CAPM, and subsequent research has resulted in mixed assessments. Nonetheless, the APM has continued to generate much interest.

Implementation Issues

Regardless of whether one is building a portfolio based on Markowitz's full model, the CAPM, or the APM, there are substantial estimation problems. For example, if a person wanted to use the Markowitz model to estimate an efficient frontier of a portfolio made up of n assets (see figure 4-8B), then one would first have to develop estimates of n means, n variances, and n(n − 1)/2 covariances. The next step involves incorporation of weights. This step is potentially unmanageable because the number of possible weights is nearly infinite. In practice, a few standard weights are chosen. Even with this simplification, the computational demands made the calculation of portfolio variance an extremely demanding process, given the nascent state of computing in the 1950s. Fortunately, today the construction of such an efficient frontier is not a problem with regard to computer capacity, but one would still need good estimates for all of the necessary variables.

The CAPM is a little more user friendly in that one would only have to have estimates of n covariances, the variance of the market portfolio, the expected return of the market portfolio, and the risk-free rate. The APM is also a little less daunting in that one would need estimates of the alphas and the betas for the M factors used in the model for the n securities (that is, n x M betas).

Approaches to Portfolio-Risk Estimation

Model	Requirements to Analyze Portfolio of n Securities
Markowitz's full model	n expected returns, n variances, and n(n − 1)/2 covariances
CAPM	(n + 1) expected returns and n betas (n covariances and the market variance as inputs)
APM	(n x M) betas corresponding to M factors

IMPACT OF MODERN PORTFOLIO THEORY[3]

Uniform Principal and Income Act prudent man rule

After reading the foregoing material, a practitioner may be prone to say, "That's nice, but what impact does it have on how I do business?" One area in which modern portfolio theory has had a significant effect is in the management of trusts. The key law affecting the management of trust assets is the *Uniform Principal and Income Act* (UPIA). This law was passed in 1931. At that time, it laid out the principle known as the *prudent man rule*. This rule stated that each security or asset in a trust must meet the standard that it is one in which a prudent man who wanted first and foremost to ensure the preservation of his assets would invest. The emphasis here is that this rule applied to each holding separately. Hence, even if there were 100 separate investments in a trust account, and 99 of them performed well, the trustee could be held at fault if the 100th asset did not perform well. This legal position had the effect of almost mandating that trustees invest only in the most conservative of investments. This meant that rates of return on such portfolios were low, reflecting the conservative nature of these investments.

Many trusts have two beneficiaries: the income beneficiary and the remainder beneficiary who receives the principal of the trust at its termination. The best interest of the income beneficiary is maximization of current income. The best interest of the remainder beneficiary is growth in the value of the assets. Obviously, the best interest of both parties cannot be served simultaneously.

prudent investor

The UPIA was revised in 1962, and again in 1997. The act now says that the trustee must act as a prudent investor, rather than a prudent man. The difference is that a *prudent investor* can invest using the principles of modern portfolio theory. Hence, what counts now is the total return on the portfolio, which is both income and price appreciation, and not the return on each holding separately. Trustees are allowed to recognize that some assets have low or even negative correlation coefficients, and so holding them in tandem with more risky assets may produce reasonable returns at substantially less risk.

SUMMARY AND CONCLUSIONS

This chapter presents key points of modern portfolio theory. Understanding the theory is critical to understanding the research and applications being done today in the field of portfolio management.

The portfolio theory discussed in this chapter yields a number of important conclusions. First, the covariance and the correlation coefficient are critical when combining securities because the lower the correlation coefficient (or the smaller the covariance relative to the product of the two standard deviations), the greater the risk reduction that can be achieved when two securities are combined. Even when the correlation coefficient is positive (but less than 1), the risk in the combination of two securities can be less than the risk of the less risky of the two securities. If the correlation coefficient is –1, it is possible to create a risk-free portfolio from two otherwise risky securities.

When two or more securities are combined into a portfolio, two features become critical: There is always a minimum variance portfolio (MVP) and an efficient frontier. The tangency point between the efficient frontier and the highest possible indifference curve determines the optimal portfolio for an investor to hold. This optimal portfolio would be the MVP for only the most risk-averse investors.

When a risk-free asset is combined with n risky assets, the result is a new efficient frontier that is a straight line emanating from the risk-free asset and passing through portfolio M, the market portfolio. This new efficient frontier is the capital market line (CML). Lending portfolios are to the left of M on this line, and borrowing portfolios (that is, buying on margin) are to the right. In theory, all investors would end up only holding some combination of the risk-free asset and portfolio M, regardless of their degree of risk aversion. In practice, only efficient portfolios lie on the CML.

The CML does not describe the expected returns on individual securities or inefficient portfolios. This is provided by the capital asset pricing model (CAPM), which measures the riskiness of a security by its impact on the overall riskiness of a portfolio. The key to the CAPM is the beta coefficient for each security. Beta shows the volatility of a particular security relative to the volatility of the market. The quality of the estimate of a beta coefficient is measured by the coefficient of determination (R^2).

The arbitrage pricing model (APM) states that an asset's expected return is a function of its volatility (as measured by beta coefficients) to what are believed to be the key factors that drive market returns. In theory, the APM is superior to the CAPM, but no one has really demonstrated how to determine the number of factors, and what those factors are.

Finally, modern portfolio theory has had the effect of even changing the legal concepts as to the appropriate objective for a trustee. A trustee should now act as a "prudent investor" rather than a "prudent man."

CHAPTER REVIEW

Answers to the review questions and the self-test questions start on page 733.

Key Terms

covariance
correlation coefficient
efficient frontier

utility function
indifference curve
separation theorem

market portfolio	characteristic line
capital market line (CML)	coefficient of determination (R^2)
capital asset pricing model (CAPM)	nonmarket risk
beta	arbitrage pricing model (APM)
security market line (SML)	Uniform Principal and Income Act
market model	prudent man rule
index model	prudent investor

Review Questions

4-1. For each pair of portfolios, identify which one dominates the other, or if neither dominates the other.

a. X ($E(R) = 4\%$, $\sigma = 8\%$); Y ($E(R) = 4\%$, $\sigma = 10\%$)

b. X ($E(R) = 8\%$, $\sigma = 12\%$); Y ($E(R) = 10\%$, $\sigma = 12\%$)

c. X ($E(R) = 6\%$, $\sigma = 10\%$); Y ($E(R) = 8\%$, $\sigma = 14\%$)

4-2. a. Compute the covariance estimate for the following ex post observations (assume equal probabilities):

$(R_{i1}, R_{j1}) = (.04, .05)$

$(R_{i2}, R_{j2}) = (.06, .03)$

$(R_{i3}, R_{j3}) = (-.01, -.05)$

b. Repeat part a., but assume that the three pairs of returns are ex ante data, and that the probability of each pair of returns are: 50 percent, 30 percent, and 20 percent.

4-3. a. After running the statistics for two companies, you conclude that the covariance of returns is .0020, and that the standard deviations of returns are .06 and .08. What is the correlation coefficient?

b. The correlation coefficient between two securities is –.5, and the standard deviations are .06 and .08. What is the covariance between them?

c. If the standard deviations for two securities are .06 and .08, what are the minimum and maximum values of the covariance?

4-4. Securities A and B have expected returns of 4 and 10 percent, and standard deviations of 5 and 16 percent. Compute the expected returns and standard deviations for the following six portfolios for two scenarios: First assume a correlation coefficient of .5, and then assume one of –.5.

a. 100% A and 0% B

b. 80% A and 20% B

c. 60% A and 40% B

d. 40% A and 60% B

e. 20% A and 80% B

f. 0% A and 100% B

4-5. You want to create a two-security portfolio. One of those holdings will be company A. The second will be B, C, or D. All three of these companies have identical expected returns and standard deviations. However, they differ in terms of correlation coefficient with company A. The three correlation coefficients are .2, .6, and −.2. Which company should you choose and why?

4-6. Explain why the SML differs from the CML.

4-7. a. Define the efficient frontier, first without borrowing or lending allowed and then with both allowed at the risk-free rate.

     b. What does the efficient frontier look like with risk-free lending only (no borrowing)?

4-8. a. Describe what is meant by market risk and nonmarket risk.

     b. What determines the effect of market risk for an individual security?

4-9. Using the CAPM, calculate expected portfolio returns for the following sets of risk-free rates, expected market returns, and portfolio betas.

Expected Portfolio Returns					
		β_p			
Risk-Free Rates	Expected Market Return	0.7	1	1.3	1.6
0.07	0.14				
0.09	0.16				
0.05	0.10				

4-10. What is the difference between a "prudent man" investment objective and a "prudent investor" investment objective?

Self-Test Questions

T   F   4-1. The riskiness of a portfolio is greater than the riskiness of the securities it contains.

T   F   4-2. A correlation coefficient of 0 does not necessarily mean no relationship between two sets of returns, only that there is no obvious linear relationship.

T   F   4-3. A portfolio's return is the arithmetic average of the returns of the assets included therein.

T   F   4-4. A correlation coefficient of −1 between two assets would result in an increased variability of the portfolio's return.

T   F   4-5. If investors are to hold only risky assets, they should hold a portfolio of assets that lies on the efficient frontier.

T F 4-6. A correlation coefficient between the returns on two securities is the covariance divided by the product of the two standard deviations.

T F 4-7. The covariance of a security's returns with itself is by definition equal to 1.

T F 4-8. When the correlation coefficient between two securities is 1, the minimum variance portfolio is 50 percent of each security.

T F 4-9. When the correlation coefficient between two securities is –1, there is one portfolio that can be created which is risk-free.

T F 4-10. When the correlation coefficient between two securities is –1, all possible combinations of the two securities are on the efficient frontier.

T F 4-11. When two assets are being combined into a portfolio, the most desirable combination is always the MVP.

T F 4-12. The same formulas are used whether one is computing covariance with ex ante data or ex post data.

T F 4-13. As one moves to the right along an indifference curve, the portfolios become more desirable as the expected return increases.

T F 4-14. The locus of portfolios that are possible when three or more securities are considered is a solid figure.

T F 4-15. The optimal portfolio to hold is the one that places the investor on the highest possible indifference curve.

T F 4-16. Indifference curves are based on one's marginal utility for wealth, and may differ dramatically among investors.

T F 4-17. The introduction of a risk-free asset enables every investor to choose the same risky portfolio.

T F 4-18. Any portfolio on the CML is an undiversified portfolio.

T F 4-19. The problem with constructing diversified portfolios is that diversification always means a reduction in expected returns.

T F 4-20. The separation theorem says that everyone would hold a combination of the risk-free asset and portfolio M.

T F 4-21. The most common surrogate for the market portfolio is the S&P 500 index.

T F 4-22. The realized return received by an investor is, by itself, the appropriate measure to assess and compare the performance of several investments.

T F 4-23. Just because one portfolio dominates another with respect to both expected return and risk does not mean one should not consider the dominated portfolio.

T   F   4-24.   Investors seeking the highest possible expected return should seek out investments with negative betas.

T   F   4-25.   If the beta of a stock is 1.1, the risk-free rate is 4 percent, and the return on the market is 10 percent, then according to the CAPM, the expected rate of return for the stock is 15.4 percent.

T   F   4-26.   The most commonly used model to analyze a security's performance is the CAPM.

T   F   4-27.   The multifactor asset pricing model lacks definition as to how many factors there should be, and what those factors are.

T   F   4-28.   The APM treats the required return to a stock as a function of its correlation with various economic factors.

T   F   4-29.   The prudent man rule is much more lenient in the evaluation of portfolio management than the prudent investor rule.

T   F   4-30.   The key law affecting the management of trust assets is the Uniform Principal and Income Act.

NOTES

1. There are two solutions because solving for the answer involves taking the square root of a positive number (for example, 4), and the answer could be either a positive number or a negative number (that is, 2 or –2).
2. It is possible to solve for the weights for the risk-free portfolio, but the mathematical complexity of this calculation is beyond the scope of this book.
3. This section draws on material presented in "The TRU Debate: The Pros and Cons of Using Total Return Unitrusts," by Gerard J. Monchek, JD, LLM, *Journal of Financial Service Professionals*, Vol. 57, No. 3 (May 2003), pp. 41–53.

5

Evaluating Portfolio Performance

Learning Objectives

An understanding of the material in this chapter should enable the student to

5-1. Compute time-weighted and dollar-weighted rates of return, and explain why they differ and which should be used for which purposes.

5-2. Describe various indices that are used for benchmarking purposes, and compute a price-weighted and value-weighted index.

5-3. Describe the different tools for evaluating portfolio performance (i.e., the Sharpe ratio, the M^2 measure, the Treynor ratio, and Jensen's alpha), and compute each of them.

5-4. Discuss the issues associated with deficiencies in the capital asset pricing model (CAPM) that render it questionable as an evaluation tool.

Chapter Outline

The measurement and evaluation of portfolio performance can involve some tricky conceptual issues and some moderately complex calculations. In this chapter, we will look first at the issue of measurement of portfolio performance, and then at the issue of evaluation. Because the process of evaluation of portfolio performance often involves comparisons with indices, we will also review the more popular indices and the problems in interpreting them. The discussion of measurement requires knowledge of the topic of the time value of money. Students who are unfamiliar with this topic, or need a refresher, should read appendix 5A.

WHY EVALUATING PORTFOLIO PERFORMANCE MAY NOT BE SIMPLE

Let us consider the situation of two portfolio managers, Lucky Lou and Unlucky Huey. On January 1, both men have $1,000 in assets under management. Lucky Lou receives an additional $1,000 to manage. During the year, Lou achieves a 20 percent rate of return on his portfolio. Not bad, but Huey achieves a 25 percent rate of return. At the end of the year, $1,000 is removed from Lou's portfolio and transferred to Huey's portfolio. During the second year, Lou has a loss of 10 percent, and Huey has a loss of 8 percent. At the end of the second year, the $1,000 is withdrawn from Huey's portfolio. The portfolio values are shown in the following table.

The impact of the deposits and withdrawals is as follows. At the end of the first year, the value of Lou's portfolio is $1,400. Because of the extra $1,000 given to him, Lou actually had $2,000 under management at the start

	Lucky Lou				Unlucky Huey			
Year	% Return	Subtotal	Deposit/ With- drawal	Value	% Return	Subtotal	Deposit/ With- drawal	Value
0			$1,000	$2,000				$1,000
1	20	$2,400	−1,000	1,400	25	$1,250	$1,000	2,250
2	−10	1,260		1,260	−8	2,070	−1,000	1,070

of the year. The 20 percent rate of return put his portfolio at $2,400, and the $1,000 withdrawal reduced the portfolio's value to $1,400. Huey's first year is much simpler. His 25 percent rate of return on the $1,000 under management resulted in a portfolio value of $1,250. The cash inflow increased assets under management to $2,250.

In the second year, Lou's portfolio falls to $1,260 ($1,400 x [1 − .10]). Huey's portfolio fall to $2,070 ($2,250 x [1 − .08]). The $1,000 is then removed from his portfolio, and the ending portfolio value is $1,070.

Who is the better portfolio manager? If the evaluation focuses just on the rates of return achieved by the portfolio managers each year, then one would conclude that Huey did better. He did better the first year, earning 25 percent versus 20 percent, and he did better the second year, losing only 8 percent versus 10 percent for Lou.

One could also argue that Lou was the better manager because both men started with $1,000 under management, both men had an extra $1,000 for 1 year, and Lou ends up with $1,260 while Huey ends up with $1,070. Of course, the counterargument in this scenario is that Huey was unlucky first to have not had the extra money during the year that both managers did well, and then second to have had the extra money in a year when both managers had negative rates of return. However, we have not established whether or not Lou or Huey had any control over when they had the extra money available to them. For example, if each manager had the ability to control during which year he had the extra cash, then Lou was more skillful in obtaining the money in the first year, and Huey was ineffective in choosing to have the extra money during the second year. Thus, in the combined skills of portfolio performance and managing cash flows, Lou did better.

Our next step is to look at two techniques for measuring portfolio performance: geometric mean rate of return and internal rate of return. Depending on the circumstances, each could be an appropriate tool to use in measuring performance. Remember, the following discussion assumes a working knowledge of time value of money. Students unfamiliar with or vague on this topic should jump to appendix 5A before proceeding to the next section.

MEASURING THE PERFORMANCE OF PORTFOLIOS WITH INTERIM CASH FLOWS

Interim Cash Flows

An interim cash flow is cash added to or removed from a portfolio during a specified holding period, such as the 2-year holding period we discussed with the example of Lou and Huey. Interim cash flows are quite common. For example, investors may contribute annually to retirement accounts such as traditional IRAs and Roth IRAs, although the rules limit the amount that may be contributed in any single year. Similarly, investors may make annual contributions to Coverdell accounts and 529 plans.[1] Many investors have automatic deposits set up for one or more accounts, particularly with mutual funds and direct-purchase plans. (Mutual funds are discussed in chapter 10, and direct-purchase plans in chapter 14.) Finally, many investors regularly add and remove money from their personal accounts as they have excess cash or need cash for particular purposes.

Note that the receipt of dividends and interest in a portfolio is not an interim cash flow as long as the cash is kept in the portfolio. That is, whether the cash from these payments is simply left in the form of cash, or it is used to purchase another security, it is still part of the portfolio, and would be counted as part of the portfolio's ending value in order to determine portfolio performance. The only circumstance under which dividends or interest would be considered an interim cash flow is if the investor withdrew them from the portfolio for purposes of consumption.

Example:	A client has a portfolio that is worth $122,000 at the start of the month. During the month, the securities in the portfolio are credited with $3,000 in dividend income and $500 in interest income. On the last day of the month, the client withdraws $1,000 from the portfolio. In this case, there is an interim cash outflow represented by a withdrawal $1,000. There are no interim cash flows represented by deposits in this example. If the rest of the dividend and interest income were simply left in the portfolio, this cash position would be added to the value of the securities to determine the end of the month value of the portfolio. If this cash had been used to purchase other securities, then the market value of these newly purchased securities would be included in the ending value of the portfolio.

For illustrative purposes, consider two portfolios (A and B) where each has an initial value of $1,000. Let's further assume that over the next 4 years, portfolio A has successive annual per-period returns (PPRs) of 30 percent, 20 percent, 10 percent, and 0 percent, and portfolio B has the same return, but in the opposite order: 0 percent, 10 percent, 20 percent, and 30 percent. Let's assume that equal deposits of $1,000 are added to each portfolio at the beginning of each of the 4 years. The values of the portfolios at time zero and at the end of each of the 4 years, including the interim cash flows, are as follows:

	A				B			
Year	% Return	Subtotal	Deposit	Value	% Return	Subtotal	Deposit	Value
0			$1,000	$1,000			$1,000	$1,000
1	30	1,300	1,000	2,300	0	1,000	1,000	2,000
2	20	2,760	1,000	3,760	10	2,200	1,000	3,200
3	10	4,136	1,000	5,136	20	3,840	1,000	4,840
4	0	5,136	0	5,136	30	6,292	0	6,292

Note that something fascinating has happened. Although portfolios A and B have had identical rates of return over the 4-year period (just in a different sequence), and both have had the same amount of deposits and at the same points in time, portfolio B nonetheless ends up with a substantially higher terminal value. In other words, portfolio B is similar to the portfolio owned by Lucky Lou in the earlier example, and portfolio A is similar to that owned by Unlucky Huey. The reason is that portfolio A has its high returns in the early years when fewer deposits have been made, so the higher rates are applied to smaller balances. Portfolio B's higher returns are in the later years, and they are applied to higher balances.

Geometric Mean Return

The easiest way to measure the performance of portfolios A and B is to simply ignore the interim cash flows. This means that we would compute the portfolio's rate of return for each period, and then use these PPRs to solve for the geometric mean return (GMR). The GMRs for these portfolios are as follows:

$$A: R = (1.30 \times 1.20 \times 1.10 \times 1.00)^{0.25} - 1 = 0.1445, \text{ or } 14.45\%$$
$$B: R = (1.00 \times 1.10 \times 1.20 \times 1.30)^{0.25} - 1 = 0.1445, \text{ or } 14.45\%$$

Note that the calculation is the same for both sets. We simply change the order of the per period relative returns (PPRRs) within the brackets, which, of course, does not change their product or the GMR.

Internal Rate of Return

The other technique for evaluating portfolio performance is known as the internal rate of return. (See appendix 5A for the definition and a detailed discussion of this term.) The internal rate of return (IRR) is the discount rate that equates the present value of the cash flows and the ending value of the investment with the beginning value. In mathematical notation, the IRR is the discount rate that makes the following equation valid:

$$0 = \text{Value}_0 + \sum \text{CF}_t/(1+R)^t - \text{Value}_n/(1+R)^n \qquad \text{(Equation 5-1)}$$

where Value_0 = value of the portfolio today (i.e., at time zero)
CF_t = cash flow in period t (inflows are positive, outflows are negative)
Value_n = value of the portfolio at the end of the holding period

For portfolio A, this equation works out to the following:

$$0 = \$1,000 + \$1,000/(1+r) + \$1,000/(1+r)^2 + \$1,000/(1+r)^3 - \$5,136/(1+r)^4$$

Note that in the above formulation, the initial value of the portfolio is treated like a cash inflow, and the ending value of the portfolio is treated like a cash outflow. In other words, we are treating the portfolio as if the market value of the portfolio were received at time zero and the cash invested in whatever assets are in the portfolio. Similarly, at the end of the time horizon, we are treating the portfolio as if it was being liquidated, and the cash distributed. Neither situation is usually the case. However, both concepts are critical to the mathematical definition of the IRR.

This equation cannot be solved algebraically. Hence, to solve for r, one would have to use some software designed for this purpose, or a calculator. For the HP-10BII calculator, the keystrokes for solving for the IRR for the two portfolios are as follows:

Portfolio A	Portfolio B
SHIFT, C ALL	SHIFT, C ALL
1000, CFj	1000, CFj
1000, CFj	1000, CFj
3, SHIFT, Nj	3, SHIFT, Nj
5136, +/–, CFj	6292, +/–, CFj
SHIFT, IRR/YR	SHIFT, IRR/YR
(display: 10.25[%])	(display: 18.97[%])

Note that when entering the number "3" to indicate that there are three consecutive deposits of $1,000 each, the "Nj" refers to the gold lettering on the CFj key. It is NOT the "N" indicated by the white lettering on the far left key of the top row.

When the performance of the two portfolios is measured using the GMR and the interim cash flows ignored, both provided a 14.45 percent rate of return. When the performance of the deposits (that is, the interim cash flows) is considered, portfolio A's rate of return is 10.25 percent and portfolio B's is 18.97 percent, as measured by the IRR.

One way to think about the above example is that portfolios A and B are each actually four portfolios that are held over the 4-year investment period. The first portfolio consisted of the initial $1,000 portfolio (let's call this portfolio A1). The rates of return on this portfolio were 30, 20, 10, and 0 percent. The second portfolio (A2) came into existence at the end of the first year. Its rates of return were 20, 10, and 0 percent. The third portfolio (A3) came into existence at the end of the second year, and its rates of return were 10 and 0 percent. The fourth and last portfolio (A4) came into existence at the end of the third year, and its rate of return was 0 percent. The IRR can be thought of as the average GMR on these four portfolios, weighted by how long each one was held and the relative size of each portfolio.[2] Note that the GMRs for the other three portfolios are 9.7, 4.9, and 0 percent, respectively.

First Deposit	$1,000	$[(1 + .20) \times (1 + .10) \times (1 + 0)]^{1/3} - 1 = .097$
Second Deposit	$1,000	$[(1 + .10) \times (1 + 0)]^{1/2} - 1 = .049$
Third Deposit	$1,000	$(1 + 0)^{1} - 1 = 0$

Hence, when a portfolio that has a GMR of 14.45 percent is combined with three other portfolios whose rates of return are 9.7, 4.9, and 0 percent, the weighted average rate of return would be expected to be below 14.45. In this case, it is 10.25 percent.

Conversely, the portfolios formed by the additional deposits to portfolio B have rates of return of 19.7, 24.9, and 30 percent.

First Deposit	$1,000	$[(1 + .10) \times (1 + .20) \times (1 + .30)]^{1/3} - 1 = .197$
Second Deposit	$1,000	$[(1 + .20) \times (1 + .30)]^{1/2} - 1 = .249$
Third Deposit	$1,000	$(1 + .30)^{1} - 1 = .30$

Hence, the rate of return on the combination of these portfolios would be expected to be higher than 14.45 percent.

Computing the Rate of Return for a Single Period with an Interim Cash Flow

In the above example, the rate of return was provided for each time period. In many cases, a financial planner will have to compute the rate of return, and this is always more complicated when there are interim cash flows. If the cash flows are at the start or the end of the period, then the formulas for solving for the rate of return are relatively straightforward. Regardless of whether the cash flow is at the start or the end of the period, the numerator for the holding period return (HPR) calculation is the change in the value of the portfolio, minus the deposit. Note that the income received on the portfolio is not included, as it is assumed that the income is retained in the portfolio and thus shows up as part of the change in the value of the portfolio. If the cash flow is at the start of the period, the denominator is the beginning value of the portfolio plus the deposit. If the cash flow is at the end of the period, then the denominator is simply the beginning value of the portfolio. Keep in mind that deposits are positive numbers and withdrawals are negative numbers. Thus, the formulas are as follows.

For a cash flow at the start of a period:

HPR = (Change in value – Deposit)/(Beginning value + Deposit)

For a cash flow at the end of a period:

HPR = (Change in value – Deposit)/(Beginning value)

Example 1:	A portfolio is worth $100,000 at the start of the year, and another $5,000 is deposited in the portfolio at this time. During the year $3,000 in dividends and interest are paid into the portfolio, and the ending value is $110,000. What is the HPR?

$$HPR = \frac{(\$110{,}000 - \$100{,}000) - \$5{,}000}{\$100{,}000 + \$5{,}000}$$

$$= .0476 \text{ or } 4.76\%$$

	Note that the $3,000 in income is not directly incorporated into the answer, as it is part of the ending value of $110,000.
Example 2:	A portfolio is worth $100,000 at the start of the year. At the end of the year it is worth $115,000, after a year-end withdrawal of $5,000. What is the HPR?

$$HPR = \frac{(\$115{,}000 - \$100{,}000) - (-\$5{,}000)}{\$100{,}000}$$

$$= .20 \text{ or } 20\%$$

Time-Weighted and Dollar-Weighted Rates of Return

The GMR is referred to as a time-weighted rate of return. The reason is that each time period's return has the same weight in the calculation. No adjustment is made for the amount of money invested at any point in time; therefore, periods with large balances are not overweighted and periods with smaller cash balances are not underweighted. If a portfolio manager has absolutely no control over interim cash flows, then this is the appropriate rate of return for measuring portfolio performance.

The IRR measure of portfolio performance is known as the dollar-weighted rate of return. More weight is given to the performance of the portfolio when it is larger in absolute dollar size, and less weight is given to the performance when the portfolio is smaller. To illustrate this point, let's consider an extreme example.

Example: A portfolio has $100 in assets. During the first year, the portfolio has a –10 percent rate of return, and so ends up being worth $90. At the end of the first year, $1,000,000 is added to the portfolio, bringing the total assets to $1,000,090. The next year, the portfolio has a 10 percent rate of return, and ends up being worth $1,100,099. What are the time-weighted and dollar-weighted rates of return?

The time-weighted rate of return is –.5 percent, computed as follows:

$$[(1+.10) \times (1 - .10)]^{1/2} - 1 = -.005 \text{ or } -.5\%$$

The dollar-weighted rate of return is defined as the discount rate that makes the following equation true:

$$0 = 100 + 1,000,000/(1+r)^1 - 1,100,099/(1+r)^2$$

The answer is 9.9978 percent, and the keystrokes are:

SHIFT, C ALL
100, CFj
1,000,000, CFj
1,100,099, +/–, CFj
SHIFT, IRR/YR
(display: 9.9978[%])

In the above example, the fact that the geometric mean provides a rate of return of –.5 percent is about what we would expect given that the arithmetic mean return is 0 percent (that is, the average of 10 percent and –10 percent would be 0), and we saw earlier that the geometric mean is always slightly less than the arithmetic mean unless the returns are all the same. We would also expect that because the IRR is dollar weighted, its value would be virtually identical to the 10 percent rate of return achieved on the portfolio in the second period (that is, 9.9978 percent is virtually the same as 10 percent).

Which Rate Should be Used?

There are several uses for the measure of a portfolio's rate of return over time, and it is important to understand why one measure may be more appropriate under certain circumstances than another. Note, however, that in the absence of interim cash flows, these two different rate of return measures will be the same, and there would be no need to pick one over the other. Circumstances in which one rate is more relevant than the other involve the answers to the following two questions:

1. How did my portfolio perform?
2. What rate of return did my financial planner achieve in managing my portfolio?

Return to an Investor

When an investor wants to know how well his or her portfolio has done, the IRR (that is, the dollar-weighted rate of return) is the true rate of return. Interim cash flows are a real part of most portfolios. Thus, the impact of withdrawals and deposits on the performance of the portfolio is just as real to the investor as the rate of return on the securities in the portfolio. Hence, an investor wanting to know how well he or she has done should use the IRR.

It should be noted that saying an individual should measure his or her performance with the IRR is extremely idealistic. Unless an individual investor has training in time value of money computations, he or she will not have the foggiest idea how to make such a computation. A secondary issue is that we have implicitly assumed in all of our examples that interim cash flows occur only at the end of each period (and each period represents a year in our examples). In practice, interim cash flows will occur at any point during a period, and it would not be unusual to have multiple interim cash flows during a period, especially if a period spans a year. The math necessary for a precise calculation of the IRR when there are multiple interim cash flows at random times is quite complex, and well beyond the scope of this textbook. However, some software programs, such as Excel, allow an investor to compute a reasonably accurate estimate of portfolio performance in the presence of interim cash flows.[3]

Since the market goes up the majority of years, and since the majority of people hold investment assets for growth, the balances in these portfolios usually grow over time not only because of earnings on the account, but also because of periodic contributions. Hence, when the IRR measure of performance is used, the portfolio's performance is implicitly weighted to reflect the most recent years (that is, when the portfolio is the largest).

Return by a Portfolio Manager

When the portfolio's performance is assessed to evaluate the performance of a financial advisor, one should keep in mind that the advisor may well have not had all that much control over interim cash flows, or the interim cash flows may be the result of other type of decisions and not just the decision of whether now is a good time to add or withdraw cash from the portfolio. For example, a client might be retiring from a job and the advisor recommends moving the money from the client's defined-contribution pension plan to a rollover IRA. Hence, the movement of what is potentially a large amount of cash into a portfolio managed by the financial advisor is a result of the client's decision to retire and the advisor's decision to take more direct control of the pension monies via the rollover, and not a result of how the advisor thinks the market will perform in the next year or two. Simply put, unless a financial advisor is deliberately influencing the timing of the movement of cash into and out of a portfolio for the purpose of improving overall performance (a practice known as timing), the financial advisor should present his or her portfolio management results using the time-weighted rate of return.

The reader will note that in the preceding paragraphs, we have indicated that an individual investor should use the dollar-weighted rate of return to measure the performance of his or her portfolio, but if that same portfolio were managed by a financial planner, the time-weighted rate of return should be used to measure performance. These two rates of return will almost never be the same. Nonetheless, it is an irony of the investment process that the measurement of performance when there are interim cash flows will involve the calculation of different numbers depending on the circumstances of the computation.

BENCHMARKS

In the previous section we discussed how one measures the performance of a portfolio. Once one has measured a portfolio's performance, the next question is: "How do I evaluate the quality of that performance?" For example, if a financial advisor achieves a 10 percent rate of return in a portfolio over the last 5 years, is that a good performance, or a weak performance? To answer this question, one needs benchmarks. Benchmarks are simply standards of comparison for managing and evaluating portfolio performance. There are several sophisticated techniques to evaluate portfolio performance that are based on portfolio theory and incorporate risk and opportunity costs. These include the Sharpe and Treynor ratios, M^2, and Jensen's alpha. We will discuss these techniques later in the chapter. For now, let us focus on what most people do when they evaluate a portfolio's performance. Specifically, most people look at how the portfolio did compared to how a benchmark portfolio did over the same period of time.

Benchmarks should be chosen for their similarity in risk characteristics to the portfolio under consideration. For example, a portfolio manager may have a goal of beating the Standard & Poor's 500 Index. If the portfolio has similar risk characteristics to the S&P 500 and outperforms it, then the portfolio has beaten the benchmark. Of course, portfolio theory tells us that if the portfolio has a higher beta that the S&P 500, it should outperform it; thus honest risk comparisons are important.

Comparing a bond portfolio to a stock index benchmark would make no sense. Even comparing a bond portfolio of AAA bonds to a broad benchmark of all bonds would make no sense. Good benchmarking means apples-to-apples comparisons.

It is also possible to create benchmarks from multiple indices. For example, consider a portfolio that consists of 60 percent in stocks with a risk profile similar to the S&P 500 and 40 percent in investment-grade bonds similar in risk to the Lehman Brothers Corporate Bond Index. The equity portion of the portfolio can be compared to the S&P 500, and the bond portion can be compared to the Lehman Brothers Corporate Bond Index. Furthermore, a combined benchmark (.60 x S&P 500 + .40 x Lehman Brothers Corporate Bond Index) can be created. It is possible to match the combined benchmark while outperforming in one sector and underperforming in another sector. Thus, it is helpful to break down the performance.

MARKET INDICES

As indicated in the previous section, many of the popular market indices are used to evaluate performance. A myriad of market performance indicators are available to investors for benchmarking and general market observations. Each indicator has its own unique characteristics, and investors should be aware of those characteristics before selecting the appropriate indicator or benchmark.

Description of Indices

Dow Jones Averages

The Dow Jones Industrial Average (DJIA) is the most widely referenced stock market indicator. There are several reasons for this, including the following:

1. Dow Jones and Company owns the index as well as the *Wall Street Journal,* which is arguably the dominant daily business publication.
2. The Dow Jones Industrial Average began in 1884 with 11 stocks and increased to 30 stocks in 1928. Simply put, it was the first widely published index.
3. Use of widely held and frequently traded companies in the Dow Industrial listing provides an important feature of timeliness—that is, the Dow represents major, frequently traded stocks. Therefore, this average represents the direction of current transactions at any point in time, which may not always be the case with broader indices. The broader indices, such as the NASDAQ/OTC Index, include less frequently traded stocks or stocks that are not widely owned and therefore include price quotes that are not as timely.

Today, the DJIA still consists of 30 of the largest American companies in major industries, and it is often referred to as representing the performance of strong, financially secure companies. All of the 30 companies are traded on the New York Stock Exchange except for Intel and Microsoft, which are traded on the NASDAQ.

As described in chapter 2, there are over 3,000 common stock issues listed on the NYSE, not to mention thousands more traded on the American Stock Exchange, regional exchanges, and OTC (listed in financial pages as NASDAQ). One might ask what good the Dow Jones Industrial Average is with only 30 stocks. Remember, the 30 companies listed for the Dow Jones Industrial are representative of the broad market and of U.S. industry. Except for the utility, transportation, and financial sectors, the companies are chosen because they are major players in their industries and their stocks are widely held by both individual and institutional investors. The 30 stocks in the Dow Industrials represent a fifth of the $1 trillion-plus market value of all stock traded, and about a fourth of the value of stocks on the NYSE.

Research has shown the Dow closely mirrors broader stock market indicators. By its nature, however, the Dow represents the blue chip or large-capitalization stocks, such as AT&T, Coca-Cola, DuPont, GE, and IBM (and more recent additions, including Microsoft, Intel, and Wal-Mart). Other broader market indices, such as the S&P 500 Industrial Index, represent a much wider array of stocks. Whenever the broader indices move in a direction opposite from Dow averages, there is a divergence between top-tier, high-capitalization stocks and second-tier, lower-capitalization stocks. For instance, if the Dow average moves up while broader indices fall or remain the same, these conflicting changes may indicate insecurity by market participants and a tendency to seek the security of larger, well-known firms (sometimes called a *flight-to-quality effect*).

flight-to-quality effect

In spite of its dominating presence, the DJIA has serious flaws as a market indicator. It only includes a small percentage of stocks available in the market, and industries are not represented in the same proportions as they are in the overall economy. The thirty DJIA companies are large and mature relative to most companies, and thus the index is not necessarily representative of the market as a whole. Furthermore, the DJIA is a price-weighted index, which can give a misleading impression of market performance. (Price weighting is discussed at greater length in a later section.) Like other indicators, the DJIA reflects that part of return that relates to price changes; it does not consider dividend returns.

Flaws in the DJIA

- Small number of stocks
- Industries not proportionally represented
- Focuses only on large, mature companies
- Ignores dividends
- Price weighted

Other Dow Jones averages include the Dow Jones Transportation Average, which represents 20 stocks of the airline, trucking, railroad, and shipping business; and the Dow Jones Utility Average, which includes 15 stocks and is geographically representative of the gas and electric utilities industries.

Standard & Poor's 500 Index

The Standard & Poor's 500 Index (S&P 500) includes 500 large-capitalization companies representing about 80 percent of the total market value of the United States stock markets. The index includes almost 400 companies that are listed on the NYSE, about 75 that are listed on NASDAQ, a few that are listed on the Amex, and a few foreign corporations whose operations are well represented in the United States. The S&P 500 is a much broader indicator than the DJIA, represents a much larger portion of the total market, and much more closely reflects the industry allocation that exists in the total market. The S&P 500 and all the indicators listed below, with one exception, are value weighted, or "market capitalization weighted."

Advantages of the S&P 500 Index

- Large percentage of total market capitalization
- Includes stocks from multiple markets
- Industry representation more typical of economy
- Value weighted

Other Standard & Poor's indicators include the S&P MidCap 400, which represents companies from the 501st to the 900th largest on all three major exchanges, and the S&P SmallCap 600, which represents the 901st to the 1,500th largest.

NASDAQ

The NASDAQ 100 Index includes 100 of the largest domestic and international nonfinancial companies listed on the NASDAQ market, based on market capitalization. The index reflects companies across major industry groups, including computer hardware and software, telecommunications, retail/wholesale trade, and biotechnology. The NASDAQ Composite Index measures all NASDAQ domestic and international-based common-type stocks listed on the NASDAQ market.

Other Indices

The NYSE Composite Index includes all common stocks listed on the New York Stock Exchange. The AMEX Composite Index includes the common stocks, American depository receipts, real estate investment trusts (REITs), master limited partnerships (MLPs), and closed-end investment vehicles that are listed on that exchange.

The Russell 3000 Index measures the performance of the 3,000 largest U.S. companies, and represents approximately 98 percent of the U.S. equity market. The Russell 1000 Index measures the performance of the 1,000 largest companies in the Russell 3000 Index, and the Russell 2000 Index measures the performance of the 2,000 smallest companies in the Russell 3000 Index.

The Wilshire 5000 Equity Index measures the performance of all U.S.-headquartered equity securities with readily available price data, which includes over 7,000 securities. (It is clearly a misnamed index!) The Wilshire 4500 Index includes all the stocks in the Wilshire 5000 except those included in the S&P 500. The Wilshire Mid Cap 750 Index includes the largest 750 among the 4,500.

The Value Line Index is one of the more unique indices. It contains 1,700 stocks, drawn from the NYSE, American Stock Exchange, NASDAQ, and over-the-counter (OTC) markets. The uniqueness is derived from the fact that it is an equally weighted index, not a value-weighted index, like most others, or a price-weighted index, like the DJIA. Because of this difference in computation, the Value Line Index is more indicative of how smaller companies have performed than the larger ones. Thus, there are times in the market when the Value Line Index is moving in an opposite direction to the rest of the market indices, which means that the smaller companies are performing in a manner different than the larger, better-known ones.[4]

Foreign Indices

Since the investment world is increasingly international, investment returns in foreign markets are followed in the United States. The FTSE 100 (pronounced "footsie") is an index of the top 100 most highly capitalized companies traded on the London Stock Exchange. The Hang Seng Index includes 33 companies representing 70 percent of the market capitalization of the Hong Kong stock market. The Nikkei Index includes 225 of the largest market capitalization companies based in Japan.

A major foreign market index is the MSCI EAFE index. It is made up of 21 MSCI country indices that represent the developed markets outside of North America. The MSCI Index is published daily by MSCI through multiple vendors, and is updated every 60 seconds through Reuters and Bloomberg. As of July 31, 2002, the MSCI EAFE Index contained 1,021 securities with a total market capitalization of over $5.5 trillion.[5]

Bond Indices

Although bond indices are not followed as closely as stock market indices, they are still important, especially in benchmarking. Among the most commonly watched bond indices are those maintained by Lehman Brothers, a global investment bank.

The Lehman Brothers Aggregate Bond Index consists of the Lehman Brothers Government/Corporate Bond Index, Mortgage-Backed Securities Index, and Asset-Backed Securities Index, including securities that are of investment-grade quality or better, have at least 1 year to maturity, and have an outstanding par value of at least $100 million.

The Lehman Brothers Corporate Bond Index includes all publicly issued, fixed-rate, nonconvertible, dollar-denominated, SEC-registered, investment-grade corporate debt.

The Lehman Brothers Government Bond Index consists of the Treasury Bond Index and the Agency Bond Index as well as the 1–3 Year Government Index and the 20+ Year Treasury Index.

The Lehman Brothers Government/Corporate Bond Index consists of the Lehman Brothers Government and Corporate Bond indices, including U.S. government Treasury and agency securities as well as corporate and Yankee bonds.[6]

The Lehman Brothers Mortgage-Backed Securities Index consists of 15- and 30-year fixed-rate securities backed by mortgage pools of the Government National Mortgage Association (GNMA), Federal Home Loan Mortgage Corporation (FHLMC), and Federal National Mortgage Association (FNMA).

The Lehman Brothers Municipal Bond Index consists of investment-grade, tax-exempt, and fixed-rate bonds with long-term maturities (greater than 2 years) selected from issues larger than $50 million.

Computation of Indices

A *price-weighted index,* such as the DJIA, means that the index is equal to the sum of the prices of the securities in the index, divided by a specified divisor. The simplest price-weighted index is an arithmetic average. Thus, if an index has three stocks in it, one would simply add up the three stock prices and divide by 3. For example, consider a price-weighted index that includes three stocks—David Corporation, Peggy Corporation, and Vail Corporation—whose prices are $30, $80, and $100 respectively. A simple, arithmetic index would add these three prices together and divide by 3, which gives an average of $70.00 ([$30 + $80 + $100]/3).

A serious problem develops for price-weighted indices whenever there is a stock split or a stock dividend. A stock split occurs whenever a corporation decides to substantially increase the number of shares outstanding. The most common reason for a stock split is to reduce the absolute dollar value at which the stock trades. In the case of stock splits, the old shares are replaced with new shares whose par values are different. The trading price of the new shares reflects the percentage increase in the number of shares outstanding. A stock dividend occurs whenever a company wants to make a slight increase in the number of shares outstanding. An example of a stock dividend would be a two percent dividend. For every 100 shares a person owned, he or she would receive an additional two shares. The stock would subsequently trade at a price approximately 2 percent less than would otherwise be the case.

Suppose that in the above example, Vail Corporation has a 2-for-1 stock split. On the effective date of the split, the new shares would trade at a price of $50, assuming no other events occurred that caused the value of the company to change. Suppose that on the same day, David falls to $29, Peggy rises to $82, and Vail rises to $51 (due to some other news about the company). If no adjustment were made in the computation of the index, the new average would be $54.00 ([$29 + $82 + $51]/3), which is a substantial drop in the value of the index and would mislead one into thinking that there has been a substantial drop in stock prices, which is not the case.

To neutralize the effect of the stock split on the index, the common adjustment is to redefine the divisor. The procedure for calculating the new divisor is to hold all the stock prices constant except for the stock that has the split or stock dividend. That stock's price is adjusted mathematically as would be expected to adjust for the split or dividend. Then we find the divisor that would cause the new average to equal the old average. Finally, we apply the new divisor to the actual prices at the end of the day.

In our example, the original index was computed as:

$$I_{pwt} = \frac{30 + 80 + 100}{3} = 70.00$$

To calculate a new divisor, we hold the price of David at $30 and the price of Peggy at $80, and we adjust the price of Vail to $50 because of the split. Since no economic changes have taken place, the average should not change. Thus, we hold the average at 70, and find the divisor that will calculate an average of 70.

$$70.00 = \frac{30 + 80 + 50}{\text{new divisor}}$$

$$\text{new divisor} = \frac{160}{70}$$

$$= 2.2857$$

Now we add the actual closing prices of the stocks and divide by the new divisor to calculate the average for the end of the day as follows:

$$I_{pwt+1} = \frac{\sum_{i=1}^{n} P_{it+1}}{\text{divisor}_{t+1}}$$

$$= \frac{29 + 82 + 51}{2.2857}$$

$$= 70.88$$

When the DJIA was first created, the denominator equaled the number of securities in the index. Because of the number of stock splits and stock dividends over the years, the DJIA divisor is now approximately .2! Note that a similar divisor adjustment occurs whenever a change is made in the 30 stocks that constitute the DJIA. Suppose another company whose stock trades at $80 per share replaces a company whose stock trades at $5 per share. Without an adjustment in the divisor, there would be the appearance of a dramatic increase in stock prices the first time the new stock was used in the calculations.

value-weighted index

A *value-weighted index,* as the name implies, considers the total market value (price times number of shares) of each stock in the index, not just their prices. The index calculation consists of three parts: the sum of the current market values of all the stocks in the index, the sum of the market values of all the stocks in the index in the base year, and the index value arbitrarily assigned to the base year, such as 100. The mathematical formulation for a value-weighted index is as follows:

$$I_{vwt} = \frac{\sum_{i=1}^{n} P_{it} Q_{it}}{\sum_{i=1}^{n} P_{iB} Q_{iB}} \times I_{vwB}$$

where I_{vwt} = value-weighted index at time t

P_{it} = price of security i at time t

Q_{it} = number of shares outstanding of security i at time t

P_{iB} = price of security i in the base time period

Q_{iB} = number of shares outstanding of security i in the base period

I_{vwB} = index value assigned for the base period (for example, 100.00)

Continuing the previous example, assume the following numbers of shares associated with the three companies in the base period.

Name	Price	Shares	Market value
David	$30	100,000	$3,000,000
Peggy	$80	5,000	400,000
Vail	$100	10,000	1,000,000
Total			$4,400,000

Thus the base market value is $4,400,000, and we will assume that the base index value is 100.00. Now consider the new stock prices, and note especially the change in the price and number of shares for Vail Corporation.

Name	Price	Shares	Market value
David	$29	100,000	$2,900,000
Peggy	$82	5,000	410,000
Vail	$51	20,000	1,020,000
Total			$4,330,000

Unlike a price-weighted index, no intermediate calculation of a new divisor is required. The index for the end of the second time period would be as follows:

$$I_{vwt} = \frac{4,330,000}{4,400,000} \times 100.00$$

$$= 98.41$$

Comparing Price-Weighted and Value-Weighted Indices

As presented in the examples above, the price-weighted index showed an increase in the index value from 70.00 to 70.89, while the value-weighted index showed a decline from 100.00 to 98.41. The reason for this disparity is that David Corporation has a relative low price, but it also has the largest market value because of the large number of shares. David Corporation counts heavily in a value-weighted index, but modestly in a price-weighted index.

An equal but opposite change in the prices of two stocks would offset each other in a price-weighted index because it considers only the price of the stock without regard to the total size of the company. However, if one stock has far more shares outstanding, its change will be more significant in a value-weighted index.

Financial Planning Issue

Financial advisors may want to compare the performance of a client's portfolio with some market index. When an advisor selects an index for comparative purposes (that is, benchmarking), he or she should understand how that index is computed, and whether or not it is an appropriate benchmark. For clients with large diversified stock portfolios, large value-weighted indices are clearly more appropriate.

EVALUATING PORTFOLIO PERFORMANCE

Comparing a portfolio's performance with a benchmark portfolio is inappropriate unless the objectives of that particular portfolio and the measurement of that portfolio's performance are essentially the same as for the benchmark portfolio. Any comparison of returns is incomplete if it does not consider risk and opportunity cost.

As noted in the previous chapters, there are two measures of risk that are relevant. The broadest measure of risk is standard deviation. As described earlier, standard deviation is a measure of the variability of an investment's return with respect to the expected return of that investment. The larger the standard deviation is, the riskier the investment is because the investment's

---

Financial Planning Issue[7]

As indicated at the start of this section, many people like to evaluate portfolio performance by comparing the rate of return on their portfolios with the rate of return on an index. This is an inappropriate practice for several reasons. First, indices reflect portfolios that are constructed with absolutely no transaction fees or advisory fees. No individual can obtain such beneficial treatment. Second, most portfolios involve trades over time, and unless the portfolio is in a tax-protected account (for example, an IRA), taxes will be due. The payment of taxes involves a removal of cash from the portfolio, thus reducing the year's rate of return.[8] Indices pay no taxes. Third, most indices have a large number of securities in them, making them extremely diversified (except for the sector indices). As such, they are likely to have less volatility than an individual's portfolio. Fourth, most people hold some cash and/or fixed-income securities in their portfolios. Comparing the returns on these portfolios directly with an index will more often than not be unfavorable. Finally, as discussed in the next section, the beta coefficients for most indices are likely to be different than those for the portfolios of most individuals.

return is more variable. An investment's actual return is within one standard deviation of its expected return approximately 68 percent of the time, and it is within two standard deviations approximately 95 percent of the time.

The other critical measure of risk is beta. Beta is a measure of the volatility of an investment's return relative to the market, usually represented by the Standard & Poor's 500 Index, which by definition has a beta of 1.0.

Almost all stocks tend to move up when the market is moving up, and down when the market is moving down. Investments that tend to move up and down less than the market have a beta less than 1.0 and are relatively conservative. Investments that tend to move up and down more than the market have a beta greater than 1.0 and are relatively aggressive. Although beta is not a reliable risk measure for individual stocks, it is relatively reliable for portfolios and mutual funds.

Whenever one uses beta as a risk measure, one should remember to consider the coefficient of determination (R^2) associated with the computation of that beta. R^2 measures the so-called "goodness of fit"; thus it is a measure of the relative reliability of the beta. R^2 has a maximum value of 1.0 and a minimum value of 0. If the relationship between a portfolio's return and the market return is strong, the R^2 will be high. Beta and R^2 are independent in the sense that it is possible to have a high R^2 regardless of whether the beta is high or low. Most mutual funds have R^2 values between 0.80 and 0.90, which means that the estimates of their betas are quite reliable.

Let's consider first the two performance measures that are based on the portfolio's standard deviation, and then look at the two performance measures that are based on a portfolio's beta.

Standard Deviation–Based Measures of Performance

Sharpe Ratio

reward-to-variability ratio (RVAR)

The Sharpe ratio, or the *reward-to-variability ratio (RVAR)* as it is sometimes called, is defined as follows:

$$S_p = \frac{R_p - R_f}{\sigma_p} \qquad \text{(Equation 5-2)}$$

where S_p = the Sharpe ratio
   R_p = arithmetic mean return on the portfolio being evaluated
   R_f = risk-free rate over the sample time period
   σ_p = the standard deviation of the portfolio being evaluated

This formula is provided on the CFP® Certification Exam formula sheet.

Note that the numerator of this ratio is the portfolio return in excess of the risk-free rate of return, while the denominator is simply the standard deviation of the portfolio's return. The value of this ratio is best understood in the context of the capital market line (CML). Recall from chapter 4 that the CML is the efficient frontier created when n risky assets are held in combination with a risk-free asset. The one portfolio of all risky assets that plots on the CML is the market portfolio, M. Hence, the slope of the CML can be defined as the difference between the expected return on the market portfolio and the risk-free rate, divided by the standard deviation of the market portfolio. The performance of the market portfolio can then be measured ex post by using the actual returns. Thus, over any time period, the performance of the market portfolio can be measured with the Sharpe ratio as:

$$S_M = \frac{(R_M - R_f)}{\sigma_M}$$

So, when one computes the Sharpe ratio for a portfolio, one could compare this ratio to that of the market portfolio to conclude whether the portfolio being analyzed has "beaten" the market or underperformed the market. A Sharpe ratio for a portfolio that is higher than that of the market would indicate the portfolio has outperformed the market. Similarly, the Sharpe ratio for any two portfolios can be compared directly to determine which has generated the better performance.

M^2

The most recently popularized tool for evaluating portfolio performance has been dubbed M^2, for Leah Modigliani and her grandfather Franco Modigliani.[9] The rationale for the ratio lies in the observation that a Sharpe ratio is not really meaningful in terms of its numerical value. For example, if the Sharpe ratio for the market were .55, and the ratio for a particular portfolio were .52, we would know that this portfolio underperformed the market, but we don't have a sense for the significance of the underperformance. Is a ratio difference of .03 (.55 – .52) a lot, or a trivial amount? This is not clear from the Sharpe ratio.

The basic idea of the M^2 measure is that a portfolio's rate of return is first adjusted to what it would have been if it had the same degree of risk exposure as the market portfolio. This is done by determining what combination of the risk-free asset and the portfolio being analyzed would be necessary to have the same standard deviation as the market portfolio. The return on this hypothetical portfolio is then computed, where the weights are as follows:

$$W_p = \sigma_M / \sigma_p \quad \text{and} \quad W_{Rf} = 1 - W_p$$

The return on this hypothetical portfolio is computed as:

$$R_{p*} = (W_p \times R_p) + (W_{Rf} \times R_f)$$

Then the M^2 is computed as the difference between this risk-adjusted return and the market's return. That is:

$$M^2 = R_{p*} - R_M \qquad \text{(Equation 5-3)}$$

where M^2 = the M^2 measure of risk-adjusted return
R_{p*} = a risk-adjusted rate of return created by a combination of portfolio p and the risk-free asset
R_M = the rate of return on the market portfolio

An M^2 that is positive is good news, and one that is negative is bad. An M^2 of 0 indicates the portfolio has performed comparably to the market portfolio.

Example: The World's Greatest Mutual Fund had an annual average rate of return over the last 5 years of 12 percent, and a standard deviation of return of 15 percent. Over that same time period, the market portfolio's (for example, the S&P 500 Index) numbers were 8 percent and 10 percent. The risk-free rate during this period was 4 percent. Given the performance of the World's Greatest Mutual Fund, one could have combined an investment in this fund with an investment in T-bills to have produced a portfolio with risk identical to that of the market portfolio by using the following weights:

$$W_p = 10/15 = 2/3 \quad \text{and} \quad W_{Rf} = 1 - 2/3 = 1/3$$

The return on this portfolio would have been:

$$R_{p*} = 2/3 \times 12\% + 1/3 \times 4\% = 9\ 1/3\%$$

Thus, this mutual fund outperformed the market by:

$$M^2 = 9\ 1/3\% - 8\% = 1\ 1/3\%$$

The Sharpe ratio and the M^2 measure are good tools, but they are really only applicable for portfolios that are represented to be fully diversified because the CML equation is relevant only for fully efficient portfolios, which means ones that are believed to be fully diversified. For single securities and undiversified portfolios, we have to turn to the security market line framework for measures of performance. This means using the beta coefficient as a measure of diversification.

Estimated Beta–Based Measures of Performance

Treynor Ratio

reward-to-volatility ratio (RVOL)

The Treynor ratio, also called the *reward-to-volatility ratio (RVOL),* is defined as follows:

$$T_p = \frac{R_P - R_f}{\beta_p}$$
(Equation 5-4)

where T_p = Treynor ratio of the portfolio
β_p = beta of the portfolio being evaluated

This formula is provided on the CFP® Certification Exam formula sheet. Note that the numerator is the same as in the Sharpe ratio, but the denominator's measure of risk is now the beta of the security—which means that only market-related risk is considered. That is, the Treynor ratio looks at the return achieved relative to the amount of systematic risk exposure of the investment.

As with the Sharpe ratio, an easy comparison can be made between any particular security or portfolio and the market index in that the beta of the market portfolio is 1 by definition. Thus, the Treynor ratio for the market portfolio is simply the return on the market portfolio minus the risk-free rate, which is also known as the market risk premium. Any security or portfolio with a Treynor ratio greater than the market risk premium can be considered to have outperformed the market. Treynor ratios less than the market risk premium have underperformed the market.

Example: Suppose that over the last year the market's return was 12 percent and the risk-free rate was 4 percent. The market risk premium was 8 percent (12% – 4%). The RFD Fund over the same period achieved a return of 10 percent but had a beta of .8. Did it beat the market?

The Treynor ratio for the market was:

$$T_M = \frac{12 - 4}{1} = 8\%$$

$$T_{RFD} = \frac{10 - 4}{.8} = 7.5\%$$

Thus the RFD Fund underperformed the market.

Jensen's Alpha

Jensen's alpha uses the capital asset pricing model (CAPM) to evaluate the risk-adjusted rate of return of the fund. If a fund generates a return that is exactly what would be expected of a fund with its beta, the alpha for the fund will be 0. Positive alphas indicate positive risk-adjusted rates of return, and negative alphas indicate negative risk-adjusted rates of return. The CAPM is stated as follows:

$$R_p = R_f + \left(R_M - R_f \right) \beta_p$$

where R_p = expected return of portfolio
$\quad\quad R_f$ = risk-free rate
$\quad\quad R_M$ = expected return of market portfolio
$\quad\quad \beta_p$ = beta of the portfolio

Actual returns are then compared to the returns that could have been expected given the risk-free rate and the beta coefficient. The difference is the alpha.

$$\alpha_p = R_p - \left[R_f + \left(R_M - R_f \right) \beta_p \right] \quad\quad \text{(Equation 5-5)}$$

Jensen's alpha has the same attractive feature as the M^2 measure, namely, its interpretation is easily understood. For example, if a security or portfolio has an alpha of 2 percent, then one can say that the security or portfolio being analyzed has outperformed the market by 2 percent. Positive alphas are good and negative alphas are bad!

Example of Performance Measurement

Suppose the following data are available for the 1984–2003 period for several mutual funds. (The S&P 500 Index and the 90-day T-bill rate will serve as proxies for the market return and the risk-free rate, respectively.)

Mutual Fund	Average Return	Standard Deviation	Beta	R^2
Julia Fund	19.20	18.50	.83	.472
Frances Drake Fund	31.92	18.57	1.08	.532
Wong Fund	15.19	9.57	.65	.877
S&P 500 Index	17.16	13.18	1.00	1.000
90-day T-Bill rate	8.31	2.56	0.00	—

Using the formulas for the Sharpe and Treynor ratios, M^2 measure, and Jensen's alpha, we can derive the following:

Mutual Fund	Sharpe	M^2	Treynor	Jensen's Alpha
Julia Fund	.589	−1.09	13.120	3.545
Frances Drake Fund	1.271	7.90	21.861	14.052
Wong Fund	.719	.625	10.585	1.127
S&P 500 Index	.671	0	8.850	0

The interpretation of these results is that Frances Drake Fund is clearly superior among the funds on all four measures of risk-adjusted performance.

However, the Julia Fund and Wong Fund have different rankings, depending on the measure chosen. When total risk is considered as measured by the standard deviation, as with the Sharpe ratio and the M^2 measure, the Wong Fund is superior to the Julia Fund. In addition, the Wong Fund has outperformed the market and the Julia Fund has underperformed it. However, when the beta measure of risk is chosen, which reflects market risk only, the Julia Fund has outperformed the Wong fund, and both have beaten the market. It is important to note that the Wong Fund did not achieve as high an average return as the market, but because the return it achieved involved less risk on a risk-adjusted basis, its performance is superior to the market. In the example shown, the Wong Fund appears to have the highest degree of coincidence with the market as measured by R^2.

THE RISK PREMIUM ON NONMARKET RISK

According to the CAPM, the risk premiums applied to the expected returns of individual investments should be solely determined by each asset's market exposure risk, as measured by beta. Thus, two assets with the same beta coefficient should have equal expected returns, even if they have different levels of nonmarket risk. A number of studies have found, however, that risk premiums are also related to nonmarket risk. This apparent conflict between the theory and the evidence has spawned a number of hypotheses.

If, for instance, effective diversification were relatively difficult or costly, many investors would diversify incompletely rather than incur the high costs of achieving a fully diversified portfolio. Because nonmarket risk would contribute to overall portfolio risks for these investors, they would consider it relevant.

Studies have found that various possible sources of estimation error could account for the price effect of nonmarket risks. The results suggest two factors: inefficiently estimated betas and a positive correlation between actual betas and nonmarket risk. If betas are inefficiently estimated, the true effect of market risk will not be fully captured by the beta estimate. If the true beta and the estimate for nonmarket risk are correlated, the nonmarket risk variable may act as a second proxy for market risk.

Estimates of beta are based on a firm's historical correlation with the market. But the nature of the firm's business, competitors, sources of supply, customer base, influence of government regulation, and other factors that influence its riskiness change over time. In some more extreme examples, a company can merge with another firm, diversify into another line of business, acquire a foreign subsidiary, divest itself of an unprofitable division, or undergo a complete change of management. In such cases, the historical beta might not even be a close approximation of current beta.

Another explanation for the apparent premium paid for nonmarket risk relates to the borrowing and lending assumption: If investors cannot borrow and lend at the same risk-free rate, one of the CAPM assumptions, effective diversification of nonmarket risk may be impossible.

The possibility that returns are not normally distributed provides yet another possible explanation. The mean and variance completely specify the shape of normal distributions. All normal distributions have the same basic shape. Normal distributions differ from each other only in scale. Nonsymmetrical or *skewed distributions*, in contrast, may have identical means and variances and yet have different shapes. Portfolio theory assumes that expected returns are normally distributed. When expected returns are not normally distributed, the model's implications may not apply. For example, distributions A and B (figure 5-1) have the same mean (M) and standard deviation (σ), yet they offer markedly different return possibilities.

skewed distributions

Distribution A's returns have some reasonable chance of being high and almost no chance of being more than one standard deviation below the mean. This type of distribution is said to have positive skewness. Distribution B's returns could well be more than one standard deviation below the mean but are unlikely to be even one standard deviation above its mean. This distribution is said to be negatively skewed. The mode (point of greatest probability) of B exceeds the mode of A, however. While individual preferences vary, most investors prefer positive skewness. Stocks with highly variable returns also tend to have highly skewed returns. An investor preference for skewness may

FIGURE 5-1
Skewed Distributions

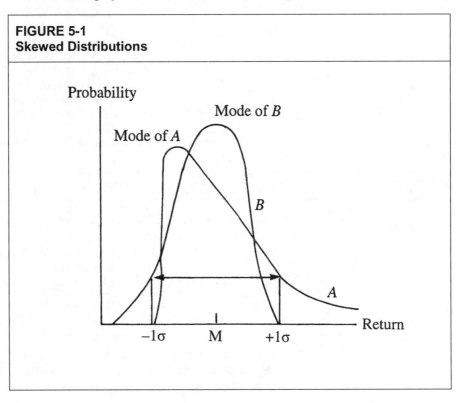

cause high-risk stocks to be priced to offer a lower expected return than less risky stocks. Moreover, investors who seek to achieve their desired skewness level might hold too few securities to be fully diversified.

Real-world distributions of returns may differ from the normal distribution in manners other than skewness. Normal distributions are symmetrical; skewed distributions are not. Another area of potential difference relates to the relative distribution of the probabilities. All normal distributions have the same probability associated with each distance (scaled in standard deviations) from the mean: 68 percent within one standard deviation of the mean; 95 percent within two standard deviations; and 99.9 percent within three deviations. There are some distributions that are symmetrical like the normal distribution but do not have its famous "bell shape." Such distributions may have as little as 50 percent to as much as 80 percent of the returns within one standard deviation. These distributions are known as leptokurtic and platokurtic.

Factors Contributing to Rewards for Nonmarket Risk

- Errors in estimated betas may be correlated with non-market risk contributing to an apparent empirical relationship.
- Estimates of beta are based on the past and fail to take major changes in the company or its business environment into account.
- Investors who are unable to lend and borrow at the risk-free rate may find that inefficient portfolios are the most effective way of achieving their desired risk levels.
- Nonnormal expected return distributions, coupled with an investor preference for skewness, may further compound the difficulty of assembling efficient portfolios and thus increase the relevance f nonmarket risk.

ESTIMATED BETAS AND SUBSEQUENT PERFORMANCE

As should be apparent to the reader, one of the critical keys to applying modern portfolio theory to portfolio management is to know the beta of a particular security. Unfortunately, betas can only be estimated—they are not knowable. Investors who expect the market to move in a particular direction would like to assemble a portfolio that takes full advantage of the expected market move. If the market is expected to rise, the portfolio manager would like to be concentrated in high-beta stocks. Alternatively, if a market decline were anticipated, the portfolio manager would prefer to be invested in low-beta stocks, if the manager cannot otherwise convert the portfolio to cash.

A large number of advisory services are happy to sell their beta estimates to investors and portfolio managers. Betas are normally estimated by regressing historical security returns on market returns. Investors who use these beta estimates as a guide to sensitivity to market moves need to know how well they explain individual security performance. A number of tests have been developed to assess the usefulness and accuracy of beta estimates.

Properties of Beta Estimates

For most publicly traded stocks, estimated betas have an average value of 1, and most beta estimates are relatively close to 1. The vast majority of estimates of beta are between 0 and 2. Individual beta estimates have been found in several different tests to be relatively unreliable. Portfolio betas, in contrast, appear to be much more stable. Apparently, errors inherent in individual company beta estimates are largely offsetting. The inconsistency between actual returns and those implied by individually estimated betas could be due to instability in the underlying betas and/or errors in the estimation process. An important question to consider: Does the estimation process introduce systematic errors, and if so, can an improved process be devised?

Improved Beta Estimates

A number of statistical phenomena, including beta estimates, exhibit a tendency to move toward the grand mean (regression toward the mean). For example, in baseball, individual high and low first-month batting averages generally move toward the overall all-player average. Note, however, that this phenomenon describes the behavior of extreme values, not the entire population. Thus, batting averages and betas near the mean tend to move randomly away from the mean with sufficient frequency to repopulate the extremes as the prior-period extremes move in. Several estimation techniques take account of the regression-toward-the-mean phenomena.

M.E. Blume suggests adjusting the beta for next year as follows:[10]

Blume-adjusted beta

Blume-adjusted beta = .35 + .68 x beta estimate [(based on data for the past 3 years)]

For example, if the stock's 3-year beta were 1.2, Blume's adjusted beta would equal .35 + .68(1.2) = 1.166. Others have proposed more sophisticated adjustments. Extensive study of these various beta-adjustment techniques shows that they are better than naively assuming no change in future betas. On the other hand, beta adjustments appear to be less necessary for large portfolios even though several mutual fund advisory services create adjusted betas for each fund as a regular part of their service. Substituting fundamental factors for or combining them with historically estimated betas are further efforts to generate more reliable beta estimates. Although all of these efforts may have improved the resulting beta estimates, the best estimates are still not perfect.

Barr Rosenberg was able to predict betas for companies using fundamental operating data—that is, accounting numbers taken from either historical or projected income statements and balance sheets.[11] Rosenberg argues that the problems with applications of the CAPM arise from the unrealistic assumptions of the simple model based on the efficient market hypothesis (discussed in the next chapter). For instance, the standard version of the CAPM is based on the clearly unrealistic assumption that investors have immediate access to all information needed to establish a security's price.

Fama and French posited the most recent significant attack on the use of market beta in an article in 1992.[12] They found evidence that the CAPM does not explain why returns of different types of risky stocks differ, and they argued that beta is not sufficient to describe the risk-return relationship in markets. They examined securities traded on the major U.S. stock exchanges between 1963 and 1990 and found that better predictors of stock returns were the size of the firm and the ratio of the firm's book value to its market value. Critics of the Fama-French results argue that investors may simply have a preference for large capitalization firms not explained by economic rationality or that investors may not have sufficient capital to diversify risk completely, so that systematic risk may not fully explain market returns.

The Market Index

The market index used in the beta estimating equation may also introduce error into the estimation process. The theoretical model assumes that betas are estimated with an index that reflects all capital assets in proportion to their relative contribution to investor wealth. In practice, however, the NYSE composite or an even less broad index (such as the Standard and Poor's 500 Index) is usually employed. The NYSE index is an acceptable measure of U.S. stock movements, although the smallest firms are omitted from the index. NYSE-listed securities are a large part of the total U.S. stock market, and NYSE, NASDAQ, AMEX, regional, and OTC stocks all tend to move together. Moreover, option, warrant, and convertible prices also tend to change in the same direction as stock prices. Thus, the NYSE composite reflects the movements of U.S. stocks reasonably well.

The NYSE index's acceptability declines, however, as the relevant universe expands progressively to include U.S. debt securities, real estate, futures contracts, foreign securities, collectibles, precious metals, and so on. Even though the U.S. equity market influences the returns on many of these assets, correlations are relatively weak for most assets and essentially zero for others. Investments other than U.S. stocks (especially home ownership) represent an appreciable part of most investors' total wealth. Accordingly, using only U.S. stocks in the market index may result in bias in the resulting beta estimates.

Indices of varying quality do exist for debt securities, foreign securities, commodities, some collector's items, real estate, and non-NYSE equities.

Implications of Statistical Tests

As a whole, the research presents a relatively discouraging picture for these implications of statistical tests, because (1) the markets are not as efficient as the theory implies; (2) contrary to the theory, nonmarket risk may affect prices; and (3) relative return forecasts based on the market model are unreliable. In view of these shortcomings, why does the theory continue to receive so much attention? The answer to this question has three parts.

First, portfolio theory is an elegant simplification of complex phenomena. The theory's defenders can make useful explanations of a great deal of stock market behavior, and a huge amount of literature (and correspondingly huge investment of time, money, and reputations) backs up the theory. Not surprisingly, portfolio theory proponents would prefer to preserve as much of that investment as they reasonably can.

Second, the theory offers a useful point of departure. Economists, for example, need to understand the model of pure competition to better understand the economy, even though few markets are perfectly competitive. Similarly, most physicists are quite familiar with the properties of a frictionless world and perfect gas. These idealized models yield interesting insights and testable predictions. A particular nonidealized effect may be observed in the difference between the model forecast and the actual event (ex post forecast analysis) and thereby yield useful information for the next (ex ante) forecast period. Remember, for rational investment, forecasting is unavoidable. Therefore, finance theorists and empiricists are expected to know the implications of portfolio theory even if the real world often behaves differently.

Third, and most important, there is no better alternative model for the relationship between risk and expected return. If we do not use the portfolio theory framework to think about and analyze security returns, then the investment world becomes nothing but a huge collection of meaningless observations.

Of course, we need to keep in mind that one of the original reasons for developing portfolio theory—especially the CAPM—was to evaluate the risk-adjusted past performance of professional portfolio managers. Prior to the CAPM approach, there was no formal way to evaluate the performance of a portfolio of securities relative to the risks taken to earn those returns. Thus, the CAPM approach may be best suited to evaluating past performance, rather than as a predictive model. In this respect, the model performs well.

Finally, the beta estimates for diversified portfolios are relatively reliable, even though the estimates for individual stocks are imprecise. Until a demonstrably superior theory is devised, therefore, the standard form of portfolio theory will continue to provide the foundation for the study of finance.

SUMMARY AND CONCLUSIONS

If there are no interim cash flows, then determining the rate of return on a portfolio is easy. The introduction of interim cash flows creates two ways to measure a portfolio's performance. The first is the time-weighted or geometric mean return (GMR), which ignores the effect of the cash flows and uses the rate of return for each period. The other is the dollar-weighted or internal rate of return (IRR), which incorporates the effect of the timing of cash flows on the final portfolio value. The return to an investor would normally be measured by the IRR. The performance of a financial advisor should be based on the GMR, providing the advisor has no control over the timing of interim cash flows.

After measuring the rate of return on a portfolio, there is frequently a desire to then qualify whether such performance is good or bad. The simplest tool for qualifying is to compare the performance to an appropriate benchmark. Various stock and bond market indices can be used, including the DJIA and the S&P 500. A financial advisor should understand the differences among these indices when using them for benchmarking. The two biggest differences are the composition (what types of stocks and how many) and the mathematical process of constructing the index (for example, price weighting versus value weighting).

More sophisticated evaluation of portfolio performance includes an adjustment for risk. The two measures that use standard deviation for risk comparison are the Sharpe ratio and M^2. The two measures that use beta for risk comparison are Treynor ratio and Jensen's alpha. The former two should be used when the portfolio being analyzed is intended as a fully diversified holding. The latter two should be utilized when one is analyzing a single security or an undiversified portfolio.

Although most evaluations of performance involve the use of beta for measuring risk, there are a substantial number of problems with so doing. First, it appears that there is a risk premium for nonmarket risk. Second, there are many conceptual problems with calculating betas. One of the more significant problems is what the appropriate market index should be in such computations. Adjustment techniques have been developed to allow for improved forecasts of beta over the assumption of no change. Some of the most recent research even questions whether beta is a relevant measure of risk at all. The problem is that there is no alternative model for describing security and portfolio returns that allows for logical and systematic thinking about performance and evaluation.

CHAPTER REVIEW

Answers to the review questions and the self-test questions start on page 733.

Key Terms

time-weighted rate of return	reward-to-variability ratio (RVAR)
dollar-weighted rate of return	Treynor ratio
flight-to-quality effect	reward-to-volatility ratio (RVOL)
price-weighted index	Jensen's alpha
value-weighted index	skewed distributions
Sharpe ratio	Blume-adjusted beta

Review Questions

5-1. A new client comes to you and provides you with her portfolio information for the last 4 years, as shown in the table below. Assume that all deposits (shown by positive numbers) and withdrawals (shown by negative numbers) occur at the end of each indicated time period.

a. Compute the rate of return for each period, keeping in mind that the value of the end of the period incorporates any deposit or withdrawal. (Hint: The rate of return for the first period is 10%.)

b. Compute the time-weighted rate of return.

c. Compute the dollar-weighted rate of return.

Year	Value at Start of Period	Deposit/ Withdrawal	Value at End of Period
1	50,000	10,000	65,000
2	65,000	0	60,000
3	60,000	−10,000	55,000
4	55,000	0	55,000

5-2. a. Explain why there can be substantial differences between the time-weighted and dollar-weighted rates of return.

b. If there are no interim cash flows, what is the relationship between the two rates of return?

5-3. You are constructing an index with two stocks. Stock A has prices over a 3-day period of $20, $19, and $20. Stock B has prices of $40, $41, and $20, because on the third day a 2-for-1 stock split became effective. Stock A has 100,000 shares outstanding, and stock B has 10,000 shares outstanding, before the split. What would be the price-weighted index for the two stocks for the 3 days? What would be the value-weighted index for the two stocks for the second and third days if the first day's prices are used as the base period and the initial index value is 100?

5-4. a. Why is it usually inappropriate to compare a client's portfolio rate of return with an index like the S&P 500 or the DJIA?

b. How does the Russell 3000 Index relate to the Russell 2000 and Russell 1000?

c. What is unique about the Value Line Index compared to all of the other indices?

d. What is the most comprehensive index of international securities?

e. Which company provides a large number of bond market indices?

5-5. Calculate the Sharpe and Treynor ratios for the market index and the three funds in the chart below. Use a risk-free rate of 4.7 percent. Rank the funds according to each method. (Hint: Although the student should calculate at least one of the standard deviations, the four standard deviations are 13.97, 7.31, 31.31, and 15.72.)

	Good Fund	Bond Fund	Go Fund	Market Index
Beta	1.1	0.6	1.3	1.0
Return Year 1	10.5	8.8	17.7	12.5
Return Year 2	−8.5	6.0	−21.6	−5.3
Return Year 3	15.7	11.4	31.4	18.9
Return Year 4	14.3	9.6	23.4	16.2
Return Year 5	−21.3	−9.1	−32.7	−20.2
Return Year 6	12.2	10.3	53.4	24.3
Return Year 7	9.0	11.5	−12.3	14.5

5-6. During the last year, you have been recommending that your clients invest in the Rocket Science Corporation. During the year, the stock went up 12 percent. The risk-free rate of return during the year was 3 percent, the stock's beta is 1.5, and the market was up 10 percent. Based on Jensen's alpha, did this stock outperform or underperform the market?

5-7. Why might there be a risk premium for nonmarket risk?

5-8. a. If a beta were estimated at 1.2, what value would Blume's adjustment formula suggest for a forecasted beta?

b. Why is there a need for this adjustment process?

c. What are the implications of this adjustment process for the use of beta?

Self-Test Questions

T   F   5-1. If two portfolios start with the same amount of assets, then one can evaluate their relative performance at any point in time by simply seeing which has more assets.

T   F   5-2. The GMR of a fund that earns 10 percent the first year and loses 10 percent the second year will be larger than that for a fund that loses 10 percent the first year and earns 10 percent the second year.

T   F   5-3. An example of an interim cash flow is the receipt of dividends in a portfolio.

T   F   5-4. A dollar-weighted rate of return gives more weight to the rates of return when the portfolio is larger.

T   F   5-5. A time-weighted rate of return gives more weight to more recent performance than earlier performances.

T   F   5-6. An investor who is evaluating the performance of his or her portfolio should use the time-weighted rate of return.

T   F   5-7. A portfolio manager should normally be evaluated on the basis of time-weighted rate of return.

T   F   5-8. Dividend and interest income are not treated as interim cash flows if they are left in one's account.

T   F   5-9. If the arithmetic average of a portfolio's rates of return is 0, the GMR will most likely be negative.

T   F   5-10. If the arithmetic average of a portfolio's rates of return is 0, the IRR could be positive or negative, depending on the interim cash flows.

T   F   5-11. To compute a value for the DJIA, sum up the prices of the 30 stocks and divide by 30.

T   F   5-12. The S&P 500 Index is a price-weighted index.

T   F   5-13. The Wilshire 5000 Index has 5,000 stocks in it, and its composition changes almost weekly.

T   F   5-14. Financial planners should encourage their clients to compare the performance on their portfolios with that of the DJIA.

T   F   5-15. The oldest stock market index is the S&P 500.

T   F   5-16. All of the stocks in the S&P 500 are listed on the NYSE.

T   F   5-17. The FTSE 100 index represents the 100 largest stocks on the French Stock Exchange.

T   F   5-18. The MSCI EAFE is updated every 60 seconds.

T   F   5-19. When there is a stock split for a stock in a price-weighted index, that stock's price has to be adjusted forever thereafter to undo the effect of the split.

T   F   5-20. The most critical part of a value-weighted index is the initial value.

T   F   5-21. The Sharpe ratio measures excess returns relative to total risk as measured by the standard deviation.

T   F   5-22.   The Treynor ratio and Jensen's alpha measure excess returns relative to market risk as measured by beta.

T   F   5-23.   The M^2 measure has the advantage over the Sharpe index in that its interpretation is much more intuitive.

T   F   5-24.   Jensen's alpha has the advantage over the Treynor index in that its interpretation is much more intuitive.

T   F   5-25.   Because the different evaluation measures can provide different rank orderings, it is important to use the most appropriate measure.

T   F   5-26.   When evaluating the performance of two mutual funds, different evaluation tools can give different rank orderings.

T   F   5-27.   Fama and French found that the size of the firm and the ratio of the firm's book value to its market value were better predictors of stock returns than was the beta coefficient.

T   F   5-28.   Although there is no theoretical basis for risk premiums being related to non-market risk, there is a clear empirical relationship.

T   F   5-29.   Investors appear to be neutral with regard to the skewness of a distribution.

T   F   5-30.   Estimates of betas for both portfolios and individual stocks are relatively stable.

NOTES

1. Coverdell accounts were previously known as educational IRAs, and they are used to accumulate assets to pay for educational expenses. A 529 plan is another vehicle for accumulating money to pay for college. Most, if not all, states now offer 529 plans, as do many universities.
2. This statement is offered as an approximation to help the reader conceptualize this issue, and is not meant to be a mathematical definition.
3. Excel's XIRR function calculates an IRR based on cash flows and actual dates.
4. See, for example, quote.bloomberg.com/apps/news?pid=10000006&sid=aBTdPto5zSQM.
5. See http://www.cboe.com/micro/efa/msci_eafe.pdf.
6. Bonds of foreign-based companies that are sold in the U.S. are known as Yankee bonds.
7. Material in this section is drawn from "Fire Your Index," by Len Reinhart, *Financial Planning,* vol. 34, no. 2 (February 2004), pp. 41–42.
8. In practice, the taxes may be paid from other sources, but the net effect is the same as if the taxes are paid out of the account where the tax liability is generated.
9. Franco Modigliani has received the Nobel prize in economics, and is world famous for a multitude of significant contributions in the fields of economics and finance. They apparently were not the originators of this measure, but have done quite a bit to popularize its usage.
10. M. E. Blume, "On the Assessment of Risk," *Journal of Finance,* March 1971, pp. 1–10.
11. Barr Rosenberg, "The Capital Asset Pricing Model and the Market Model," *Journal of Portfolio Management,* Winter 1981, pp. 5–16.
12. E. Fama and K. French, "The Cross-Section of Expected Stock Returns," *Journal of Finance,* June 1992, pp. 427–465.

Appendix 5A

Time Value of Money

Learning Objectives

An understanding of the material in this appendix should enable the student to

---

5A-1.   Compute the future value of a lump sum of cash.

5A-2.   Compute the present value of a lump sum of cash.

5A-3.   Compute the effect of compounding more than once per year.

5A-4.   Compute an effective annual interest rate.

5A-5.   Compute the future value of an annuity.

5A-6.   Compute the present value of an annuity.

5A-7.   Compute a net present value.

5A-8.   Compute an internal rate of return.

5A-9.   Value a perpetuity.

The primary tool in finance is the concept of the *time value of money (TVM)*. TVM is used to calculate how much some lump sum or series of payments will accumulate to at some later time. This tool is also used to determine how much money should be set aside today to fund a future payment or cash flow. Finally, TVM is used to price securities by determining the present value of all cash flows expected to be paid to the owners of those securities.

Although many of these applications of TVM can be derived quickly and simply by using a financial calculator, a basic understanding of these concepts will help the user avoid errors of application and interpretation.

Basics Concepts of Time Value of Money

compound interest

Money grows over time to some future value as a result of compounding interest. *Compound interest* is interest on both the original principal and the interest that has been credited throughout the period. As a result of compounding, the future value will always exceed the present value, as long as the interest rate exceeds 0 percent.

opportunity cost

Interest accrues as compensation for delay in using the money. This compensation can be referred to as *opportunity cost*—the interest that could have been earned if the money had been invested elsewhere. For example, if you deposit $1,000 in a savings account and leave it there for one year, you expect your account to earn interest as compensation for your opportunity cost.

discounting

Likewise, some value in the future can be reduced to an equivalent value as of today using *discounting*. When a future value is discounted at some interest rate greater than 0 percent, the resulting present value is less than the future value. For example, in order to have $1,000 one year from today, you would expect to be able to deposit less than that $1,000 in your bank account today.

There are two important variables you will need to determine the future value or present value of some sum. The first is the number of periods over which compounding or discounting occurs. The greater the number of periods an amount is compounded, the higher the future value. Likewise, the greater the number of periods that an amount is discounted, the lower the present value.

The second important variable is the interest rate used in the compounding or discounting process. The higher the interest rate for compounding, the higher the future value. Likewise, the higher the interest rate for discounting, the lower the present value.

Let's summarize these relationships. The future value is higher than the present value. The future value *increases* when the number of periods (n) *increases* or the interest rate (i) *increases*. The present value has an inverse relationship with these variables—that is, the present value *decreases* when the number of periods (n) *increases* or the interest rate (i) *increases*.

So far, we have talked about relationships among variables for compounding and discounting. The four key variables in simple time value of money problems are the number of periods, the interest rate, the present value, and the future value. Given three of the variables, we can always solve for the fourth.

Future Value of Single Sums

Let's consider a specific example of how to compute the future value of some single sum today. Let's say that we deposit $100 in a savings account that earns 3 percent annually and leave it there for 4 years. Each year, the account will earn 3 percent on the principal sum of $100 plus the interest that has accrued on that principal. Each year our account will accrue interest as follows, starting from today, year 0:

Year 0	Deposit $100
Year 1	$100 + 3%(100) = $103
Year 2	$103 + 3%(103) = $106.09
Year 3	$106.09 + 3%(106.09) = $109.27
Year 4	$109.27 + 3%(109.27) = $112.55

This approach can quickly become tedious when a lot of years are involved. We can determine the future value more directly by using a general equation that takes into account each year of compounding. The general equation for future value is

$$FV = PV \times (1 + i)^n$$

where FV = future value
PV = present value
i = interest rate for compounding
n = number of periods of compounding

Let's use the equation to verify the results of our example. In this case, FV is unknown, PV is $100, i is .03, and n is 4 years. We will round our result to two decimal places.

$$FV = PV \times (1 + i)^n$$
$$FV = \$100 \times (1.03)^4$$
$$FV = \$100 \times (1.125509)$$
$$FV = \$112.55$$

Example: Calculate the future value of $8,000 today, invested
for 19 years at 7 percent.

$$FV = PV \times (1 + i)^n$$
$$FV = \$8,000 \times (1.07)^{19}$$
$$FV = \$8,000 \times (3.616528)$$
$$FV = \$28,932.22$$

Solving for Future Value with the HP-10BII

The Hewlett-Packard HP-10BII will provide a precise answer to these types of problems within just a few keystrokes. After turning on the calculator, adjust the number of payment periods per year from 12 to 1. This step is critical or all subsequent calculations will be incorrect.

To make the change, press the 1 key, followed by the gold SHIFT key, followed by the P/YR key, which is the fourth key from the left on the top row. Note that after you press the gold SHIFT key, the next key pressed will effect the operation indicated by the gold label on that key rather than the white label. As a test, press the SHIFT key, then put your finger on the C ALL key (left column, next-to-bottom row). Before you press the key, focus on the display. When you press the C ALL key, you will see "1 P-Yr" flash on the display.

1, SHIFT, P/YR

Virtually all time value of money problems have answers that are in one of two forms. Either the answer is in dollars and cents, or it is in percentage (or decimal) notation. When the answer being sought is in dollars and cents, the display should be set to show two decimal places, because the penny is the smallest coin in our currency. When the answer being sought is in percentage or decimal notation, the display should be set to show four decimal places.

As this particular problem involves an answer measured in dollars and cents, adjust the number of decimal places shown on the display to two using the following instructions:

SHIFT, DISP, 2

Like most financial calculators, the HP-10BII is programmed to show opposite signs for present and future values. The convention is to enter outflows as negatives and inflows as positives. In this problem, $8,000 is an investment—an outflow.

Now enter the data from the problem.

SHIFT, C ALL
8000, +/–, PV (+/– is the change sign key)
19, N
7, I/YR
FV   (display: 28,932.22)

Note that if you forget to enter the change of sign key (that is, the +/– key), then the answer will be –$28,932.22. Again, the calculator is programmed to analyze these problems with the assumption that at least one of the cash flows will have an opposite sign to the other. Hence, when you change the sign of the $8,000 to negative, you are telling the calculator that the investor is paying out (that is, investing) $8,000. Hence, it is a negative cash flow (that is, a cash outflow) to the investor. The positive answer then indicates how much money comes back to the investor. By entering $8,000 as a positive number, you are telling the calculator that the investor is receiving the $8,000 today, and solving for how much the investor would have to pay back at the end of the time horizon. Hence, the answer would be a negative number representing a payment by the investor.

One other item that should be mentioned is that when entering and reading display numbers that involve calculations using the financial calculator keys, the calculator is programmed to interpret any percentage numbers as being in percentage notation. In the above problem, 7 percent can be expressed as either 7 percent or .07. Because we are using the financial calculator button market "I/YR", the calculator will interpret the number entered as being in percentage notation rather than decimal notation.

Compounding More Than Once Per Year

So far, we have assumed that compounding takes place once per year (annually). Unless told otherwise, you can assume that compounding or discounting takes place on an annual basis. However, compounding or discounting may take place more frequently than annually. When that occurs, the same equation can be used, but the n and i variables must be adjusted. The following relationships apply to the frequency of compounding. First, the more frequent the compounding, the higher the future value. The more frequent the discounting, the lower the present value. Let's take a look at calculating a future value when compounding occurs more frequently than annually.

Let's say that your $100 will receive 3 percent interest, but this time compounding will be on a monthly basis, or 12 times a year. We can expect that after a 4-year period, we will end up with more than $112.55—the amount we would receive when compounding is on an annual basis. Before we begin, remember that we will need to make adjustments both to n and to i. The adjustments can be expressed as follows:

> n = number of years multiplied by the frequency of compounding
> i = annual interest rate divided by frequency of compounding

In this case,

$$n = 4 \times 12 = 48$$
$$i = .03/12 = .0025$$

Now we can use our formula as usual:

$$FV = PV \times (1 + i)^n$$
$$FV = \$100 \times (1.0025)^{48}$$
$$FV = \$100 \times (1.127328)$$
$$FV = \$112.73$$

The HP-10BII keystrokes are:

> SHIFT, C ALL
> 100, +/−, PV
> 4, x, 12, =, N
> 3, ÷, 12, =, I/YR
> FV   (display: 112.73)

An alternative approach to solving this problem is that one could set one's calculator to assume monthly compounding, then enter the number of months as 48, and the annual interest rate as 3 percent, and obtain the same answer. The keystrokes would be as follows:

12, SHIFT, P/YR, SHIFT, C ALL
100, +/–, PV
4, x, 12, =, N
3, I/YR
FV   (display: 112.73)

If compounding had been semiannual (twice a year), we would have multiplied the number of years by 2, and divided the interest rate by 2. If compounding had been quarterly (four times a year), we would have multiplied the number of years by 4, and divided the interest rate by 4. Adjustments to n and i are the same, regardless of whether you are calculating a future value or a present value. If one were working a series of problems (for example, on an exam), in which the frequency of compounding changes from one problem to the next, there would probably be less chance for error if the student picks one compounding period (such as annual), and then adjusts the time period and interest rate to reflect that programming selection, rather than having to constantly remember to reset the compounding frequency and remember which interest rate should be entered.

Example: Determine the future value of $8,000 invested for 19 years at 7 percent quarterly.

$$n = 19 \times 4 = 76$$
$$i = .07/4 = .0175$$
$$FV = PV \times (1 + i)^n$$
$$FV = \$8,000 \times (1.0175)^{76}$$
$$FV = \$8,000 \times (3.737797)$$
$$FV = \$29,902.38$$

Note that the quarterly compounding has increased the future value by $970.16 ($29,902.38 – $28,932.22), compared to the annual compounding in the example shown on page 231.

The HP-10BII keystrokes are:

SHIFT, C ALL
8000, +/–, PV
19, x, 4, =, N
7, ÷, 4, =, I/YR
FV   (display: 29,902.38)

If one wanted to solve this problem by resetting the compounding frequency of the calculator, the key-strokes would be:

4, SHIFT, P/YR, SHIFT, C ALL
8000, +/–, PV
4, x, 19, =, N
7, I/YR
FV   (display: 29,902.38)

Effective Annual Rate

In some cases, when compounding occurs more than once per year, we are interested in computing the effect of this process on the interest rate. When interest is compounded multiple times per period, it creates a distinction between what is known as the *nominal interest rate*—the stated rate—and the effective annual rate. The effective annual rate is the true annual interest rate in a problem.

nominal interest rate

The concept we use in computing an effective annual interest rate requires us to break down the period of one year into the number of periods that interest is compounded. We then determine the compounding effect of these multiple periods. The formula for this is

$$r_{ear} = \left(1 + \frac{r_{nom}}{m}\right)^m - 1$$

where r_{ear} = effective annual interest rate
r_{nom} = stated nominal annual interest rate
m = number of times per year compounding occurs

As an example, suppose you look at your credit card statement and note that the interest rate is 18 percent. As the interest on credit cards is charged each month on the unpaid balance, the interest is being compounded monthly, or 12 times per year. The effective annual rate would then be computed as

$$r_{ear} = \left(1 + .18/12\right)^{12} - 1 = 1.015^{12} - 1 = .1956, \text{ or } 19.56\%$$

Example: You are considering two different banks for your savings account. The first bank pays 4 percent compounded daily, and the second bank pays 4 1/4 percent compounded annually. Which bank offers the higher effective annual rate?

Answer: For the bank that pays interest compounded annually, no adjustment is necessary. Any interest rate compounded annually is automatically stated as an effective annual rate. To adjust the interest rate that is compounded daily, we start by noting that daily compounding means 365 times per year. We can thus compute the effective annual rate for the first bank as

$$r_{ear} = (1 + .04/365)^{365} - 1 = .0408 \text{ or } 4.08\%$$

This makes it clear that the bank offering 4 and 1/4 percent compounded annually has a much better deal in terms of the interest rate paid.

Any calculator with an exponent key (y^x) is capable of computing the effective interest rate. The following keystrokes are used to calculate the effective rate on the example above with the HP-10BII calculator:

SHIFT, C ALL
.04, ÷, 365, =   (this is $r_{nom}/365$)
+, 1, =, SHIFT, y^x, 365, =, –, 1, =   (display: 0.0408)

Calculating the effective annual rate is especially easy with most financial calculators. With the HP-10BII, the exponent key isn't even required. In the keystroke sequence, 4 (not .04) is entered as the nominal rate (NOM%), and the number of periods per year (P/YR) is entered as 365. Of course, the EFF% key refers to the effective rate. The keystrokes for the example above are as follows:

4, SHIFT, NOM%, 365, SHIFT, P/YR, SHIFT, EFF%   (display: 4.0808)

IMPORTANT: Remember to change the number of periods per year back to 1. Failing to make this change will cause subsequent time value of money calculations to be incorrect.

1, SHIFT, P/YR

Present Value of Single Sums

So far, we've taken single sums of today's dollars and compounded them to various amounts in the future. Now we will work in the opposite direction, discounting future values back to the present. Let's say that we expect to receive $100 four years from now and we would like to discount it at 3 percent annually. We may select that discount rate because we could have earned this rate in an investment if the money were available to us now, rather than 4 years from now. We will discount our future value back to today, year 0, as follows:

Year 4 $100
Year 3 $100/(1 + .03) = $97.09
Year 2 $97.09/(1 + .03) = $94.26
Year 1 $94.26/(1 + .03) = $91.51
Year 0 $91.51/(1 + .03) = $88.84

We can obtain the same result using an equation based on the future value equation. Remember that FV = PV x $(1 + i)^n$. We can restate this equation for the present value by solving for PV:

$$FV = PV \times (1+i)^n$$

$$\frac{FV}{(1+i)^n} = PV$$

$$PV = \frac{FV}{(1+i)^n}$$

Let's use the equation to verify the results of our example. In this case, PV is our unknown, FV is $100, i is 3 percent, and n is 4 years. We will round our result to two decimal places. You will notice that our answer is one cent different from our answer using the prior method. This difference is due to rounding and should not be a concern.

$$PV = \frac{FV}{(1+i)^n}$$

$$PV = \frac{\$100}{(1+.03)^4}$$

$$PV = \frac{\$100}{1.125509} = \$88.85$$

The HP-10BII keystrokes are:

SHIFT, C ALL
100, FV
3, I/YR
4, N
PV   (display: –88.85)

Example 1:   Discount an asset promising $100 3 years from now back to today at a discount rate of 6 percent.

$$PV = \frac{\$100}{1.06^3} = \frac{\$100}{1.1910} = \$83.96$$

The HP-10BII keystrokes are:

> SHIFT, C ALL
> 100, FV
> 6, I/YR
> 3, N
> PV   (display: –83.96)

Example 2:   Determine the present value of $10,000 to be received 9 years from now, discounted semiannually at an annual rate of 5 percent.

$$n = 9 \times 2 = 18$$

$$i = .05 / 2 = .025$$

$$PV = \frac{FV}{(1+i)^n}$$

$$PV = \frac{\$10,000}{(1+.025)^{18}}$$

$$PV = \frac{\$10,000}{1.559659} = \$6,411.66$$

The HP-10BII keystrokes are:

> SHIFT, C ALL
> 10000, +/–, FV
> 9, x, 2, =, N
> 5, ÷, 2, =, I/YR
> PV   (display: 6,411.66)

Alternatively, the calculator could be set for semi-annual compounding, in which case the keystrokes would be:

> 2, SHIFT, P/YR, SHIFT, C ALL
> 10000, +/–, FV
> 9, x, 2, =, N
> 5, I/YR
> PV   (display: 6,411.66)

Periodic Cash Flows

So far, we have talked about compounding and discounting a single payment. We can also compound or discount a series of payments made at the end of each period. These cash flows may be of equal or different amounts. Let's consider first the case of the future value of a series of unequal cash flows.

Uneven Cash Flows

We can solve for the future value or series of cash flows by using the previous equations for each payment and totaling the results:

$$FV_N = CF_1 x(1 + i)^{n-1} + CF_2 x(1 + i)^n + ... + CF_{n-1} x(1 + i)^1 + CF_n x(1 + i)^0$$
(Equation 5A-1)

where FV_N = future value N periods from today of the cash flows
CF_t = cash flow in time period t

Note in the above equation that although the cash flows are number from 1 to N, the exponents of the interest rate terms are numbered from n-1 to zero. This is because the cash flow is invested at the end of each time period. Hence, a cash flow that is received one year from today will have only n-1 time periods in which to accrue interest. The cash flow that is received n periods from today will have no time to accrue interest as it is received at the same time we are determining the future value. Remember when an exponent is zero, the value of the term is one, regardless of what the expression might be. Thus, the last compounding term of $(1 + i)^0$ equals one, and so the future value of the last cash flow is simply CF_n.

Example: A client is considering funding a Coverdell IRA.[1] The client can set aside $500 the first year, $1,000 the second year, and $2,000 the third year. If you believe the client will earn 6 percent in this account, how much will the account be worth at the end of 3 years?
Answer:

$$FV_N = CF_1 x(1 + i)^2 + CF_2 x(1 + i)^1 + CF_{n-1} x(1 + i)^0$$
$$FV_N = \$500 \ x \ (1 + .06)^2 + \$1,000 \ x \ (1 + .06)^1 + \$2,000 \ x \ (1 + .06)^0$$
$$FV_N = \$500 \ x \ (1.1236) + \$1,000 \ x \ (1.06) + \$2,000 \ x \ (1)$$
$$FV_N = \$3,621.80$$

Let's now consider the present value of a series of uneven cash flows. The concept is basically the same as for the future value of such a series. Namely, the present value is the sum of the present values of each of the cash flows.

$$PV = CF_0 + CF_1/(1+i)^1 + CF_2/(1+i)^2 + \ldots + CF_{n-1}/(1+i)^{n-1} + CF_n/(1+i)^n$$

(Equation 5A-2)

In this case, the subscripts of the cash flows and the exponents of the interest rate term match up nicely. Note, also, that the first cash flow is identified as occurring at time period zero. Because it occurs immediately, there is no discount term associated with it. The present value of an immediate cash flow is the cash flow itself. Consider the following example:

Example: Your client has a small, privately owned business. He is approached with a buy-out offer. The offer is $1,000,000 to be paid in one year, $2,000,000 in 2 years, and $3,000,000 in 3 years. You confer with your client and conclude that an appropriate discount rate is 10 percent. What is the value in today's dollars of this offer?

Answer (in millions):

$$PV = CF_0 + CF_1/(1+i)^1 + CF_2/(1+i)^2 + CF_3/(1+i)^3$$
$$= \$0 + \$1/(1+.10)^1 + \$2/(1+.10)^2 + \$3/(1+.10)^3$$
$$= 0 + \$.9091 + \$1.6529 + \$2.2539 = \$4.8159$$

The keystrokes would be as follows:

0, CFj
1, CFj
2, CFj
3, CFj
10, I/YR
SHIFT, NPV   (display: 4.8159)

Note in the above keystrokes that a zero is entered as a cash flow at time period zero. That is, the calculator is programmed to assume that the first cash flow occurs immediately. Similarly, it is programmed to assume that all cash flows are entered consecutively by period. This means that if there is no cash flow in one of the periods, a zero must be entered for that cash flow.

Example: Let's continue the previous example by assuming that your client makes a counter offer that involves the payment of $3 million immediately, and a second payment of $3 million in 3 years. This involves the same total amount of cash payments, but an adjustment as to timing. How much has this adjustment altered the present value of the buy-out offer?

Answer (in millions):

$$PV = CF_0 + CF_1/(1 + i)^1 + CF_2/(1 + i)^2 + CF_3/(1 + i)^3$$
$$= \$3 + \$0/(1 + .10)^1 + \$0/(1 + .10)^2 + \$3/(1 + .10)^3$$
$$= \$3 + \$0 + \$0 + \$2.2539 = \$5.2539$$

This has increased the value of the buy-out by \$.438 or \$438,000.

The keystrokes would be as follows:

> SHIFT, C ALL
> 3, CFj
> 0, CFj
> 0, CFj
> 3, CFj
> 10, I/YR
> SHIFT, NPV   (display: 5.2539)

Annuities

An annuity is a series of equal, consecutive payments. Annuities occur frequently in the investments world. First, they can be sold as a product by themselves. Second, many instruments such as bonds and preferred stock offer an annuity as a component of the benefit of owning these securities.

When calculating annuity values, a critical factor is whether payments occur at the beginning of each period or at the end. An annuity with payments occurring at the beginning of each period is called an *annuity due*. An annuity with payments occurring at the end of each period is called a *regular annuity*. On the HP-10BII, the normal setting is for a regular annuity (that is, cash flows at the end of each period). To set the calculator for an annuity due, use the following keystrokes: SHIFT, BEG/END. The word BEGIN should appear in the display. To switch back to a regular annuity, use the same keystrokes and the word BEGIN will disappear from the display. Most problems in investments involve regular annuities rather than annuities due.

annuity due
regular annuity

Mathematically, annuities have the benefit that a simpler computation process can be used. Consider first the future value of a regular annuity, using equation 5A-1. Because all of the payments are equal, we can replace the cash flow for each period with the common term PMT.

$$FV_N = PMT \times (1 + i)^{n-1} + PMT \times (1 + i)^n + \ldots + PMT \times (1 + i)^1 + PMT \times (1 + i)^0$$
(Equation 5A-3)

This equation can manipulated by factoring out all of the PMT terms:

$$FV_N = PMT \times [(1 + i)^{n-1} + (1 + i)^n + \ldots + (1 + i)^1 + (1 + i)^0]$$

This produces an expression that says the future value of an annuity equals the payment per period times the sum of the future value terms for each payment. It turns out that the summation of terms in the brackets can be written with the following short-cut formula:

$$FV_N = PMT \times \left(\frac{(1 + i)^n - 1}{i} \right)$$

Example: Your client has just become a proud parent. He decides to fund a Coverdell IRA for the child with $2,000 per year for 18 years, starting one year from today. How much will the account be worth in 18 years if he earns 8 percent per year?
Answer:

$$FV_N = PMT \times \left(\frac{(1 + i)^n - 1}{i} \right)$$

$$FV_N = \$2,000 \times \left(\frac{(1 + .08)^{18} - 1}{.08} \right)$$

$$FV_{18} = \$2,000 \times 37.4502$$

$$FV_{18} = \$74,900.40$$

The HP-10BII keystrokes are:

SHIFT, C ALL, set for end-of-period payments
2000, PMT
8, I/YR
18, N
FV   (display: –74,900.49)

Please note: The difference of 9 cents in this answer and the calculations shown above is due to rounding.

Next, let's consider the present value of a regular annuity. For the mathematics of this present value, we can substitute PMT for the cash flows in equation 5A-2.

$$PV = PMT/(1+i)^1 + PMT/(1+i)^2 + \ldots + PMT/(1+i)^{n-1} + PMT/(1+i)^n$$

(Equation 5A-4)

Because we are considering a regular annuity, the immediate payment is omitted from the equation. As with the future value equation, we can factor out the PMT terms. This produces the following expression:

$$PV = PMT \times [(1+i)^1 + (1+i)^2 + \ldots + (1+i)^{n-1}(1+i)^n]$$

The term in the brackets then can be simplified to the following:

$$PV = PMT \times \left(\frac{1 - \dfrac{1}{(1+i)^n}}{i} \right)$$

Example: Your client has won a state lottery and is offered the choice between $800,000 cash in hand, and a payout of $60,000 per year for 20 years starting one year from today. After consulting with your client, you believe the appropriate discount rate to value the annuity is 6 percent. Should your client take the immediate payout?

Answer: We need to determine the present value of the above annuity, and see if its value is greater or less.

$$PV = PMT \times \left(\frac{1 - \dfrac{1}{(1+i)^n}}{i} \right)$$

$$PV = \$60,000 \times \left(\frac{1 - \dfrac{1}{(1+.06)^{20}}}{.06} \right)$$

$$PV = \$60,000 \times \left(\frac{1 - \dfrac{1}{(3.2071)}}{.06} \right)$$

$$PV = \$60,000 \times \frac{(1 - .3118)}{.06}$$

$$PV = \$60,000 \times \frac{(.6882)}{.06}$$

$$PV = \$60,000 \times (11.4699) = \$688,194.00$$

The fact that the present value of the annuity is substantially less than the $800,000 lump sum award today indicates the lump sum should be chosen.

The HP-10BII keystrokes are:

> SHIFT, C ALL, set for end-of-period payments
> 60000, PMT
> 6, I/YR
> 20, N
> PV   (display: −688,195.27)

Please note: The difference of $1.27 in this answer is due to rounding.

Net Present Value

Virtually all investment decisions can be reduced to a simple question: Do the cash flows justify the price that would be paid for the investment? Two techniques that are commonly used to answer these questions are net present value (NPV) and internal rate of return (IRR). Let us consider the NPV calculation first.

For NPV purposes, an investment is defined solely in terms of the cash flows it is expected to produce. NPV normally is thought of as an expenditure of cash today followed by a series of cash inflows. A NPV calculation is quite similar to the present value of a series of uneven cash flows. The formula for NPV is:

$$NPV = -\,Cost + CF_1/(1+i)^1 + CF_2/(1+i)^2 + \ldots + CF_{n-1}/(1+i)^{n-1}$$
$$+\ CF_n/(1+i)^n \qquad\qquad \text{(Equation 5A-5)}$$

The only difference between equation 5A-2 (present value of a series of uneven cash flows) and equation 5A-5 (NPV) is that in the first equation the first term was defined as the cash flow at time period zero (CF_0), and in the second equation it is defined as the cost of the project, which occurs at time period zero. In practical terms, there really is no difference between the two equations.

The selection of the discount rate is, obviously, critical in computing a net present value. The discount rate should be set at a value that reflects the riskiness of the cash flows being discounted. Many people like to use the capital asset pricing model to ascertain the appropriate discount rate. It is not always the case that a beta coefficient for an investment is readily available or easily determined. Selection of an appropriate discount rate in many situations may be more of an art than a technical skill.

Example: An investment offers the following expected cash flows: $CF_1 = \$110$, $CF_2 = \$121$, $CF_3 = \$133.10$. It costs $250. As a financial advisor considering whether or not to recommend this investment for your client, you review this investment and conclude that based on the riskiness of the cash flows, a 10 percent discount rate is appropriate. What is the investments' NPV?

Answer:

$$NPV = -\text{Cost} + CF_1/(1+i)^1 + CF_2/(1+i)^2 + CF_3/(1+i)^3$$
$$= -\$250 + \$110/(1+.10)^1 + \$121/(1+.10)^2 + \$133.10/(1+.10)^3$$
$$= -\$250 + \$100 + \$100 + \$100 = +\$50$$

Because the NPV is positive, the investment should be undertaken. The keystrokes for this calculation are

SHIFT, C ALL
250, +/–, CFj
110, CFj
121, CFj
133.10, CFj
10, I/YR
SHIFT, NPV   (display: 50.00)

Some people find the concept of net present value unclear because they are not sure how to interpret it. The easiest interpretation is that it tells a person the instantaneous impact upon his or her wealth from undertaking that particular investment. In the above example, there is no difference between walking down the street finding $50 lying on the ground, picking it up, and putting it one's pocket, and purchasing the investment. In both cases, the individual is immediately wealthier by $50.

Many students like to argue this interpretation by saying there is a difference. The $50 on the ground is a perfect certainty, and the investment contains risk. Although this statement is true, it is also misleading. The reason is that in computing the NPV, an adjustment was made for risk, along with an adjustment for the timing of the cash flow. The sum of the future cash flows in the above project is $364.10. To acquire these cash flows, one only has to pay $250 today. So, if we ignore risk and the timing of the cash flows, the investment will leave us richer by $114.10 ($364.10 - $250). However, in analyzing the investment and adjusting for differences in timing and allowing for risk, we have concluded that this investment will make us wealthier by $50, not $114.10. The difference in these two numbers completely compensates us for the fact that the investment is risky. Hence, it is equivalent in value to a perfectly certain $50. If one still feels that the $50 on the ground is a better deal, then one has not chosen the correct discount rate.

Internal Rate of Return

Some people are uncomfortable with computing an NPV calculation because they are unsure of what discount rate to use. When this is the case, an alternative approach is to solve for the internal rate of return (IRR). An IRR is the discount rate that causes the NPV of an investment to equal zero.

$$NPV = 0 = -Cost + CF_1/(1 + IRR)^1 + CF_2/(1 + IRR)^2 + \ldots$$
$$+ CF_{n-1}/(1 + IRR)^{n-1} + CF_n/(1 + IRR)^n \qquad \text{(Equation 5A-6)}$$

If the investment has only one or two cash flows, then one could actually solve for the IRR. But, as soon as the investment has a life of 3 years or more, one cannot mathematically solve for the IRR.[2] However, IRRs are easily computed on a calculator.

Example: An investment offers the following expected cash flows: $CF_1 = \$110$, $CF_2 = \$121$, $CF_3 = \$133.10$. It costs $250. As a financial advisor, you are not sure what the appropriate discount rate is to value this investment. So, you decide to compute its IRR.

Answer:

$$NPV = 0 = -Cost + CF_1/(1 + IRR)^1 + CF_2/(1 + IRR)^2$$
$$+ CF_3/(1 + IRR)^3$$
$$IRR = 20.67\%$$

The keystrokes for this calculation are:

    SHIFT, C ALL
    250, +/–, CFj
    110, CFj
    121, CFj
    133.10, CFj
    SHIFT, IRR/YR   (display: 20.67)

As with NPV, some people are not quite sure what the appropriate interpretation is for the internal rate of return. The easiest way to think of an IRR is that purchasing the investment is equivalent to putting one's money into a savings account that pays an interest rate equal to the IRR. The proof is that if one did so, one could exactly reproduce the cash flows of the investment.

As proof of this point, consider the investment in the previous example. Let's assume that a person could invest the $250 in a savings account that paid exactly 20.67 percent. If so, could they make withdrawals that would match the cash flows of the investment? Proof that this is the case is shown in table 5A-1.

TABLE 5A-1
Proof of Meaning of an IRR

Time Period (1)	Balance at Start of Time Period (2)	Interest Earned During the Period (3) = (1)x.2067	Withdrawal at the end of the Period (4)	Balance at the End of the Period (5) = (2) + (3)–(4)
1	$250	$51.68	–$110.00	$191.67
2	$191.68	$39.62	–$121.00	$110.30
3	$110.30	$22.80	–$133.10	$.00

In the above table, the investor starts with $250. During the first year, this generates an interest income of $51.68 ($250 x .2067). At the end of the year, the investor draws out $110. The balance at the end of the year is then $191.68 ($250 + $51.68 − $110). This figure becomes the opening balance for the second year. In like manner, the investor is able to draw out $121 at the end of the second year, and $133.10 at the end of the third year. At that time, there is exactly nothing left in the account. Hence, investing $250 at 20.67 percent will permit a person to provide cash flows of exactly $110, $121, and $133.10 over the next 3 years. Thus, there is conceptually no difference between saying this project has an IRR of 20.67 percent, and investing the cost of the project ($250) at a rate of 20.67 percent.

Unfortunately for the financial advisor in the above example, the determination that the IRR is 20.67 percent does not really solve his or her problem in deciding if this is a good investment or not. The question remains whether or not this is a sufficiently good rate of return to compensate for the riskiness of the cash flows. If the investment were considered so risky that it should not be purchased unless the IRR is at least 25 percent, then one would have to turn down the investment because the IRR is inadequate. If the investment is considered moderately risky and it should not be purchased unless the IRR is at least 10 percent, then one would have to say that this is a very attractive investment. In the discussion of NPV, we specified an appropriate discount rate of 10 percent for this investment. Thus, we would reach the same conclusion after computing the IRR: the investment should be purchased.

It can be mathematically proven that a decision maker will always reach the same conclusion whether he or she computes an NPV or an IRR, as long as the IRR is compared to the discount rate that is used in the NPV calculation. The point here is that although some people prefer to compute an IRR rather than an NPV because they are uncomfortable selecting a discount rate for the NPV calculation, they are really not bypassing the problem. The reason is that they have to select a discount rate to determine whether or not an IRR is reasonably attractive.

Now, it is true that a negative IRR would mean automatic rejection of a project, and an extremely low IRR (such as 1 or 2 percent) would mean almost certain rejection. A negative IRR would occur whenever the sum of the future flows are less than the cost of the project, even before the discounting process. It is also true that unusually high IRRs such as 100 percent or more would likely mean certain acceptance. An IRR of 100 percent would mean you are doubling your money every time period! In truth, most investments do not produce such extreme values of IRRs, and thus the decision maker must still identify the appropriate comparison rate for an IRR calculation.

Perpetuity

There is a very simple formula in finance that occasionally has practical applications. It is the formula for valuing a perpetuity. A perpetuity is an annuity that goes forever. For example, if someone were to offer an investor the opportunity to receive $1,000 per year, forever, starting next year, then the investor is being offered a perpetuity. The initial reaction to perpetuities is that they must be extremely valuable if they will pay forever. In fact, they are never as valuable as they might first seem.

So far, no individual has lived forever, and thus, one might question whether there is any value to the receipt of cash flows after one's death. In practice, this does not matter. The reason is that, in theory, a perpetuity can be sold at anytime. As such, its value is not dependent upon the life of the investor, but upon the expectation that the payments will always be made.

The formula for valuing a perpetuity is

$$\text{Value of a perpetuity} = PMT/i$$

In the example mentioned earlier, if the annual payment were $1,000, and if the appropriate discount rate were 5 percent, then the value of this perpetuity would be $20,000 ($1,000/.05). This is easy to prove. Suppose a person had $20,000 cash in hand and invested it at a guaranteed rate of 5 percent forever. After one year, the interest income from this investment would be $1,000. Let's assume the investor drew out the $1,000 accumulated interest and left the balance on deposit for another year at 5 percent. At the end of the second year, the investor could draw out another $1,000 and leave the $20,000 on deposit at 5 percent. This process could be repeated forever as long as one is willing to assume the interest rate on this investment paid 5 percent. Hence, as with our IRR example, the point is that if $20,000 invested at 5 percent can produce a perpetuity for its investor of $1,000 per year, then a perpetuity of $1,000 per year discounted (that is, valued) at 5 percent must be worth $20,000.

As we will see later, the most common example of perpetuity in practice is preferred stock. Preferred stock has no expiration or termination date, and usually promises to pay a fixed dividend forever. Some governments around the world have issue bonds that are perpetuities. They are promising to pay the bondholder interest forever. These would be analogous to loans that never mature.

A final use of the perpetuity formula is that it always sets an upper limit on value. For example, supposed one was offered an investment opportunity that would pay $1,000 per year for 20 years. If a 10-percent discount rate were appropriate, how much is this investment worth? As seen above, one can value this as a present value of annuity. However, before any calculations are done, it should be clear to the analyst that the value of this annuity has to be less than $10,000. If the $1,000 per year were a perpetuity, then discounting these cash flows at 10 percent would make them worth $10,000 (that is, $1,000/.10). However, because the payments will only run for 20 years and not forever, they have to be worth less than the $10,000 value of the perpetuity.

A perpetuity can be converted to an internal rate of return number. This is accomplished by dividing the annual payment by the initial value of the perpetuity. For example, if you could buy a perpetuity that pays $1,000 forever, for $20,000, your IRR would be 5 percent ($1,000/$20,000).

SUMMARY AND CONCLUSIONS

One of the most basic tools of finance is the time value of money (TVM). It is the basis for the determination of intrinsic value. TVM involves either compounding (figuring wealth at a future point in time) or discounting (figuring wealth today based on future cash flows). The simplest TVM application is the future value of a lump sum:

$$FV = PV \times (1 + i)^n$$

The present value of a future cash flow is directly derived from this relationship:

$$PV = FV/(1 + i)^n$$

When interest is compounded more than once per year, all TVM problems require the annual interest rate to be divided by the number of times per year compounding occurs, and the number of years to be multiplied by the number of times per year compounding occurs to determine the effective interest rate and number of time periods. Similarly, an effective annual rate can be derived from a nominal rate via the following adjustment:

$$r_{eair} = \left(1 + \frac{r_{nom}}{m}\right)^m - 1$$

A series of uneven cash flows are treated as the sum of separate lump sum calculations for both present and future value calculations.

An annuity is a series of consecutive, equal cash flows. The present and future values of an annuity are defined as:

$$PV = PMT \times \left(\frac{1 - \dfrac{1}{(1+i)^n}}{i} \right)$$

$$FV_N = PMT \times \left(\frac{(1+i)^n - 1}{i} \right)$$

The net present value of a project is the present value of future cash flows less the cost of the project. A positive NPV project should be accepted, and a negative one should be rejected. An internal rate of return (IRR) is the discount rate that causes the NPV of a project to equal zero. A project should be accepted whenever its IRR is greater than the discount rate used in determining a project's NPV, and rejected whenever it is less.

A perpetuity is an annuity that runs forever. Its value is the annual payment divided by the appropriate discount rate. Its IRR is the annual payment divided by its value.

APPENDIX REVIEW

Answers to the review questions and the self-test questions start on page 733.

Key Terms

compound interest	annuity due
opportunity cost	regular annuity
discounting	internal rate of return (IRR)
nominal interest rate	perpetuity

Review Questions

5A-1. a. A 35-year-old client comes to you with $50,000 that he has just inherited. He wants to invest this money to finance his retirement. If you believe you can conservatively earn an average of 8 percent per year, and the client wants to retire in 30 years, how much should his account be worth at that time?

b. Your client states that when he retires, he wants this portfolio to provide an income of $50,000 per year for 20 years. If you believe that the portfolio would be adjusted during his retirement years to earn a more conservative 6 percent, can he achieve this goal?

c. Let's go back to part a. Suppose the client has no inheritance, but says he is willing to set aside $6,000 per year (at the end of each year) for the next 30 years. If you still plan to earn at least 8 percent on this portfolio, will the client be better or worse off in 30 years than if he had started with the inheritance?

d. After further consideration, your client indicates that he is willing to set aside $500 at the end of each month for the next 30 years. By how much would this change from annual investing to monthly investing be expected to increase his final portfolio?

e. Finally, suppose you convince your client to make his contribution at the beginning of each month rather than the end. By how much would this be expected to increase his final portfolio?

5A-2. a. A 25-year-old client walks into the office and says he wants to retire at age 60 with $1,000,000. He wants an aggressive portfolio, which means he wants to achieve at least a 10 percent rate of return, and he wants to fund this portfolio today with a single deposit. How much would he have to deposit today to expect to achieve his objective?

b. The client in part a suddenly realized he has no cash with which to immediately fund his retirement plan. Instead, he will have to fund it with equal annual deposits, beginning one year from today. If he still wants an aggressive portfolio that would be expected to yield a 10 percent rate of return, what would the size of each deposit have to be?

5A-3. As part of an overall portfolio recommendation, your client wants to put some money into a 5-year CD. If you call around to four different banks and get the following rates, which is the best deal?

a. 4% compounded daily

b. 4.1% compounded monthly

c. 4.15% compounded quarterly

d. 4.2% compounded annually

5A-4. Your client's business is looking at three mutually exclusive projects. They can be described as follows:

a. The first costs $100,000, and is expected to produce net cash inflows over the next 3 years of $30,000, $40,000, and $50,000. The appropriate discount rate is 8 percent.

    b. The second costs $150,000, and is expected to produce net cash inflows of $30,000 at the end of each year for the next 10 years. The appropriate discount rate is 10 percent.

    c. The third costs $75,000, and is expected to produce net cash inflows of $10,000 at the end of each year, forever. The appropriate discount rate is 10 percent.

        i. What is the NPV for each project?

        ii. Based on the NPVs, which of the three projects should be accepted?

        iii. What is the IRR for each project?

Self-Test Questions

T   F   5A-1. The present value of a cash flow depends on how much is to be received, when it is to be received, and the discount rate.

T   F   5A-2. The intrinsic value of a security may be more or less than the present value of payments expected to the owner of that security.

T   F   5A-3. Compounding refers to interest accruing on interest.

T   F   5A-4. If the interest rate were zero, everyone would be indifferent between $100 today and $100 in one year.

T   F   5A-5. The higher the interest rate, the higher the present value of a future cash flow.

T   F   5A-6. When computing a future value number, the appearance of a negative number on the calculator means you made a mistake.

T   F   5A-7. When compounding occurs more than once per year, you only have to remember to adjust the interest rate before doing any computations.

T   F   5A-8. If compounding occurs more than once per year, the effective annual rate will always be greater than the nominal rate.

T   F   5A-9. If the NPV of an investment is positive, the IRR will be greater than the discount rate used in the NPV calculation.

T   F   5A-10. A series of cash flows described as identical payments every other period (for example, odd numbered years) is an annuity because the payments are equal.

NOTES

1. A Coverdell IRA is for funding educational expenses. The profits in the account can accrue tax-free and the withdrawals are tax free if they are used to pay for qualified educational expenses. The maximum contribution is $2,000 per year, but only if the person making the contribution does not exceed certain income limits.

2. There actually is a formula for solving for the IRR when there are three cash flows, but said formula is sufficiently complex that few people know it and how to apply it, and most have never heard of it.

Market Efficiency

Learning Objectives
An understanding of the material in this chapter should enable the student to

6-1. Explain the three forms of the efficient market hypothesis (EMH).

6-2. Describe various tests of each of the forms of the EMH.

6-3. Describe some of the anxious trader effects and potential adjustment lags.

6-4. Describe the more common technical market indicators.

6-5. Describe how a bar chart and point-and-figure chart are constructed, and how one interprets a chart pattern (such as a head-and-shoulders formation).

Chapter Outline

The development of modern portfolio theory and the assumptions contained therein eventually led researchers to develop what has come to be known as the efficient market hypothesis (EMH). It should be remembered that this is a hypothesis; it is not a statement of fact. The purpose of the EMH is to provide a framework for thinking about the issues of market efficiency and the research that is done to shed light on the empirical question of market efficiency. One can almost think about the EMH as if it is a religion. Some people believe it literally, some people reject all of it out-of-hand, and some people accept some of it and reject other aspects. It is critical that any investments professional understand the EMH and its various implications. After that, each person is, of course, free to approach investments with whatever philosophy he or she wants. However, for an investments professional, that philosophy should be grounded in his or her understanding of the evidence of how the stock market works, where that understanding comes from knowledge of empirical research on the subject.

The chapter starts with a definition of the EMH, then proceeds to a review of some of the empirical research that has focused on validating or refuting the EMH. Because part of the EMH deals with the issue of the value of technical analysis, the chapter concludes with a review of some of the techniques of technical analysis.

TYPES OF INVESTMENT ANALYSIS

fundamental analysis

To discuss the EMH in a meaningful fashion, we need a basic understanding of the two primary types of investment analysis: fundamental analysis and technical analysis. *Fundamental analysis* consists of analyzing the factors that affect the amount and value of the expected future income streams of a security. Thus, fundamental security analysts assess a firm's earnings and dividend prospects by evaluating such factors as its sales, costs, and capital requirements. Fundamental commodity analysts base their futures forecasts on the relevant demand and supply factors. Fundamental real estate analysts generate price and rental value expectations from anticipated future construction costs and demand growth estimates.

technical analysis   *Technical analysis*, in contrast, concentrates on past price and volume relationships of a security or commodity (narrow form) or technical market indicators applicable to that security or commodity (broad form). Both types of technical analysis attempt to identify evolving investor sentiment, but neither has a sound theoretical base. Technical analysts are not particularly concerned with a theoretical justification for their method. They would argue that results are what ultimately matter. A wealth of available data facilitates the application of technical analysis to the security and commodity markets.

One major distinction between technical and fundamental analysis is that technical analysis looks at prices and volume of trade in isolation without concern for the type of company whose stock is being traded (its financial strength, the quality of its management, the nature of its competition, and so on). Technical analysis could be performed on data, without any knowledge of the company with which that data is associated. Fundamental analysis requires a thorough understanding of the specific company, the nature of its products, and its method of operation. Fundamental analysis is more inclusive and takes into account both quantitative and qualitative factors.

THE EFFICIENT MARKET HYPOTHESIS

The EMH simply contends that the market is extremely proficient at pricing securities. Thousands of security analysts and portfolio managers, with unlimited computer time, ample resources, and access to corporate management, are well compensated for their ability to identify mispriced securities. As a result of their activity, when new information appears, the market as a whole reacts quickly to incorporate that information by bidding the security's price up or down. Thus, for an individual to identify mispriced securities becomes extremely difficult, even futile.

Ironically, the EMH implies that because analysts as a group are so effective, the efforts of an individual in trying to find mispriced securities may be a waste of time. Instead, analysts (and especially financial planners) should direct their activity toward selecting securities that are suitable for the client's desired risk-return profile.

Random Walk Hypothesis

Many natural phenomena follow a random walk, or what the physical sciences call a Brownian motion. When applied to stocks, the random walk concept implies that the next price change of a randomly moving stock is unrelated to past price behavior. Obviously, if prices move randomly, the repeating price patterns that technical analysts claim to observe have no predictive ability.

One can think of Brownian motion in the following manner. Think of flipping a coin, where heads is a buy order and tails is a sell order. If you flip this coin 20 times, then you have what would represent the random arrival of buy and sell orders. Let's further say that the price of a security goes up 10 cents any time there are three heads in a row, and it goes down 10 cents any time there are three tails in a row. Clearly, such a process will produce price changes, but these price changes will be random. It is not obvious that a stock's price in this process would always end up where it started.

Of course, stock prices tend to rise over time, so it might be more accurate to describe their movement as a "random walk with upward drift." That is, in the previous example, think of the coin that is being flipped as having a slight bias to it, such that it comes up heads 52 percent of the time and tails 48 percent of the time. In this case, the stock would probably rise over time, but significant downward movements are still possible. In other words, it seems pretty safe, based on historical evidence, to predict that the market will be higher 10 years from now than it is today, but it is unrealistic to argue that one could predict with any certainty that the market will be higher (or lower) tomorrow than it is today.

Price movements need not be precisely random for past price data to lack predictive ability. Marginally associated relations between past and future price changes may be either too small or too unreliable to generate returns that consistently exceed transaction costs. Indeed, commissions, search costs, and bid-ask spreads would generally offset any expected price change of less than 2 or 3 percent.

Weak Form of the EMH

The weak form of the EMH states that current stock prices fully reflect all historical information concerning stock prices and trading volume. The implication is that knowledge of past price behavior has no value in predicting future price movements. That is, such knowledge cannot be used to construct a portfolio that consistently outperforms the market on a risk-adjusted basis.

The weak form implies that once we know the most recent price quote, we know as much about possible subsequent returns as those who know the full price history up to that point. That is, prices do not move in predictable patterns. Weak-form adherents further argue that, if prices did move in dependable patterns, the reactions of alert market participants would rapidly eliminate any resulting profit opportunities. If a particular price pattern were thought to forecast a rise, many market participants would react to take advantage of the move. Such actions would eliminate the value of any recognized patterns, because the market would very quickly be driven to its predicted value.

Example:	Suppose a stock sells for $6 per share. Also suppose that based on some technical formula, it is possible to predict that next month the price of the stock will be $10 per share. Other people would also use that formula and make the same prediction. Therefore, everyone would want to buy the stock, and nobody would want to sell it. The stock would move immediately to almost $10 per share. (To be exact, it would move to the present value of $10 discounted 1 month at the risk-free interest rate.)
	Simply put, if it were really possible to find trends and predict future stock prices, the forces of supply and demand would immediately bring present prices in line with expected future prices.

Semistrong Form of the EMH

The weak form of the EMH implies that technical analysis is useless, but it does not address the effectiveness of fundamental analysis. The semistrong form of the EMH, on the other hand, asserts that current stock prices reflect all publicly available information.

Implicit in the semistrong form is the assumption that investors and analysts have an expectation regarding future events and information that would affect a company's stock price. Hence, when that event or information becomes public knowledge, the real question is not whether that information or event is favorable in absolute terms. The real question is how that information compares to the expectations of that information or event. For example, if a company announces that its quarterly earnings are up 20 percent from the same quarter a year ago, then one might initially assume that this is good news for the stock. However, if everyone had an expectation that because of recent trends in the economy and the industry that earnings were going to be up 25 percent, then the announcement that they went up only 20 percent would be considered disappointing news, and thus the stock price would likely decline. Conversely, if everyone had been anticipating only a 15 percent increase in earnings, then the 20 percent increase would be considered a highly favorable result.

Another aspect of the semistrong form is the concept of the adjustment process. A strict interpretation of the semistrong form would be that as soon as a new event occurs or new information becomes available, everyone (or at least a large number of people) simultaneously becomes aware of this event or information. Furthermore, either everyone processes this information in the same way, or at least they all process it in an unbiased manner. This means that there is no subset of individuals that is consistently able to assess the information more quickly or analyze it more effectively than others. As a result, the next trade in a stock after a significant event occurs or new information comes out will be at a price that reflects the new value of the stock, as both buyer and seller are aware of the information and its effect on the stock's price.

Strong Form of the EMH

According to the strong form of the EMH, current stock prices fully reflect all information, whether it is publicly available or not. This version asserts that the market also incorporates information that so-called monopolists of information (usually called insiders) have about security prices.

Corporate insiders constitute the main group of information monopolists. Corporate insiders—defined as managers, board members, and those who own 10 percent or more of the stock of a company—certainly have access to information that is not yet made public. However, SEC rules and federal law prohibit them from profiting from that information or sharing it with outsiders selectively prior to a public announcement. Insiders are permitted to trade the stocks of their own companies, but they are subject to some restrictions. For example, they are prohibited from engaging in short-term trading and from selling short. Strong-form efficiency maintains that even the information known by these monopolists quickly gets reflected in security prices, thus eliminating the potential for abnormal gains.

Professional money managers, such as mutual fund managers or investment advisory services, are one group alleged to have special knowledge

---

Forms of the EMH

- Weak form: Current stock prices fully reflect all historical information concerning stock prices and trading volume. Future returns are unrelated to past return patterns. (Charting and other types of technical analysis do not result in superior returns.)
- Semistrong form: Current stock prices fully reflect all publicly available information. Future returns are unrelated to any analysis based on public information. (Fundamental analysis does not result in superior returns.)
- Strong form: Current stock prices fully reflect all information. Future returns are unrelated to any analysis based on public or nonpublic data. (Insider trading does not result in superior returns.)

about companies they follow. Specialists who make a market in stocks on the organized exchanges are also believed to have knowledge of their stocks. Since they are granted a monopoly in making a market in specific stocks, they have short-term knowledge about the flow of buy and sell orders on those stocks. In particular, knowing what orders are outstanding may give them insight into future price movements.

Market Success and the EMH

There are two issues with regard to market success and market efficiency that need to be clarified:

1. If the EMH is true, does this mean that no one can beat the market?
2. If someone beats the market, does this automatically invalidate the EMH?

It is possible for an investor to earn an abnormally high return, just as it is possible to make money at a gambling casino. Some people make the mistake of thinking that if the market is efficient then no one can earn an abnormally high return. That is not the case. Market efficiency simply means that technical and fundamental analysis should not *consistently* earn an investor an abnormally high return once risk and transaction costs are taken into account. (The costs of obtaining information, including the opportunity cost of forgoing other productive uses of one's time, should also be taken into account when deciding whether to use fundamental analysis techniques.)

To illustrate the fact that some people do appear to consistently beat the market requires only the following illustration. Let's define flipping heads as beating the market, and flipping tails as underperforming the market. Over any time period, one-half of investors would be expected to "beat" the market (that is, perform better than some market index), and one-half of them would be expected to underperform the market (that is, do worse than the same index). Let's say that we start with 1,024 investors and their performance is defined by flipping coins. If all the coins are fair, then we would expect one-half of them (that is, 512 of them) to flip heads and beat the market in the first time period. If those 512 investors flipped their coins again, then we would expect 256 of them to beat the market for a second time period. Similarly, we would expect 128 of them to beat the market three periods in a row, 64 to beat it four periods in a row, 32 for five, 16 for six, 8 for seven, 4 for eight, 2 for nine, and 1 investor to beat the market ten times in a row. Now, does this mean that this one investor is incredibly skillful? Or does it mean that out of the 1,024 investors who started out, this person was the only one lucky enough to flip ten heads in a row? Similarly, in the actual market, because of the large number of people who are investing, there will be an occasional few who put together an amazingly large number of consecutively successful years. However, we have no way of telling if they are truly superior investors or if they just happen to be the lucky ones.

It should also be pointed out that many portfolio managers, financial advisors, stockbrokers, and financial planners claim consistent, superior performance but do not provide independently validated evidence of that performance. In addition, as we saw in the previous chapter, there are many ways to evaluate performance. One can compare one's results to a simple benchmark, such as any of the many indices described; one can use a standard deviation-based measure or one can use a beta-based measure. Without knowing how a person is measuring his or her own performance, and whether or not that person is doing it properly, it is impossible to know if claims of superior performance are valid. Finally, even the best portfolio managers have occasional poor years, and even the worst portfolio managers have occasional good years.

TESTING THE EFFICIENT MARKET HYPOTHESIS

Tests of the EMH always boil down to this rather simple concept: Is there a strategy that could consistently be applied that would allow an investor to outperform the market by a statistically significant amount? It is well established that any and all tests of the EMH are really a dual hypothesis test. The first is a test of the model that is used to adjust for risk (usually the capital asset pricing model, or CAPM), and the second is a test of the efficiency itself.

To be judged successful, a trading strategy needs to generate returns that, after an appropriate adjustment for risk, exceed in the aggregate the market returns of the corresponding periods. Thus, the techniques of both technical and fundamental analysis need to be tested against real-world data. This testing is done by forming portfolios that one would have selected based on buy signals from a particular tool. The hypothetical portfolios are then compared to an actual market index for the same period. Normally, a stock market index, such as the S&P 500 Index or the New York Stock Exchange Composite, is used to represent overall market performance. Virtually all academic studies of market efficiency utilize such risk-adjusted returns data.

Weak-Form Tests of the EMH

Two of the most basic tests of technical analysis are serial correlations and filter rules. If past price patterns help forecast future price change, past and future price changes should be related, and filter rules should help identify profitable trading opportunities.

Serial Correlation

Some studies have examined the serial correlation of stock returns over consecutive time periods. For example, one could compute the serial correlation coefficient between returns for each day and returns for the previous day. If stocks tended to move in the same direction on consecutive days more frequently than they reversed direction, the serial correlation coefficient would be a statistically significant positive number. But serial correlation coefficients are not statistically different than zero.

Other studies have investigated runs of price changes. A run is an uninterrupted series of price increases or decreases. To understand a runs test, think of designating every trade in a stock with either a + if the trade represents a price increase, a − if the trade represents a price decline, and a 0 if the trade results in no price change. Next, ignore all of the zeros. One is then left with a series of plusses and minuses. Next, count the number of times there are two consecutive plusses or minuses, the number of times there are three consecutive plusses or minuses, and so on up to the maximum number of consecutive plusses or minuses. This distribution is then compared to the number of consecutive plusses or minuses that one would expect to see if the sequence of plusses and minuses had been generated by coin flips. Many different studies have consistently failed to find any significant relationship in successive price changes. Thus, past price patterns do not appear to forecast future price movements.

chartist *Chartists* are people who create and/or study charts for patterns in price movements. A chartist would say that these statistical tests look largely for linear relations and that they are much too crude to capture subtleties. Moreover, chartists assert that their "craft" is as much art as science because it depends heavily on judgment, interpretation, and experience; that is, beneath the apparent randomness of stock price movements is a distinct nonrandom pattern that can be discerned from charts. They argue that these patterns are difficult to quantify by standard statistical methods. Nonetheless, most nonlinear dependencies that they claim to see should show up in tests as linear approximations. Chartists have offered no convincing counterevidence (to academicians) as to why standard statistical proofs of forecast reliability cannot be applied.

Filter Rules

Filter rules attempt to capture the momentum/resistance-level factors that **momentum** technical analysts claim are important. *Momentum* indicates the tendency of a stock price to continue to rise or fall, whereas resistance level refers to a stock price at which either a large number of sell orders (upper resistance level) or a large number of buy orders (lower resistance level) would be expected to appear. Filter rules mechanically identify supposed buy and sell situations.

The standard filter rule flashes a buy signal whenever a stock increases by x percent. After an x percent decline from a subsequent high, a sell signal is given. For instance, a 5 percent filter would signal to buy whenever a stock rose 5 percent from the previous low. Really small filters actually appear to work. Thus, if an investor set a filter of, say, one-half of 1 percent (.5 percent), then the investor could expect to outperform the market. Unfortunately, these results occur only when transaction fees are ignored. When any reasonable transaction fees are incorporated into the analysis, even small filters result in losses for investors because the number of transactions is extremely large.

Market Overreaction

A widely held view that investors tend to overreact to information has been tested directly by N. Jegadeesh and S. Titman. They found that the trading strategy of buying stocks that have performed well in the past and selling stocks that have performed poorly in the past appeared to generate significant positive returns over 3- to 12-month holding periods during 1965 through 1989. The abnormal returns generated in the first year after portfolio formation, however, dissipated during the following 2 years.[1] The initial positive and later negative relative returns (returns reversals) may be evidence of overreaction.

But there could be other explanations. For instance, one interpretation is that transactions by investors who buy past winners and sell past losers move prices away from their long-run values temporarily and this causes prices to overreact. Another interpretation is that the market underreacts to information about the short-term prospects for firms, but it overreacts to information about their long-term prospects. This is plausible because information available for a firm's short-term prospects, such as earnings forecasts, is different in nature from the more ambiguous information that is used by investors to assess a firm's longer-term prospects.

Dow Theory

The Dow theory is one of the oldest and best-known approaches to market timing. Its originator, Charles Dow, was also the founder and first editor of *The Wall Street Journal*. Dow developed the key averages quoted widely in the financial pages: the Dow Jones Industrial Average (DJIA), the Dow Jones Transportation Average (DJTA), and the Dow Jones Utility Average (DJUA). The DJIA is commonly referred to as the Dow. As discussed in detail in chapter 5, it is composed of the stock prices of 30 leading industrial companies chosen from sectors of the economy that represent America's largest capitalization industrial (that is, nonfinancial) companies; it is a price-weighted average of these companies' stock prices adjusted for stock splits and dividends.

Three Basic Ideas Behind the Dow Theory

- To make a profit in the stock market, investors should take advantage of the primary market trend, which is the generally upward movement of the market over a period of 1 to 4 years.
- Whenever a primary trend is up, each secondary trend (a cycle around the basic trend) will produce a peak higher than the last one (vice versa for a down trend).
- Any true indicator of a primary market trend will be confirmed relatively quickly by similar action in the different stock price averages.

The Dow theory asserts that a continuing trend can be identified by looking first for a new high in a market average defined as primary (such as the DJIA), and then seeking confirmation from a second high (such as the DJTA). Thus, if the DJIA reaches a new high at approximately the same time a new high is set for the DJTA, an up trend is said to be intact.

A study by Brown and Goetzmann appears to confirm some validity to the Dow theory.[2] The original developers of the Dow theory did not provide an easily testable theory besides the simple rules listed above. Later research using state-of-the-art artificial intelligence software to identify the precise technical trading patterns associated with the buy and sell signals, applied the patterns over 70 years of data. The study found some merit in the Dow theory. For instance, a portfolio that followed the signals to buy or sell identified by the Dow theory software, using an index fund with no transaction costs, would have outperformed a buy-and-hold strategy by about 2 percentage points per year. In addition, the Dow theory portfolio would have incurred one-third less volatility (the researchers' proxy for risk). Brown and Goetzmann found that their version of the Dow theory portfolio beat the market indexes during such bearish periods as the 1970s and even the 1930s. Their model, however, showed the least favorable results during strongly bullish periods, such as the 1980s and the 1990s.

According to the *Hulbert Financial Digest* (a service that monitors performance of investment advisory letters), a portfolio that switched in and out of the market on signals from Dow theorist Richard Russell in the "Dow Theory Letters" would have underperformed a buy-and-hold strategy by about 2.7 percentage points per year since 1980. *Hulbert* found, however, that a Russell-guided portfolio would also have been 35 percent less volatile than the market as a whole. Thus, on a risk-adjusted basis (using volatility as a proxy for risk), the Dow theory–guided portfolio would have beaten the market.

Most academics and practitioners remain highly skeptical of technical analysis. The main reason for this skepticism is that much of the research on technical analysis techniques has failed to confirm their consistency and validity, given all the transaction costs involved, relative to a simple buy-and-hold strategy. Furthermore, it seems that every time someone identifies and publishes a mechanical rule that would allow a person to outperform the market, that rule ceases to work from that point onward! Also, as with our 1,024 coin flippers, if enough trading rules are tested some will be shown to be statistically significant in beating the market, when in fact such rules were just "lucky."

In addition, there are other troubling features of technical analysis. First, several interpretations of a particular technical tool or chart pattern are possible, giving rise to numerous different assessments or recommendations. For instance, those who interpret the signals of the Dow theory are notorious for their multiple interpretations.

A second troubling factor is if a technical trading rule (or chart pattern) proves truly successful and is made public, it will become widely adopted by market participants. If any rule or pattern is widely adopted, it will often prove to be self-defeating. Therefore, stock prices will reach their equilibrium value quickly, taking away profit opportunities from most market participants. Moreover, some market observers may start trying to act before the rest on the basis of what they expect to occur; thus, the prices of affected stocks will tend to reach equilibrium even more quickly. Eventually, the value of any such rule or pattern will be negated entirely.

According to Burton Malkiel, there are three potential flaws in technical analysis.[3] One, the information and analysis may be incorrect. Two, the security analyst's estimate of "value" may be faulty. Three, the market may not correct its mistake, and the stock price might not converge to its value estimate.

It is impossible to test all the techniques of technical analysis and their variations and interpretations. The techniques are too numerous, and new ones are developed all the time. Therefore, absolutely definitive statements about their validity cannot be made.

Example: Despite the strong refutation of technical analysis by academic researchers, there is no lack of businesses that are anxious to sell technical analysis. A current example of such a firm is Channeling Stocks.com. In this case, the firm appears to promise to identify for its customers at least 12 stocks that demonstrate a channeling pattern. A channeling pattern appears to be one in which a stock bounces around within a fairly well-defined range. The strategy would appear to be that one should buy at the bottom of the range and sell at the top.

Semistrong- and Strong-Form Tests of the EMH

General tests of the semistrong and strong forms are difficult to devise and perform. Moreover, test procedures are not all that powerful in identifying market efficiency. Market efficiency cannot be directly proven. Rather, we can only infer efficiency by showing that specific inefficiencies do not exist. The market pricing process generates so much random movement, or "noise," that prices can stray quite a bit from their intrinsic values without detection by tests that are commonly used. Nevertheless, various subhypotheses of the EMH have been examined. Many studies have found market anomalies or imperfections. An *anomaly* suggests that a specific type of analysis is profitable in consistently outperforming the market on a risk-adjusted basis.

anomaly

For instance, a number of studies suggest that stocks with low price-earnings ratios, small market capitalizations, low per-share prices, or related characteristics tend to outperform the market. With so much conflicting evidence, the extent of semistrong-form efficiency is decidedly debatable. Some academicians suggest that, since institutional investors—with all their professional expertise—rarely outperform the market on a risk-adjusted basis, individual investors are unlikely to do better. Others claim that there are enough market imperfections that talented investment analysts can outperform the market. Even if the market eventually evaluates public information accurately, they claim that some investors and/or analysts may be able to take advantage of lags in the price-adjustment process.

Many strong-form supporters concede that insider information is sometimes useful, but they contend that such instances are rare and therefore the conclusions of the strong form generally hold up. Research on the profitability of insider information is somewhat mixed. Several of the early studies found little evidence of excess returns to insiders. More recent studies showed that insiders earned more than outsiders on the same purchase or sale transaction in the same company's stock; results also indicated that, as the information became public knowledge, excess insider returns decreased as the length of the holding period increased.

The mixed results may be due to different definitions of "insiders." The advantages of professional money managers and specialists may be somewhat limited. However, such corporate insiders as senior managers and directors clearly have access to information about a company's prospects that is not available to the general public. In the absence of laws against insider trading, they would be able to reap excessive profits from that information.

Dogs of the Dow

One of the more famous strategies for beating the market that has emerged in recent years is known as "the dogs of the Dow." The strategy is simple. At the start of each year, the investor should rank the 30 stocks in the

DJIA based on dividend yield (from high to low). The investor should then buy the top ten stocks on the list (that is, the ten stocks with the highest dividend yields). These stocks are held for 1 year, at which time a new portfolio is constructed in the same manner.

Not all of the research on the dogs of the Dow has been consistent in proving whether or not it actually works in terms of beating the market. High-dividend-yielding stocks are usually considered above average in risk. Thus, a strategy that involves holding high-dividend-yielding stocks would be expected to produce rates of return greater than the market. The real question is whether the returns are sufficient given the higher degree of risk. Recent research by Domian, Louton, and Mossman[4] found that prior to 1987, the selection criterion truly selected stocks that had performed poorly the prior year; hence they deserved the title of "dogs." After 1987, the selection criterion actually ended up selecting stocks that had done well the previous year, even though their dividend yields ended up being high. Hence, the selection process no longer selected "dogs." It has been since 1987 that this strategy has ranged from being less effective to an outright failure. Domian, Louton, and Mossman conclude that at the time of publication, this selection rule was consistent with the overreaction hypothesis. Since 1987, the rule has no longer functioned as a surrogate for this hypothesis, and has no longer worked. This means that there was no legitimacy to the rule in the first place, but it provided more support for the overreaction hypothesis.

Market Efficiency Debate

Although some academicians hold extreme positions, few who have examined the issue believe that the market is strong-form efficient or is always semistrong-form efficient. On the other hand, virtually all serious finance scholars agree that the weak form of the EMH is essentially correct. The principal disagreements relate to the importance, extent, and causes of the imperfections of the semistrong form. These imperfections are largely viewed as departures or exceptions to normal behavior defined by portfolio theory.

Example:	A client approaches you to say he has heard about a technique for beating the market. The technique is to buy the ten stocks in the DJIA that have the highest dividend yields. He suggests that you adjust his portfolio to hold mostly these stocks. How might you respond?
	The empirical evidence for such techniques is always weak at best. Frequently, once a technique that has worked in the past is publicized, it subsequently ceases to work.. In addition, none of the techniques for beating the market would work well enough to offset the benefits from appropriate diversification and asset allocation. None-

theless, if the client truly believes this to be the case, the advisor would be happy to make some of the future stock selections based on this criterion. After all, even if this technique has no value, if markets are efficient then no harm should come from using it.

Causes of Persistent Market Imperfections

Why, if the market contains many talented rational investors, do imperfections persist? As yet, there is no consensus on the issue. These imperfections can have numerous causes.

Conventional theory assumes that market prices are formed by a homogeneous group of investors who analyze the same sources of information in identical fashions. Although market efficiency does not require perfect homogeneity of investor expectations, marginal investors must behave as if they accurately analyze all relevant public information and are unaffected (or identically affected) by such matters as tax status, costs of trading, risk orientation, borrowing power, liquidity preference, familiarity with local markets, and total available funds. In the business world, however, the resources of investors who are best positioned to profit may be insufficient to eliminate some mispricings.

Because investment analysts and periodicals concentrate on the larger, better-known firms, the security prices of many smaller firms may depart from the values that a careful analysis would yield. These firms generally trade in localized markets; therefore, few investors are positioned to observe **small firm effect** the mispricings. This is known as the *small firm effect.*

Only investors who can purchase control of a company may exploit some types of mispricings. An investor who acquires control of a firm that is worth more out of business than in business could liquidate its assets for more than the firm's value as a going concern. Such takeovers, however, are not usually easy to accomplish. The effort tends to bid up prices and provoke vigorous defensive efforts by those whose interests are threatened. Investors with the necessary resources to eliminate the mispricing may frequently have inadequate incentives to do so. Still other imperfections (arbitrage opportunities) may require quick and low-cost access to several markets. Only if enough investors are able to take advantage of these imperfections will their actions correct the price imbalances.

SPECIALIZED DEPENDENCIES

Anxious Trader Effects

Block trades, secondary distributions, informed trading, intraday dependencies, and tax-loss trading may lead to temporary supply-demand imbalances. Initially, the price may be disturbed away from its equilibrium level. Later, as the effects dissipate, the price may move back toward its prior level.

Block Trades and Secondary Distributions

As discussed in chapter 2, block trades are transactions involving 10,000 or more shares. Most block trades reflect a relatively large trader's desire to buy or sell. Sell trades may put some downward pressure on the market. If this pressure is temporary, an investor might profit from it. Most block trades, however, do not depress prices by enough to permit after-commission trading profits on the typical rebound, although those with the greatest price declines offer the most attractive trading prospects.

Several researchers have found price declines that are associated with large secondary distributions on the day of the sale and subsequently.[5] They have also found that secondary distributions of corporate insiders, investment companies, and mutual funds are followed by appreciably greater price changes than when the sellers are banks, insurance companies, estates, trusts, or individuals. Quite possibly, corporate insiders, investment companies, and mutual funds are more likely to base their decisions to sell on fundamental grounds to which they are privy but others are not, whereas banks, insurance companies, and others may simply need liquidity.

General Intraday Dependencies: Specialists and Limit Orders

It has been argued that stock prices closely resemble a random walk for daily movements. However, temporary intraday barriers to price movements and non-random overnight price changes have been observed, which may be ascribed to the interaction of specialists' trading and publicly placed limit orders.

Specialists are charged with keeping an orderly market (that is, avoiding excessive volatility) in their assigned stocks. They rely on a combination of limit orders and buying and selling with their own inventory to keep their markets orderly. Limit orders tend to collect at even values (generally whole numbers and halves). A collection of these limit orders at even values may act as temporary barriers to price movements. Once the market has executed a stack of whole-number limit orders, only a few orders may be necessary to generate substantial price movement. Continued buying (selling) activity may lead to a rather rapid price increase (decrease) until a new barrier is encountered.

Example:	Buying pressure may move a stock price from 18.80 to 19.00. Once 19 is reached, a slew of limit sale orders may stop the price surge. Once these limit orders are exhausted, continued buying could quickly propel the price to 19.90, with 20 becoming the next barrier.

Informed Trading

Markets sometimes reflect the activity of informed traders executing transactions with a public that does not know what the informed traders know. For example, someone accumulating a position prior to a takeover attempt will, at the outset, generally have information that is kept secret from the rest of the market. Similarly, an insider may have a much better assessment of the company's prospects than the rest of the market does. Sophisticated traders and investors—particularly specialists—are always aware of the possibility that an informed trader may be on the other side of the market. Accordingly, they become cautious when persistent buying or selling moves a price outside of its recent trading range.

Tax-Loss Trading

Yet another area of possible anxious trader impact involves year-end selling to establish a tax loss. Tax-loss trading is believed to have dramatically affected some year-end stock prices. The end of the year, therefore, may be an attractive time to purchase stocks that are under tax-loss selling pressure. (Tax-loss trading is discussed in detail in chapter 13.)

Several studies have refined our knowledge on tax-loss trading, especially as it relates to seasonality. A number of studies have found that most of the turn-of-the-year effect—stocks that decline by the largest amounts in December are most likely to rise in January—occurs at the small-firm level.[6] One study tests the hypothesis that tax-loss trading by individual investors is responsible for the January effect. The study examines the ownership structure of a large sample of firms over a 4-year-period and finds that the small firms that usually exhibit high January returns have low institutional ownership. Thus, the study indicates that individual ownership is significantly related to abnormal returns in January. One reason that the January effect may be concentrated in small firms is because investors who are motivated in part by

---

Anxious Trader Effects

- Block trades: Prices tend to decline with block trades and regain most of the loss by day's end.
- Large secondary distributions: Prices show modest declines on the day of and following a secondary distribution.
- Intraday dependencies: Bunching orders at certain price points may slow and then exaggerate/accelerate price movements.
- Informed trading: Persistent buying or selling moves the price outside of its recent trading range.
- Tax-loss trading: Issues under year-end tax selling pressure may rise at the beginning of the year; small-firm and low-priced issues are particularly likely to be affected in this way.

the tax consequences of their trades hold these firms.[7] Remember, many institutional investors, such as pension funds and endowment funds, do not pay taxes. Other institutional investors, such as many of the mutual funds, do not consider the tax consequences of their trades.

Adjustment Lags

Adjustment lags are another category of specialized dependencies. Remember, true market efficiency requires that as soon as a significant piece of information becomes publicly available, all or nearly all investors are immediately aware of it and properly analyze it. Thus, the next trade would occur at a price that reflects this information. This assumption is obviously extreme. In reality, prices may take time to react to such factors as earnings announcements, dividend changes, additions to the S&P 500 Index, bond rating changes, corporate crime disclosures, insider trading reports, media recommendations, stock splits, stock dividends, tender offers, mergers, liquidations, share repurchases, rights offerings, equity sales, debt-for-equity swaps, forced conversions, divestitures, and spin-offs.

Earnings and Dividend Announcements

According to several studies on earnings and dividend announcements, although prices may not adjust instantly to these announcements, the lags appear to be quite short. The reactions seem to be faster for firms with listed options. Firms without listed options take longer to react to quarterly earnings announcements. Moreover, several studies found a relatively slow market reaction to unexpected earnings changes. Similarly, studies that focused on dividends have generally found that dividend increases often result in substantial positive price reactions that are usually completed by the day of the announcement or soon thereafter.

Studies that have looked at the timing of earnings and dividend announcements have found that favorable announcements tend to be made in a timely fashion. Unfavorable announcements tend to be made later than they were expected to be made. In this case, expectations would be based on how long after the end of the quarter or fiscal year it takes other firms in the same industry to report, as well as how long it has taken a particular firm to report in past years. Put simply, good news travels fast, bad news travels slowly. Thus, even the lack of an earnings and/or dividend announcement on an expected date may be a news event in itself!

Additions to the S&P 500

Additions to Standard & Poor's 500 Index are widely followed by the market. Because the S&P 500 is a much broader-based index than the Dow

Jones Industrial Average, and it is quoted in the media almost as frequently, it is the index on which many other financial instruments are based. For example, most stock index futures, options on index futures, and indexed mutual funds utilize the S&P 500. Stocks are regularly added to and deleted from the index by Standard & Poor's in order to preserve or enhance its representativeness. The announcement that a stock is to be added to the index tends to cause that stock's price to rise, whereas a deletion has the opposite tendency.

Bond Rating Changes

According to research on stock price reaction to bond rating changes, there is an appreciable reaction to rating downgrades, but upgrades have an insignificant effect. That may be because the stock's market price already takes into account the positive information about the company that provided the basis for the bond rating upgrade.

Corporate Crime Disclosures

There is a significant negative market reaction to disclosures or allegations of illegal corporate behavior. Virtually all of this reaction occurs at the time of the announcement.

Insider Trading

Often, insider information appears to facilitate a relatively accurate stock evaluation. People who are not insiders must generally wait until the information is publicly released, but traders can observe insiders' trading decisions and act accordingly. The insider trades of CEOs and directors appear to be better predictors of subsequent performance than those of vice presidents and beneficial owners.[8] Apparently, CEOs and directors have better access to information.

Insiders must report their trades to the SEC. Thus, investors can consult SEC records to determine insiders' trading on a particular stock. Moreover, some investment services report SEC insider trading data to subscribers. Certain periodicals, including *Barron's* and *Value Line*, report on insider trades, and insider-trading activity is sometimes discussed in the financial press, at least on an ad hoc basis. However, there can be a time lag of several days or weeks between the time insider trades take place and the time they become known by the investing public. During the intervening time, the market price of the company's stock might change sufficiently so that investors who are not insiders would find it difficult to profit after taking transaction costs into consideration.

There have been several cases related to alleged misused insider information by outsiders who made trades based on it. An important

Supreme Court decision in 1997 clarified what constitutes illegal insider trading. The decision upheld the so-called misappropriation theory of insider trading, which states that traders may not trade on nonpublic information even if they are not corporate insiders.[9] One of the most recent cases of insider trades has involved Martha Stewart. Although she was not accused of insider trading, she was accused of lying to investigators about trading on what is effectively insider information. Specifically, she was accused of trading on the tip from her stockbroker that the president and CEO of another company was selling a large block of his own shares in that company. If true, subsequent stock price movement validated that Martha made what most people would consider a huge profit on that trade.

Media Recommendations

According to a study of the daily "Heard on the Street" column in *The Wall Street Journal,* which highlights specific companies' and analysts' opinions of specific stocks, the market appears to react efficiently to published takeover rumors in that column.[10] According to the study, excess returns could not be earned, on average, by purchasing rumored takeover targets at the time the rumor appeared. No significant excess returns occurred on the day the takeover rumor was published, although a positive cumulative excess of about 7 percent occurred in the calendar month *prior* to the appearance of the rumor in the "Heard on the Street" columns.

A 1992 study examined the impact of the insider information scandal related to R. Foster Winans' "Heard on the Street" column in 1984. Winans was giving to a friend advance notice of information that was to appear in the column. The friend was making money on trades involving these stocks. Following the scandal, the column had a reduced impact on stock prices for both buy and sell recommendations. Several months into the postscandal period, stock price response to information prior to the column's publication day was less. The results seem to indicate that the editors of *The Wall Street Journal* may have become more cautious in guarding against information leaks concerning the column. The scandal did not appear, however, to have altered the column's impact on trading volume.[11]

Another study focused on stock price behavior of firms that were favorably mentioned in the "Inside Wall Street" column in *Business Week.* The study found positive excess returns for favorably mentioned stocks on the day prior to the publication date, the publication date, and the days immediately after publication. There were positive, significant excess returns for long-term holding periods prior to the publication date but significant negative returns for long-term postpublication holding periods.

The study's findings are consistent with the price performance of firms that might have been the subject either of rumors or recent recommendations by analysts or brokerage firms. These results, along with those of earlier studies, suggest that secondary information is valuable only to low-transaction-cost, short-term traders. Investors who buy stock for the longer term based on secondary information generally receive below-market rates of return.[12] By secondary information, we mean the information that tells us how others perceive the stock. This should be distinguished from new information about the firm itself, such as information about the firm's product line or earning potential.

Analysts' Recommendations versus Market Efficiency

The question of whether following analysts' recommendations can consistently lead to superior returns brings us back to the debate over the semistrong form of the EMH versus the efficacy of fundamental analysis. Analysts' recommendations are based on evaluating information that is publicly available, so efficient market adherents would argue that such recommendations should not systematically yield superior risk-adjusted returns.

In a recent study,[13] analysts' recommendations were reviewed for a sample of 3,600 listed companies over a 10-year period. The study constructed hypothetical portfolios based on the consensus recommendations of the analysts. The authors found that an investor who consistently bought stock with the most favorable consensus ratings and sold stock with the least favorable consensus ratings would have outperformed the market on a risk-adjusted basis.

However, due to rating changes, such a portfolio would have had substantial turnover, resulting in substantial transaction costs. Therefore, the study found that once transaction costs are taken into account, one could not consistently earn superior risk-adjusted returns by following analysts' consensus recommendations.

Tender Offers, Mergers, and Liquidations

Tender offers, mergers, and liquidations may present investors with still other attractive trading opportunities. Stockholders often profit when their stock (a target) is tendered for and/or merged into another company. The offering price almost always exceeds the price at which the company's stock has been trading, usually by a substantial margin.

Yet another strategy is to acquire a large position in what is believed to be an undervalued company and then have the company buy out most or all of the small public shareholders. Taking a company private in this way may even allow the acquiring firm to buy out most shareholders at possibly depressed prices. Of course, the stock may not stay depressed if the public shareholders realize there is new demand for their shares. If the company succeeds in buying out all small public investors, it eliminates much of the stockholder relations cost. Finally, a company whose assets are worth more than the market price of its shares may be bought as a liquidation prospect.

Although these various maneuvers may yield handsome returns, traders need either inside information of planned takeovers (and a willingness to break the law) or the resources to influence the relevant firms. The only realistic strategy for individual investors is to try to anticipate forthcoming acquisitions. They can then be in the right place at the right time when the target company is put in play. Moreover, once a takeover looks like a success, tendering the remaining publicly held shares is almost always advisable. Small holdings of subsidiaries usually have little speculative appeal and no active secondary market.

While some mergers actually occur, others are merely rumored. Stock prices are often influenced by these rumors. Once the real situation is known, the stock will react appropriately. If the stock is truly a target, the announcement will tend to move the price toward the level of the offer. If the rumor is incorrect, the stock will probably go back to or near its price prior to the rumor. Some investors will already own stock of a company that is rumored to be a takeover target. They would like to know whether to hold the stock until the anticipated event occurs or to sell before the rumor turns out to be merely unfounded speculation. Investors who are contemplating buying do not want to be influenced by rumors that turn out to be false. Trading on takeover rumors is clearly a risky strategy.

Financial Planning Issue

Any investor who holds a reasonable number of stocks will sooner or later receive a tender offer for a stock. Sometimes, the tender offer is with the current management's blessing, and sometimes it is with a strong protest by the current management that the offer is unreasonable. Tender offers always involve a premium over the price prior to the announcement of the tender offer. Sometimes there is even a premium after the tender offer is announced because of the uncertainty as to whether the tender offer will be successful. Tender offers almost always are made contingent on a certain number of shares being tendered.

When current management gives its blessing, accepting the tender offer is an easy, obvious choice. When current management advocates rejecting the offer, they usually make one of three arguments:

1. The offer is too low, and by rejecting the current offer the suitor will make a higher offer.
2. The offer is too low, and other suitors can be found to make a higher offer later.
3. The offer is too low, and given some time, the company will grow to be more valuable on its own merits.

It is possible the rationale given for rejecting the tender offer is valid; it is also possible that the current management is just trying to protect their jobs as they would likely be let go after a merger. There are lots of famous examples where shareholders rejected attractive tender offers based on one or more of the above arguments, only to see their own company's share price drop substantially after the rejection of the offer. A good general rule is to accept all tender offers.

It is certainly possible that investors with large positions who are looking to liquidate their holdings sometimes start takeover rumors. Normally, the liquidation of a large position would involve downward price pressure. Thus, a false rumor would allow the investor liquidating to sell into a market surge in demand and possibly liquidate with a price gain.

Share Repurchases and Equity Sales

Earnings retention and minor debt decisions continually alter capital structures. Other actions can appreciably alter the number of shares outstanding and/or the firm's debt ratio. (The debt ratio is discussed in chapter 8.) These actions can dramatically affect the shareholders' expected income streams and risks. Moreover, capital structure changes that affect the relative amounts of dividend and interest payments have important tax implications. Thus, the market may well react to such events as share repurchases (which decrease outstanding shares), rights offerings, and forced conversions (both of which increase outstanding shares). According to one study, market reactions to capital structure changes are as follows:

- Changes that affect expected taxes and/or the relative values of stocks versus bonds are associated with significant security price moves in the predicted directions.
- Different classes of security holders are often affected differently by the shift.
- Shareholders are generally adversely affected by a decrease in leverage.[14]

Other studies report that firms use share repurchases to signal their belief that their stocks are undervalued. The studies also found that common shareholders usually benefit from such repurchases and that market reaction to repurchases occurs within 1 day of the announcement.[15] More recent studies indicate that the announcement of share repurchase programs may be little more than window dressing. This is because most firms end up buying back fewer shares than they indicated as their intention to repurchase. Thus, a firm that announces it intends to buy back 10 million shares may end up buying back only 1 million. For this reason, many investors may well ignore such announcements.

The repurchasing of shares decreases shares outstanding and tends to increase per-share prices, while a rights offering and other types of equity sales tend to have the opposite effect. One study has found a negative market reaction to the announcement and implementation of equity sales (including the sale of convertible securities).[16] Another study found that management requests to increase authorized shares had little or no effect.[17] The impact of

---

Adjustment Lags

- Earnings and dividend announcements: The market reacts quickly to earnings and/or dividend news.
- Additions/deletions to S&P 500 Index: Stocks tend to rise when added to the index and fall when deleted.
- Bond rating changes: Price reaction is appreciable for downgrades but not for upgrades.
- Alleged corporate crime: The market reacts quickly to news of alleged illegal activity.
- Insider trading: Reports of insider trades appear to provide profitable trading signals.
- Media recommendations: There are short-term positive excess returns for recommended stocks prior to media coverage.
- Tender offers, mergers, and liquidations: Returns can be significant, but investors must anticipate the event.
- Share repurchases: Repurchases often indicate that management believes the stock is undervalued.
- Rights offerings and equity sales: Shareholders generally react negatively to announcements of rights offerings and equity sales.

---

the offering on the market price of the firm's stock may depend on the firm's disclosure (required by SEC regulation) of how the proceeds of the offering are to be applied. Still another study indicated that equity carve-outs (partial sales of subsidiaries) and announcements of capital expenditures had generally positive effects.[18]

Assessment of Adjustment Lags

The market appears to adjust quickly to most new information. Reactions generally occur within a day or so of the following types of announcements: earnings reports, dividend changes, additions to the S&P 500, bond rating changes, allegations of corporate crimes, share repurchases, and rights offerings. Stock price adjustments actually tend to precede the announcement or event for splits, tender offers, and mergers. Thus, trading based on these relationships normally requires prior knowledge or accurate forecasts. On the other hand, revisions of earnings forecasts and insider trading signals may produce usable price relationships (that is, those that take place over a long enough period to be exploited).

TECHNICAL ANALYSIS

Although empirical research testing the EMH is fairly consistent about market efficiency with regard to the weak form (that is, technical analysis), technical analysis is still widely practiced and believed in by many market participants. It is crucial that a financial planner understand the jargon and concepts of technical analysis so that he or she can respond knowledgeably to questions and comments concerning technical analysis. This material is NOT being presented herein as concepts a financial planner should use in his or her practice. It is only being presented so that a planner will be familiar with the techniques when he or she encounters them, and will therefore have enough knowledge of these practices not to be taken in by them.

Market Timing

market timer

For investors who are trying to beat the market, there are only two strategies: market timing and security selection. *Market timers* attempt to make their profit by timing their moves into and out of the market. Hence, they will load up on stocks when they anticipate a bull market, and convert many holdings to cash when they anticipate a bear market. On a historical basis, there is no question that one can achieve phenomenal rates of return with effective timing. The only real question is, is it doable? One of the biggest costs to market timing is the opportunity cost of being out of the market at the time of a major move. One of the best studies on market timing found that market timers had to be right about the future direction of market moves at least 70 to 80 percent of the time to outperform a buy-and-hold strategy. For additional observation on market timing, see Appendix A to this chapter.

The relatively unspectacular performance of most mutual funds illustrates the difficulty of anticipating major market moves. Brinson, Singer, and Beebower found that among well-qualified institutional portfolio managers, market timing could account for only 1.8 percent of the average return differential, whereas security selection could account for 4.6 percent.[19] Portfolio allocation at 91.5 percent is far and away the most significant cause of the average return differential among these sophisticated investors. (The residual interaction term accounts for the other 2.1 percent.)

Market Behavior during Recession

Investors would like to buy when the market has completed most of its downward movement but has not yet risen much above its low. If the precise bottom is not usually identifiable in advance, perhaps buying can at least be concentrated in depressed periods. This strategy requires some idea of when stocks are near their cyclical lows.

In 1991, Jeremy Siegel examined the reliability of the relationship between stock prices and the business cycle. The stock market has frequently given false signals about future economic activity, particularly with regard to impending recessions. For instance, since 1946, there were seven periods during which the cumulative stock returns index fell at least 8 percent and a recession did not occur. The stock market appears to have been a better indicator of coming economic expansions, turning upward on average about 5 months before the economy hits bottom and starts to turn around.[20]

Traditional Technical Indicators

sophisticated investor rationale

contrarian rationale

Much of technical analysis consists of defining and measuring technical indicators. Associated with a technical indicator is a theory or rationale as to why that particular indicator should work. Many of the indicators can be classified into some broad categories based upon similar rationales for success. The two most common rationales are the "sophisticated investor" and the "contrarian." The *sophisticated investor rationale* takes the position that some investors are more sophisticated or knowledgeable than other investors. These sophisticated investors are right more often than they are wrong. Hence, all that a clever person has to do is to identify an indicator that reveals whether these sophisticated investors are buying or selling, and do the same.

The *contrarian rationale* says that certain investors are wrong more often than they are right. The most common type of investor who is wrong is the individual investor who only has a limited amount of resources—the small guy. Hence, the best strategy is to figure our what the small guys are doing, and do the opposite.

It would be nice to categorize each technical indicator as being either a sophisticated investor or a contrarian indicator, but that is difficult to do as there are sometimes multiple rationales to support specific indicators. That is, different people will agree that a particular indicator is a good forecasting tool, but they will disagree as to why that is the case. In fact, sometimes the same indicator is treated as either bullish or bearing depending on the rationale used to support the legitimacy of the indicator!

Short Interest

As discussed earlier, short sellers sell borrowed stock that they hope later to replace at a profit. At one time, short sellers were thought to be sophisticated traders who were able to anticipate market turns. Thus, an increase in the cumulative short interest position (uncovered short sales) was said to forecast a market decline. Others, in contrast, argued that short interest reflects potential demand from short traders who will need to buy back the stock to cover the position. According to this view, a rise in short interest forecasts a market rally. Studies show, however, that short interest is largely unrelated to market rises and falls. Short interest data are published monthly in *The Wall Street Journal*.

Odd-Lot Activity

According to some analysts, odd-lot (fewer than 100 shares) traders tend to buy at tops and sell at bottoms. The rationale is the assumption that people who trade in odd lots, which have a higher per-share commission than round lots, tend to be inexperienced and unskilled traders. Thus, when odd-lotters are buying on balance, the market may be about to fall; when odd-lot investors are mostly selling, the market may be ready to turn up.

There are a lot of different ways to measure what the odd-lot traders are doing. Probably the most direct way of doing this is the ratio of odd-lot purchases to odd-lot sales. Both numbers are provided for each day of the week and the sum for the week in *Barron's*. For example, on January 15, 2004, there were 10,903,200 shares purchased on an odd-lot basis, and there were 9,160,000 shares sold on an odd-lot basis.[21] Thus, the ratio of purchases to sales is 1.190 (rounded to three decimal places). The ratio has fluctuated historically between 0.50 and 1.45, but tends to be above 1. The reason is that some investors accumulate holdings through odd-lot purchases until they have a round lot, simply because they lack the cash to make a round-lot purchase. However, when they sell, they tend to sell their entire holding, thus making them a round-lot sale rather than an odd-lot sale.

Although the odd-lot theory appeared to have some validity during the 1950s and 1960s, it has failed to be a useful predictor since then. For instance, odd-lotters outperformed many professional money managers by selling on or before the stock market collapses of the 1970s and late 1980s, and they began buying in advance of a recovery during the early 1990s.

As noted above, one of the rationales for the odd-lot theory rests on the traditional observation that odd-lot trades have a higher commission on a per-share basis. This used to be true, and was known as the odd-lot differential. Nowadays, brokerage firms charge a commission primarily on the basis of a trade, rather than the number of shares in a trade. Thus, whether one buys 40 shares of a $50 stock for $2,000, or 100 shares of a $20 stock for $2,000, the commission will be the same. Thus, there is no real incentive for an investor with $2,000 to avoid what would be an odd-lot purchase if he or she likes a particular stock.

Specialists' Short Selling

Some people consider specialists to be especially sophisticated investors who have access to nonpublic trading intention information (the limit order book) and are positioned to react quickly to any emerging developments. Because their profits are largely derived from trading their assigned stocks, much of their success depends on effectively managing their inventory. Specialists generally are supposed to sell short when they expect a price decline and buy when their expectations are positive. Studies have not confirmed, however, that this is a reliable market indicator.

Mutual Fund Cash Position

Equity mutual funds usually maintain a modest cash reserve to meet redemption demands and other needs for cash. Sometimes their cash position becomes a relatively large percentage of their portfolio. This may happen for one of two reasons. First, they may be anticipating a market decline and are thus trying to move as much of their portfolio to cash as possible to avoid market losses. Second, they may also hold on to cash when they are undecided about where to invest it. If so, at such time as they make up their mind, there will be a lot of buying power that is suddenly entering the market place. In other words, large cash positions represent pent-up demand for stocks, nothing more. If one believes that mutual fund portfolio managers are in the group of sophisticated investors and are attempting to engage in timing, then a large cash investment would be a bullish indicator. In fact, some studies do show that some mutual funds attempt to time their trading to take advantage of market swings. However, the extent to which a mutual fund attempts to engage in timing is highly correlated with the longevity of its portfolio manager. Newer managers are more likely to try timing. The more experienced the manager, the less likely he or she is to try to engage in timing.

One could also note that mutual funds do not, however, successfully alter the composition of their portfolios over the market cycles. (See chapter 10 for more information on mutual funds.) This fact suggests that the mutual fund cash position is a contrary indicator. If mutual fund cash balances are high, fund managers must think that it is not a good time to be in the market. If fund managers were not very good at market timing, the contrarian would consider this to be a buy signal.

Barron's Confidence Index

The Barron's Confidence Index (BCI) is the ratio of ten high-grade corporate bond rates relative to the more speculative Dow Jones Bond Index rates. A high value for the ratio indicates that high-grade yields are relatively close to the yields on more speculative issues. At such times, the market is unwilling to pay much of a premium for quality (or, stated differently, does not require a large premium to hold lower-grade issues). Alternatively, a low ratio implies a substantial premium for quality. The ratio appears in *Barron's* "Market Laboratory" section. This section is a source of many of the underlying data used to compute market indicators. Users of the BCI believe that sophisticated investors will move toward quality bonds when the market

---

Traditional Technical Market Indicators

- Odd-lot activity: When odd-lot sales are abnormally high (low), the market is said to be near a bottom (top).
- Specialists' short selling: High (low) specialist short selling is thought to forecast a market decline (rise).
- Mutual fund cash position: Mutual fund cash is an indication of potential future demand for stocks; a large cash position indicates a bullish market.
- Barron's Confidence Index: The ratio of high-grade to average-grade bond yields reflects confidence of "sophisticated investors."

---

outlook is unfavorable and toward speculative bonds when the market outlook is favorable. In other words, the risk premium on riskier bonds will increase when the overall outlook for the market is unfavorable. As with most of the indicators discussed so far, the evidence is suggestive but not conclusive. Even in forecasting market peaks, the results are not especially encouraging or useful.

Other Technical Indicators

Although the indicators discussed in the previous section are quite traditional, they are by no means exhaustive. Let us consider some of the more recent indicators that have developed a following.

Some analysts argue that the market's strength may be gauged by the ratio of the number of stocks advancing to the number declining (the advance-decline ratio), especially if there is a tendency for the ratio to persist over some time period.

short-term trading index

The *short-term trading index*, which is derived from the advance-decline ratio, attempts to measure the degree to which volume is concentrated in declining and advancing stocks, and it is defined as the ratio of two other ratios. The first ratio (A) is the *number* of advancing stocks divided by the *number* of declining stocks. The second ratio (B) is the *volume* of advancing stocks divided by the *volume* of declining stocks. The short-term trading index is A divided by B. The indicator is available on most stock quotation machines and on the Internet. A little manipulation reveals that the index is the average volume of declining stocks (that is, the volume of declining stocks divided by the number of declining stocks) relative to the average volume of advancing stocks (that is, the volume of rising stocks divided by the number of rising stocks). The lower the ratio, the greater the average volume in advancing stocks relative to the average volume in declining stocks. Hence, a low ratio is bullish.

January indicator (January effect)

The *January indicator (January effect)* is a rather simplistic tool that often receives a good bit of attention at the beginning of each year. A market that rises in January is expected to rise during the year; a market that falls in January is expected to fall during the year. Because the market generally rises both in January and for the year, the success of the January indicator may easily be overstated. Several other months seem to do about as well.

Regarding the January effect, Donald Keim found that small stocks outperformed large ones during the first several weeks almost every year between 1926 and the mid-1970s. One explanation for this was that hard-to-trade small stocks tend to be depressed by investors' tax-related year-end selling. But then small stocks bounce back as investors rebuy them early the next year.[22] However, according to Prudential Securities, small stocks underperformed the market averages each January for the period 1993–1998. One explanation is that fund managers buy stocks of small companies in December in anticipation of the January effect, thus offsetting individual investors' tax-loss selling.

Unusual price behavior has been found for Mondays and Fridays. In the past, the market was consistently more likely to be up on Friday than on Monday. The frequent practice of withholding unpleasant economic news until the market's Friday close might account for this phenomenon. This day-of-the-week price effect suggests that, if no overriding considerations intervene, investors might as well sell on Friday and wait until late in the day on Monday to buy. The Monday after a Friday decline may offer somewhat more attractive buying opportunities.

S. Penman's study of stock market seasonality found that the market tends to be particularly strong in the first half of the first month of quarters two, three, and four.[23] This result appears to be due to a tendency for good earnings reports to be issued at that time; poor reports are released later in the first quarter after most total fiscal year results are fully known. In other words, firms act as if they are hoping to delay bad news until the last moment when it becomes legally impossible (due to reporting requirements) to delay any further.

Other Technical Indicators

- Advance-decline ratio: High values are bullish if they persist.
- Short-term trading index: A low value is bullish.
- January indicator: January performance is said to forecast the year, but the evidence is unimpressive.
- Monday-Friday price pattern: The market tends to rise on Fridays and fall on Mondays.
- Monthly pattern: The market tends to rise in the first half of each month, with much of that tendency concentrated in the months of April, July, and October.

CHARTING

Charting is a common tool of technical analysis used to assess the overall mood of the market, or the market's mood toward specific stocks. Although controversial, chart reading (or its modern-day equivalent, momentum modeling) is still widely practiced. There is a substantial industry built around the development and interpretation of charts.

Types of Charts

Bar Charts

The most common type of chart is the bar chart. The vertical axis of a bar chart is dollars, usually on a logarithmic scale so that price movements of equal percentage amounts will be the same size. The horizontal axis represents trading days. For each trading day, a line is drawn connecting the high and low price of the day. An example of this is the bar chart shown in figure 6-1 (although the vertical axis in this chart is arithmetic and not logarithmic). A more elaborate bar chart would show the closing price each day by a cross mark or tic on the vertical line representing each day's price range. Some charts will also add the daily volume at the bottom (obviously added with a different vertical axis).

FIGURE 6-1
Typical Bar Chart

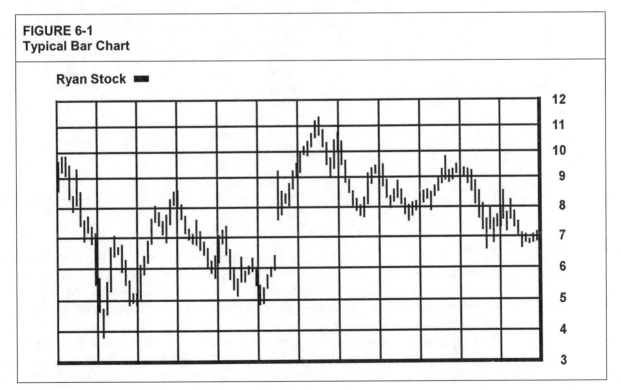

relative strength line

The basic format of the bar chart may be supplemented with a moving average line (for example, the average stock price for the past 50 days) and a relative strength line. The *relative strength line* plots the ratio of the stock's price to that of the S&P 500 average or to some other appropriate average or index.

Example:	Suppose Standard Widget's daily closing prices are as follows:

May 1, 2004	$30
May 2, 2004	$31
May 3, 2004	$32
May 4, 2004	$31
May 5, 2004	$31
May 8, 2004	$32
May 9, 2004	$31
May 10, 2004	$30
May 11, 2004	$29
May 12, 2004	$30

Assume we wish to calculate the moving average for the past 5 trading days. On May 8, our moving average would be based on the closing prices of May 1 through 5, or ($30 + $31 + $32 + $31 + $31)/5, or $31. On May 9, our moving average would be based on the closing stock prices for May 2 through 8, and so on. For the second week in May, our daily 5-day moving average would be

May 8, 2004	$31
May 9, 2004	$31.40
May 10, 2004	$31.40
May 11, 2004	$31
May 12, 2004	$30.60

Point-and-Figure Charts

A point-and-figure chart diagrams stock movements only and has no time dimension. The vertical axis measures the stock price, and the horizontal axis is used to note a change in the direction of price movement. To start a chart, one looks for a price movement of a minimum magnitude, usually $3. Price changes are measured based on highs and lows, and closing prices have no relevancy to the chart. Thus, the first column in a chart would be measured either from a low to a high that represents at least a $3 movement, or a high to a low that represents a $3 movement. Using figure 6-2, let's say that the chart is started with an upward price movement that goes from a low of $26 to a subsequent high of $29. Hence, X's are entered in the chart denoting the trading has occurred at $27, $28, and $29. Once this initial entry has been made, then the chartist is looking to see what occurs next, an upward price movement of at least $1, or a downward price movement of at least $3. In other words, no more entries are made on the chart until the stock trades at a high of at least $30, or a low of at least $26. It is certainly possible that both could occur on the same day, and the chartist would have to look at the ending price to see which likely occurred first, the new high or the new low. For the new low to occur, the low of the day must be at least $26 exactly or lower. Thus, a price of $26.05 would be treated as a price of $27, not $26. Similarly, a price of $25.95 is treated as $26, not $25.

If the price of $30 occurs first, then the chartist looks to see whether $31 occurs next (a continuation in the same direction), or $27 occurs next to indicate a reversal in price movement. If the $30 occurs first, the chartist adds another X to the vertical column of X's that has been started. If the price of $27 occurs first, the chartist will start a new column of O's to signal the new price direction.

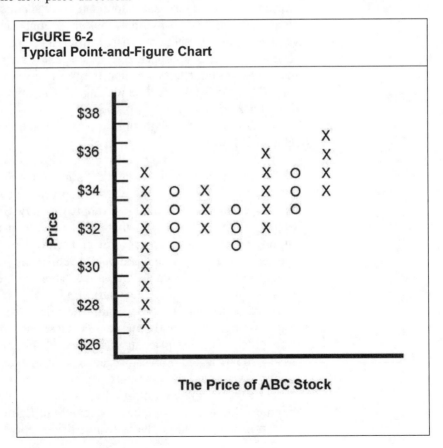

FIGURE 6-2
Typical Point-and-Figure Chart

The Price of ABC Stock

Note also that several days, weeks, or even months could go by in which there are no entries on a chart. To a point-and-figure chartist, this simply means that no significant price movement has occurred, and thus there is nothing to record. Put another way, by eliminating time, a point-and-figure chart is meant to provide a picture of only the significant price movements.

Major Premises of the Chartist's Approach

Chartism is based on one basic premise: Stock price movements occur in patterns that are consistent enough to provide some predictability. One rationale for this might be as follows. Assume that there exist some superior investors. Such investors develop a sense that a stock is underpriced (overpriced). They will begin a process of accumulation (distribution). They will attempt to do it in a manner that does not cause an immediate jump up (down) in the stock's price. This process of accumulation (distribution) will then typically produce a series of price movements that will result in a chart pattern that is recognizable and signals to other investors what is occurring.

resistance level

support level

The second major premise of the chartist's approach hypothesizes the existence of resistance and support levels. A *resistance level* emerges as a significant number of investors look to get out when a certain price level is reached. The number of shares offered increases dramatically as this resistance level is approached. Similarly, at a *support level*, a support price may exist at about the level that the most recent rise began. Investors who missed the first move may be waiting for a second chance to buy if the stock drops back down to that level.

An alternative way to think about resistance and support levels is as upper and lower price barriers. In other words, suppose a stock trades at $38 per share. Suppose further that most people believe this is *approximately* a fair price for the stock. Note the emphasis on "approximately." This is because no one knows exactly what the true fair price of the stock is, but many are comfortable that it is approximately $38. The stock will trade around this price as long as this belief holds that $38 is approximately the fair price of the stock. Because buy and sell orders arrive randomly, the price will move randomly above and below $38. However, if the stock price starts to get too far away from $38, then the "sophisticated" investors will start to enter the market. If the price starts trading significantly below $38, these investors will enter buy orders until the price returns to the $38 range. If it starts trading significantly above $38, these investors will enter sell or sell short orders until the price again returns to this range. The prices at which these "sophisticated" investors enter the market are the resistance and support levels, as shown in figure 6-3.

Note that at some point in time, as shown in the figure, the belief about the true value will change. In the example in figure 6-3, there is an increase in what is believed to be the fair value of the stock. Hence, at the time of the

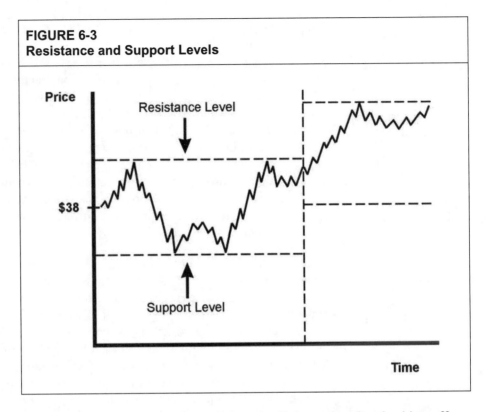

FIGURE 6-3
Resistance and Support Levels

shift, the price approaches the resistance level, but rather than backing off as before, it moves to a new, higher trading range. Unfortunately, there is nothing in the market place that allows an investor to know when an upward price movement is simply a random movement that will be corrected if it goes to far, or the start of a shift to a new price range.

A third tenet of chartists (in the case of bar charts) is the belief that volume goes with the trend. Thus, in a major up trend, volume will increase as the price rises and decrease when the price declines.

The Head-and-Shoulders Pattern

Technical analysts seek to identify favorable buying and selling opportunities from repeating price patterns. These patterns include chart formations, such as triangles, coils, rectangles, flags, pennants, gaps, line-and-saucer formations, and V-formations. Perhaps the best-known pattern is the head-and-shoulders formation on bar charts, as shown in figure 6-4. This pattern, which resembles the human form, shows the following stages of development for a bearish signal:

- Left shoulder—The left shoulder builds up when there is a strong rally, accompanied by significant volume. Thereafter, when a profit-taking reaction occurs, the shoulder slopes downward. Volume is noticeably reduced.

- Head—Rising prices and increased volume initiate the left side of the head pattern, followed by a contraction, or reduced volume, which extends to the neckline. In this configuration, the head always extends well above the left shoulder.
- Right shoulder—When there is another price rally, the left side of the right shoulder slopes upward; finally, when the rally breaks up and prices slide downward, the right side of the right shoulder slopes downward. Volume action is usually decidedly smaller than it was under the left shoulder and head. The right shoulder tends to be roughly equal in height with the left shoulder and it is always well below the head.

neckline

Note that the bottom of each shoulder is at about the same price. This price is referred to as the *neckline*. As shown in the graph, the formation is complete, and the pattern is screaming that an investor should sell. The expectation is that after the right shoulder is completed, the price is expected to drop significantly.

A variation of this pattern is the upside-down head and shoulders. Think of this as a person standing on his or her head. The description of the volume as it relates to each "leg" of this pattern is the same. The only difference is that the upside-down formation is bullish, and the forecast is that there will be a major upward price movement once the price breaks the neckline.

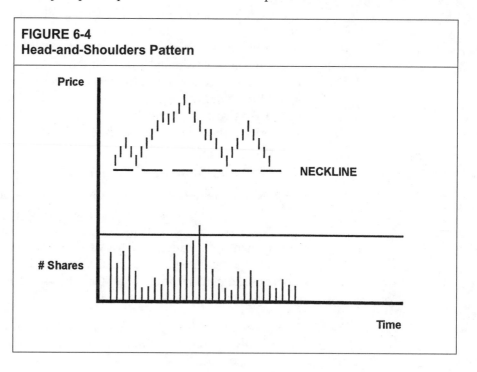

FIGURE 6-4
Head-and-Shoulders Pattern

SUMMARY AND CONCLUSIONS

The earliest research on stock price movements documented that security prices tended to follow a Brownian motion. This led to the development of the efficient market hypothesis (EMH), which has three forms. The weak form states that knowledge of past price changes or other trading statistics is useless in predicting future stock prices (charting is of no value). The semistrong form states that knowledge of any publicly available information is useless in predicting future stock prices (fundamental analysis is of no value). The strong form states that knowledge of any privately held information is useless in predicting future stock prices (insider information is of no value).

For the last 40 years, a great deal of research in the stock market has focused on testing the validity of the EMH. Unfortunately, the EMH cannot be proved. Rather, we can only prove that specific strategies which might allow an investor to beat the market do not work. It is always possible that there exists a strategy that would allow anyone using it to beat the market.

Weak-form tests include an examination of serial correlation coefficients, runs, and filter rules, as well as such strategies as the Dow theory. Semistrong-form tests cover all sorts of strategies. Tests of the strong form are more limited because of the difficulty of accessing privately held information. The majority of tests all suggest that the market is efficient, at least in the weak and semistrong forms, once one allows for the presence of transaction fees.

A substantial number of studies have looked at the issue of the speed with which information spreads throughout the market and thus becomes fully incorporated in the stock price. There is some evidence of the ability to profit from being the first to access certain types of information.

Technical analysis includes the use of technical market indicators as well as charting techniques. The indicators discussed in this chapter include short interest, odd-lot activity, specialists' short selling, mutual fund cash positions, Barron's Confidence Index (BCI), advance-decline patterns, short-term trading, and the January indicator. The two most common types of charting techniques are bar charts and point-and-figure charts. The analysis of charts depends on the ability of the analyst to recognize such patterns as the head-and-shoulders formation. The success of charting depends on the consistency of such patterns in predicting future price movements.

CHAPTER REVIEW

Answers to the review questions and the self-test questions start on page 733.

Key Terms

fundamental analysis	efficient market hypothesis (EMH)
technical analysis	random walk

weak form of the EMH
semistrong form of the EMH
strong form of the EMH
chartist
filter rule
momentum
Dow theory
anomaly
dogs of the Dow
small firm effect
market timer
sophisticated investor rationale

contrarian rationale
short-term trading index
January indicator (January effect)
charting
bar chart
relative strength line
point-and-figure chart
resistance level
support level
head-and-shoulders pattern
neckline

Review Questions

6-1. Discuss the three forms of the EMH. What does each imply about the types of investment analysis? Summarize the relevant evidence on each.

6-2. Discuss the possible causes of persisting market imperfections.

6-3. Discuss the relevance of short interest and odd-lot behavior in market timing. What is the theory, and what is the evidence?

6-4. Identify the hypothesized relationships for the following indicators:
   a. specialists' short selling
   b. mutual fund cash position
   c. BCI

6-5. Compute the BCI for the following values for high-grade and average-grade bond rates: 5.67 percent and 6.01 percent; 10.34 percent and 13.89 percent.

6-6. Identify the hypothesized relationships for the following indicators:
   a. advance-decline ratio
   b. short-term trading index
   c. January indicator
   d. Monday-Friday price pattern

6-7. a. Compare the positions of chartists and those who subscribe to the random walk hypothesis.
   b. What is the role of the market efficiency concept in this discussion?

Self-Test Questions

T   F   6-1. The efficient market, as the term is used in investments, is concerned with making security transactions at the lowest unit cost.

T   F   6-2.   Characteristics of efficiency in the market are that information is widely available and that it is generated in a random fashion.

T   F   6-3.   The weak form of the EMH states that the history of price information is of no value in assessing future changes in stock prices.

T   F   6-4.   The semistrong form of the EMH states that stock prices reflect all public and nonpublic information.

T   F   6-5.   In a semistrong-efficient market, investors cannot act on new public information after its announcement and expect to earn above-average returns.

T   F   6-6.   A market that is semistrong-form efficient is also weak-form efficient.

T   F   6-7.   The semistrong form of the EMH refutes technical analysis but supports fundamental analysis.

T   F   6-8.   If someone were to successively predict the direction of the stock market 10 years in a row, this would be absolute proof that this person is a superior investor and the EMH is invalid.

T   F   6-9.   Most tests of the EMH are also joint tests of the validity of the capital asset pricing model (CAPM).

T   F   6-10.   Occasional stock market overreaction is inconsistent with the weak form of the EMH.

T   F   6-11.   Tests of technical trading rules generally conclude that a strategy based on past price and volume strategies cannot consistently outperform a simple buy-and-hold strategy.

T   F   6-12.   Results of studies concerning the trading activities of corporate insiders always support the validity of the strong form of the EMH.

T   F   6-13.   If the stock market is efficient, then money (portfolio) managers need not be concerned with portfolio diversification and risk.

T   F   6-14.   A market anomaly is an exception to what is expected in a totally efficient market.

T   F   6-15.   Adjustment lags demonstrate that the stock market is not perfectly efficient in adjusting instantaneously to new information.

T   F   6-16.   Tender offers, mergers, and liquidations may present investors with attractive trading opportunities.

T   F   6-17.   For the purpose of the Dow theory, the most important price movement is that of day-to-day fluctuations.

T   F   6-18.   The Dow theory is still used by technical analysts and chartists.

T   F   6-19. One problem with the short interest technical indicator is that more than one interpretation is possible.

T   F   6-20. The odd-lot activity indicator is based on the presumption that odd-lotters are relatively unsophisticated investors.

T   F   6-21. The ratio of odd-lot purchases to odd-lot sales tends to be less than 1.

T   F   6-22. The January effect denotes that the market's performance in January is indicative of how it will do the rest of the year.

T   F   6-23. Chart reading is a type of fundamental analysis.

T   F   6-24. Profitable exploitation of chart reading and other technical analysis is inconsistent with the weak form of the EMH.

T   F   6-25. Moving average prices are sometimes shown on bar charts.

T   F   6-26. The amount of time it takes for a pattern to develop in a point-and-figure chart is a key part of the analysis.

T   F   6-27. In a point-and-figure chart, a new column can be generated with as little as a $1 reversal.

T   F   6-28. Volume numbers are always shown at the bottom of a point-and-figure chart.

T   F   6-29. The resistance level is the price level at which a significant number of investors start buying stock.

T   F   6-30. An upside-down head-and-shoulders chart pattern is a bearish indicator.

NOTES

1. N. Jegadeesh and S. Titman, "Returns to Buying Winners and Selling Losers: Implications for Stock Market Efficiency," *Journal of Finance,* vol. 48, no. 1 (March 1993), pp. 65–91.
2. S. Brown and W. Goetzmann, "Mutual Fund Styles," *Journal of Financial Economics,* vol. 43, no. 3 (March 1997), pp. 373–399.
3. B. Malkiel, *A Random Walk Down Wall Street*, 6th ed. (New York: W.W. Norton, 1995), chapter 5.
4. D. Domian, D. Louton, and C. Mossman, "The Rise and Fall of the 'Dogs of the Dow'," *Financial Services Review,* vol. 7, no. 3 (1998), pp. 146–160.
5. M. Scholes, "The Market for Securities: Substitution versus Price Pressure and the Effects of Information on Share Prices," *Journal of Business* (April 1972), pp. 179–211; and W. Mikkelson and M. Partch, "Stock Price Effects and Costs of Secondary Distributions," *Journal of Financial Economics* (June 1985), pp. 165–194.
6. M. Blume and R. Stambaugh, "Biases in Computed Returns: An Application to the Size Effect," *Journal of Financial Economics* (November 1983), pp. 387–404; W. Kross, "The Size Effect Is Primarily a Price Effect," *Journal of Financial Research* (Fall 1985), pp. 169–179.
7. S. Eakins and S. Sewell, "Tax-Loss Selling, Institutional Investors, and the January Effect: A Note," *The Journal of Financial Research,* vol. 16, no. 4 (Winter 1993), pp. 377–384. See also

J. R. Ritter, "The Buying and Selling Behavior of Individual Investors at the Turn of the Year," *Journal of Finance*, vol. 43, no. 3, pp. 701–717.

8. K. Nunn, G. Madden, and M. Gombola, "Are Some Insiders More 'Inside' Than Others?," *Journal of Portfolio Management* (Spring 1983), pp. 18–22.

9. E. Felsenthal, "Big Weapon against Insider Trading Is Upheld," *The Wall Street Journal* (June 26, 1997), p. C1.

10. J. Pound and R. Zeckhauser, "Clearly Heard on the Street: The Effect of Takeover Rumors on Stock Prices," *Journal of Business* (July 1990), pp. 291–308.

11. P. Liu, S.D. Smith, and A.A. Syed, "The Impact of the Insider Trading Scandal on the Information Content of *The Wall Street Journal*'s 'Heard on the Street' Column," *Journal of Financial Research*, vol. 15, no. 2 (Summer 1992), pp. 181–188.

12. I. Mathur and A. Waheed, "Stock Price Reactions to Securities Recommended in *Business Week*'s 'Inside Wall Street," *Financial Review*, vol. 30, no. 3 (August 1995), pp. 583–604.

13. B. Barber, R. Lehavy, M. McNichols, and B. Trueman, "Can Investors Profit from the Prophets? Security Analyst Recommendations and Stock Returns," *Journal of Finance*, vol. 56, no. 2 (April 2001), pp. 531–563.

14. R. Masulis, "The Effects of Capital Structure Change on Security Prices: A Study of Exchange Offers," *Journal of Financial Economics* (June 1980), pp. 139–177.

15. T. Vermaelen, "Common Stock Repurchases and Market Signaling: An Empirical Study," *Journal of Financial Economics* (June 1981), pp. 139–183; L. Dann, "Common Stock Repurchases: An Analysis of Returns to Bondholders and Stockholders," *Journal of Financial Economics* (June 1981), pp. 113–138.

16. P. Asquith and D. Mullins, "Equity Issues and Offering Dilution," *Journal of Financial Economics* (January/February 1986), pp. 61–89.

17. S. Bhagat, J. Brickley, and R. Lease, "The Authorization of Additional Common Stock: An Empirical Investigation," *Financial Management* (Autumn 1986), pp. 45–53.

18. K. Schipper and A. Smith, "A Comparison of Equity Carve-outs and Seasoned Equity Offerings: Share Price Effects and Corporate Restructuring," *Journal of Financial Economics* (January/February 1986), pp. 153–186.

19. G.P. Brinson, B.D. Singer, G.L. Beebower, "Determinants of Portfolio Performance II: An Update," *Financial Analysts Journal* (May/June 1991), pp. 40–48.

20. J.J. Siegel, "Does It Pay Stock Investors to Forecast the Business Cycle?," *Journal of Portfolio Management,* vol. 18, no. 1 (Fall 1991), pp. 27–34.

21. *Barron's*, January 18, 2004, p. MW23.

22. D.B. Keim, "Size-Related Anomalies and Stock Return Seasonality: Further Empirical Evidence," *Journal of Financial Economics*, vol. 12, no. 1 (June 1983), pp. 13–32; "A New Look at the Effects of Firm Size and E/P Ratio on Stock Returns," *Financial Analysts Journal*, vol. 46, no. 2 (March/April 1990), pp. 56–67.

23. S. Penman, "The Distribution of Earnings News over Time and Seasonalities in Aggregate Stock Returns," *Journal of Financial Economics*, vol. 18, no. 2 (June 1987), pp. 199–228.

Appendix 6A

The Evidence on Timing

Larry E. Swedroe[*]

One bit of conventional wisdom held by investors is that there are smart people who can somehow be invested when the market is in its bull phase and yet manage to hibernate when the historically inevitable bear market arrives. The airways and publications are filled with recommendations on which direction the market is headed. And market timing is the endeavor to which many investors devote most of their efforts, despite the fact that many academic studies have all come to the same conclusion: Market timing (as well as stock selection) has almost no impact on the returns of a portfolio. Here is what Bernard Baruch said about market timing: "Only liars manage to always be out during bad times and in during good times." And here is what John Bogle, Vanguard's founder, had to say: "The idea that a bell rings to signal when investors should get into or out of the stock market is simply not credible. After nearly fifty years in this business, I do not know of anybody who has done it [market timing] successfully and consistently. I don't even know anybody who knows anybody who has done it successfully and consistently. Yet market timing appears to be increasingly embraced by mutual fund investors and the professional managers of fund portfolios alike." These legendary investors believe so strongly that market timing is likely to produce negative results not only because of their own experiences but also because the historical evidence is so powerful. By going to our videotape we can discover just how great are the odds a market timer must overcome in order to be successful in his or her effort to outperform.

One study, "A Market Timing Myth" *(Journal of Investing,* Winter 2000), covered the period 1991–1998 and examined the market returns for the period when eliminating the best and worst ten, twenty, thirty, and forty days of market performance out of the entire 2,023 trading days. The author, John D. Stowe, calculated the returns of such a successful strategy, after expenses (though not after taxes). He also calculated the odds of such a successful effort. The return of the market for the entire period was 19.87%.

Because an active strategy has costs, those costs must be considered. Stowe assumed a one percent cost of a round-trip buy and sell trade. The implication for returns was astounding. The return figures are annualized returns,

---

first before and then after expenses (though not taxes). In summary, here is what he found.

- If you missed the best ten days (0.5% of the trading days), your return dropped to 15.06% before expenses/13.62% after expenses. Thus, if you missed out on the best ten days you missed out on 24%/32% of the available returns.
- If you missed the best twenty days (1% of trading days), your return dropped to 11.98%/9.2%, and you missed out on 40%/54% of the available returns.
- If you missed the best thirty days (1.5% of the trading days), your return dropped to 9.4%/5.35% and you missed out on 53%/73% of the available returns.
- If you missed the best forty days (2% of the trading days), your return dropped to just 7.15%/1.9%, and you missed out on 64%/90% of the available returns.

Stowe also looked at the impact on returns if you somehow were able to avoid the worst market days.

- If you missed out on the ten worst days, your return improved to 25.85%/24.28%. However, 26% of the improvement in returns was eaten up by the expense of the effort.
- If you missed out on the twenty worst days, your return improved to 29.56%/26.35%. However, 33% of the improvement in returns was eaten up by the expense of the effort.
- If you missed out on the thirty worst days, your return improved to 32.76%/27.85%. However, 38% of the improvement in returns was eaten up by the expense of the effort.
- If you missed out on the forty worst days, your return improved to 35.74%/29.09%. However, 42% of the improvement in returns was eaten up by the expense of the effort.

Since a market timing strategy, at least for taxable investors, would likely convert most of the market's gain from long term to short term, such a strategy would have a very significant negative impact on any potential value added.

Stowe then calculated the odds of success of any such market timing strategy. Here is what he found.

- The odds of being able to avoid the ten worst days are $1:3.094 \times 10^{26}$.
- The odds of being able to avoid the twenty worst days are $1:4.93 \times 10^{47}$.
- The odds of being able to avoid the thirty worst days are $1:4.596 \times 10^{66}$.
- The odds of being able to avoid the forty worst days are $1:1.444 \times 10^{84}$.

Here is some further evidence that the most likely winning strategy is passive investing. Legendary investor Peter Lynch, in a September 1995 *Worth* article, pointed out that an investor who stayed fully invested in the S&P 500 over the forty-year period beginning in 1954 would have achieved an 11.4% rate of return. If that investor missed just the best ten months (2%), the return dropped (by 27%) to 8.3%. If the investor missed the best twenty months (4%), the return dropped (by 54%) to 6.1%. Finally, if the investor missed the best forty months (8%), the return dropped (by 76%) all the way to 2.7%.

Let's take a look at the results of market timing "experts." Mark Hulbert, publisher of *Hulbert's Financial Digest,* studied the performance of thirty-two of the portfolios of market timing newsletters for the ten years ending in 1997, as reported in the March 9, 1998, *Business Week.* During this period, the S&P 500 Index was up over 18% per annum. Here is what he found:

- The timers' annual average returns ranged from 5.84% to 16.9%.
- The average return was 11.06%.
- None beat the market.

Two researchers, from Duke University and the University of Utah, respectively, collaborated on a study examining the performance of the stock selections of 237 market-timing newsletters over the 12.5-year period June 1980 to December 1992 (National Bureau of Economic Research Working Paper 4890, October 1994). They used a database supplied by Mark Hulbert. If an investor held an equally weighted portfolio of all the newsletters, he or she would have earned an 11.3% rate of return. This compared to the 15.8% return earned by the S&P 500 index fund. If we considered the costs associated with the trading recommendations of these financial tout sheets, the results would look even worse: transaction costs would have to be subtracted; the negative impact of the taxes generated by trading must be considered; and, adding insult to injury, the cost of the newsletters themselves would have to be subtracted from returns.

Perhaps more telling is that only 5.5% (13 of 237) of the newsletters survived the entire 12.5-year period. How would an investor, at the start of the period, have known which thirteen would survive? (W. Scott Simon, *Index Mutual Funds*)

Another study, in the October 1999 *Journal of Finance,* found similar results. Andrew Metrick studied the equity portfolio recommendations of 153 newsletters covering the 17-year period ending December 1996. His conclusions: There was no evidence of stock-picking ability and no evidence of abnormal short-term performance persistence ("hot hands" didn't stay hot).

Let's look at another form of market timing, tactical asset allocation (TAA). TAA is an investment strategy that gained great popularity in the 1980s and 1990s. The objective of TAA is to provide better-than-benchmark returns with (possibly) lower volatility. This would be accomplished by forecasting returns of two or more asset classes and varying the exposure (percent allocation) accordingly. The varying exposure to various asset classes that TAA depends on is based on economic and market (technical) indicators. A TAA fund would then be measured against their benchmark. Although the benchmark might be 60% S&P 500 Index and 40% Lehman Bond Index, the manager might be allowed to have his or her allocations range from 50% to 5% for equities, 20% to 50% for bonds, and 0% to 45% for cash.

In reality, TAA is just a fancy name for market timing. By giving it a fancy name, however, Wall Street seems able to charge high fees. Let's see if the high fees are worth the price of admission. For the twelve years ending 1997, while the S&P 500 on a total return basis rose 734%, the average equity fund returned just 589%, but the average return for 186 TAA funds was a mere 384%, about half the return of the S&P 500 Index, reported David Dreman in his book, *Contrarian Investment Strategies.*

One more myth debunked.

7

Equities

Learning Objectives

An understanding of the material in this chapter should enable the student to

7-1. Describe the valuation process for common stock, and solve both simple and complex constant-dividend-growth-rate problems.

7-2. Discuss the various market-price-based ratios, and the advantages and disadvantages of each.

7-3. Distinguish between value and growth stocks, and discuss some of the issues associated with analyzing each group.

7-4. Use price/earnings (P/E) ratios to forecast the market or a specific stock.

7-5. Discuss the theory and evidence of the effect of inflation on stock prices.

7-6. Describe the key characteristics of other equity instruments, including preferred stock, warrants, and rights.

7-7. Describe the mechanics of dividend payments.

Chapter Outline

The major task for a financial planner is to ensure the optimal asset allocation for a client. (Asset allocation is discussed in chapter 14.) A planner may occasionally recommend specific stocks. Many times, new clients will come to planners with specific stocks in their portfolios. Thus, it is important that a planner understand the basics of equity valuation. If the planner wants to make valuations and recommendations of equities a primary part of his or her job, he or she should obtain a chartered financial analyst (CFA) designation. This chapter and the next one are simply introductions to the material that constitutes the program of study of equities for the CFA exams.

STOCK VALUATION

intrinsic value (stock)   The *intrinsic value* of any security is the present value of the expected net cash flows that accrues to the owner of that security. The intrinsic value is the market value at which a security should trade based on proper expectations and the correct discount rate. In the case of equities, there are two sources of net cash inflow: cash dividends and the proceeds from the sale of the stock. Thus, the most general statement that can be said with regard to the price that someone is willing to pay for a share of stock is that it equals the discounted values of each of the projected dividends received during the holding period plus the discounted value of the projected price of the stock when it is sold.

$$V_o = \frac{d_1}{(1+r)} + \frac{d_2}{(1+r)^2} + \frac{d_3}{(1+r)^3} + \cdots + \frac{d_H}{(1+r)^H} + \frac{P_H}{(1+r)^H}$$ (Equation 7-1)

where d_t = dividend during period t
       r = required rate of return
       H = holding period
       P_H = price of the stock at the end of the holding period

The above equation appears to be based somewhat on circular logic in that the value (or price) of a share of stock today is defined using its value (or price) at a future time period. This raises the rather interesting question, what will determine the price that someone would be willing to pay for the stock at time period H? Well, the same concept can be applied, namely, P_H will equal the discounted value at time H of all the projected dividends and projected future price during the second owner's holding period. This raises the question of what determines the price that the third owner would be willing to pay for this share of stock. Again, the answer is that he or she would be willing to pay the present value of projected dividends during the expected holding period, plus the present value of the selling price. This scenario can be repeated infinitely. When it is, and the mathematical substitutions are made, we end up with the general model for stock valuation, which is:

$$V_o = \frac{d_1}{(1+r)} + \frac{d_2}{(1+r)^2} + \frac{d_3}{(1+r)^3} + \cdots + \frac{d\infty}{(1+r)^\infty}$$ (Equation 7-2)

$$= \sum_{t=1}^{\infty} \frac{d_t}{(1+r)^t}$$

dividend discount model
dividend valuation model

This model is known as the *dividend discount model*, or *dividend valuation model*.

Some people find the above model confusing and even counterintuitive in that selling price is no longer represented. It is critical to understand that selling price is nothing more than a surrogate for the dividends expected to be paid after a share of stock is sold. Thus, if I plan to sell some stock in 5 years, the selling price will be based on all of the dividends expected to be paid after 5 years from today. Hence, the above equation does not deny the relevance of the selling price; it simply is looking beyond that to what determines that selling price.

Why Isn't Value Based on Earnings?

Some people find the above arguments confusing in that it would seem more intuitive that a stock's price should be based on the profits or earnings of a company, rather than its dividends. The reason that value is not based on earnings is that there would be double counting involved. When a company generates earnings, its board of directors must make a choice as to what percentage of the earnings to pay out as dividends, and what percentage to reinvest in the company. Those earnings that are reinvested will presumably lead to increased earnings in the future. If one bases value on earnings, then one is giving value to both the original earnings that were reinvested and to the incremental earning being generated by that reinvestment.

This double-counting argument can be demonstrated mathematically. Let's start with the concept of a company whose dividends are expected to take the form of a perpetuity. Recall that in appendix 5A, a perpetuity was defined as an annuity that runs forever. The valuation formula for a perpetuity is the annual cash flow divided by the discount rate. Thus, in the case of a company whose dividends are expected to be constant forever, the value of the stock would be expressed as:

$$V = \frac{d}{r}$$

where V = intrinsic value of a stock whose dividends are
expected to form a perpetuity
d = the constant annual dividend
r = discount rate

For example, suppose a company was expected to earn and pay a dividend of $1 per year, forever, starting 1 year from today. Further assume that the appropriate discount for this stock is 10 percent. Thus, the value of the stock would be $10 ($1/.10). Note that in the above assumption, there is no reinvestment of any earnings. The company is paying out all of its earnings as dividends, and that is why there is no growth in future dividends.

Now let's suppose that an investment opportunity comes along that promises a 10 percent rate of return, but financing this project will mean that the company will have to skip its dividend for 1 year. The earnings per share will still be $1, but all of the earnings will be reinvested in the coming year. As a result, there will be no dividend for this year. However, future earnings and dividends will be $1.10 rather than $1 as a result of this project. Remember, this project provides a 10 percent rate of return. Thus, the one-time investment of $1 per share will provide a return of $.10 per share forever thereafter.

For purposes of our dividend discount model, there is no dividend for the coming year, but there will be a dividend of $1.10 forever thereafter. To value this stock using the dividend discount model, we need first to consider what the price of the stock will be 1 year from now. At that point in time, an investor will be looking at a perpetuity of $1.10 forever. Given a discount rate of 10 percent, this means that the stock 1 year from today will be worth $11 ($1.10/.10). As there is no dividend to be paid 1 year from today, the stock price today is simply the present value of the stock price in 1 year. The present value of $11 discounted at 10 percent for one time period is

$$\$11/(1 + .10) = \$10$$

Note that the price of the stock has not changed as a result of this investment decision. Nor should it! If investors are requiring a 10 percent rate of return, and the company invests in a project that pays exactly a 10 percent rate of return, then there should be no change in the value of the stock. Investors are giving up the $1 dividend they would have received in 1 year for an increase in future dividends from $1 to $1.10 forever thereafter.

Now, suppose we had argued earlier that the price of stock equaled the present value of future earnings. Before the investment decision, one would say that the value of the stock was $10 ($1/.10). However, after the investment in the new project, one would have to think that the value of the firm had increased. Undertaking the new project does not affect the earnings for the coming year. The earnings will remain at $1 per share. Furthermore, after the investment the earnings will increase to $1.10 each year (at which time the firm returns to paying out all of its earnings as dividends). If we continue to use 10 percent as the appropriate discount rate, then the value of the stock would be $11 in 1 year (same computation as with the dividends). However, the price of the stock today would be based on the present value of the price in 1 year, plus the $1 in earnings the firm would report 1 year from now. This would produce a stock price today of

$$(\$11 \text{ price in one year} + \$1 \text{ earnings in one year})/(1 + .10) = \$10.91$$

In other words, taking the present value of earnings would cause one to believe the stock price should increase in value by $.91, when in fact the firm's decision to invest in a project that provides exactly the rate of return required by shareholders would have no impact on the value of the firm. The increase in the value results simply from the double counting that has occurred when reinvestment of earnings takes place.

The Valuation of Stocks that Don't Pay Dividends

The most immediate objection to the dividend discount model is, how can it make sense for stocks that do not pay dividends? The answer is simple. There has to be an expectation of future dividends. In the prior discussion, we considered a firm that reinvested all of its earnings into a project. For the current year, this firm would have no dividends. But, the expectation that there would be dividend payments starting in 2 years was sufficient to give the stock value today. In fact, let's rework the above example to show not only why current dividends may not be relevant to valuation, but also why most investors would actually prefer the firm not to pay dividends.

Example 1:   The WJC Corporation's dividend is a perpetuity of $1 per year, forever, as the company pays out 100 percent of its earnings as dividends. The company plans to undertake a project that has a one-time investment equal to $1 per share. The investment pays a return of 20 percent forever, beginning 2 years from today. Hence, if the firm undertakes this project, the value of the stock should change from the current $10 to $10.93. The price in 1 year, when the dividends return to a perpetuity, is $12 ($1.20/.10). The present value today of a stock worth $12 in 1 year (given no dividends will be paid in the coming year) is $10.93 ($12/[1 + .10]).

The fact that in the above example the firm is investing the shareholder's money at a rate greater than what the shareholders require creates, for the shareholders, what is tantamount to a windfall gain in the value of their stock. This simple example is easily extrapolated to make the following point. As long as the firm can invest its earnings at a rate of return greater than what the shareholders require, the shareholders are better off and the firm should do so. It is only when the firm is no longer able to find projects that provide rates of return greater than that required by shareholders that it should pay out its earnings in the form of dividends. For a non-dividend-paying company it is these future dividends that are being valued. Thus, a firm may pay no dividends today, and may not be expected to pay any dividends for many years, and still have substantial value. Let's consider a more elaborate example:

Example 2:   The WJC Company now believes that it can reinvest all of its earnings over the next 10 years at a rate of return of 20 percent. Beginning 11 years from today, it will resume paying 100 percent of its earnings as dividends. If the earnings per share for the year just ended was $1, and if the required rate of return is 10 percent, what should the value of the stock be?

First, let's figure the earnings of the stock 10 years from today. This is a future value calculation in which $1 grows at the rate of 20 percent per year for 10 years. At that time, the earnings per share will be:

$$\$1 \times (1 + .20)^{10} = \$6.19$$

From this point on, the firm will pay a perpetuity of $6.19 per year, starting in the eleventh year. Hence, the value of the stock 10 years from today should be $61.90 ($6.19/.10). The value today of stock that is worth $61.90 in 10 years, based on a 10 percent discount rate, is

$$\$61.90/(1 + .10)^{10} = \$23.87$$

Thus, this 10-year investment program means that the value of the stock today should be $23.87, rather than the $10 price if there was no investment program.

The key in the above example is the investment of earnings at a 20 percent rate of return when investors are only requiring a 10 percent rate of return. Clearly, most investors should always be happy to see a company omit its dividends when it is able to reinvest the profits at such attractive rates.[1]

Constant Growth Model

The major problem with the dividend discount model as presented in equation 7-2 is that it is essentially unusable. A literal interpretation says that one should specify the projected dividends of a firm for all eternity, and then take their present value! We were able to use this model in the prior discussion only because we assumed that all future dividends took the form of a perpetuity. For common stock, a perpetuity is wonderful for illustrative purposes. But a perpetuity is a bust with respect to any attempt to model real situations. What is needed is a model or assumption that is more realistic but is still mathematically easy to use.

Years ago, Myron Gordon popularized just such a model. The one simple assumption of this model is that dividends are expected to grow at a constant rate, g, forever. Thus, the dividend for any year, t, is expected to equal the prior year's dividend times 1 plus that growth rate. Thus, $d_1 = d_0(1 + g)$, $d_2 = d_1(1 + g) = d_0(1 + g)^2$, and so on. This relationship can be defined as

$$d_t = d_{t-1}(1+g) \text{ or } d_t = d_0(1 + g)^t$$

where d_t = dividend in year t
d_{t-1} = dividend in year prior to year t
d_0 = dividend just paid
g = growth rate in dividends

If we are willing to make this one assumption with regard to future dividends, then we can rewrite equation 7-2 as follows:

$$V_0 = \frac{d_1}{(1+r)} + \frac{d_2}{(1+r)^2} + \frac{d_3}{(1+r)^3} + \ldots$$

$$= \frac{d_0(1+g)}{(1+r)} + \frac{d_0(1+g)^2}{(1+r)^2} + \frac{d_0(1+g)^3}{(1+r)^3} + \ldots$$

Gordon growth model

It turns out that some nifty mathematical manipulation can reduce this complex formula to a rather simple formula, called the constant growth model or *Gordon growth model:*

$$V_0 = \frac{d_1}{(r-g)} = \frac{d_0(1+g)}{(r-g)} \text{ for } g < r \qquad \text{(Equation 7-3)}$$

In this equation, V_0 is the intrinsic value of the stock today (at year 0), d_1 is the dividend projected for the coming year (year 1), r is the required rate of return, and g is the growth rate. Note that this formula is on the formula sheet provided by the CFP® Board of Standards for its exam.

Based on this constant growth model, we can make the following statements regarding a stock's value:

- An increase in next year's expected dividend (d_1) will cause the value of the stock to be higher.
- An increase in the expected growth rate of dividends (g) will cause the value of the stock to be higher.
- A decrease in the required rate of return (that is, the discount rate) will cause the value of the stock to be higher.

Bear in mind that this formula applies only when expected growth rates are below the discount rate. Stocks with dividends that have expected growth rates exceeding the discount rate in perpetuity would have theoretically infinite prices. That nonsensical result would occur because each successive expected dividend would have a higher present value than the one before it. Clearly, stock prices are finite.

Example 1:	Assume that Acme Corp. experiences constant dividend growth at a rate of 5 percent per year. Its required rate of return (discount rate) is 15 percent. The dividend that was just paid was $2/share. Using the constant growth model, we can value Acme Corp. common stock as follows:

$$d_1 = d_0(1+g) = \$2(1.05) = \$2.10$$

$$V_0 = \frac{d_1}{r-g} = \frac{\$2.10}{.15-.05} = \$21.00$$

Example 2: Use the same assumptions as in Example 1, except assume that Acme's dividend growth rate is now 7 percent. To find the value:

$$d_1 = d_0(1+g) = \$2(1.07) = \$2.14$$

$$V_0 = \frac{d_1}{r-g} = \frac{\$2.14}{.15-.07} = \$26.75$$

Example 3: Use the same assumptions as in Example 1, except assume that now Acme's required return is 20 percent. To value the security:

$$d_1 = d_0(1+g) = \$2(1.05) = \$2.10$$

$$V_0 = \frac{d_1}{r-g} = \frac{\$2.10}{.20-.05} = \$14.00$$

One aspect of the above model that is important to remember (particularly as it shows up on various exams) is that it turns out the value of g is also equal to the expected annual increase in the price of the stock. This can be shown in two different ways. First, we can rewrite the constant growth model to solve for the discount rate. When we do, we obtain the following:

$$r = (d_1/V_0) + g \qquad \text{(Equation 7-4)}$$

This says that the required rate of return is the expected dividend yield (d_1/V_0) plus the growth rate of dividends. Note that this formula is also on the CFP® Board of Standards Formula Sheet for its exam.

As an equilibrium condition in markets, the required rate of return will equal the expected rate of return. After all, if the required rate differs from the expected rate, then investors will buy or sell securities, causing the appropriate price changes to occur, until such time as equilibrium is reestablished. The expected rate of return for stock consists of two components, the projected dividend yield plus the price appreciation. That is:

$$\text{Expected return} = (d_1/V_0) + \text{percentage price change} \qquad \text{(Equation 7-5)}$$

If equations 7-4 and 7-5 are then set equal to each other (that is, required return equals expected return), then we get:

$$(d_1/V_0) + g = (d_1/V_0) + \text{percentage price change}$$

This reduces to the observation that g equals the expected rate of change in the price of the security.

A second way to see this same relationship is to compute the percentage change in price, using the constant growth model. That is, the constant growth model tells us that the value of the stock now and in one period would be defined as:

$$V_0 = d_0 \times (1 + g)/(r - g)$$
$$V_1 = d_0 \times (1 + g)^2/(r - g)$$

Thus, the percentage change in the price of the stock would equal:

$$(V_1 - V_0)/V_0 = ([d_0 \times (1 + g)^2/(r - g)] - [d_0 \times (1 + g)/(r - g)])/[d_0 \times (1 + g)/(r-g)]$$

After some mathematical manipulation, we obtain the following:

$$(V_1 - V_0)/V_0 = g \qquad \text{(Equation 7-6)}$$

Again, not only does g represent the expected growth rate in dividends, it also represents the expected percentage change in the price of the security.

Example: The stock of the Surefire Corporation currently trades at $20. The expected annual dividend is $.50. If your required rate of return on the stock is 10 percent, what is your expected annual price appreciation?

We can use the constant growth model to solve for g:

$$V_0 = d_1/(r - g)$$

$$\$20 = \$.50/(.10 - g)$$

$$.10 - g = \$.50/\$20 = .025$$

$$g = .075 \text{ or } 7.5\%$$

For short periods of time, companies may grow more rapidly than their market-determined discount rate. These growth rates are, however, temporary phenomena that exist only when a company is in a stage of rapid growth. In the long run, dividends are always expected to grow more slowly than the rate at which they are discounted. A modification of the constant growth model, referred to as the supernormal growth model, can be used to price such a security. The supernormal growth model is presented in appendix 7A.

d_0 versus d_1

When solving problems using the constant growth model, many students are confused about what number to put into the numerator. Sometimes, a problem gives the student the value of d_0, in which case the student needs to compute d_1 for the numerator. The rest of the time, the student will simply be told the value of d_1, in which case any attempt to manipulate this number will result in an incorrect answer. The clue is always in the wording. When the student is being given such wording as "the company just paid a dividend equal to" or "the company has paid a dividend of," then these are strong clues that the dividend number being given is d_0, and the student needs to multiply this by 1 plus the growth rate to obtain the correct value for the numerator. However, when the wording is something like "the company expects to pay" or "the company will pay," then these are strong clues that the dividend number being given is d_1, and the student should plug this number directly into the numerator without any additional computation.

Example 1:	Assume that Acme Corp. experiences constant dividend growth at a rate of 5 percent per year. The company's projected dividend is $2/share and the security sells for $25 per share. What is the discount rate being used to value the stock?

$$d_1 = \$2.00$$

$$r = \frac{d_1}{V_0} + g$$

$$= \frac{2.00}{25} + .05$$

$$= .13$$

Example 2:	Smith and Daltrey Corp. will be paying a dividend of $5.00. The company's projected dividend growth rate is 10 percent, and the required rate of return is 15 percent. What is the stock's intrinsic value?

$$V_0 = \frac{d_1}{r - g}$$

$$= \frac{5.00}{.15 - .10} = \frac{5.00}{.05}$$

$$= \$100$$

Zero Growth Model

In our earlier discussion in this chapter, we used as an example a common stock whose expected dividend was a perpetuity. The reader should note that the perpetuity is nothing more than a special case of the constant growth rate model. In this case, the growth rate is zero. Thus, if the student uses a value of zero for g in equation 7-3, the constant growth rate model reduces to the formula for valuing a perpetuity.

Although the concept of a perpetuity is highly unrealistic for common stock, it is the perfect formula for valuing preferred stock. Remember, preferred shares are usually expected to pay a stream of equal dividend payments. The expected stability of the income stream is similar to the expected stability of the coupon payment of bonds. However, as noted earlier, preferred stocks do not mature as do bonds, and they are expected to continue dividend payments in perpetuity.

Example 1:　　A preferred stock pays a dividend of $1.50 annually. If the appropriate discount rate is 5 percent, what is the value of the stock?

$$V = \frac{d}{r} = \frac{\$1.50}{.05} = \$30.00$$

Example 2:　　A preferred stock has an annual dividend of $5. If it trades at a price of $50, what is the expected or required rate of return?

$$r = d/V = \$5/\$50 = .10 \text{ or } 10\%$$

Selection of the Discount Rate

In the above problems, the selection of the discount rate to calculate the present value of anticipated cash flows is clearly critical. The investor should select this rate based on the risk of the security as well as the returns available in the market for other securities.

There are two general approaches to selection of a discount rate. The first is based on the use of some formal model that incorporates a specification for risk. The second is traditional security analysis.

The most common risk-based model used to determine an appropriate discount rate is the capital asset pricing model (CAPM), which was presented in chapter 4. The model stated:

$$r_i = r_f + (r_m - r_f) \beta_i \qquad \text{(Equation 4-15a)}$$

where r_i = required rate of return
     r_f = risk-free rate of return
     r_m = return on the market portfolio
     β_i = the beta coefficient of the security

Example: After analyzing the LB Corp., you conclude that next year's dividend is likely to be \$1.00 and that the long-term growth rate in dividends is 4 percent. You also conclude that the beta for the stock is .80, the risk-free rate is 4 percent, and the expected return on the market portfolio is 10 percent. What should be the value of the stock?

We must start by determining the appropriate discount rate, which we obtain by plugging the necessary numbers into the CAPM as follows:

$$r_i = r_f + (r_m - r_f)\ \beta_i$$

$$= 4\% + (10\% - 4\%)\ .80 = 8.8\%$$

Next, we use this number as the discount rate in the constant growth model:

$$V_0 = d_1/(r - g) = \$1.00/(.088 - .04) = \$20.83$$

The second approach involves doing a full traditional security analysis of the company and then, with that information, identifying the appropriate discount rate. The basic techniques of security analysis are presented in chapter 8, and so will not be elaborated on here. However, it must be emphasized that there is no formal model that relates traditional security analysis to a particular discount rate.

MARKET-PRICE-BASED RATIOS

One aspect of security analysis and valuation of publicly traded securities is that the conclusion frequently is seen as already incorporated into the price of the stock. Specifically, when an analysis indicates a company is strong and has high growth potential, then the analyst will usually find that this company's stock is trading at a relatively high price. Similarly, when a company looks dismal and has poor prospects, the analyst will find it to be trading at a rather low price. Therefore, one might like to start the valuation process by knowing which companies are already considered attractive and which are considered "dogs." There are several market-price-based ratios that will immediately provide this information. They include the price/earnings, the price/free cash flow, the price/sales, and the price/earnings/growth ratios.

Price/Earnings Ratio

The most common ratio used today to get a quick read on how the market place likes a stock is the price/earnings (P/E) ratio. The more optimistically the market views the prospects for a particular stock, the more likely it is prepared to bid up the price of the stock relative to its current earnings. Thus, the stocks of companies with favorable growth opportunities (often called growth stocks) tend to have high P/E ratios. Stocks with less promising earning potentials have lower P/Es.

The P/E ratio can be expressed as follows:

$$P/E = \frac{\text{Price per share}}{\text{Earnings per share}} = \frac{P_0}{\text{EPS}} \qquad \text{(Equation 7-7)}$$

In this equation, P_0 represents the price of the security today. The denominator may represent either last year's (actually the sum of the last 4 quarters) earnings per share, or next year's earnings per share. If the historical earnings are used, the number is referred to as the past P/E ratio, price-to-current-earnings ratio, or even the price-to-past-earnings ratio. If the future earnings are used, it is the price-to-future-earnings ratio or future P/E ratio. Most people are sloppy when using this term and simply say "P/E ratio." An investor should always be sure he or she understands which ratio is being described or discussed.

The problem with using the future P/E ratio is that it depends on whose forecast of earnings is being used. Forecasting earnings 1 year ahead is extremely complex. Ample research suggests that anyone who can accurately forecast a company's earnings 1 year in advance would make an incredible fortune in the market. So if all forecasts of future earnings are suspect, a price-to-future-earnings ratio has to be even more suspect. The preferred P/E ratio is the one that uses the prior year's earnings. There should never be any debate as to what the value of the price-to-past-earnings ratio is at any point in time.

To help us understand the meaning of the P/E ratio, let us relate it to the constant growth rate model. Let's start by restating the model to incorporate earnings in the numerator. Noting that by definition multiplying the earnings per share by the payout ratio produces the dividends per share easily does this. That is, the *payout ratio* is defined as the percentage of earnings that is paid out as dividends. In mathematical notation:

payout ratio

$$V_0 = E_0 \times m \times (1 + g)/(r - g)$$

where E_0 = last year's earnings
m = the payout ratio

Dividing through by last year's earnings produces the price-to-past-earnings ratio:

$$V_0/E_0 = m \times (1 + g)/(r - g) \qquad \text{(Equation 7-8)}$$

There are three critical observations to be noted in this equation. First, the lower the discount rate, all other things equal, the higher the P/E ratio. Remember, a low discount rate means that the company is considered less risky. Hence, the less risky a company is believed to be, the higher its P/E ratio will be.

Second, the higher the growth rate, all other things equal, the higher the P/E ratio. A higher growth rate means both a larger numerator and a smaller denominator. Simply put, the faster that investors see future earnings as growing, the more they are willing to pay today for a dollar's worth of current earnings.

The third observation is that the absolute values of the discount rate and the growth rate do not really matter so much as the spread between the two. It is this spread that is the primary driver of the P/E ratio. A small spread would likely indicate a company that is considered less risky than most and/or has unusually high prospects for rapidly growing its dividends. Who wouldn't like to own a stock like this! Of course, everyone would. Hence such a stock would have an unusually high P/E ratio.

As a practical matter, note that a P/E ratio cannot be computed when earnings equals zero. However, it would be incredibly rare for a company to have earnings of exactly zero, although it surely happens occasionally. Another practice is that the P/E ratio is normally not computed when a company loses money. A negative P/E is a nonsense number. Finally, some companies occasionally report earnings of one or a few pennies per share. Unless the company's stock price is also in the range, its P/E ratio may be extremely large.

There are lots of caveats associated with examining P/E ratios. For example, two companies that are otherwise identical may have different P/E ratios because they have different accounting procedures (both legitimate). One company may use FIFO (first-in, first-out) to value its inventory and cost of goods sold, and another may use LIFO (last-in, first-out). During inflationary periods, these two methods can dramatically alter a company's income statement (as well as their balance sheets).

Characteristics of Company's with High P/E Ratios

- Lower discount rate (that is, less risky)
- High growth rate
- Small spread between the discount rate and growth rate

Secular Trends in P/E Ratios

Another issue associated with P/E ratios is the fact that recognized blips in earnings may affect the ratio dramatically but not really affect the stock's price. Consider a company that has the following sequence of earnings:

2000	$2.45
2001	$2.52
2002	$2.48
2003	$ .22

Let's suppose that the low earnings in 2003 were due to a strike. The strike was resolved before the end of the year, and labor relations are now good at the company. In a situation such as this, the stock price may well not adjust much to the drop in earnings because the drop is considered unique, with no long-term consequences. If the stock price makes no significant change during the year 2003, then the P/E ratio would likely show a big jump. The jump is not due to investors suddenly thinking the company is a better deal. In fact, their overall opinion of the company may not have changed. The big jump would be due to the transitory drop in earnings. If expectations are correct, and earnings return to their normal level in the following year (2004), the P/E ratio would likely "fall" back to its original level. Naturally, the same scenario would apply in the reverse situation if there were a one-time windfall jump in earnings (say a huge lawsuit settlement) that was not expected to be repeated or have any effect on future earnings. In this case, the P/E would be lower in the current year, and then "rise" back to its normal level as earnings return to the normal level.

Price/Cash Flow Ratio

One of the problems with using a P/E ratio to get a sense of the relative value of a share of stock is that earnings can be relatively easily manipulated, particularly with the use of noncash expenses. Many security analysts argue that what matters more for a firm is the amount of cash flow the firm is generating, rather than what management says its earnings are. In this case, cash flow is defined as operating net cash flow, and is found on the statement of cash flows (discussed in the next chapter). The cash flow number in this case is obviously defined as cash flow per share.

cash flow

The major item that distinguishes earnings from cash flow is depreciation. Thus, many people simply think of *cash flow* as the sum of earnings plus depreciation. Naturally, any other noncash expenses would also be added to earnings.

Price/Free Cash Flow Ratio

An alternative to looking at share price relative to cash flow is to focus on share price relative to free cash flow. Free cash flow is defined as operating cash flow net of new investment.

Price/Sales Ratio

Another way of thinking about value that has become popular in recent years is the price/sales ratio, which is share price divided by sales per share (that is, annual sales divided by the number of shares outstanding). The advantage of this ratio over the P/E ratio is, as we noted above, that P/E ratios are meaningless when earnings are negative. The price/sales ratio is always positive (although in theory it could be negative if a company had more product returns in a year than it had in new sales). The price/sales ratio may also be more meaningful for start-up companies, which typically have negative earnings but a lot of growth potential. For start-up companies, market share may be more important than earnings, especially in markets where there is the potential for huge growth.

The major drawback to the price/sales ratio is that profit margins may vary by industry. Thus, industries with big profit margins would be expected to have higher price/sales ratios, and industries with small profit margins would have lower price/sales ratios. In fact, it is certainly possible to get a variety of price/sales ratios within the same industry that reflect differences in business strategy rather than differences in value. For example, one firm may have a high-volume, low-margin strategy (such as Kmart), and another firm in the same industry may have a low-volume, high-margin strategy (for example, Neiman Marcus). All other things being equal, one would expect the former to have the lower price/sales ratio. The lower ratio does not necessarily mean it is a better or worse strategy, just different.

Price/Earnings/Growth Ratio

PEG ratio

Another valuation ratio that has become popular in recent years is the ratio of the price/earnings ratio to a projected growth rate *(PEG ratio)*. The ratio is somewhat redundant in the sense that over time, dividends are expected to grow at the same rate as earnings. Hence, the same or similar growth rate is showing up in both the numerator (as the growth rate in dividends) and the denominator (as the growth rate in earnings). One of the major proponents of the PEG ratio has been Peter Lynch (former portfolio manager of the Fidelity Magellan Mutual Fund and considered by many as one of the most brilliant portfolio managers of the 20th century), in his book *One Up on Wall Street*.

VALUE STOCKS VERSUS GROWTH STOCKS

Many people like to use the above valuation ratios to help select stocks for investment consideration. Proof of this is that most stock screening calculators on the Internet include these ratios as some of the screening criteria. An example of such a calculator is shown in table 7-1.

TABLE 7-1
Sample Stock Screening Calculator

Company Name	Curr. Price	Price/ Book Value	Price/ Cash Flow	Price/ Free Cash Flow	Trailing P/E	Forward P/E (Curr. Yr.)
Meckler Corp.	26.23	7.5	15.73	31.97	19.04	14.65
Remcun Inc.	37.09	4.2	12.87	92.45	14.21	7.78
McLavich AG	13.50	5.2	14.22	51.99	16.45	45.51
Cornine Inc.	6.64	4.9	7.68	11.16	9.77	9.32
Nunwell Corp.	2.34	3.6	4.43	19.03	4.56	4.55

Of all of the market-price-based ratios discussed in the previous section, the P/E ratio is by far the most dominant in the minds of many people. In fact, a popular terminology that focuses strictly on P/E ratios has emerged among investors. That is, stocks with high P/E ratios are referred to as *growth stocks,* and stock with low P/E ratios are referred to as *value stocks.*[2]

growth stocks
value stocks

Growth is sometimes interpreted to mean growth in stock price, but it technically means growth in earnings. Thus, to say something is a growth stock simply means that it is a stock whose earnings are expected to grow at a high rate over the next few years. Such a stock is readily identifiable because it has a high P/E ratio.

The association of high growth in earnings with a high P/E ratio is easy to understand. In the formula for the trailing P/E ratio, repeated below, the growth rate term g stands for the expected growth rate of dividends.

$$V_0/E_0 = m \times (1 + g)/(r - g) \qquad \text{(Equation 7-8 repeated)}$$

However, as mentioned before, there is a strong correlation between earnings and dividends over time, and so the growth rate of dividends must necessarily follow the growth rate of earnings.

A value stock is one whose assets and earning capacity can be bought cheaply. Such a stock is readily identifiable because it has a low P/E ratio.

As with much of the stock market terminology, the above definitions for value and growth stocks are not necessarily universally agreed to. It is certainly possible for someone to proclaim a stock with a low P/E as being a growth stock, and another with a high P/E as being a value stock. Ultimately, the characteristics of value and growth are in the eye of the beholder.

The classification of what is a value stock and what is a growth stock is only the first step in an ongoing debate as to how well the market prices securities relative to their actual potentials for each of these two groups. That is, should investors concentrate on value stocks or growth stocks?

According to such well-known fundamental analysts as Benjamin Graham and John Templeton, the market frequently goes to extremes. These two suggested that the market tends to overestimate the growth prospects and underestimate the risks of some stocks (especially the highly touted growth stocks). As a result, the market accords them higher P/Es than their fundamentals warrant. The stocks of less exciting companies, in contrast, may be viewed by the market as having less attractive prospects than they actually do. Stocks that the market views too pessimistically would then end up with unrealistically low P/Es. Once the market realizes the true potentials of these stocks, the prices of low-P/E stocks should rise at a faster rate than the market averages, whereas the high-P/E stocks should do less well. Those who accept this line of reasoning prefer a portfolio that is heavily weighted toward low-P/E stocks and largely avoid stocks with high P/Es.

Growth-stock advocates, in contrast, have contended that stocks with rapid growth potentials are attractive investments even at relatively high prices. A high current P/E may not seem overpriced relative to future earnings, whereas low P/Es may accurately reflect poor potentials.

value investing
growth investing

These two views have alternated in popularity. For the period 1975 through year-end 1995, *value investing* (investing in below-average P/E stocks) as measured by the S&P/Barra indices led *growth investing* (investing in above-average P/E stocks) as measured by average annual returns. The average annual return for value investing came to 16.5 percent, compared to 14.0 percent for growth investing. In the latter 1990s, however, the trend shifted, and growth stocks have moved ahead of value stocks, with a 29.9 percent average annual return versus 25.9 percent for value stocks for the period 1995–1999.

One explanation for value investing's lagging performance is that the payoffs from these two investment disciplines tend to move in opposite directions as investor sentiment shifts. That is, value investing is the preferred style in some years, and in other years, growth investing is preferred.

Growth Investing

The companies that tend to grow the fastest are relatively young companies and companies whose products are new or who are in the process of developing new technologies. Yet these are also the companies that tend to be quite risky. While a fair number of new companies may grow at a rate of 20 percent or more during their first few years of existence, a sizable number also go bankrupt. Thus, the same companies that are potentially high-growth companies are also high-risk companies.

Furthermore, very high rates of growth are not sustainable over the long haul. Although it may not be too unusual for a company to grow at 20 percent or more during its first few years of existence, it is unrealistic to expect that rate of growth to persist. As businesses mature, their rate of growth tends to level off. On average, businesses tend to grow at the same rate as the overall economy.

Therefore, while it makes sense for growth stocks to have higher P/E multiples than other stocks, these multiples should be based on realistic assumptions about the firm's long-term growth prospects. If a P/E ratio appears to be based on the assumption that a new company's high earnings growth rate will persist indefinitely, it seems logical to conclude that the stock is overvalued. The two-stage growth-rate model presented in appendix 7A shows the mathematics behind this point.

Much of the fluctuation in stock prices reflects a change in the consensus P/E ratio. The change in P/E ratios, in turn, reflects changing views within the market regarding each firm's growth potential. Let us therefore examine more closely just how much differing growth expectations can affect a firm's P/E ratio. The following example focuses on the impact of growth.

Example: Assume a firm's payout ratio (m) is .5 and the appropriate discount rate is 12 percent; a long-term growth rate (g) of 7 percent (3 percent real and 4 percent inflation) would produce an average P/E of $0.5/(.12 - .07) = 10$. If a particular company's g is 8 percent, its P/E would be 12.5. A company with a g of 9 percent would produce a P/E of 16.7, and a g of 10 percent would imply a P/E of 25. If a firm's g is as high as 11 percent, the P/E would rise to 50.

As the example shows, relatively small changes in the expected long-term growth rate can have a dramatic impact on the P/E ratio. This impact is particularly great when the P/E is already relatively large. A more realistic example would take account of the tendency for higher values of g to correspond to lower payouts and greater risk premiums (and thus higher discount rates). In his extensive research on security valuation approaches, Aswath Damodaran discusses a number of problems associated with uses of P/E ratios, noting that the volatility of earnings can cause the P/E ratio to change dramatically from period to period.[3]

Value Investing

Advocates of low-P/E stocks note that stock prices rise dramatically when both earnings and P/E multiples increase. Quite possibly, a P/E multiple may more easily increase from 5 to 10 than from 10 to 20, and it will have an easier time growing from 10 to 20 than from 20 to 40. That is, the market may well become more nervous about the price of a stock as its P/E rises. Thus, low-P/E stocks may have a better chance of achieving truly outstanding performances than high-P/E stocks, which may be more likely to be fully priced already.

Example:	Suppose a company that sells initially at a P/E of 5 experiences per-share earnings growth of 20 percent per year for 10 years. Its earnings will be six times as high as when it started. Such an earnings growth is likely to lead to an increase in the P/E multiple. Rapid past growth often leads to expectations of rapid future growth. If the P/E of this company doubles, its stock will sell for more than 12 times its earlier price.

The advocates of low-P/E stocks further contend that high-P/E stocks are particularly vulnerable to disappointing news.

Example:	Suppose a growth stock currently earns $2 per share and sells for $50 (P/E of 25). If in the following year it earns only $1.50, a continuation of its P/E of 25 would correspond to a price of $37.50. On the other hand, if the poor earnings led to lower growth expectations and a lower P/E, the price decline would be much steeper. Thus, for example, a fall to a P/E of 10 would imply a price of $15, or a decline of 70 percent.

Combining P/E Ratios with Other Factors

Although evidence suggests that low-P/E stocks tend to be underpriced, a more basic relationship may be at work. For example, a disproportionate number of low-P/E stocks may be the issues of relatively small companies.

Firm Size

Suppose that the stocks of relatively small companies tend to outperform the market as many believe. Size, not P/E, might then be the true factor to explain the apparent effect of a low P/E. Indeed, Reinganum found that portfolios selected on both P/E and firm size tended to generate abnormal returns (above the risk-adjusted market level). The P/E effect largely disappeared, however, when there was a control for size.[4] Other studies found similar results.

The studies hypothesized that the small-firm effect was due to a misspecification of the CAPM because CAPM formed the basis for adjusting returns for risk. The positive abnormal returns may simply have been a reward for the extra effort of analyzing small firms (the basis of the neglected-firms hypothesis discussed below). The apparent abnormal returns may have been due to underestimating their risks, or due to lower trading activity (a measure of liquidity). Still other researchers have reported that the magnitude of the small-firm effect was reduced but could not be fully explained away when adjustments were made for the effects of risk premium, tax effects, benchmark error, incorrect assumptions about investor risk aversion, nonsynchronous trading, and earnings yield.

Analyst Neglect (Neglected-Firm Effect)

The abnormal returns of small firms could be due to either (1) superior performance relative to their fundamentals (current profitability, apparent growth potential, and so on) or (2) underpricing relative to those fundamentals.

Most institutional investors prefer to invest in large firms. They can make meaningful investments in large firms without having an undue effect on these companies' stock prices. Similarly, analysts tend to concentrate on larger firms and therefore draw attention to such stocks. Several studies have found that stocks which analysts ignore (whether large or small) tend to outperform the more closely followed issues. Accordingly, a number of mutual funds have sought to exploit this small-firm/neglected-firm effect by assembling portfolios of these companies.

The Low-Price Effect

low-price effect

The results of several studies imply that stocks with low per-share prices tend to generate returns above the market averages. Moreover, this *low-price effect* may well be stronger than both the P/E and the size effects. Exactly why low-priced stocks seem to perform so well is subject to much debate. There are three rationales offered to support this phenomenon. The first is that low-priced stocks are generally believed to be more risky than the average stock. Thus, their higher average return may reflect greater risk. Still, the returns of these stocks continue to be higher when standard risk adjustment procedures are applied. Perhaps low-priced stocks are even more risky than their estimated betas imply. In particular, they may contain a substantially greater amount of nonmarket, and thus diversifiable, risk. We have already seen that, contrary to capital market theory, nonmarket risk is generally accorded a premium. That is, stocks with high levels of nonmarket risk are priced to offer higher expected returns than otherwise similar stocks with lower levels of nonmarket risk.

Furthermore, the market-determined risk premium is a function of perceived risk. If investors collectively believe that, all else being equal, low-priced stocks are riskier than higher-priced stocks, then their risk premium and required rate of return will reflect that belief.

The second rationale is that low-priced stocks are also more expensive to trade. The bid-ask spread of low-priced stocks tends to be relatively high. Stocks that are more expensive to trade probably need to offer higher expected returns to attract investors. In addition, the market for low-priced stock may be thinner, so low-priced stock will be less liquid than higher-priced stock.

The third reason is the general aversion of many investors, especially institutional investors, to low capitalization and low-priced shares. The perceived quality of a stock is thought to be associated with the level of its per-share price. If many investors shun a significant segment of the stock market, that group of stocks may tend to be underpriced. The financial performance of some of the group may eventually lead them to achieve quality status and institutional acceptance.

Research by Fama and French in 1995 found that stocks of small firms and those with high book-to-market ratios (which will be discussed in chapter 8) provided above-average returns. They point out, however, that there was evidence that risk factors may have been left out of the simple capital asset pricing model. Fama and French suggest a three-factor model in which the expected return on a stock depends on its exposure to market risk, size, and book-to-market value.[5]

Takeover Candidates

Buying a stock just before it becomes an acquisition target is one of the few ways of making a quick profit in the stock market. Acquiring firms almost always offer a substantial premium over the preannouncement price of the target firm. Moreover, takeover candidates are sometimes bid up in a competition between would-be owners. At times, stock market activity tends to focus on the possibility of a takeover. In the 1980s a number of investors (often called raiders) became well known for their records of attempted takeovers. Only a relatively small fraction, however, of takeover attempts actually succeed in wresting control from the existing management. Sometimes the target firm buys back the raider's stock at a premium over the market price *(greenmail)*. At other times, another buyer is brought into the picture by management (the *white knight*), or another raider eventually outbids the initial raider. At still other times, a friendly outsider (the *white squire*) is sold a substantial minority position. Occasionally, the target tries to acquire the raider company (the *Pac Man defense*).

greenmail

white knight

white squire

Pac Man defense

leveraged buyout (LBO)

Regardless of the buyer (white knight, target company, or another raider), the initial raider usually sells out at a profit. At still other times, the initial raider succeeds in taking control. At that point, it may do one of several things. It may, for example, seek to restructure the company in order to extract value for itself and the other shareholders. Such restructurings usually increase the firm's debt and use the borrowed funds to buy out the public shareholders, which is known as a *leveraged buyout (LBO)*. In other instances, all shareholders may be paid a substantial sum per share (partial liquidating dividend). Once in control, the raider may seek to sell the firm off a piece at a time or as a package. Sometimes selling off unprofitable divisions can make the remainder of the business more profitable, so shareholders' wealth is increased by these divestitures. In some circumstances, the raider may settle in and run the acquisition as a going concern.

Another group of investors, called risk arbitrageurs, looks to profit from potential and attempted takeovers. They assess the current stock price relative to the proposed or expected terms of the takeover and the likelihood of a successful acquisition. Depending on that assessment, they may purchase shares of the target firm in hopes of selling later at a profit.

Implications of Takeover Trading for Individual Investors

Several studies have examined the activities of raiders and risk arbitrageurs. One study found that, when a firm acquired enough stock (5 percent or more) to file a Schedule 13D, the target's price generally rose, probably in anticipation of a takeover attempt. Schedule 13D, which is required by the SEC, discloses beneficial ownership of certain registered equity securities. Any person or group that acquires beneficial ownership of more than 5 percent of a class of registered equity securities must file a Schedule 13D, reporting the acquisition, together with other information, within 10 days after the acquisition. Furthermore, the market price of the stock of a target firm acts as a rather accurate predictor of the probability that the takeover attempt will succeed. Thus, the activity of risk arbitrageurs generally drives the stock price toward the terms of a takeover that is likely to go through but not toward the terms of one that is likely to fail. Risk arbitrageurs are able to obtain useful information on the probability of a

---

Characteristics of Possibly Undervalued Securities

- Low P/E
- Small capitalization
- Neglect by investment analysts
- Low per-share price
- Unrecognized takeover candidates

successful takeover and then earn substantial returns by trading on that information. Such traders not only make profits on their own investments but also generally enhance the wealth of the other shareholders in the firms that they target by driving up the price of the stock.

FORECASTING WITH P/E RATIOS

P/E ratios are frequently used in forecasting models. One can forecast the entire market with a P/E-based model, or one can forecast an individual stock with a P/E-based model. Let us consider each.

Forecasting the Stock Market

A forecast of "the market" is actually a forecast of a specific market index. The various common indices were discussed earlier, as well as the distinctions among these indices. The level of stock prices is the product of the market's average P/E ratio and its average earnings per share (or the corresponding earnings for the index). A forecast of the market could thus be decomposed into two tasks: forecasting the earnings of the market (or an index) and forecasting its corresponding P/E ratio.

Forecasting the Market P/E

Many analysts predict the market's earnings and then derive a forecast for the market's price level by applying their earnings forecast to the current market P/E ratio.

Example:	In mid-1987, the NYSE Composite Index stood at about 180 with a P/E of about 21 and most recent 12-month earnings of $8.60. If year-ahead earnings are expected to be $10, a P/E of 21 implies an index value of 210.

Such a simple approach, however, ignores the possibility that the market P/E may change. It often does. Indeed, the market did change dramatically shortly after June 1987. The great stock market crash of October 1987 saw the market fall by more than one-third in the space of a few weeks. By late November, the NYSE index was down to around 135. That level corresponded to a P/E of 16. Had the NYSE index generated 1988 earnings of $10, a P/E of 16 would imply a value for the index of around 160.

Recall the determinants of the P/E reflected in equation 7-8:

$$V_0/E_0 = m \times (1 + g)/(r - g) \qquad \text{(Equation 7-8 repeated)}$$

Thus, the market P/E ratio is a function of m, the dividend payout ratio; r, the appropriate discount rate; and g, the expected growth rate in dividends. The overall market dividend payout ratio has averaged close to or somewhat above .5. The variations relative to that average are largely a response to departures from the normal growth in earnings.

The long-run growth rate in the economy is around 3 percent to 4 percent in real (adjusted-for-inflation) terms. Although the growth in earnings will vary greatly from year to year, the long-term growth rate will be similar to that of the economy. The growth rate in nominal terms would tend to be increased by the inflation rate. That is, the expected nominal growth rate should approximately equal the long-term real growth rate plus the expected inflation rate. In periods of rapid inflation, however, the nominal growth in earnings is likely to be somewhat less than the inflation rate plus the long-term real growth rate. Rapid inflation tends to depress the real value of earnings and discourages investment in long-term growth (discussed in more detail in the next section).

The appropriate discount rate is a function of several factors. Suppliers of capital seek a return that will compensate them for both risk and the expected rate of inflation. Thus, r should equal the real risk-free rate plus a premium for risk and a premium to compensate for expected inflation. A real risk-free rate of 3 percent and risk premium of 4 percent would produce a market discount rate of 7 percent plus the expected inflation rate.

Note that inflation plays a role in all three components of the P/E equation. A rise in the inflation rate tends to depress m, thereby reducing the P/E. For example, profit sources, such as sales from inventories carried on the books at long-out-of-date cost levels, tend to be greater at high inflation rates. Firms are unlikely to increase their dividend rates when their earnings increases are expected to be temporary.

A rise in the inflation rate also tends to increase both r and g, but the impact is greater on r. Thus, (r − g) tends to increase as inflation rises, thereby reducing the P/E. Overall, an increase in expected inflation tends to decrease the numerator and increase the denominator of the P/E ratio equation, thereby tending to lower its overall value.

It is important to remember that the risk premium and its impact on the required rate of return (discount rate) are based on perceived risk. Although it takes time for the dividend payout ratio, growth rate, or even the inflation rate to change, investors' perceptions of riskiness can change rapidly, often in response to a single piece of information, or even a rumor that turns out to have no factual basis. Investors tend to overreact to news (especially bad news), and the market sometimes reacts to events that have no economic significance. The volatility of perceived risk applies to the market as a whole, as well as to individual firms. In fact, it might be safe to say that one of the most powerful causes of rapid market declines, such as the one that occurred on October 19, 1987, was a sudden increase in investors' perception of market risk.

Steps to Obtain the Market P/E Multiple

- Estimate the market's overall dividend payout ratio (m) from past data, the stage of the business cycle, and expected inflation rates.
- Estimate the aggregate stock market discount rate (r) as the sum of the real risk-free rate, the expected inflation rate, and the market risk premium. Alternatively, add the appropriate risk premium to the current nominal (no inflation adjustment) risk-free rate (for example, the rate of return on T-bills).
- Forecast the nominal long-term growth rate in the market's earnings (g). The real long-term growth rate is largely a function of the stage of the business cycle. The nominal rate is the sum of the expected long-term real growth rate and a percentage (close to but probably less than 1) of the expected inflation rate.
- Apply the values for m, k, and g to equation 7-8 to obtain the forecasted market P/E.

Forecasting a Specific Stock

This same basic approach for forecasting the market can be applied to individual companies. That is, the investor can direct his or her analysis toward forecasting a company's earnings and its P/E ratio. The product of these forecasts is then a prediction of its stock price. These forecasts should be based on an understanding of the company's competitive position, management quality, and financial soundness, which will be discussed in the next chapter.

Various approaches can be used to forecast the company's P/E. One method examines the historical relationship between the company's and the market's P/Es. The forecasted change in the market P/E can then be applied to the company's current P/E value.

A second P/E estimate can be obtained by using the predicted change in the industry P/E. Finally, equation 7-8 can, with appropriate inputs, be used to derive a prediction for the company's P/E. That is, values for the payout ratio, required return, and expected growth can be estimated and applied to the equation to generate the forecast. Estimated values for these factors can be derived both from industry estimates and from an analysis of the specifics of the company.

Keep in mind that this is only an approximation because it assumes that the company's dividend payout ratio, growth rate, and required rate of return remain constant over time.

The forecasted P/E is then multiplied with the per-share earnings forecast. The result of this process is a forecast for the company's stock price. Several of

---

Approaches to Forecasting the Company's P/E

- Utilize the historical relation between the company's and the market's P/E, then apply the forecasted change in the market P/E to the current company P/E value.
- Apply the predicted change in the industry P/E to the current company P/E.
- Use the P/E equation (equation 7-8) to derive a prediction for the company's P/E.

---

these forecasts can be obtained by using different earnings and P/E forecasts. Comparing the current price of the stock with the forecasts should indicate whether the stock is appropriately priced.

To summarize, one logical approach to forecasting the average level of a company's stock price is to forecast its earnings and P/E multiple and take the product of the result.

INFLATION–STOCK MARKET RELATIONSHIP

In recent years, inflation has been negligible, and as a result, there has been little in the way of discussion of the impact of inflation on stock prices. However, during the 1970's through the mid-1990's, inflation rates were high and volatile, and at times were in the double-digit range. Changes in the inflation rate appeared to have dramatic impacts on market prices, and thus the relationship between inflation and market prices was a subject of keen interest. Because of the possibility of the return of high rates of inflation, it is important that the financial planner have a good understanding of the relationship between inflation and stock prices.

Some people see inflation as a purely monetary phenomenon. According to this view, inflationary pressures affect prices but little else. Those who accept this line of reasoning expect investors to seek to maximize their expected risk-adjusted real return without regard to the inflation rate. In their view, inflation just reduces the real (after-inflation) return of anything in which they invest. Thus, investors would choose their investments and manage their portfolios without taking account of the potential impact of inflation.

Others see the inflation rate as having an impact that goes well beyond just affecting the price level. These people believe that inflation plays an important role in the determination of the level of economic activity and that it can have rather different effects on the various components of the economy. As a result, investors would consider the inflation protection of various types of investments. Thus, the appeal of some assets may depend on the expected long-term inflation rate. Investors who were concerned about increases in the inflation rate would shift from less inflation-resistant to more inflation-resistant investments.

Aside from its impact on prices, volatile inflation rates may increase the uncertainty in the overall economy, and in the stock market in particular. Investors' propensity to spend (particularly on durables) would be affected by what they expect their real returns to be. Corporations would be less willing to enter into long-term contracts and to commit to long-term expansion, when there is substantial uncertainty as to what future prices and interest rates will be. This uncertainty itself can have an adverse effect on the stock market.

Simplistic Views of the Impact of Inflation

One view of the impact of inflation is that it is partially incorporated into security returns each year. To quantify this view, think of the return on stocks as being determined by the following function of inflation (measured by x):

$$r = a + bx$$

where   r = rate of return or yield
        a = a constant value
        b = some positive number less than one
        x = inflation rate

Thus, if a = 3 percent and b = .7, then an inflation rate of 5 percent would imply a nominal (no adjustment for inflation) stock market return of

$$3\% + .7\ (5\%) = 6.5\%$$

Such a nominal return corresponds to a real return of

$$(1.065/1.05) - 1 = .0143\ \text{or}\ 1.43\%$$

A real return of 1.43 percent is positive but less than the real return would be at lower inflation rates. This type of behavior relative to the inflation rate would imply that stocks acted as a partial hedge against inflation.

A more sophisticated view of the impact of inflation takes a much longer-range perspective. According to this viewpoint, average long-run stock returns will generally exceed the rise in the general price level. However, for short-run periods, nominal returns may be below the inflation rate. Eventually, however, nominal returns will catch up with and exceed the increase in the price level. If markets behave as this perspective implies, then the real value of capital would tend to be preserved in spite of the inflation rate, although the market would be affected adversely (if temporarily) by high and/or rising inflation rates. In spite of the experience in the 1970s with rapid inflation and poor stock market performance, and in the early 1990s when stock returns were mediocre, the view persists that stocks will still protect investors from inflation in the long run. The work of Jeremy Siegel at the Wharton School of the University of Pennsylvania has reinforced the view that stocks are the best investment in the long run.[6]

Theoretical Underpinnings of Stock Market–Inflation Hedge Hypothesis

To provide effective short- or long-run inflation protection, companies must increase their profits (as measured in nominal terms) or increase their efficiency (that is, lower costs). In periods of rising prices, their own costs are almost certain to be increasing unless offset by productivity gains. Thus, one way that firms might be able to sustain their profitability is by raising prices. Because inflation represents an overall increase in the price level, companies should generally be able to increase their prices commensurately with the rate of inflation without losing market share to competitors, who are likely to be raising their prices at the same time. The ability of stocks to withstand the adverse impact of an inflationary environment depends on the underlying company's ability to maintain its profitability. Stocks represent ownership of real assets. The replacement value of these assets and their ability to generate income may well rise with the price level. If firms are able to raise their prices sufficiently, the real (inflation-adjusted) value of dividends and share prices may keep pace with price-level increases. A number of considerations, however, limit firms' abilities to raise prices by enough to preserve investment values.

For example, various aspects of our tax system tend to penalize investment income at high inflation rates. First, the IRS requires that companies use historical costs in computing their profits. As a result, they must pay taxes on sums that reflect the difference between the historical cost and the replacement value of inventory, plant, and equipment.

Example 1:	Suppose a company is in a competitive environment that prevents price increases on its own products. The company produces a widget for a recorded cost of $1, based on now out-of-date materials costs. If it then sells the widget for $2, the company must report a profit of $1 ($2 – $1), even if the next widget would cost $1.50 (based on up-to-date materials prices) to produce.

Example 2:	A company's plant and equipment has a book value of $1,000,000. It would cost $3,000,000 today to replace that equipment. Nonetheless, if the plant and equipment is being depreciated on a straight-line basis over a 10-year life, then the depreciation charge that can be reported is limited to $100,000. Note that when it comes time to physically replace the assets, the cost of replacement will be much more than what is represented by this $100,000 depreciation charge.

A high inflation rate increases these differences between accounting costs of goods sold and the forward-looking replacement costs of goods sold. Similarly, a high inflation rate will tend to increase the tax on these reported (phantom) profits. As a result, the real after-tax component of reported profits tends to fall as prices increase. Of course, use of LIFO (last-in, first-out) accounting may reduce or eliminate the difference in accounting cost of goods and replacement cost of goods sold.

Second, inflation tends to push noninstitutional investors into higher marginal tax brackets, further increasing the tax penalty on investments. This effect was a severe problem when our tax system had 11 brackets with a top rate of 50 percent or even higher. The reduced number of tax brackets and lower maximum rate under the Tax Reform Act of 1986, somewhat reversed by the Budget Reconciliation Act of 1993, as well as the reductions in tax rates contained in the Tax Reform Act of 2001, lessen but do not eliminate this effect. (Taxes are discussed in chapter 13.)

Third, individuals must pay taxes on sums (dividends and capital gains) that often contain a substantial inflation component. Thus, even if the before-tax return rose point for point with the inflation rate, the after-tax return would not.

Example:	A one-third tax rate applied to a 3 percent nominal return and zero inflation (a 3 percent real return before taxes) provides a 2 percent after-tax real return. A 6 percent nominal return with a 3 percent inflation rate produces a real after-tax return of only 1 percent. A 9 percent nominal return and 6 percent inflation rate yields a real after-tax return of 0 percent. For nominal returns above 9 percent, a 3 percent before-tax real return corresponds to a negative real after-tax return.

We might suspect that cost and price increases of x percent would (neglecting tax effects) approximately maintain a firm's financial position. In fact, however, higher prices and costs generally require a contemporaneous and disproportionate increase in capital to support inventories, accounts receivables, and new plant and equipment. Moreover, if higher inflation rates are associated with higher interest rates, both the amount and the cost of financing tend to increase with inflation. Thus, to offset the effect of taxes on nominal profits and to finance the increased capital requirements at higher interest rates, prices must be raised proportionately more than the increase in the direct costs. To offset the increased retained earnings requirement (needed to support the additional borrowings) and the investor's inflation-imposed tax burden, prices may have to rise more than proportionately.

Many firms are unable to raise prices sufficiently to recapture their increased production costs, however, to say nothing of increasing them sufficiently to offset tax and financing effects. Increased competition (including that from substitute products whose costs of production may be less affected by inflation), the existence of long-term contracts with customers that lock in a purchase price, or an environment of reduced demand and excess capacity may limit a firm's ability to raise prices and retain the same volume of sales.

International competition may hold some prices down, depending on the interplay of such factors as domestic versus international inflation rates, changes in exchange rates, tariffs and import quotas, and foreign competitors' pricing responses. Similar considerations influence domestic exporters' ability to pass their higher costs on internationally.

Finally, Modigliani and Cohn argue that investors make two basic errors in pricing securities in the presence of inflation.[7] First, investors are said to

---

Inflation's Adverse Stock Market Impact

- Tax impact
  - Corporate taxes are based on historical costs of plant and equipment and inventories.
  - Investors are pushed into high tax brackets.
  - Individual taxes are applied to nominal dividend and interest income.
- Cost impact
  - Greater capital is needed for new plant and equipment and for inventories.
  - Higher interest costs are incurred on borrowings.
- Price impact
  - There is resistance to price increases.
  - Competition from substitutes may increase.
  - International competition may increase.

capitalize equity earnings incorrectly by comparing the current cash earnings of equity with nominal rather than real bond returns. Bond returns are fixed until maturity, whereas profits and dividends attributable to stocks tend to rise over time. Focusing on stock returns as if they are expected to be constant rather than rise will cause investors to undervalue them. Second, Modigliani and Cohn contend that investors have failed to take proper account of the impact of inflation on the real value of corporate debt. Over time, inflation tends to reduce the real value of outstanding debt. Thus, corporations with substantial amounts of debt outstanding will, in effect, see that debt decline (at least in real terms) in times of rapid inflation. According to Modigliani and Cohn, these two alleged mispricing effects reduced the S&P 500 stock index by 50 percent in 1977. In 1982, a low point for stocks, P. Cagan asserted that the market seemed to be as underpriced as it was alleged to be in 1977.[8] The market more than tripled over the next 5 years. Perhaps the market was mispriced and later realized its error. On the other hand, the crash of 1987 indicates that the market can also be mispriced on the upside.

Impact of Inflation on Security Returns

Table 7-2 shows how $1 would have grown, in both nominal and inflation-adjusted terms, between 1926 and 2002, if all dividend or interest income had been reinvested in each of five asset classes. Of course, these investments differ in degrees of risk, which accounts for much of the differences in their respective returns. A dollar invested in the lowest-risk investment, Treasury bills, would have grown to an inflation-adjusted value of $1.67 by 2002; in long-term Treasury bonds, to $4.28; and in corporate bonds, to $6.05 in real terms. Common stocks were far and away the best inflation-adjusted investment, with $707.44 for smaller firms and $303.09 for the large-company stocks.

We can also calculate the compound and average annual rate of return from the five asset classes for each year over the 77-year period. This rate reflects both cash receipts, such as dividends and interest, and capital gains or losses realized during the specific year. Table 7-2 also shows the average of the 77 annual rates of return for each asset class. From 1926 to 2002, the Treasury bills provided 3.79 percent per year in nominal terms and 0.71 percent in real terms. The average rate of inflation over the period was 3.05 percent per year. The average annual return on common stocks as measured by the large company stocks was a 10.2 percent nominal rate and a 6.94 percent real return. This rate of return included an average risk premium of 6.18 percent. As might be expected, the nominal rate and real returns for smaller stocks were higher, with a higher risk premium of 8.05 percent. Clearly, over the 77-year period, stocks provided a good hedge against inflation.

TABLE 7-2
Cumulative Values and Returns, 1926–2002

	Cumulative Value of $1 with All Interest and Dividends Reinvested		Mean Annual Rates of Return		
	Nominal	Real	Nominal	Real	Risk Premium
Treasury bills	$ 15.64	$ 1.67	3.79%	0.71%	—
Long-term government bonds	40.22	4.28	5.45	2.33	1.60
Corporate bonds	56.77	6.05	5.90	2.76	2.03
Large-company stocks	2,845.63	303.09	10.20	6.94	6.18
Small-company stocks	6,640.79	707.44	12.15	8.83	8.05
Inflation	9.39	—	3.05	—	—

Source: Calculated using information and data presented in Ibbotson Investment Analysis Software, © 2003 Ibbotson Associates, Inc. All rights reserved. Used with permission.

Table 7-3 shows nominal and real returns for a recent 20-year period (1983–2002), 10-year period (1993–2002), and 5-year period (1998–2002). Most notable in the table is the negative return for large-company stocks in both real and nominal terms for the 5-year period. Although stocks have been an effective inflation hedge—earning a rate higher than inflation—in the vast majority of 5-year periods, the 1998–2002 period serves as a reminder that stock is not always an effective short-term inflation hedge. Indeed, in the 77 one-year periods from 1926–2002, large-company stock has provided a negative real return in 26 years, which is about one-third of the time. The other asset categories have demonstrated comparable numbers of positive and negative real returns. Keep in mind, though, that over extended periods of time stock outperforms debt securities in both nominal and real terms.

TABLE 7-3
Rates of Return, 1983–2002, 1993–2002, 1998–2002

	1983–2002		1993–2002		1998–2002	
	Nominal	Real	Nominal	Real	Nominal	Real
Treasury bills	5.65%	2.43%	4.37%	1.83%	4.17%	1.75%
Long-term government bonds	11.12	7.72	9.67	7.01	8.85	6.31
Long-term corporate bonds	10.99	7.61	8.75	6.11	8.29	5.77
Large-company stocks	12.71	9.27	9.33	6.68	−0.59	−2.90
Small-company stocks	11.57	8.16	11.58	8.87	4.31	1.88
Inflation	3.15	—	2.49	—	2.38	—

Assessment of the Evidence

Overall, stocks tend to provide long-term inflation protection and possibly some short-term protection from anticipated inflation. For investors to know that stock price increases may eventually offset inflation is small comfort, however, if they must sell before the market rebounds. If unexpected inflation rate increases depress stock prices, the real value of investments falls both with the rise in the price level and with the decline in the position's nominal value.

OTHER EQUITY INSTRUMENTS

When the term "equity investment" is mentioned, one immediately thinks of common stock, as this is the primary equity investment. However, there are other equity and equity-related investments. These include straight preferred stock, convertible preferred stock, convertible bonds, rights, and warrants. All of these except straight preferred stock were introduced in chapter 1. Nonetheless, we will expand our discussion on each of these instruments, except for the convertibles, which are discussed in more detail in the chapter on options (chapter 11).

Straight Preferred Stock

Although preferred stock is a type of equity security, it has much in common with debt instruments. For example, a company may issue more than one class of preferred stock, just like it can have a large number of bond issues.

The issuer of the preferred stock is not required to declare dividends. However, the payment of preferred stock dividends is required before common stock dividends can be paid. Moreover, most preferreds are cumulative, which means that accumulated (unpaid) dividends must be made up before any common stock dividend can be paid. Thus, most companies' preferred stock dividends are almost as dependable as their bond interest. In addition, many preferred stock charters call for the preferred stockholders to gain voting rights if a certain number of consecutive dividend payments are missed, giving preferred stockholders some control over the management of the company. The preferreds of a weak company may, however, be almost as risky as its common stock. Some preferred issues may pay an extra dividend payment if earnings or common stock dividends are high enough, and these are known as **participating preferred stocks**. *participating preferred stocks*. Each participating preferred stock has a specific formula as to how the extra dividends would be computed.

In the event of bankruptcy, preferred stockholders are residual claimants only one step ahead of common stockholders and behind everyone else. Unless the creditors' claims are fully satisfied, nothing will be left for either class of stockholders.

Unlike corporate interest payments, 70 percent of the dividends received by a domestic corporation (incorporated in the United States) from another domestic corporation are tax-exempt. This exemption applies to both common stock dividends and preferred dividends. Moreover, the exemption may be 80 percent or even 100 percent of dividends received if the receiving corporation owns specified percentages of the stock of the paying corporation.

This tax-exemption feature has always made straight preferred stock popular with corporate investors. In fact, straight preferred stock usually trades at prices that reflect this tax exemption. Because their tax advantage is available only to corporations, one of the few things that we used to be able to say definitively in the investment world was that individual investors should avoid holding any straight preferred stock. However, the recent change in the taxation of dividend income for shareholders (to be discussed in chapter 13) may have now made it reasonable for individuals to again consider investing in straight preferred stock over bonds.

Rights

rights offering

In some states, corporations are only allowed to sell new stock with a rights offering. In the rest of the states, it is a choice. A *rights offering* to existing shareholders allows a company to raise additional capital and avoid diluting the current shareholders' positions. A rights offering begins with the company simply giving to all current investors a certain number of rights for each share held. Often, this is on a one-to-one basis. Thus, an investor holding 300 shares at the time of a rights offering would receive 300 rights from the company.

A right specifies an exercise price (the same concept as the strike price, which will be discussed in chapter 11) and an expiration date, after which the rights become worthless. Shareholders who want to maintain their proportional ownership in the company can simply exercise their rights. For everyone else, the decision of whether to exercise the rights or sell them should be based on their opinions of the attractiveness of the company for additional investment. Thus, some may prefer to sell their rights on the open market, thus effectively reducing their investment in the company. Others will exercise their rights, thus increasing their investment in the company.

When companies issue rights, it is for the explicit purpose of selling new shares of common stock. Thus, the exercise price will be set safely below the current market price. As a result, rights will trade at prices that are about the same as their intrinsic values. Rights trading is, however, relatively speculative because most rights have a short lifespan—often only a few weeks.

Although one right is usually issued for each outstanding share, each right typically provides the holder an option to acquire a fraction of a new share of stock. Thus, the holder of 100 shares of the underlying stock might receive 100 rights that would entitle him or her to buy 10 additional shares.

Cum-Rights and Ex-Rights

A rights offering announcement specifies a date of record for people who own the stock to receive the rights. Up to that day, the stock trades cum-rights. After that date, the stock sells ex-rights (no rights attached). Because it takes 3 business days to settle stock trades (that is, legally transfer the trade), the cum rights trading stops 3 days before the record date. Table 7-4 shows the typical timing of a rights offer.

TABLE 7-4 Typical Timing of a Rights Offering		
Date	Day	Event
January 14	Monday	Rights offering announced for shareholders of record on Monday, February 4
January 28	Monday	Last day to buy the shares cum-rights
January 29	Tuesday	Shares go ex-rights
February 1	Friday	Actual record date

Rights Valuation Formulas

The value of the underlying stock depends on whether it is selling cum- or ex-rights. The stock's price adjusts on the day it goes ex-rights because subsequent buyers will not receive the rights.

Valuation during the Cum-Rights Period. Assume that buying 10 shares of XYZ at $40 gives the buyer enough rights to buy one additional share at $38. Accordingly, the buyer can buy 10 + 1 shares of stock for $438:

$$(10 \times \$40) + (1 \times \$38) = \$438$$

The market will recognize that the stock price should decline since new shares are being offered below the current market price. The shares' average price is $438 divided by 11, or $39.82, and the intrinsic value of one right is $40 minus $39.82, or $.18. An owner of 100 shares should be able to sell his or her 100 rights for $18 (minus commission). Thus, the intrinsic value of one right during the cum-rights period is determined by the following formula:

$$\text{Instrinsic value of one right during cum-rights period} = \frac{\text{Market price of stock} - \text{Subscription price}}{\text{Number of rights needed to subscribe to one share} + \text{One share}}$$

Applying this formula to the above example yields

$$\text{Intrinsic value} = (\$40 - \$38)/(10 + 1) = \$2.00/11 = \$.18$$

Once the stock starts trading ex-rights, the rights will have their own market value. The initial market value is approximately equal to the intrinsic value of the right at the end of the cum-rights period. The actual market price of the rights during the ex-rights period may be slightly higher than its intrinsic value, but it would never be lower.

Continuing the example, assume that the buyer owns 100 shares of XYZ at $40 per share for a total of $4,000. The buyer has two choices with the rights offering. First, the buyer can exercise his or her 100 rights and buy 10 more shares for $38 per share for a total cash outlay of $380. At this point, the buyer has invested in this company a total of $4,380. The shares would be valued at $39.82 per share times 110 shares for a total of $4,380. In other words, the buyer's wealth would not have changed.

Second, the buyer can sell his or her rights. At a price of $.18 per right, the 100 rights would sell for $18. Meanwhile, the buyer's shares would decline in price from $40 to $39.82, making the value of the shares decline from $4,000 to $3,982. However, the $18 received for the rights exactly offsets the decline in share value, so the buyer's wealth would not have changed (omitting, of course, the impact of the commission).

Of course, there is a third option—letting the rights expire. In this case, wealth would decline from $4,000 to $3,982, or by $18, which is the value of the rights.

Note that the value of a right varies with the market price of the stock. If market forces cause the stock's price to fall below the subscription price at the subscription date, the rights will expire worthless.

Valuation during the Ex-Rights Period. As already noted, when a stock goes ex-rights, its market value will adjust for the fact that new shares are being issued at a lower price, but other factors will affect the stock's price. It will rise and fall like any other stock price. At this point, the formula for the intrinsic value of a right is as follows:

Financial Planning Issue

Joe Beamer has received 1,000 rights in the Quick Explosion Company in which he owns 1,000 shares. The rights expire in 3 weeks. He asks your advice on whether he should exercise them, sell them, or forget about them.

The worst choice is to forget about them. If Joe has no interest in them, the financial planner needs to make sure the rights are at least sold lest they die worthless.[9] If Joe has no interest in increasing his investment in the company, then this would be a good time to review if Joe is really interested in continuing to hold his 1,000 shares. If the company is still viewed as a good investment, he should exercise the rights. If Joe lacks the cash to exercise the rights, he should sell sufficient rights to raise the cash to exercise the remaining rights.

$$\text{Intrinsic value of one right during ex-rights period} = \frac{\text{Market price of stock} - \text{Subscription price}}{\text{Number of shares needed to subscribe to one share}}$$

If the stock trades at a price of $39.75 after it goes ex-rights, the intrinsic value of one right would be:

$$\frac{\$39.75 - \$38.00}{10} = \frac{\$1.75}{10} = \$.175$$

Finally, note that at the time the stock goes ex-rights, if nothing happens to cause the price of the stock to change other than the ex-rights event, then the value of a right will be the same as it cum-rights value, namely $.18. The stock will be trading at $39.82, the subscription price is $38, and 10 rights buy one new share of stock, so the price works out to $.18 per right.

Warrants

The motivation for creating warrants is different from that for creating rights. Warrants are usually attached to a bond issue for the purpose of allowing a company to obtain a lower coupon rate on the bond, and presumably for the purpose of conveniently selling new equity at a later point in time. Frequently, start-up firms or firms with somewhat risky (but optimistic) prospects are the main issuers of warrants to aid in financing. Because pure debt issues would have to carry higher yields, the firm would use the bond-cum-warrants approach to lower its initial financing costs. This approach allows the bondholders to share in the firm's growth while providing a more secure return on capital if the firm does not grow.

Warrants are similar to rights in that a subscription price is paid to the company when exercised and new shares of stock are issued. They differ from rights in that their expiration date may range from several years to perpetual, and at the time they are issued the subscription price is usually substantially above the current market value of the stock. Thus, warrants have value only to the extent the future price of the stock might exceed the subscription price.

Example: The Slow-Go Bus Company has issued some bonds, with 100 warrants attached to each bond. The warrants expire in 10 years. Each warrant allows a person to buy one new share of stock at $40 per share. The stock currently trades at $25. Without the warrants, the company would have had to pay a 8 percent interest rate on the bonds; with them, the interest rate is 6 percent.

THE MECHANICS OF PAYING A DIVIDEND

record date

payment date

ex-dividend date

When dividend income is an important component of a client's total income, the financial planner needs to understand the mechanics of dividend payments. Dividends can be paid on common stock only at such time as the company's board of directors declares them. Hence, the first date that is of critical importance is the declaration date.

At the time of the declaration, the board also establishes a record date and a payment date. The *record date* is the date on which the stockholder must own the stock on the books of the corporation in order to receive the dividend. The *payment date* is the date that company pays the dividend. When individuals own stocks directly, it is the day the checks are put into the mail. When stocks are held in street name, it is the day the company forwards the payment to the brokerage firm. Even if the stockholder sells the stock the day after the record day and well before the payment date, this stockholder will still receive the dividend check.

There is a fourth date that is critical, and it is the only date not directly controlled by the board of directors. This is the ex-dividend date. Remember, security transactions are settled 3 days after the trade is made. Hence, to own a stock as of the close of trading on the record date, one must have bought the stock at least 3 trading days prior to the record date. The next day is the *ex-dividend date*, as it is the first trading date on which one buys or sells the stock without the announced dividend trading with the stock.

Example: The Ivers Corporation's board of trustees has just met on Monday, January 15 and declared the first quarter's dividend. Hence, January 15 is the declaration date. It sets a record date of Thursday, February 15, with a payment date of Thursday, March 15. The exchange on which the stock is traded will then note that to own the stock on the record date, the buyer will have to have bought the stock by the close of business on Monday, February 12. Hence, the exchange will establish Tuesday, February 13, as the ex-dividend date.

The above discussion may make it sound as if dividends are paid haphazardly. This is far from the case. Corporations like for investors to be comfortable about when to expect the next dividend, and what that amount might be. As a result, declaration dates are approximately the same time each quarter, and record and dividend dates are almost exactly the same time each quarter, with exceptions usually being made for Saturday, and always for Sunday. Thus, a company whose record date is March 1 will likely have as its other record dates June 1, September 1, and December 1. One could likely project these dates well into the future and be fairly certain about them.

Dividend Increases

Firms like to increase their dividends on a regular basis. Some of the most successful firms like to boast of the number of years of consecutive dividend increases they have had, or at least of the number of years they have paid quarterly dividends without a reduction or an omission. The quarter in which the dividend is increased is usually the same quarter each year. Thus, not only can one predict well in advance the record dates for dividends, one can predict almost as well the date on which the dividend will be increased. Finally, many firms with solid records of steady dividend increases also like to have the dividend increase be the same amount each time. Thus, a firm that increases its dividend by one penny per share in the third quarter of each year for several years will likely be looking to make a one-penny-per-share increase in the third quarter of the coming year. Because of this consistency, the market will sometimes react to a firm not increasing its dividend in a quarter in which everyone was expecting a dividend increase, or if the firm increases it by a different amount.

SUMMARY AND CONCLUSIONS

Although it would seem logical that stock prices would be based directly on earnings, doing so causes a double counting process. Stock prices are based on the present value of all future dividends that are expected to be paid to the owners of those shares. Over long periods of time, dividends will necessarily follow earnings. For simplification, most people use the constant dividend growth rate model, which is defined as:

$$V_0 = d_1/(r - g)$$

The discount rate in this model is frequently derived from the CAPM.

To get a sense of the value of a company's stock, several market-price-based ratios are utilized, including the price-to-future-earnings, the price-to-past-earnings, the price-to-cash-flow, the price-to-sales, and the price-earnings-to-earnings-growth-rate ratios. All of these ratios are reasonable to consider when only historical values are used; they may be highly deceptive when projected values are used.

Stocks with high P/E ratios are usually considered growth stocks, and stocks with low P/E ratios are considered value stocks. There has been a long-running debate about which group of stocks provides better investment returns. It varies depending on the time period. There is also evidence that P/E ratios may reflect facts other than just value or growth. They may reflect such considerations as firm size, analyst neglect, the low-price effect, and takeover candidates.

P/E ratios provide a basis for forecasting the market as a whole, or for forecasting the prices of individual stocks. One only has to project the future P/E ratio and the future value of earnings.

The impact of inflation on stock prices has always been problematical. According to pre-1970 Wall Street wisdom, companies could offset the adverse impact of inflation on their earnings (and stock values) by raising prices. Tax effects, government anti-inflation pressure, and international competition often make implementing the necessary price increases difficult, however. Still, to induce investors to hold stock, the stock market must offer the prospect of a positive real after-tax return. Some empirical research suggests that, in the short run, unanticipated rises in inflation have been associated with adverse stock market performance. In the longer run, however, average market returns exceed the inflation rate.

There are other equity securities besides common stock. These include preferred stock, rights, and warrants. Preferred stock is characterized as having a perpetual fixed dividend. Rights are issued to facilitate the sale of new stock to existing shareholders. Warrants are issued to obtain lower interest rates on debt today and to sell stock in the future.

There are four relevant dividend payment dates: the announcement date, the ex-dividend date, the record date, and the payment date. Most firms strive for consistency in these dates over each quarter, as well as consistency in the amount and date of dividend increases.

CHAPTER REVIEW

Answers to the review questions and the self-test questions start on page 733.

Key Terms

intrinsic value (stock)	analyst neglect (neglected-firm effect)
dividend discount model	low-price effect
dividend valuation model	greenmail
constant growth model	white knight
Gordon growth model	white squire
price-earnings (P/E) ratio	Pac Man defense
payout ratio	leveraged buyout (LBO)
cash flow	participating preferred stocks
PEG ratio	rights offering
growth stocks	record date
value stocks	payment date
value investing	ex-dividend date
growth investing	

Review Questions

7-1. The American Pig Company (ticker symbol PORK) recently paid a dividend of $3.00 per share, which is expected to rise by $.25 per share for the next 5 years. The stock currently sells for $36 per share, a ratio of 12 times its current dividends. The same ratio of dividends to price is also expected at the end of 5 years. Compute the present value of PORK's expected income stream for the following discount rates:

    a. 8 percent
    b. 10 percent
    c. 12 percent
    d. 15 percent
    e. 18 percent
    f. for a constant dividend of $3.00 (at a discount rate of 8 percent)

7-2. Based on appendix 7A, evaluate the stock of ZYX Corporation using the following information:

- prospective annual dividends over the next 5 years: $1.10, $1.20, $1.30, $1.40, and $1.50
- discount rate: 16 percent
- growth rate of dividends beginning with the dividend in year 6: 4 percent

7-3. Repeat question 7-2 using the following discount rates:
    a. 10 percent
    b. 20 percent

7-4. Assuming constant growth, compute the market price for the following sets of information:
    a. $d_0 = \$1; r = 12\%; g = 10\%$
    b. $d_0 = \$2; r = 12\%; g = 11\%$
    c. $d_0 = \$1.50; r = 12\%; g = 8\%$

7-5. Distinguish between a warrant and a right.

7-6. XYZ stock is selling cum-rights at $50. The rights entitle the holder to five shares at $47 for every 100 shares owned.
    a. What is their theoretical value?
    b. Compute the theoretical value assuming that during the ex-rights period, the stock price falls by the amount implied by the dilution.

Self-Test Questions

T   F   7-1. An investor who is planning to hold stock only for a short time need not be concerned about the stock's expected dividend stream after the time he or she plans to sell the stock.

T F 7-2. The required return on stock is equal to the risk-free rate plus the stock's risk premium.

T F 7-3. The discount rate used to evaluate the expected future dividend stream is the same as the required return.

T F 7-4. A stock that was expected to pay a constant dividend forever could be valued by dividing the dividend by the appropriate discount rate.

T F 7-5. The price of common stock should reflect the present value of its expected future stream of dividends.

T F 7-6. When using the constant growth model, the price of a stock should equal its current dividend divided by $(r - g)$, where r is the required rate of return.

T F 7-7. For the constant growth model to apply, the discount rate must exceed the growth rate.

T F 7-8. The expected income stream from common stock is much more difficult to determine than that of bonds.

T F 7-9. The price-to-past-earnings ratio is just as good a number as the price-to-future-earnings ratio.

T F 7-10. Historically, large-company common stocks have provided the best rates of return.

T F 7-11. Past earnings growth is an excellent predictor of future earnings growth.

T F 7-12. An appropriate dividend payout ratio for a rapidly growing start-up company may be too low for a mature company.

T F 7-13. Any net earnings not paid out in dividends are retained earnings, which are used to finance the company's future growth and future income.

T F 7-14. One of the problems with inflation is that investors end up paying taxes on compensation for inflation.

T F 7-15. Inflation is not a major problem to corporations because they can always raise their prices.

T F 7-16. Modigliani and Cohn argued that in the past investors have capitalized earnings incorrectly, and failed to correctly incorporate the impact of inflation on debt.

T F 7-17. With participating preferred stock, the shareholders get to vote on an equal basis with common stockholders.

T F 7-18. Rights give existing shareholders the opportunity to buy additional stock at a price lower than the current market price of the shares outstanding.

T   F   7-19. If four rights are needed to purchase a new share of stock, the shares are currently trading at $50, and the subscription price for a new share is $42, each right has an approximate value of $2 if the stock is ex-rights.

T   F   7-20. In the event of bankruptcy, preferred stockholders are only ahead of common stockholders in the queue for payoffs.

T   F   7-21. Historically, individuals have had to pay little or no income tax on dividends from preferred stocks.

T   F   7-22. Companies issue rights as a substitute for dividend payments.

T   F   7-23. The only inappropriate response to a rights offering is to let the rights expire.

T   F   7-24. The primary reasons for creating warrants is for the firm to obtain a lower interest rate on its debt and to sell stock at a later date.

T   F   7-25. When a warrant is issued, the subscription price is almost always below the current market price, so that they will have an intrinsic value.

T   F   7-26. Dividend payments on common stock tend to remain constant over time.

T   F   7-27. The ex-dividend date is the only date set directly by the company's board of directors.

T   F   7-28. The ex-dividend date is the last day one can buy stock and still receive the next dividend.

T   F   7-29. The ex-dividend date is the day following the record date.

T   F   7-30. A firm is most likely to increase its dividend in the first quarter of each year.

NOTES

1. The above discussion is oversimplified to the extent that it implies the firm finances its new projects only with profits. Most firms borrow money as part of their financing. Although the interest rate on debt is always less than the required rate of return on equity, the relevant number becomes the weighted average of the cost of debt and the required rate of return on equity. This number is known as the cost of capital. As long as the firm earns more on its projects than the cost of capital, the price of the value of the stock would increase in a manner described herein.

2. C. Jones, *Investments: Analysis and Management,* 6th ed. (Hoboken, NJ: John Wiley & Sons, 1998), p. 401.

3. A. Damodaran*, Damodaran on Valuation: Security Analysis for Investment and Corporate Finance* (New York: John Wiley & Sons, 1994).

4. M. Reinganum, "Misspecification of Capital Asset Pricing: Empirical Anomalies Based on Earnings' Yields and Market Values," *Journal of Financial Economics* (March 1981), pp. 19–46; "Abnormal Returns in Small Firm Portfolios," *Financial Analysts Journal* (March/April 1981), pp. 52–56; "Portfolio Strategies Based on Market Capitalization," *Journal of Portfolio Management* (Winter 1983), pp. 29–36.

5. E. Fama and K. French, "Size and Book-to-Market Factors in Earnings and Returns," *Journal of Finance,* vol. 50, no. 1 (March 1995), pp. 131–155.

6. J. Siegel, *Stocks for the Long Run,* 3rd ed. (New York: McGraw-Hill, 2002).
7. F. Modigliani and R. Cohn, "Inflation, Rational Valuation and the Market," *Financial Analysts Journal* (March/April 1979), pp. 24–44.
8. P. Cagan, *Stock Prices Reflect the Adjustment of Earnings for Inflation,* NYU Monograph Series in Finance and Economics (New York: New York University, 1982).
9. Even if the commission equals the value of the rights, if the client does not want to exercise the rights they should be sold to establish a verifiable record for tax purposes.

Appendix 7A

Complex Growth Models

In chapter 7, we considered the case of the constant dividend growth rate model. The model has a wonderful simplicity to it, provides critical insights into stock pricing, but is not realistic in its scenario. That is, few companies are envisioned as having dividends that grow at a constant rate forever. In this appendix, we will consider what might be referred to as complex dividend growth rate models. They are more realistic in terms of application, but create more mathematical complexity in terms of solutions.

Case I: Deferred Dividend

Let's start by considering the case of a company that pays no dividend today. For the stock to have value, there must be an expectation of a dividend some time in the future, even if it is only a liquidating dividend. So, let's suppose that the company plans to reinvest all of its earnings for at least 20 years. However, at that time, the opportunities for reinvestment will diminish, and the company will begin to pay out part of its earnings as dividends, although it will keep the rest to finance a slower rate of growth. Thus, the company expects to pay a dividend of $25 per share, beginning 21 years from today, and that dividend is expected to grow at a 4 percent rate forever thereafter. Finally, let's assume that an appropriate discount rate is 10 percent.

A two-step process is required to solve this problem. First, we have to value what the price of the stock will be in 20 years. Second, we must then value what that stock is worth today, given that there are no dividends to be paid over that time.

Step 1: $V_{20} = d_{21} / (r - g) = \$25 / (.10 - .04) = \$416.67$
Step 2: $V_0 = V_{20} / (1 + r)^{20} = \$416.67 / (1 + .10)^{20} = \$61.94$

[**Keystrokes**: Step 1: SHIFT, C ALL, 25, ÷, .06, =

Step 2: 416.67, FV, 10, I/YR, 20, N, PV (DISPLAY: –61.93)]

In step 1, keep in mind that if you want to value the stock 20 years from today using the constant growth rate model, you have to use in the numerator the dividend that will be paid one year from the point in time to which you are valuing the stock. In step 2, you are simply discounting the price back 20 years. Note that $61.93 per share is a nice price for a share of stock that currently pays no dividend, and is not expected to pay any for 20 years.

Case II: Flat Dividend, Followed by Constant Growth

Next, let's assume that the company in question is expected to pay a constant dividend of $1.00 per share for three years. Beginning four years from today, the dividend will grow at a rate of 4 percent forever. Let's also assume a 10 percent discount rate.

Now, a four-step process is required to determine the price of the stock today. Step 1 is to compute the present value of the dividends during the flat years. Step 2 is to value the stock once the constant growth starts, step 3 is to compute the present value of this stock price, and step 4 is to add together the present value of the dividends from step 1 and the present value of the stock price from step 3.

Step 1: $\$1/(1+.10)^1 + \$1/(1+.10)^2 + \$1/(1+.10)^3 = \$2.49$
Step 2: $V_3 = d_4/(r - g) = \$1.04 / (.10 - .04) = \$17.33$
Step 3: $V_0 = V_3 / (1 + r)^3 = \$17.33 / (1 + .10)^3 = \$13.02$
Step 4: Value of stock today = $\$2.49 + \$13.02 = \$15.51$

[Keystrokes: Step 1: SHIFT, C ALL, 3, N, 10, I/YR, 1, PMT, PV (DISPLAY: –2.49)

Step 2: SHIFT, C ALL, 1.04, ÷, .06, = (DISPLAY: 17.33)
Step 3: SHIFT, C ALL, 17.33, FV, 10, I/YR, 3, N, PV (DISPLAY: –13.02)
Step 4: SHIFT, C ALL, 13.02, +, 2.49, = (DISPLAY: 15.51)]

Note that in this problem we are able to treat the first three payments as an ordinary annuity. This greatly simplifies the keystrokes!

Case III: Irregular Dividend Followed by Constant Growth

The next situation to consider is where the initial dividends vary, rather than form a nice, smooth annuity. An example might be this: the projected dividends for the next three years are $1, $1.50, and $2. Thereafter, the dividends will grow at a constant rate of 4 percent forever. Assume a discount rate of 10 percent. Once again, to price the stock today requires the same four-step process that we used in Case II. That is, step 1 is to compute the present value of the first three dividends; step 2 is to value the stock in three years; step 3 is to find the present value of the stock price in three years; and step 4 is to add together the results from steps 1 and 3. Here are the calculations:

Step 1: $\$1/(1+.10)^1 + \$1.50/(1+.10)^2 + \$2/(1+.10)^3 = \$3.65$
Step 2: $V_3 = d_4 / (r - g) = \$2 \times (1 + .04) / (.10 - .04) = \$34.67$
Step 3: $V_0 = V_3 / (1 + r)^3 = \$34.67 / (1 + .10)^3 = \$26.05$
Step 4: Value of stock today = $\$3.65 + \$26.05 = \$29.70$

[Keystrokes: Step 1: SHIFT, C ALL, 0, CFj, 1, CFj, 1.5, CFj, 2, CFj, 10, I/YR, SHIFT, NPV (display: 3.65)

Step 2: SHIFT, C ALL, 2, x, 1.04, =, ÷, .06, = (DISPLAY: 34.67)

Step 3: SHIFT, C ALL, 34.67, FV, 10, I/YR, 3, N, PV (DISPLAY: –26.05)

Step 4: SHIFT, C ALL, 26.05, +, 3.65, = (DISPLAY: 29.70)]

Note that in the above calculations, we are treating the first three cash flows as a series of uneven cash flows, and using the NPV function key that was discussed in Appendix 5A.

Case IV: Rapid Growth Followed by Slow (Constant) Growth

What is probably the most popular version of complex growth models is the one known as fast (or supernormal) growth, slow growth. What makes this model interesting is that the first growth rate is defined as being greater than the discount rate. The second growth rate, of necessity, must be less than the discount rate. There is only one way to solve this type of problem. The student must first define each of the dividend payments during the rapid growth period. Then the model is solved exactly the same way as in Case III. Consider the following situation: assume that the dividend just paid was $1.00, and that dividends will grow at a rate of 20 percent per year for three years. After that, they will slow to an annual growth rate of 4 percent. Finally, let us continue to use the 10-percent discount rate. This now becomes a five-step process. Step 1 is to project out the dividends during the rapid growth period. Steps 2–5 then become identical to what had been steps 1–4 in Case III. Here are the calculations:

Step 1: $d_1 = \$1 \times (1 + .20)^1 = \$1.20$
$d_2 = \$1 \times (1 + .20)^2 = \$1.44$
$d_3 = \$1 \times (1 + .20)^3 = \$1.73$
$d_4 = d_3 \times (1 + .04) = \$1.73 \times 1.04 = \$1.80$
Step 2: $\$1.20/(1+.10)^1 + \$1.44/(1+.10)^2 + \$1.73/(1+.10)^3 = \$3.58$
Step 3: $V_3 = d_4/(r - g) = \$1.80/(.10 - .04) = \$30.00$
Step 4: $V_0 = V_3 / (1 + r)^3 = \$30.00 / (1 + .10)^3 = \$22.54$
Step 5: Value of stock today = $3.58 + $22.54 = $26.12

[Keystrokes: Step 1: SHIFT, C ALL, 1, x, 1.2, = (DISPLAY:1.20), x, 1.2, = (DISPLAY: 1.44), x 1.2, = (DISPLAY: 1.73), x, 1.04, = (DISPLAY: 1.80)
Step 2: SHIFT, C ALL, 0, CFj, 1.20, CFj, 1.44, CFj, 1.73, CFj, 10, I/YR, SHIFT, NPV (DISPLAY: 3.58)

Step 3: SHIFT, C ALL, 1.80, ÷, .06, = (DISPLAY: 30.00)
Step 4: SHIFT, C ALL, 30.00, FV, 10, I/YR, 3, N, PV (DISPLAY: −22.54)
Step 5: SHIFT, C ALL, 22.54, +, 3.58, = (DISPLAY: 26.12)]

Fundamental Analysis

Learning Objectives

An understanding of the material in this chapter should enable the student to

8-1. Explain the components of fundamental analysis.

8-2. Define a business cycle, and explain what is meant by leading, coincident, and lagging indicators.

8-3. Describe the tools of fiscal policy and the economic issues associated with fiscal policy.

8-4. Describe the tools of monetary policy and the economic issues associated with monetary policy.

8-5. Explain the process of industry analysis.

8-6. Perform a simple company analysis based primarily on financial ratios.

8-7. Discuss the relationship between fundamental analysis and semistrong market efficiency.

Chapter Outline

In chapter 7, we looked at the theory of equity valuation, which requires estimates of future income and identification of an appropriate discount rate. For people who believe in market efficiency, all prices are fair, and no further analysis is necessary. However, one of the requirements of market efficiency is that a sufficiently large number of people have examined each security to ascertain what each of them thinks it is worth. This process is known as fundamental analysis.

This chapter surveys the issues associated with fundamental analysis. It discusses both macroeconomic analysis and industry analysis and presents specific approaches to economic and industry analysis. It then considers company analysis, giving particular attention to the evaluation of a company's competitive position, management quality, financial strength, and profitability.

OVERVIEW OF FUNDAMENTAL ANALYSIS

Fundamental analysis traditionally takes a "top down" approach, which consists of breaking the analysis into three parts: (1) macroeconomic analysis,

macroeconomic analysis

industry analysis
company analysis

(2) industry analysis, and (3) company analysis. *Macroeconomic analysis* seeks to evaluate the current economic setting and its effect on industry and firm fundamentals. *Industry analysis* assesses the outlook for particular industries. *Company analysis* examines a firm's relative strengths and weaknesses within its industry or industries.

These three categories correspond to the three principal influences on stock performance. Clearly, each is important, although studies show that, in terms of both firm profits and the total return on stocks (dividends plus price changes), market/economy and firm-specific factors are the dominant influences.

Three Steps of Fundamental Analysis

- Macroeconomic analysis: Evaluates current economic environment and its effect on industry and company fundamentals
- Industry analysis: Evaluates the outlook for particular industries
- Company analysis: Evaluates a company's strengths and weaknesses within its industry or industries

---

MACROECONOMIC ANALYSIS

As we saw in the previous chapter, stock valuation is based on an assessment of a company's future dividends. Dividends, in turn, are based on a company's current and prospective earnings. Earnings, in turn, are based on a company's sales. Finally, for most companies, particularly the largest ones, the single most important factor influencing sales is the general level of economic activity. Economic activity is reflected in such data as the gross domestic product (GDP), industrial production, and the employment and unemployment rate.

Business Cycles

If the economy behaved like the weather in the Sahara desert, forecasting would be easy. The Sahara meteorologist most likely forecasts a hot and dry day every day of the year, and is correct virtually all the time. What complicates forecasting the economy is the existence of business cycles. There are four phases to a cycle: expansion, peak, contraction, and trough. These are illustrated in figure 8-1, which shows three peaks and two troughs. The economy is referred to as being in a *recession* or *contraction* when it is moving from a peak to a trough, and in an *expansion* when it is moving from a trough to a peak.

TABLE 8-1
Historical Information on Business Cycles

Business Cycle Reference Dates		Duration in Months			
Peak	**Trough**	**Contraction**	**Expansion**	**Cycle**	
Quarterly Dates Are in Parentheses		*Peak to Trough*	*Previous Trough to This Peak*	*Trough from Previous Trough*	*Peak from Previous Peak*
	December 1854 (IV)	—	—	—	—
June 1857 (II)	December 1858 (IV)	18	30	48	—
October 1860 (III)	June 1861 (III)	8	22	30	40
April 1865 (I)	December 1867 (IV)	**32**	**46**	**78**	**54**
June 1869 (II)	December 1870 (IV)	18	18	36	50
October 1873 (III)	March 1879 (I)	65	34	99	52
March 1882 (I)	May 1885 (II)	38	36	74	101
March 1887 (II)	April 1888 (II)	13	22	35	60
July 1890 (III)	May 1891 (II)	10	27	37	40
January 1893 (I)	June 1894 (II)	17	20	37	30
December 1895 (IV)	June 1897 (II)	18	18	36	35
June 1899 (III)	December 1900 (IV)	18	24	42	42
September 1902 (IV)	August 1904 (III)	23	21	44	39
May 1907 (II)	June 1908 (II)	13	33	46	56
January 1910 (I)	January 1912 (IV)	24	19	43	32
January 1913 (I)	December 1914 (IV)	23	12	35	36
August 1918 (III)	March 1919 (I)	**7**	**44**	**51**	**67**
January 1920 (I)	July 1921 (III)	18	10	28	17
May 1923 (II)	July 1924 (III)	14	22	36	40
October 1926 (III)	November 1927 (IV)	13	27	40	41
August 1929 (III)	March 1933 (I)	43	21	64	34
May 1937 (II)	June 1938 (II)	13	50	63	93
February 1945 (I)	October 1945 (IV)	**8**	**80**	**88**	**93**
November 1948 (IV)	October 1949 (IV)	11	37	48	45
July 1953 (II)	May 1954 (II)	**10**	**45**	**55**	**56**
August 1957 (III)	April 1958 (II)	8	39	47	49
April 1960 (II)	February 1961 (I)	10	24	34	32
December 1969 (IV)	November 1970 (IV)	**11**	**106**	**117**	**116**
November 1973 (IV)	March 1975 (I)	16	36	52	47
January 1980 (I)	July 1980 (III)	6	58	64	74
July 1981 (III)	November 1982 (IV)	16	12	28	18
July 1990 (III)	March 1991 (I)	8	92	100	108
March 2001 (I)	November 2001 (IV)	8	120	128	128

TABLE 8-1 (continued)
Historical Information on Business Cycles

Business Cycle Reference Dates		Duration in Months			
Peak	Trough	Contraction	Expansion	Cycle	
Quarterly Dates Are in Parentheses		*Peak to Trough*	*Previous Trough to This Peak*	*Trough from Previous Trough*	*Peak from Previous Peak*
Average, all cycles:		17	38	55	56*
1854–2001 (32 cycles)		22	27	48	49**
1854–1919 (16 cycles)		18	35	53	53
1919–1945 (6 cycles)		10	57	67	67
1945–2001 (10 cycles)					
Average, peacetime cycles:		18	33	51	52***
1854–2001 (27 cycles)		22	24	46	47****
1854–1919 (14 cycles)		20	26	46	45
1919–1945 (5 cycles)		10	52	63	63
1945–2001 (8 cycles)					

   * 31 cycles
  ** 15 cycles
 *** 26 cycles
**** 13 cycles

Figures printed in ***bold italic*** are the wartime expansions (Civil War, World Wars I and II, Korean War, and Vietnam War), the wartime contractions, and the full cycles that include the wartime expansions.

Sources: NBER; the U.S. Department of Commerce, *Survey of Current Business, October 1994*, Table C-51. Reprinted from www.nber.org/cycles.html, January 27, 2004.

The forecasting problem arises from the fact that the amount of time for a cycle varies, as well as the extent of fluctuation in economic activity during a cycle. For example, the longest cycle on record lasted 128 months, measured from peak to peak (that is, 10+ years), and the shortest cycle was 17 months (see table 8-1). Cycles are officially defined by the National Bureau of Economic Research (NBER) Business Cycle Dating Committee. The current definition of a recession is "a significant decline in economic activity spread across the economy, lasting more than a few months, normally visible in real GDP, real income, employment, industrial production, and wholesale-retail sales."[1]

Leading, Coincident, and Lagging Indicators

The primary tools used by the NBER to identify business cycles are the leading, coincident, and lagging indicators. Beginning in the 1940s and based

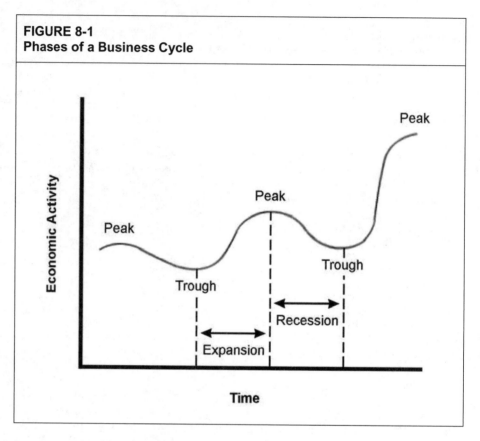

FIGURE 8-1
Phases of a Business Cycle

on observations going back to the 1920s, NBER and the U.S. Commerce Department identified 10 monthly data series that tended to lead the business cycle. Today, the monthly data series are quite similar to the original selection and are shown in table 8-2.

In addition to the 10 leading indicators, there is a coincident indicator series (four components) and a lagging series (seven components). Both of these are also shown in table 8-2. The list of indicators has been expanded and revised over time and is now published by the Conference Board. Under normal circumstances, updates to the leading, coincident, and lagging indicators incorporate revisions to data only over the previous 6 months. Longer-term revisions that cover changes in components that fall outside the moving 6-month window are incorporated in December of each year.

The Impact of the Business Cycle on Assets

In an expanding economy, sales increase, inventory moves more quickly, employment and personal income increase, and corporate profits and dividends rise. In a weak economy, the opposites occur.

Let's consider what typically is happening to stocks, bonds, cash, and real assets during the phases of the business cycle. Before doing so, remember that when dealing with real economic activity, there are always many exceptions to general rules.

As we have already seen, stocks tend to be a leading indicator. Therefore, the stock market precedes movement in the economy. In fact, the stock market has predicted every major turn in economic activity. The problem is that the stock market also gives many false signals. Paul Samuelson, Nobel laureate and one of the most famous economists of the twentieth century, once noted that "the stock market has predicted eight of the last five recessions!"

TABLE 8-2
The Conference Board US Business Cycle Indicators

Leading Indicators (10 Series)
- Average weekly hours, manufacturing
- Average weekly initial claims for unemployment insurance
- Manufacturers' new orders, consumer goods and materials (inflation adjusted)
- Vendor performance, slower deliveries diffusion index
- Manufacturers' new orders, nondefense capital goods (inflation adjusted)
- Building permits, new private housing units
- Stock prices, S&P 500 Index
- Real money supply, M2 (includes currency and checkable deposits in the hands of the public, plus savings and small-time deposits, repurchase agreements, and money market deposit accounts)
- Interest rate spread, 10-year Treasury bonds less federal funds
- Index of Consumer Expectations, University of Michigan Survey Research Center

Coincident (4 Series)
- Employees on nonagricultural payrolls
- Personal income less transfer payments
- Industrial production
- Manufacturing and trade sales

Lagging (7 Series)
- Average duration of unemployment
- Inventories to sales ratio, manufacturing and trade
- Labor cost per unit of output, manufacturing
- Average prime rate
- Commercial and industrial loans
- Consumer installment credit to personal income ratio
- Consumer Price Index for services

Source: The Conference Board, 2004, www.globalindicators.org

Interest rates (and hence bond prices) also move with the economy. Interest rates tend to rise when the economy is expanding, and decline when the economy is falling. Intuitively, we might think it would be the opposite. After all, if the economy is expanding, then businesses are less likely to default and lenders should be willing to accept lower interest rates due to the lower likelihood of defaults. We might also think that businesses are more likely to fail during recessions and lenders should charge a higher interest rate to compensate for the higher default risk.

However, the reality is just the opposite. Interest rates tend to rise (and bond prices fall) during expansions, and the reverse occurs during contractions. The reason is that the demand for loans moves with the business cycle. Thus, during expansion periods, businesses have a huge appetite for money for new projects, and because of the rosy economic outlook, are willing to pay increasingly higher interest rates for loans. Conversely, during contractions, businesses see substantially few attractive investment opportunities and thus curtail their demand for loans.

During contractions, there is usually a scramble for liquidity. This means many businesses begin hoarding cash by delaying payments and attempting to accelerate receivables. Finally, the prices of real assets, such as land and buildings, tend to be highly pro-cyclical. This sometimes creates dramatic boom and bust cycles in real estate. Because of the time lag associated with planning, financing, and constructing buildings, many building projects are initiated during economic expansions and then become available for occupancy during economic contractions. Real estate, particularly commercial real estate, can be a feast or famine investment.

FISCAL POLICY

It is one thing to understand where the economy is in terms of the business cycle. Anybody can look like a genius if he or she happens to invest at the trough of a business cycle, and nearly everyone looks foolish if he or she happens to invest at the peak. Nonetheless, picking the peaks and troughs is complex enough as it is. Remember, even the NBER defines the business cycle turning points only with clear and sufficient hindsight, and even then, it occasionally changes its mind later as to the exact dates of the peaks and troughs. Complicating an analysis of business cycles is the fact that Congress, through fiscal policy activities, and the Federal Reserve Board, through monetary policy activities, are constantly trying to change what would be the natural course of a business cycle. Hence, they are trying to slow expansions in order to extend them, and to dampen and/or shorten all contractions. Thus, a financial planner has to have an understanding about what is occurring with regard to fiscal and monetary policy.

There are three tools associated with fiscal policy. The most common is the adjustment of the government's revenues and expenditures to control the economy. This may happen in several ways. First, when the economy has room to expand, increased government expenditures (whether this is deficit spending or reducing what would have been a surplus) may call forth additional production. Thus, starting a new public works project (for example, a highway, school, or dam) will put people to work to produce the structure and the required inputs (cement, steel, and so on). These newly employed workers will likely spend most of their income on consumer goods and services, thereby creating demands that put others to work. This fiscal multiplier process increases employment and production. At each stage, however, a portion of the extra income does not go directly back into the domestic economy. It is saved, taxed, or spent on imported goods. These leakages reduce the multiplier's power. Moreover, the additional spending forces the government to increase its borrowing or taxes, thereby crowding out other borrowers and/or reducing other disposable incomes. Thus, proportionately less goes to each succeeding round.

The second tool of fiscal policy is changes in the tax code. The most fundamental way to change the tax code is to raise or lower the marginal tax brackets.[2] The effect of a tax decrease is similar to a government spending increase. Lower tax rates and reduced withholding increase households' after-tax income, causing consumer spending to rise. This spending increase, in turn, leads to additional production, employment, and income, which cause further increases in spending. Thus, either a government spending increase or a tax decrease stimulates the economy, whereas a government spending decrease or a tax increase restrains the economy. According to Keynesian theory (Keynesians are discussed later in this chapter), a change in government spending has a greater economic impact than a tax change of equivalent size. The multiplier acts on the full amount of the change in government spending to affect the GDP, whereas a portion of the tax change affects savings, leaving the multiplier a lesser amount on which to act.

debt management policy

The third tool of fiscal policy is the management of the maturity of the government's outstanding debt, which is referred to as *debt management policy*. The goal of debt management policy is to change the shape of the

---

Tools of Fiscal Policy

- Government spending: More spending stimulates the economy; less spending slows the growth rate.
- Tax revenues: Less taxation stimulates the economy; more taxation slows the growth rate.
- Debt management: Changes in maturity of outstanding Treasury debt influence the yield curve.

yield curve, which is the relationship between yield to maturity and term to maturity for bonds of like quality. (Yield curves are discussed in chapter 9.) Debt management consists of raising or lowering short-term interest rates relative to long-term rates.

MONETARY POLICY

Federal Reserve Board (Fed)

The *Federal Reserve Board* (*Fed*) has primary authority over our nation's monetary policy.[3] By largely determining the rate at which the money supply expands or contracts, the Fed exercises a considerable amount of influence over the supply of and demand for credit (that is, loanable funds). Interest is the price paid for the use of such funds. Interest rates are determined by the intersection of these supply and demand functions. (Appendix 8A discusses supply and demand curves.)

M1

M2

There are multiple definitions of the money supply. The most common is known as *M1*, which is all cash and coin in circulation outside banks, plus all accounts in depository institutions that are subject to withdrawal by check. The second most common is *M2,* which is M1 plus savings, small time-deposits, and retail-type money market mutual fund balances.

There are three tools of monetary policy. In order of frequency of use, they are open-market operations, changes in the discount rate, and changes in reserve requirements. Before we discuss these tools, let's consider the process by which banks alter the money supply and the role of reserve requirements.

How a Bank Increases the Money Supply

When a bank grants a loan, it funds the loan by depositing to the borrower's account. In effect, it implicitly creates the money that it loans. The money that is thereby created is initially retained in an account at the lending bank. Checks written against these loan-created deposits will, in turn, be deposited into the accounts of the people or firms receiving the payments. In this way, most of the money flows into other bank accounts, but some of the funds remain with the bank that made the loan. A relatively small portion of the loan money may go into additional cash holdings. Thus, most of the new money resulting from granting the loan ends up as deposits somewhere in the banking system. The corresponding increase in deposits throughout the banking system creates additional lending power. When this lending power is utilized, more deposits and still more lending power result.

Reserve Requirements

Most of M1 is held in the form of checkable deposits. Federally chartered banks and state banks with Fed memberships are required to maintain reserves (that is, cash and certain near-cash assets) equal to a certain percentage of their deposits. This percentage is called the reserve ratio or reserve requirement. Under the Depository Institution Deregulation and Monetary Control Act of 1980, the Fed's Board of Governors must set the reserve requirements in the range of 8 to 14 percent on transaction balances. To avoid being punitive toward smaller banks in setting this ratio, the act also sets the reserve ratio at 3 percent on the first $25 million of transaction balances, and it mandated that this be adjusted regularly for changes in the amount of transaction balances in U.S. banks (by 2001, this figure was up to $41.3 million). The Garn-St. Germain Act of 1982 later provided for a 0 percent reserve requirement for the first $2 million of a bank's deposits, and also mandated adjustments in this figure for deposit growth. By 2002, the exempted deposits totaled $5.7 million. As of February 2002, the reserve requirement for transaction deposits above the exempted amounts was 10 percent; there continue to be no reserve requirements for time deposits.[4] A bank's required reserves are determined by multiplying its deposits by the required reserve ratio.

Example:	What would the required reserves in 2003 be for a bank with $100 million in transactions deposits? The requirement can be computed in three steps:

Balance	Reserve Requirement	Reserves
$ 5.7 million		0%
$35.6 ($41.3 – $5.7) million	3%	$1.068 million
$58.7 ($100 – $41.3) million	10%	$5.870 million

The total required reserves are then $6,938,000, which must be held either as vault cash or deposits at the bank's regional Federal Reserve bank.

Open-Market Operations

Open-market operations consist of the Fed's buying and selling government bonds in the open market. Two things happen when the Fed buys bonds. First, the purchase of bonds will, other things being equal, result in increases in the price of the bonds. Higher bond prices, by definition, mean lower interest rates. Lower interest rates, as will be explained more fully later, stimulate the economy. The second thing that happens is those selling bonds to the Fed receive drafts (checks) that increase the sellers' banks' reserves. In many cases, the seller is a bank, in which case the increase in reserves is direct.

If the Fed sells government bonds, the reverse happens. First, the selling causes the prices of the bonds to decline, which slows economic growth.

Second, the sales remove cash from the economy, which means there is less cash for consumption purchases.

What makes open-market operations so effective for the Fed is that they can be done without formal announcement. The Fed buys and sells Treasury securities virtually on a daily basis. In fact, the Fed will sometimes place offsetting buy and sell orders with different bond traders just to create some confusion among market traders as to whether the Fed is a net buyer or seller of bonds. Nonetheless, many Wall Street analysts carefully monitor the Fed's open-market operations and the resulting changes in the money supply. The Fed generally prefers to exercise its influence on the banking system through open-market operations rather than changing the reserve requirements because the latter may disrupt the financial markets more than is desirable.

Changes in the Discount Rate

One of the activities the Fed engages in is lending cash (reserves) to member banks. The Fed does this because it is charged by Congress to protect the integrity of the banking system. However, borrowing from the Fed is a privilege, not a right. It extends these loans only on a short-term basis and only to applicants that it views as not abusing the borrowing privilege. This lending process is referred to as discounting, so the interest rate the Fed charges is known as the *discount rate*.

discount rate (monetary policy)

Compared with the Fed's other tools, discounting plays a relatively minor role. Changes in the discount rate are used principally to signal changes in Fed policy. At its meeting in February 1994, the Federal Open Market Committee (FOMC) began the practice of immediately disclosing its decisions upon making them, rather than waiting until the next meeting to disclose the minutes of the previous meeting. When the Fed announces a decision that it is lowering the discount rate, it is signaling to the financial markets that it is easing (or continuing to ease) monetary policy in order to stimulate the economy. The lower discount also encourages banks to borrow from the Fed, for the purpose of lending out the money. Increases in the discount rate are intended to slow the growth rate of an economy that is at risk of getting overheated and thus creating problems like inflation.

The effectiveness of the discount rate is limited by its relationship to the federal funds rate. As discussed in chapter 1, this is the rate that banks charge each other for overnight use of federal reserves in the so-called federal funds market. Federal funds are deposits that commercial banks hold at Federal Reserve banks. Beginning in October 1997, the Fed announced that its FOMC directive would henceforth specify an explicit target for the federal funds rate. In addition, the directive would express a bias to possible future action in terms of the rate. For a long time prior to the announcement, the Fed had implemented monetary policy by making discrete and frequent small adjustments to its federal funds rate target. Often, changes in the federal funds rate are simultaneous with other changes in the marketplace, such as changes in the various market-determined interest rates.

Changes in Reserve Requirements

The least used tool of the Fed is changes in the reserve requirement. The last change made to the reserve requirement was in April 1992, when it was lowered from 12 percent to 10 percent of transaction deposits. If the reserve requirement is decreased, banks do not need the same amount of reserves to support their existing deposits. To the extent that banks loan out this cash that they had previously had to hold as reserves, the money supply expands. The catch is that banks are not forced to lend this money. They may take the freed-up reserves and buy Treasury securities, thus defeating the Fed's attempt to stimulate the economy. An increase in the reserve requirement should have the effect of forcing banks to forgo loans because of the additional cash that must be kept on hand. The problem here is that some banks hold more reserves than are necessary; these are called *excess reserves*. Excess reserves are computed as

excess reserves

$$\text{Excess reserves} = \text{Actual reserves} - \text{Required reserves}$$

For these banks, an increase in reserve requirements may only convert the nature of the reserves from excess to required, and thus have no effect on the economy.

Example: Suppose a bank has $5 million in transactions deposits, actual reserves of $300,000, and required reserves of $300,000 (assume that the reserve requirement is a flat 6 percent). If the Fed lowers the reserve ratio to 4 percent, the bank is now required to have only $200,000 in reserves ($5,000,000 x .04). The bank now has excess reserves of $100,000 and is able to make an additional $100,000 in loans.

The Fed's Policy Tools

- Open-market operations: Fed purchases (sales) of government securities increase (decrease) the bank deposits available to support the money supply.
- Discount loans: Decreasing (increasing) the discount rate signals greater (less) willingness to grant discount loans.
- Reserve requirement: Increasing (decreasing) the required percentage reduces (raises) the amount of money that a given reserve base can support.

The Money Multiplier

The ratio between the change in money supply (numerator) and the initial change in the reserves (denominator) is called the money multiplier. For example, if the Federal Reserve Board purchases $100 million in government securities through open-market operations, and the resulting increase in the money supply is $500 million, we conclude that the money multiplier is $500 million/$100 million, or 5. Although this is something of a simplification, we can say that the maximum value of the money multiplier is the reciprocal of the reserve requirement. For example, if the reserve requirement is 20 percent, or one-fifth, then the maximum value of the money multiplier is approximately 5.

Example: Imagine that the Fed buys $100 million in government bonds from Bank A. This reduces Bank A's security balances and increases its cash. With a 20 percent reserve requirement, Bank A will have to keep $20 million of the $100 million in reserve, but it can loan out $80 million. The borrowers of that $80 million will use the money to purchase a variety of goods and services. The sellers of those goods and services will deposit their proceeds in a bank, or they will spend it on other goods and services, in which case other people will receive the money and most likely deposit it in a bank.

     Sooner or later, a very large part (almost all) of that $80 million will find its way into a bank deposit. For simplicity, let's assume that the $80 million is deposited in Bank B. Bank B must now put $16 million (20 percent of $80 million) in reserve and can lend out $64 million. Once again, an extra $64 million worth of goods and services will be purchased, and the sellers of those goods and services will have $64 million at their disposal. Again, for simplicity, let's assume that the entire $64 million is deposited at Bank C. Bank C can now lend out 80 percent of $64 million, or $51.2 million. The process then repeats itself again and again, increasing the amount of money in circulation each time.

Mathematically, if the Fed makes an open-market purchase of P dollars, and the reserve requirement is r, the increase in the money supply is

$$P + P \times (1-r) + P \times (1-r)^2 + P \times (1-r)^3 + \ldots$$
$$= P \times [1 + (1-r) + (1-r)^2 + (1-r)^3 + \ldots]$$
$$= P \times 1/r$$

Therefore, 1/r is called the money multiplier.

The above discussion is a bit of a simplification for two reasons. First, the reserve requirement is the *minimum* percentage of deposits that banks are required to keep in reserve. Remember, some banks hold excess reserves. However, banks generally prefer to lend money out in order to earn interest, rather than to hold it as reserves. Second, not all money ultimately winds up in banks. Some money is kept in the form of currency or held in brokerage accounts.

When the Fed makes open-market purchases or sales, it increases or decreases the money supply by the amount of the open-market transaction times the money multiplier. When the Fed changes the reserve requirement, it changes the money multiplier itself. For example, if the Fed changed the reserve requirement from 20 percent to 25 percent, it would reduce the money multiplier from 5 to 4 (1/.25), thus decreasing the money supply.

Economic Impact of Monetary Policy

How does an increase in deposits and loans affect the economy? The supply of money in the form of transactions balances (for example, checkable deposits) and the corresponding amount of the banking system's outstanding loans play key roles in the economy. An increase in the supply of money and loans outstanding tends to reduce interest rates (at least in the short run). The increased supply and lower cost (interest rate) of loanable funds encourage many people to spend more on consumption. For example, households are more inclined to purchase a new car or a new home if it is easier to finance. Similarly, businesses are encouraged to invest more in plant and equipment expenditures and in other long-term projects (for example, research and development). These additional consumption and investment expenditures tend to create more income and jobs and to stimulate even more spending. A reduction in deposits and loans, in contrast, tends to reduce spending and income.

Economic Effect of Deposits and Loans

- Increase in deposits and loans: Stimulates spending and income; can increase inflation
- Decrease in deposits and loans: Restrains spending and income; can reduce inflation

As with fiscal policy, stimulative monetary policy tends to increase real (noninflationary) output when the economy has slack resources, and it tends to increase prices when bottlenecks appear or when the economy is already operating near full employment or capacity utilization. Thus, stimulative monetary policy is often favorable to the economy and stock market. That is, it is likely to increase demand for goods and services and thereby increase profits.

Additionally, an increase in the availability of loanable funds may reduce real interest rates. As we shall see, a decline in interest rates is particularly bullish (favorable) for stock prices. When the economy is already operating near its capacity, however, further stimulation is particularly likely to be inflationary.

Why Monetary Policy Is So Important

Stock market analysts pay particular attention to monetary (as opposed to fiscal) policy for several reasons. First, monetary policy has different industry effects. This is because some industries are particularly sensitive to changes in interest rates.

Second, monetary policy is considered easier to track—and perhaps easier to predict. The Fed's weekly monetary data releases are intensively analyzed by some members of the financial press.

monetarists

Third, an influential group of economists (called *monetarists,* many of whom are associated with the University of Chicago) assert that money drives the economy, while fiscal policy plays a more modest role.

Fourth, monetary policy directly affects the stock market through its influence on interest rates. We will consider each of these matters in greater detail.

Factors Affecting Likelihood of Shift in Monetary and Fiscal Policy

A shift toward greater stimulation is more likely if	A shift toward greater restrictiveness is more likely if
• The inflation rate is near its target, or inflation is decreasing.	• The inflation rate is far above its target, or inflation is increasing.
• Unemployment is far above its target, or unemployment is increasing.	• Unemployment is near its target, or unemployment is decreasing.
• The dollar is strong.	• The dollar is weak.
• The trade deficit is small, or there is a trade surplus.	• The trade deficit is large.
• Substantial amounts of capital are flowing into the U.S.	• Foreign capital is threatening to withdraw from or slow its flow into the U.S.

Disproportionate Impact of Monetary Policy

Monetary policy works by rationing credit. Restrictive monetary policy not only raises interest rates (at least in the short run), but it also tends to limit availability of credit to borrowers who represent greater credit risks and thereby influences the allocation of funds among the financial intermediaries.

Savings and loan associations and mutual savings banks (thrift institutions) may be particularly hard hit when interest rates increase. The thrifts have historically maintained a large percentage of their portfolios in long-term fixed-rate mortgages.

The thrifts' deposits, in contrast, have tended to be available to their depositors on demand or to be represented by CDs with relatively short maturities. This type of situation implies an imbalance between the maturity structure of thrifts' assets (long-term) and their liabilities (short-term). The imbalance has tended to make the thrifts more vulnerable to rising interest rates than other lending institutions that do not have a high concentration of assets in fixed-rate mortgages. As interest rates rise, the costs of funds tend to go up, while the rates that the thrifts earn on existing fixed-rate mortgage loans remain relatively constant. The larger the proportion of their assets tied up in fixed-rate loans, the more vulnerable the thrifts are to rising interest rates. Having experienced the adverse effects of rising interest rates a number of times, the thrifts have sought to limit their exposure. Their sensitivity to increasing interest rates adds to the real estate, construction, building materials, and major appliance industries' vulnerability to tight money.

Over time, a shift to adjustable-rate mortgages and the appropriate use of various instruments for hedging interest rate risks (financial futures, options, and interest rate swaps) have inclined to reduce this vulnerability.[5] Nonetheless, many thrifts (particularly the smaller ones) remain vulnerable to adverse interest rate moves.

Relative Ease of Tracking Monetary Policy

Monetary policy is easier to follow than the lengthy, uncertain path of fiscal policy that includes authorizations, appropriation, and implementation of government expenditures. Tax legislation, the other side of fiscal policy, is equally difficult to follow. Moreover, the greater volatility of monetary policy provides more signals than is the case with fiscal policy.

Monetarists versus Keynesians

Keynesians

Since John Maynard Keynes published his *General Theory of Employment, Interest, and Money* in 1936, the monetarists have debated with those who emphasize the importance of fiscal policy (*Keynesians*). Although the Keynesians dominated economic thinking throughout the 1940s and 1950s, by the early 1960s, the debate was again in full swing. The dispute continues, but the issues may be narrowing. During much of the post-1936 period, the Keynesians were far more influential in and out of government. Since the late 1960s, however, both groups have had substantial influence.

Most economists now agree that both monetary and fiscal policy affect the economy but disagree on their relative importance, although the "rational expectations" school (originating at the University of Chicago, based on the work of Robert Lucas) argues that both monetary and fiscal policy are useless in the long run.

Direct Effect of Monetary Policy on the Stock Market

Monetary policy indirectly influences the stock market through its effect on the economy and on corporate profits. Moreover, the impact of monetary policy on interest rates has a direct effect on the stock market in three related ways.

First, stock prices reflect the present value of their expected future income streams. The rate at which these expected incomes are discounted is affected by the market rates of interest.

Second, investors find bonds relatively more attractive as their yields to maturity increase. As a result, some investors will shift from stocks to bonds when interest rates rise and from bonds to stocks when interest rates fall.

Finally, higher interest rates mean increased borrowing costs for margin investors. These investors will require a higher expected return to justify the greater cost of financing their margin purchases and, as such, may place fewer buy orders than they otherwise would have. Falling interest rates have the opposite effect.

How the Impact of Monetary Policy on Interest Rates Affects the Stock Market

- The market rate of interest affects the rate at which stocks' expected future income streams are discounted.
- As bonds' yields to maturity increase (fall), some investors may switch from stocks (bonds) to bonds (stocks).
- High interest rates result in increased borrowing costs for margin investors, who need a higher expected return to justify their greater financing costs.

MONETARY AND FISCAL POLICY: QUALIFICATIONS AND GOALS

Some Qualifications

As we have seen, the economy may be stimulated by increased government spending, lower taxes, and an increase in the money supply, and it may be restrained by the reverse processes. Now let us introduce some qualifications.

First, the impacts of changes in tax rates and government spending (fiscal policy) or in the reserve requirement, discount rate, and open-market operation (monetary policy) take time to work their way through the economy. As a result, changes in the direction of monetary and fiscal policy generally precede changes in the direction of economic activity. This is particularly true of fiscal policy, because it takes considerable time for Congress to enact a new budget or to change the tax rates.

Second, monetary and fiscal policy are both subject to political pressures. Their degree of sensitivity differs, however. Monetary policy is formulated by the Federal Reserve Board of Governors and its FOMC. Members are appointed by the President and confirmed by the Senate for long (14-year), staggered terms. Furthermore, the Fed is not dependent directly on Congressional appropriations. Its own interest income is more than adequate to cover its operating expenses. The Fed, therefore, is generally able to pursue a relatively independent monetary policy.

Congress and the President jointly formulate fiscal policy. Many diverse interest groups may affect the decision-making process. As a result, short-term pressures increase the difficulty of implementing long-run fiscal policies.

Third, the stock market already incorporates an expectation of the direction of economic policy. Thus, to obtain an advantage relative to that incorporated in the market, investors need to have a superior understanding of economic policy/economy-stock market relationships. In other words, investors need to be able to outguess the market in its forecast for the economy's future.

Goals

The primary economic goals of monetary and fiscal policymakers are price stability and full employment. Most people have a general idea of what price stability and full employment mean. Nonetheless, the concepts are sufficiently complex and confusing to warrant some discussion.

price stability

Price stability is the absence of either a sharply rising (inflation) or falling (deflation) trend in overall prices. Inflation is a general rise in the price level. Thus, for example, a 6 percent annual inflation rate implies that $1.06 is required to buy the same diverse market basket of goods and services as could have been acquired a year earlier for $1. Inflation of 6 percent does not mean that *all* prices rise by 6 percent. In fact, some prices may actually fall, while other prices rise dramatically. An inflation rate of 6 percent simply means that, *on average,* prices rise by 6 percent. Deflation, in contrast, is a general fall in the price level. During most of our history, actual inflation and potential inflation have been much more of a problem than the threat of deflation. Furthermore, policymakers (especially at the Fed) frequently state the problem of achieving price stability as a

disinflation

matter of lowering the rate of inflation (rate of change of prices upward), rather than the complete elimination of all price increases. One sign of a successful monetary policy would be *disinflation*, which means that prices are going up at a slower rate than the rate at which they had previously been going up.

It might be logical to think that full employment would be defined as 100 percent of the labor force's having jobs. Realistically, however, some people (not necessarily the same people) will always be unemployed, even in the best of times. People change jobs (frictional unemployment), work at seasonal jobs (seasonal unemployment), or are unemployed because of location, background, or training (structural unemployment). These various classes of unemployed people create an almost irreducible floor for reported unemployment. In fact, the absence of frictional unemployment would probably not be a good thing. Frictional unemployment often occurs because some percentage of people are looking for better jobs, where their talents, skills, and training can be better utilized and where they can be more productive and earn more money. Society as a whole benefits when individuals work at jobs that maximize their productivity. The height of this floor, however, changes as the economy evolves (see figure 8-2). Full employment, therefore, is generally defined as corresponding to some acceptable level of unemployment. The *unemployment rate* itself is defined as the percentage of the labor force that is out of work and actively seeking a

unemployment rate

FIGURE 8-2
Unemployment, Labor Force Participation, and Employment Rates

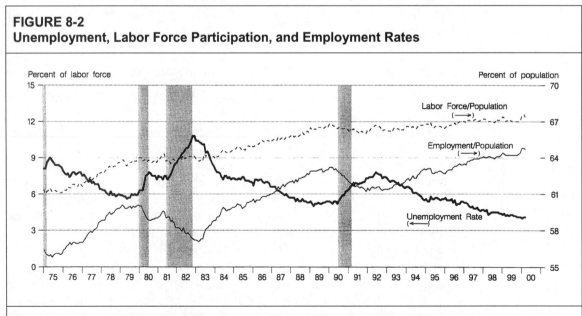

Reprinted with permission of the Federal Reserve Bank of St. Louis, *National Economic Trends.* The chart appeared on page 10 of the May 2000 issue. Michael R. Pakko wrote the lead article.

job. The labor force consists of those who are employed or actively seeking employment. Extensive government statistics are compiled on both employment, unemployment, and inflation.

Currently, the relationship of the U.S. to the international economy is increasing in importance. Thus, as the world economy has grown more interdependent, such matters as the relative exchange value of the dollar (exchange rate), the amount of imports relative to exports (*balance of trade*), and international capital flows (which may take the form of foreigners investing in U.S. securities or U.S. citizens investing in foreign businesses) have become increasingly important to economic policymakers. Moreover, the actions of foreign and other international investors are having an increasingly large impact on U.S. financial markets.

balance of trade

Some of the government's additional economic and quasi-economic goals and concerns include economic growth, freedom, and opportunity; increased productivity; a higher standard of living; environmental protection; energy independence; consumer protection; and product safety. Policies designed to achieve some of these goals may frequently conflict with other goals.

Virtually everyone agrees that price stability and full employment are desirable. Policies to reduce unemployment may, however, accelerate inflation. When the economy is already near full employment and further stimulated by an increase in the money supply, those bidding for the limited supply of labor will cause wages and other prices to rise. However, some stimulation may be administered to a slack economy before the inflation rate is driven upward.

The international situation adds a further complication. During the 1980s, maintaining the value of the dollar and seeking to attract capital to help reduce the budget and trade deficits may have led to a relatively restrictive monetary policy. Such a policy tends to raise U.S. interest rates relative to rates abroad. However, higher interest rates usually lead to reduced domestic economic activity. Thus, policymakers may at times have to choose between doing what is best for the domestic economy and doing what is best with respect to foreign trade.

Inflation rates in the U.S. have been basically downward from their peaks in the early 1980s, as measured by the Consumer Price Index (CPI). This trend has been matched by other leading industrial countries and regions, including the European Union, Canada, and Japan. Figure 8-3 shows the rate of inflation in the U.S. measured by the CPI and inflation expectations as measured by the quarterly Federal Reserve Bank of Philadelphia, the monthly University of Michigan Survey Research Center, and the FOMC ranges as reported to Congress in the annual Humphrey-Hawkins testimony each year. The downward trend is clearly noted in each of the time series and variables shown since 1990. The CPI inflation rate shown in figure 8-3 is the percentage change from the previous year.

FIGURE 8-3
Inflation and Inflation Expectations

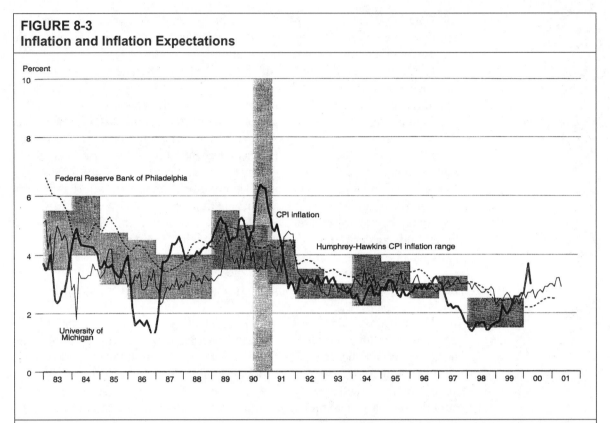

The shaded region shows the Humphrey-Hawkins CPI inflation range. Beginning in January 2000, the Humphrey-Hawkins inflation range was reported using the PCE price index and therefore is not shown on this graph.

Used with permission from Surveys of Consumers, University of Michigan. Reprinted from *Monetary Trends*, June 2000.

INDUSTRY ANALYSIS

Economic analysis assesses the general environment and its impact on firms and industries. Industry analysis, in contrast, examines the specific environment of the markets in which different industries compete. Investors might begin a search for attractive investments by either evaluating the component companies of a selected industry or analyzing a particular firm first and then its industry and competitors. With either scenario, both company and industry analysis are undertaken. In the discussion that follows, the process is assumed to begin with industry analysis. (This is consistent with the top-down approach.)

Before proceeding, we should establish the relevance of industry analysis to investors. The evidence is rather clear on one point: Individual industries have, over time, provided very different returns to investors. On the other hand, there is wide dispersion in the performance of individual firms within particular industries. Furthermore, when assessing a firm's financial data, it is important to see how the firm performs relative to other firms in the same industry in order to make a meaningful comparison.

Research by Michael Porter indicates that a critical factor affecting the profit potential of an industry is the intensity of competition in the industry.[6] He believes that the competitive environment of an industry determines the firm's ability to sustain above-average rates of return on invested capital. Porter discusses five competitive forces that determine the intensity of competition among firms: rivalry among existing competitors, threat of new entrants, substitute products or services, bargaining power of customers, and bargaining power of suppliers. These factors can vary greatly among industries.

In some industries, global competition is more significant than domestic competition. Clearly, the U.S. automobile industry faces competition from firms in Japan, Germany, and Korea. Thus, any analysis of the auto industry must be extended to include global factors.

Their independent movements notwithstanding, attractively performing industries contain a disproportionate number of profitable investments. Therefore, we would like to know how to identify industries with the best economic prospects. One possibility might be to select industries with strong recent records. This assumes that the same forces that produced the past record will continue, at least for a while longer. Projecting past industry performance, however, involves uncertainties similar to those of extrapolating past earnings growth. The central issue is whether past growth reflects the industry's stage of development or isolated circumstances. Knowing the industry's stage of development is a good indicator of whether its recent rate of growth is likely to continue. Thus, identifying an industry's development stage may help assess its growth prospects.

Stages of Industry Development

Industries are thought typically to pass through several developmental stages. Initially, many new firms are established (start-up stage), and growth is rapid. A shakeout then reduces the number of firms (consolidation stage) as the less efficient firms tend to merge or go bankrupt. After the adjustment, growth slows to that of the economy (maturity stage). Finally, new industries begin to grow at the expense of the existing industry (decline stage). Predicting evolution from one stage to another is not easy. In fact, some industries follow different schemes from the typical one just described. For example, the solid waste disposal industry experienced modest performance until the ecology movement brought it to life.

Some experts question the validity of the life cycle approach to industry analysis. They note, for instance, that the Coca-Cola Company has been a successful competitor, deriving much of its revenues from a product that has changed relatively little in 100 years. However, Coca-Cola has achieved its most recent profit momentum through the effects of globalization and international growth. As of 2003, Coke derives over 70 percent of its income from outside the United States.[7]

In general, globalization may offer new life to some mature and declining industries. Products that have already saturated the market in the United States and other industrialized countries might find substantial new marketing opportunities in less developed nations.

Sometimes, companies or even whole industries reinvent themselves with invention or innovation. Thus, what had been a mature or declining industry may suddenly be an industry that has jumped back to the start-up stage.

Life Cycle of an Industry

- Start-up stage: Many new firms; growth is rapid (example: genetic engineering)
- Consolidation stage: Shakeout period; growth slows (example: video games)
- Maturity stage: Growth parallels growth of the economy (example: automobile industry)
- Decline stage: Growth is slower than that of the economy (example: railroads)

As with market analysis, investors should bear in mind the relative nature of the process. Although the prospects of individual industries need to be evaluated, the most attractive industries for investment are not necessarily the ones with the greatest stock appreciation potential. Rather, investors seek investments with greater potentials than the market recognizes. In other words, the market may have already taken account of these prospects in the prices of stocks of companies in an attractive industry, so that investors cannot earn superior risk-adjusted returns by investing in that industry. Thus, an industry with bleak prospects may contain attractive investments if the market is even more pessimistic than the true outlook justifies.

It is easy to identify a "hot" industry and a mature or dying industry. All we have to do is to look at the P/E ratios for the various industry indexes. The industry indexes with the highest P/E ratios are the hot industries, and those with the lowest are the mature and dying industries. The real issue is whether or not the hot industries over- or undervalued relative to their prospects; the same goes for the mature and dying industries.

COMPANY ANALYSIS

Once industry analysis has identified a potentially attractive area for investment, the companies within that industry need to be evaluated. Three important company characteristics are competitive position, management quality, and financial soundness. Each relates to how successful a firm is likely to be within its industry or industries.

Competitive Position

Although it is somewhat more difficult to evaluate than its financial strengths and weaknesses, a company's competitive position is an important performance determinant. How able is the firm to withstand competitive pressures? How vigorous are its rivals? What is the government's treatment of the company?

Management Quality

A perceptive, aggressive, forward-looking management improves the odds of a company's realizing its full potential. The following characteristics are relevant: motivation, research and development activity, willingness to take risks, long-term orientation, success in integrating merged firms, effectiveness in delegating authority, use of information systems, utilization of the board of directors as a resource, and relations with financial analysts.

agency problem

Several studies note that managers who are especially interested in stockholder welfare generally outperform those more concerned with their own well-being. This is the issue known as the *agency problem,* which is that when someone is hired as an agent to represent the interests of someone else, incentives must be in place to ensure that the agent puts the interests of the person being represented ahead of the agent's own interests. In this case, the agents are the officers and directors of the firm, and the people being represented are the shareholders. The solution to the agency problem is to align the interests of the agent and the person represented. In this case, stock options are one obvious vehicle, although accounting for these options is a pending regulatory issue and a potential drain on corporate earnings.

Financial Soundness

An attractive industry environment, strong competitive position, and effective management are all-important components of a company's fundamental position. Only companies with adequate financial resources, however, can fully exploit their opportunities. Accordingly, much of fundamental analysis involves assessing the company's financial strengths and weaknesses.

ACCOUNTING CONCEPTS AND FINANCIAL ANALYSIS

Because accounting data are utilized extensively in financial analysis, we shall briefly review the three principal financial statements: the balance sheet, the income statement, and the statement of cash flows.

Financial Statements

Balance Sheet

The balance sheet reflects the financial status of a company at a point in time. It is a listing of what the company owns and what it owes. The assets are traditionally listed on the left-hand side of the balance sheet; these are what the company owns. The right-hand side of the balance sheet indicates where the money came from to buy the assets. There are basically two sources of money: debt (money that is borrowed) and equity (money that the owners have provided).

current assets

Assets are listed in decreasing order of liquidity. The first group of assets listed are known as the current assets. *Current assets* are cash and items that are expected to be converted to cash within the next year. They include cash (which encompasses money market instruments), accounts receivable, and inventory. Prepaid expenses are sometimes shown as an additional entry in current assets.

The remainder of the asset side of the balance sheet is fixed assets. The major item is almost always plant and equipment. Plant and equipment are valued at cost less depreciation, whereas most other assets are valued at the lower of cost or market value.

current liabilities

Liabilities are listed first on the right-hand side of the balance sheet. They are listed in increasing order of maturity. Thus, the standard balance sheet has current liabilities first and long-term debt second. The owner's equity is located at the bottom of the right-hand side of the balance sheet. *Current liabilities* are debts due within one year. This includes accruals and payables, such as accrued wages and accounts payable, as well as short-term debt and any payments of principal on long-term debt that are due within the next year.

The equity section is primarily the money represented by the shareholders' purchase of newly issued stock and retained earnings. The purchase of newly issued stock by shareholders is usually broken into two subcategories: par value and paid-in surplus.

par value

Most stocks have a number associated with them known as *par value*. Although at one time the par value for stock had legal and practical significance, it no longer does. Hence, some common stock is designated as "no par," and some common stocks have a par value of one cent. When an investor buys stock from the company, the purchase price is allocated to the two accounts based on the amount paid. For example, suppose a company has common stock with a par value of $10, and a new share is sold to an investor for $15. The $15 received shows up on the asset side as an increase in the cash balance. In the equity section, $10 is added to the common stock, par value account; the remaining $5 is added to the paid-in surplus account.

The retained earnings account is the sum of the profits the company has accumulated since it was incorporated but not paid to shareholders in the form of dividends. A common mistake is to look at the retained earnings account and assume that it represents a pool of cash. Any cash implicit in the retained earnings account is already a part of the assets. Some of it may be in the form of cash, but the rest of it is invested in one or more of the assets. There is no direct link between most right-hand-side entries (where money comes from) and specific assets on the left-hand side (how the money is used).

**net worth
(equity)**

The *net worth*, or *equity*, section of the balance sheet is the sum of the common stock, paid-in surplus, and retained earnings accounts. It represents the aggregate of how much money the shareholders have put into the firm. It is always analyzed as a single number, because it is the total that matters—the breakdown between the individual accounts is immaterial.

The most important fact to keep in mind is that the total of the assets always equals the sum of the liabilities and stockholders' equity. This is because all money raised has been invested in one or another asset. Conversely, we could say that all assets owned have some source of financing. Figure 8-4 is an example of a typical balance sheet.

**FIGURE 8-4
Example of a Balance Sheet**

Assets		Liabilities and Stockholders' Equity	
Current assets		Current liabilities	
Cash	$10,000	Wages payable	$ 8,000
Accounts receivable	27,000	Accounts payable	29,000
Inventory	61,000	Total current liabilities	$37,000
Total current assets	$98,000		
		Long-term liabilities	
Fixed assets		Note	$ 53,000
Plant and equipment	$187,000	Mortgage	60,000
Less accumulated		Total long-term liabilities	$113,000
depreciation	62,000		
Net fixed assets	$125,000	Stockholders' equity	
		Common stock (par value)	$ 40,000
Total assets	$223,000	Paid-in surplus	10,000
		Retained earnings	23,000
		Total stockholders' equity	$ 73,000
		Total liabilities and	
		stockholders' equity	$223,000

Income Statement

The income statement (see figure 8-5) reflects the results of operations for a period of time. It starts with total sales or revenues. From this, the cost of goods sold is subtracted to obtain the gross profit of the business. Next, both cash and non-cash operating expenses are totaled. The sum of these expenses is subtracted from the gross profit to obtain *earnings before interest and taxes (EBIT)*. EBIT is frequently referred to as operating income or operating profit. The interest expense is then subtracted from the EBIT to obtain the company's *taxable income*. Finally, income taxes are subtracted from taxable income to produce the *net income* number. The income statement helps answer the most basic question about the firm: Did the company make or lose money in the recent period, and how much? Every year (unless the company sells or buys back some stock) the company's net worth will change by the amount of net income that is retained—that is, the net income less any dividends paid. The income statement and balance sheet are thus connected by changes in net worth.

earnings before interest and taxes (EBIT)

taxable income

net income

FIGURE 8-5
Basic Income Statement

Net sales	$200,000
Cost of goods sold	120,000
Gross profit	$ 80,000
Operating expenses	
Wage expense	$40,000
Depreciation expense	10,000
Other	10,000
	$60,000
Earnings before interest and taxes	$20,000
Interest expense	8,000
Earnings before taxes	$12,000
Income taxes	5,000
Net profit	$ 7,000

Statement of Cash Flows

The statement of cash flows is similar to the income statement, but it focuses on where and how cash came into the business, and where and how it left. It shows how the changes in the accounts of the balance sheet contributed to the net change in the cash position for the year.

Preparing accounting statements necessarily involves many subjective judgments, and subjectivity opens up opportunities for abuse. Unfortunately, the temptation is too great for some managers. Permissible accounting

---

Types of Accounting Statements

- Balance sheet: Picture of resources (assets), obligations (liabilities), and net worth (equity) at a certain point in time
- Income statement: Earnings, calculated as revenues less expenses, over a period of time
- Statement of cash flows: A list of how cash entered and left the firm over a period of time

---

conventions can be misused to distort a company's financial appearance. Nevertheless, the vast majority of accounting statements reflect a meaningful financial picture.

Ratio Analysis

When we look at financial statements (for example, figures 8-4 and 8-5), what we see is a lot of numbers. A financial analyst of a firm wants to go to the next step to ask: Are these numbers good? Are they bad? What do they mean? The traditional technique to answer these questions is to create financial ratios. There are hundreds of ratios that can be, and are, used. Many of them are so closely related that they are really not providing additional information. The trick is to identify a relatively small number of ratios that provide critical information, and stick with these. Furthermore, because many of the ratios are closely related, they are always grouped together in terms of the characteristic of the firm on which they focus. Unfortunately, the myriad of books published on the subject of financial analysis do not agree on how many ratios to consider, what the most critical ratios are, or even how they should be grouped together. Thus, the discussion that follows is representative, not definitive, of ratios and classification categories. The classification categories we will use are liquidity, debt, profitability, and efficiency.

Liquidity Ratios

The purpose of the liquidity ratios is to evaluate a business's ability to meet its cash obligations in the near future. The most commonly used (and oldest) liquidity ratio is the *current ratio*. It is defined as current assets divided by current liabilities. As with all ratios, the optimal value varies from company to company, industry to industry, and over time. Stable incomes and reliable sources of short-term credit lessen the need for liquid assets and therefore reduce the optimal current ratio level. Indeed, a high current ratio may indicate that resources are being tied up unnecessarily.

current ratio

The *quick ratio,* or *acid test ratio,* focuses on the most liquid of the liquid assets—cash and receivables—and is defined as cash plus receivables

quick ratio
acid test ratio

divided by current liabilities. Some people define the numerator as current assets minus inventory. The two definitions should produce the same number. The argument for evaluating liquidity without counting inventory is that if the company is having financial difficulties, it may well be that inventory is not selling. Hence, high inventory may be a sign of a liquidity problem, not a source of liquidity. Simply put, a high current ratio and low quick ratio might be a warning sign indicating that the firm is experiencing difficulty moving its inventory.

inventory turnover ratio

The quality of the inventory can be measured directly with the *inventory turnover ratio*. There are several different definitions for this ratio; the most common is the cost of goods sold divided by average yearly inventory.[8] The reciprocal of the inventory turnover ratio, multiplied by 360, represents the average number of days that goods are held in inventory.[9] Normally, we would say that a high inventory turnover suggests brisk sales and well-managed inventories. However, a high inventory turnover ratio might also indicate inadequate inventories. A low inventory turnover ratio may reflect idle resources that are tied up in excess inventories and/or a large obsolete inventory component. It might also indicate that the company uses a marketing strategy of assuring customers that there will always be adequate inventory.

One way to interpret the industry turnover ratio is to divide the value into 12 (the number of months in a year). This indicates how long (in months) the inventory is in the business before it is sold. Thus, an inventory turnover ratio of 6 could be interpreted as having inventory on hand an average of 2 months, and a turnover ratio of 2 would mean the inventory is sitting around for 6 months.

average collection period (ACP)

The quality of a firm's accounts receivable is usually measured by *average collection period (ACP)*, which is defined as the net accounts receivable divided by daily sales. Daily sales is defined as annual net sales divided by 360. The ratio should be compared with the company's stated credit policy. For example, a manufacturer might have a credit policy based on an expectation of receiving payments within 30 days of billing. If the ACP is longer than 30 days, the firm may have a problem with credit extensions. Some firms make easy credit a key part of their marketing program. Such firms would likely have large ACPs, and this would simply reflect their business strategy. An unusually low average collection period might suggest that the firm is losing potential customers by maintaining an overly stringent credit policy.

Liquidity Ratios

- Current: Current assets/current liabilities
- Quick (or acid test): (Current assets – inventories)/current liabilities
- Inventory turnover: Cost of goods sold/average yearly inventory
- Average collection period: Net accounts receivable/daily sales

---

Example :   Using figures 8-4 and 8-5, what are the liquidity ratios for this firm?

$$\text{Current ratio} = \frac{\$98,000}{\$37,000} = 2.65$$

$$\text{Quick ratio} = \left(\frac{\$98,000 - \$61,000}{\$37,000} \right) = 1.0$$

$$\text{Inventory turnover} = \frac{\$120,000}{\$61,000} = 1.97$$

$$\text{Average collection period} = \frac{\$27,000}{\left(\dfrac{\$200,000}{360} \right)} = 48.6 \text{ days}$$

Debt Ratios

debt ratio

debt-equity ratio
equity multiplier

times-interest-earned
ratio

Debt ratios are used to measure the extent to which a company uses debt financing, and the impact of that debt financing on the firm's overall profitability. The four most common debt ratios are the debt, the debt-equity, and the times-interest-earned ratios. The *debt ratio* is total debt divided by total assets. It tells the analyst in the simplest possible terms the percentage of assets that are financed by debt. Many people like to use variations of the debt ratio. The most common variation is the *debt-equity ratio*,[10] which is total debt divided by total equity. Another is the *equity multiplier*, which is total assets divided by total equity.

The final debt ratio is the *times-interest-earned ratio,* sometimes called the earnings-coverage ratio, which is computed as EBIT (earnings before interest and taxes) divided by interest. Unlike the other three ratios, it relates the company's interest obligation to its earning power. The higher the ratio, the greater the safety of a company's interest payments.

Interpreting the debt ratio can be tricky, because some debt is good, but too much debt is bad. Unfortunately, it is never clear when a business has moved from "some" debt to "too much" debt. There are two reasons that some debt is good. The first is that interest payments are tax deductible for a business. The second is the benefit of financial leverage. Specifically, if a company can borrow at X percent and earn (X + Y) percent on the money, the difference is like a windfall gain. Debt becomes a problem as soon as a firm is unable to make its interest and/or principal payments. This failure could well force a company into bankruptcy. (Financial default and bankruptcy are discussed in appendix 9-B.)

A company's appropriate debt ratio varies primarily with its earning stability. A rapid rise in the ratio can suggest potential problems. It is of less concern if the increased debt still leaves the firm with a substantial cushion

debt capacity

of equity and the firm has profitable operations; the company may simply be taking advantage of heretofore unused debt capacity. *Debt capacity* is the firm's ability to borrow money. Having underutilized debt capacity is a wonderful resource because it means that if a problem or opportunity arises for which a lot of cash is immediately needed, the firm should be able to borrow it. However, underutilized debt capacity would also mean the firm is not currently taking full advantage of the two benefits of using borrowed money.

Debt Ratios

- Debt: Total debt/total assets
- Debt-equity: Total debt/total equity
- Equity multiplier: Total assets/total equity
- Times-interest-earned: EBIT/interest expense

Debt is not the only type of fixed payment obligation. In particular, leases can complicate accounting statement analysis. Purchasing assets with borrowed funds increases the debt ratio, whereas leasing the same assets does not increase debt *per se*. The long-term obligations are similar, however, whether new assets are leased or purchased with borrowed money. Thus, debt ratios do not always accurately reflect a company's total financial commitments. Investors need to look beyond the debt ratios of companies that lease a large fraction of their assets. Companies must show their capitalized long-term lease obligations on their balance sheets.[11]

Example: Using figures 8-4 and 8-5, what are the debt ratios for this firm?

$$\text{Debt ratio} = \frac{(\$37,000 + \$113,000)}{\$223,000} = .67$$

$$\text{Debt-equity ratio} = \frac{(\$37,000 + \$113,000)}{\$73,000} = 2.05$$

$$\text{Equity multiplier} = \frac{\$223,000}{\$73,000} = 3.05$$

$$\text{Times-interest-earned} = \frac{\$20,000}{\$8,000} = 2.5$$

Profitability Ratios

return on equity (ROE)
return on assets (ROA)
net profit margin (NPM)

The three most important profitability ratios are *return on equity (ROE)*, *return on assets (ROA)*, and *net profit margin (NPM)*. ROE is net income divided by total equity, ROA is net income divided by total assets, and NPM is net income divided by net sales.

The net income number should be for a full-year period, as a shorter time frame could allow seasonal influences to distort the results. The total equity and total asset numbers should be for the beginning of the year, rather than the end of the year, because the end-of-the-year numbers would incorporate the earnings that were retained during the year. However, if the beginning-of-the-year numbers are not available, the end-of-year numbers are used. The net sales number should be for the same time period as the net income number.

Profitability Ratios

- Return on equity (ROE): Net income/total equity
- Return on assets (ROA): Net income/total assets
- Net profit margin (NPM): Net income/net sales

The ROE ratio indicates the profits generated relative to shareholders' investments. In theory, a firm could pay out all of its net income as dividends. If it did, then the return on the investors' money would literally be the ROE. The higher the ROE number, the better for the shareholder.

The ROA formula indicates how profitable the firm is relative to the investment in assets. It provides a measure of operational efficiency. As with the ROE, the larger this number, the stronger the firm is financially.

The net profit margin indicates the percentage of profit in each dollar of sales. It is also a measure of efficiency.

Example: Using figures 8-4 and 8-5, what are the profitability ratios for this firm?

$$\text{Return on equity} = \frac{\$7,000}{\$73,000} = .096$$

$$\text{Return on assets} = \frac{\$7,000}{\$223,000} = .031$$

$$\text{Net profit margin} = \frac{\$7,000}{\$200,000} = .035$$

Efficiency Ratios

total asset turnover ratio
fixed asset turnover ratio

The efficiency ratios measure how efficient the business is with certain assets, or with all of its assets. Some textbooks include the average collection period and the inventory turnover ratio as efficiency ratios, but we included them as measures of liquidity. The two other common efficiency ratios are the total asset turnover ratio and the fixed asset turnover ratio. The *total asset turnover ratio* is net sales divided by total assets, and the *fixed asset turnover ratio* is net sales divided by net fixed assets.

Efficiency Ratios

- Total asset turnover: Net sales/total assets
- Fixed asset turnover: Net sales/net fixed assets

The total asset turnover ratio is interpreted as the amount of sales generated per dollar of total assets. Thus, a ratio of 2.0 means the firm is generating $2.00 in sales per $1.00 invested in assets. Larger ratios mean more efficiency. However, an extremely large ratio may signify a firm is underinvested in assets and would do well to expand its assets.

Similarly, the fixed asset turnover ratio is interpreted as the amount of sales generated per dollar of fixed assets. Thus, a ratio of 3.5 means the firm is generating $3.50 in sales per $1.00 invested in fixed assets. Larger ratios mean more efficiency, but too large a ratio may signify a problem. Remember, the denominator is *net* fixed assets, which means that it is the amount paid for the fixed assets less the accumulated depreciation charges against these assets. Older assets will have substantial accumulated depreciation charges, and thus will tend to produce large fixed asset turnover ratios. Similarly, new assets (and more technologically efficient assets) will tend to have little in the way of accumulated depreciation, and thus may produce low turnover ratios. Thus, the fixed asset turnover ratio may say as much about the age of the fixed assets as it says about their efficiency in generating sales.

Example: Using figures 8-4 and 8-5, what are the efficiency ratios for this firm?

$$\text{Total asset turnover} = \frac{\$200,000}{\$223,000} = .90$$

$$\text{Fixed asset turnover} = \frac{\$200,000}{\$125,000} = 1.6$$

Du Pont Analysis

decomposition analysis

Many people like to use the Du Pont analysis, also called *decomposition analysis*, to analyze a firm's financial statements. The Du Pont analysis can be done in a short-form or long-form version. In the short-form version, the ROE is shown as the product of ROA (operational profitability) and the equity multiplier (leverage).

$$\text{ROE} = \text{ROA} \times \text{Equity multiplier} \qquad \text{(Equation 8-1)}$$

$$\frac{\text{Net income}}{\text{Equity}} = \frac{\text{Net income}}{\text{Total assets}} \times \frac{\text{Total assets}}{\text{Equity}} \qquad \text{(Equation 8-2)}$$

Notice in equation 8-2 that multiplying the ROA by the equity multiplier causes the denominator of the ROA and the numerator of the equity multiplier to cancel out, yielding net income divided by equity, which is the definition of ROE. However, note that calculating ROE from the other two factors is not the point of decomposition analysis. Rather, the point is to break down the ROE value into its critical components.

By breaking down ROE into the ROA and the equity multiplier, we can determine the extent to which ROE is a function of operational profitability—which is a positive concept—and leverage—which can be either positive or negative but certainly implies greater risk. In other words, to the extent that a high ROE results from a large equity multiplier rather than a large ROA, it is due to taking more risk rather than operating more profitably.

Example: You are analyzing a client's business and notice its ROE has been fairly constant over the last few years. However, you decompose the ROE into its ROA and equity multiplier and notice that the ROA is steadily decreasing and the equity multiplier is steadily rising. The obvious conclusion is that the firm is headed for trouble, as there are limits to how high it can increase its equity multiplier.

ROA can be broken down further into NPM and asset turnover.

$$\text{ROA} = \text{NPM} \times \text{Asset turnover} \qquad \text{(Equation 8-3)}$$

$$\frac{\text{Net income}}{\text{Total assets}} = \frac{\text{Net income}}{\text{Total revenues}} \times \frac{\text{Total revenues}}{\text{Total assets}} \qquad \text{(Equation 8-4)}$$

NPM is a measure of profitability, and asset turnover is a measure of operating efficiency. Again, the point is to evaluate the factors that contribute to ROA, not simply to calculate ROA from them. By plugging the value of ROA from equation 8-3 into 8-1, we obtain

$$ROE = NPM \text{ x Asset turnover x Equity multiplier} \qquad \text{(Equation 8-5)}$$

$$\frac{\text{Net income}}{\text{Equity}} = \frac{\text{Net income}}{\text{Total revenues}} \text{ x } \frac{\text{Total revenue}}{\text{Total assets}} \text{ x } \frac{\text{Total assets}}{\text{Equity}} \quad \text{(Equation 8-6)}$$

Equation 8-6 is the long version of the Du Pont analysis. Figure 8-6 shows graphically how the Du Pont ratios fit together. Equation 8-6 states that ROE is a function of profitability (NPM), efficiency (asset turnover), and leverage (equity multiplier). Breaking down the critical ROE ratio into the other ratios and comparing them to industry averages allows the manager or analyst to evaluate the sources of performance.

Example: Consider the following three firms.

Firm	Net Profit Margin	Total Asset Turnover	Equity Multiplier	ROE
XYZ	2%	4.0	1.25	10%
JKL	5%	2.0	1.0	10%
PQR	2%	1.0	5.0	10%

All three firms have the identical returns on equity (10 percent). We can readily see, however, that they have followed three different strategies to achieve this result. The XYZ Company has a low profit margin but a high turnover ratio. Thus, it is probably a discount type operation, which slashes prices and then makes it up on volume. The JKL firm has a high profit margin but a low turnover ratio. It is probably charging higher prices so that what it loses in volume, the firm makes up on profit margin. The PQR firm has both a low profit margin and a low turnover ratio, but it compensates for these by heavily leveraging the company. The PQR firm is clearly the riskiest of the three firms. It is not completely obvious which of the other two firms is the stronger.

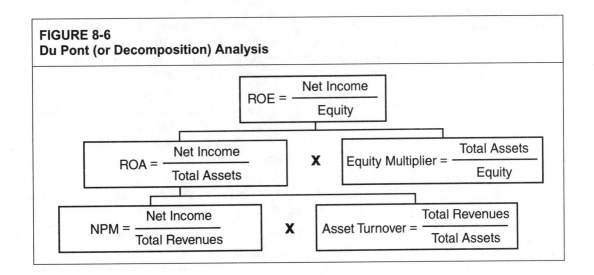

FIGURE 8-6
Du Pont (or Decomposition) Analysis

$$ROE = \frac{Net\ Income}{Equity}$$

$$ROA = \frac{Net\ Income}{Total\ Assets} \qquad X \qquad Equity\ Multiplier = \frac{Total\ Assets}{Equity}$$

$$NPM = \frac{Net\ Income}{Total\ Revenues} \qquad X \qquad Asset\ Turnover = \frac{Total\ Revenues}{Total\ Assets}$$

Other Ratios

earnings per share (EPS)

In addition to liquidity, debt, profitability, and efficiency ratios, investors may find several other ratios useful. *Earnings per share (EPS)* is the company's total earnings (less any preferred dividends) divided by the number of shares of common stock outstanding. Several different earnings numbers are often reported. Fully diluted EPS assumes the exercise of all outstanding warrants and rights and conversion of any outstanding convertible bonds and convertible preferred stock. In other words, to calculate fully diluted earnings per share, we divide net earnings by the number of shares of stock that would be outstanding if all warrants, rights, and conversion privileges were exercised. In a sense, fully diluted earnings per share provides a worst-case-scenario analysis. Earnings figures may include or exclude extraordinary items and the results from noncontinuing operations.

dividend yield
dividend payout ratio

The current annual dividend divided by the price per share is the *dividend yield*. The *dividend payout ratio* is the dividends paid during the year divided by the company's earnings during the year. It can also be computed as dividends per share divided by EPS. A low dividend payout ratio may indicate a desire to finance growth internally, or it may be a sign of a struggling company. A high dividend payout ratio may suggest few attractive investment opportunities.

cash flow per share

Cash flow per share is the sum of after-tax profits and depreciation and other non-cash expenses divided by the number of shares of common stock outstanding. The cash-flow-per-share figure reflects an important source of discretionary funds.

book value per share

Book value per share equals the company's net worth (after subtracting that attributable to preferred shareholders) divided by the number of shares of common stock outstanding. The per-share book value is typically compared

**price-book value
ratio**

with the current stock price, and the ratio is known as the *price-book value
ratio*. A high book value relative to the stock's price may indicate either
unrecognized potential or overvalued assets. The book values of railroad
companies, for example, are often many times the market price of the stock.
Unless the assets can be sold for close to their book values, however, the
railroads' modest profit rates justify their low stock prices. For most
companies, the per-share book value is much lower than the price of the
stock. In other words, most firms are worth more than just the combined
value of their assets. Book value is based on historical costs and generally
fails to take into account the impact of inflation. It also ignores intangible
assets such as the quality of R&D that the firm is currently undertaking or the
value of well-trained and highly motivated employees.

Other Useful Ratios

- Earnings per share (EPS): (Net income after taxes –
  preferred dividends)/number of shares
- Dividend yield: Indicated annual dividend/price per share
- Dividend payout: Dividends per share/EPS
- Cash flow per share: (After-tax profits + depreciation and
  other noncash expenses)/number of shares
- Book value per share: Net worth attributable to common
  shareholders/number of shares
- Price-book value ratio: Price per share/(net worth
  attributable to common shareholders/number of shares)

Sources of Ratios

A ratio by itself means nothing. It is simply a number. It takes on
meaning only when compared to something else. There are two sources of
comparison. One is to look at each ratio over time. Depending on data
availability, analysts look at anywhere from 2 to 5 years worth of data. The
other source is to compare ratios with those of similar companies. Thus,
averages of industrywide ratios are helpful. Robert Morris Associates
collects data and computes ratios for a large group of industries. Other
sources include Dun & Bradstreet, Standard & Poor's, and Margent
Corporation. Individual industry ratios may be computed with appropriate
data from several similar companies. The most effective comparison may be
to compare a company's ratios over time against industry averages over the
same time period.

Comprehensive Example

Suppose a client comes to you, and his major holding is a small business
for which he is the sole shareholder. Your recommendations for a financial

plan for the client will depend, in part, on your analysis of his business. You request and receive his financial statements for the last 3 years (see figures 8-7 and 8-8). Your client indicates that the sales of his firm are growing nicely, the net income was off a little last year, but overall he generates a good dividend income from the business. Despite this summary, you compute the relevant financial ratios (figure 8-9) and you obtain the industry averages for these ratios (also shown in figure 8-9).[12]

The current and quick ratios show a slight downward trend, and both are below industry averages at the end of 2003. The inventory turnover has declined significantly from 5.12 to 3.64, which means that the inventory is sitting around a lot longer before it is sold. In 2001, the inventory was on hand about 2 1/3 months (12/5.12), and by 2003, it was sitting around for nearly 3 1/3 months (12/3.64). Unless there has been a deliberate decision to increase inventory, this would suggest a slight problem. Similarly, the average collection period has grown from 22.25 days to 42.07 days, well above the industry average of 30 days. Again, unless there was a deliberate decision to give customers more generous credit terms, this suggests

---

FIGURE 8-7
Client's Balance Sheet for the Last 3 Years

	(All Numbers in Thousands)		
	2001	2002	2003
Cash	50	37	25
Accounts receivable	34	52	68
Inventory	75	92	114
Current assets	159	181	207
Plant and equipment	250	250	250
Less: accumulated depreciation	150	160	170
Net fixed assets	100	90	80
Total assets	259	271	287
Accrued wages	10	10	10
Accounts payable	15	25	35
Notes payable	45	55	75
Current liabilities	70	90	120
Long-term debt	100	100	100
Common stock (par)	20	20	20
Paid-in-surplus	10	10	10
Retained earnings	59	51	37
Total liability and equity	259	271	287

FIGURE 8-8			
Client's Income Statement for the Last 3 Years			
	(All Numbers in Thousands)		
	2001	2002	2003
Sales	550	582	590
− Cost of goods sold	384	400	415
= Gross profit	166	182	175
− Cash expenses	100	110	115
− Depreciation	10	10	10
= EBIT	56	62	50
− Interest expenses	11	12	13
= Taxable Income	45	50	37
− Taxes	9	10	7
= Net income	36	40	30
− Dividends paid out	35	48	44

problems with collections. Overall, this firm is developing a liquidity problem as evidenced by the decline of the current and quick ratios, especially in light of the apparent deterioration of the quality of inventory and receivables.

The firm is increasing its reliance on the use of debt and financial leverage. It has gone from financing 66 percent of its assets with debt to financing 77 percent of its assets with debt. The firm had more debt financing than the typical firm in the industry to start with, and the situation has deteriorated. The deterioration in the times-interest-earned ratio indicates that the firm is not doing a good job of supporting the incremental debt financing. If this business needed to find an additional lender for future financing, it would probably not be able to locate one. The increased reliance on debt financing either has exhausted or soon will exhaust the firm's debt capacity. The only source of new financing would be the sale of equity, which means either the owner would have to invest more of his own money in the firm, or he would have to give up part of the ownership of the firm to a new investor.

The strength of the firm is its attractive return on equity, which has remained well above industry average. The return on assets is deteriorating, as is the net profit margin.

The total asset turnover ratio is comparable to the industry average. However, given the deterioration in the quality of the receivables and inventory (as noted by the decline in the inventory turnover ratio and the growth in the average collection period), the total asset turnover ratio is

FIGURE 8-9
Ratios and Industry Averages

	(All Numbers in Thousands)			
	2001	2002	2003	Ind. Avg.
<u>Liquidity ratios</u>				
Current ratio	2.27	2.01	1.73	2.5
Quick ratio	1.20	.99	.78	1.0
Inventory turnover	5.12	4.35	3.64	4.0
Average collection period	22.25	32.16	41.49	30.0
<u>Debt ratios</u>				
Debt ratio	.66	.70	.77	.50
Equity multiplier	2.91	3.35	4.28	2.00
Times-interest-earned	5.09	5.16	3.85	6.00
<u>Profitability ratios</u>				
Return on equity	40.4	49.4	44.8	30.0
Return on assets	13.9	14.8	10.5	15.0
Net profit margin	6.5	6.9	5.1	7.5
<u>Efficiency ratios</u>				
Total asset turnover	2.12	2.15	2.06	2.00
Fixed asset turnover	5.50	6.47	7.38	4.00
<u>Other ratios</u>				
Dividend payout	97.2	120.0	146.7	30.0
<u>Du Pont analysis</u>	<u>NPM</u>	<u>TAT</u>	<u>Eq. Mul.</u>	<u>ROE</u>
2001	6.5	2.12	2.91	40.4
2002	6.9	2.15	3.35	49.4
2003	5.1	2.06	4.28	44.8
Industry average	7.5	2.00	2.00	30.0

Note: Inventory turnover is based on the cost of goods sold and year-end inventory.

suspect. The firm is doing a good job with its fixed asset turnover ratio, but note that the accumulated depreciation is well over one-half of the total investment in plant and equipment. This would suggest aging fixed assets, which itself may be a source of problems. The strong fixed asset turnover ratio would certainly explain why the total asset turnover ratio is about equal to the industry average despite the overinvestment in accounts receivable and inventory.

Because there is no stock price available and we do not know the number of shares outstanding, the only "other ratio" that can be computed is the dividend payout ratio. But this tells an incredible story. The owner has moved from paying out almost all of his earnings as dividends (97.2 percent in 2001), to paying out substantially more in dividends than the firm earned (146.7 percent in 2003). These excessive dividend payments are showing up on the balance sheet in two places. One is the dramatic decline in cash, and the other is the steady decline in the retained earnings. (When a dividend is paid, the accounting entries are to reduce cash on the left-hand side of the balance sheet and to reduce retained earnings on the right-hand side.) It is the decline in the retained earnings that is producing a reduction in equity, which in turn creates the rise in the debt ratio.

Finally, the Du Pont analysis emphasizes the above points. Profitability (as measured by the net profit margin) is a little weak, and efficiency (as measured by the total asset turnover) is on the stronger side. The primary reason the firm's ROE is so much stronger than the industry average is the increased financial leverage (as measured by the equity multiplier).

As a conclusion, the firm is clearly deteriorating. Unless the client is able to get the inventory and receivables under control, improve the profit margin, and most important, substantially reduce dividend payments over the next few years, the firm will likely collapse. This client needs to start worrying about alternative sources of income, as well as about how to straighten out his business.

FUNDAMENTAL ANALYSIS VERSUS MARKET EFFICIENCY

Fundamental analysis of *private* companies is an important skill for many people (for example, a bank loan officer or a financial planner). However, the value of performing fundamental analysis on *publicly* traded companies is not as obvious. After all, if markets are relatively efficient (semistrong form), the (known) fundamental strengths and weaknesses of companies are already accurately reflected in their market prices. Under these circumstances, it could be argued that fundamental analysis of a publicly traded company is a waste of time. If, however, the market at least occasionally misvalues securities vis-à-vis the available public information, fundamental analysis of publicly traded companies may be worthwhile. Although the degree of market efficiency is a controversial topic, whatever level is achieved occurs because some important market participants, such as brokerage firms and other investment houses, analyze fundamentals. In other words, fundamental analysts tend to make markets more efficient than they would otherwise be. Remember, a requirement of market efficiency is that there be a sufficient number of informed investors. Indeed, many investors (both large and small) devote considerable amounts of time and money to undertake or buy such research. Moreover, several firms (for example, IBES International) regularly publish consensus estimates of earnings by industry analysts. When actual earnings differ from these consensus estimates, the market reacts quickly to raise or lower stock prices, depending on the direction of the surprise.

A study by H. Russell Fogler (1993) showed that the crucial factor in stocks that enjoyed the best versus the worst price performance during given years was the relationship between expected earnings estimates of professional analysts and the firm's actual earnings (earnings surprise).[13] He found that stock prices increased if actual earnings exceeded expected earnings (positive earnings surprises), and they fell if earnings did not reach expected levels (negative earnings surprises). Thus, if investors or analysts can do a superior job of projecting earnings and their expectations differ from the consensus, they will probably have a superior investment record.

In analyzing the possible superior returns to performing fundamental analysis, it is important to consider the costs as well as the benefits. Obtaining the information necessary to forecast a company's future sales, profits, and dividends is both costly and time consuming. Even if an investor "beats the market" by performing a detailed fundamental analysis, it might be worthwhile to ask how much time and expense were devoted to that analysis and how much that individual could have earned during that time. It might also be worthwhile to ask whether the investor's methods of analysis result in *consistently* superior returns or whether there have been only a few exceptionally good, perhaps lucky, investments.

SUMMARY AND CONCLUSIONS

Traditional fundamental analysis begins with an analysis of the economy (macroeconomic analysis), continues with an industry analysis, and concludes with an analysis of specific firms. Macroeconomic analysis focuses on the current position in the business cycle (expansion, peak, contraction, and trough), as well as what is being done with monetary and fiscal policy to manage the economy. The tools of fiscal policy are the size of the budget deficit or surplus, changes in the tax code, and debt management policy. The key to monetary policy is that banks are required to hold reserves, and the amount of reserves they have is the basis for the amount of loans they are willing to extend. The Fed has three tools for conducting monetary policy. The one used daily is open-market operations—the purchase and sale of government bonds. Occasionally, the Fed uses a change in the discount rate. Rarely, it uses changes in reserve requirements. Monetary policy can disproportionately affect specific industries, but it has the attractive feature that it is easy for people to track. The goals of monetary and fiscal policy are price stability and full employment.

Evaluating the industry's stage in its life cycle may be helpful. The stages of development in an industry are start-up, consolidation, maturity, and decline.

Company analysis involves assessing a company's relative strengths and weaknesses within its industry(ies). Competitive position, management quality, and financial soundness are critical.

An opinion as to the financial soundness of a firm is based on its financial statements. These include the balance sheet, the income statement, and the statement of cash flows. The traditional technique for understanding financial statements is ratio analysis. One way to evaluate ratios is by grouping them into categories. Liquidity ratios evaluate the ability of the firm to meet near-term liquidity needs. Debt ratios evaluate the extent to which the company uses debt financing (that is, financial leverage), and the impact of that debt financing on the firm's profitability and default risk exposure. The three critical profitability ratios are the return on equity, return on assets, and net profit margins. Efficiency ratios consider the ability of the company to generate sales with its assets.

Other ratios to be considered are the EPS, dividend yield, dividend payout ratio, and price-book value ratio. The relative impact of the different components of operation can be examined with a Du Pont analysis. The long version states that the return on equity equals the product of the net profit margin (a measure of profitability), total asset turnover (a measure of efficiency), and the equity multiplier (a measure of the use of financial leverage). Ratios should be considered only in the context of a trend over time, or in comparison to industry averages.

If the market is at least semistrong efficient, the value of fundamental analysis is debatable for a publicly traded security. However, a requirement for semistrong efficiency is that a reasonable number of people have performed a capable fundamental analysis and thus have a good sense of the value of each company. For privately owned firms, however, fundamental analysis is critical for understanding their strengths and weaknesses.

CHAPTER REVIEW

Answers to the review questions and the self-test questions start on page 733.

Key Terms

macroeconomic analysis	monetary policy
industry analysis	Federal Reserve Board (Fed)
company analysis	M1
leading indicators	M2
coincident indicators	reserve requirements
lagging indicators	open-market operations
fiscal policy	discount rate (monetary policy)
debt management policy	excess reserves

money multiplier
monetarists
Keynesians
price stability
disinflation
unemployment rate
balance of trade
agency problem
balance sheet
current assets
current liabilities
par value
net worth (equity)
earnings before interest and taxes
   (EBIT)
taxable income
net income
current ratio
quick ratio
acid test ratio

inventory turnover ratio
average collection period
   (ACP)
debt ratio
debt-equity ratio
equity multiplier
times-interest-earned ratio
debt capacity
return on equity (ROE)
return on assets (ROA)
net profit margin (NPM)
total asset turnover ratio
fixed asset turnover ratio
decomposition analysis
earnings per share (EPS)
dividend yield
dividend payout ratio
cash flow per share
book value per share
price-book value ratio

Review Questions

8-1. Explain how fiscal policy operates through taxes and through government spending.

8-2. How would the stock market be expected to react to each of the following developments?
   a. The Fed, fearing that a recession is threatening, lowers the federal funds rate and expands the money supply. Long-term interest rates fall by over 200 basis points.
   b. Congress finally gets serious about reducing the budget deficit and raises taxes across the board by $100 billion. The Fed cushions the blow by expanding the money supply. Interest rates fall dramatically, while the GDP continues to grow.
   c. The Third World countries form a debtors' cartel and offer to negotiate. When the bargaining gets nowhere, they announce a total moratorium on interest and principal payments. The creditor nations respond by cutting off all credit.

8-3. What are the goals of monetary and fiscal policy? What do these goals indicate is the appropriate action during each stage of the business cycle?

8-4. Discuss the Fed's three principal tools and how they are used to affect the economy. Address the degree of use and effectiveness of each method.

Balance Sheet for Review Question 8-7 (Amounts in Millions, except Share Data)

	January 28, 2003	January 30, 2002
Assets		
Current assets		
Cash and cash equivalents	$ 167	$ 168
Short-term investments, including current maturities of long-term investments	10	2
Receivables, net	835	587
Merchandise inventories	6,556	5,489
Other current assets	209	144
Total current assets	7,777	6,390
Property and equipment, at cost		
Land	4,230	3,248
Buildings	6,167	4,834
Furniture, fixtures, and equipment	2,877	2,279
Leasehold improvements	665	493
Construction in progress	1,032	791
Capital leases	261	245
	15,232	11,890
Less accumulated depreciation and amortization	2,164	1,663
Net property and equipment	13,068	10,227
Long-term investments	15	15
Notes receivable	77	48
Cost in excess of the fair value of net assets acquired, net of accumulated amortization of $41 at January 28, 2001, and $33 at January 30, 2000	314	311
Other	134	90
Total Assets	$21,385	$17,081
Liabilities and Stockholders' Equity		
Current liabilities		
Accounts payable	$1,976	$1,993
Accrued salaries and related expenses	627	541
Sales taxes payable	298	269
Other accrued expenses	1,402	763
Income taxes payable	78	61
Current installments of long-term debt	4	29
Total current liabilities	4,385	3,656
Long-term debt, excluding current installments	1,545	750
Other long-term liabilities	245	237
Deferred income taxes	195	87
Minority interest	11	10
Stockholders' Equity		
Common stock, par value $0.05. Authorized: 10,000,000,000 shares; issued and outstanding—2,323,747,000 shares at January 28, 2001, and 2,304,317,000 shares at January 30, 2000	110	108
Paid-in capital	4,810	4,319
Retained earnings	10,151	7,941
Accumulated other comprehensive income	(67)	(27)
Total stockholders' equity	15,004	12,341
Total Liabilities and Stockholders' Equity	$21,385	$17,081

Income Statement for Review Question 8-7 (Amounts in Millions, except Per Share Data)	Fiscal Year Ended	
	January 28, 2003	January 30, 2002
Net Sales	$45,738	$38, 434
Cost of merchandise sold	32,057	27,023
Gross profit	13,681	11,411
Operating expenses		
Selling and store operating	8,513	6,819
Pre-opening	142	113
General and administrative	835	671
Total operating expenses	9,490	7,603
Operating Income	4,191	3,808
Interest income (expense)		
Interest and investment income	47	37
Interest expense	(21)	(41)
Interest, net	26	(4)
Earnings before Income Taxes	4,217	3,804
Income taxes	1,636	1,484
Net earnings	$2,581	$2,320
Basic Earnings Per Share	$ 1.11	$ 1.03
Weighted average number of common shares		
outstanding	2,315	2,244
Diluted Earnings Per Share	$ 1.10	$ .99
Weighted average number of common shares		
outstanding, assuming dilution	2,352	2,342

8-5. Why do stock analysts generally give so much attention to monetary (as opposed to fiscal) policy? Discuss its effects on the stock market and the role in investment analysis.

8-6. Briefly summarize the three principal types of accounting statements.

8-7. Using the balance sheet and income statement for this question, find the current ratio, quick (acid test) ratio, inventory turnover ratio (based on average inventory), debt-equity ratio, net profit margin, asset turnover ratio, return on assets, equity multiplier, and return on equity for the fiscal year ended January 2003.

8-8. a. Why might a dramatic growth rate in a company's sales, accompanied by an even more dramatic growth in its average collection period, be a bad sign?

  b. Why might an increase in the current ratio accompanied by a decline in the inventory turnover ratio by a bad sign?

  c. What is wrong with a company offsetting a decline in its net profit margin with increases in its equity multiplier?

Self-Test Questions

T   F   8-1.   Fundamental analysis rests on the premise that a security has an intrinsic value that is based on the firm's underlying variables.

T   F   8-2.   The fact that business cycles have approximately the same duration each time helps to forecast the overall economy.

T   F   8-3.   Data series on the average work week, average unemployment claims, and new building permits are examples of leading economic indicators.

T   F   8-4.   The unemployment rate refers to the percentage of the labor force that is out of work and actively seeking employment.

T   F   8-5.   Increases in either government spending or tax collections will stimulate the economy.

T   F   8-6.   Restrictive monetary policy has no effect on the allocation of funds in the economy.

T   F   8-7.   An increase in the discount rate signals a restrictive monetary policy.

T   F   8-8.   If its open-market operations are resulting in a net purchase of securities, the Fed has an expansionary monetary policy.

T   F   8-9.   Monetary policy affects the stock market through its influence on interest rates.

T   F   8-10. Monetary policy is a function of the Treasury Department.

T   F   8-11. The M1 definition of the money supply includes checkable deposits and cash and coin in circulation outside the banks.

T   F   8-12. Reductions in the reserve requirement enables banks to increase their loans.

T   F   8-13. The money multiplier is the ratio of the resulting increase in the money supply to the initial increase in funds (open-market purchases).

T   F   8-14. The federal funds rate is the rate charged by the Fed when it lends reserves to banks.

T   F   8-15. Fiscal policy attempts to influence the level of economic activity by changing reserve requirements and open-market operations.

T   F   8-16. The primary economic goals of monetary and fiscal policy are in conflict.

T   F   8-17. Monetary policy is formulated by the Federal Reserve's Open Market Committee.

T   F   8-18. Price stability implies that individual prices remain the same during the year.

T   F   8-19. An increase in required reserves signals a restrictive monetary policy.

T   F   8-20. During the consolidation stage, any firm in a "hot" industry is a good investment.

T   F   8-21.   The basic balance sheet equation is as follows: Assets + liabilities = net worth.

T   F   8-22.   The quick ratio is used to assess the capital structure of the firm's balance sheet.

T   F   8-23.   Raising the debt ratio will lower return on equity, all other things being equal.

T   F   8-24.   Fully diluted earnings per share are not affected by outstanding convertible debt.

T   F   8-25.   The short-form of Du Pont analysis breaks ROE into the two components of ROA and equity multiplier.

T   F   8-26.   A high fixed asset turnover ratio may indicate aged assets.

T   F   8-27.   If the total asset turnover ratio is consistent with industry averages, there is no need to evaluate the quality of individual assets.

T   F   8-28.   A firm with consistently high payout ratios is likely to have weak prospects for growth.

T   F   8-29.   The more stable a company's earnings, the less concern one should have about a high debt ratio.

T   F   8-30.   According to the semistrong form of the efficient market hypothesis, fundamental analysis should not consistently provide superior returns for an investor.

NOTES

1. NBER's Business Cycle Dating Committee memo dated 07/17/03.
2. The tax code is discussed in chapter 13.
3. For additional discussion on monetary policy, see www.newyorkfed.org education/add pub/pdf/ch2.pdf.
4. www.newyorkfed.org/aboutthefed/fedpoint/fed45.html, January 27, 2004.
5. Every now and then, an officer at a thrift will decide to use these hedging instruments (that is, futures and options) for speculative purposes rather than for hedging. Incorrect guesses can easily bankrupt an institution, as has occurred several times. These instruments are discussed in chapters 11 and 12.
6. M. Porter, *Competitive Advantage: Creating and Sustaining Superior Performance* (New York: McMillan, Inc., 1985), chapter 1.
7. www.coca-cola.com/our company/around the world. html, July 15, 2004.
8. The most common alternative to this ratio is sales divided by average yearly inventory. Also, many people use either beginning-of-year inventory, or end-of-year inventory, rather than average inventory in the denominator. A common way to measure average yearly inventory is to add the beginning-of-year inventory and the end-of-year inventory together and divide by 2 (that is, take the arithmetic average of the two numbers).

9. There are, of course, 365 days in a year. However, the industrywide definitions for many of these ratios were established long before the arrival of calculators and computers and thus used 360 for ease of computation.

10. Note that, because total debt + equity = total assets, the debt-equity ratio can be written as total debt/(total assets − total debt). If we divide each term in this last definition by total assets, we get yet another version of the debt-equity ratio, which is debt ratio/(1 − debt ratio). Thus, if we know the debt ratio, we can quickly derive the debt-equity ratio without even knowing the actual dollar figures.

11. Several ratios have been developed to incorporate the impact of lease payments, but these ratios are beyond the introductory level of this discussion.

12. For simplicity, we will assume that the industry averages are the same for all 3 years.

13. H. Russell Fogler, "A Modern Theory of Security Analysis," *Journal of Portfolio Management,* vol. 19, no. 3 (spring 1993), pp. 6–14.

Appendix 8A

The Elements of Supply and Demand

The economic forces determining the quantity supplied and the quantity demanded for a good or service are so intertwined that it is problematic to consider one element without the other when constructing an economic analysis of the pricing of a good or service.[1] The interdependent nature of supply and demand evolved in large part because they both are expressed as a function of price.

Economics is the study of unlimited wants and scarce resources. The efficient and effective use of resources in an economic system allows the members of that system to, in aggregate, live better lives. The pricing of resources, at least in a capitalistic economy, is the primary method of allocating these scarce resources among competing uses. Price, then, is the driving force in determining both the supply and demand for a good. Demand connotes both the willingness and ability to buy a good at its market price. Supply connotes being willing and able to sell the good at its market price.

It is both intuitive and correct to note that, other things being equal, the higher the price for a good, the lower the demand for that good. Also intuitive and correct is that at higher prices, more goods become available. On the supply side, the quantity of a good will rise with an increase in price and fall with a price decrease. Together these are known as the *laws of supply and demand*. At some point, the higher prices that stimulate increased supply bump up against consumers' unwillingness to pay a higher price for the good. If the quantity demanded, Q_D, equals the quantity supplied, Q_S, the market for the good is in equilibrium. If supply outstrips demand, or demand outstrips supply, the market is in disequilibrium. Figure 8A-1 shows a simple supply/demand relationship for a product.

Demand, as a single point on the demand curve (or function) represents the quantity of a good required by consumers at a particular price. The function itself represents how quantity demanded changes with changes in price. If the function does not change, then we expect movement along the curve to accurately describe the relationship between price and quantity demanded. A change in the quantity demanded along the existing demand curve is related solely to a price change. Demand can be either defined as the function or a point along that function.

The demand curve does not remain static over time. The forces behind the pricing of a good can change. A simple example is the relationship between

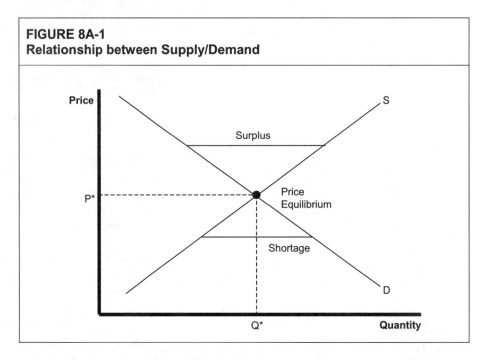

FIGURE 8A-1
Relationship between Supply/Demand

weather and crops. Ideal growing conditions, like good weather, increase crop yields. Increased crop yields mean increased supply. The increased supply can drive down prices, thereby increasing demand. A shift in the demand curve results in a new equilibrium price as consumers and producers adjust to the changes in market dynamics for the good.

A shift in the demand curve represents a change in the demand for the good and a new demand curve. If the demand curve shifts to the left on the graph, it represents a decrease in demand; a shift to the right represents an increase in demand. Figure 8A-2 shows a demand curve shifting to the right for an unnamed good. For the same price, P_0, the quantity demanded increases from Q_0 to Q_1 because of the shift in the demand curve.

Take a can of mixed nuts as an example. What drives the mixture of nuts in the can? Supply and demand is, of course, the right answer but not in-depth enough to demonstrate the issues involved. A bumper crop of almonds would lower the price of almonds. A producer could reduce the cost of a can of mixed nuts by increasing the percentage of almonds in the mix. Put all almonds in the mix, however, and we no longer have a can of mixed nuts, so there are limits to the nut manufacturer's ability to substitute nuts into the mix.

The availability of close substitutes is one factor in the pricing of a good. A good with no close substitutes is said to have an *inelastic demand* since consumers cannot replace the good with an alternative if its price rises too

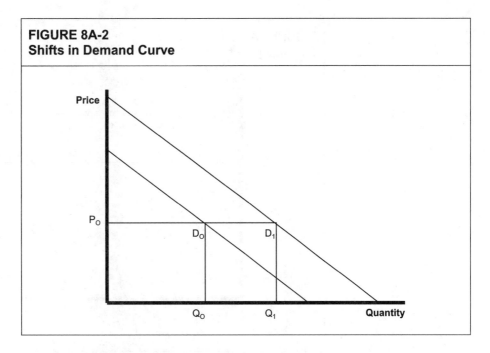

FIGURE 8A-2
Shifts in Demand Curve

high. Goods that have close substitutes will have a more elastic demand function because consumers can move from the expensive good to the less expensive good if prices get too high.

Figure 8A-3 shows two demand functions, D1 and D2. The function represented by line D1 shows a good with a perfectly inelastic demand. Regardless of the price for the good, the quantity demanded remains the same. Function D2 shows a perfectly elastic demand schedule. The quantity demanded cannot be adequately explained by price. A small shift downward in price will result in a huge (infinite) increase in demand, while a small shift upward in price will result in demand dropping off precipitously.

In the current market, the precious metal platinum is off its recent high of $936/troy ounce, retreating to about $800/troy ounce. Consumers have the choice of continuing to buy platinum jewelry, with jewelry representing 56 percent of the demand for that metal,[2] or switching to white or yellow gold. Industrial users, like high-tech electronics, may not have the flexibility to substitute platinum for other metals in the manufacturing process. Thus, the elasticity of the demand for platinum is different for jewelry makers than it is for electronics manufacturers. The elasticity of demand is a measure of how responsive the quantity demanded is to a change in price. How, for example, does a 10 percent increase (decrease) in the price of platinum change the demand for the metal? If a 10 percent increase in price has no effect on the quantity demanded, then demand for the good is inelastic.

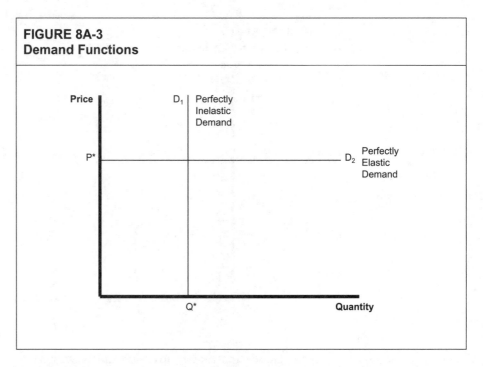

FIGURE 8A-3
Demand Functions

The degree of product differentiation among producers of a good determines the type of market for the good. A perfectly competitive market has a standardized commodity and numerous buyers and sellers. Products that are commodities—classically products like corn, wheat, pork bellies, and lumber—have minimal product differentiation among producers. Auction markets work well for these goods because the auction process can establish a market clearing price that will match supply with demand. The commoditization of financial securities also allows for a degree of standardization that makes an auction market practical for these goods.

Figure 8A-4 shows two supply functions, S1 and S2. The function represented in the graph by line S1 shows a good with a perfectly inelastic supply. Regardless of price, the amount of the good supplied does not change. In contrast, the supply function represented by line S2 shows a good with a perfectly elastic supply. Small changes in price will dramatically affect the amount of the good supplied.

Perfectly elastic (or inelastic) supply or demand functions are rare. Most goods have some substitutes available, and the price relationships between these goods, called cross elasticity, influences the price elasticity of the individual good.

Estimating the supply and demand functions for a good is as much art as it is science. Once the functions have been estimated, though, finding the intersection of the two functions is a fairly straightforward matter. It is the intersection that determines the market equilibrium price where supply equals demand.

FIGURE 8A-4
Supply Functions

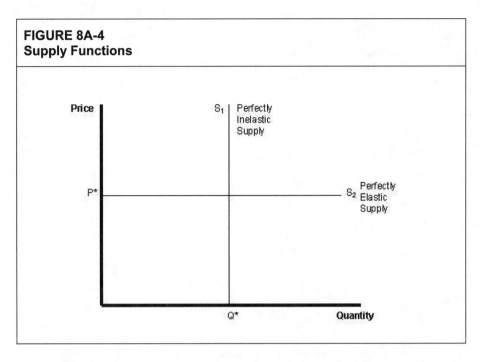

Market forces will continually exert pressure on this relationship, causing either movement along the curve with changes in price, or a change in one or both of the functions, resulting in a shift. In either case, the market will move toward a new equilibrium price.

NOTES

1. For simplicity during the remainder of this section, the term good is used instead of using the term good or service.
2. New York Mercantile Exchange information. http://www.nymex.com/jsp/markets/pla_pre_agree.jsp

9

Debt Instruments

Learning Objectives

An understanding of the material in this chapter should enable the student to

9-1. Describe the basic features of corporate debt obligations, including income bonds, floating rate notes, caps and collars, zero-coupon bonds, consols, Eurobonds, and private placements.

9-2. Compute the price of a bond, given the discount rate; the yield to maturity, given the price; the current yield; the realized compound yield to maturity; the yield to call; and the realized rate of return.

9-3. Compute a bond's duration statistic.

9-4. Explain the duration statistic's uses as an index number, its use to estimate bond price changes, and its use as a tool for immunizing a portfolio.

9-5. Discuss bond swaps, ladders, barbells, and riding the yield curve as strategies for managing a bond portfolio.

9-6. Describe the term structure of interest rates, and explain the investment implications of the term structure.

9-7. Describe several factors that affect bond prices and yields.

9-8. Show how an immunized portfolio allows an investor to achieve the targeted yield to maturity.

9-9. Describe the parameters of the default risk facing debt security instruments, and explain how rating services assess the risk.

Chapter Outline

The terms fixed-income security and debt security are often used interchangeably. This is because the initial interest rate or coupon rate on debt instruments, such as bonds, is stated in a contractual agreement at the time the debt instrument is issued. Although there are other types of debt instruments, most debt takes the form of bonds. Therefore, unless stated otherwise, the terms *bond yield, debt security yield,* and *fixed-income security yield* can be used interchangeably.

BOND CHARACTERISTICS

Corporate Debt Obligations

debenture

Corporations are the largest issuers of bonds. They issue both secured bonds (bonds backed by specific collateral) and *debentures* (bonds backed only by the issuer's full faith and credit). Corporate bonds, like government and municipal bonds, have a coupon rate and mature on a specified date. In addition, some corporate bonds may, at the owner's option, be exchanged at some fixed ratio for stocks of the issuing corporation. These corporate bonds, known as convertibles, are discussed in greater detail in chapter 11.

Most bond trades involve both the price of the bond and an adjustment for accrued interest. The buyer pays and the seller receives monies to reflect the portion of interest that has already been earned but not yet paid.

Example:

A bond that is quoted at 93 would initially cost the buyer $930 in principal plus the pro rated amount of accrued but unpaid interest. If the bond has a 10 percent coupon paid semiannually and made its last coupon payment 3 months ago, unpaid interest would have accrued as follows:

$$(1/2 \times .10) \times \$1,000 \times 3/6 = .05 \times \$1,000 \times 1/2 = \$25$$

That is, because the bond pays interest every 6 months and 3 months have elapsed, half of one coupon payment has accrued. This corresponds to one-half of the semiannual interest payment.

As with dividends on stock, interest is paid to the holder of the bond on the day of record. When the issuer makes the coupon payment, the new owner of record will receive the entire amount of interest for that period.

flat

Bonds trading for a net price that does not reflect any accrued interest are said to be trading *flat*. Typically, bonds that are in default or whose interest payments are considered uncertain trade flat. In bond quotations, bonds that trade flat have an "f" following their name.

Most trading of bonds takes place in the over-the-counter (OTC) market. Bond quotations usually include the name of the company issuing the bond, along with the coupon rate and year of maturity, the current yield, volume, closing price, and net change. The price and volume numbers are as of 4 p.m. Eastern time (when exchanges close).

Examples of Corporate Bond Quotations

Bonds	Cur. Yld.	Vol.	Close	Net Chg.
Att6s09	6.6	4	90 1/2	−1/8
Hilton5s06	cv	130	82	−1
Polaroid11 ½ f		489	14 1/2	−1/2

- Bonds: The name of the company issuing the bond, the interest or coupon rate as a percentage of the face or par value (typically $1,000), and the year in which the bond will be paid off (the s that sometimes appears between the interest rate and the year of maturity has no significance other than to separate the interest rate from the year of maturity when the interest rate does not include a fraction—read the explanatory notes given in the financial media for the meaning of other letters used)
- Cur. Yld.: The current yield, calculated by dividing the coupon amount by the current price. Flat bonds show no current yield, and convertible bonds have the letters cv listed here.
- Vol.: The actual number of bonds traded
- Close: The final trading price of the day, which is stated as a percentage of par value
- Net Chg.: The difference between the closing price as listed in the close column (see Close above) and the closing price from whatever day the bond previously traded, which is usually the previous trading day

Call Feature

call price

call premium

Most bonds include a call feature. The first component of a call feature is the *call price,* which is a price at which the issuer can buy back the bond from the bondholder. Some bonds are callable from the day they are issued, and others are noncallable initially. The call price is the sum of par value, a *call premium* that is defined in the indenture, and accrued interest up to the day of the call. The call premium is sometimes set at a fixed number (for example, 3 percent of par), and other times it is set at a higher number initially and then the value is amortized over time. Bonds are called in for one of the following three reasons:

- The issuer can issue new bonds at a substantially lower coupon rate, such that the issuer can pay the call premium, the costs of processing the new issue, and still save money. This is known as refinancing. It is essentially the same process as a homeowner's refinancing his or her mortgage for a lower interest rate.

forced conversion

- The bond is convertible and the issuer wants to issue the common stock and terminate the interest payments, which is known as *forced conversion*. It can be successful only when the market value of the stock received upon conversion is greater than the call price.
- The terms of the indenture have become a serious constraint for a company, and it wants to get out from under the indenture.

If a bond is called for either of the first two reasons, it is a sure bet that the investor is worse off as a result of the call feature's being invoked. On the rare occasions when a bond is called for the third reason, the investor may receive a windfall gain.

Income Bonds

Most bonds must either pay the agreed upon interest (coupon rate) or go into default. Income bonds, on the other hand, pay interest only if the issuer earns it. Passed coupons do not accumulate. Specific indenture provisions indicate when earned income is sufficient to require an interest payment. Most income bonds originate in a reorganization exchange (that is, bankruptcy). Some, however, are sold initially as income bonds. At any given time, there are relatively few income bonds outstanding.

Floating-Rate Notes (FRNs)

Notes can be issued with variable or floating rates of interest. These floating-rate notes are a form of long-term debt, but they are subject to short-term interest rate changes. The floating or variable rate feature of these bonds generally allows their prices to remain relatively close to their par values. Just how close their prices remain to their par values is a function of how frequently the coupon rate is adjusted, as well as the rate to which it is pegged. Because the changes in the interest rate tend to reflect changes in the inflation rate, these bonds keep their *real* rate of return relatively constant. Thus, their prices can stay relatively constant as interest rates fluctuate.

The characteristics of these floating-rate notes vary somewhat. Some adjust their coupon rates once every 6 months; others adjust them weekly. Some peg the coupon rates to one percent over the index rate; others peg them to .75 percent over the index rate or even lower. Some use as the index rate the yield on 90-day T-bills; others use the prime rate or the federal funds rate. Although floating-rate notes do appear in the United States, they appear more often in the international market, especially in Asia. A few companies even issue floating-rate preferred stock.

Caps and Collars[1]

When a borrower issues a floating rate security, it exposes itself to potentially catastrophic losses. For example, if a lender issues a floating rate bond with an initial interest rate of 5 percent, and the index to which that rate is tied jumps dramatically and causes the new rate on the reset date to be, say, 30 percent, then the borrower may have difficulty making the interest payment. To deal with this potential problem, some borrowers will purchase caps. A cap is an arrangement to limit the maximum amount of interest paid. A cap is based on a strike rate, which is the price at which an option to buy or sell can be exercised. The seller of the cap agrees that at any time the interest rate on the loan, as determined under the indenture, exceeds the strike rate, the seller will pay the incremental interest expense.

Example:	Big Chance Corporation has issued some floating rate notes. The initial interest rate is 4 percent for the first year, but on the first anniversary, the interest rate will be reset to LIBOR (London Interbank Offered Rate, which was discussed in chapter 1) plus 2 percent. The bond issue is for $100 million. The company buys a cap with a strike rate of 6 percent. On the first anniversary, LIBOR is at 5 percent, so the reset rate becomes 7 percent. The seller of the cap will have to pay Big Chance $1 million, which is the difference between the floating rate and the strike rate, times the principal of the loan. When Big Chance has to make its interest payment, the net interest charge will be $2 million.

To reduce the cost of buying a cap, borrowers will sometimes opt for a *collar* arrangement. A collar combines a cap with an interest rate floor. With a floor, the borrower agrees to pay the seller of the collar any of the interest savings achieved if the floating rate falls below the floor.

Example:	In the previous example, Big Chance opts for a collar rather than a cap. The price of the collar is lower than the price of the cap. The interest rate floor is set at 3 percent. On the first reset date, the interest rate on the loan resets to 2.5 percent. Because this is .5 percent below the floor, Big

Chance owes the seller of the collar $500,000. Big Chance will recoup this money through what it saves on its interest payment to the bondholders.

A collar has the benefit of converting a floating rate bond to a semi-fixed-rate note. The purchase of a cap is analogous to the purchase of insurance. The purchase of a collar is analogous to the purchase of insurance with large deductibles. In the second example, the buyer of the insurance (that is, the collar) may have to pay some money out of his or her own pocket, but the savings on the premium may more than offset these payments.

An alternative arrangement for a bond issuer to transfer the risk exposure of fluctuating interest rates is to enter into a swap arrangement. Bond swaps will be discussed in more detail later.

Zero-Coupon and Other Types of Original-Issue Discount Bonds

zero coupon bonds (zeros)

As mentioned previously, most bonds' coupon rates are initially set so that the price of the bonds will be close to their face or par value when the bonds are insured. Original-issue discount bonds, however, are sold for appreciably less than their par value. These bonds either pay no coupon or have a coupon rate that is well below the market rate. Bonds that do not make coupon interest payments are called *zero-coupon bonds (zeros)*. The return on these securities is derived from the difference between their purchase price and selling price or maturity value.

Zero-coupon bonds have precisely identifiable maturity values. This feature has an appeal for IRA and Keogh accounts. Investors in zeros know at the outset exactly what the value will be at maturity. The end-period value of funds invested in coupon-yielding bonds, in contrast, is uncertain, because it depends on the rate earned on the reinvested coupon payments.

The uncertainty associated with the return on reinvested coupon payments is called reinvestment rate risk. Because of their lack of reinvestment rate risk and relative scarcity, zero-coupon bonds have tended to sell for somewhat lower yields than equivalent-risk coupon bonds.

Like other long-term bonds, long-term zero-coupon bonds lock both the buyer and the issuer into a long-term rate. If rates go up after the purchase, the buyer will end up receiving a below-market return. The issuer, in contrast, will pay an above-market rate if market interest rates decline after the issue is sold. Moreover, for a given change in interest rates, the prices of zeros change more than those of most coupon bonds. Owners of coupon bonds are at least able to reinvest their coupon income at higher rates when market interest rates rise. Owners of zeros receive no coupon payments and thus have no interim payments to reinvest.

Consols

The vast majority of debt obligations promise to repay principal at some future date. Britain, however, has issued some bonds without maturity, called consols. They can be valued in a manner similar to preferred stock, which was discussed in chapter 7.

Eurobonds

Eurobonds are bonds that are offered outside the country of the borrower and outside the country in whose currency the bonds are denominated. Therefore, if a U.S. corporation issues bonds that are denominated in U.S. dollars (or in Japanese yen, for that matter) but sold in France (and perhaps some other countries as well), the bonds are considered Eurobonds. These foreign bonds differ from U.S. or foreign bonds that are traded in only one country. The Eurobond issuer benefits from the wider distribution and the absence of restrictions and taxes that are placed on single-country bonds. Eurobond buyers may obtain greater diversification than is available from U.S. bonds alone. Moreover, bonds denominated in a foreign currency offer investors an opportunity to speculate on exchange rate fluctuations.

One of the most attractive features of Eurobonds (at least for some investors) is the ease with which some of these bonds allow investors to avoid taxes. Two features of many Eurobonds facilitate tax evasion. First, unlike domestic bonds, no backup withholding is applied to Eurobond interest payments. Second, many Eurobonds have been issued in bearer (unregistered) form. Without either registration or backup withholding, Eurobond owners find that taxes are relatively easy to avoid. Because of this appeal, Eurobonds tend to yield less than domestic bonds of comparable risk. More recently, however, Eurobonds have generally been issued in registered form, and thus the tax evasion opportunity has disappeared for newer issues.

Multinational corporations, governments, and international organizations issue most Eurobonds, and most are denominated in dollars, yen, or deutsche marks. They may take on any of the forms of regular bonds: straight bonds, convertibles, floating-rate notes, zero-coupon bonds, and so on.

Private Placements

Approximately one-third of the debt instruments sold are placed privately to a few large buyers (often insurance companies) and publicly announced in the financial press. Announcements are generally referred to as "tombstones" because of the large amount of white space and small amount of lettering. Even if the size (tens of millions of dollars) of typical private placements rules out direct purchases, individuals may participate indirectly through one of the closed-end funds (to be discussed in chapter 10) that specialize in such investments.

Private placements generally yield one-half percent to one percent more than equivalent-risk bonds because they lack liquidity. Private placements offer greater flexibility to issuers. They can be tailored for specific buyers and do not require a prospectus. Moreover, the underwriting cost savings largely offset their somewhat higher coupon. Finally, the relatively small number of owners makes it easier to renegotiate the terms of the indenture if necessary.

Private placements do not have to comply with the standards of disclosure that the SEC requires of public offerings. The absence of disclosure of material risk factors makes the investment more risky to potential investors. Therefore, private placements can be suitable investments only for those with both the know-how and financial resources to discover risk factors for themselves.

THE MATHEMATICS OF BONDS: PRICES AND YIELDS

Pricing a Bond

Computing a price for a bond is more complicated than doing a simple present value calculation because a bond provides periodic interest (coupon) payments and then the par or face value at maturity. As mentioned in chapter 1, the par or face value for corporate bonds is almost always $1,000. For the vast majority of bonds, the periodic interest payment is fixed at a set amount, called the coupon rate.

The mathematically purest way to present the formula for pricing a bond is as

$$P = \sum_{t=1}^{n} \frac{C_t}{(1 + i)^t} \qquad \text{(Equation 9-1)}$$

where C_t = the cash flow in period t (coupon, principal, or both)
      t   = the time period when the cash flow is to be received
      i   = appropriate discount rate
      n   = the term to maturity of the bond

The appropriate discount rate is frequently referred to as the bond's yield to maturity.

An alternative mathematical representation of the formula for pricing a bond is

$$P = \left[\sum_{t=1}^{n} \frac{C_t}{(1+i)^t}\right] + \frac{PAR}{(1+i)^n} \qquad \text{(Equation 9-2)}$$

where C_t = coupon payment in period t
  PAR = par or face value of the bond

Equation 9-2 clearly illustrates that the price of a bond consists of two elements: the present value of the coupon payments plus the present value of the par value. Most people now solve for bond prices on financial calculators. Therefore, rather than work through the steps of equation 9-2, let's look at the keystrokes for pricing a bond. Before doing so, however, note that most bonds pay interest every 6 months. This fact makes the process of pricing a bond a little more complicated. To facilitate a basic understanding of the bond pricing process, let's first consider an example in which interest is paid annually.

Example: A $1,000 (face value) bond with a 2.5 percent coupon rate will mature in 6 years. Thus, the bond will pay annual coupons of $25 (2 ½ % x $1,000). The appropriate discount rate is 4 percent. The price of the bond is calculated as follows:

$$P = \sum_{t=1}^{n} \frac{C_t}{(1+i)^t} + \frac{PAR}{(1+i)^n}$$

$$P = \left[\sum_{t=1}^{6} \frac{\$25}{(1+.04)^t}\right] + \frac{\$1,000}{(1+.04)^6} = \$921.37$$

The HP-10BII keystrokes are

SHIFT, C ALL
set for end-of-period payments
1000, FV
1000, x, .025, =, PMT
3, x, 2, =, N
4, I/YR
PV (display: −921.37)

Now let's be more realistic and consider the process of pricing a bond when interest payments are made every 6 months. When this is the case, we must make these three adjustments before we calculate the price of the bond:

- Convert the coupon payment to a semiannual basis, which is done by dividing the coupon rate by 2.

- Adjust the number of time periods to reflect the fact that a time period is now 6 months, which is done by multiplying the maturity of the bond by 2.
- Adjust the discount rate to a semiannual basis, which is done by dividing the discount rate by 2.

In terms of the valuation formula, the price of a bond that pays interest semiannually is defined as

$$P = \left[\sum_{t=1}^{2n} \frac{\left(\frac{C_t}{2} \right)}{\left(1 + \frac{i}{2} \right)^t} \right] + \frac{PAR}{\left(1 + \frac{i}{2} \right)^{2n}} \qquad \text{(Equation 9-3)}$$

Let us consider an example of how to price a bond when interest is paid *semiannually*.

Example: A $1,000 (face value) bond with a 5 percent coupon rate will mature in 3 years. Therefore, the bond will pay semiannual coupons of $25 (1/2 x 5% x $1,000). The present value of this income flow at an 8 percent discount rate is

$$P = \left[\sum_{t=1}^{2n} \frac{\left(\frac{C_t}{2} \right)}{\left(1 + \frac{i}{2} \right)^t} \right] + \frac{PAR}{\left(1 + \frac{i}{2} \right)^{2n}}$$

$$P = \left[\sum_{t=1}^{6} \frac{\frac{\$50}{2}}{\left(1 + \frac{.08}{2} \right)^t} \right] + \frac{\$1,000}{\left(1 + \frac{.08}{2} \right)^6}$$

$= \$921.27$

The HP-10BII keystrokes are

  SHIFT, C ALL
  set for end-of-period payments
  1000, FV
  1000, x, .05, ÷, 2, =, PMT
  8, ÷, 2, =, I/YR
  3, x, 2, =, N
  PV (display: –921.37)[2]

Note that the present value of the bond in the example is less than its $1,000 face value. Any bond with a coupon rate below its discount rate sells at a discount, meaning for less than $1,000. Any bond with a coupon rate exceeding the discount rate sells at a premium, meaning for more than $1,000. Finally, any bond with a coupon rate equal to the discount rate will sell at par, meaning for $1,000.

When people discuss and analyze bonds, there are several different rates and yields that may be relevant, depending on an investor's objectives and expectations. The simplest two are the coupon rate and the current yield. The single most important yield is the yield to maturity, followed by the yield to call. Holding period yields (or returns), as well as realized compound yield to maturity, are also important. We will first examine coupon rate and current yield to illustrate these various rates and yields.

Coupon Rate and Current Yield

Suppose an XYZ bond pays an annual coupon of $40 and matures at a par value of $1,000 in 6 years. The bond is callable for $1,040 in 3 years. The current price of the bond is $950. (Although bond coupons are typically semiannual, we will assume annual coupons to simplify the calculations.)

coupon rate

The *coupon rate* for the bond equals the annual interest payment divided by the par value and is fixed for the life of the bond. Therefore, it is 4 percent for the XYZ bond, calculated as follows:

$$\text{Coupon rate} = \frac{\text{Annual interest payment}}{\text{Par value}} = \frac{\$40}{\$1,000} = 4\%$$

The coupon rate is a descriptive statistic only and has no real relevance for a financial planner. Although the income provided by a bond can be quite important, knowing the income paid by a bond without knowing the price at which the bond trades is meaningless. This leads us to a more relevant yield:

current yield

the current yield. The *current yield* is the annual interest divided by the current price. Although the coupon is fixed, the price varies; thus, the current yield will vary during the bond's life. For the XYZ bond, the current yield is 4.21 percent, determined as follows:

$$\text{Current yield} = \frac{\text{Annual interest payment}}{\text{Market price}} = \frac{\$40}{\$950} = 4.21\%$$

If a financial planner is creating a bond portfolio for a client, a critical component is usually the current yield.

Example: George Jones has $2 million in assets and is 73 years old. After extensive discussions with George, you decide to put $1.5 million in bonds and $.5 million in stocks. George would like to generate $100,000 in current income from his investments. You believe that the average dividend yield on his stock holdings will be 1 percent, which, based on $.5 million invested would be $5,000. What is the current yield you must obtain on the bond portfolio?

If George's stocks generate $5,000 in income, and he needs $100,000 total income, then his bonds must provide current income of $95,000. Based on an investment of $1.5 million, the current yield for the portfolio needs to be .0633 or 6.33 percent ($95,000/$1,500,000). If such a holding is not sufficiently safe, then George needs to adjust his income needs, or an alternative investment plans needs to be constructed.

Yield to Maturity (IRR)

yield to maturity
(promised yield)

Yield to maturity (YTM), or *promised yield,* is a much more difficult calculation. It is equivalent to the internal rate of return[3] in other investments. Yield to maturity is the rate that would discount all the future cash flows (coupons and par value) so that this present value equals the market price. Continuing our example of the XYZ bond that pays $40 interest annually, has a maturity of 6 years, and a current price of $950, the yield to maturity is the discount rate *i* that makes the following equation valid:

$$\text{Price} = \sum_{t=1}^{n} \frac{\text{coupon}}{(1+i)^t} + \frac{\text{par}}{(1+i)^n}$$

$$950 = \frac{40}{(1+i)} + \frac{40}{(1+i)^2} + \frac{40}{(1+i)^3} + \frac{40}{(1+i)^4} + \frac{40}{(1+i)^5} + \frac{40}{(1+i)^6} + \frac{1000}{(1+i)^6}$$

Unfortunately, we cannot solve this equation by simply putting *i* on one side and everything else on the other. Although computing yield to maturity requires many iterations, financial calculators make it easy to determine the correct answer, 4.9846 percent.

The HP-10BII keystrokes are

SHIFT, C ALL
950, +/–, PV
40, PMT
1000, FV
6, N
I/YR (display: 4.9846)

To understand why the YTM is also called the promised yield, as well as what is meant by an internal rate of return number, consider the scenario of someone who deposits $950 today into an account that pays an interest rate of 4.98 percent. Let's suppose that this person wants to replicate the cash flows from the bond. To do so, he or she would draw out $40 at the end of each year for 6 years, and then at the end of the sixth year draw out $1,000 (the bond's par value). As shown in table 9-1, this person would have exactly zeroed out the account with the last withdrawal.

Note in the table that this person starts with $950 at time zero. During the first year, he or she accrues $47.35 in interest, giving an end-of-year balance of $997.35. The person then withdraws $40 to match the interest payment on the bond. This withdrawal reduces the end-of-year balance to $957.35, which becomes the beginning-of-year balance for the second year. After the sixth and last withdrawal, there is nothing left in the account. To emphasize the above point, one interpretation of a yield to maturity (or any internal rate of return calculation) is that it is the interest rate at which we could invest the price of the asset and exactly reproduce the cash payments of that asset, with nothing left over.

Finally, note that if we want to price the bond used in this example, and we are given a discount rate of 4.9846, then the price would be $950.

TABLE 9-1
Internal Rate of Return Proof

Time Period (1)	Beginning-of-Period Balance (2)	Interest Accrued for Period (3)=(2)x .049846	Balance before Withdrawal (4)=(2)+(3)	Withdrawal (5)	Balance after Withdrawal (6)=(4) – (5)
0					$950.00
1	$950.00	$47.35	$ 997.35	$ 40.00	957.35
2	957.35	47.72	1,005.07	40.00	965.07
3	965.07	48.11	1,013.18	40.00	973.18
4	973.18	48.51	1,021.69	40.00	981.69
5	981.69	48.93	1,030.62	40.00	990.62
6	990.62	49.38	1,040.00	1,040.00	0.00

The HP-10bII keystrokes are

SHIFT, C ALL
set for end-of-period payments
1000, FV
1000, x, .04, =, PMT
6, N
4.9846, I/YR
PV (display: –950.00)

Simply stated, given the price of a bond, we can compute its yield to maturity. Given a bond's yield to maturity, we can compute its price. For this reason, people often use the term yield to maturity as the name for the discount rate to use when solving for a bond's price. More important, *price and yield-to-maturity are interchangeable terms in discussions of bond values.*

Another important aspect of this relationship is that because price and yield to maturity automatically define each other, a change in one automatically defines a change in the other. Hence, it would be silly to say that bond prices fell because interest rates rose. It would be silly because interest rates rising is defined by bond prices falling.

To solve for the YTM on a bond that pays interest semiannually requires the same sort of adjustments, except in reverse, as we made when we discussed how to compute the price of a bond that pays interest semiannually. The steps are as follows:

- Determine the semiannual payment by dividing the annual payment by 2.
- Compute the effective number of periods by multiplying the term to maturity by 2.
- After solving for the YTM, multiply the answer by 2 because the calculator solution is the YTM per 6-month period.

Example: The YTM of a bond with a 4 percent coupon rate that pays interest semiannually, matures in 6 years, has a par value of $1,000, and trades for $950 is calculated as follows:

First, compute the semiannual payment to be $20, then compute the number of time periods to be 12, and then enter the FV and PV of the bond as $1,000 and –$950. After solving for the YTM (I/YR), multiply the answer by 2. In this case, the YTM is 4.9741 percent.

The HP-10bII keystrokes are

SHIFT, C ALL
set for end-of-period payments
1000, x, .04, /, 2, =, PMT
6, x, 2, =, N
1000, FV
950, +/–, PV

I/YR (display: 2.4871), x, 2, = (display: 4.9741)

Relationship between Coupon Rate, Current Yield, and Yield to Maturity

Note that in our example of the XYZ bond, the coupon rate of 4 percent is less than the current yield of 4.21 percent, and both are less than the yield-to-maturity of 4.9846 percent. In retrospect, this result was to be expected because the yield to maturity (promised yield) is greater than the coupon rate. Hence, the bond must trade at a discount to provide the incremental return expected by investor. Because the current yield is the coupon divided by the price, and the coupon rate is the coupon divided by par, we can make the following statement:

For all discount bonds, the current yield will be greater than the discount rate.

The reverse will hold for bonds trading at a premium. Finally, we should note that if a bond trades exactly at par, the coupon rate and the current yield will be identical.

The yield to maturity is greater than the current yield for discount bonds because the current yield considers only the coupon payments relative to the current price. The yield to maturity considers both the coupon payment and the change in the price of the bond between now and maturity, at which time the price will equal par. For discount bonds, the change in price will be positive. Hence, we can make the following statement:

For discount bonds, the yield to maturity will always be greater than the current yield.

As before, the relationship will be the reverse for premium bonds, and when a bond trades at par, the two will be identical. This relationship is shown graphically in figure 9-1.

Realized Compound Yield to Maturity

One aspect of the yield to maturity is that it incorporates no assumptions about the coupon payments.[4] In general, we can make two assumptions about

FIGURE 9-1
Relationship between Yield to Maturity and Current Yield

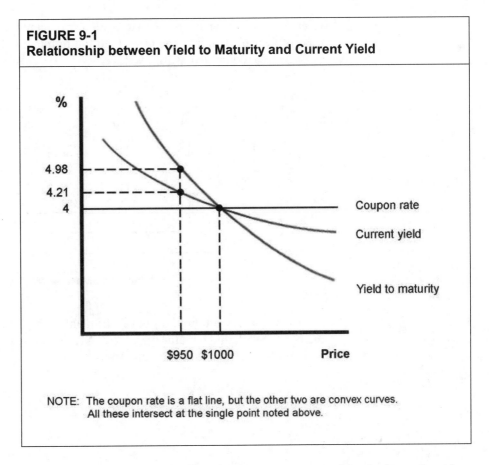

NOTE: The coupon rate is a flat line, but the other two are convex curves.
        All these intersect at the single point noted above.

the coupon payments. The first is that they are consumed by the investor at the time of receipt. If this is the case, then the YTM is a sufficient calculation.

The alternative is to assume that they are reinvested at some specific rate of return. This reinvestment rate may or may not be the same as the yield to maturity. When an explicit assumption is made about the rate of return on reinvested coupon payments, we need to be aware of the realized compound yield to maturity (RCYTM). The RCYTM is essentially a weighted average of the return on the bond itself and the return on the reinvested coupon payments.

The only way to solve for a RCYTM is to explicitly solve for the future value of what the reinvested coupon payments will be worth when the bond matures, and add this to the maturity value of the bond. Then we must solve for the internal rate of return that equates the present value of the combined ending values of the bond and the reinvested coupons to today's price of the bond.

Let's continue the previous example of the XYZ bond, and assume, for illustrative purposes, that the cash flows (that is, the coupon payments) are reinvested at the yield to maturity (4.9846 percent) until the maturity date (end of year 6). If this is the case, then the terminal value of this investment is $1,271.96, computed as follows:

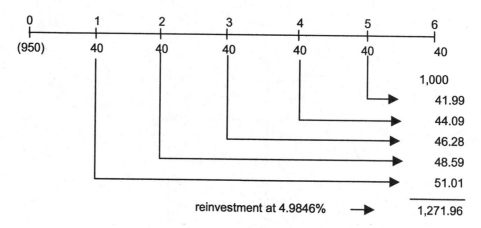

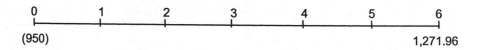

Now imagine a pure discount instrument with a price identical to that of the bond ($950) and a maturity value of $1,271.96—the terminal value of the bond with the reinvestment assumptions.

If we calculate the internal rate of return for this synthetic instrument, we find that it is identical to the bond's yield to maturity except for a tiny difference due to rounding.

The HP-10BII keystrokes are

    SHIFT, C ALL
    950, +/–, PV
    1271.96, FV
    6, N
    I/YR (display: 4.9844)

Recall from earlier discussions that interest rate risk includes price risk and reinvestment rate risk. For example, if the bond's yield to maturity falls instantaneously to 4.50 percent, the owner would happily see an increase in price from $950 to $974.21.

The HP-10BII keystrokes are

SHIFT, C ALL
40, PMT
1000, FV
6, N
4.5, I/YR
PV (display: –974.21)

Let's see, however, what happens if the owner retains the bond until maturity with coupons reinvested at the new yield to maturity of 4.50 percent.

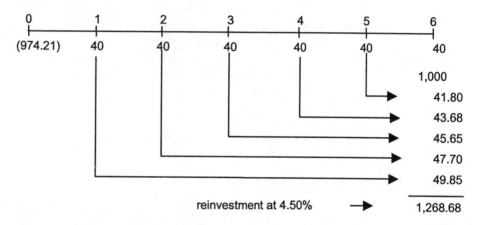

Again, if there were a synthetic, pure discount instrument paying $1,268.68 in 6 years and costing $974.21 today, the yield to maturity would equal 4.5 percent, the same as the bond's YTM.

If the bond had been purchased before the drop in yield—when the price was $950 and the yield was 4.9846 percent—and if the bond is retained to maturity, what would the RCYTM be over the life of the bond? Again, we can create a synthetic instrument to calculate an internal rate of return of 4.9393 percent.

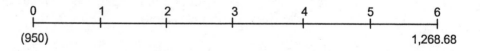

The HP-10BII keystrokes are

SHIFT, C ALL
950, +/–, PV
1268.68, FV
6, N
I/YR (display: 4.9393)

In other words, because of the drop in interest rates, the rate of return over the life of the bond would fall from 4.9846 percent to 4.9393 percent.

Yield to Call

Yield to call computations are identical to yield-to-maturity calculations except the call price is substituted for the par, and N equals the number of periods until the earliest call date. Note that because the yield to call is the discount rate that equates the present value of the call price and the coupon payments to today's price, it too is an internal rate of return calculation. The call price equals par plus some type of call premium. This call premium may be as high as one year's worth of interest. Continuing the previous example, the following timeline shows the cash flows for a call price of $1,040 and a period to first call of 3 years.

$$Price = \sum_{t=1}^{N} \frac{\text{coupon payment}}{(1+i_c)^t} + \frac{\text{call price}}{(1+i_c)^N}$$

$$950 = \frac{40}{(1+i_c)} + \frac{40}{(1+i_c)^2} + \frac{40}{(1+i_c)^3} + \frac{1040}{(1+i_c)^3}$$

where N = time to earliest call
i_c = yield to first call

Again, computing the answer of 7.15 percent is made simple with a financial calculator where PV = 950, PMT = 40, FV = 1040, and N = 3 (remember, we are assuming annual payments for simplicity).

The HP-10BII keystrokes are

    SHIFT, C ALL
    950, +/–, PV
    40, PMT
    1040, FV
    3, N
    I/YR (display: 7.1529)

Example: Suppose the callable bond pays interest semiannually rather than annually. The calculation of the yield to first call of a bond with a 4 percent coupon rate that pays interest semiannually, is called in 3 years for $1,050, and trades for $950 is as follows:

Compute the semiannual payment to be $20, and the number of time periods to be 6 (6 half-years), and enter the FV and PV of the bond as $1,050 and $950. Then solve for the YTM (I/YR), and multiply the answer by 2 to annualize it. In this case, the answer is 7.4082 percent.

The HP-10bII keystrokes are

SHIFT, C ALL
set for end-of-period payments
1000, x, .04, ÷, 2, =, PMT
3, x, 2, =, N
1050, FV
950, +/–, PV
I/YR (display: 3.7041), x, 2, = (display: 7.4082)

Realized Returns

We can use the same approach to calculate an investor's realized rate of return. For example, if our $950 bond investment is sold 2 years later for $980, and the sale is immediately after the (annual) coupon payment, what is the rate of return for the 2 years? Just as with yield to maturity and yield to earliest call, we can show the cash flows on a timeline and calculate the answer as 5.7454 percent.

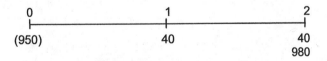

HP-10BII keystrokes
SHIFT, C ALL
950, +/–, PV
40, PMT
980, FV
2, N
I/YR (display: 5.7454)

BOND PRICE VOLATILITY

There are several theorems about bond pricing with which every financial planner should be familiar. The three most fundamental ones are as follows

- Theorem 1: Bond prices and interest rates are inversely related.
- Theorem 2: The longer a bond's term to maturity, the greater the percentage change in its price for a given change in interest rates. (The is known as the *maturity effect*.)
- Theorem 3: The lower a bond's coupon rate, the greater the percentage change in its price for a given change in interest rates. (This is know as the *coupon effect*.)

maturity effect

coupon effect

The first theorem follows from the mathematical formulation of a bond's price presented in the previous section. The second and third theorems are illustrated with the following two examples.

Example 1: The Short Circuit Corp. has two bonds outstanding: A and B. Both have a 5 percent coupon rate (with annual payments) and a 5 percent yield to maturity, but Bond A has a 5-year maturity, and Bond B has a 20-year maturity. What is the percentage change in each bond's price if interest rates change from 5 percent to 6 percent?

Because the coupon rate matches the YTM, both bonds initially trade at par. At a 6 percent YTM, the price of Bond A is $957.88, and the price of Bond B is $885.30. Thus, the percentage changes in the two bond prices are –4.21 percent and –14.70 percent. The bond with the longer maturity, all other things being equal, has the greater percentage price change.

Example 2: The Live Wire Corp. has two bonds outstanding: A and B. Bond A was issued many years ago, has 10 years to maturity, and has a 3 percent coupon rate. Bond B was just issued, has 10 years to maturity, and has a 10 percent coupon rate. The YTM on both bonds is 5 percent. What is the percentage change in each bond's price if interest rates change from 5 percent to 6 percent?

The initial prices of the two bonds are $845.57 for Bond A and $1,386.09 for Bond B. After the change in interest rates, the prices are $779.20 for Bond A and

$1,294.40 for Bond B. The percentage price changes are –7.85 percent for Bond A ([$779.20 – $845.57]/ $845.57) and –6.62 percent for Bond B. The bond with the lower coupon rate has the greater percentage price change, if all other things are equal.

A less common, but still important, bond theorem is as follows:

yield-to-maturity effect

- Theorem 4: For a given change in interest rates, bonds with lower YTMs have greater percentage price changes than bonds with higher YTMs, all other things being equal. (This is known as the *yield-to-maturity effect*.)

Again, let's demonstrate this with an example.

Example: Consider two bonds: A and B. Both have a 5 percent coupon rate and 20 years to maturity. However, Bond A has a 3 percent YTM, and Bond B has an 8 percent YTM. What is the percentage change in each bond's price if the YTMs fall by 1 percent (that is, from 3 to 2 percent for A and 8 to 7 percent for B)?

The initial prices of the two bonds are $1,297.55 for Bond A and $705.46 for Bond B. If each YTM drops by 1 percent in absolute terms, the new prices will be $1,490.54 for Bond A and $788.12 for Bond B. The percentage changes are +14.87 percent for Bond A and +11.72 percent for Bond B. The bond with the lower YTM has the greater percent price change.

This last theorem has serious implications for the financial planner. It means that when market interest rates are low, not only will the client have less income from the portfolio, but the prices of the client's bonds will also be more volatile in percentage terms.

Based on theorems 2, 3, and 4, we can now pose a simple question: Which of the following three bonds will have the greatest price volatility?

Bond X: 25 years to maturity, 10% coupon rate, and a 6% YTM
Bond Y: 10 years to maturity, 2% coupon rate, and a 6% YTM
Bond Z: 17.5 years to maturity, 6% coupon rate, and a 4% YTM

Theorem 2 indicates that Bond X will have the greatest price volatility because it has the longest maturity. Theorem 3 indicates that Bond Y will have the greatest price volatility because it has the lowest coupon rate.

Theorem 4 indicates that Bond Z will have the greatest price volatility because it has the lowest YTM. In other words, although we have identified three excellent theorems about bond price volatility, they cannot really help us answer the simple question of which of the three bonds will have the greatest percentage change in price for a given change in YTM.

DURATION

Fortunately, there is a statistic for bonds that can be computed, which will answer the question of which of the three bonds, X, Y, or Z, will have the greatest percentage price change for a given change in interest rates. This statistic is known as the bond's duration. Like maturity, duration is a measure of time. Duration is defined as the weighted average of the lengths of time until the present values of all remaining payments are made. In other words, it is the weighted average time until recovery of the present value of the bond's future cash flows (principal and interest). The most common formula for calculating duration (and the one provided on the formula sheet for the CFP® certification examination) is the following:

$$D = \frac{\displaystyle\sum_{t=1}^{n} \frac{C_t \times (t)}{(1+i)^t}}{\displaystyle\sum_{t=1}^{n} \frac{C_t}{(1+i)^t}} \qquad \text{(Equation 9-4)}$$

where C_t = the cash flow in period t (coupon, principal, or both)
t = the time period when the cash flow is to be received
i = yield to maturity (discount rate)
n = the term to maturity of the bond

Note that the above formula can be written more simply as

$$D = \frac{\displaystyle\sum_{t=1}^{n} \frac{t \times C_t}{(1+i)^t}}{P_0} \qquad \text{(Equation 9-4a)}$$

where P_0 = price of the bond today

Macaulay's duration

The values produced by these formulas are known as *Macaulay's duration,* in honor of Frederick Macaulay, who first published and promoted this concept.[5] The weight of each promised payment's time to receipt is based on its present value relative to the sum of the present values of the entire payment stream (the intrinsic value of the bond). That is, each weight equals the present value of that payment divided by the bond's market price.

The total of the present values of expected future cash flows equals the bond's market price. Duration thereby captures the impact of differing coupon rates and recognizes that the earlier coupon payments have a higher present value than later coupon payments.

Consider the durations of two bonds maturing in 7 years. Bond A has a 6 percent coupon, and bond B has a 10 percent coupon; both pay interest on an annual basis. Table 9-2 shows the results of computing the durations of both bonds when the market-determined interest rate for new bonds of comparable risk is 8 percent. Column (1) lists the time period in which a cash flow (that is, interest payment or principal) will be received, and column (2) shows the cash flow (that is, C_t). Column (3) provides the present value of the cash flow, discounted at the current market rate (that is, the yield to maturity). Note that the total for the third column is the price of the bond. Finally, column (4) is the product of the time until a cash flow is received and its present value (that is, the product of columns (1) and (3)). The duration of the bond is computed by dividing the sum of column (4) by the price of the bond, which was the sum of column (3). In this example, the duration for Bond A is 5.85 years, and the duration for Bond B is 5.44 years.

Duration can be calculated with an HP-10BII calculator, although the process is cumbersome, especially for long periods. Keystrokes are as follows for Bond A:

> SHIFT, C ALL
> 60, FV, 8, I/YR, 1, N, PV, M+
> 2, N, PV, x, 2, =, M+
> 3, N, PV, x, 3, =, M+
> 4, N, PV, x, 4, =, M+
> 5, N, PV, x, 5, =, M+
> 6, N, PV, x, 6, =, M+
> 1060, FV, 7, N, PV, x, 7, =, M+
> RM, +/–, ÷, 895.87, =   (display: 5.85)

Another formula on the CFP® formula sheet for computing duration[6] is

$$D = \frac{1+i}{i} - \frac{(1+i)+n(C-i)}{C\left[(1+i)^n - 1\right] + i} \qquad \text{(Equation 9-5)}$$

> where i =   yield to maturity
> C =   coupon rate
> n =   term to maturity

Using this alternative formula, the duration statistics for Bonds A and B can be computed as

TABLE 9-2
Durations of Two Bonds Maturing in 7 Years
(Assume Annual Interest Payments)

Bond A

(1) Year(s) Until Receipt t Where N = 7	(2) Cash Flow	(3) Present Value at 8%	(4) Year(s) x Present Value [Column (1) x Column (3)]
1	$ 60	$ 55.56	$ 55.56
2	60	51.44	102.88
3	60	47.63	142.89
4	60	44.10	176.40
5	60	40.83	204.15
6	60	37.81	226.86
7	1,060	618.50	4,329.50
Total	$1,420	$895.87	$5,238.24

Duration for Bond A is equal to $5,238.24/$895.87 = (5.8470984 years rounded to) 5.85 years

Bond B

(1) Year(s) Until Receipt t Where N = 7	(2) Cash Flow	(3) Present Value at 8%	(4) Year(s) x Present Value [Column (1) x Column (3)]
1	$ 100	$ 92.59	$ 92.59
2	100	85.73	171.46
3	100	79.38	238.14
4	100	73.50	294.00
5	100	68.06	340.30
6	100	63.02	378.12
7	1,100	641.84	4,492.88
Total	$1,700	$1,104.12	$6,007.49

Duration for Bond B is equal to $6,007.49/$1,104.12 = (5.4409756 years rounded to) 5.44 years

$$D_A = \frac{1+.08}{.08} - \frac{(1+.08)+7(.06-.08)}{.06\left[(1+.08)^7 - 1\right]+.08}$$

$$= 5.85$$

$$D_B = \frac{1+.08}{.08} - \frac{(1+.08)+7(.10-.08)}{.10\left[(1+.08)^7 - 1\right]+.08}$$

$$= 5.44$$

Duration as an Index Number

For anyone who has never heard of the term duration until now, the first question that arises is, what does this number mean? There are several interpretations and uses for the duration number, but the simplest one is that it is an index number. The larger the duration statistic, the greater the percentage change in the price of the bond for a given change in interest rates. In our previous example, we can definitively say that the price of Bond A will be more volatile to a change in market interest rates than the price of Bond B, because it has a larger duration statistic. We can also say that the difference in the price volatility will not be great because the duration statistics are relatively close. In this particular example, we knew that the duration statistic for Bond A would be the larger of the two because the two bonds have the same term to maturity and the same yield to maturity, but different coupon rates, so all of the conditions of theorem 3 are met.

There is an alternative way to think about the duration statistic. It is that a bond's price volatility will be the same as that of a zero-coupon bond whose maturity equals that duration. A zero-coupon bond will always have a duration equal to its remaining life n because it has only one payment, the principal, associated with the bond. In other words, since $P_0 = C_n/(1 + i)^n$ for a zero-coupon bond, equation 9-4a reduces to

$$D = \frac{n \times [C_n/(1+i)^n]}{P_0} = n \times \frac{P_0}{P_0} = n \times 1 = n$$

This same result can be obtained from the simplification formula if we substitute the value of zero for C, as follows:

$$D = \frac{1+i}{i} - \frac{(1+i) + n(C-i)}{C\left[(1+i)^n - 1\right] + i}$$

$$= [(1+i)/i] - [(1+i) - ni]/i = [(1+i)/i] - [(1+i)/i] + [ni/i] = n$$

Because zero-coupon bonds have no coupons, the only volatility theorem that applies is the maturity effect. Hence, the maturity is an immediate index of bond price volatility for all zero-coupon bonds. In our above example, we can say that Bond A would have the identical duration to a zero-coupon bond whose term to maturity is 5.85 years.

It is not obvious in table 9-2 or in the equations above, but the duration of a bond that has coupons will always be less than its remaining life n. In other words, the duration statistic of a coupon bond will always be less than the bond's maturity. It can also be easily proved with calculus that there is an inverse relationship between the coupon rate of a bond and the duration statistic, and between the yield to maturity and the duration. These are the coupon and the yield-to-maturity effects noted above in theorems 3 and 4.

Major Characteristics of Duration

- The duration of a zero-coupon bond is equal to its term to maturity.
- The duration of a coupon bond is always less than its term to maturity.
- There is an inverse relationship between coupon rate and duration.
- There is an inverse relationship between yield to maturity and duration.

Most of the time, there is a direct relationship between a bond's maturity and its duration statistic. However, we do not offer this as a universally true statement because there are some exceptions. Oddly enough, some bonds with low coupon rates, extremely long terms to maturity, and high yields to maturity may actually increase in price volatility with the passage of time. However, these are really obscure exceptions to the concept that a bond's duration statistic is directly related to its term to maturity. About the only place we would actually run into such bonds would be on an exam!

Example: Consider two bonds, both of which have coupon rates of 2 percent, yields to maturity of 10 percent, and terms to maturity of 40 and 50 years. Their duration statistics are

$$D = \frac{1+.10}{.10} - \frac{(1+.10) + 40(.02 - .10)}{.02\left[(1+.10)^{40} - 1\right] + .10} = 13.13$$

and

$$D = \frac{1+.10}{.10} - \frac{(1+.10) + 50(.02 - .10)}{.02\left[(1+.10)^{50} - 1\right] + .10} = 12.19$$

Simply put, the bond with the longer term to maturity has the shorter duration (and therefore less price volatility), despite the fact that all other things are equal. This means that there are some exceptions to theorem 2 (the one on the maturity effect) stated above.

Earlier in this section, we considered three bonds—X, Y, and Z—and pondered which would have the greatest price volatility. The answer was complicated by the fact that none of our three basic theorems perfectly applied. The duration statistics for the three bonds are 12.37, 8.96, and 11.99. So the answer is that bond X would have the greatest price volatility, as it has the largest duration, although bond Z is a close second.

Estimating a Bond's Price Volatility

modified duration

A second use of the duration statistic is to actually estimate the percentage change in a bond's price. To do this calculation, we must first compute the modified duration. To find a bond's *modified duration,* calculate its duration using equation 9-4a or 9-5, and adjust it for the bond's yield to maturity as follows:

$$D^* = \frac{D}{1+i} \qquad \text{(Equation 9-6)}$$

where D^* = the bond's modified duration
D = the bond's duration
i = the bond's yield to maturity

Having determined a bond's modified duration, it is relatively easy to estimate that bond's percentage price change resulting from a small change in the market interest rate. Thus, the bond's modified duration is first multiplied by -1 (to reflect the inverse relationship between bond prices and interest rates) and then by the percentage change in market interest rates. In equation form, this is expressed as follows:

$$\frac{\Delta P}{P} = -D \times \left(\frac{\Delta(1+i)}{1+i} \right)$$
$$= -D^* \times \left[\Delta(1+i) \right] \qquad \text{(Equation 9-7)}$$
$$= -D^* \times \Delta i$$

where P = price of the bond
ΔP = change in the price of the bond
$\Delta(1 + i)$ = change in bond's yield to maturity

This formula is also on the formula sheet of the CFP® certification exam.

| *Example:* | Continuing with the previous discussion of duration and the calculations in table 9-2, Bond A's modified duration would be |

$$D^* = \frac{5.85 \text{ years}}{1 + .08} = 5.42 \text{ years}$$

where 5.85 years is Bond A's duration, calculated using a yield to maturity of 8 percent (the market-determined interest rate for new bonds of comparable risk) when its coupon rate is 6 percent.

Assuming the market interest rate for new bonds of comparable risk increases from 8 to 8.5 percent, the price of Bond A would decrease by approximately 2.71 percent, or $24.28 (2.71% x $895.87) in value. This is computed as follows:

$$\text{Percent change in bond price} = -5.42 \times 0.5\% = -2.71\%$$

The estimated dollar change in the price of the bond can then be computed by multiplying this percentage change by the current price. This is computed as follows:

$$\begin{aligned} \text{Dollar change in price} &= 2.71\% \times \$895.87 \\ &= -\$24.28 \\ \text{New bond price} &= \$895.87 - \$24.28 = \$871.59 \end{aligned}$$

The actual dollar value decline in price is $23.83 (to $872.04). Had the magnitude of the change in the discount rate been smaller, the approximation would have been even more accurate.

Convexity

Note in this example that the modified duration formula overestimates the dollar decline in the price of the bond. Had we considered a decrease in interest rates, the modified duration formula would have underestimated the increase in the price of the bond. It is important to understand why this happens. The answer can be seen in figure 9-2, which shows the price of a bond on the vertical axis and the yield to maturity on the horizontal axis. The curved line defines the price of the bond for any given yield to maturity. Note that this curve is convex. *Convex* means that the curvature of the relationship is away from the horizontal axis.

convex

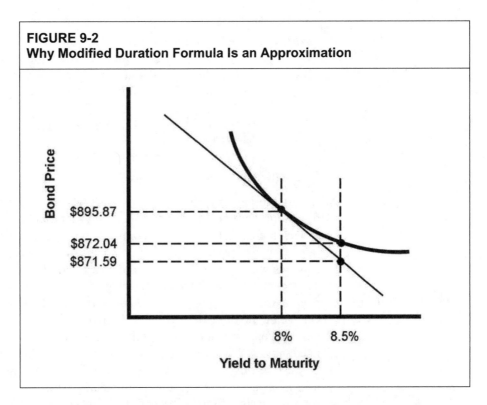

FIGURE 9-2
Why Modified Duration Formula Is an Approximation

The other line in the figure is a straight-line tangent to the curved line at the point where the yield to maturity equals 8 percent and the price of the bond is $895.87. The modified duration is the slope of this straight line. The modified duration formula is a linear approximation of the change in the price of the bond, and it is not exact because the relationship is curvilinear. It is for this reason that all discussions of the use of the modified duration approximation formula emphasize that it works best when the change in yield to maturity is small. "Small" in this case actually means a few basis points (a basis point is one-hundredth of one percent, or .01 percent). The larger the change in yield to maturity, the more error in the approximation, as noted by the vertical difference between the approximation line and the curved line in figure 9-2.

Duration of a Portfolio

From the calculation of the duration of individual bonds like Bonds A and B, it is a simple matter to calculate the duration of a whole portfolio of bonds. The duration of a bond portfolio is equal to the weighted average of the durations of the individual bonds in the portfolio, where the weights are based on market values.

Example: If a two-security portfolio has one-fourth of its funds invested in Bond A with a duration of 5.85 years and three-fourths in Bond B with a duration of 5.44 years, then the portfolio itself has a duration of 5.54 years [$D_p = (1/4 \times 5.85) + (3/4 \times 5.44) = 1.46 + 4.08 = 5.54$ years, where D_p is the duration of the portfolio].

Immunization of a Portfolio

As we have mentioned previously, when interest rates change in either direction, there is always both good news and bad news for a bond investor. When interest rates rise, the coupon payments can be reinvested at higher rates, but the price of the bond falls. When interest rates fall, reinvested coupons will receive lower rates of return, but the price of the bond will rise. The impact of the interest rate change on the yield of reinvested coupon payments is known as *reinvestment rate risk.* The impact of this interest rate change on the price of the bond is known as *price risk.*

reinvestment rate risk
price risk

The opposite impacts of reinvestment rate risk and price risk raise an interesting question. Namely, is there a way to use these opposite effects so that they can be offsetting? The answer turns out to be yes, and the concept is referred to as *immunization.* A portfolio is immunized when the benefits from one of these changes exactly offset the losses from the other change.

immunization

Components of Interest Rate Risk

- Price risk: The risk of an existing bond's price changing when market interest rates change. If rates increase, the bond's price decreases, and if rates decrease, the bond's price increases.
- Reinvestment rate risk: The risk associated with reinvesting coupon payments as market interest rates change. If rates increase, the coupons are reinvested at higher rates than previously expected, and if rates decrease, the coupons are reinvested at lower rates than previously expected.

Immunization allows an investor to earn a specified rate of return from a bond portfolio over a given period of time, regardless of what happens to market interest rates. Immunization is accomplished by setting a bond's duration (or as is more likely, the duration of a bond portfolio) equal to the investor's planning horizon.

There are two methods available to the investor for immunizing his or her portfolio. The easier of these methods is to purchase a series of zero-coupon bonds that mature at times and in amounts that correspond to the investor's need for funds. This strategy encounters two basic problems, however. First, the need for funds can rarely be forecast precisely, and second, zero-coupon bonds may not be available in the exact maturities needed.

Example: Your client has a daughter who will be going to college in 10 years. She has $30,000 in a Coverdell IRA (formerly known as an educational IRA). If this $30,000 were invested in zero-coupon bonds that mature in 10 years, your client would know the value of the account with perfect certainty, provided the issuer does not default on the bonds.

The typical method of immunizing involves assembling and appropriately managing a diversified portfolio of bonds. The portfolio is structured and managed with the objective of keeping its duration equal in length to the investor's planning horizon. This requires continual portfolio rebalancing for two reasons. The first is that, unless the bonds are all zero-coupon bonds, the duration of a bond changes at a slower rate than the investor's planning horizon.

Example: Consider Bond B that we discussed earlier, which had a duration of 5.44 years. Suppose that an investor has a planning horizon of 5.44 years. Bond B provides the necessary immunization. However, after one year, the investor's planning horizon will be 4.44 years, but the duration of the bond will be 4.85 years. Thus, the investor will no longer be immunized. The reason this occurs is that the bond's duration will go to zero over the term to maturity, which in this case was initially 7 years. To decline from a value of 5.44 to zero over a period of 7 years requires that the reduction in the duration statistic each year has to be less than a full year.

The second reason that regular rebalancing is necessary is that every time interest rates change, the duration of the portfolio changes, but the investor's time horizon is unaffected. Because immunization requires that the portfolio have a duration equal to the remaining time in the investor's planning horizon, the composition of the investor's portfolio must, in theory, be rebalanced every time interest rates change. When an imbalance occurs, the investor would likely replace some portfolio components with others whose durations more closely matched the planning horizon target.

Moreover, as cash flows are received from coupon payments, the proceeds can be used to purchase new bonds to maintain the target duration. These cash inflows, however, may not be adequate to rebalance the portfolio. To accomplish rebalancing under these circumstances, the investor may have to sell some bonds in the secondary market to obtain the additional funds.

As is evident from the discussion, portfolio immunization is a powerful investment tool that is clearly not a passive strategy.[7] Under the typical immunization method, a portfolio requires frequent rebalancing to keep its duration equal to the remaining time horizon. Finally, the effectiveness of immunizing a portfolio must take transaction costs into account. Frequent rebalancing can be very expensive. A discussion of how exactly immunization works can be found in appendix 9-A.

Immunizing a Portfolio

- Purchasing a series of zero-coupon bonds whose maturities correspond with the planning horizon
- Assembling and managing a bond portfolio whose duration is kept equal to the planning horizon

---

It should be emphasized that immunization is only one strategy for managing a portfolio. It is not necessarily clear that a financial planner should always seek to immunize a bond portfolio. For example, an investor may not have a well-defined time horizon of when he or she wants to cash out his or her investment. Another possibility is that the investor may want to speculate on interest rate movements. For example, if an investor expects interest rates to fall and wants to benefit from this decline, he or she should hold a portfolio whose duration is longer than the desired time horizon. Conversely, if an investor expects interest rates to rise and wants to benefit from this, he or she should hold a portfolio whose duration is less than the time horizon. In theory, if an immediate increase in interest rates is expected,

---

Uses of the Duration Statistic

- As an index number to compare the relative price volatility of bonds or bond portfolios
- To compute the modified duration, which allows an investor to estimate the percentage change in the price of a bond for a given change in the yield to maturity
- To immunize a portfolio by setting the portfolio's duration equal to the investor's time horizon

---

then the investor should hold a portfolio whose duration is zero (that is, an all-cash portfolio). After interest rates rise, the investor can then purchase the bonds at a lower price and benefit from higher reinvestment rates.

ASSEMBLING AND MANAGING A BOND PORTFOLIO

Bond portfolios are similar to stock portfolios in that the most important characteristic is diversification. A good portfolio contains bonds that are issued by firms in different industries that have different basic attributes (for example, size and location of company). Bonds should also be selected to produce the desired level of maturity/duration, default risk/quality rating (this topic will be discussed in a later section), coupon/price appreciation, and taxable income.

Bond Swaps

Portfolio managers frequently seek to improve their portfolios by buying a bond with the funds freed up by liquidating another position. These bond swaps may be designed to increase yield to maturity, increase current yield, adjust duration or risk, or establish a tax loss.

Many swaps are not executed simultaneously. Thus, swap traders risk making one side of the swap (say, the sell) only to encounter an adverse price move before the other side of the swap is accomplished. Moreover, transaction costs absorb some of the anticipated benefits of the swap. Nonetheless, a variety of circumstances make swaps attractive. Bond swaps generally fall into the following four categories:[8]

- *substitution swap.* In this case the bond sold and the one bought are considered near perfect substitutes. The motivation for such a swap might be either the recognition of a loss for tax purposes (this topic is discussed in chapter 13) or an attempt to move from a fairly priced or overpriced bond to an underpriced bond. For example, if an investor owns the XYZ bond and notes that the ABC bond has the same coupon rate, same maturity, same quality rating, and is in the same industry but trades for $20 less than the XYZ bond, the investor might expect a $20 windfall gain from selling the XYZ bond and buying the ABC bond.
- *intermarket spread swap.* The basis of this swap is that there is an equilibrium relationship in the spreads between yields of bonds in different markets or sectors. For example, suppose the yield on top-rated bonds of utilities tends to be about one-quarter of one percent below that on top-rated bonds of transportation companies, but that currently the two yields are the same. This suggests that either utility bonds are underpriced (that is, the yield is too high) or the

transportation bonds are overpriced (that is, the yield is too low). To the extent that the investor holds transportation bonds, an intermarket spread involves selling the transportation bonds and buying utility bonds.

- *pure-yield pick-up swap*. In this case, the investor sells a bond with a lower current yield or yield to maturity and buys another bond with a higher current yield or yield to maturity. This differs from the intermarket spread swap in that the intermarket swap has an expectation of bond price changes. The pure-yield pick-up swap has no expectation of price changes; it is simply an action to increase the yield of the portfolio, even if it means moving into lower-quality bonds.

- *rate anticipation swap*. This trade involves moving money between short- and long-duration bonds in anticipation of general movement of interest rates. When an investor expects interest rates to fall, the rate anticipation swap entails selling bonds with short durations and buying bonds with long durations. Conversely, when the investor expects interest rates to rise, this swap involves selling bonds with long durations and buying bonds with short durations.

Other Aspects of Bond Portfolio Management

Managing a bond portfolio effectively can involve much more than the swaps mentioned above. The investor might, for example, speculate on a bond upgrade by buying an issue that the market views pessimistically. Margin borrowing may be used to magnify potential gains and/or to leverage a high yield. Some bonds may have higher promised long-term yields than the current cost of margin money. Whether to exploit such apparently attractive yield spreads depends on both the likelihood that they will persist and the default risk of these high-yielding issues. If market interest rates rise, the margin-borrowing rate will increase and the bond prices will decline.

Bond Ladders

In some cases, the appropriate strategy for managing a bond portfolio might simply be a bond ladder.[9] A bond ladder spreads the value of the portfolio evenly across some time horizon. If the investor's time horizon is 10 years, a pure bond ladder has one-tenth of the portfolio maturing at the end of the first year, one-tenth maturing in the end of the second, and so on until the end of the tenth year. As each bond matures, it is reinvested with a 10-year maturity. Note that what had previously been 10-year bonds will now have a 9-year maturity. Rolling over the maturing bonds each year into another set of 10-year bonds keeps the ladder pure.

A bond ladder may also serve a client well if the purpose is to liquidate a portfolio over time. A 10-year ladder allows a client to have 10 years worth of steady cash inflow. Alternatively, the client may simply want the choice each year of whether to liquidate none, some, or all of the maturing bonds. A ladder allows this to occur with minimal disruption to the portfolio.

Barbells

Some people prefer the barbell strategy to a ladder. A *barbell* bond portfolio puts a disproportionate percentage of the portfolio into the shortest-term and longest-term bonds in the portfolio. The rest of the portfolio is evenly distributed to maturities between these two. For example, with a 10-year time horizon, the portfolio may have 40 percent allocated to one-year bonds, 40 percent allocated to 10-year bonds, and 2.5 percent allocated to each of the in-between maturities (that is, 2-year to 9-year maturities). The rationale for a barbell strategy is that the heavy allocation to the short-term bonds increases the liquidity of the portfolio, and the heavy allocation to the long-term bonds increases the interest income from the portfolio. This is because most of the time, long-term bonds provide higher current yields than short-term bonds (this relationship is discussed in the next section).

Bond Returns Compared with Stock Returns

Many investors keep both stocks and bonds in their portfolios. There are advantages and disadvantages to each. Stocks' expected returns are higher, but bonds are less risky. A balanced portfolio of stocks and bonds may offer the risk-expected return tradeoff appropriate to the needs and risk-tolerance levels of many investors.

TERM STRUCTURE OF INTEREST RATES

The relationship between a bond's time to maturity and its yield to maturity (assuming all other factors, such as default risk, are equal) is known as the term structure of interest rates. To understand why bonds of different maturities have different yields, let us first consider how differences in maturity can affect the value of bonds.

Impact of Maturity on Bond Prices

As noted in our second bond theorem (and in the discussion on duration), the longer the maturity of a bond (all other things being equal), the greater the bond's price sensitivity to changes in market interest rates. Therefore, any change in market interest rates, such as an overall increase in the rate of inflation, will have a larger impact on the price of a bond with 10 years remaining to maturity than on a bond with only one year remaining to maturity. Thus, risk-averse investors would, other things being equal, prefer short-term bonds to long-term ones.

Borrowers (bond issuers) may prefer the security of a fixed long-term rate and therefore find distant-maturity issues less risky. If they issue shorter-maturity debt, they factor in the risk that interest rates will have risen when the debt matures and they will have to pay a higher rate of interest to refinance the debt when it comes due.

Term to maturity is a major determinant of a debt security's yield to maturity. The relationship between term to maturity and yield to maturity is **yield curve** illustrated with a yield curve. A *yield curve* is the graphic representation of the term structure of interest rates—that is, the relationship between yield to maturity and term to maturity for debt securities with otherwise similar characteristics (default risk, coupon, call feature, and so on). The yield curve reveals a pattern that at various times rises, falls, does not vary, or rises and then falls (see figure 9-3). It is critically important that any investor understand why the yield curve takes on different shapes at different times.

Term Structure Hypotheses

Although there are different yield curves for different classes of bonds, the most commonly discussed yield curve is the one for Treasury bonds. This is probably because Treasury bonds have virtually no risk of default, and thus any difference in yield between two Treasury bonds results solely from the difference in their maturities. Hence, this discussion will focus on the Treasury bond yield curve.

The following term structure hypotheses are all designed to explain the various shapes of the yield curve:

- market segmentation
- preferred habitat
- liquidity preference
- unbiased expectations

market segmentation hypothesis

The *market segmentation hypothesis* asserts that supply and demand within each market segment, as defined by maturities, determine interest rates for that maturity class. According to this hypothesis, the yield curve simply reflects the supply and demand for each maturity class. Because most investors are thought to prefer short-term investments, and most borrowers prefer to borrow long term, we would expect to see upward-sloping yield curves almost all of the time.

preferred habitat hypothesis

According to the *preferred habitat hypothesis*, borrowers and lenders prefer certain maturities. They can be induced to accept other maturities only

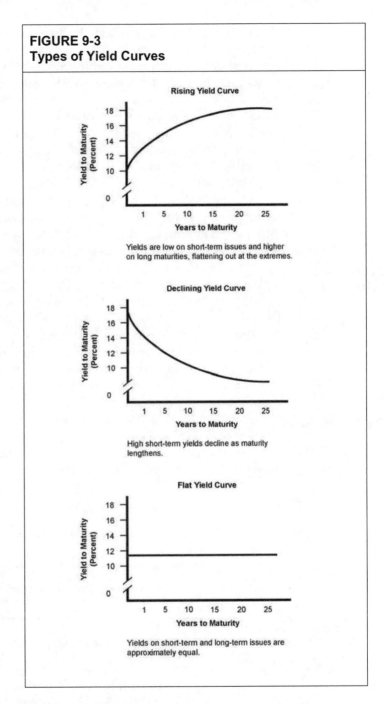

FIGURE 9-3
Types of Yield Curves

Rising Yield Curve

Yields are low on short-term issues and higher on long maturities, flattening out at the extremes.

Declining Yield Curve

High short-term yields decline as maturity lengthens.

Flat Yield Curve

Yields on short-term and long-term issues are approximately equal.

if the rates are significantly more attractive. This hypothesis is related to the market segmentation hypothesis, but it is somewhat less restrictive. The preferred habitat hypothesis provides more likelihood for any shape of yield curve. The difference between the two theories is that the market segmentation hypothesis states that there are completely separate markets for debt instruments of different maturities. Therefore, the interest rates of bonds of one maturity should have no effect on the interest rates of bonds of another maturity. By contrast, the preferred habitat hypothesis allows for the possibility of substitution of maturity by the borrower and lender if the interest rates on debt instruments of various maturities differ sufficiently, although it recognizes that there are limits to the extent by which those rates can differ. Under the market segmentation hypothesis, there can be substantial differences in the yields of bonds of different maturities.

As long as there is an active secondary market for bonds and other debt instruments, it is difficult to argue that the markets for debt instruments of different maturities are distinct, and that investors cannot be attracted to bonds of different maturities by interest rate differentials.

liquidity preference hypothesis

The *liquidity preference hypothesis* assumes that because price risk (the impact of interest rate changes on the bond price) increases with maturity, investors demand a premium to hold longer-term securities. Borrowers are willing to pay a premium to borrow for a longer term because it reduces the frequency, and therefore risk, of refinancing. Because lenders demand a premium for longer-term lending and borrowers are willing to pay a premium, the yield curve will always be upward sloping. The difference between long-term and short-term interest rates due to liquidity preference is called the *liquidity premium*.

liquidity premium

unbiased expectations hypothesis

According to the *unbiased expectations hypothesis,* long-term rates are a function of current and expected future short-term rates in a geometric mean relationship. For example, the current 2-year rate is a function of the current one-year rate and the expectation of next year's one-year rate, as follows:

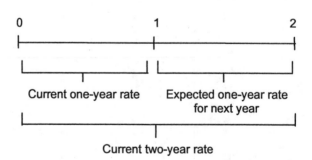

$$\left(1 + \begin{array}{c} \text{Current} \\ \text{2-year} \\ \text{rate} \end{array}\right) = \left(\left(1 + \begin{array}{c} \text{Current} \\ \text{one-year} \\ \text{rate} \end{array}\right)\left(1 + \begin{array}{c} \text{Expected} \\ \text{one-year} \\ \text{rate for} \\ \text{next year} \end{array}\right)\right)^{0.5}$$

Since we can find the current 2-year rate and current one-year rate in the newspaper or online, we can manipulate the formula above to solve for the expected one-year rate for next year.

$$\begin{matrix}\text{Expected}\\\text{one-year}\\\text{rate for}\\\text{next year}\end{matrix} = \left(\left(1 + \frac{\text{Current}}{\text{2-year}\atop\text{rate}}\right)^2 \div \left(1 + \frac{\text{Current}}{\text{one-year}\atop\text{rate}}\right)\right) - 1$$

Example: Consider a current 2-year rate of 10 percent and a current one-year rate of 8 percent.

Using the formula above, we can determine what the market expects next year's one-year rate to be according to the unbiased expectations hypothesis.

$$\begin{matrix}\text{Expected}\\\text{one-year}\\\text{rate for}\\\text{next year}\end{matrix} = \left(1.10^2 \div 1.08\right) - 1$$

$$= 1.1204 - 1$$

$$= 12.04\%$$

The HP-10BII keystrokes are

SHIFT, C ALL
1.10, SHIFT, y^x, 2, =
÷, 1.08, =, −, 1, =
(display: 0.1204)

The unbiased expectations hypothesis asserts that the market's expectations for future short-term interest rates are reflected by the rates it establishes for debt securities of various maturities. According to this view, potential arbitrage activity (riskless buying and selling to gain a profit) always drives the yield curve into the shape that is appropriate for that set of expectations.

If long-term rates seem too high compared to expected future short-term rates, some short-horizon investors will move toward longer-term issues while some longer-horizon borrowers will switch toward shorter-term borrowing. This activity should quickly drive rates into the appropriate relationship. Although the preferred habitat, liquidity preference, and unbiased expectations hypotheses all recognize the existence of this arbitraging activity, only the unbiased expectations hypothesis asserts its overriding power.

Each hypothesis explains the various yield curve shapes slightly differently and has somewhat different implications. According to liquidity preference, yield curves are typically rising because of investor risk aversion. Market segmentation and preferred habitat are also consistent with a tendency for yield curves to rise. Lenders may be relatively more numerous at the short end of the maturity spectrum, and borrowers more numerous at the long end.

The unbiased expectations hypothesis, in contrast, asserts that yield curves rise only when short-term interest rates themselves are expected to increase over time. A flat yield curve indicates neutral expectations—that is, expectations that short-term interest rates will remain constant. A falling yield curve reflects an expectation that short-term rates will fall. This expectation causes borrowers (bond issuers) to rely on short-term financing until the expected fall occurs. Accordingly, borrowers anticipating a decline in interest rates tend to shift demand from the long- to the short-term market. As a result, short-term rates tend to be bid up relative to long-term rates.

Term Structure of Interest Rate Hypotheses

- Market segmentation: Yields reflect supply and demand for each maturity class.
- Preferred habitat: Investors and borrowers can be induced out of their preferred maturity structures only by significantly more attractive rates.
- Liquidity preference: Borrowers are risk averse and demand a premium for buying long-term securities. As a result, yield curves tend to be upward sloping.
- Unbiased expectations: Long-term rates reflect the market's expectation of current and future short-term rates.

Lenders' expectations have a similar effect. Lenders (bond buyers) want to profit from the expected interest rate decline by owning long-term bonds. Falling rates would cause the prices of outstanding long-term bonds to rise relative to shorter-term issues. Thus, investors who expect rates to fall will tend to favor the longer maturities, thereby pushing long-term rates downward and short-term rates upward.

None of the term structure hypotheses have gained overwhelming acceptance or been completely ruled out by research. On theoretical grounds, the unbiased expectations hypothesis is generally favored. Liquidity preference may also be useful in explaining the data. Most academicians believe that modern debt markets are not segmented *per se* but that appreciable numbers of borrowers and lenders may have preferred habitats. More than one hypothesis may be useful in explaining the relationship between yield and maturity.

Investment Implications of the Term Structure

Yield curve relationships may give bond traders two opportunities. First, securities whose yields are some distance from curves plotted with otherwise similar issues may well be misvalued. Thus, bonds whose yields exceed their respective yield curve values may be underpriced. If their market prices adjust more quickly than the curve itself shifts, they could produce an above-market return. Of course, a trader who detects such underpriced bonds will need to act very quickly because other investors will be following the same strategy, thus driving the price of undervalued bonds up to their intrinsic value. Also, the trader should make certain that the underpricing does not represent a risk premium, perhaps for a risk that has only recently been discovered and is not yet reflected in the bond's rating. (This assumes, of course, that the bond in question is not a Treasury bond, which has virtually no default risk.)

riding the yield curve

A second strategy involves what is called *riding the yield curve*. A steeply rising yield curve may offer an attractive trading opportunity. To ride the yield curve, an investor buys a bond whose term to maturity corresponds to the "top" of the curve, and then holds this bond as the maturity shortens to a flatter part of the curve. The holding period return from such a strategy may dramatically exceed the yield to maturity of the bond that was purchased. The only way one "loses" on this strategy is if the yield curve rises dramatically or flips to a declining slope during the investment period.

Example:	Let's assume the existence of 2-year T-bills, and that they have a yield to maturity of 7 percent. Let's also assume that one-year T-bills have a yield to maturity of 5 percent. If the investor buys the one-year T-bill and holds it to maturity, the annual return is 5 percent. If the investor buys the 2-year T-bill and holds it to maturity, the annual return is 7 percent. But if the investor buys the 2-year T-bill, holds it one year, and then sells it at a 5 percent yield (which means the yield curve has not shifted), the investor's purchase price is \$873.44 (\$1000/1.07^2), the selling price is \$952.38 (\$1000/1.05), and the annual return is 9.04 percent [(\$952.38 − \$873.44)/ \$873.44)].

FACTORS THAT AFFECT BOND PRICES AND YIELDS

As should be obvious, the discount rate is critical to bond valuation. The appropriate discount rate varies both over time and from investment to investment. Many factors influence discount rates for bond valuation. The characteristics already discussed (general interest rate levels, term structure, and maturity/duration) constitute the principal price/yield determinants of specific bonds. Other relevant characteristics include default risk, marketability, seasoning, call protection, sinking fund provisions, and "me-first" rules.

Factors That Influence a Bond's Discount Rate

Default Risk

A particular asset's appropriate discount rate depends on the perceived risk of the investment. In general, the more certain the expected outcome, the lower the appropriate discount rate. Default risk is the risk that the issuer will not fulfill the obligation to pay all coupons and/or the maturity value. The default risk of municipal and corporate debt securities depends on the income-producing and/or liquidation values of the issuers' assets and on the amount of other debt outstanding. Additional discussion on default risk is provided in appendix 9-B.

The federal government guarantee of Treasury-issued securities results in virtually no default risk for these securities. The market trusts the federal guarantee because the government has extensive taxing power, and the Federal Reserve Board (the Fed) can facilitate sales of government securities.[10]

Bond Ratings

The best way to avoid the uncertainty and potential losses from a default and possible bankruptcy is to invest in bonds with low default risk. This strategy requires a method to assess the default risk level. Bond ratings offer just such an assessment. The default risks of both municipal and corporate bonds are rated by several rating services. The best-known services are Standard & Poor's and Moody's Investors Service. Two other important ratings firms are Duff & Phelps and Fitch Investors Service. Each service's ratings are based on its evaluation of the firm's financial position and earnings prospects. Table 9-3 describes the primary rating categories of these four agencies. Pluses and minuses are used to discriminate within a rating category.

Rating services do not release their specific rating formulas or analyses, but a number of academic studies do reveal a rather predictable pattern. Ratings tend to rise with profitability, size, and earnings coverage (earnings before interest and taxes, divided by total interest expense). They decrease with earnings volatility, leverage, and larger pension obligations; they vary with industry classification. Ratings sometimes differ among the rating agencies; these differences usually reflect a close call on fundamentals.

TABLE 9-3
Bond Rating Categories

Moody's	Standard & Poor's	Fitch	Duff & Phelps	Definition
Aaa	AAA	AAA	AAA	Prime, maximum safety
Aa1 Aa2 AA3	AA+ AA AA–	AA+ AA AA–	AA+ AA AA–	High grade, high quality
A1 A2 A3	A+ A A–	A+ A A–	A+ A A–	Upper medium grade Medium grade
Baa1 Baa2 Baa3	BBB+ BBB BBB–	BBB+ BBB BBB–	BBB+ BBB BBB–	Lower medium grade Minimum investment grade
Ba1 Ba2 Ba3	BB+ BB BB–	BB+ BB BB–	BB+ BB BB–	Noninvestment grade
B1 B2 B3	B+ B B–	B+ B B–	B+ B B–	Highly speculative
Caa	CCC+ CCC CCC–	CCC	CCC	Substantial risk, in poor standing
Ca				Extremely speculative
C				May be in default
	D	DDD DD D	DD DP	In default

investment grade

The top four ratings categories (which range from BBB to AAA for Standard & Poor's and from Baa to Aaa for Moody's) are referred to as *investment grade* bonds. This is because some financial institutions are restricted to invest only in these better-rated bonds, and other investors also restrict themselves to invest only in these. A financial planner who keeps a client in investment grade bonds is clearly acting prudently with regard to safety of principal. Bonds rated less than Baa or BBB are known as *junk bonds* and will be discussed shortly.

junk bond

For issues of the same company, a subordinate issue usually receives a lower rating than a senior security. The rating agencies follow the fortunes of issues over time and change ratings on occasion. These rating changes occur

Financial Planning Issue

Bonds worth $50,000 have matured in your client's portfolio. You are following a ladder strategy, and want to reinvest this money into bonds with a 10-year maturity. Your goal is to have all of the bonds in the portfolio be rated A or better. You have identified three bonds, all rated A, that have yields to maturity of 6.1, 6.2, and 7.3 percent. Which bond is the best deal?

Naturally, an advisor would initially be tempted to buy the issue with the 7.3 percent YTM. However, the pricing of this bond suggests that the company is not in as good shape as the others and is at risk of having its bond rating lowered. Although the announcement of a lower rating does not usually have an immediate price impact (the price impact has already occurred), nonetheless you would not want to end up with a lower-rated bond. From a safety perspective, one of the other two bonds is more likely a better choice.

relatively infrequently, however, and often take place long after the underlying fundamentals change.

Other Factors

Seasoned issues are established in the marketplace. They have been traded for at least a few weeks beyond completion of the initial (offering)

Factors Affecting Bond Yields

- General credit conditions: Credit conditions affect all yields to one degree or another.
- Default risk: Riskier issues require higher promised yields.
- Duration: The weighted average of the amount of time until the present value of the purchase price is recouped.
- Term structure: Yields vary with maturity, reflecting expectations of future interest rate changes.
- Marketability: Actively traded issues tend to be worth more than otherwise equivalent issues that are less actively traded.
- Seasoning: Newly issued bonds may sell at a slight discount to otherwise equivalent established issues.
- Call protection: Protection from an early call tends to enhance a bond's value.
- Sinking fund provisions: Sinking funds reduce the probability of default, thereby tending to enhance a bond's value.
- Me-first rules: Bonds protected from the diluting effect of additional borrowings are generally worth more than otherwise equivalent unprotected issues.

sale. As with new stock issues, new issues of bonds tend to be priced a bit below equivalent seasoned issues.

Call protection varies appreciably from issue to issue. Some bonds are callable beginning the day they are sold. Many others may not be called for the first 5 or 10 years of their life. Callable issues that are reasonably likely to be redeemed due to their high yields should be evaluated on their yield to call rather than on their yield to maturity.

A sinking fund's presence increases demand slightly and reduces the probability of default. Thus, a sinking fund generally adds modestly to the value of a bond.

Me-first rules are designed to protect existing bondholders. These rules prevent the bondholders' claims from being weakened by the issuance of additional debt with a priority higher than or equivalent to theirs. Research has found that these rules significantly enhance the market values of the protected bonds.[11]

Yield Differentials

As interest rates change over time, the yields on all bonds, regardless of their rating, change. However, they do not change at the same rate. Table 9-4 provides the annual average yields to maturity on Aaa and Baa bonds from 1976 to 2003. Note that with the exception of 1982, the direction of change from one year to the next is the same for both ratings. Note also that the difference between the two yields varies substantially over the years. The explanation for this varying spread has to do with investors' willingness to accept risk. When investors become more anxious than usual, they want to hold safer securities. Thus, they will sell lower-rated securities and buy higher-rated ones. The result is that the prices of lower-rated bonds fall *relative* to those of higher-rated ones. This means the yield differential widens. This process is known as a *flight to quality*, which means movement into less risky securities associated with an increase in the yield differential. The yield differential tends to narrow when the economy is expanding, and to widen when the economy is struggling.

flight to quality

High-Yield Corporates

Years ago, most new bond issues were well rated. Junk bonds (issues rated lower than BBB) were primarily the result of their issuers having financial difficulties. Hence, poorly rated bonds were often referred to as *fallen angels*. Since the 1980s' merger and acquisition wave, the issue volume and marketability of junk bonds have grown dramatically as investment bankers concluded that investors were actually willing to buy newly issued high-risk bonds. Junk bonds, of course, provide substantially higher yields than the

fallen angel

TABLE 9-4
Historical Yields on Moody's Aaa and Baa Rated Bonds

Year	Yield on Aaa	Yield on Baa	Difference (Baa— Aaa)
1976	8.43	9.75	1.32
1977	8.02	8.97	0.95
1978	8.73	9.49	0.76
1979	9.63	10.69	1.06
1980	11.94	13.67	1.73
1981	14.17	16.04	1.87
1982	13.79	19.11	5.32
1983	12.04	13.55	1.51
1984	12.71	14.19	1.48
1985	11.37	12.72	1.35
1986	9.02	10.39	1.37
1987	9.38	10.58	1.20
1988	9.71	10.83	1.12
1989	9.26	10.18	0.92
1990	9.32	10.36	1.04
1991	8.77	9.80	1.03
1992	8.14	8.98	0.84
1993	7.22	7.93	0.71
1994	7.97	8.63	0.66
1995	7.59	8.20	0.61
1996	7.37	8.05	0.68
1997	7.27	7.87	0.60
1998	6.53	7.22	0.69
1999	7.05	7.88	0.83
2000	7.62	8.37	0.75
2001	7.08	7.95	0.87
2002	6.49	7.80	1.31
2003	5.66	6.76	1.10

Source: www.federalreserve.gov/releasesH15/data.htm, January 22, 2004

well-rated bonds. Figure 9-4 shows the spread differential between the Merrill Lynch junk bond index and 7-year constant maturity Treasuries from September 1986 to September 2001. As with the yield differential between AAA and BBB bonds, we note that there is substantial variation in this yield differential. An underlying factor but not apparent from the graph is that this yield differential tends to decline during economic expansions and rise during economic contractions.

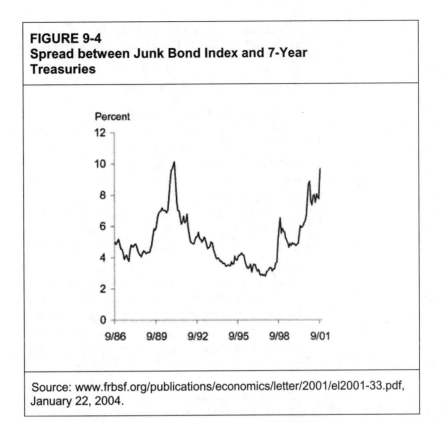

FIGURE 9-4
Spread between Junk Bond Index and 7-Year Treasuries

Source: www.frbsf.org/publications/economics/letter/2001/el2001-33.pdf, January 22, 2004.

There is a simple lesson to be learned from bond yields: The higher the "promised" yield, the greater the default risk is likely to be. Although junk bonds are ill-suited to the needs of more cautious investors, many investors with a greater tolerance for risk are attracted to them. Risk and potential return can be comparable to that of many stocks. Indeed, a risky firm's bonds sometimes offer a more attractive way of speculating than its stock does, because the bonds represent a stronger claim on the firm's assets in case of liquidation or bankruptcy. To realize an attractive return, the junk bond investor needs only for the troubled firm to avoid bankruptcy or to maintain substantial value in reorganization. The stockholder's return may not be attractive unless the firm becomes relatively profitable, because stocks represent only a residual claim on the firm's assets.

During the late 1980s and early 1990s, rates of return on junk bonds were often low and sometimes even negative. Although it is always an important investment goal, diversification is crucial for junk bond investors. A defaulting issue may eventually pay off, but the wait can be long and nerve-racking. Having a diversified bond portfolio substantially dilutes the impact of a single default. Junk bond mutual funds give small investors an effective diversification vehicle. In fact, these funds' growth has encouraged some firms with relatively low credit ratings to return to the bond market.

Transaction Costs for Bonds

Brokers' commissions affect the cost of trading bonds and the bid-ask spread. Accrued interest also needs to be taken into account.

Compared to commissions on stock trades, commissions on bond trades are relatively low as a percentage of the principal amount involved. This is because most bonds are fairly marketable, which makes it easier for brokers to find counterparties to the trades.

Small trades may be particularly costly to an investor. Brokers generally have a minimum commission that they charge. For a particularly small trade, such as five or fewer bonds, this minimum charge could be a sizable percentage of the value of the bonds traded. Also, a trade involving deep-discount bonds may incur a high commission relative to the dollar value of the trade.

Bid-ask spreads are important to consider as well. On actively traded bonds, these spreads tend to be quite narrow. For example, on government bonds, the spread can be less than one-10th of one percent of the price of the bond. On the other hand, a small, inactively traded corporate bond may have a spread of 5 percent of the bond's price.

SUMMARY AND CONCLUSIONS

There are many variations in bonds, including income bonds that pay the promised interest only if its is earned; floating rate notes, where the borrower can limit its interest rate risk exposure through the use of caps or collars; zero-coupon bonds and original-issue discount bonds; consols; and Eurobonds. Many bonds are sold through private placement

The price of a bond equals the present value of its coupon payments and its par value, discounted at the appropriate risk-adjusted discount rate, which is referred to as the yield to maturity. Given the bond's price, we can compute the YTM. Given the YTM, we can calculate the bond's price. Each automatically defines the other. When investing in bonds, the investor needs to be aware of the coupon rate, current yield, yield to maturity, realized compound yield to maturity, and yield to call, as well as the prospective holding period return.

The potential volatility of a bond's price can be measured by its duration. Duration is the weighted average of the time it takes to receive the present value of the bond's expected stream of future payments. Duration can be a basis for investment strategy, including immunization. Other bond investment strategies include laddered portfolios and barbells.

Active management of bond portfolios includes bond swaps, such as substitution swaps, intermarket spread swaps, pure-yield pick-up swaps, and rate anticipation swaps. Managing a bond portfolio also includes ensuring that there is adequate diversification and rebalancing the portfolio to match the portfolio's duration with the investor's desired time horizon.

There are four hypotheses that attempt to explain the term structure of interest rates. The market segmentation and preferred habitat hypotheses argue that both borrowers and lenders (investors) have specific planning horizons, so there are, in effect, different supply-and-demand functions for bonds of different maturities. The liquidity preference hypothesis argues that investors prefer to invest short term, while borrowers prefer to borrow long term, so long-term interest rates tend to be higher than short-term rates in order to attract investors. The unbiased expectations hypothesis holds that long-term interest rates are based on the average of present and expected future short-term rates.

There are a number of factors that influence bond yields. General market conditions, especially the inflation rate and expectations about inflation rate changes, affect both the level of yields in general and the term structure of interest rates. For any given market environment, default risk plays the largest role in determining the interest rate of a particular issue of bonds.

Other factors that influence the price and yield of bonds are marketability, call provisions, priority in the event of default, collateral, and sinking funds.

CHAPTER REVIEW

Answers to the review questions and the self-test questions start on page 733.

Key Terms (including terms in appendix 9B)

debenture	Macaulay's duration
flat	modified duration
call price	convex
call premium	reinvestment rate risk
forced conversion	price risk
zero-coupon bonds (zeros)	immunization
coupon rate	bond swap
current yield	yield curve
yield to maturity (promised yield)	market segmentation hypothesis
maturity effect	preferred habitat hypothesis
coupon effect	liquidity preference hypothesis
yield-to-maturity effect	liquidity premium

unbiased expectations hypothesis	call provision
riding the yield curve	call price
investment grade	call premium
junk bond	trustee
flight to quality	sinking fund
fallen angel	technical default
indenture	Chapter XI
subordination	Chapter VII
senior debt	absolute-priority-of-claims principle

Review Questions (including questions from appendixes 9A and 9B)

9-1. What are the key features of the following bonds: income bonds, floating rate bonds, zero-coupon bonds, and consols?

9-2. What is the difference between a cap and a collar?

9-3. Hayes-L Corporation bonds recently paid the annual interest payment of $35. The bonds mature in 12 years and have a market price of $975. They are callable in 3 years at a price equal to par plus one year's interest.
  a. What is the coupon rate of the Hayes-L bonds?
  b. What is the current yield of the Hayes-L bonds?
  c. What is the yield to maturity of the Hayes-L bonds?
  d. What is the yield to earliest call of the Hayes-L bonds?
  e. If the bonds are purchased today and sold for $990 immediately after the coupon payment 5 years from today, what will the investor's realized yield be? (Ignore reinvestment rate issues.)

9-4. Recompute the duration for bonds A and B in table 9-2 using an appropriate discount rate of 20 percent. Compare the results with those derived from the 8 percent rate.

9-5. What is immunization? Explain the two methods of immunization.

9-6. a. What should be considered when assembling a bond portfolio?
  b. What are bond swaps?
  c. What are three simple strategies that an advisor can use to set up a bond portfolio?

9-7. Describe the four proposed explanations for the term structure of interest rates and how each explains the normal (rising) yield curve.

9-8. Discuss the impacts on yields of
  a. marketability
  b. seasoning
  c. call protection
  d. sinking fund provisions

9-9.   Your client, Johanna Tyson, has an investment-planning horizon of 7 years. Current interest rates are 4 percent and she would like to minimize the risk of not receiving this yield. You are considering an immunization strategy that involves the purchase of a bond with a term to maturity of 9 years and a coupon rate of 8 percent. The YTM is, of course, 4 percent.
   a.   What is the price of this bond today?
   b.   What would her annual HPR be if interest rates jump to 6 percent immediately after buying the bond and she sells the bond after 7 years?
   c.   What would her annual HPR be if interest rates drop to 2 percent immediately after buying the bond?

9-10.   What is a default? How does it relate to bankruptcy?

9-11.   What is meant by the absolute-priority-of-claims principle? What is its relevancy to most bankruptcies? How is it generally applied in practice?

Self-Test Questions

T   F   9-1.   The indenture is a detailed contract between the bond's issuer and the bondholders.

T   F   9-2.   With income bonds, the greater the income earned by the issuer, the more interest that is paid each year.

T   F   9-3.   When a bond is traded flat, the seller does not receive the accrued interest on the bond.

T   F   9-4.   A call provision gives the bondholder the option of receiving the principal amount of the bond prior to maturity.

T   F   9-5.   A call provision is most likely to be exercised if market interest rates decline appreciably while the bond is outstanding.

T   F   9-6.   The terms *fixed-income security* and *debt security* can be used interchangeably.

T   F   9-7.   The yield to maturity on a debt instrument is based on both its market price and its coupon rate.

T   F   9-8.   The current yield is the contractually stated interest rate on a bond.

T   F   9-9.   A bond's coupon rate and yield to maturity are always equal.

T   F   9-10.   The yield to maturity will always be higher than the current yield.

T   F   9-11.   The duration of a zero-coupon bond is equal to its maturity.

T   F   9-12.   Bonds with longer terms to maturity always have greater price volatility than otherwise identical bonds with shorter terms to maturity.

T   F   9-13.   Maturity is a better measure of a bond's sensitivity to interest rate changes than duration.

T   F   9-14.   For bonds of the same maturity and yield to maturity, the lower the coupon rate, the greater the duration.

T   F   9-15.   Immunizing a portfolio reduces the investor's interest rate risk exposure.

T   F   9-16.   A rate anticipation swap involves buying bonds with higher durations if the investor believes rates are about to rise.

T   F   9-17.   A pure-yield pick-up swap has an expectation of bond price changes, whereas an intermarket swap does not.

T   F   9-18.   The expected return to stocks tends to be higher than the expected return to bonds, but stocks also tend to be more risky than bonds.

T   F   9-19.   A barbell investment strategy involves putting heavy weights on bond rather than stock holdings.

T   F   9-20.   Bond ladders have higher weights for those bonds with longer terms to maturity.

T   F   9-21.   The term structure of interest rates describes the relationship between maturity and market interest rates.

T   F   9-22.   The yield curve is a graphic representation of the term structure of interest rates.

T   F   9-23.   Under the liquidity preference hypothesis, borrowers prefer to borrow in the short term rather than the long term.

T   F   9-24.   Under the unbiased expectations hypothesis, if long-term interest rates are higher than short-term interest rates, we can conclude that the consensus expectation is that short-term interest rates will increase in the future.

T   F   9-25.   Riding the yield curve refers to buying intermediate-term bonds when the yield curve is downward sloping and holding them for several years.

T   F   9-26.   The market segmentation hypothesis says that certain segments will consistently outperform other segments.

T   F   9-27.   A bond's sinking fund reduces the risk of default.

T   F   9-28.   Aside from general credit conditions, the most significant factor that influences the coupon rate of a bond is duration.

T   F   9-29.   In the case of liquidation, the claims of senior creditors must be satisfied before any money is paid to the holders of subordinate debt.

T   F   9-30.   The market uses Moody's and Standard & Poor's ratings, among others, to assess the default risk of bonds.

NOTES

1. Some of this section is based on www.cdfa.net/cdfa/press.nsf/pages/800, January 22, 2004.

2. A sharp-eyed reader will notice that the calculations in this example are *almost* the same as the calculations in the prior example, and that the answer is identical to the prior example. In other words, we are saying that a 2.5 percent coupon bond that pays interest annually, has 6 years to maturity, and an appropriate discount rate of 4 percent is of equal value to a 5 percent coupon rate bond that pays interest semiannually for 3 years, and has an appropriate discount rate of 8 percent.

3. An internal rate of return is a discount rate that causes the present value of future cash flows to equal the price someone has to pay today to obtain those cash flows. There is a full discussion on the internal rate of return in appendix 5A.

4. Some investments textbooks, including earlier editions of this book, make the erroneous statement that the YTM formula assumes that the coupon payments are reinvested at the YTM rate. An examination of the mathematical notation for the YTM clearly shows this not the case.

5. Frederick Macaulay, *Some Theoretical Problems Suggested by the Movements of Interest Rates, Bond Yields, and Stock Prices in the United States Since 1856* (New York: National Bureau of Economic Research, 1938).

6. On the formula sheet, "Y" is used in lieu of "i," and "T" in lieu of "n." Thus, it appears there as

$$D = \frac{1+Y}{Y} - \frac{(1+Y) + T(C-Y)}{C\left[(1+Y)^T - 1\right] + Y}$$

7. With bond portfolios, a passive strategy involves buying the bonds and holding them to maturity.

8. The definitive statement on bond swaps is found in Sidney Homer and Martin Leibowitz, *Inside the Yield Book* (Englewood Cliffs, NJ: Prentice Hall, 1972).

9. For a simple discussion of bond ladders, see www.fool.com/retirement/retireeport/2000/retireeport000724.htm

10. We could argue that there is some infinitesimally small default risk to Treasury securities as there is always the possibility that prior to their maturity, the U.S. government would be overthrown and the successor government repudiate the debt, or that the U.S. government might declare bankruptcy as a result of an inability to collect the necessary taxes or borrow additional monies to pay off the current debt.

11. G. Brauer, "Evidence of the Market Value of Me-First Rules," *Financial Management,* spring 1983, pp. 11–18; M. Brody, "Controversial Issue: A Leveraged Buy-Out Touches Off a Bitter Dispute," *Barron's,* September 19, 1983, pp. 15, 19–22.

Appendix 9A

Proof That Immunization Works

Consider the case of a client who has a 7-year time horizon. If the client wants to be immunized, then he or she should hold a bond portfolio whose duration is 7 years. The best candidate is a zero-coupon bond with a 7-year maturity. However, to make the example interesting, let's choose a bond with a maturity of 10 years, a coupon rate of 10 percent with annual payments, and a yield to maturity of 8 percent. The price of this bond is \$1,134.20 (SHIFT, C ALL; set for end-of-period payments; 1000, FV; 1000, x, .10, =, PMT; 10, N; 8, I/YR; PV (display: −1,134.20)). The duration statistic is 6.97 years, computed as

$$D_A = \frac{1 + .08}{.08} - \frac{(1 + .08) + 10(.10 - .08)}{.10\left[(1 + .08)^{10} - 1\right] + .08}$$
$$= 6.97$$

Although this duration statistic is not exactly 7.0, it is close enough for our purposes, and it makes for a more realistic example.

The first point to make is that if interest rates do not change, regardless of the holding period, the client will receive a rate of return of 8 percent. That is, if the yield to maturity stays at 8 percent and if all of the reinvested coupons earn 8 percent, the client's rate of return will be 8 percent, regardless of whether he or she sells the bond in 7 years or holds it for all 10 years.

What Happens When the Interest Rate Goes Up

Let's say that the day after the client buys the bond, interest rates rise to 10 percent. The immediate impact of this event is that the price of the bond will fall to \$1,000 (remember, whenever the coupon rate equals the yield to maturity, the price will equal par, regardless of any other conditions that apply). The bad news is the increase in interest rates. The good news is that the client can now reinvest his or her coupon payments at a higher interest rate. To see the impact of the higher interest rate, let's look at the value of the client's holding after 7 years. Remember, the client has a 7-year holding period, and thus intends to liquidate his or her investment at that time. Let's consider first the value of the coupon payments. The client will have received seven annual payments of \$100 each, beginning one year from today and ending 7 years from today, and will have reinvested these at a rate of 10 percent. This is a future-value-of-annuity problem. To solve it on a HP-10BII calculator, use the following keystrokes:

> SHIFT, C ALL
> set for end-of-period payments
> 1000, x, .10, =, PMT
> 7, N
> 10, I/YR
> FV (display: –948.72)

This next step is the tricky part. At the end of 7 years, the client will sell the bond. Therefore, we have to figure out what the price of the bond will be at that time. Seven years from today, this bond will have 3 years to maturity and a 10 percent yield to maturity. The price will be $1,000, the same as it is today (for the same reason). The total value of the investment from the liquidation of the reinvested coupons and the bond is $1,948.72. The initial investment by the client is $1,134.20 (that is, the price of the bond today). The one question remaining is, what is the rate of return of an investment worth $1,134.20 today and $1,948.72 in seven years? The keystrokes to solve this problem are

> SHIFT, C ALL
> 1134.20, +/–, PV
> 1948.72, FV
> 7, N
> I/YR (display: 8.0389)

The answer is 8.04 percent. The yield to maturity at the time of the bond purchase was 8 percent. So the client has actually exceeded the expected yield of 8 percent by 4 basis points. More important, however, is to understand why. The answer is that the bond chosen for immunization had a duration of 6.97 years, not 7.0 years exactly. Thus, the immunization was only near perfect, not perfect.

What Happens When the Interest Rate Goes Down

Let's now consider the other possibility, namely that market interest rates drop to 6 percent the day after the client buys the bond. Once again, the immediate impact of the bond purchase is that the price will increase to $1,294.40 (SHIFT, C ALL; set for end-of-period payments; 1000, FV; 1000, x, .10, =, PMT; 10, N; 6, I/YR; PV (display: –1,294.40)). This, of course, will make the client quite happy, but unfortunately the client now faces the prospect of reinvesting the coupon payments at a lower than expected rate (6 percent versus 8 percent). Once again, let us compute the future value of this annuity of $100 per year for 7 years. The keystrokes are

> SHIFT, C ALL
> set for end-of-period payments
> 1000, x, .10, =, PMT
> 7, N
> 6, I/YR
> FV (display: −839.38)

Note that the future value of these reinvested coupons is about $109 less than their future value when the reinvestment rate was 10 percent.

Again, the tricky part is to determine the price at which the client can sell the bond in 7 years. As before, at that time, the term to maturity will be 3 years. But in this case, the YTM will be 6 percent. The price will be $1,106.92 (SHIFT, C ALL; set for end-of-period payments; 1000, FV; 1000, x, .10, =, PMT; 3, N; 6, I/YR; PV (display: −1,106.92)). The combined value of the reinvested coupon payments and the proceeds from selling the bond is $1,946.30 ($1,106.92 + $839.38). Finally, we again have to solve for the HPR for an investor who starts with an investment of $1,134.20 and ends with $1,946.30. The answer is 8.02 percent, and the keystrokes are

> SHIFT, C ALL
> 1134.20, +/−, PV
> 1946.30, FV
> 7, N
> I/YR (display: 8.0197)

Once again, the final answer is near perfect, but it is not exactly perfect because the bond selected did not have the perfect immunization number.

Implications for Portfolio Management

Note that the preceding analyses are simplistic in nature. They assume that interest rates change once during the client's time horizon, and that the change occurs immediately after the bond is purchased. They also assume that the coupon payments can be reinvested at the same rate as the new yield to maturity on the bond. In fact, implicit in the analysis is the assumption that the yield curve is flat. This should be apparent because we assumed that after the initial change in interest rates, the yield to maturity on the bond and the reinvested coupons did not change, despite the fact the bond was moving toward maturity. Furthermore, we did not provide any specification as to the maturity of the instruments in which the coupons were invested.

To say the least, all of these assumptions are highly unrealistic. Nonetheless, they provide the basis for an immunization strategy. Clearly, an actual immunization strategy can work better for a large bond portfolio than for a single bond, because the coupon payments would be of sufficient size to reinvest at the same yield and term to maturity as the client's holding period. Furthermore, immunization requires active monitoring. Because interest rates have the potential to change on a regular basis, an immunized portfolio must be adjusted regularly. Research on the optimal frequency of monitoring and adjusting the portfolio suggests that quarterly monitoring is sufficient.

Appendix 9B

Understanding Default Risk

No investor wants to buy bonds in what appears to be a secure company and later see the company get into financial difficulty, because the market price of these bonds will adjust downward to reflect this increased risk. Unless the financial problems facing the firm are corrected quickly, the issuing company may default on its debt obligation. The bonds might eventually pay off part or all of the principal amount plus accrued interest, but that is uncertain when default occurs. It is even possible that the bondholders will be left with nothing. On the other hand, it is possible for an investor to achieve high yields from investing in a portfolio of risky bonds. Some investors even invest in a diversified portfolio of bonds that are near default, because they can purchase these bonds at a substantial discount below their face value. To understand how bonds differ in riskiness, let us start with the bond *indenture*, which is the issuer's contract with the bondholders.

indenture

Indenture Provisions

Bond indentures are contracts and, as such, contain a variety of provisions. Most important are those specifying the coupon rate and the maturity date. The indenture may also contain a number of other provisions. For example, some debt obligations are backed by specific collateral. The indenture for such a security will specify the nature of the collateral obligation. The provision will typically state that the issuer agrees to maintain any pledged assets in good repair.

Most corporate bonds, known as *debentures,* do not have specific property serving as collateral but, rather, are backed by the full faith and credit of the issuer. In the event of bankruptcy, holders of debentures are treated the same as any other general creditors of the issuer.

Some other fairly common indenture provisions include subordination, a sinking fund, call or conversion provisions, and restrictions on the company, such as restrictions on the amount of dividends that can be paid. *Subordination* means that the company's obligation to the bondholders is subordinate to some other specified financial obligations called *senior debt.* The company's obligations to the holders of senior debt take precedence over its obligations to the holders of subordinate debentures. This means that if the company becomes insolvent and unable to pay all of its debts, the holders of the subordinated bonds will not be paid even a penny until after the holders of the senior debt are paid in full.

subordination
senior debt

To protect the bondholders from the risk of default, it is not uncommon for an indenture to contain a provision that restricts the amount of additional debt the issuing firm can incur. For example, an indenture might restrict the total amount of long-term debt to a specified percentage of the company's total assets.

call provision
call price
call premium

A *call provision* gives the issuer the option of redeeming the bonds prior to maturity, usually at a specified amount above the par value, called a *call price*. The difference between the call price and par is the *call premium*. When a bond has a call provision, the indenture generally specifies when the company may call the bond and what the call premium will be at any given point in time. There is no common rule as to how a company will set the call premium.[1]

> *Example:*   A hypothetical bond has an initial maturity of 30 years. The indenture specifies that the issuer may call the bond 20 or more years after the date of issue and that the call premium is 1 percent of the face value for each remaining year until the bond matures. If the company issued a $1,000 bond in 1999, the soonest the bond can be called is 2019, in which case the company will have to pay bondholders $1,100 per bond. If the company redeems the bonds in 2024, the call price will be $1,050 per bond.

Usually, a company will call bonds prior to maturity only if market interest rates decline sufficiently that it will be cost effective for the company to call the bonds, even with a call premium, and refinance at a lower interest rate. Although less likely, there are also situations in which a company will become less risky over time, so that even if market conditions do not change, the company will be able to issue bonds with a lower coupon rate than before. There have even been cases in which companies have called mortgage bonds because the corporations want to sell the assets that are pledged as collateral. Some bond indentures contain a provision stipulating that when bonds are called because of the sale of the mortgaged property rather than to refinance, the bonds are callable at par rather than at the call price. Convertible bonds are an exception to this because the call feature on a convertible bond exists so that the company can force conversion.

> *Example:*   Imagine a start-up company with very little operating history. Because the company's financial performance is uncertain, the market may require a substantial risk premium on the company's debt obligations. But 20 years later, if the company establishes an admirable track record of profitable operations and financial stability, its debt might be regarded as quite safe.

Therefore, it may be able to borrow money at a much lower interest rate. It might then make sense for this company to call its outstanding bonds and issue new bonds at a lower interest rate.

An investor who is considering purchasing a bond should be careful of call provisions, especially if the bond is paying a high coupon rate and trading at a price greater than the call price. An early call will cost the bondholder the difference between the bond's market price and the call price. Therefore, in such situations, the investor should make sure he or she will be comfortable receiving the yield to call if the worst case happens (from the investor's perspective) and the company calls the bond at its first opportunity.

Some restrictions in the indenture are intended to ensure that the company remain solvent and able to make interest and principal payments when due. For example, an indenture may specify that a company limit its dividend payments to a specified percentage of its net income. The indenture may also specify that the company maintain at least a certain current ratio (current assets divided by current liabilities) or that its total debt be limited to a specified percentage of its total assets.

trustee

The indenture also specifies a *trustee,* usually the trust department of a large bank, who is appointed to represent the bondholders and ensure that the company abides by the provisions of the indenture.

sinking fund

Some indentures require a sinking fund. A *sinking fund* is an escrow fund into which the company periodically deposits a portion of its debt obligation to the bondholders. The purpose of this fund is to make certain that when the bonds mature, the company will have accumulated enough money to repay the bonds' principal at maturity. Another approach is to buy back some of the bonds on the open market or call some randomly selected bonds (assuming the indenture contains a call provision), gradually reducing the debt over the life of the bond issue. Municipal issuers use serial maturities instead of a sinking fund to retire debt over the life of the obligation.

Defaults and Near Defaults

technical default

A firm is in *technical default* whenever any of the indenture provisions of its bonds are violated. Many technical defaults, however, involve relatively minor matters. For example, if the current ratio falls below the stipulated minimum, the firm is technically in default of the relevant indenture provision. Rarely, if ever, does a default in such a matter in itself lead to a bankruptcy filing. The trustee may grant a waiver for the violation, or the matter may be quickly cured.

Even a failure to make an interest payment on time does not necessarily lead to bankruptcy. The firm may rectify the situation within a grace period;

the indenture usually provides for such grace periods. In addition, defaults and near defaults generally result in a mutually acceptable resolution that stops short of bankruptcy and liquidation.

Typical Indenture Provisions

- Principal and maturity: Specifies amount and timing of principal payment
- Coupon: Specifies amount and timing of each coupon (interest) payment
- Collateral (first mortgage bond, equipment trust certificate, or other collateralized bond): Identifies pledged collateral and specifies obligation of the issuer to maintain collateral's value
- Full faith and credit (debenture): Backs bond with the pledge of the issuer
- Subordination: Gives interest payment and liquidation priority to specified senior debt
- Call provision: Specifies length of no-call protection and call premiums payable over life of the bond
- Dividend restrictions: Restrict dividend payments, based on earnings and/or amount of equity capital
- Current ratio minimum: Requires that the ratio of current assets to current liabilities not fall below a specified minimum
- Me-first rule: Restricts the amount of additional (nonsubordinated) debt that may be issued (usually as a percentage of total assets)
- Trustee: Specifies the institution responsible for enforcing the indenture provisions
- Sinking fund: Provides for periodic redemption and retirement over the life of the bond issue, or for an escrow account to ensure repayment of the principal amount when due
- Grace period: Specifies the maximum period that the firm has to cure a default without incurring the risk of a bankruptcy filing

---

When a few large creditors (such as banks who have extended substantial loans) can be identified, the troubled borrower may seek concessions that will give it a reasonable chance of avoiding a bankruptcy filing. Big lenders have an important stake in their debtors' survival. An interesting oversimplification of the borrower-lender relationship is seen in the following two sentences:

- A borrower who owes $1,000 and cannot pay is in trouble.
- A borrower who owes $1 million and cannot pay puts the lender in trouble.

Accordingly, lenders with large exposures are likely to be asked to accept a payment stretch-out, an interest rate reduction, a swap of debt for equity or tangible assets, a reduction in loan principal, or a change or waiver of certain default provisions. Lenders often agree to such restructurings in the hope of eventually recovering more than they would have in a formal bankruptcy.

Although the stock price of firms that are struggling will generally already be quite low, when a firm formally files for bankruptcy, there is usually an additional substantial drop in stock value.

Example:	Enron Corporation, an interstate marketer of natural gas, electricity, and related products, was trading as high as $84.87 in December 2000. The stock's price began a gradual decline in 2001 as bad news about the company circulated. In August 2001, Enron's CEO resigned, and the stock price declined from $42.80 to $36.80 (a 14 percent drop) during the subsequent 11-day period.
	The stock price decline continued in October and November as news about the company's financial difficulties hit the market. On October 31, there was a news release to the effect that the SEC had begun an investigation into the company's financial dealings with affiliated partnerships. The decline in stock price accelerated in November.
	On November 28, Enron's stock opened at $3.69, which was the low for the year until that point. On November 28, there was news to the effect that Standard and Poor's had lowered Enron's bond rating from BBB– (the lowest rating that is still considered investment grade) to B– (a speculative grade bond rating).
	Enron Corporation formally filed for Chapter XI on November 29. Its stock price reached a low of $.25 on November 30. This was a drop of over 93 percent in just 2 days.

Bankruptcy Filings

Even though bankruptcy should be avoided if at all possible, the reorganization of a financially troubled firm is not always doable without filing for bankruptcy. Bankruptcy proceedings may begin with a petition from a creditor, a creditor group, an indenture trustee, or the defaulting firm itself.

Chapter XI

If the firm chooses to file for reorganization under *Chapter XI,* it intends to emerge from bankruptcy as a continuing entity. Chapter XI permits the firm to retain its assets and to restructure its debts under a plan of reorganization. A Chapter XI proceeding can give the firm respite from creditors' claims, because the firm has 120 days after filing the petition to formulate a plan of reorganization.

Reorganizations under Chapter XI, however, are not always successful in salvaging financially troubled firms; they are also very expensive. An unsuccessful Chapter XI reorganization effort usually leads to Chapter VII liquidation proceedings.

Chapter VII

absolute-priority-of-claims principle

If a defaulting firm is thought to be worth more dead than alive, bankruptcy proceedings may begin as a *Chapter VII* liquidation. Under Chapter VII, the bankruptcy trustee is responsible for selling the firm's assets and distributing the proceeds according to the *absolute-priority-of-claims principle.* Under this principle, the valid claims of each priority class are fully satisfied before the next class receives anything. The marginal priority group receives proportional compensation. The classes below the marginal priority class receive nothing because the funds available for distribution will have already been exhausted.

Filing for Bankruptcy

- Chapter XI reorganization
  - The proceeding is designed to preserve potentially profitable elements of the business in a recapitalized form.
  - It permits the firm to keep its assets and restructure its debts, provided a plan of reorganization is drafted within 120 days after filing the petition.
  - During that 120-day period, the company is protected from the claims of creditors.
- Chapter VII liquidation
  - A bankruptcy trustee, appointed by the court, is given the responsibility for selling the firm's assets and distributing the proceeds under the absolute-priority-of-claims principle. Following this principle, the valid claims of each priority class must be satisfied in full before the next priority class receives any proceeds.
  - To regain possession of the company from the trustee, the debtor firm must file an appropriate bond.

A few companies do successfully emerge from Chapter XI bankruptcy proceedings after a careful review of their financial and competitive situation. The process is designed to preserve the potentially profitable elements of their businesses in a recapitalized form. Unproductive assets are liquidated. The bankruptcy trustee and courts seek to retain as much value as possible for distribution to the creditors. They also try to minimize the risk that the firm will have to return for court protection or seek additional lender concessions.

Many troubled firms would be financially viable if their debt load were sufficiently reduced. Thus, an objective of many Chapter XI bankruptcy proceedings is to reduce the company's debt load, and since bankrupt firms generally have little or no excess cash to distribute to creditors, most creditors are prevailed upon to accept lower-priority securities of the reorganized firm as payment. Senior creditors may receive subordinated debentures or preferred stock, whereas junior creditors could be given common stock and warrants.

Several factors, however, limit the applicability of the absolute-priority-of-claims principle. The going-concern value of a firm that is experiencing a bankruptcy process is subjective. The securities to be issued by the reorganized firm will not have an established market price until it emerges from bankruptcy. Therefore, the relevant values are rather uncertain at the time (in the course of the bankruptcy proceeding) the securities distribution is set. Not surprisingly, the ability of these securities to satisfy claims is often subject to dispute.

Generally, the lower-priority claimants argue for a higher overall valuation for the company and its securities. In this way, they seek to increase the estimated value of the securities that are available for distribution to their priority class. The greater the firm's overall estimated value, the greater the proportion of that estimated value available to satisfy the lower-priority claimants.

Example: Suppose a company's high-priority claimants have claims of $95 million and the company's value is estimated at $100 million. The high-priority claimants will be awarded securities representing 95 percent of the firm's value. Only 5 percent will be available to the lower-priority claimants. Now suppose that the lower-priority claimants are able to get the company's estimated value raised to $110 million. At that valuation, the higher-priority claimants will receive about 86 percent (95/110) of the firm's value. The lower-priority claimants will, in contrast, see their share rise to about 14 percent (15/110).

Unless the low-priority claimants are given something, however, they may use various legal maneuvers to delay the proceedings. As a result, most informal workouts and reorganizations ultimately allocate lesser-priority claimants somewhat more than what the absolute-priority-of-claims principle requires. In practice, unsecured and subordinated creditors can usually make enough noise to obtain some share of the assets even when senior creditors' claims exceed the firm's remaining asset value. When a company emerges from Chapter XI bankruptcy, the reduced debt burden generally permits it to remain solvent.

NOTE

1. Many textbooks erroneously state that the call premium is initially equal to one year's worth of interest. A quick review of the call premiums on several bonds will show this is not the case.

10

Investment Companies

Learning Objectives

An understanding of the material in this chapter should enable the student to

---

10-1. Explain the various characteristics of mutual funds, including their sales fees, benefits, and disadvantages.

10-2. Describe several types of pooled portfolio arrangements that are similar to but differ from mutual funds.

10-3. Identify the various factors associated with mutual fund selection.

Chapter Outline

An alternative to the direct purchase of stocks, bonds, and money market instruments is the purchase of shares in an investment company. An investment company is a pooled portfolio in which multiple investors pool their cash and this cash is then used to buy securities. The investors own shares that are claims on the portfolio. Investment companies are structured in many different ways. The major distinction among investment companies is whether they are open-ended or closed-ended. Open-ended investment companies are known popularly as mutual funds.

There are many good reasons why nearly every investor will have at least some of his or her money in investment companies. In defined-contribution-type pension plans, employees are given a menu of mutual funds from which to choose. Small accounts, such as those managed on behalf of children, have insufficient resources to hold a diversified portfolio through direct investing. In addition, some investors like to have a single-decision investment that provides convenience, diversification, record keeping, safekeeping of securities, and professional portfolio management.

The most common holding by investors of investment companies is mutual funds. Today, about 95 million Americans have about $7 trillion invested in mutual funds.[1] For this reason, the majority of this chapter focuses on mutual funds. Much of what it says about mutual funds also applies to the other types of investment companies.

MUTUAL FUNDS

open-end investment company

The distinction between an *open-end investment company* (that is, a mutual fund) and a closed-end one is that the only way an investor can buy shares in a mutual fund is from the fund itself through the creation of new shares. The only way an investor can sell shares of a mutual fund is back to the fund through the redemption (that is, liquidation) of shares. Shares in a

closed-end investment
company

closed-end investment company can be bought only from another investor.[2] Shares in a closed-end investment company can be sold only to another investor.

Because all trades in a mutual fund's shares can be only with the fund itself, there must be a mechanism that determines the price. The prices for all mutual fund shares are based on the net asset value (NAV) of those shares, which is calculated as follows:

$$NAV = \frac{\text{Total assets } - \text{ Total liabilities}}{\text{Number of shares outstanding}}$$

Example: The Holy Grail Mutual Fund reported total assets at the end of the trading day of $322,738,516, and total liabilities of $2,517,683. Prior to the sale of new shares and the redemption of old shares, there are 4,698,245.633 shares outstanding. The NAV at this point in time is computed as

$$\frac{\left(\$322,738,516 - \$2,517,683\right)}{4,698,245.633} = \$68.16$$

Types of Mutual Funds

The major task of an investment advisor is to make sure the client holds a portfolio whose objectives and risk exposure match the client's objectives and risk tolerance. The great thing about mutual funds (and investment companies in general) is that there probably exists at least one (if not several) fund that can match almost any objective or risk tolerance. After establishing portfolio objectives, investors and their advisors can begin by identifying the general type of mutual fund that will help them accomplish their goals. Many different organizations classify funds based on objectives, but there is no universal categorization paradigm. Thus, exactly how a fund is characterized sometimes depends on who is doing the classifying. To complicate matters, subcategories exist for most of the portfolio categories. To provide some framework for discussion, we will use the classification scheme used by the Investment Company Institute, which is provided in figure 10-1.

Although figure 10-1 is fairly self-explanatory, a few comments are appropriate. *Money market mutual funds* (MMMFs) own portfolios of short-term interest-bearing securities and are used by investors as an alternative to cash. They operate only as open-end funds and include subcategories, such as funds that focus mainly on nontaxable securities. Bond funds own portfolios of bonds. Subcategories include funds that invest only in U.S. government issues,

money market
mutual funds

FIGURE 10-1
Mutual Fund Investment Objectives

The Investment Company Institute classifies U.S. mutual funds in 33 investment objective categories.

EQUITY FUNDS

Capital appreciation funds seek capital appreciation; dividends are not a primary consideration.
- *Aggressive growth funds* invest primarily in common stocks of small, growth companies.
- *Growth funds* invest primarily in common stocks of well-established companies.
- *Sector funds* invest primarily in companies in related fields.

Total return funds seek a combination of current income and capital appreciation.
- *Growth-and-income funds* invest primarily in common stocks of established companies with the potential for growth and a consistent record of dividend payments.
- *Income-equity funds* invest primarily in equity securities of companies with a consistent record of dividend payments. They seek income more than capital appreciation.

World equity funds invest primarily in stocks of foreign companies.
- *Emerging market funds* invest primarily in companies based in developing regions of the world.
- *Global equity funds* invest primarily in equity securities traded worldwide, including those of U.S. companies.
- *International equity funds* invest primarily in equity securities of companies located outside the United States.
- *Regional equity funds* invest in companies based on a specific part of the world.

HYBRID FUNDS

Hybrid funds may invest in a mix of equities, fixed-income securities, and derivative instruments.
- *Asset allocation funds* invest in various asset classes, including, but not limited to, equities, fixed-income securities, and money market instruments. They seek high total return by maintaining precise weightings in asset classes. Global asset allocation funds invest in a mix of equity and debt securities issued worldwide.
- *Balanced funds* invest in a mix of equity securities and bonds with the three-part objective of conserving principal, providing income, and achieving long-term growth of both principal and income. These funds maintain target percentages in asset classes.
- *Flexible portfolio funds* invest in common stocks, bonds, other debt securities, and money market securities to provide high total return. These funds may invest up to 100 percent in any one type of security and may easily change weightings depending on market conditions.
- *Income-mixed funds* invest in a variety of income-producing securities, including equities and fixed-income instruments. These funds seek a high level of current income without regard to capital appreciation.

TAXABLE BOND FUNDS

Corporate bond funds seek current income by investing in high-quality debt securities issued by U.S. corporations.
- *Corporate bond funds—general* invest two-thirds or more of their portfolios in U.S. corporate bonds with no explicit restrictions on average maturity.
- *Corporate bond funds—intermediate-term* invest two-thirds or more of their portfolios in U.S. corporate bonds with an average maturity of 5 to 10 years. These funds seek a high level of income with less price volatility than longer-term bond funds.
- *Corporate bond funds—short-term* invest two-thirds or more of their portfolios in U.S. corporate bonds with an average maturity of one to 5 years. These funds seek a high level of income with less price volatility than intermediate-term bond funds.

FIGURE 10-1—Continued
Mutual Fund Investment Objectives

High-yield funds invest two-thirds or more of their portfolios in lower-rated U.S. corporate bonds (Baa or lower by Moody's and BBB or lower by Standard and Poor's rating services).

World bond funds invest in debt securities offered by foreign companies and governments. They seek the highest level of current income available worldwide.

- *Global bond funds—general* invest in worldwide debt securities with no stated average maturity or an average maturity of one to 5 years. These funds may invest up to 25 percent of assets in companies located in the United States.
- *Global bond funds—short-term* invest in debt securities worldwide with an average maturity of one to 5 years. These funds may invest up to 25 percent of assets in companies located in the United States.
- *Other world bond funds,* such as international bond and emerging market debt funds, invest in foreign government and corporate debt instruments. Two-thirds of an international bond fund's portfolio must be invested outside the United States. Emerging market debt funds invest primarily in debt from underdeveloped regions of the world.

Government bond funds invest in U.S. government bonds of varying maturities. They seek high current income.

- *Government bond funds—general* invest two-thirds or more of their portfolios in U.S. government securities of no stated average maturity. Securities utilized by investment managers may change with market conditions.
- *Government bond funds—intermediate-term* invest two-thirds or more of their portfolios in U.S. government securities with an average maturity of 5 to 10 years. Securities utilized by investment managers may change with market conditions.
- *Government bond funds—short-term* invest two-thirds or more of their portfolios in U.S. government securities with an average maturity of one to 5 years. Securities utilized by investment managers may change with market conditions.
- *Mortgage-backed funds* invest two-thirds or more of their portfolios in pooled mortgage-backed securities.

Strategic income funds invest in a combination of U.S. fixed-income securities to provide a high level of current income.

TAX-FREE BOND FUNDS
State municipal bond funds invest primarily in municipal bonds issued by a particular state. These funds seek high after-tax income for residents of individual states.

- *State municipal bond funds—general* invest primarily in single-state municipal bonds with an average maturity of greater than 5 years or no specific stated maturity. The income from these funds is largely exempt from federal as well as state income tax for residents of the state.
- *State municipal bond funds—short-term* invest primarily in single-state municipal bonds with an average maturity of one to 5 years. The income of these funds is largely exempt from federal as well as state income tax for residents of the state.

National municipal bond funds invest primarily in bonds of various municipal issuers in the United States. These funds seek high current income free from federal tax.

- *National municipal bond funds—general* invest primarily in municipal bonds with an average maturity of more than 5 years or no specific stated maturity.
- *National municipal bond funds—short-term* invest primarily in municipal bonds with an average maturity of one to 5 years.

FIGURE 10-1—Continued
Mutual Fund Investment Objectives

MONEY MARKET FUNDS
Taxable money market funds invest in short-term, high-grade money market securities and must have average maturities of 90 days or less. These funds seek the highest level of income consistent with preservation of capital (that is, maintaining a stable share price).

- *Taxable money market funds—government* invest primarily in U.S. Treasury obligations and other financial instruments issued or guaranteed by the U.S. government, its agencies, or its instrumentalities.
- *Taxable money market funds—nongovernmental* invest primarily in a variety of money market instruments, including certificates of deposit from large banks, commercial paper, and bankers' acceptances.

Tax-exempt money market funds invest in short-term municipal securities and must have average maturities of 90 days or less. These funds seek the highest level of income—free from federal and, in some cases, state and local taxes—consistent with preservation of capital.

- *National tax-exempt money market funds* invest in short-term securities of various U.S. municipal issuers.
- *State tax-exempt money market funds* invest primarily in short-term securities of municipal issuers in a single state to achieve the highest level of tax-free income for residents of that state.

Source: *2003 Mutual Fund Fact Book,* © 2003 by the Investment Company Institute (www.ici.org). Reprinted with permission.

---

municipal issues, corporate issues, or low-quality (junk) bonds. Further subcategories can be short-term (up to 5 years), intermediate-term (5 to 10 years), or long-term (10+ years) bond funds.

common stock funds

Common stock funds hold portfolios that consist primarily of common stocks and perhaps a small number of preferred stocks. Subcategories include funds that invest primarily in conservative (defensive) stocks, growth stocks, aggressive growth stocks, or foreign stocks. *Mixed portfolio funds* have portfolios of bonds, stocks, and other investment instruments. Subcategories include balanced funds and growth and income funds. The characteristics of funds in some of the more common mutual fund categories are shown in table 10-1.

mixed portfolio funds

There are some other types of funds that are not captured in figure 10-1. These include the following:

- *Index funds* own portfolios of either common stock or bonds that replicate a major market index, such as the S&P 500 or the Lehman Brothers Aggregate Bond Index. Index funds are low-cost funds that are especially useful in passive investment strategies in which the investor is satisfied to match the performance of the index.

TABLE 10-1
Characteristics of Funds in Selected Categories

Type of Fund	Primary Goal	Potential Price Appreciation	Potential Current Income	Safety
Aggressive growth funds	Maximum price appreciation	Very high	Very low	Lowest
Growth funds	High price appreciation	High to very high	Very low	Low
Growth and income funds	Moderate price appreciation and current income	Moderate	Moderate	Low to moderate
Balanced funds	Current income and some growth	Low	Moderate	Moderate
Fixed-income and equity income funds	High current income	Very low	High	Moderate
Money market funds	Current income and maximum safety	None	Low to high	Highest
Tax-free money market funds	Tax-free income and safety	None	Low to moderate	High
Municipal bond funds	Tax-free income	Not applicable	Low to moderate	Moderate

- *Specialty funds* have a unique focus to them. Both index and sector funds are sometimes categorized as specialty funds, but true specialty funds may be characterized as having a gimmick. For example, there is a "race car" fund that invests in companies tied to the sport of auto racing. This is not really a sector fund because auto racing is not an industry; it is more like a subindustry. Hence, it is a specialty fund.
- *Sector funds* concentrate on one investment sector or industry. For example, a fund may limit its portfolio to health care companies, technology companies, or energy companies. Obviously, the emphasis on one sector means that these funds are not well diversified and are appropriate only for relatively small portions of an individual's portfolio.

- *International funds* specialize in investments outside of the United States and help the investor to further diversify his or her portfolio. International funds may specialize in specific countries or regions, such as the Pacific Rim.
- *Global funds* invest in the United States and foreign markets. The general philosophy is that we live in a global economy and capital should flow toward those regions that offer optimal risk-return combinations.
- *Asset allocation funds* allow managers considerable flexibility in allocating the portfolio among the three major asset categories (stocks, bonds, and money market instruments) as market conditions change.
- *Life-cycle funds* are designed to appeal to investors in specific phases of the life cycle by providing different asset allocations. For example, one fund may be oriented toward growth investments and intended for young investors, while another may be oriented toward current income and intended for older investors. Some life-cycle funds come with a retirement date, and the portfolio will steadily move toward a more conservative stance as that date approaches and is passed.
- *Socially responsible funds* invest only in corporations or other entities that maintain social and/or ethical principles that are consistent with those the fund advocates. For example, a fund may elect not to invest in any company that produces tobacco products or other products associated with potential health hazards, or in any company that is considered environmentally unfriendly. Or a fund may avoid companies that invest in countries the fund managers deem oppressive. A problem with socially responsible funds is that it is difficult to find one that has standards that exactly match the standards of the investor. Although these funds eliminate many investment opportunities, compromising their potential to obtain an optimal risk-return profile, there has been no evidence developed to date to indicate that they do any worse than other funds.

Price Appreciation, Dividends, and Capital Gain Distributions

When investors buy a mutual fund, they are effectively buying a pro rata share of the portfolio. As with any holding, investors are looking for price appreciation and/or dividend and interest income. If the values of the securities in the portfolio appreciate, the NAV of the fund will rise. An increase in the NAV is analogous to the price of any other security rising. Over time, the securities in the fund will accrue dividend and interest income. On a regular basis (usually quarterly but sometimes monthly, semiannually, or annually), the mutual fund distributes this dividend and interest income to investors on a

regular dividend

per share basis. This is known as a *regular dividend*.

Over time, the portfolio manager will trade the securities in the portfolio. Each trade will generate a capital gain or capital loss (these will be discussed in detail in chapter 13). In most years, the capital gains exceed the capital losses, and the net capital gain must be distributed to shareholders. This is known as a capital gain distribution.[3] When dividends and distributions are made, the NAV of the shares will automatically adjust for the distribution of cash from the portfolio.

Mutual funds as operating entities do not pay income taxes, provided they operate as a conduit. For tax purposes, a conduit is simply an organization that passes taxable income through to another taxable entity. To be recognized as a conduit, Subchapter M of the Internal Revenue Code specifies that mutual funds must distribute to shareholders at least 90 percent of the dividends and interest received by the fund.

Although dividends and capital gain distributions are taxed to the investor, many mutual fund shareholders direct that these payments be reinvested. Note that the reinvestment process does not alter the treatment as taxable income. The reinvestment process is always optional, as investors can elect to implement it or discontinue it at any time. Some investors elect to take the dividends as cash and reinvest only the capital gain distribution. The appeal of this strategy is that taking the capital gain distribution as cash is analogous to dipping into principal. It is certainly possible to reinvest the dividends and take the capital gain distribution as cash, although this is less appealing intuitively. In addition, the dividends do not fluctuate as much as the capital gain distributions from year to year, and when investors opt for income, they usually prefer stable sources. Note that when there has been a serious bear market, many funds simply have no capital gain distribution because their capital losses have exceeded their capital gains.

Fund Families

One of the most dramatic changes in the mutual fund industry over the last quarter of the twentieth century has been the growth in the family structure. A mutual fund family is created any time one management company manages more than one fund. For example, Fidelity currently offers investors over 150 funds to from which to choose.[4] There is a distinct advantage—the opportunity for switching—to investing within a family framework. *Switching* is when an investor moves funds from one fund to another fund within the same family. It represents the only opportunity in the investments world wherein an investor can move substantial sums of money from one large diversified portfolio to another such portfolio with minimal or no transaction fees.

switching

Load Charges

The mutual fund industry can generally be divided into two types of funds: load and no-load. For reasons that will be explained shortly, the distinction is not always clear. The term load is industry jargon for commission. The general idea is that load funds are sold through salespeople who work with the individual investor and generate a commission for their efforts, whereas no-load funds are marketed directly to individuals and thus there is no salesperson to compensate. Traditionally, when investors buy shares in a load fund they pay the NAV price plus the load charge, and when they redeem their shares they receive back only the NAV price per share. Investors in no-load funds both buy and redeem at the NAV price.

The legal maximum load charge is 8.5 percent. Note that this is 8.5 percent of the total investment, not the investment in the fund's shares. Thus, if an investor writes a check for $10,000 to buy shares in a fund charging an 8.5 percent load, the salesperson will receive a commission of $850 ($10,000 x .085), and the remaining $9,150 will go toward the purchase of shares at the NAV. Because we traditionally think of the commission as a percentage of the money actually placed in the investment, this 8.5 percent maximum rate actually works out to a 9.29 percent ($850/$9,150) commission rate. Nowadays, the maximum charged by most equity funds is 5.75 percent, and the maximum charged by most bond funds is 4.75 percent.

Consider the following two examples.

Example 1:   The Pegasus Mutual Fund is listed in the newspaper as having a bid price of $20 and an ask price of $21. The bid price is the price the investor will receive for the redemption of any shares, and the ask price is the price the investor must pay for new shares. The difference in the two prices is a load charge of $1. The load charge as a percentage of the NAV is $1/$20 = 5.00 percent.

Example 2:   The Victory Mutual Fund has an NAV of $50. If it has a 3 percent load, the NAV must be divided by (1 – load percentage) to calculate the gross price.

$$P_L = NAV/(1 - L)$$

where P_L =   gross price including load
L =   load percentage

Thus, the gross price is $50/(1 – .03) = $51.55. The load is $51.55 – $50 = $1.55.

Breakpoints

Many load funds offer investors what are known as breakpoints. These are analogous to volume discounts in which a lower load is charged for larger investments. An example of a breakpoint schedule is shown in table 10-2.

TABLE 10-2
Sample Breakpoint Schedule

Investment Amount	Sales Load
Less than $25,000	5.0%
$25,000 but less than $50,000	4.25%
$50,000 but less than $100,000	3.75%
$100,000 but less than $250,000	3.25%
$250,000 but less than $500,000	2.75%
$500,000 but less than $1 million	2.0%
$1 million or more	0.0%

Source: www.nasd.com. © 2004 National Association of Securities Dealers (NASD). Reprinted with permission of NASD.

Using table 10-2, suppose an investor has $24,000 to invest. The load charge is $1,200 ($24,000 x .05). However, if the investor opts to invest $25,000, the load charge declines to $1,062.50. In other words, by putting up an additional $1,000, the investor is *actually saving* $137.50 in commission.

Ethical Issue in Financial Planning

The January 2004 issue of the *Journal of Financial Planning* reports that in 2001, of all the mutual fund transactions that should have received a breakpoint charge, 20 percent did not. Either some financial planners are deliberately cheating their clients, or planners clearly need to double check these critical details.

Right of Accumulation

Many load funds provide for a right of accumulation. This means that when an investor is making an additional purchase of a load fund, the load charge is based on the accumulated total purchases.

Example: Johnnie Johnson has previously invested $20,000 in the XYZ Growth Fund. The load charge schedule is that shown in table 10-2. Johnnie now wants to invest an additional $10,000. Although her commission rate was 5 percent on the first purchase, with the right of accumulation it will be 4.25 percent on this incremental purchase, because the sum of the prior and current purchases exceeds the $25,000 breakpoint.

Some funds add the feature that the right of accumulation will be based not only on purchases in one specific account, but also on other accounts the same person owns. For example, if the investor has both a retirement account and an ordinary account, the breakpoint is based on combined purchases. Other funds even allow an investor to include in the right of accumulation other accounts his or her spouse or children own. Finally, some fund families allow the right of accumulation to apply to all purchases of load funds within that family of funds.

Letter of Intent

Certainly, in the above example, Johnnie would have liked to have had the benefit of the breakpoint on her first purchase. Some funds will allow the use of a letter of intent. A letter of intent states a schedule of future (planned) share purchases. This letter then allows the investor to receive the commission rate for the total of planned purchases, beginning with the first purchase. In the above example, if Johnnie had signed a letter of intent for the second purchase at the time of the first purchase, her load fee on the first purchase would have been $850 ($20,000 x .0425) rather than the $1,000 ($20,000 x .05) she actually paid.

Naturally, investors might be tempted to sign letters of intent to get lower load charges, even if they had no actual intent to make subsequent purchases. At the very least, in this case the mutual fund would retroactively charge the higher load fee on the first purchase if the date of the intended investment came and went without an actual investment occurring.

Back-End Loads

contingent deferred sales charge

Although the original load charges were always front-end load charges, many funds now incorporate back-end load charges. The technical name for a back-end load is *contingent deferred sales charge*. Other names include rear load and reverse load. These charges usually decline over time. A typical back-end load is 5 or 6 percent the first year, and then it usually declines by 1 percent per year until in the sixth or seventh year it is eliminated. A contingent load is attached to each deposit in such an account, not just the first deposit. The maximum back-end load that can be charged is 7.2 percent.

Some funds will impose a redemption fee of something like 1 percent if the shares are redeemed within a relatively short period such as 6 months. The purpose of this load is to discourage investors from quickly moving money into and out of that particular fund. The maximum redemption fee that is allowed is 2 percent.

Dividends and capital gain distributions are exempt from the deferred sales charge, and some funds actually allow withdrawals each year of up to 12 percent of the principal without triggering the load charge. When an

---

Ethical Issues in Financial Planning

Consider the following five scenarios:

- A husband and wife have $100,000 and want to buy a mutual fund. If you recommend two separate accounts of $50,000, rather than a joint account, you will receive a substantially greater commission.
- A client has a large account invested in a fund with a right of accumulation that includes family members. The client wants to open three small accounts for her children. If you forget to indicate her account on the applications, you will receive a substantially larger commission.
- A client wants to open a small account today but will be receiving a substantial windfall in 6 months. If you forget to mention the letter of intent, you will receive a substantially larger commission today.
- A client has $99,000 to invest in the fund whose breakpoints are shown in table 10-2. If you neglect to mention the breakpoint of $100,000, you will generate nearly $500 in additional commission.
- A year ago, a client invested $200,000 in a load fund. The fund is fine, but if you switch the client to a similar fund with a different company, you will generate what is essentially a double commission.

All of the above are not only morally and ethically wrong, but they are also illegal.

---

investor does make a withdrawal subject to a back-end fee, the fund normally assumes the withdrawal is on a FIFO (first-in, first-out) basis so that the lowest possible redemption fee would apply.

Many back-end load funds refer to themselves as no-load funds. This may be technically true in that the load charge is avoidable, but to an investor who ends up paying a sales fee, it would have a really bad smell.

Ethical Issue in Financial Planning

Sally Gardner, a 72-year old widow, comes to you as a new client. Her biggest asset is $500,000 she invested just last year in the Great Growth Mutual Fund on the recommendation of her stockbroker. She says it is a no-load fund, but when you look up the fund, you find it is, in fact, a back-end load that had a first-year redemption rate of 6 percent. The current load is 5 percent. After analyzing Sally's finances, you believe she needs to cash out most of this holding and buy an annuity for two reasons. One is that based on her age, level of wealth, and risk tolerance, she needs a substantially lower percentage of her portfolio in equities. The second is that she needs to substantially increase her expected annual income. How do you explain to her that her "no-load" fund has a $25,000 back-end load?

Operating Expenses

All funds, whether they are load or no-load, have operating expenses. These fees are usually deducted from the interest, dividend, and capital gain income before distribution to the shareholders. There are three components to operating expenses: the management (or investment advisory) fee, marketing (12b-1) fees, and other expenses. All of these are computed as a percentage of net assets. The *investment advisory fee* is the fee paid to the mutual fund's managers for portfolio supervision and other managerial activities. Many funds place this on a declining scale, whereby a lower fee is charged on incremental assets. For example, the management fee may be .75 percent on the first $100 million in assets, .70 percent on the next $25 million, and so on. Management fees are generally between 0.50 and 1 percent of average fund assets.

investment advisory fee

Not all funds charge a *12b-1 fee*, which pays the marketing expenses of the fund. The fee cannot exceed 0.75 percent of average net assets per year plus another 0.25 percent service fee (*trail commission* or "trailer") that can be paid to salespeople, presumably for providing ongoing service and information.

12b-1 fee

trail commission

When the mutual fund industry originally sought approval to charge a 12b-1 fee, it argued that the fee would actually benefit investors. The argument was that such marketing would sufficiently increase a fund's total assets so that the management fees (which will be discussed in the next section) could be spread over more assets and would be lower for each investor. The reduction in the management fee was supposed to have been greater than the direct cost of the 12b-1 fee. There is no proof this has happened, and there is some proof that investors are actually worse off as a result of the 12b-1 fees.[5] Most mutual funds with 12b-1 fees in excess of 0.25 percent are classified as load funds. A recent trend in the industry has been for funds to lower or eliminate the load charges and replace them with 12b-1 fees.

Other expenses include various administrative costs such as keeping shareholder records, sending out financial reports, filing documents with the SEC, and generally paying for the service department.

The sum of all of the operating expenses charged to shareholders equals the management expense ratio. For equity funds, these ratios can easily be as high as 1.5 percent. They tend to be lower for bond funds, and they are extremely low for money market funds. Research has consistently shown that funds, on average, underperform market averages by an amount equal to the management expense ratio. In other words, the typical mutual fund is not effective enough to outperform the market in a manner sufficient to cover the fees charged to the fund.

Brokerage Fees

Although these fees are readily available in the funds' financial statements, the funds' transaction costs (brokerage fees incurred when buying and selling securities) are not listed as operating expenses because they are netted

portfolio turnover ratio

out in each transaction. However, they can represent a significant drag on performance for funds with high portfolio turnover rates. Portfolio turnover refers to the relative frequency of trading by the fund. The *portfolio turnover ratio* equals the lesser of annual purchases or annual sales (excluding securities with less than one-year maturities) divided by the average monthly net assets. Equity funds may have turnover ratios as high as 100 percent or more in any one year. Funds with turnover ratios of 300 percent or more for several years in a row are spending a substantial amount of investor monies on brokerage commissions.

Other Expenses

Because each fund has the ability to create some fees that are unique to it, a comprehensive listing of all the different fees an investor might encounter is impossible. Appropriate investment advising requires that the advisor be familiar with the prospectus issued by the fund. The Investment Company Act of 1940 requires that each new investor in a mutual fund be provided with a prospectus that details all of the potential expenses associated with fund ownership. Nonetheless, some of the other fees that an investor might encounter in mutual fund investing include

- *exchange fees.* Although some funds do not charge for switching, others do. In fact, because some investors engage in switching trades multiple times per month, and because such fast movements of cash in and out of a fund make it more difficult to manage the fund, most funds impose some sort of fee for a switch, or they place a limit on the amount of switching that is permitted in an account. The purpose of the fee is to discourage investors from using the funds to engage in timing trades.
- *account maintenance fees.* A common practice of mutual fund families is to charge an annual fee for every account the investor holds. This fee, which may be as little as $10, defrays the cost of account record keeping. As a percentage, this fee is much higher for small accounts than for large accounts, and it may be waived for accounts above a certain size.
- *reinvestment loads.* Some funds charge a load even for automatic reinvestment of dividends.

Classes of Shares

multi-class funds

Once 12b-1 fees started to become common, some funds, to allow investors to choose how they would pay for marketing fees, created classes of shares, and these are known as *multi-class funds*. The categorization now used by many funds is that investors can choose between Class A, Class B, and Class C shares.[6] The common distinctions are as follows:

- *Class A shares* typically have a large (front-end) load fee but have a minimal or no 12b-1 charge. The load fee can range from 4 percent to as much as 8.5 percent, which is the legal maximum that can be charged.
- *Class B shares* typically have a back-end load and 12b-1 fees. The shares usually convert to Class A shares after a certain amount of time such as when the back-end load has been waived. This time period is usually in the range of 4 to 7 years. Class B shares are usually excluded from any right-of-accumulation rules.
- *Class C shares* can have either a front-end or back-end load, but these charges are substantially lower than those associated with Class A or B shares. Class C shares usually have the highest 12b-1 fees of the three classes, and they typically do not convert. Hence, investors are stuck with the 12b-1 fee for as long as they hold these shares.

Some funds also offer Class I shares, which are for institutional investors only. Because institutional investors typically put substantially larger amounts of money into a fund (for example, millions of dollars versus thousands of dollars), the entire fee structure is likely to be different.

Ethical Issue in Financial Planning

In August 2002, the NASD affirmed a hearing panel decision that a broker made unsuitable recommendations to a customer. The broker had sold $2.1 million in Class B shares in two mutual fund families to the customer. The amount invested in one fund family was enough to entitle the customer to obtain Class A shares with no front-end load. The amount invested in the second fund family would have entitled the customer to obtain the largest breakpoint discount on Class A shares. NASD's National Adjudicatory Council held that a broker's suitability obligation includes the requirement to minimize the sales charges paid for mutual fund shares, when consistent with the customer's investment objectives. The broker's recommendation was unsuitable because the customer's purchase of Class B rather than Class A shares resulted in significantly higher commission costs, including the payment of contingent deferred sales charges upon sale of the shares. The broker was fined $40,000, suspended in all capacities for one year, and ordered to pay restitution of $55,567, plus interest, to the customer's estate. See *Department of Enforcement v. Wendell D. Belden.*

Source: www.nasd. © 2004 National Association of Securities Dealers (NASD). Reprinted with permission from NASD.

What conditions favor the selection of each class? Class A is favored by investors who intend to make a large purchase (provided there are breakpoints), already hold other funds in the same family (provided this is covered in the right of accumulation), plan to make regular purchases (provided a letter of intent is allowed), and/or have family members who hold funds in the same family of funds (provided these can be included in the right of accumulation). Class C shares are usually preferred by anyone with a limited time horizon for the investment such as no more than a few years. For investors with longer time horizons, Class A or B is preferable, depending on the terms of the shares.

Distribution Systems

Distribution systems for marketing mutual funds take one of four different forms:

- *direct marketing.* Many mutual funds market shares directly to the public. They attract investors through advertising and word of mouth. Both load and no-load funds are available through direct marketing.
- *captive sales force.* Some mutual funds are marketed by salespeople who are employed by management of a mutual fund family and are allowed to sell mutual funds only in that family. Funds sold through captive sales forces are typically load funds.
- *broker-dealers.* Individuals who are appropriately registered with the National Association of Securities Dealers (NASD) through securities broker-dealers often sell load mutual funds.
- *financial planners.* Financial planners who are appropriately registered with broker-dealers may sell load mutual funds. Increasing numbers of financial planners are charging asset-based fees for selection and management of the investor's mutual fund holdings. They may use either load or no-load mutual funds.

revenue sharing   Note that many mutual funds engage in a practice known as *revenue sharing*, which means that they pay brokers for promoting their funds' shares to investors. A recent study by the Securities and Exchange Commission found that 14 of 15 brokers examined had received such payments; 13 of the 15 appeared to tilt their advice toward these funds. The SEC also noted that the funds would also direct brokerage to reward these brokers. In addition, about one-half of brokerage firms reviewed paid brokers more for selling in-house funds or funds with whom the brokerage firm had a revenue-sharing agreement.[7]

Benefits of Mutual Fund Ownership

Although there are drawbacks to investing in mual funds, there are also significant advantages. Let's consider these benefits.

Professional Management

Many investors lack the time to properly select securities and can better delegate this responsibility to others. Professional portfolio managers typically have extensive education in investments and portfolio management. They have ready access to professional analysts and quantitative techniques to evaluate financial statements, market conditions, management quality, research and development, competition, and other relevant factors. Portfolio managers can speak directly to corporate management because of the quantity of shares that the portfolio managers control, and they can also speak directly to competitors, suppliers, and customers.

Diversification

Small investors are effectively precluded from diversifying their portfolios through purchase of individual securities. One reason is that many investments have relatively large minimum denominations. In addition, the structure of transactions costs makes diversification more expensive for small investors. Mutual fund portfolios typically include 50 to 200 securities. Their size provides the opportunity for diversification among different asset categories (such as stocks versus bonds), among different industries (such as energy versus entertainment), among different companies (such as Ford versus General Motors), among different economies (such as United States versus Japan), among different credit qualities (such as AAA bonds versus BBB bonds), and among different interest rate risks (such as long maturity versus short maturity). Mutual funds offer a wide range of investment opportunities.

Convenience

Almost all mutual funds offer the following services:

- automatic reinvestment programs for dividends and capital gains
- automatic checking account debits
- check writing privileges for money market funds
- telephone and electronic account transfers between funds in the same family

Another convenience of mutual funds is that an investor does not need to worry about buying full shares to match an exact dollar amount. Funds track shares to at least three decimal places. Thus, when an investor makes a purchase of shares, the fund divides the dollar amount of the purchase (less any load charge) by the NAV to obtain the number of shares purchased. For example, suppose an investor makes a purchase for $5,000 and at the close of business that day, the NAV is computed to be $23.18. The investor will be credited with 215.703 shares (that is, $5,000/$23.18).

Record Keeping

Among the account data provided are the following:

- statements to confirm transactions
- periodic statements (monthly, quarterly, or annually)
- documentation for tax calculations
- shareholder newsletters
- shareholder reports (at least semiannually)
- telephone and on-line access to account information

Other Factors

The following factors also encourage mutual fund ownership:

- *liquidity.* Because the account value is based on the NAV, fund balances can be redeemed, and thus converted into cash, on short notice with no concern about affecting the market price. As long as any order to redeem shares is placed by 4 p.m. (Eastern time), the shares will be liquidated that day at the closing NAV.
- *minimal investment requirements.* Some investments are sold in denominations that are too large for small investors. For example, the minimum denomination for a bond may be as high as $10,000. However, most mutual funds are available in much smaller amounts, especially for monthly automatic investment plans.
- *regulation.* The recent scandals in the mutual fund industry notwithstanding, the extensive regulation of the industry by the National Association of Security Dealers and the Securities and Exchange Commission should provide some comfort to investors that they will not be abused. Complaints about abuse can be directed to either organization.

Drawbacks of Mutual Fund Ownership

The major drawbacks to mutual fund ownership are the various fees and expenses discussed earlier, and we will comment more on these later in the chapter. A more subtle drawback is that the investor loses control over the timing of capital gains. When the fund manager declares a capital gain distribution, it triggers a taxable event for the owner of a taxable account. Of course, the investor still has control over the timing of gains generated by the sale of the fund shares themselves.

Another disadvantage—particularly for funds with large portfolios—is that mutual funds sometimes adversely affect the market prices of the stocks that they trade. Sizable purchases tend to trade above the most recent market price, and large sales tend to trade below it. Small investors, in contrast, can generally purchase up to several round lots (or even more for an actively traded stock) with no price effect. Funds sometimes attempt to counteract this problem by assigning portions of their portfolio to several different managerial groups. Subdividing may reduce, but is unlikely to eliminate, the adverse price effects of their large trades. Furthermore, subdividing may increase management and administrative costs.

Many institutional investors, which includes mutual fund managers, must restrict their analysis to a small percentage of traded stocks, thus limiting the universe of available securities. Institutions frequently focus on as few as 100 to 500 companies, compared with about 5,000 listed securities and at least 20,000 traded over the counter. Institutional holdings are clearly concentrated among the larger firms. The institution is reluctant either to acquire a small-dollar-value position (because it will have little effect on the institution's overall portfolio) or to take too large a percentage position in a small company (because the institution will then risk owning too large a percentage position to be classified as a passive investor). This reluctance tends to remove a large number of stocks from the institution's choice set. Consequently, institutional attention on the large-capitalization segment of the market may reduce the likelihood of finding undervalued stocks. Many smaller-capitalization stocks may remain misvalued because some institutional investors are forced to ignore them. Individual investors are unconstrained when it comes to investing in such stocks.

Mutual Fund Price Quotations

Daily price quotes for mutual funds can be found in most major newspapers. The information varies from paper to paper. Individual funds are listed under the fund family. For example, the fictitious funds managed by The Woerheide Group would be listed under Woerheide Funds.

The New York Times Sunday edition includes the following information:

- fund family
- fund name
- type of fund
- rating
- NAV
- weekly percentage return
- year-to-date percentage return
- 1-year percentage return
- 3-year percentage return

For example, the Woerheide Index 500 Fund would be listed as follows:

Fund Family							
Fund Name	Type	Rating	NAV	Wkly % Ret.	YTD % Ret.	1-Yr % Ret.	3-Yr % Ret.
Woerheide Index							
500 Idx	LB	3/4	135.22	+5.0	−0.1	+14.2	+23.2

The meaning of various symbols and footnotes is explained in the newspaper. For example, LB indicates that the fund is a domestic general stock fund that invests in a portfolio described as large blend—the selected stocks are generally large capitalization and the portfolio is a blend of both growth and value stocks.

The Prospectus

Under the federal laws that regulate security transactions, a prospectus (a document produced by the mutual fund management that provides relevant information about the fund) must be delivered to prospective investors before the purchase. The prospectus offers a large amount of information about the fund, including the following:

- *the fund's investment objectives.* For example, the prospectus may state that the primary objective is long-term growth of capital, and the secondary objective is current income.
- *the fund's investment policies.* The prospectus may state, for example, that the fund invests primarily in common stocks, but that it may also invest in bonds or money market instruments, or even stock futures and options.
- *general information* about the risks of investing in the fund
- *tables showing the loads and other expenses* associated with the purchase, retention, and sale of the fund's shares
- *additional information* concerning performance, management, purchase and redemption procedures, minimum initial purchase and subsequent amounts, and more

With regard to information concerning performance, the SEC requires mutual funds that advertise past financial performance to use a standard calculation method, which is defined in Form N-1A, the registration statement that investment companies must file with the SEC under the Investment Company Act of 1940. For a money market fund, the calculation provides the effective yield for the most recent 7-day period covered by the fund's filings with the SEC. For all other mutual funds, the calculation provides the average annual total returns for the most recent 1-, 5-, and 10-year periods (or at least since the fund's inception) covered by the fund's filings with the SEC. Sales loads or other charges, as well as the fund's expenses, are deducted from the average annual total return figure. Dividends and distributions by the fund are assumed to be reinvested.

Statement of Additional Information

Another document, the *Statement of Additional Information*, also called Part B of the prospectus, is available upon request. It provides details about the mutual fund's portfolio. Mutual funds also issue annual and semiannual reports.

OTHER POOLED INVESTMENTS

Closed-End Investment Companies

The second most common type of investment company after mutual funds is the closed-end investment company. The number of a closed-end investment company's shares outstanding is basically fixed. The shares outstanding for a closed-end fund change only if the fund has a public offering, a dividend reinvestment plan (DRIP), a direct purchase plan (DPP), or a share buy-back program. (DRIPs and DPPs will be discussed in chapter 14.)

Unlike purchasers of mutual funds, buyers of shares in a closed-end fund do not receive a prospectus when they consider a purchase. Investors buy and sell their shares in the secondary market in much the same way as with stock in a publicly traded corporation. Like publicly traded stock, their share prices are determined by supply and demand. The shares may sell for a premium or a discount relative to their NAV. Most of the time, closed-end funds trade at a discount, and these discounts can often be 15 percent to 20 percent or more.

Some investors believe the purchase of closed-end funds at substantial discounts is a "free lunch" available in the marketplace. Others believe there are real reasons for these discounts. Some of the more commonly listed reasons for these continuing discounts include the following:

- *embedded tax liabilities.* To the extent that portfolios of closed-end funds contain unrecognized capital gains, a buyer of these shares is buying future tax liabilities. Stated another way, the portfolio cannot be liquidated at the NAV because of the capital gains taxes the shareholder would owe.
- *lack of marketability of some holdings.* Just as closed-end funds do not have to worry about share redemptions, they do not have to worry about the marketability of all of their holdings. This lack of market-ability may even extend to the point where they have holdings for which daily price quotations are not available. As a result, the NAV that is computed each day may represent no more than a best guess.

Many people find it a strange phenomenon that a closed-end company will sometimes trade at a premium. Indeed, no economically sound explanation has ever been offered in the literature. At best, we could argue that occasionally a closed-end company holds a portfolio that is concentrated in a sector that is "hot" and for which no other sector funds might exist. Hence, this company is a unique investment opportunity for which investors are willing to pay a premium. In view of the overwhelming tendency for closed-end companies to trade at discounts, investment advisors should be wary of placing clients in one that trades at a premium.

Conversions

It occasionally happens that some closed-end funds convert to an open-end format. There was an average of about 10 conversions per year in the late 1990s,[8] although that was an unusually high rate compared to the rate at most other times. To the extent that the fund's discount was an irrational phenomenon, such a process would generate a windfall gain for the shareholders. To the extent that there was a legitimate reason for the discount, it is not clear that investors would benefit from such an action.

lifeboat provisions

Nonetheless, many closed-end funds adopt for their investors what are known as *lifeboat provisions*. These provisions usually require that the funds take some action to bolster their shares if they sell at a discount exceeding 10 percent for a specified period of time. One downside to this conversion process is that some funds create an exit fee after the conversion. This fee usually amounts to about 2 percent and typically lasts for about 6 months to one year. The revenue this generates can be substantial, as the average asset decline during the 6 months following conversion is 28.2 percent.[9]

Dual-Purpose Investment Companies

income share
capital appreciation share

Dual-purpose investment companies (DPICs) are closed-end funds with two classes of shares. One is the *income share*, and the other is the *capital appreciation share*. The income share is like a preferred stock with a maturity date. It promises a fixed rate of return and par value back at maturity. The capital appreciation share promises no dividends during the life of the income shares. At the maturity of the income shares, the fund has several choices.

One is that the fund may liquidate its entire portfolio, and pay the capital appreciation shareholders whatever is left over after the income shareholders are paid off. If the fund has performed well, the capital appreciation shareholders could do quite well in their investment. If the fund has done poorly, it is possible that the income shareholders would end up with the better rate of return. It is certainly possible that at the maturity of the income shares, the fund portfolio might not have enough assets to pay the income shareholders in full. In this case, the capital appreciation shares would be worthless. An alternative to liquidating the capital appreciation shares at the maturity of the income shares is to convert these shares into either a mutual fund or a closed-end company with only the one class of shares outstanding.

Closed-End Fund Price Quotations

Closed-end fund quotations can be found in *The Wall Street Journal*, *The New York Times*, and *Barron's,* as well as on the Internet. Funds are grouped into categories similar to those of mutual funds. These quotations typically contain the following information:

- name of fund and symbol
- market where traded
- NAV
- market price
- premium or discount of share price relative to NAV
- 52-week market return

An example is as follows:

Fund Name Symbol	Stock Exchange	NAV	Market Price	Premium or Discount	2-Year Market Return
Exwhyzee (XYZ)	N	27.40	25.10	–8	16.7
Abeecee (ABC)	O	42.15	44.20	5	–3.2

In the above example, the N refers to the New York Stock Exchange and the O to the over-the-counter market. Note that the premium or discount percentage is a number that could readily be computed, and so is provided for the reader's convenience. Some investors seek out funds with the largest discount. Inclusion of this facilitates an investor's ability to quickly find his or her desired investment choices.

REITs

Real estate investment trusts (REITs) provide indirect ways to invest in property. Each REIT offers the opportunity to participate in the market without having management responsibility while limiting risk. REITs assemble and manage portfolios of real estate and real estate loans. By law, at least 75 percent of REIT assets must be invested in real estate, and no less than 75 percent of income must be derived from real estate. In addition, to be recognized as a conduit and thus avoid taxation, REITs must pay out at least 95 percent of their income annually.

Based on investment objectives, REITs fall into one of three general categories:

- Equity REITs invest in properties that produce income or have growth potential, such as office buildings, apartments, shopping malls, and hotels.
- Mortgage REITs are in the business of making both construction loans and mortgage loans.
- Hybrid REITs are a combination of equity and mortgage REITs.

Equity REITs are typically the most popular type with investors who want to participate in the growth of real estate values. Dividends should rise if rents increase more than expenses, and share prices generally reflect changes in property values. Mortgage REITs are similar to bonds. Like all interest-rate-sensitive investments, their prices rise when interest rates fall, and fall when interest rates rise.

RELPs and Unlisted REITs

More aggressive investors looking for equity positions in real estate might consider RELPs and unlisted REITs. RELPs were popular in the 1980s until the passage of the Tax Reform Act of 1986. This act reduced or eliminated many limited partnership holders' ability to deduct partnership losses. Another drawback is that RELPs are often sold with large loads. RELPs usually have a provision that they will be liquidated at a point 8 to 12 years from the time of creation. Similarly, most unlisted REITs today carry a provision that promises the REIT will become listed by a certain date, or it will be liquidated. Investors who want out of unlisted REITs or RELPs before some step is taken to provide marketability will likely have to pay a high price to get their cash back. For example, one study found that the discount from NAVs on the sale of RELPs was as high as 60 percent.[10] Unlisted REITs have for the most part taken the place of RELPs.

Unit Investment Trusts

The next most common type of investment company is the unit investment trust (UIT). There are two key features to a UIT: The portfolios are unmanaged, and they are usually created to have finite lives. The minimal management of these trust means there are no management expenses. These trusts are typically set up and marketed by a brokerage firm that receives an underwriting fee from the proceeds of the sale and manages the trust until it is liquidated. Investors technically buy units rather than shares. There are two types of UITs: debt and equity.

Debt UITs

Once assembled, most debt security portfolios can be left unmanaged until the last holding in the portfolio matures. Interest payments and principal payments for maturing securities are paid to UIT investors as they occur, net of any administrative costs. Once all of the cash flows have been paid out, the trust is dissolved. One problem that can occur with such a portfolio is that if there is a default on one of the bonds, it can take years for final resolution. In such situations, the portfolio manager will usually sell the defaulted bond and distribute the proceeds or reinvest, depending on what seems more appropriate.

Debt UITs have maturities that range from 5 years to 30 years. They contain either taxable or tax-exempt bonds. The minimum investment in a debt UIT is usually $1,000.

Equity UITs

Equity UITs may or may not have a termination date, at which time the portfolio is liquidated and the proceeds distributed. Most of those without a termination date are the exchange-traded funds (discussed in one of the next sections). There is usually a strategy or theme to an equity UIT. One popular theme has been "dogs of the Dow," which we discussed in chapter 6. Recall that this strategy is based on the belief that the 10 stocks in the DJIA with the highest dividend yields will outperform the other 20 stocks over the next 12 months. These UITs are assembled for 12-month holding periods. Hence, an investor who believes in this strategy could regularly repeat it by buying a UIT based on this theme, then rolling the proceeds over into a similar UIT when the old one matures.

Advantages and Disadvantages of UITs

There are several advantages to UITs, although many of these are similar to the advantages and disadvantages of other investment companies. The advantages are

- *convenience.* One purchase allows the investor to obtain a fully diversified portfolio that meets a particular objective.
- *minimum investment size.* The minimum investment requirements are substantially less than if an investor attempted to create such a portfolio directly.

- *portfolio stability.* The investor knows from the date of purchase what the underlying portfolio should be over the life of the investment.
- *tax efficiency.* In the case of debt UITs, there should be minimal capital gains or losses. Equity UITs have a known date on which the capital gain or loss will be recognized.
- *no management fees.* Due to the lack of any active management, there are no management fees.

The disadvantages are as follows:

- UITs are not as common as other forms of investment companies. Thus, an investor is less likely to find a UIT that seeks to fill a particular investment goal, especially with equity trusts.
- Front-end loads vary from 3 to 5 percent.
- There is a lack of a resale market. For most UITs there is no active secondary market. Thus, an investor may have to give up a substantial discount to sell the units.

Exchange-Traded Funds

There has been a substantial growth in recent years in exchange-traded funds (ETFs). An ETF is a closed-end index fund. The portfolio of the ETF is essentially a composite of whatever index it is meant to replicate. Because of its closed-end nature, the fund's portfolio manager does not have to worry about cash inflows and outflows from the sale of new shares or liquidations. As such, these are essentially buy-and-hold portfolios.

At the end of 2001, there were 102 ETFs with total assets of $83 billion. At this same time, index mutual funds held $366 billion in assets.[11]

ETFs come with many intriguing names. The most widely advertised is the SPDR, which stands for the Standard & Poor's Depository Receipt. This was the first ETF, created in 1993, but it did not really become popular until the late 1990s. Other appealing ETFs include DIAMONDS, which tracks the Dow Jones Industrial Average, and iShares, which stands for index shares and tracks indexes used in countries all around the globe. [12]

The most heavily traded ETF is known by the nickname Qubes, because its ticker symbol is QQQ. Qubes is an ETF that tracks the technology-laden NASDAQ 100 index.

One of the unique features of ETFs is that most allow in-kind creation and redemption of shares. In fact, ETFs are sometimes created only through in-kind contributions. In this case, the investor (a financial institution) holds a portfolio that is a match for the index targeted by the ETF. The investor contributes the shares and receives back a block of ETF shares. Although this is limited to really large share holdings, it means that the market price cannot wander too far from its NAV. For example, the investor can redeem a 50,000 shareholding of SPDRs with the actual stocks of the index.

Although we might think an investor would be indifferent between an index fund and an ETF, there are real advantages and disadvantages to each. The advantages of ETFs over index funds include the following:

- ETFs are traded on a daily basis like any other stock and thus give investors the ability to buy or sell at any time during the trading day. Index funds can be bought or redeemed only at the end of a trading day.
- The investor can buy an ETF on margin or even take a short position in such a fund. Index funds require the full purchase price and absolutely cannot be shorted.
- ETFs can have extremely low management fees, because once the fund has been created and the stock sold, there is not all that much for management to do as the portfolio is fixed.
- ETFs are extremely tax efficient in that the lack of trading in the portfolio means that there are few, if any, capital gain distributions on which an investor has to pay taxes.
- ETFs more readily track an index. It is more difficult for an index fund to track an index due to transaction costs, fund cash flows, dividends, and index composition changes.[13]

The advantages of index funds over ETFs include the following:

- Most index funds are no-loads, whereas ETFs are normally bought through a broker, thus requiring a commission.
- Like other stocks, ETFs trade on a bid-ask spread, thus creating an implicit cost to buy and sell these shares.
- Index funds always trade at the NAV, but ETFs will sometimes trade at a discount from the NAV.

Financial Planning Issue

When should an advisor recommend an ETF, and when should he or she recommend an index fund? If the client (or the planner) wants to engage in market timing trades, then index funds are preferable. Timing involves frequent trades. Although index funds can be bought or redeemed only at the end of the day, the transaction is cost free. The commissions and bid-ask spreads make ETFs less appealing for this strategy, although there are some ETFs that actively solicit this type of investor.

Conversely, investors with long-term objectives should prefer ETFs, because the low annual expenses of managing the fund will easily offset commissions over a period of several years.

Holding Company Depository Receipts (HOLDRs)

In recent years, *Holding Company Depository Receipts (HOLDRs),* a variation of ETFs, have become popular. HOLDRs are analogous to sector funds—that is, they are ETFs that, instead of mimicking an index, hold selected stocks (frequently 20) in a particular industry.

Hedge Funds

Hedge funds are a type of pooled portfolio instrument organized for maximum flexibility for the portfolio manager. For example, hedge funds may invest in derivatives, sell short, use leverage, and invest internationally. Most hedge funds are organized offshore to avoid the regulations imposed on U.S. funds, and most of them take substantial risks. They are typically organized as limited partnerships and allow only "qualified investors" to participate. These investors must demonstrate both the sophistication and the financial resources to understand and take the risks associated with such investments. Nonetheless, in 2002, approximately 15 percent of advisors were putting their clients into hedge funds.[14]

Statistics on the returns of hedge funds are always quite exciting, but they are also misleading. About 20 percent of the 6,000 to 7,000 active hedge funds cease operations every year due to poor returns.[15] Any return indexes will clearly suffer from survivorship bias and selection bias.

Hedge funds can have a substantial impact on the securities markets. Consider the near collapse in October 1998 of Long Term Capital Management—a large and previously high-flying hedge fund that at its peak value was leveraged to the tune of more than $100 billion against a capital base of $3 billion. Another example is the collapse of the EiFuki Master Fund, which lost its entire $300 million market value in a mere 7 trading days.

Variable Annuities

Yet another form of investment company is the variable annuity. (The mechanics of annuities were discussed in chapter 1.) An individual buys an annuity with the insurance company, which places the premiums into its own pooled portfolio. The value of the annuity contract then depends on the performance of the insurance company's portfolio. The policyholder may opt for a variable annuity during either or both the accumulation period and the payout period. Some policyholders select a variable annuity during the accumulation period, and then during the payout period switch at least part of the funds to a fixed annuity. For example, upon retirement, an individual might switch from a 100 percent variable annuity to 50 percent variable and 50 percent fixed. This gives the individual some assurance as to a minimum fixed income and an opportunity for income growth. The NAVs of variable annuities are reported in the financial press.

The drawback to a variable annuity is that the sale of the annuity involves a relatively high load, and the individual still has to pay the management fees of the portfolio. In addition, if the policyholder is unhappy with the performance of the insurance company's portfolio, there may be a substantial fee to cancel the policy.

Because of their separate accounts, variable annuities are considered securities under federal law. This means the seller must have a life insurance license and be registered with the National Association of Securities Dealers to sell variable annuities. The seller must also obtain state licensing powers or authorization to sell variable annuities within each jurisdiction they are sold. Also, any potential buyer of a variable annuity must be given a prospectus. Furthermore, the seller must take steps to determine that a variable annuity is a suitable product choice for the purchaser. Suitability involves assessing a potential investor's investment objectives, time horizon, and risk tolerance.

Reasons to Recommend a Variable Annuity

Whether or not a financial planner recommends a variable annuity depends on the client's risk tolerance and how long the money will be invested before it must be withdrawn. People with short investment time horizons and low investment risk tolerance will generally be happier with a fixed annuity. If they have long time horizons and moderate risk tolerance, a planner might recommend an equity-indexed annuity. The advantage of both the variable annuity and the equity-indexed annuity over the fixed annuity is that they are more likely to keep up with inflation because of their link to the financial markets. An advantage of all annuities is that the assets accumulate on a tax-deferred basis, although the policyholder has to pay income taxes on the gain in value either at the time of withdrawal or as the payments are received during the payout phase. (This topic is covered in more detail in chapter 13.)

The variable annuity is for the senior client who realizes that gains and losses may occur, but who wants the investment flexibility that comes from being able to move funds among subaccounts within the separate account. This flexibility allows annuity owners in the seniors market to change their investment focus in response to changes in the financial markets or in their personal situations at the different stages of their retirement.

Pooled Funds

Many people have personal accounts that are managed by trust companies, trust departments within banks, and insurance companies. It would be nearly impossible for a large trust operation to manage each account separately. To facilitate the management of these accounts, the company creates its own in-house portfolios (that is, mutual funds), which are also known as pooled funds. The assets in a trust account can then either be sold and the proceeds used to buy shares in the pooled funds, or the assets can be given in-kind to the pooled fund and allocated shares based on their market value. To facilitate such trades, the pooled funds compute a daily NAV and function pretty much as any other mutual fund.

Types of Pooled Portfolio Funds by Organizational Structures

- Mutual funds: Open-ended; price based on NAV
  - Load funds: Sold through salesperson for a commission
  - No-load funds: Sold directly without a commission
- Closed-end investment companies: Corporation owned; managed portfolio; stock trades on an exchange or OTC, usually at a discount from NAV
- Unit investment trusts: Unmanaged; self-liquidating; largely consisting of short-term debt securities
- ETFs and HOLDRs: UITs with infinite lives; match either an index or an industry or market sector
- Hedge funds: Typically organized as offshore limited partnerships for qualified investors; maximum investment flexibility
- Variable annuities: Can be used in either the accumulation period or the payout period
- Pooled funds: In-house mutual funds used by trust operations and insurance companies

---

Other Types of Pooled Portfolios: Corporations, Partnerships, and Blind Pools

Several other types of pooled portfolios are available to the investor. For example, some ordinary companies hold such large portfolios of stock in other companies that they are, in effect, investment companies in all but name. Among the better known of these firms is Berkshire Hathaway. Berkshire Hathaway was once in textiles but now is primarily an owner of stocks. Its CEO, Warren Buffett, is highly respected for his adroit portfolio management.

Perhaps the most risky pooled portfolio device is the blind pool. With a blind pool, the investor agrees to finance a venture whose precise purposes are to be revealed later. The prospective investor will, however, be told the pool's general purpose (that is, to finance a program of risk arbitrage). Most people who invest in blind pools do so on the basis of their faith in the investor or group of investors they are bankrolling. In some instances, the investors are given a clue, such as the intended industry or investment approach. At other times, the investors are truly blind. Blind pools may be organized as shares of stock (usually of a closed-end fund), limited partnership interests, or debt securities (often to be used in as yet undisclosed takeover attempts). Somewhat surprisingly, many people are quite willing to buy these "pigs in a poke."

SELECTING A MUTUAL FUND

Now that we have discussed the nature of mutual funds and other investment companies, we turn to the practical question of how to select a mutual fund or investment company[16] from among the multitude available. As mentioned earlier, the first step in the investment process is to identify the appropriate category of funds to be considered. This is based on understanding the client's objectives and risk tolerance. Once this has been accomplished, then the task becomes one of picking a particular fund within that investment category.

Example:	Problem: Your client is an 80-year old widow with a portfolio of $700,000. It is clear that preservation of principal is a critical need, which implies safety. However, like most older clients, she worries about the ravages of inflation, and she is willing to forgo some current income if she can feel that she has some inflation protection. Is there an appropriate mutual fund for her?
	Solution: Safety and low income are automatically synonymous. However, protection from inflation with a willingness to sacrifice current income suggests only one particular type of instrument—TIPS (Treasury Inflation Protection Securities). Funds whose objective is to hold a diversified portfolio of TIPS are an excellent investment vehicle for this senior client.[17]

Third-Party Evaluation

A good starting point to selecting funds for further consideration is third-party evaluation. This process entails compiling a list of funds in a particular category and seeing what others have to say about these funds. Three of the more popular third-party evaluators are Morningstar (www.morningstar.com), Wiesenberger,[18] and Lipper, Inc.[19] (www.lipperweb.com/). In addition to ob-taining factual information on a fund (such as load charge, management fees, portfolio turnover ratios, and so on) from these companies, we can acquire a rating for each particular fund. Unfortunately, the authors know of no research to indicate that the quality ratings have any predictive value to them. Nonetheless, it would behoove a financial planner to attempt to keep his or her clients in well-rated funds as a normal part of due diligence, unless there is a particular reason to pick a fund that is poorly rated.

Investment Style

To better understand exactly what the objective and nature of a fund's portfolio are, many people resort to the concept known as investment style. If an investor understands what is meant by style, he or she can more effectively pursue investment goals by investing in a mutual fund that consistently maintains the desired style. One popular approach to categorizing investment style for stock portfolios uses the following two descriptive factors:

- *the relative market capitalizations of the companies that the fund invests in.* (Market capitalization is the total market value of a corporation's outstanding stock.) Some analysts divide this factor into three categories: large cap, mid cap, and small cap.
- *the relative emphasis of growth stocks versus value stocks.* In general, growth stocks are expected to increase in price due to projected growth in earnings, while value stocks are considered to be undervalued by the market. Factors used to classify stocks in these two categories include the price-earnings ratio (price per share divided by earnings per share) and the market-to-book ratio (price per share divided by accounting book value per share)—both of which are presumably higher for growth stocks than for value stocks. Another classification factor is dividend yield (dividend per share divided by price per share), which is typically lower for growth stocks. Funds are classified as growth oriented, value oriented, or blended. Combining the two factors generates a matrix of nine possibilities as shown below:

large cap value oriented	large cap blended	large cap growth oriented
mid cap value oriented	mid cap blended	mid cap growth oriented
small cap value oriented	small cap blended	small cap growth oriented

For fixed-income portfolios, the most appropriate factors are interest rate risk—primarily the price risk aspect—and credit quality. The interest rate sensitivity can be captured by the duration or weighted average maturity of the bond portfolio and can be characterized as long term, intermediate term, or short term, corresponding to high, medium, and low price risk, respectively. Credit quality can be captured by the average credit rating of the bonds in the portfolio. Presumably, a continuum of credit worthiness is possible, but one simplified approach limits the classifications to high, medium, and low credit quality. Combining the two factors also generates a matrix of nine possibilities:

high quality short term	high quality intermediate term	high quality long term
medium quality short term	medium quality intermediate term	medium quality long term
low quality short term	low quality intermediate term	low quality long term

Other Selection Factors

style drift

One issue that many financial planners worry about is what is known as *style drift,* which means that the portfolio is drifting away from what had been an established style. The problem with drift is that the investor ends up with a holding different from what the financial planner intended. An example of style drift is when a fund manager, in anticipation of a bear market, increases his or her cash holdings from 2 percent of the portfolio to 30 percent of the portfolio. The portfolio manager's forecast may or may not be right, but in the meantime, the manager may be significantly altering the investor's total portfolio away from what the investor wants to hold.

A second factor is the degree of concentration within a portfolio. A quick review of the top 10 holdings provides some indication of concentration. Simply adding the percentages of the top 10 holdings in the portfolio gives a comparative measure of concentration. Looking at the nature of the industries of the top 10 holdings is another indicator of concentration. If the top 10 holdings are in 10 different industries, then there is good diversification. If they are all in one industry, there is a significant lack of diversification. A lack of diversification is not necessarily bad. If the investor wants a sector fund for a particular component of his or her portfolio, a concentrated fund is good. If the fund is meant to provide market diversification, however, concentration in a single industry is bad.

As we have previously mentioned, portfolio turnover is a statistic that reveals something about the frequency of trading. More trading means more commissions paid. In addition, trades may mean more in the way of capital gains taxes to be paid and may be an indication of style drift. If an investor is holding the mutual fund in a tax-deferred account (see chapter 14), then the size of the capital gains distribution is immaterial, although the magnitude of commissions and style drift is still a concern.

Two factors that many financial planners seriously consider are (1) the age of the fund and (2) the experience, qualifications, and longevity of the fund's manager. Many planners prefer several years of history before selecting a fund and thus will simply ignore newer funds. In addition, some planners will ignore funds in which the portfolio manager is relatively new to the job. No matter how great that fund's past performance, it is not the performance generated by that particular manager. That manager has little or no track record with the fund; therefore, for all intents and purposes, a fund with a new manager is no different from a new fund.

If the fund is in a fund family with a broad selection and solid performance, clients will have a good set of alternatives for reallocation of assets, and they may be able to avoid loads when transferring between funds in the same family. Service issues, which can be a source of satisfaction or aggravation, are also important. Funds differ in the timeliness, responsiveness, and clarity of correspondence and statements. Some funds have established reputations for helpful telephone service, while others have developed less enviable reputations. Funds also vary in the availability and user friendliness of their online account information and services.

Some financial planners deliberately choose funds from different families. This is not unreasonable when there are no load charges and no breakpoints involved. There is a certain element of diversification in using funds from different families. For example, if another scandal develops that involves a fund in a particular family, a client who owns only funds in the family may get nervous, and with good reason. Family diversification, therefore, can offer safety from scandals and other forms of inappropriate or illegal activity. In addition, not every family will have what a planner considers to be the best fund in a particular area. It is unwise to opt for a family fund just to "keep it in the family" when another fund appears to be better suited for the client.

Finally, many financial planners visit the offices of various funds to check out their culture and professionalism. Some planners regularly talk to the portfolio manager or at least to some of a fund's analysts to get a feel for the direction of the fund and to see if the decisions the fund is making seem reasonable.

SEC Yield

When a bond fund or other fixed-income mutual fund is being analyzed, the investor should consider the SEC yield. This quotation is based on the most recent 30-day (or one month) period covered by the fund's filings with the SEC. The yield figure reflects the dividends and interest earned during the period after deducting the fund's expenses for the period. The SEC computes this yield as follows:

Based on a 30-day (or one month) period ending on the date of the most recent balance sheet included in the registration statement, calculate the fund's yield by dividing the net investment income per share earned during the period by the maximum offering price per share on the last day of the period, according to this formula:[20]

$$\text{Yield} = 2\left[\left(\frac{a-b}{cd}+1\right)^6 - 1\right]$$

where   a   =   dividends and interest earned during the period
        b   =   expenses accrued for the period (net of reimbursements)
        c   =   the average daily number of shares outstanding during the period that were entitled to receive dividends
        d   =   the maximum offering price per share on the last day of the period

Note that the return relative is taken to the 6th power and not the 12th power as we would normally expect when dealing with what is ostensibly an annualization of monthly data. This is because the final answer is multiplied by 2. In other words, the formula is computing a 6-month rate of return, and then doubling it.

Example: The Overblown Stats Mutual Fund calculates that its dividends and interest during the last 30 days are $300,000, and its accrued expenses for the period (net of reimbursements) are $50,000. The average daily number of shares outstanding during this period was $10 million, and the maximum offering price per share on the last day of the period was $10. The SEC yield is

$2\ [\{(\$300{,}000 - \$50{,}000)/\ (10{,}000{,}000 \times \$10) + 1\}^6 - 1] = 2[\{.0025 + 1\}^6 - 1] = 2\ [1.0151 - 1] = .0302$, or 3.02%

HP-10BII keystrokes	Display
SHIFT, C ALL	
300,000, –, 50,000, =	250,000
10,000,000, x, 10, =	100,000,000
250,000, divided by, 100,000,000, =	.0025
+, 1, =	1.0025
SHIFT, y^x, 6, =	1.0151
–, 1, =, x, 2, =	.0302

When to Sell a Mutual Fund

Certain factors are appropriate to consider in the buy or sell decision for any investment (and they are discussed in chapter 14), but there are certain factors unique to mutual funds.

One is style drift, which we explained earlier. For example, an aggressive growth fund may grow so large that it has difficulty finding enough investments with characteristics appropriate for an aggressive growth fund. The fund may even make a conscious effort to change its investment style because of other pressures, including the manager's own assessment of the immediate prospects for funds with the original style. One indication of a change in style might be if a fund merges into another fund or acquires another fund. Also, if the fund manager is replaced, there is reason to be concerned that the fund's characteristics will change.

A second factor is a significant change in a fund's asset allocation. For example, suppose the planner wants the client's Roth IRA account to be 100 percent in equities, but notices that the fund in which the IRA is invested has shifted to holding 30 percent of its assets in money market instruments. The fund's manager is obviously anticipating a bear market, but the client's asset allocation scheme has been compromised.

Another factor, although not unique to mutual funds, is poor performance over an extended period of time, especially if the poor performance is related to high expenses.

Reasons to Sell a Mutual Fund

- Style drift
- Inappropriate asset allocation
- Extended periods of poor performance

It would be inappropriate to sell a fund based on subpar performance over a short period. Most managers feel that at least a 3-year time frame is necessary to validate a manager's performance. If underlying characteristics of the fund are unchanged, switching to a similar fund with slightly better performance in an attempt to "chase returns" frequently causes the client to generate a tax liability without improving the portfolio.

Why Mutual Funds Usually Underperform the Market

All sorts of research over the last 40 years has consistently shown that most mutual funds do not earn positive abnormal risk-adjusted returns, and many regularly provide negative abnormal risk-adjusted returns. Outperforming a relatively efficient market (such as the U.S. stock market) is difficult. Still, mutual funds do have the resources to hire the best talent, collect the most useful information, and analyze it with the most sophisticated techniques. Furthermore, their large size should facilitate operational efficiency—especially when securities are bought in quantities that qualify for commission discounts. Why then, with all these advantages, do the funds as a group so rarely outperform the market? There are several reasons:

- *Institutional investors constitute a large part of the market.* Outperforming the average would be difficult for any group of investors that makes up a large part of the average. Institutions hold at least 40 percent of the total value of U.S. stocks; a still higher percentage of the larger listed issues makes up most of the market indexes.

- *Some other types of large investors have advantages similar to those of the institutions.* Each type of institutional investor (mutual funds, insurance companies, pension funds, college endowments, foundations, and bank trust departments) has access to similar managerial talent, sources of information, and types of analysis. Furthermore, private investment managers, individuals with large sums to invest, and nonfinancial corporations with large stock portfolios all have equivalent advantages. Thus, mutual funds must compete with other similarly positioned institutional and noninstitutional investors.

- *Mutual funds have a number of disadvantages relative to many other types of investors.* Although mutual funds offer several advantages to investors, they also have a number of disadvantages (described earlier) that tend to lower their return by outweighing any likely advantage they may have over small investors. The primary disadvantage is their fee structure.

Are Mutual Funds Appropriate Investments?

If funds do not generally outperform market averages, should individuals invest in mutual funds (other than index funds)? In other words, should they pay for active professional management that does not increase the risk-adjusted expected return?

This is a really good question. Currently, there are over 10,000 mutual funds from which investors can choose. Many in the financial services industry believe that in the foreseeable future this number will collapse to something on the order of 5,000 funds, with a good number of these being index funds. There will always be a place for funds with objectives other than indexing, just as there will always be investors who want to specialize in a particular industry or style but do not have a sufficient portfolio to achieve the necessary degree of diversification. Other investors may want diversification but would rather construct it themselves by holding a variety of funds with different objectives.

Investors in mutual funds will find relatively few reliable selection guidelines. Even the most avid practitioners of fund selection readily agree it is an art, not a science. For believers in the EMH, there are a few obvious criteria to consider. Clearly, investors should prefer a fund with a risk level corresponding to their preferences. Also, a fund that has a favorable past performance and a low portfolio turnover, a low expense ratio, no load, and no 12b-1 fee may generate a bit better performance than the average fund. Most investors should probably give serious consideration to index funds.

Should an Investor Buy a Load Fund?

One final question is whether anyone should consider buying a load fund. There is no evidence that load funds perform any differently than no-loads (before consideration of the load). After all, the load charge pays the person who sells the shares, not the person who manages the portfolio.

There are several reasons why load funds should not be automatically rejected in any analysis. First, many investors should be in mutual funds, but they lack the knowledge or financial sophistication to get there. To borrow a phrase from the insurance industry, some funds are sold, not bought. This means that a financial advisor needs to educate a client as to the benefits of funds and help the client understand how funds work. Financial planners who do such work are entitled to fair compensation for it. Compensation can be on a fee basis or commission basis. If it is on a commission basis, then load charges can be fair compensation.

As we saw with classes of shares, some load funds carry little or no 12b-1 fees, and others may have unusually low management expense ratios. Others may have relatively low portfolio turnover ratios. In other words, some load funds may provide other cost savings to an investor that could make paying the load fee a reasonable charge.

There may be some funds that are unique in their objective and not any no-load funds that provide the same objective. If that is the objective the investor really wants, then he or she may have to pay the load charge.

SUMMARY AND CONCLUSIONS

Mutual funds, also known as open-end investment companies, are the most common investment company. The return is provided in the form of changes in the NAV, dividends, and capital gain distributions. Most funds belong to a mutual fund family, and the family structure provides some benefits to investors. The most significant expense to buying a mutual fund can be the load charge. When working with load charges, planners should be aware of breakpoints, the right of accumulation, letters of intent, and back-end loads. Other expenses of a fund include operating expenses, brokerage fees, and miscellaneous charges. There are a variety of distribution systems that are used to sell funds. The major benefits of mutual funds as an investment vehicle include professional management, diversification, convenience, record keeping, liquidity, reasonable minimal investment requirements, and extra regulation. Their major drawback is the commissions and fees. Everyone buying mutual fund shares must receive a prospectus and is entitled to receive a Statement of Additional Information.

The most common alternative to mutual funds is the closed-end fund. REITs and RELPs provide the opportunity for investors to have equity or debt participation in the real estate market. ETFs are a rapidly growing segment of the closed-end menu, and they have advantages and disadvantages when compared to index funds. Hedge funds can be extremely risky, and variable annuities carry potentially high commissions and fees. Some people—for example, trust beneficiaries—find they are effectively holding pooled funds.

The selection of an investment company starts with identifying funds whose objectives and risk exposure match the needs of the client. It is critical that a financial planner be familiar with third-party evaluations of any fund, such as those provided by Morningstar, Wiesenberger, and Lipper, Inc. A planner should also be aware of the fund's investment style, as well as the fund's objective. Other factors include the potential for style drift, the degree of concentration in the fund's portfolio, (including industry concentration), portfolio turnover ratios, the age of the fund, the longevity of the fund's manager on the job, fund family membership, and the quality of customer service. When buying fixed-income funds, a planner should be familiar with the SEC yield. Good reasons to liquidate a position in a fund are style drift, significant changes in promised allocation of assets, and extended poor performance. On average, funds underperform market averages, primarily due to their fees. Mutual funds are unquestionably an appropriate investment for many people, but it is not so clear that everyone should be in funds other than index funds.

CHAPTER REVIEW

Answers to the review questions and the self-test questions start on page 733.

Key Terms

open-end investment company	mixed portfolio funds
closed-end investment company	regular dividend
money market mutual funds	switching
common stock funds	contingent deferred sales charge

investment advisory fee
12b-1 fee
trail commission
portfolio turnover ratio
multi-class funds
revenue sharing
Statement of Additional Information
lifeboat provisions

income share
capital appreciation share
Holding Company Depository
    Receipts (HOLDRs)
blind pool
investment style
style drift

Review Questions

10-1. The $$$ Mutual Fund has a portfolio valued at $652 million, $2 million in liabilities, and 30 million shares outstanding. Suppose over the next 12 months the fund's portfolio value increases to $802 million, liabilities remain the same, and shares outstanding increase by 2 million.
   a. What is the initial NAV?
   b. What is the percentage increase in the NAV?

10-2. Assume that the $$$ Mutual Fund in question 10-1 is a load fund that charged a 3 percent front-end load and paid a distribution of $.70 per share over the past year. What would the one-year return for an investor in the $$$ Fund be?

10-3. Compare loads with 12b-1 fees.

10-4. Using table 10-2 as the structure for load fees, compute the following:
   a. If an investor has $495,000 to invest, how many shares would he or she buy if the NAV were $52.76?
   b. How much more cash would go to buy shares if the investor wrote a check for $500,000?
   c. If an investor pays $100,000 today to buy shares and signs a letter of intent to buy another $100,000 on the next four anniversary dates, how much commission does he or she save over the 5 years, as opposed to making the same purchases but not signing a letter of intent?

10-5. You are considering buying some shares in the Sure Growth Mutual Fund whose current NAV is $10.00. You plan to sell the shares in 2 years; the NAV will increase by 10 percent each year (ignore dividends and capital gain distributions in this problem). You can buy Class A shares, which have a 5 percent front-end load and no 12b-1 charges; Class B shares, which have a .25 percent 12b-1 charge (based on the year-end NAV) and a back-end load that will be 3 percent in 2 years; or Class C shares, which are no load but have 12b-1 charges of 1 percent. Which is the cheapest in terms of total fees?

10-6. What advantages and disadvantages do mutual funds have relative to other investors?

10-7. a. What types of investors are most likely to find mutual funds attractive?
       b. What mutual fund attributes are valuable to all investors?

10-8. a. What is meant by a sector fund?
       b. What are families of funds, and what are their benefits?

10-9. Why are there no closed-end money market funds?

10-10. Briefly describe and contrast open-end investment companies and closed-end investment companies.

Self-Test Questions

T   F   10-1. Mutual funds (open-end investment companies) stand willing to buy and sell the funds' shares on demand at a price based on their net asset value (NAV).

T   F   10-2. No-load mutual funds are typically sold to investors by salespeople.

T   F   10-3. Most load mutual funds charge an 8.5 percent fee on the sale of shares to the public.

T   F   10-4. To purchase a fund with an NAV of $20 a share and a 5 percent load, an investor has to pay $21.05 per share.

T   F   10-5. All funds charging 12b-1 fees are technically classified as load funds.

T   F   10-6. To qualify as a regulated investment company, a fund must distribute at least 80 percent of its gross income to its owners.

T   F   10-7. Index funds typically have lower expenses and fees than those charged by actively managed funds.

T   F   10-8. Institutional investors generally focus their analysis on all traded stocks.

T   F   10-9. Most stock mutual funds are consistently able to beat the returns on S&P 500 Index funds.

T   F   10-10. A holding of mutual fund shares is usually computed to the third decimal place.

T   F   10-11. Mixed portfolio funds hold stocks in a variety of industries.

T   F   10-12. Specialty funds have a unique focus.

T   F   10-13. Some socially responsible funds hold stocks that other funds find objectionable.

T   F   10-14. Switching is when an investor moves money from one fund in a family to another fund in that same family.

T   F   10-15. Sometimes, an investor can actually save substantial money if he or she can slightly increase his or her investment in a load mutual fund to the point where the next breakpoint is hit.

T   F   10-16. A right of accumulation applies only to one account.

T   F   10-17. A portfolio turnover ratio is the lesser of a portfolio's annual purchases or sales (excluding securities with maturities less than one year) divided by average total net monthly assets.

T   F   10-18. Class A shares are usually no-loads but have large 12b-1 fees.

T   F   10-19. Placing a customer in the wrong class of shares can be a serious legal and ethical violation for a broker.

T   F   10-20. REITs do not have to pay corporate income taxes if they distribute at least 95 percent of their profit as dividends.

T   F   10-21. A REIT is an open-end mutual fund that redeems its shares when investors sell.

T   F   10-22. Hybrid REITs invest exclusively in office buildings, apartments, and shopping malls.

T   F   10-23. The shares of closed-end investment companies typically sell at their NAV.

T   F   10-24. Closed-end funds are not permitted to convert to open-end funds.

T   F   10-25. Unit investment trusts are typically unmanaged investment portfolios composed of debt securities.

T   F   10-26. Variable annuities generate tax-free returns to investors.

T   F   10-27. Hedge funds are usually organized as limited partnerships and take large risks in seeking large returns.

T   F   10-28. Blind pools may be organized as limited partnerships or closed-end funds.

T   F   10-29. Third-party evaluations are useful in selecting a mutual fund, but they are not a guarantee.

T   F   10-30. Past performance is far more important to consider in the selection of a fund than fees.

NOTES

1. http://global.factiva.com/en/arch/print_results.asp, January 16, 2004.
2. Some closed-end investment companies, such as unit investment trusts, do not have an active market in their shares. Thus, they technically do not trade.
3. Some people mistakenly refer to this as the capital gain dividend. It is a distribution and not a dividend because it will be taxed to the investor as capital gain income and not dividend income.
4. http://personal.fidelity.com/products/funds/, January 9, 2004.
5. The classic study on 12b-1 fees is "The Effects of 12b-1 Plans on Mutual Fund Expense Ratios: A Note," by S. Ferris and D. Chance, *Journal of Finance*, vol. 42 (1987), pp. 1077–1082.
6. There is no legal requirement for the definition of what is meant by each class of shares, but the nomenclature presented herein seems to be nearly universal. The legal requirements with

respect to classes of shares are covered in Rule 18f-3 of the SEC, adopted under the Investment Company Act of 1940.

7. //online.wsj.com/article/0,SB107401775870784300,00.html?mod=home_whats_news_us, January 13, 2004.

8. Aaron Lucchetti, "Scudder is at Center of Fight over Fees," *Wall Street Journal* (Eastern edition). New York: July 14, 1999, p. 1.

9. *Medical Economics*, December 14, 1998, p. 24.

10. www.appraisals.com/articles/demystifying.htm, January 12, 2004.

11. http://partners.financenter.com/businessweek/learn/guides/investmutfund/invfundexchange.fcs, January 12, 2004.

12. www.msci.com/licensing/eafe_factsheet.pdf_, May 4, 2004.

13. Leonard Kostovetsky, "Index Mutual Funds and Exchange-Traded Funds: A Comparison of Two Methods of Passive Investment," *The Journal of Portfolio Management*, summer 2003, p. 81.

14. B. Kelley, "Hedge Use Rises amid Concerns," *Investment News,* July 2003, p. 1.

15. S.J. Brown, W.N. Goetzmann, and R.G. Ibbotson, "Offshore Hedge Funds: Survival and Performance: 1989–1995," *Journal of Business*, vol. 72, 1999, pp. 91–117.

16. Some of the material for this section is based on "The Art and Science of Mutual Fund Selection," by Nancy Opiela, *Journal of Financial Planning,* vol. 17, issue 1 (January 2004), pp. 36–41.

17. "Mutual Gains," *Senior Market Advisor*, vol. 4, issue 11 (November 2003), pp. 29–30, 32, 34.

18. Wiesenberger is now a subsidiary of Thomson Financial. It can be accessed through www.thomsoninvest.net/funds/mfmonitor_analysis.sht.

19. Lipper, Inc., has recently changed its name from Lipper Analytical Services.

20. See item 21 at www.sec.gov/rules/final/33-7512f.htm#formn1a, January 13, 2004.

11

Options and Other Derivative Securities

Learning Objectives

An understanding of the material in this chapter should enable the student to

---

11-1.   Describe the basic terminology used by option traders.

11-2.   Describe the two reasons options have value.

11-3.   Construct a profit function and a payoff function for any of the simple combinations of options and stocks.

11-4.   Describe how the variables used in the Black-Scholes and binomial option pricing models affect the value of a call option.

11-5.   Explain the put-call parity relationship and solve for the value of an option using this model.

11-6.   Explain the mechanics of the options markets.

11-7.   Describe how stock index options, interest rate options, and LEAPS® differ from listed puts and calls on common stock.

11-8.   Discuss the differences between rights and warrants, and how these two differ from traditional call options.

11-9.   Explain the advantages and disadvantages of convertibles and compute conversion values and conversion premiums.

11-10. Describe some of the other types of convertible or option-related securities available to an investor.

Chapter Outline

People regularly create options. For example, if someone rents a house with an option to buy and the purchase price for the option is clearly defined, the owner and renter have created an option. Whenever someone leases a car with an option to buy, the lessor and lessee have created an option. Options also exist for financial assets.

Although option trading has been around for many, many years, options became a significant part of the financial markets when the Chicago Board of Options Exchange (CBOE, pronounced Cee-bow) opened its doors in the early 1970s for the formal trading of options. The trick was the standardization of the terms on option contracts, such that people wanting to trade in options had a limited number of choices. This created the necessary marketability to make option trading interesting to a large number of people for a variety of reasons.

LISTED OPTIONS

option

An option is basically what its name implies: a choice. An *option* gives the owner the choice of whether or not to engage in a specified transaction, which would involve either buying or selling some underlying asset at a specified price at some future time. The choice itself has value, and people are willing to pay a price in order to have the choice of whether or not to engage in a specified transaction in the future.

Option Terminology

writer

call option (call)

A call option comes into existence when the order to buy a call option is matched on the floor of the exchange with an order to sell a call option with the exact same terms that has been placed by someone who does not currently own the option. The seller is referred to as a *writer* because by selling something he or she does not currently own, he or she is creating or writing the option. A *call option* gives the owner the privilege (or choice) to buy a <u>specified</u> number of shares of a <u>specified</u> asset at a <u>specified</u> price prior to an <u>expiration date</u>. For example, a call option on Xerox common stock gives the holder of the option the right to purchase from the writer 100 shares of Xerox at a specified price anytime up until the option's expiration date.

put option (put)

A *put option* permits the owner to sell a <u>specified</u> number of shares of a <u>specified</u> asset at a <u>specified</u> price prior to an <u>expiration date</u>. For example, the holder of a put option on Xerox stock has the right to sell 100 shares of Xerox stock to the writer of the put at the specified price anytime up until the option's expiration date. Buying a put or a call is referred to as *going long* in the put or call. Writing an option is referred to as *going short.*

premium (option)

There are three prices associated with an option. To avoid confusion, special names are assigned to each price. The first is, obviously, the price of the option itself, and this is usually known as the *premium*. Normally, we think of a premium as the price we pay for an insurance contract, and in some of the trading strategies involving options, the option is used as a form of insurance.

exercise price
strike price

The second price is the price at which the underlying asset is bought or sold if the option is exercised. This is referred to as the *exercise price* or *strike price*. It is a part of the option contract, and cannot be changed once the option comes into existence. The third price is the price at which the underlying asset trades. Unfortunately, there is no simple name for this price; it is known as the *price of the underlying* asset.

in the money

     An option is said to be *in the money* if it could be exercised immediately to produce a cash inflow. For the call option, this means that the market price of the underlying asset is higher than the exercise price of the option. Conversely, for the put option, it means that the exercise price of the option is higher than the market price of the underlying asset. When the strike price of a call option exceeds the market price of the underlying stock, or when the market price of the underlying stock exceeds the strike price of a put, the option is *out of the money*. When the exercise price of the option is equal to the market price of the underlying stock, both the put and the call option are *at the money*.

out of the money

at the money

Expiration Dates

     It is incredibly important for the owners of options that said options be exercised if the options are in the money just before the close of business on the expiration date. After the close of business on the expiration date, all options become worthless (it would be like trying to sell tickets to the Super Bowl on the day after the game is played). This need to exercise is so important for in the money options that are dying that many brokers demand from their customers the right to exercise these options on the expiration date if the customer has failed to do so. Obviously, this would be one of the benefits to a having a discretionary account at least for option trading.

Example: About 3 months ago, RG stock traded at $72 per share. At that time, you bought a RG call option and paid a premium of $2.50 per share. The option has a strike price of $75 per share. The option expires tomorrow; the stock currently trades at $76 per share, and the option trades at $1.06 per share. If you take no action by the close of trading the next day, the option becomes worthless (expires). What should you do?

     Answer: You have three choices. First, you could exercise the option and buy the stock for $75 per share (and pay the standard commission for the purchase of stock). Second, you could sell the option today (and pay the standard commission for the sale of an option). Third, you could wait to see what happens on the expiration date. If the price of RG goes up, you could make a fantastic percentage gain. If the price goes down (below $75), the option would become worthless.

Why Options Have Value

**intrinsic value
(option)**

Puts and calls always have an intrinsic value. For an in the money call, *intrinsic value* is the difference between the market price of the underlying stock and the strike price, and for an at the money or out of the money call it is zero. Similarly, for an in the money put, this is the difference between the strike price and the market price of the underlying stock, and for an out of the money put it is zero. In equation format:

Intrinsic Value of a Call = P – X   if P > X, and
$\qquad\qquad\qquad\qquad$ = 0   if X > P.

Intrinsic Value of a Put = X – P   if X > P, and
$\qquad\qquad\qquad\qquad$ = 0   if P > X.

where   P = market price of underlying stock
$\qquad$ X = exercise or strike price

At any point during the life of an option, said option may be cashed out or sold for its intrinsic value (less commissions, of course). Thus, an option can never be worth less than its intrinsic value.

Options also have a speculative or time value. To understand this, consider a simple example. Let's say that the price of the stock of Big Fox Corp. trades at $50 per share. Let's further assume that there is an option on this stock with a striking price of $50. At this point in time, the intrinsic value of the option is clearly zero (why would anyone pay for the privilege to buy something for $50, when that item can be bought directly for $50!). However, let's assume that the investor believes that on the option expiration date, the stock will either trade at a price of $60 per share, or a price of $40 per share. Let's further assume that that these events are equally likely (that is, a 50 percent probability of either price). If this is the case, then on the expiration date, the call option will have an intrinsic value of either $10 (that is, $60 – $50) or zero (if the market prices closes at $40). The expected value of the option on the expiration date is then computed as:

Expected value of the option = .50 x $10 + .50 x $0 = $5.

The speculative or time value is then based on this expected value of $5.

Note in this above example that the expected price of the stock on the expiration date is $50:

Expected price of the stock = .50 X $60 + .50 x $40 = $50.

We indicated that the current price of the stock is $50. Hence, the expected rate of return from owning the stock in this case is 0 percent. Despite the 0 percent expected rate of return, the option has value.

Options are a form of leveraged investing, somewhat akin to buying on margin. As such, they provide a magnification of the percentage gain or loss for the investor, compared to what would have been achieved with a direct purchase of the common stock.

Example: Assume that an investor can choose between buying a stock outright for $50 per share today and buying a call option for $8 per share with an exercise price of $50. If the stock price falls to $30, the call option would not be exercised, and the $8 price of the option would be a complete loss (–100%). If the investor had purchased the stock outright, the loss would be –40 percent [($30 – $50)/$50 = –40%]. Conversely, if the stock price rises to $80, the option could be exercised for a gain of $22. The option holder would receive a return of 275 percent [($30 – $8)/$8 = 275%], while the shareholder would earn a return of 60 percent [($80 – $50)/$50 = 60%].

In both the gain and the loss situations above, the percentage return on the option has a larger absolute value than that of the stock, meaning that the option is inherently and significantly more risky than the stock.

Financial Planning Issue

When are options appropriate for clients? Generally, there are three motivations for engaging in option trading. The first is purely speculative. If a client has a strong belief a particular stock will go up or down, a call or a put are effective ways to speculate on these price movements.

There are many variations of this speculative motivation. For example, suppose a client is expecting a cash windfall in the near future, but wants to buy a particular investment today. The client could buy call options at a fraction of the future purchase price, and then use the cash windfall to exercise the options (assuming the stock has gone up). Another possibility is the client wants to sell a stock, but for tax reasons (see chapter 13), needs to postpone the sale until next year. If the client is concerned the stock price might fall in the meantime, he or she can buy a put. More elaborate forms of speculation include straddles, strangles, and bullish and bearish spreads.

A second motivation is some sort of hedging activity. Covered call writing trades off incremental income with potential opportunity losses in price appreciation. Similarly, married puts provide an investor at times with a sense of insurance protection.

A third motivation is to arbitrage. Arbitrage occurs when one believes one or more options are mispriced relative to other options, and places orders in an attempt to profit from the mispricing. The mispricing belief may be based on a model such as the Black-Scholes or binomial option pricing models, or just on historical relationships between various prices.

PROFIT FUNCTIONS AND PAYOFF FUNCTIONS

Profit Functions and Payoff Functions for Single Positions

It is a lot easier to understand the risk exposure and the return potential of options if one can graph either the profit function or the payoff function for a particular position. The profit function shows the potential prices of the underlying asset on the expiration date (which range from zero to infinity) on the horizontal axis and the profit derived from a particular investment associated with each price on the vertical axis. The payoff function has the same horizontal axis (that is, the price of the underlying asset on the expiration date), but the vertical axis shows the payoff of the option position associated with each potential price. In formula notation:

Profit function: Profit = f (price of underlying asset on the expiration date),

and

Payoff function: Payoff = f (price of underlying asset on the expiration date).

For simplicity, both functions are usually on a per share basis, and transactions costs, dividends, and taxes are ignored. The difference between the two functions is that the profit function combines the initial cash flows of the investment (that is, the cost of the investment) with the payoffs, and the payoff function focuses only on the cash flows on the expiration date.

Payoff and Profit Functions for Being Long and Short Stock

Before looking at options, let's look at the profit and payoff functions for owning stock and holding a short position. When we are dealing with only stock, there is, of course, no expiration date, so let's substitute the term holding period for expiration date. For a long position (that is, purchasing stock), the payoff and profit functions are defined as follows:

Payoff function (long the stock) = PS

Profit function (long the stock) = PS − Purchase price

where PS = price of the stock on the expiration date

The payoff function, shown in figure 11-1a, will be a line emanating from the origin at a 45-degree angle. Simply put, the payoff for long a share of stock will be whatever the stock price is on the payoff date (that is, the end of the holding period).

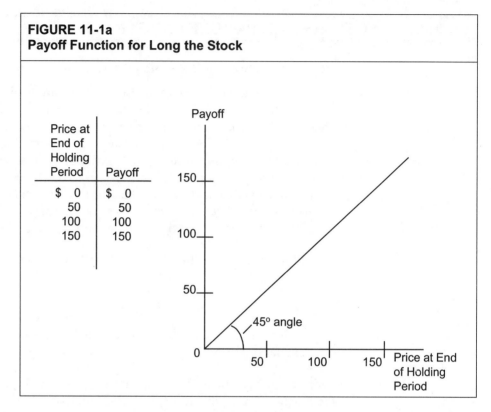

FIGURE 11-1a
Payoff Function for Long the Stock

Price at End of Holding Period	Payoff
$ 0	$ 0
50	50
100	100
150	150

Profit functions are usually a little trickier. Although anyone who works with options on a regular basis can visualize these graphs without effort, the rest of us usually require the identification of a few points on the function before we are able to "connect the dots." This is done by arbitrarily picking a few prices on the expiration date (or at the end of the holding period) and identifying the payoff or profit associated with that ending price. Let's consider an example.

Example: Assume that a stock's current price is $100. If the stock is purchased at this price, the profit or loss equals the change in the price. A market price of $105 equates to a profit of $5; a market price of $110 equates to a profit of $10. On the down side, a price of $95 equates to a loss of $5 and a price of $90 equates to a loss of $10. The break-even point is at $100—where the market price equals the purchase price. Figure 11-1b displays the profit function for this stock's purchase. Notice that, as with the payoff function, the slope of the line is still 45 degrees. The

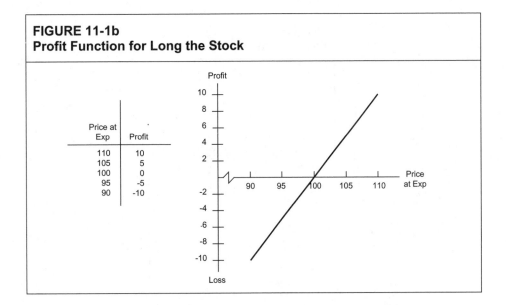

FIGURE 11-1b
Profit Function for Long the Stock

Price at Exp	Profit
110	10
105	5
100	0
95	-5
90	-10

only difference is that this function intersects the horizontal axis at the current price of the stock, and the payoff function intersects it at the origin.

Now let's consider the two functions for a person who is short a share of stock. The equations for the two functions are:

$$\text{Payoff function (short the stock)} = -\ PS$$

$$\text{Profit function (long the stock)} = \text{Sale price today} -\ PS$$

The graph for the payoff function, shown in figure 11-2a, will be a line emanating from the origin at a negative 45-degree angle. In other words, whatever is the price of the stock at the end of the holding period, the short seller must pay out that price to cover his or her short position. The graph for the profit function of someone who shorts a stock, shown in figure 11-2b, is similarly a negative 45-degree angle, but intersects the horizontal axis at the current price of the stock rather than at the origin.

Payoff and Profit Functions for Being Long a Call

Now let's look at the payoff and profit functions for someone who buys a call option (that is, goes long in a call). The payoff function for long a call is the intrinsic value on the expiration date. This can be stated as:

FIGURE 11-2a
Payoff Function for a Short Sale

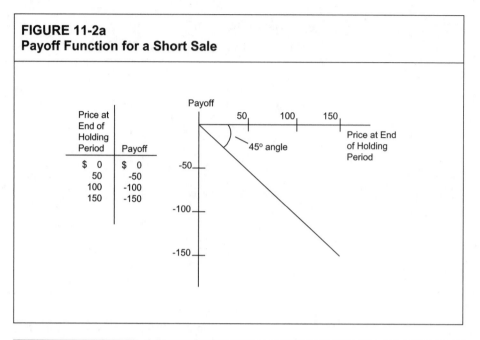

Price at End of Holding Period	Payoff
$ 0	$ 0
50	-50
100	-100
150	-150

FIGURE 11-2b
Profit Function for a Short Sale

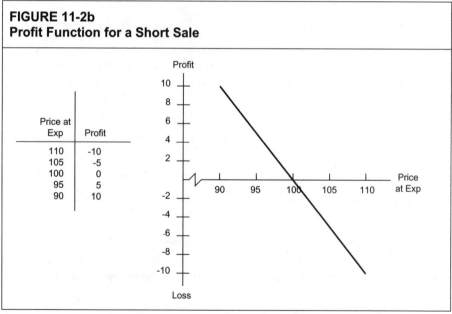

Price at Exp	Profit
110	-10
105	-5
100	0
95	5
90	10

$$\text{Payoff function (long a call)} = PS - X \qquad \text{if } PS > X$$
$$= 0 \qquad \text{if } X > PS$$

Figure 11-3a shows this payoff function for a call option with a strike price of $100.

FIGURE 11-3a
Payoff Function for Long a Call with a Strike Price of $100

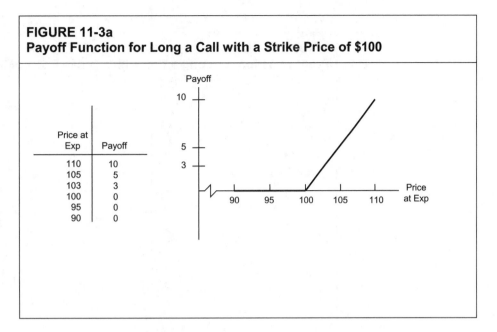

Price at Exp	Payoff
110	10
105	5
103	3
100	0
95	0
90	0

The formula for the profit function is:

$$\text{Profit function (long a call)} = PS - X - C \qquad \text{if } PS > X$$
$$= -C \qquad \text{if } X > PS$$

where C = the price of the call option

Consider the following example:

Example: The premium for a call option with a strike price of $100 for TK stock trades at a $3 per share. The current price of the stock does not matter. If the price of the stock is $100 or less at expiration, the option expires worthless because there is no benefit to the call owner to exercise the call, buying stock for $100 that is readily available in the market at that price or less. Since the premium was $3, the call owner has lost $3. Thus, the maximum loss is the call premium, and the horizontal portion of the function in figure 11-3b shows this. If the price at expiration is between $100 and $103, then the option will equal its intrinsic value, although this value will be less than $3. So the buyer of the option incurs a loss on the holding, but this loss is lessened by the intrinsic value of the option on the expiration date. If the stock closes at exactly $103 on the expiration date, the option holder

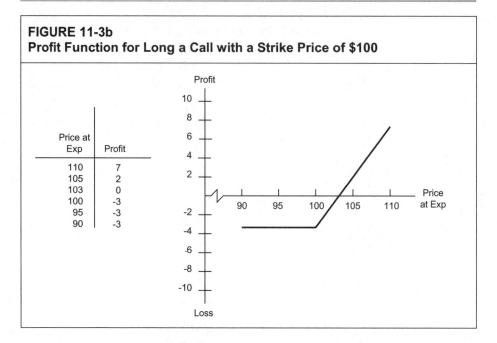

FIGURE 11-3b
Profit Function for Long a Call with a Strike Price of $100

Price at Exp	Profit
110	7
105	2
103	0
100	-3
95	-3
90	-3

would break even as he or she could exercise the option for $100 and sell the stock for $103, for a gain of $3. This would exactly offset the $3 premium paid for the option. If the stock price closes at any price above $103, the profit is then the intrinsic value of the option less the premium paid. For example, if it closes at $105, the profit is $2 ($105 – $100 – $3). If the price increases to $110, the profit is $7 ($110 – $100 – $3). Notice in figure 11-3b that the profit function is a 45-degree angle in the right-hand section of the graph—a dollar increase in price leads to a dollar increase in profit. The amount of profit is theoretically unlimited.

Why would someone buy a call option? The simple answer can be stated as a description of the profit (or payoff) function. The owner of a call option has a security that provides unlimited potential gain (because there is no upper limit on the stock price), and limited loss (the maximum loss is the premium). Unlimited potential gain and limited loss does sound attractive! The only drawback is that the limited loss is 100 percent of the initial investment. Many options expire worthless. An analogy would be the purchase of a lottery ticket. If you pay $1 to buy a lottery ticket, you have a limited loss ($1), and what usually sounds like an almost unlimited gain (big ticket winners get checks of 7 digits or more).

Another way to look at a call option is that it is a convenient way to speculate on the future price of the underlying asset. For example, if a client believes that some major announcement is about to occur for a company that will cause the price of the stock to jump dramatically, a larger percentage gain can be made in the call option than by buying the stock directly.

Profit Function for Being Short a Call

We mentioned above that the person who sells a call option not previously owned is known as a writer. The exact description of a writer depends on whether or not the writer owns the underlying security at the time of writing. If he or she owns the underlying security, he or she is referred to as a *covered writer*, and the position is known as a covered call. If the writer does not own the underlying stock, he or she is referred to as a *naked writer*, and the position is known as a naked call. It is certainly possibly for someone to be a naked writer and then later buy the underlying stock to change the position to a covered call. Similarly, a covered writer may sell the underlying shares while still being short the call, thus converting the position to a naked call (provided his or her account qualifies for holding naked calls).

covered writer

naked writer

Let's consider the profit function for a naked call writer. (The reader should now have a good concept of the payoff function and its relationship to the profit function, so continued discussion of both would seem redundant.) The mathematical notation for this function is:

$$\text{Profit function (naked call)} = C \qquad \text{if } X \geq PS$$

$$= (X - PS) + C \qquad \text{if } PS > X$$

Let's consider an intuitive interpretation of the above equations. Remember, a naked writer is taking on a risk exposure. This person is guaranteeing to sell the stock to the option buyer at the strike price, no matter how high the price might go, and the writer has no protection. If the stock price ends up less than the strike price, the naked writer has pocketed the premium, essentially as a windfall gain. However, if the stock price ends up greater than the strike price, then the writer will either have to buy the option back or buy the stock in the market and deliver it to the holder of the call. If the writer buys back the option, he or she will pay the intrinsic value on the expiration date (that is, $PS - X$). If the writer has to buy the stock in the market and sell it under the option, then he or she will sustain a loss equal to $PS - X$. The profit function of the naked writer, shown in figure 11-4, will thus be a flat line representing the premium income if the stock prices ends up between 0 and the strike price. From that point on, the profit function turns down at a 45-degree angle, representing the fact that the writer loses one dollar for each one-dollar increase in stock price.

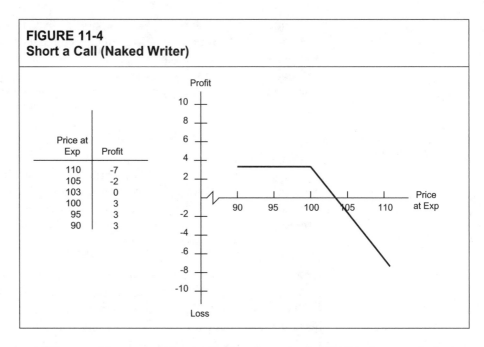

FIGURE 11-4
Short a Call (Naked Writer)

Price at Exp	Profit
110	-7
105	-2
103	0
100	3
95	3
90	3

Why would someone be a naked writer of a call? This is a particularly good question when it is pointed out that the graph shows that the profits on a naked call are limited, but the potential loss is unlimited. That is, the maximum profit is the premium income. But as the upside potential of a stock's price is unlimited, the potential loss to the writer is unlimited. Clearly, a naked writer is someone who strongly believes that the price of the underlying stock will drop, or at worst will not rise.

Long a Call and Naked Writer as Mirror Images

It is extremely important that the reader note the relationship between figures 11-3b and 11-4. If one rotates one of the figures around the X-axis, one will obtain the other figure. The reason this is the case is that a call buyer and a naked writer essentially have a bet with each other about the ultimate price of the stock, and no other parties are involved. Thus, what one gains on the transaction, the other loses, and vice-versa. The economic term for this process is that it is known as a *zero-sum game*. (It's a negative-sum game when transaction costs are considered.) Stated another way, the sum of the two profit functions is always zero.

zero-sum game

Example: Is it appropriate for your clients to buy call options or to engage in naked writing? It depends on the objectives and risk tolerance of your client. Really aggressive clients with a high tolerance for risk could reasonably look to be long on *some* call options. However, even these clients should not have an undue investment in these instruments. A sudden downturn in the markets could cause most options to become worthless, thus wiping out most if not all of that part of the client's portfolio. For conservative clients, going long on calls is incredibly inappropriate.

Similarly, although some people see naked writing as a chance to enhance the income to a portfolio (when the options expire worthless), every now and then there is a large jump in stock prices and naked writers could get severely burned. Neither aggressive nor conservative clients should engage in naked writing.

Profit Function for Long a Put and Short a Put

Now let's consider the profit function for purchasing a put option (that is, long a put), shown in figure 11-5. The formula for this function is:

$$
\begin{aligned}
\text{Profit function (long a put)} \quad &= X - PS - P && \text{if } X \geq PS \\
&= -P && \text{if } PS > X
\end{aligned}
$$

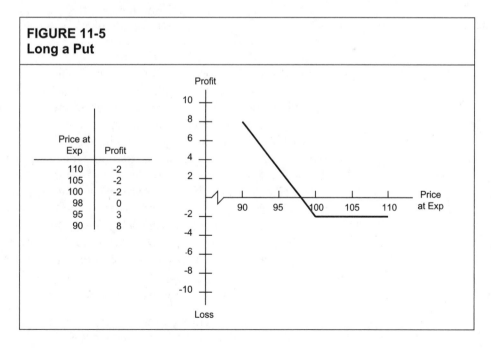

FIGURE 11-5
Long a Put

Price at Exp	Profit
110	-2
105	-2
100	-2
98	0
95	3
90	8

Example: Suppose an investor buys a put option with a strike price of $100 and pays a premium of $2. If the price of the underlying stock is $100 at expiration, the option expires worthless because there is no benefit to the put owner to sell stock for $100 if the put owner would have to pay $100 to obtain the stock intended for the sale. Since the premium was $2, the put owner has lost $2. Indeed, if the stock price rises, it makes no sense for the put owner to exercise the option because doing so is unprofitable. Why would the put owner force someone to buy stock for $100 if the same shares could be sold in the market at, for example, $108? Thus the maximum loss on the put purchase is the put premium of $2, as represented by the horizontal part of the profit function.

If the price falls to $98, the put owner can buy the stock in the market for $98, and force the put writer to buy it from him or her for $100, for a $2 gain. However, the $2 gain is exactly offset by the $2 option premium, so $98 is the break-even point. A market price of $95 equates to profit of $3 ($100 – $95 – $2). A market price of $90 equates to a profit of $8 ($100 – $90 – $2). For every dollar that the market value falls below $98, the profit function increases by a dollar, as indicated by the diagonal part of the function shown in figure 11-5.

Why would anyone want to buy a put? The characteristics of long a put are that it has limited loss (limited to the premium) and large potential gain. As with the position of long a call, there is a bit of an analogy here to buying a lottery ticket. The buyer of a put must strongly believe there is a significant chance of a decline in the price of the underlying stock. We mentioned in chapter 2 that one way to profit from an expected price decline in a stock is to sell the stock short. The problem with selling short is that one's loss was potentially unlimited if one is wrong (see figure 11-2b). Thus, for anyone who is betting on the underlying assets, buying puts may be a less risky way to try to make money on an expected price decline.

What happens to the put writer (that is, the person who is short a put)? Again because of the zero-sum nature of options, the writer of the put option has the opposite profit function to the put purchaser's function, as shown in figure 11-6. The equation for the function is:

$$\text{Profit function (writing a put)} = + P \qquad\qquad \text{if } PS \geq X$$
$$= PS - X + P \qquad\qquad \text{if } X > PS$$

The holder of a put option with a strike price of $100 can force the put writer to buy the stock for $100—whether the actual value is $99 or $2. Figure 11-6 shows the profit function for a writer of a put with a strike price of $100 and a premium of $2. At $98, the put writer loses $2 on the stock transaction, exactly offsetting the put premium received. At $95, the put writer must allow the put purchaser to put the stock into the writer's portfolio for $100, for a net loss of $3 ($95 − $100 + $2). For every additional dollar of market price decline, the loss increases by one dollar, as represented by the diagonal line in figure 11-6. If the market price of the stock rises, the put purchaser will not "put" the stock to the put writer at the strike price, because he or she would incur a loss in doing so. Thus, if the stock price rises, the put writer receives the maximum profit of $2.

Why would someone want to write a put? Since the essence of writing a put is that one can have only limited profit (limited to the premium) and almost unlimited loss (the maximum loss is if the stock price goes to zero), the concept of writing a put sounds rather bizarre. Clearly, the writer of a put has a strong belief that the price of the underlying asset will go up. If this were the case, the writer would likely be better off buying a call option.

Profit Functions for Combination Positions

Heretofore, we have discussed the profit functions for six different holdings: long stock, short stock, long a call, short a call, long a put, and short a put. When people trade options, it is much more likely that they will establish combination positions. A *combination position* is any position in

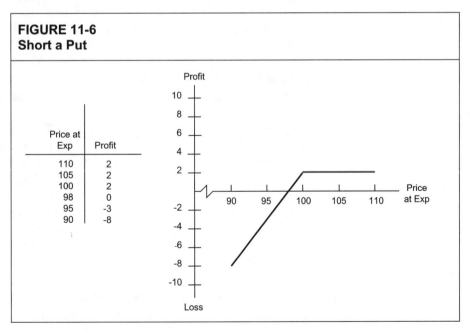

FIGURE 11-6
Short a Put

Price at Exp	Profit
110	2
105	2
100	2
98	0
95	-3
90	-8

Financial Planning Issue

Should a financial planner have a client buy puts or write puts? As was the case with calls, a limited program of the purchase of puts may be appropriate for aggressive investors with a good capacity for handling risk. For conservative investors, the purchase of puts is totally inappropriate. Similarly, the writing of puts is sometimes seen as a way to generate incremental income (from the premiums) for investors, but sooner or later, a big price drop in an underlying asset will occur, generating a substantial loss for the investor. Hence, the incremental income is probably not worth the risk.

---

which more than a single put, single call, or single position in the underlying stock is held. Combination positions can create much more interesting strategies for investors.

Profit Function for a Covered Call Writer

What is probably the most common example of a combination position is that of the covered writer. A covered writer owns the stock (or simultaneously buys it) on which he or she writes a call option. The profit function for a combination position is simply the sum of the profit functions for the two positions separately. In this case, we would combine the profit function for owning stock with the profit function for writing a call.

To illustrate how this is done, lets assume a stock trades for $100, a call option on the stock has a strike price of $100, and the call's premium is $3. Based on these numbers, the combined profit structure will look like figure 11-7. As an example of how to plot a particular point on the graph, suppose the stock price closes at $105. The profit on the stock is $5, as the writer either owned at the time of writing or bought the stock for $100 and it appreciated $5 during the life of the option. Unfortunately, the writer will either have to buy back the call option, or deliver the stock. If he or she buys back the call option at that time, its price will be the intrinsic value. Hence, the price to repurchase the option is $5. This is offset by the original premium of $3. So there is a net loss on the option of $2. When this loss of $2 on the option is combined with the $5 profit on the stock, the net gain is $3. If the writer delivers his or her own stock, then the profit on the stock is zero as he or she sells stock for $100 that was originally worth $100 and the profit on the option is the premium income of $3, hence the net profit is $3.

Notice that the upside potential of owning the stock is cut off because of selling the call. On the other hand, if the stock price falls, one is better off by the amount of the premium received than if one simply retained the stock without selling the call.

For example, if you bought the stock at $100 and it closes at $95, you have a $5 per share loss. However, if you write the covered call for a $3 premium, your loss if the stock closes at $95 is only $2, as you have the profit of the $2 in premium to offset the $5 loss on the stock.

Who would want to be a covered call writer? Notice that the profit function for a covered call writer (figure 11-7) has the identical *shape* as the profit function for writing a put. Thus, the position can be characterized as one offering limited gain and nearly unlimited loss (the maximum loss is if the stock goes to zero). Thus, it would appear that only someone who is bullish on the stock should establish it.

There are some other ways of viewing covered call writing. Suppose a client were considering selling a stock anyway. Then writing an in-the-money call option might be a way to generate a slightly higher price for the stock than selling it outright. Another issue might be that a client needs to sell a particular stock, but for tax reasons (taxes will be discussed in chapter 13) the client needs to have the sale be assigned to next year rather than the current year. In this case, a deep-in-the-money call option would normally allow the investor to postpone the sale of the stock until the expiration of the call option.

Profit Function for a Married Put

A married put is a put acquired on the same day the investor acquires the corresponding number of shares of the underlying stock, although this description would likely still apply even if one already owned the underlying stock. As with the covered call option, we can plot the profit function for a

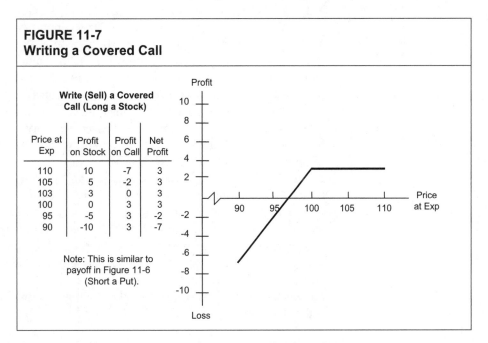

FIGURE 11-7
Writing a Covered Call

Write (Sell) a Covered
Call (Long a Stock)

Price at Exp	Profit on Stock	Profit on Call	Net Profit
110	10	-7	3
105	5	-2	3
103	3	0	3
100	0	3	3
95	-5	3	-2
90	-10	3	-7

Note: This is similar to payoff in Figure 11-6 (Short a Put).

Financial Planning Issue

Should clients be encouraged to write covered call options? There may be some situations where this is an appropriate strategy. Many financial planners see covered call writing as a way to generate extra income for the client. If the alternative to a covered call position is to be long the stock, then the covered call position clearly provides extra income. The only risk from a covered call position compared to long the stock is an opportunity cost. Suppose in the above example (figure 11-7), the underlying stock were to double to $200 after the call was written. Without the call, the client would have doubled his or her money. With the covered call in place, the client will still receive only the limited gain of $3 per share. The benefit here is that when the planner presents the portfolio returns to the client, he or she will still show a profit. Opportunity losses are never shown on any financial statements. So, with a covered call position, if the stock goes down the client is always better off than he or she would have been without the covered calls, and if the stock goes up, the client will see that he or she has made money.

The real issue is whether a consistent program of covered call writing outperforms or underperforms the portfolio that consists of only the underlying stocks. The research on this point has rather mixed results, so there is no clear-cut answer.

---

married put by combining the function for owning the stock with the function for buying a put. Again, assuming a stock price of $100, a put strike price of $100, and a put premium of $2, the profit function will look like figure 11-8. Note that a married put (figure 11-8) profit function has the exact same *shape* as the profit function for long a call (figure 11-3b).

Who should buy married puts? Married puts should be analyzed as an alternative to being long the stock. Many people see the purchase of puts as analogous to buying insurance protection against a price decline. This is not a bad analogy. The real issue is if one made the purchase of puts (insurance premiums) a regular part of one's portfolio over a long period of time, then would the premiums paid for this insurance be worth the safety provided? It may well be that over long periods of time for a diversified portfolio that the losses sustained from price declines would work out to be less than the sum of premiums paid for this insurance protection.

It should now be apparent that for any option position that could be established, the opposite position could just as easily be established by going short wherever one had gone long, and going long wherever one had gone short. Thus, an investor could just as easily take the opposite side of a married put by going short the stock and short the put. The profit function would then be the mirror image of a married put, rotated around the x-axis. It is the same shape as that for being short a call. Thus, being short a married put means one has limited gain (if the stock goes down), and unlimited losses if the stock goes up.

FIGURE 11-8
Buying a Married Put

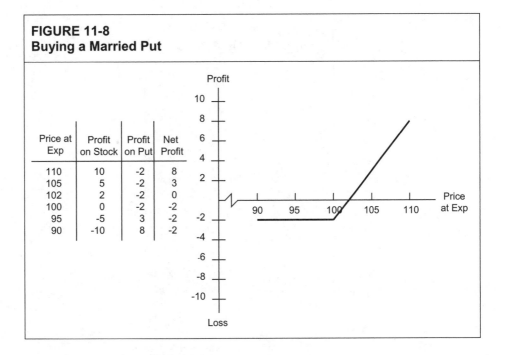

Price at Exp	Profit on Stock	Profit on Put	Net Profit
110	10	-2	8
105	5	-2	3
102	2	-2	0
100	0	-2	-2
95	-5	3	-2
90	-10	8	-2

Profit Function for a Straddle

One of the most popular combinations of options is called the straddle. In a straddle, the investor simultaneously buys or sells a call option and a put option with the same underlying asset, same exercise price, and same expiration date. The purchase of both options is called going long a straddle. To generate the profit function for a long straddle position, we merely combine the profit functions of the call and put that make up the straddle.

Continuing the previous examples, consider a stock for which a call has a strike price of 100 and a premium of $3, and a put with the same expiration date and strike price trades for $2. Going long a straddle—buying both the call and the put—will generate the profit function shown in figure 11-9. It is shaped like a large letter V. It has limited loss (the sum of the two premiums, which is $5 in this case), almost unlimited gain on the downside (if the stock goes to zero), and unlimited gain on the upside. Note that the breakeven points (that is, where the profit function intercepts the horizontal axis) of $95 and $105 equal the exercise price plus or minus the sum of the two premiums.

As the graph shows, with a long straddle, the investor loses if the underlying asset price ends up near the exercise price of the two options but gains if the underlying asset price is highly volatile (makes a big jump one way or the other). Investors frequently use this strategy to profit when they

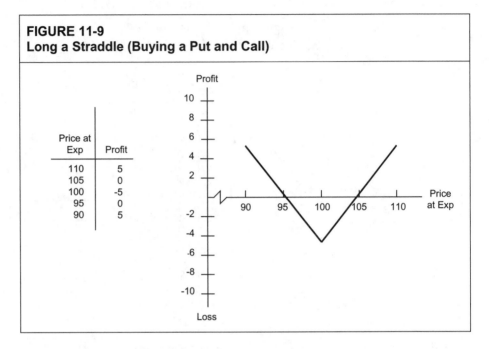

FIGURE 11-9
Long a Straddle (Buying a Put and Call)

Price at Exp	Profit
110	5
105	0
100	-5
95	0
90	5

expect unusual volatility in a particular stock. For example, suppose a company's stock were getting bid up because of speculation that it is a takeover target. If the takeover happens, the purchase price will exceed the current stock price. If it does not, the stock price will fall back to its prior level. Thus, one can speculate on this by going long a straddle. However, in such a case, one will usually find that the prices of both the puts and calls have already both increased as other investors have hit upon the same strategy!

Naturally, one can just as easily short a straddle. As may be anticipated from previous examples, it is a mirror image of going long a straddle and is shaped like an inverted letter V. Figure 11-10 demonstrates graphically that the straddle writer benefits if the stock stays in a narrow trading range, but loses if the stock moves significantly in either direction. The maximum gain occurs if the stock closes on the expiration date at exactly the exercise price (and thus both options are worthless). In our example, this gain is $5. The breakeven points are still the exercise price plus or minus the sum of the premiums, or $95 and $105.

Profit Function for a Strangle

A strangle is similar to a straddle, except that the options have different strike prices.[1] Specifically, the strike price of the call option is above the strike price for the put option. A profit function for long a strangle, where the call option has a strike price of $105 and a premium of $2 and the put option

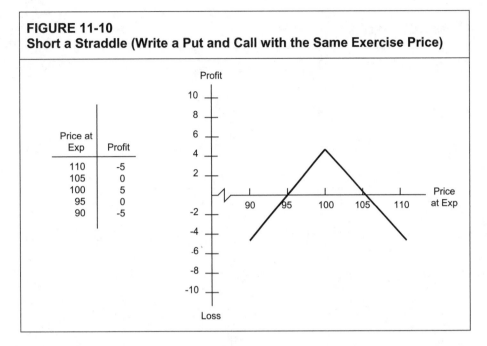

FIGURE 11-10
Short a Straddle (Write a Put and Call with the Same Exercise Price)

Price at Exp	Profit
110	-5
105	0
100	5
95	0
90	-5

has a strike price of $100 and a premium of $1, is shown in figure 11-11. The shape is somewhat like a cereal bowl. It has the advantage over the long straddle that the maximum loss is less. In this case, the maximum loss is $3, compared to $5 in our long straddle example. But the breakeven points are now wider, they are now $108 (the call exercise price plus the cost of both premiums) and $97 (the put exercise price less the cost of both premiums). As with long a straddle, long a strangle has limited losses and almost unlimited gain (if the stock price goes to zero). Naturally, one can go short a strangle by writing rather than buying the same two options. This short position has limited gain and large or unlimited potential losses.

Profit Function for a Bullish Call Spread

There is yet another entire class of strategies that can be pursued with options. These are known as spreads. In a spread, one option is purchased and the other is sold, with each option having a different exercise price or a different expiration date. Spreads can be constructed with either two puts or two calls. Let's look at the profit function of a bullish call spread that involves two call options with different striking prices.[2]

Suppose a call is available with a strike price of $100 and a premium of $3. Another call is available with the same underlying stock, the same expiration date, a strike price of $110, and a premium of $1. A bullish call

FIGURE 11-11
Long a Strangle (Long a Put with a $100 Strike Price and Long a Call with a $105 Strike Price)

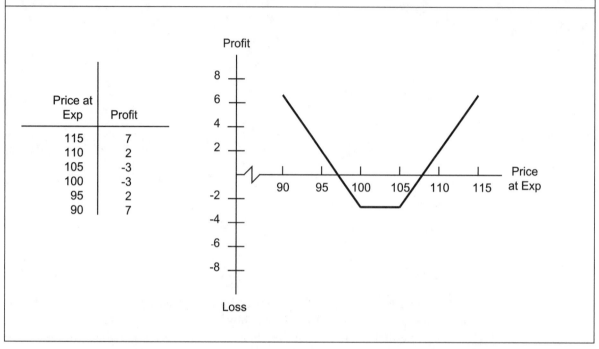

Price at Exp	Profit
115	7
110	2
105	-3
100	-3
95	2
90	7

spread would involve a long position in the option with the lower strike price, and a short position in the option with the higher strike price. To think about the graph, let's start by considering the profit at two key points: $100 and $110. If the underlying stock closes at $100 on the expiration date, the investor's own option is worthless, and the option he or she sold would also be worthless. The investor paid $3 for the first option, and sold the second for $1, so there is a loss of $2. In fact, if the stock price ends up at anything less than $100, the same discussion would apply, and the net loss would be the same, minus $2.

Financial Planning Issue

Should a financial planner recommend straddles and/or spreads to his or her clients? For more aggressive clients who are willing to take double or nothing type bets, going long on straddles and strangles would seem reasonable. In fact, they are better than the racetrack because at least the losses are tax deductible (see chapter 13 for a discussion of taxes). Although one might look at the short side of these positions as an opportunity to generate extra income, especially for conservative, income-oriented investors, the potential risk of loss is so great that taking short positions in either strategy would seem inappropriate for almost any type of client.

If the stock closes at $110, the investor can sell his option at its intrinsic value of $10 (or exercise the option, buy the stock for $100 and sell it to the option writer for $110). However, he or she will not have to worry about honoring his shorted call, as there is no intrinsic value to it at this time. The net profit at this price is the net gain on the option bought of $7 (the $10 intrinsic value less the $3 purchase price), plus the $1 premium for the option sold that is now worthless, or a total of $8. For any closing price above $110, the incremental profit on the long call will exactly be offset by a loss on the short call, leaving a net profit of $8. For closing prices between $100 and $110, the profit will range from minus $2 to a profit of $8. The breakeven point will be $102. These points are all shown in figure 11-12.

Why would an investor go long a bullish spread? This strategy is used by the same investors who would use a regular call option but prefer not to pay for the unlimited potential profits of the call option with the $100 strike price. In other words, although the upside potential of the bullish spread is less, the cost of creating the position (which is also the maximum loss) is also less. By itself, the call option costs $3, while the bullish spread costs only $2. The break-even point occurs where the underlying asset price is equal to the lower exercise price plus the difference in premiums between the two options. As with the purchase of an individual call, the downside risk is limited.

Alternatively, the investor who would like to purchase a put option but does not want to pay for the high profit potential of the put option may create a *bearish spread*. The bearish spread can also be constructed with two puts or two calls. The version with two calls can be constructed by buying a call with

bearish spread

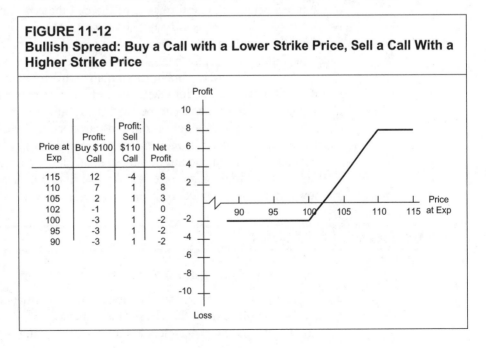

FIGURE 11-12
Bullish Spread: Buy a Call with a Lower Strike Price, Sell a Call With a Higher Strike Price

Price at Exp	Profit: Buy $100 Call	Profit: Sell $110 Call	Net Profit
115	12	-4	8
110	7	1	8
105	2	1	3
102	-1	1	0
100	-3	1	-2
95	-3	1	-2
90	-3	1	-2

a higher strike price and selling a call on the same underlying asset and with the same expiration date, but with a lower strike price. This is simply the opposite side of the bullish spread construction.

As an example, let's say that there is another call option with a strike price of $90 and a premium of $11. Since this call is in the money, it will have value at expiration unless the stock price falls to $90 or less. However, the intrinsic value now is only $10. (The $11 premium also reflects the time value of the option—the fact that there is still time left before expiration for the stock price to rise.) Selling this call brings in $11. To lose money from writing this call, the stock price at expiration will have to be above $101, which would mean an intrinsic value at expiration of $11. For every dollar that the stock price rises above $101, the investor loses a dollar. If the stock falls below $90, the option will expire worthless, and the investor will gain $11—the income from sale of the call. In the range from $90 to $101, the potential $11 profit declines one dollar for every dollar that the stock price rises above $90.

Now, let's complete the bearish spread by buying the call from earlier examples with the $100 strike price and the $3 premium. We have already discussed its profit function. Again, we combine the two profit functions to see the total effect. If the stock price at expiration is below $90, the profit is the difference between what was received for the call the investor sold and what was paid for the call the investor bought—$8 ($11 – $3). The net profit declines by one dollar for every dollar of stock price increase between $90 and $100. As the stock price at expiration rises above $100, every dollar of improvement in the performance of the call that was purchased is offset by a dollar of loss in the performance of the call that was sold. The graphical depiction of the profit function for a bearish spread appears in figure 11-13. Similar to the bullish spread, the bearish spread is cheaper than a related put option.

There are a large number of combinations involving options that produce all sorts of profit functions with all sorts of risk exposures and return opportunities. An entire book can be (and many are) devoted to option strategies. However, our purpose here is only to introduce the reader to option strategies and the appropriate techniques (profit function or payoff function) by which one can understand and analyze these strategies. So far, we have focused only on looking at trading strategies that can be implemented with options. We will now turn to a related question: How does one value an option?

VALUATION OF OPTIONS

Valuation of an Option: Black-Scholes Model

The valuation of options has long intrigued financial theorists. F. Black and M. Scholes wrote the classic theoretical option pricing work,[3] which is now known as the Black-Scholes model. Black and Scholes began with the

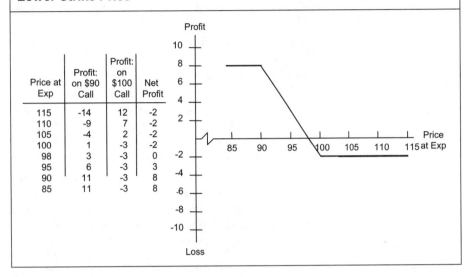

FIGURE 11-13
Bearish Spread: Buy a Call with a Higher Strike Price, Sell a Call with a Lower Strike Price

Price at Exp	Profit: on $90 Call	Profit: on $100 Call	Net Profit
115	-14	12	-2
110	-9	7	-2
105	-4	2	-2
100	1	-3	-2
98	3	-3	0
95	6	-3	3
90	11	-3	8
85	11	-3	8

assumption that investors could buy the underlying non dividend-paying stock and write (sell) calls to maintain a riskless hedge. In this case, a riskless hedge position is defined as one in which an investor would neither make nor lose money. For stock price increases, writing calls is similar to short-selling the stock. Thus, one could identify a hedge in which any change in the value of the stock's price would be offset by an equivalent but opposite change in the value of the short position in calls.

Example: Suppose that a $1 change in the stock price was known to cause a $.50 change in the call price. Investors could then construct a fully hedged position by writing calls on twice as many shares as are held. If the investor is short two calls, a $1 increase in the stock price would be matched by a $1 decrease in the value of the call position. Similarly, a $1 decrease in the stock's price would be offset by a $1 increase in the value of the call position. In fact, any small move in the stock price would be precisely offset by a change in the value of the option position.

hedge ratio

In the above example, the ratio of the change in stock price to the associated change in option price is defined as a *hedge ratio*. As time passes and stock and call options prices change, the appropriate ratio for hedging will vary. For example, the hedge ratio of two calls to one share of stock might later change to a ratio of three calls to one share of stock. The investor can maintain a fully hedged position by adjusting the ratio of shares to calls whenever necessary. Thus, if the required ratio changes from two calls per share to three calls per share, the hedger can write (sell) an additional call for each share held. The result of this process is called a *riskless hedge*—designed to insulate the investor from market moves in the underlying stock's price. Selling the calls provides a form of insurance against the contingency of market changes in the price of the stock.

In an efficient market, an investment in the combined riskless position should earn the riskless interest rate (approximately the rate on T-bills). Using a model based on the assumptions stated earlier, Black and Scholes developed a mathematical call valuation formula that is a function of five variables. The precise form of the model, shown in appendix 11-A, is rather complex, but the most important results are as follows: Call values *increase* with increases in: time to maturity, interest rates, the price of the underlying stock, and volatility (or variance) of the underlying stock; they *decrease* as the strike price increases.

Five Variables in the Black-Scholes Model

- Time to maturity: the longer the time to maturity, the more valuable the call
- Interest rate: the higher the interest rate, the more valuable the call
- Price of underlying stock: the higher the stock price, the more valuable the call
- Volatility: the more volatile the price of the underlying stock, the more valuable the call
- Strike price: the higher the strike price, the less valuable the call

---

The Black-Scholes formula is more than just an interesting theoretical exercise. Option traders often compute Black-Scholes prices to follow a strategy of buying undervalued options (vis-à-vis the model) and writing overvalued ones. The importance of Black-Scholes and its later extensions, therefore, cannot be overstated. It gave investors confidence in fair values for options.

Example: At the start of this chapter, we noted that options had value based on both intrinsic value (as identified in payoff functions) and speculative value (as identified in the Black-Scholes model). The example at the time was that a stock trades at $50 per share, and has an equally likely chance of going to $60 per share or dropping to $40 per share. Although the expected price of the stock was $50 and the expected rate of return was 0 percent, the option had value. Let's expand upon that example by assuming that on the option's expiration date, the price of the stock would either be $70 or $30. The expected price of the stock on the expiration date and the expected rate of return are unchanged, yet the expected intrinsic value of the option on the expiration is now $10. Clearly, increases in the variability of a stock's price will increase the value of the option, even if the expected rate of return of the stock is unaffected.

Binomial Option Pricing Model

There is an alternative to the Black-Scholes option-pricing model, and it is known as the binomial option-pricing model. When the model is used in a realistic manner, it is extremely mathematically complex. Therefore, we will content ourselves with a relatively simple, if unrealistic, presentation of the model so that the reader can understand the basic ideas of the model.

It starts with the same type of scenario we used for our intrinsic value presentation. Let's assume a stock currently trades at $50, and that at the end of the year it will have a value of either $60 or $40. Let's now value a call option with a strike price of $50. To do so, we need an interest rate at which the investor could borrow money today. Let's assume a 10-percent interest rate and that there are no initial margin requirements.

Now, in one year the intrinsic value of the call option will be either $10 or zero, and the value of the stock will be either $40 or $60. Let's assume that an individual can borrow just enough money to buy one share of stock so that in the worst-case scenario the price of the stock is the exact amount needed to pay back the loan with interest. As the worst-case price is $40, and as the interest rate is 10 percent, taking the present value of $40 discounted at 10 percent for one year indicates the investor would borrow $36.36 ($40/(1+.10)). As the stock is trading at a price of $50, the individual would have to put up the difference between the price and the loan amount of $13.64 ($50 − $36.36).

The purchase of stock with borrowed money will result in a value one year from now of either $20 (if the stock goes to $60 and the loan is repaid with interest), or $0 (if the stock goes to $40 and the loan repaid with interest). Note that this is exactly double what the payoff of the option would be (that is, $10 if the stock ends up at $60 and $0 if the stock ends up at $40). Hence, the investor should be able to buy two calls (because the stock payoffs are two times the call option payoffs) for the same out-of-pocket cost of buying one share of stock. The share of stock costs $13.64. Hence, dividing this by two (because there are two options), means each option should be worth $6.82 ($13.64/2).

Example: Consider a similar scenario. Suppose the stock trades for $100 today, and the only two possible prices a year from now are $125 and $80. Further assume an interest rate of 8 percent with no restriction on initial margin requirements. What is the value of an option with a striking price of $100?

Answer: The option payoffs are $25 or $0. To replicate the $0 payoff for the option, let's assume just enough can be borrowed so that in the worst-case scenario, the sale of the stock just pays off the loan with interest. At an 8-percent interest rate, this means a loan of $74.07 ($80/(1 + .08). Hence, one share of stock could be bought for only $25.93 of out-of-pocket cash ($100 - $74.07). The payoffs for the share of stock are $45 or $0. To equilibrate the payoffs, one would need to buy 1.8 call options. This is obtained by dividing $45 by $25. Thus, 1.8 call options must be worth $25.93. If this is the case, then one call option must be worth $14.41 ($25.93/1.8).

As with the Black-Scholes option-pricing model, the binomial option-pricing model provides certain insights into option valuation. Specifically, the five variables we identified as affecting the value of a call option in the Black-Scholes framework will have the exact same effect in a binomial option-pricing model. Specifically, call values *increase* with increases in these four variables: time to maturity, interest rates, the price of the underlying stock, and volatility (or variance) of the underlying stock; they *decrease* as the fifth variable—strike price—increases.

Put-Call Parity

The Black-Scholes and binomial option-pricing models provide insights into the pricing of call options. Unfortunately, they do not directly tell us how to price a put option. However, another concept has evolved along with the option-pricing models that allows valuation of put options. This concept is known as put-call parity.

The basic argument for put-call parity is simple. If there are two ways to create the same profit function, then the cost of creating them should differ by no more than a risk-free rate of return. This is because investors will buy the less expensive combination and sell the more expensive one until the value of doing so is no more than can be obtained by investing in a risk-free asset.[4]

When we discussed combinations of holdings in the previous section, we noted many instances where different combinations produced the same shaped profit function. For example, a call-like position was created from going long the stock and long a put. This combination is sometimes called a *manufactured* or *synthetic call*. Synthetic puts could also be created. The ability to create a profit function for a put in two different ways leads to the following formula:

manufactured (synthetic) call

$$C_0 = P_0 + S_0 - \frac{X}{e^{r_f t}}$$

where C_0 =   call value
P_0 =   put value
r_f =   risk-free rate
e =   2.718 (the natural logarithmic constant)
S_0 =   initial stock price
X =   strike price
t =   time to expiration of the option as a fraction of the year

The use of the value "e" for discounting is associated with continuous discounting, a concept we have not addressed herein. Thus, the put-call parity formula may be modified to discrete compounding with the following adjustment:

$$C_0 = P_0 + S_0 - \frac{X}{(1 + r_f)^t}$$

One can actually interpret the put-call formula by noting that it says that going long a call (the left-hand side of the equation) should be the same as going long a put, long the stock, and borrowing just enough cash to pay the exercise price at maturity (the right-hand side of the equation).

Example: Suppose a stock has a market price of $25, and both put and call options have a strike price of $24 and 6 months to expiration. The annual risk-free rate is 4 percent. If the put option has a price of $2, the price of the call can be determined as follows:

First, determine the discount factor for 6 months:

$(1 + .04)^{1/2} = 1.02$

Then plug this factor into the models

$C_0 = \$2 + \$25 - \$24/1.02 = \$3.47$

Traders normally prefer to buy puts or calls directly, but some people choose to manufacture puts from calls, or *vice versa*, when prices get out of line. Moreover, some brokerage firms try to profit from apparent price disparities by taking offsetting positions in the synthetic and actual puts and calls. This arbitrage activity tends to drive the prices back toward their proper parity.

OPTION MARKETS

Most put and call trading takes place on option exchanges. Unlisted puts and calls and less actively traded warrants and rights are traded over-the-counter. Before listed options appeared, all option trading was in the over-the-counter market. OTC options had expiration dates and strike prices that varied greatly. Secondary market trading in OTC options was haphazard. Virtually all option contract trading now takes place with listed puts and calls traded under rules of the Chicago-based Options Clearing Corporation (OCC). The OCC was founded in 1973, and is now equally owned by the five participant exchanges that trade options: American Stock Exchange, Chicago Board Options Exchange, International Securities Exchange, Pacific Exchange and the Philadelphia Stock Exchange.

The OCC acts as an intermediary between the two principals in every option trade. Each put and call buyer and seller is actually contracting with the OCC, rather than directly with the opposite party to the transaction; thus it is not necessary to seek out the person or entity with whom the a transaction was originally done. Thus, the writer of a call option who wants to liquidate his or her position does not need to go back to the original buyer in that trade to buy back the contract. The writer simply places an order to buy a call option with identical terms, and upon purchase, the OCC cancels the original writer from that contract. Because of the presence of the OCC, no option participant need ever worry about whether or not the other party in the trade will honor the terms of the contract. The OCC ensures the integrity of the traded option—if one party to the option transaction defaults on its position in the transaction, the OCC stands ready to fulfill the terms of the defaulted side of the option contract. The OCC management and guarantee-of-option contracts have dramatically improved the efficiency of the options market.

When listed option trading began in 1973, new option contracts were introduced every 3 months and had an initial maturity (time to expiration) of 9 months. Three sets of expiration dates were traded at any particular time. For example, a company might have options on a January cycle. Its options would be set to expire every 3 months, beginning with January, then in April, July, and October. When the nearest expiration month is January, the other listed options would be April and July. Once the January option expired, a new set of options would be listed for October. Other companies' options were set for February and March cycles.

Some companies' options still expire only every 3 months. Most companies with listed options, however, now have additional expiration times that fill in the 2 nearest months. Consider, for example, a company with a January basic cycle. In early January, there would be options expiring in January, April, and July. In addition, an option expiring for February would be listed.

Thus, most companies now have a total of four options expirations. Two are in the nearest 2 months; two more distant expirations occur at 3-month intervals. Listed options are set to expire on the Saturday following the third Friday of their month of expiration. The value of the options traded often exceeds the value of the stocks traded for the underlying shares.

Setting Strike Prices

Strike prices are initially set at levels that are divisible by 5 or 10 (or in some cases 2½) depending on the stock's market price. Thus, a stock trading at 43 would typically have options listed at 40 and 45. Similarly, a stock trading at 21 would have options listed at 20 and 22.50. If a stock price moves out of this range on either the up or down side, the listing exchange will add trading in options with additional strike prices. Thus, a stock might be trading at $20 per share, but have call options listed with strike prices all the way up to $75 or more. This would indicate that at one time this stock traded in the $75 range, but its price has since dropped.

Note that when there is a stock split, all contracts are automatically adjusted to incorporate the split. Thus, the announcement that a company was preparing to have a 2 for 1 split would not be cause to buy puts on the company's stock!

As a stock price moves away from the available strike prices, trading becomes less attractive in the out of the money or the deep in the money options. For example, a call with a strike of $30 on a stock selling for $50 will be priced too high to offer very much leverage. Similarly, a call with an $80 strike on a stock trading at $30 is a near certainty to expire worthless. Thus, these options have little speculative appeal because one side of the market or the other has few likely buyers or sellers. About the only trading that will take places in these circumstances is by investors who want to terminate their positions before the expiration date.

Example: Sally Jones has written five calls on AK Steel Corporation. The strike price of the options is $15, and the stock now trades at $30. It is a near-perfect certainty that the options will be exercised. Suppose Sally wants to sell her stocks today. If her account is not approved for naked writing, she cannot simply sell the shares. Hence, to sell the shares, she must first buy back the options (and take what is likely a large capital loss on the options). She is then free to sell her underlying shares.

American, European, and Bermuda Options

Options are distinguished by when they can be exercised. Options that may be exercised anytime up to the expiration date are called American options. Options that may be exercised only on the expiration date are called European options. All of the discussion in this chapter has focused on American options. Options that can be exercised on a multiple set of predetermined dates (the last being the expiration date) are called Bermuda options. The typical Bermuda option has an exercise period once per month.

Assuming no dividends or tax effects, it would not make sense to exercise an American or Bermuda option prior to their expiration dates. Before the expiration date, the option has more value when it is sold than when it is exercised. This must be true because exercising the option eliminates any time value that the option could have retained had it been sold instead. However, cash flows from the underlying asset and tax incentives may induce an investor to exercise early.

OPTIONS ON OTHER ASSETS

Virtually any standardized asset can be subject to the option writing and holding process, provided enough investors are interested in trading these instruments. Assets on which standardized options are written include the following:

- foreign currencies
- stock indexes
- industry indexes
- interest rates (Treasury securities)
- futures contracts

Discussions of stock index, industry index, and interest rate options follow. Futures contracts are covered in chapter 12.

Stock Index Options

Users of stock index options are able to buy or sell an entire stock market index, such as the S&P 500 (SPX) or the NASDAQ (NDX) stock exchange index, for the premium paid for the option. Instead of selecting either an index mutual fund (whose portfolio replicates a specific stock market index) or specific stocks (with which to go long if a prolonged market rise seems imminent), the investor "buys" the market by acquiring a call option on the index. Since the gain from the rise in the market is captured for a minimal outlay, the value of the option will rise with the increase in the index. Bearish investors, on the other hand, hold puts to profit from an expected decline in the market index.

As with stock options, standardized expiration dates and strike prices have been established for index options. Settlement between the writer and the holder takes place on the expiration date (that is, they are European options). Strike prices are written with 5-point increments on the underlying index. For example, if the SPX (the most popular of the indexes used for option trading) stands at 1141, put and call options at 1140 and 1150 and in ± 5- or 10-point increments from there could be written and traded. When the index rises to new highs or lows, options for new strike prices around those levels are written and traded—often for months to come. The options exchanges will trade index options at strike prices well beyond any recent levels of the indexes (even well above historical highs) as long as buyers and sellers can be matched.

Table 11-1 shows sample premium quotations for the SPX and NDX options from a typical financial page. The actual price of the contract is computed by multiplying the premium quotation by 100. For example, assume that the SPX stands at 1141 and the premium asked for a December call option with a strike price of 1150 on that specific index is $29. For an index option, the normal lot is 100 units. Therefore, the price for this call option is $2,900 ($29 x 100). Because the index is 1141, this call is currently out of the money and thus the intrinsic value is zero, but it has a time value of $2,900.

TABLE 11-1
Sample Chicago Mercantile Exchange Index Options Quotes

S&P 500 Index (SPX)			Close 1141	
	Calls		Puts	
Strike Price	Nov	Dec	Nov	Dec
1130	15.50	. . .	3.80	
1140	11	35.50	8.50	32
1150	4.10	29	12	36

NASDAQ-100 (NDX)			Close 3997	
	Calls		Puts	
Strike Price	Nov	Dec	Nov	Dec
1100	41	61	1	18.40
1175	.50	18	33.50	50

As with a company-specific naked call writer, writers of index options place margin deposits with their brokers for the period of the option or until the option position is closed out through purchasing an offsetting contract. Unlike the stock options in which settlement of exercised options includes the delivery of the common stocks to the call holder (or to the put writer), settlement for stock index options is made in dollars. The amount of money that will be paid on the settlement date depends on the difference between the exercise price and the closing value of the index on the expiration date. Multiplying this difference by $100 determines the amount that will be paid by the option writer if it is exercised.

Example:　　　Referring to the above table, suppose that on the above date a December call on the NDX with a strike price of $1100 is purchased at the closing price of $61. Suppose also that the index closes at 1175 on the expiration date—a difference of 75, or approximately 6.4 percent. In this case, the writer's obligation requires payment of $7,500 ([$1,175 – $1,100]) x 100) to the holder of the option. As the holder acquired the call at a price of $61 from the writer for a cost of $6,100 ($61 x 100), the buyer's gain is $1,400, and the holding period return is 23 percent ([75 – 61]/61) over one month. The writer, of course, loses $1,400.

A similar put option at a strike price of $1,100 would not be exercised because the index value in the example above exceeds $1,100. Holders of puts exercise their options only when the strike price exceeds the index value on the day the option expires. However, if the purchaser of the put had bought the put at the same time as the call buyer, the put purchaser would have paid $18.40 per put and would have lost it all (–100%).

Industry Index Options

Industry options work pretty much the same way as index options. There are at present a large number of industry index options. The semiconductor index option (SOX) probably has the most number of options and volume associated with it of any of the industry index options. Examples of other industry index options include pharmaceuticals, high tech (MS HITECH), and oil service.

Interest Rate Options

Puts and calls on specific U.S. Treasury securities are called interest rate options. Usually, these options are written for a relatively large dollar amount of a particular issue, such as $100,000. These options are based on the average yield of the most recently auctioned 7-, 10-, and 30-year U.S. Treasury bonds, and they are European style. One unique aspect of these options is that their duration is only one trading cycle of 3- and 6-month options. Once these expire, no new options can be written on the Treasury bonds on which these options are based. The rationale for this practice is that most of the bonds are in portfolios that are not actively traded. Sufficient secondary trading does not exist to justify a continuing market for these options.

LEAPS®

Long-term Equity Anticipation Securities (LEAPS®)

Puts and calls are normally written for relatively short periods (9 months is typically the longest available); however, a 1990 innovation in the options market called *Long-term Equity Anticipation Securities (LEAPS®)* with expiration dates as long as 3 years—and covering both calls and puts—was introduced on the CBOE and the AMEX. They are now traded on all the options exchanges. There are no differences in the terminology or strategy involved with LEAPS® and those of regular options, other than that LEAPS® can have a substantially longer time to expiration.

There are two types of LEAPS®, Equity LEAPS® and Index LEAPS®. All equity LEAPS® are American style, and expire in January of the designated year (actually the Saturday following the third Friday of the expiration month).

Index LEAPS® are long-term index options based either on a fractional value of one-tenth of the value of the underlying index or on the full value of the underlying index, depending on the value of the particular index. Like regular index options, Index LEAPS® are cash-settled based on the difference between the exercise settlement value of the index on the exercise date and the exercise price of the option. Some Index LEAPS® are American-style, but others are European-style options. Index LEAPS® expire in January, June, and December of each year.[5]

RIGHTS AND WARRANTS

Two securities that are quite similar to call options are rights and warrants. (Rights and warrants were discussed in detail in chapter 7.) Actively traded rights and warrants are generally listed on a stock exchange. The major difference between rights and warrants and call options is that call options do not involve the company itself, whereas rights and warrants have the company as the writer of the options. Thus, an investor who exercises his or her rights or warrants ends up acquiring newly issued shares of common stock from the company.

CONVERTIBLES

Convertible Bonds

Convertible bonds provide the option to the owner of exchanging the bonds for a fixed number of shares of common stock. The number of shares of common stock received is known as the exchange ratio or conversion ratio. In some situations, people will refer to a conversion price rather than an exchange ratio. The conversion ratio is par value divided by the conversion price. Alternatively, one could say that the conversion price is the par value divided by the conversion ratio.

$$\text{Conversion Ratio} = \frac{\text{PAR}}{\text{Conversion Price}}$$

When considering convertible bonds, an investor needs to be alert not only to the price of the bond itself, but also to the conversion value. Conversion value is the value of the common stock that would be received upon immediate conversion. It is simply the product of the conversion ratio and the price of the common stock.

At the time they are issued, the conversion value is less than par (which also means the market price of the stock is less than the conversion price). Like warrants, convertibles are analogous to out-of-the-money options at the time they are issued. Companies issue convertible bonds for much the same reasons they issue warrants: it allows them to pay a lower coupon rate on the bond, and it gives them the ability to issue new stock at a later date, provided the market price of the stock rises above the conversion price.

The difference between the market price of the convertible bond and the conversion value is known as the conversion premium. This number may be stated in absolute dollars, or as a percentage of the conversion value. With one rare exception, convertibles sell for more than their conversion value. This exception is if the price of the common stock has risen to such a high level that there is no real distinction between the convertible bond and the stock.

Example: A $1,000 par-value bond trades at $950 and has a conversion price of $20. If the underlying stock trades at $15, what are its conversion ratio and its conversion premium?

Answer: The conversion ratio is 50 (that is, $1,000/$20). The conversion value of the bond is 50 x $15 = $750. So the conversion premium in dollar terms is $200 ($950 – $750), and in percentage terms it is 26.7 percent ($200/$750).

---

straight-debt value

A third value associated with a convertible and the only one that is not directly observable is the *straight-debt value.* This is the investor's estimate of what the value of a convertible bond would be without the conversion feature. It requires ascertaining what the appropriate discount rate for the bond would be if it traded as straight debt.

Example: Suppose the convertible bond in the example above has a coupon rate of 12 percent and 5 years to maturity, and a straight bond of comparable risk trading at par pays a coupon rate of 13.5 percent. Using a discount rate of 13.5 percent and calculating the present value, we find that the straight-debt value of the convertible bond (assuming annual interest payments) is $947.88. The keystrokes are:

SHIFT, C ALL
1000, FV
120, PMT
13.5, I/YR
5, N
PV (display: -947.88)

The market price of a convertible bond is always at least the greater of its straight-debt value or its conversion value. This is because the holder has the option of either keeping the instrument as a bond or converting it into stock. The price of most convertibles exceeds these floor values because of the time value of the conversion option. Just as call options have value even when the stock is less than the strike price, convertibles trade at a premium to these floor values because of the chance that the price of the stock might increase sufficiently before the bond matures to make conversion worthwhile. Also, as with options, the size of this time value is directly related to the time to maturity and the volatility of the price of the underlying stock, and it is inversely related to the spread between the conversion price and the stock's current market price.

Advantages of Convertible Bonds

There are two advantages often cited to investing in convertibles compared with common stock. The first is that the current yield on the convertible bond is usually greater than the dividend yield on the underlying common stock. The second is the presence of the floor value defined by the straight debt value of the bond.

The higher current yield is clearly a nice advantage, although it comes with a price tag. The price tag is that if the price of the stock goes up, the conversion premium declines toward zero. Thus, the percentage price appreciation

---

Financial Planning Issue

When analyzing convertible bonds for their clients, financial planners should focus on the bond ratings for safety, but should also consider the relationship between the bond's current yield and the conversion premium percentage. Unfortunately, higher current yields are associated with higher conversion premiums. When faced with a variety of convertibles to choose from, a planner will usually be willing to give up some current yield for smaller conversion premiums.

---

from owning common stock will be greater than the percentage price appreciation in the convertible associated with the stock price movement.

The second cited advantage, the presence of a floor value, is simply not true! When a company's stock price declines precipitously, it is because the company's prospects have declined. When this happens, the prices of *all* its securities decline, not just its stock price. Thus, when a company's financial condition deteriorates, the yield-to-maturity on its debt rises, and so the straight bond value would also decline. This point is illustrated in figure 11-14 which shows the conversion premium as a function of the price of the common stock. A straight line emanating from the origin represents the conversion value, and its slope equals the conversion ratio. The straight debt value also starts at the origin, but steadily rises to the point where it becomes a flat line defined by the company's current bond rating. The actual price of the convertible bond will always be greater or equal to the larger of these two values. Thus, when the price of the stock is "low," the convertible bond's

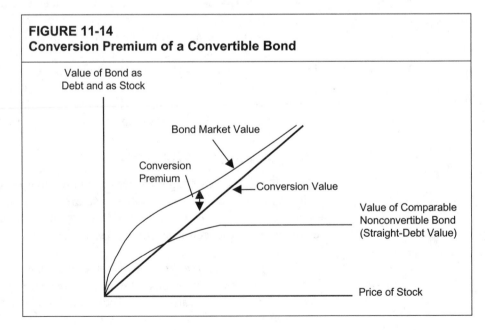

FIGURE 11-14
Conversion Premium of a Convertible Bond

price is determined primarily by the straight-debt value. When the convertible bond's price is "high," it is the conversion value that determines its value. Note that when the price of the stock is near the conversion price, the bond premium is at its maximum.

The key point in this graph is that the market value of the convertible bond will go to zero if the price of the common stock also goes to zero. At a price of zero, the company is bankrupt, and so both securities are worthless.

Call Feature

All convertible bonds are callable. Remember, the call feature allows the issuing company to buy back the bond at a predetermined call price which is always greater than par, but usually less than par plus one year's worth of interest. For straight debt, companies make bonds callable to give them the opportunity to refinance the bonds in the event market interest rates drop sufficiently such that the issuer could refinance the bonds with new bonds that have a lower coupon rate. Although the refinancing option might be a motivation for making convertibles callable, it is unlikely. This is because convertibles have lower coupon rates to start with, and therefore the drop in interest rates would have to be huge to make the refinancing option attractive for the issuer. The real motivation for making convertibles callable is the opportunity to create a forced conversion. Consider the following example.

Example: The King Company has outstanding a convertible bond with a conversion ratio of 100 (a $10 conversion price), a coupon rate of 8 percent, a call price of 110 (that is, $1,100), and 5 years left to maturity. It currently pays no dividend on its stock. The company has had a run of good news recently, and its stock price has risen from $5 per share to $15 per share. The conversion value is now $1,500, and the market price of the convertible bond is $1,505. The reason the conversion value and market value are so close is that everyone knows the company will likely call the bond in the near future to force conversion. A primary reason for forcing conversion is that the company is currently making annual interest payments of $80 per bond (8% coupon rate) and by calling the bond, all of the bonds will be converted into the common stock on which no dividends are being paid. After all, the bondholder has been given a choice of taking $1,500 worth of stocks per bond, or accepting the $1,100 call price. Thus, the company will save the annual interest payment, and only have to give up new stock that it would have to eventually give up.

After the last date of the call period passes, the investor no longer has the option to convert and will not earn any additional interest. Financial planners need to be extremely careful to not let any forced conversion calls expire for any convertible bonds held by clients. The bond's conversion value is typically at enough of a premium to the call price that rational investors feel compelled to convert the bond rather than redeem it.

Convertible Preferred Stock

There are similarities between convertible bonds and convertible preferreds, but there are also some differences. The downside value associated with the straight-debt value of the bond is less certain with convertible preferreds, because there is no legal requirement that the preferred dividends be paid. However, preferred dividends must be paid before common stock dividends are paid, so there is still some degree of downside protection.

The pricing of convertible preferreds is similar to the pricing of convertible bonds. When the market price of the underlying stock is close to or above the conversion price, the conversion value influences the price of the convertible preferreds. When the market price is far below the conversion price, the price of the convertible preferreds is closer to the straight preferred stock value.

As with convertible bonds, the number of common shares that can be obtained by converting one preferred share is known as the conversion ratio. The conversion ratio can change over time. For example, an issue of convertible preferred stock may have a conversion ratio of 4:1 for the first 10 years after issue, 2:1 for the next 10 years, and become straight preferred stock thereafter. Convertible preferreds also always have a call feature to allow forced conversion.

The conversion value of convertible preferred is the market price of the common stock multiplied by the conversion ratio.

Example: If the market price of the underlying common stock is $15/share, and the conversion ratio is 4:1, then the conversion value is $60 ($15 x 4 = $60). If the market price of the convertible preferred stock is $65/share, then the conversion premium is $5 ($65 – $60 = $5) or 8.33 percent ($5/$60).

Other Types of Convertibles

Convertible bonds and preferreds are the primary types of convertible securities, but other types of combination securities also bear mentioning.

Financial Planning Issue

Are convertibles an appropriate investment for clients? The historical rates of return on convertibles are higher than straight bonds, and lower than equities, which is what one would expect given the combined equity and debt features of this instrument. Thus, convertibles would make sense for those clients who want to hold both bonds and stocks in their portfolios. However, they should not be pitched to clients as the best of both worlds (equity appreciation with the safety of bonds). But neither do they need to be pitched as the "worst" of both worlds, less price appreciation potential than equities, and lower rates of return than straight debt.

Hybrid Convertibles

Hybrid convertibles (also called exchangeable debentures) are convertible into stock of different companies from those that issued them. Companies with substantial stock portfolios or companies that seek to divest shares of a partially owned subsidiary may find hybrids a useful source of funds.

Equity Notes

Equity notes (also called mandatory convertible notes) were developed to meet banks' capital needs. These notes are issued as debt instruments that yield a fixed coupon until maturity, when they are automatically converted into common stocks.

Liquidity Yield Option Notes

One of the most complex of the convertibles is the liquidity yield option note, or LYON. LYONs differ from ordinary convertibles primarily in being zero-coupon convertibles. In addition, they are callable and redeemable. Making the security even more complicated, both the redemption and call prices change over time.

Commodity-Backed Bonds

Commodity-backed bonds are debt instruments whose values are potentially related to the price of some physical commodity. These bonds allow the owner to speculate on a commodity price rise while earning a modest return. The bond's price will move up and down with variations in both the commodity price and market interest rates. Mexico has issued 20-year bonds with payments that depend on the price of oil. With options that specially positioned issuers can offer, commodity-backed bonds were designed to appeal to speculative investors. Additional types of innovative combination securities will probably be devised as time passes.

Types of Combination Securities

- Convertible bonds: debt securities that may be exchanged for common stock at a fixed ratio
- Convertible preferreds: preferred stock that may be exchanged for common stock at a fixed ratio
- Hybrid convertibles: debt securities of one company convertible into the common stock of another company
- Equity notes: debt securities with mandatory conversion to equity upon maturity
- Liquidity yield option notes (LYONs): zero-coupon, convertible, callable, redeemable bonds
- Commodity-backed bonds: debt securities whose potential redemption values are related to the market price of some physical commodity, such as oil

---

SUMMARY AND CONCLUSIONS

The two basic options are the put and call. The writer of the call gives the buyer the privilege of buying the stock at the strike price, and the writer of the put gives the buyer the privilege of selling the stock at the strike price. Options have value for two reasons: the intrinsic value when they are in-the- money, and the time value when there is a chance the price of the underlying asset may rise. Profit and payoff functions can be used to demonstrate the return and risk exposure of different options and combinations of holdings. Many of the positions can be characterized as either limited loss with the potential for unlimited gain, or limited gain with the potential for large or unlimited loss.

There are two models for valuing call options, the Black-Scholes model and the binomial option-pricing model. Under both models, the value of a call should increase with the underlying stock's price and volatility, time to maturity, and the market interest rate, and it should move inversely with the strike price. The put-call parity model shows the equilibrium relationship between the prices of a put, a call, the underlying stock, and the risk-free interest rate.

Although the most common underlying asset is the common stock of a company, other underlying assets can include indexes and bonds. LEAPS® constitute options with expiration dates as much as three years in the future.

Option-like securities include rights, warrants, and convertibles. Rights and warrants have the issuing corporation as the writer. The key to convertibles is the conversion price or conversion ratio (flip sides of the same coin). Convertibles have lower current yields than straight debt, and lower rates of return than direct purchase of equity. Buyers of convertibles need to consider the trade-off between current yield and conversion premium. Forced conversions are a potential problem for investors in convertibles.

CHAPTER REVIEW

Answers to the review questions and the self-test questions start on page 733.

Key Terms

option
writer
call option (call)
put option (put)
premium (option)
exercise price
strike price
in the money
out of the money
at the money
intrinsic value (option)
covered writer
naked writer
zero-sum game
combination position
married put

straddle
strangle
bullish call spread
bearish spread
Black-Scholes model
hedge ratio
binomial option-pricing model
put-call parity
manufactured (synthetic) call
American options
European options
Bermuda options
Long-term Equity Anticipation
    Securities (LEAPS®)
straight-debt value

Review Questions

11-1. The ASD Company's stock sells for $32; a 6-month option to purchase it at $35 sells for 1 3/4. (Ignore time value in a.–c. Ignore dividends in a. and b.)

a. What price must the stock reach within those 6 months for the buyer of the call option to break even?

b. What are the percentage gains for the buyer of the stock (that is, ROA) and the buyer of the call option if the stock rises to $45?

c. How would all of these results change if ASD pays one dividend of $.75 during the 6-month period?

11-2. a. Distinguish between a put option and a call option.

b. Explain the writer's obligations for each.

c. Why is purchasing a call not equivalent to writing a put?

11-3. a. Explain the meaning of the term strike price.

b. How does it relate to intrinsic value, speculative value, or being in or out of the money?

11-4. a. What kind of option would an investor purchase to protect a profit in a stock he or she owns?

b. How would such a strategy differ from simply selling the position?

    c.   What factors should an investor consider when evaluating the two strategies?

11-5. a.   What obligation does the writer of a covered call undertake?

        b.   What are the risks and prospective returns of a covered-call-writing strategy?

11-6. a.   What is a straddle?

        b.   Under what circumstances would an investor be inclined to buy a straddle?

        c.   When would a writer be inclined to write a straddle?

11-7. a.   Briefly explain a spread.

        b.   What is the motivation for holding a bullish spread?

11-8. a.   Name the five variables in the Black-Scholes option pricing model that determine the value of a call option.

        b.   Indicate how an increase in the value of each would affect the value of a call.

11-9. XYZ Corp. stock is selling for $30/share. Both a put and a call option are at the money, with exercise prices of $30 and 3 months to expiration. If the put option sells for $1, and the risk-free rate of interest is 6 percent, use put-call parity to find the value of a call option (assume annual rather than continuous compounding).

11-10. Describe the differences between rights and warrants.

11-11. a.   Why is call risk particularly relevant to convertibles?

        b.   Under what circumstances are convertibles particularly likely to be called?

11-12. What do convertible bond investors obtain and what do they sacrifice relative to investors in straight bonds and relative to investors in the underlying stock?

11-13. A share of convertible preferred selling at $100 might be exchanged for two shares of common stock trading at $40. What is the conversion premium?

11-14. The SOM Company convertible debentures sell for 105 ($1,050), while its common stock is priced at $40/share. The convertible's conversion ratio is 20; its annual coupon rate is 10 percent. Its estimated straight-debt value is 90. The stock pays a dividend of $2 per share per year. The bonds mature in 2007 and are callable at 107.

        a.   Compute the convertible's
- conversion price
- conversion value
- conversion premium (in dollar and percentage terms)
- premium over straight-debt value
- current yield

b. If you purchased the bonds at par ($1,000) and the stock subsequently rose to $55 1/2, what is the minimum profit per bond (ignoring commissions and coupon payments)?

Self-Test Questions

T   F   11-1.   The issuer of the stock writes stock options.

T   F   11-2.   The speculative value of an option is the difference between an option's price and its intrinsic value.

T   F   11-3.   If the underlying stock is trading at $31, the intrinsic value of a put with a strike price of $30 is –$1.

T   F   11-4.   The profit potential, as a percentage of the initial investment, is greater when purchasing call options than when fully margining a long position in the stock.

T   F   11-5.   The writer of a put expects the price to stay steady or perhaps fall in the near future.

T   F   11-6.   The value of a put will decline as the price of the stock rises.

T   F   11-7.   When the market price of the stock is less than the exercise price in the option, a call is in the money and a put is out of the money.

T   F   11-8.   The buyer of a put option has unlimited loss potential.

T   F   11-9.   The purchase of an out-of-the-money call when anticipating a run-up in the price of a stock would be a shrewd but aggressive investment strategy.

T   F   11-10. At a call option's expiration, the payoff to its holder is zero if the market price of the stock is equal to the exercise (strike) price.

T   F   11-11. When the stock's price is less than the exercise price, the payoff for writing a naked call remains constant at the amount of the premium paid by the option buyer.

T   F   11-12. The risk of a short sale can be reduced by the purchase of a call on the same stock.

T   F   11-13. An investor who anticipates a fall in the price of a stock might want to short the stock and purchase a put to hedge his or her risk if the price of the stock starts rising.

T   F   11-14. Writing covered calls can increase income at the expense of opportunity losses in price appreciation.

T   F   11-15. A straddle combines a put and a call option on the same stock with the same exercise price but different expiration dates.

T F 11-16. Listed options have standardized expiration dates and strike prices.

T F 11-17. Buying a protective put on a stock index ensures that the owner of a diversified stock portfolio can limit the potential loss over the duration of the holding period.

T F 11-18. When the holder of a stock-index call exercises the option, the writer must deliver a portfolio that represents the index.

T F 11-19. Stock index options differ from industry options in that stock index options are written on broad-based portfolios of stocks intended to capture the overall behavior of the stock market, whereas industry options are written on much more narrowly defined portfolios of stocks from specific industries.

T F 11-20. LEAPS® can have maturities of as much as five years.

T F 11-21. The bond value or straight-debt value of a convertible is defined as the price at which the convertible would trade if it were nonconvertible and valued at (or near) the prevailing market yields of comparable nonconvertible issues.

T F 11-22. Convertible bonds offer the issuer the opportunity to offer common stock at a price above the stock's current market price.

T F 11-23. Convertible bonds that are called must be either converted into stock or redeemed at the call price.

T F 11-24. Assuming that the stock price rises above the conversion price, eventually the conversion value and the market price of a convertible bond will equal each other because of the risk that the bond might be called.

T F 11-25. The term conversion premium refers to the difference between the market price of the bond and its par value.

T F 11-26. A convertible's conversion premium is directly (as opposed to inversely) related to the price of the underlying common stock.

T F 11-27. Because of their risk, convertible bonds carry a higher interest rate than comparable bonds without the conversion option.

T F 11-28. Most convertible bonds are callable.

T F 11-29. There is little correlation between returns on convertible bonds and returns on the underlying stocks.

T F 11-30. Hybrid convertibles, or exchangeable debentures, are convertible into common stock of a company other than the company that issued the debenture.

NOTES

1. www.optiondigest.com/stock-option-strategies.htm#Strategy10, November 10, 2004.
2. www.optiondigest.com/stock-option-strategies.htm#Strategy8, November 10, 2004.

3. F. Black and M. Scholes, "The Pricing of Options and Corporate Liabilities," *Journal of Political Economy* (May–June 1973), pp. 637–654.

4. Remember, we are assuming there are no transaction fees or taxes. To the extent that there are transaction fees and differences in tax consequences, then put-call parity is not perfectly achievable.

5. For additional information on LEAPS®, see www.cboe.com/LearnCenter/pdf/LEAPS_11-2001. pdf, November 10, 2004.

Appendix 11A

Black-Scholes Formula

Note: Knowledge of the Black-Scholes formula is not required for the CFP[TM] exam. The use of the Black-Scholes formula to estimate option values is appropriate for the more advanced student who is interested in examples of how option prices can be derived. The Black-Scholes formula for call option pricing can be derived precisely, given the following assumptions:

- The capital markets are frictionless—that is, there are no transaction costs or taxes, and all information is simultaneously and freely available to all investors.
- There are no short-sale restrictions.
- All asset prices follow a continuous stationary, lognormal, stochastic process.
- There is a constant risk-free rate over time, at which investors can borrow as well as lend.
- No dividends are paid.
- No early exercise is permitted (that is, European call options)

The resulting formula is as follows:

$$C_0 = S_0 N(d_1) \ - \ \frac{S \ N(d_2)}{e^{r_f t}}$$

$$d_1 = \frac{\ln \ (S_0 / S) \ + \ \left(r_f \ + .5 \ \sigma^2\right) \ t}{\sigma \sqrt{t}}$$

$$d_2 = \frac{\ln \ (S_0 / S) \ + \ \left(r_f \ - .5 \ \sigma^2\right) \ t}{\sigma \sqrt{t}}$$

and where C_0 = option value

r_f = continuously compound riskless annual interest rate

S_0 = stock price

S = strike price of option

e = 2.718 (the natural logarithmic constant)

t = time to expiration of option as a fraction of a year

σ = the standard deviation of the continuously compounded annual rate of return of the underlying stock

$\ln (S_0/S)$ = natural logarithm of S_0/S

N(d) = value of the standard normal distribution evaluated at d

Tables 11A-1 and 11A-2 are normal cumulative distribution tables that can be used to find the value of N(d).

TABLE 11A-1
For Values of N(x) When x ≥ 0

This table shows values of N(x) for x ≥ 0. The table should be used with interpolation. For example,

N(0.6278) = N(0.62) + 0.78[N(0.63) − N(0.62)]
= 0.7324 + 0.78 x (0.7357 − 0.7324)
= 0.7350

x	.00	.01	.02	.03	.04	.05	.06	.07	.08	.09
0.0	0.5000	0.5040	0.5080	0.5120	0.5160	0.5199	0.5239	0.5279	0.5319	0.5359
0.1	0.5398	0.5438	0.5478	0.5517	0.5557	0.5596	0.5636	0.5675	0.5714	0.5753
0.2	0.5793	0.5832	0.5871	0.5910	0.5948	0.5987	0.6026	0.6064	0.6103	0.6141
0.3	0.6179	0.6217	0.6255	0.6293	0.6331	0.6368	0.6406	0.6443	0.6480	0.6517
0.4	0.6554	0.6591	0.6628	0.6664	0.6700	0.6736	0.6772	0.6808	0.6844	0.6879
0.5	0.6915	0.6950	0.6985	0.7019	0.7054	0.7088	0.7123	0.7157	0.7190	0.7224
0.6	0.7257	0.7291	0.7324	0.7357	0.7389	0.7422	0.7454	0.7486	0.7517	0.7549
0.7	0.7580	0.7611	0.7642	0.7673	0.7704	0.7734	0.7764	0.7794	0.7823	0.7852
0.8	0.7881	0.7910	0.7939	0.7967	0.7995	0.8023	0.8051	0.8078	0.8106	0.8133
0.9	0.8159	0.8186	0.8212	0.8238	0.8264	0.8289	0.8315	0.8340	0.8365	0.8389
1.0	0.8413	0.8438	0.8461	0.8485	0.8508	0.8531	0.8554	0.8577	0.8599	0.8621
1.1	0.8643	0.8665	0.8686	0.8708	0.8729	0.8749	0.8770	0.8790	0.8810	0.8830
1.2	0.8849	0.8869	0.8888	0.8907	0.8925	0.8944	0.8962	0.9890	0.8997	0.9015
1.3	0.9032	0.9049	0.9066	0.9082	0.9099	0.9115	0.9131	0.9147	0.9162	0.9177
1.4	0.9192	0.9207	0.9222	0.9236	0.9251	0.9265	0.9279	0.9292	0.9306	0.9319
1.5	0.9332	0.9345	0.9357	0.9370	0.9382	0.9394	0.9406	0.9418	0.9429	0.9441
1.6	0.9452	0.9463	0.9474	0.9484	0.9495	0.9505	0.9515	0.9525	0.9535	0.9545
1.7	0.9554	0.9564	0.9573	0.9582	0.9591	0.9599	0.9608	0.9616	0.9625	0.9633
1.8	0.9641	0.9649	0.9656	0.9664	0.9671	0.9678	0.9686	0.9693	0.9699	0.9706
1.9	0.9713	0.9719	0.9726	0.9732	0.9738	0.9744	0.9750	0.9756	0.9761	0.9767
2.0	0.9772	0.9778	0.9783	0.9788	0.9793	0.9798	0.9803	0.9808	0.9812	0.9817
2.1	0.9821	0.9826	0.9830	0.9834	0.9838	0.9842	0.9846	0.9850	0.9854	0.9857
2.2	0.9861	0.9864	0.9868	0.9871	0.9875	0.9878	0.9881	0.9884	0.9887	0.9890
2.3	0.9893	0.9896	0.9898	0.9901	0.9904	0.9906	0.9909	0.9911	0.9913	0.9916
2.4	0.9918	0.9920	0.9922	0.9925	0.9927	0.9929	0.9931	0.9932	0.9934	0.9936
2.5	0.9938	0.9940	0.9941	0.9943	0.9945	0.9946	0.9948	0.9949	0.9951	0.9952
2.6	0.9953	0.9955	0.9956	0.9957	0.9959	0.9960	0.9961	0.9962	0.9963	0.9964
2.7	0.9965	0.9966	0.9967	0.9968	0.9969	0.9970	0.9971	0.9972	0.9973	0.9974
2.8	0.9974	0.9975	0.9976	0.9977	0.9977	0.9978	0.9979	0.9979	0.9980	0.9981
2.9	0.9981	0.9982	0.9982	0.9983	0.9984	0.9984	0.9985	0.9985	0.9986	0.9986
3.0	0.9986	0.9987	0.9987	0.9988	0.9988	0.9989	0.9989	0.9989	0.9990	0.9990
3.1	0.9990	0.9991	0.9991	0.9991	0.9992	0.9992	0.9992	0.9992	0.9993	0.9993
3.2	0.9993	0.9993	0.9994	0.9994	0.9994	0.9994	0.9994	0.9995	0.9995	0.9995
3.3	0.9995	0.9995	0.9995	0.9996	0.9996	0.9996	0.9996	0.9996	0.9996	0.9997
3.4	0.9997	0.9997	0.9997	0.9997	0.9997	0.9997	0.9997	0.0007	0.9997	0.9998
3.5	0.9998	0.9998	0.9998	0.9998	0.9998	0.9998	0.9998	0.9998	0.9998	0.9998
3.6	0.9998	0.9998	0.9999	0.9999	0.9999	0.9999	0.9999	0.9999	0.9999	0.9999
3.7	0.9999	0.9999	0.9999	0.9999	0.9999	0.9999	0.9999	0.9999	0.9999	0.9999
3.8	0.9999	0.9999	0.9999	0.9999	0.9999	0.9999	0.9999	0.9999	0.9999	0.9999
3.9	1.0000	1.0000	1.0000	1.0000	1.0000	1.0000	1.0000	1.0000	1.0000	1.0000
4.0	1.0000	1.0000	1.0000	1.0000	1.0000	1.0000	1.0000	1.0000	1.0000	1.0000

TABLE 11A-2
For Values of N(x) When x ≤ 0

This table shows values of N(x) for x ≤ 0. The table should be used with interpolation. For example,

N(−0.1234)   = N(−0.12) − 0.34[N(−0.12) − N(−0.13)]
             = 0.4522 − 0.34 x (0.4522 − 0.4483)
             = 0.4509

x	.00	.01	.02	.03	.04	.05	.06	.07	.08	.09
0.0	0.5000	0.4960	0.4920	0.4880	0.4840	0.4801	0.4761	0.4721	0.4681	0.4641
0.1	0.4602	0.4562	0.4522	0.4483	0.4443	0.4404	0.4364	0.4325	0.4286	0.4247
0.2	0.4207	0.4168	0.4129	0.4090	0.4052	0.4013	0.3974	0.3936	0.3897	0.3859
0.3	0.3821	0.3783	0.3745	0.3707	0.3669	0.3632	0.3594	0.3557	0.3520	0.3483
0.4	0.3446	0.3409	0.3372	0.3336	0.3300	0.3264	0.3228	0.3192	0.3156	0.3121
0.5	0.3085	0.3050	0.3015	0.2981	0.2946	0.2912	0.2877	0.2843	0.2810	0.2776
0.6	0.2743	0.2709	0.2676	0.2643	0.2611	0.2578	0.2546	0.2514	0.2483	0.2451
0.7	0.2420	0.2389	0.2358	0.2327	0.2296	0.2266	0.2236	0.2206	0.2177	0.2148
0.8	0.2119	0.2090	0.2061	0.2033	0.2005	0.1977	0.1949	0.1922	0.1894	0.1867
0.9	0.1841	0.1814	0.1788	0.1762	0.1736	0.1711	0.1685	0.1660	0.1635	0.1611
1.0	0.1587	0.1562	0.1539	0.1515	0.1492	0.1469	0.1446	0.1423	0.1401	0.1379
1.1	0.1357	0.1335	0.1314	0.1292	0.1271	0.1251	0.1230	0.1210	0.1190	0.1170
1.2	0.1151	0.1131	0.1112	0.1093	0.1075	0.1056	0.1038	0.1020	0.1003	0.0985
1.3	0.0968	0.0951	0.0934	0.0918	0.0901	0.0885	0.0869	0.0853	0.0838	0.0823
1.4	0.0808	0.0793	0.0778	0.0764	0.0749	0.0735	0.0721	0.0708	0.0694	0.0681
1.5	0.0668	9.9655	0.0643	0.0630	0.0618	0.0606	0.0594	0.0582	0.0571	0.0559
1.6	0.0548	0.0537	0.0526	0.0516	0.0505	0.0495	0.0485	0.0475	0.0465	0.0455
1.7	0.0446	9.9436	0.0427	0.0418	0.0409	0.0401	0.0392	0.0384	0.0375	0.0367
1.8	0.0359	0.0351	0.0344	0.0336	0.0329	0.0322	0.0314	0.0307	0.0301	0.0294
1.9	0.0287	0.0281	0.0274	0.0268	0.0262	0.0256	0.0250	0.0244	0.0239	0.0233
2.0	0.0228	0.0222	0.0217	0.0212	0.0207	0.0202	0.0197	0.0192	0.0188	0.0183
2.1	0.0179	0.0174	0.0170	0.0166	0.0162	0.0158	0.0154	0.0150	0.0146	0.0143
2.2	0.0139	0.0136	0.0132	0.0129	0.0125	0.0122	0.0119	0.0116	0.0113	0.0110
2.3	0.0107	0.0104	0.0102	0.0099	0.0096	0.0094	0.0091	0.0089	0.0087	0.0084
2.4	0.0082	0.0080	0.0078	0.0075	0.0073	0.0071	0.0069	0.0068	0.0066	0.0064
2.5	0.0062	0.0060	0.0059	0.0057	0.0055	0.0054	0.0052	0.0051	0.0049	0.0048
2.6	0.0047	0.0045	0.0044	0.0043	0.0041	0.0040	0.0039	0.0038	0.0037	0.0036
2.7	0.0035	0.0034	0.0033	0.0032	0.0031	0.0030	0.0029	0.0028	0.0027	0.0026
2.8	0.0026	0.0025	0.0024	0.0023	0.0023	0.0022	0.0021	0.0021	0.0020	0.0019
2.9	0.0019	0.0018	0.0018	0.0017	0.0016	0.0016	0.0015	0.0015	0.0014	0.0014
3.0	0.0014	0.0013	0.0013	0.0012	0.0012	0.0011	0.0011	0.0011	0.0010	0.0010
3.1	0.0010	0.0009	0.0009	0.0009	0.0008	0.0008	0.0008	0.0008	0.0007	0.0007
3.2	0.0007	0.0007	0.0006	0.0006	0.0006	0.0006	0.0006	0.0005	0.0005	0.0005
3.3	0.0005	0.0005	0.0005	0.0004	0.0004	0.0004	0.0004	0.0004	0.0004	0.0003
3.4	0.0003	0.0003	0.0003	0.0003	0.0003	0.0003	0.0003	0.0003	0.0003	0.0002
3.5	0.0002	0.0002	0.0002	0.0002	0.0002	0.0002	0.0002	0.0002	0.0002	0.0002
3.6	0.0002	0.0002	0.0001	0.0001	0.0001	0.0001	0.0001	0.0001	0.0001	0.0001
3.7	0.0001	0.0001	0.0001	0.0001	0.0001	0.0001	0.0001	0.0001	0.0001	0.0001
3.8	0.0001	0.0001	0.0001	0.0001	0.0001	0.0001	0.0001	0.0001	0.0001	0.0001
3.9	0.0000	0.0000	0.0000	0.0000	0.0000	0.0000	0.0000	0.0000	0.0000	0.0000
4.0	0.0000	0.0000	0.0000	0.0000	0.0000	0.0000	0.0000	0.0000	0.0000	0.0000

Example: Suppose we want to use the Black-Scholes formula to estimate the value of a call option, given the following information:[*]

- The current market price of the stock (S_0) is $23/share.
- The option's strike price (S) is $25/share.
- The option has 3 months until expiration (t = .25).
- The standard deviation of the stock's return (σ) is .5 (50% per year).
- The risk-free rate of interest is 4 percent (r_f = .04).

We proceed to calculate as follows:

$$S_0/S = \$23/\$25 = .92$$
$$\ln(S_0/S) = \ln(.92) = -.0834$$
$$.5\sigma^2 = .5 \times .5 \times .5 = .125$$
$$r_f + .5\sigma^2 = .04 + .125 = .165$$
$$(r_f + .5\sigma^2)t = .165 \times .25 = .0413$$
$$\sigma\sqrt{t} = .5 \times \sqrt{.25} = .25$$
$$d_1 = \left(-.0834 + .0413\right)/.25 = -.1684$$

Using table 11A-2 and interpolating, $N(d_1) = .4331$

$$(r_f - .5\sigma^2)\, t = (.04 - .125) \times .25 = -.085 \times .25$$
$$= -.0213$$
$$d_2 = (-.0834 - .0213)/.25 = -.4188$$

Using table 11A-2 and interpolating, $N(d_2) = .3376$

$$r_f t = .04 \times .25 = .01$$
$$e^{r_f t} = e^{.01} = 1.01$$

The value of the call option (C_0) is

$$C_0 = (\$23 \times .4331) - (\$25 \times .3376/1.01)$$
$$= \$9.96 - \$8.36 = \$1.60$$

11A-1. Using the Black-Scholes formula, estimate the value of a call option with 3 months to maturity and a strike price of $95 when the market price of the underlying stock is $100, the standard deviation of the stock's price is .5 (50% per year), and the risk-free rate is 10 percent.

---

[*] Calculators for pricing an option are available online. A particularly good one can be found by clicking on <u>Basic</u> under Online Options Pricing Calculators at www.theocc.com/learning_center/opt_ed/get_started. jsp. Next, click on Black-Scholes and enter the following data: Underlying price, 23; Time to expiration, 91; Interest rate, 4; Dividend yield, 0; Strike price, 25; and Volatility, 50. Then click on Finish, and the price of the call option will be displayed as 1.597.

Futures

Learning Objectives

An understanding of the material in this chapter should enable the student to

12-1.   Describe the characteristics of futures contracts, futures markets, and futures traders.

12-2.   Describe how futures contracts can be used for hedging, including the importance of the relationship between basis risk and price risk.

12-3.   Explain why some contracts have only a cash settlement, while most contracts allow delivery.

12-4.   Describe futures options and program trading.

Chapter Outline

Of all the major investment vehicles discussed in this book (that is, stocks, bonds, mutual funds, options, and futures), most people have the least familiarity with futures contracts. Futures contracts can be broadly divided into three segments: agricultural, mineral, and financial. There are two primary motives for trading futures contracts: speculation and hedging. Financial planners may have occasion to use financial futures contracts for hedging purposes (that is, the transference of risk from a client's portfolio). Financial planners may have clients who want to speculate in the futures markets, and may trade in any of the three markets. It is unlikely a financial planner would have a client who needs to use the agricultural or mineral markets for hedging, unless the planner is advising on business related strategies. In this chapter we will discuss primarily the agricultural and financial futures markets. The agricultural markets are somewhat easier to understand, so we will focus on these first. But it is the financial futures markets that a planner is more likely to use.

THE SPOT MARKET, FORWARD CONTRACTS, AND FUTURES CONTRACTS

Everyone uses the spot market, even if they don't use that name or think of it in that way. The spot market involves any transaction wherein the purchase price is paid (whether in cash or credit) and the commodity purchased is given to the buyer at the same time (that is on the spot). For example, when an individual goes to the grocery store, he or she is buying in the spot market.

The entire nature of the transaction changes, however, when both parties agree to a later delivery and later payment of the item purchased. Such a transaction is referred to as a forward contract. People regularly enter into forward contracts. For example, if Juanita Rodriguez goes to a new car dealer but can't find the exact combination of color and options she wants, she may sign a contract for delivery of the specified car at a later date. Juanita does not want to pay for the car until she receives it, and the dealer wants assurance that Juanita will show up to buy the car once it is delivered. Juanita revolves this by placing a deposit on the purchase of the car. If Juanita fails to show up, the dealer can confiscate Juanita's deposit as compensation for the lost sale. For her part, Juanita will want as precise a description as possible as to what the car will look like and when it will be delivered. Juanita and the car dealer have created a forward contract. Note that Juanita has bought a product, and the car dealer has sold a product, that has not yet been produced.

If the contract that Juanita and the car dealer had created involved standardized terms, an active market for these contracts, and a third party to guarantee both parties honor their contracts, then it would be known as a futures contract. As a futures contract, if the car dealer no longer wanted to be responsible for the delivery of the car, or if Juanita no longer wanted to buy the car, either party could sell his or her obligation under the contract to a third party.

There are always two parties to a futures contract, the person who is long (that is, the buyer), and the person who is short (that is, the seller). The person with the long position has agreed to take delivery of the particular commodity described in the contract, and pay the agreed upon price at the time of delivery. The person with a short position has agreed to make delivery of the particular product described in the contract, and will receive the agreed-upon price at the time of delivery. Each futures contract fully specifies what the commodity is that is to be delivered, where it is to be delivered, when it is to be delivered, and what the consequences are for failure to meet each of the above requirements. Simply put, when one trades in the futures market, one is trading in contractual obligations.

Futures versus Options

Futures and option contracts are sometimes confused. Both involve subsequent events. An option holder has a right but not an obligation to buy (if he or she owns a call option) or sell (if he or she owns a put option) a specified quantity of some asset at a specified price over a specified time period. The holder of a futures contract, in contrast, has the obligation to accept and pay for a specified quantity of some asset at a specified price at a specified time. Thus, those who own options have a choice to do something in the future, whereas those who own futures have an obligation to do something in the future.

Difference between Futures Owner and Option Holder

- A futures buyer has the *obligation* to accept and pay for a specified quantity of an asset at a specified price at a specified time.
- A option holder has the *right*—but not an obligation—to buy or sell a specified quantity of an asset at a specified price over a specified time period.

Forward Contracts versus Futures Contracts

As noted earlier, a forward contract is a customized contractual agreement between parties to accept delivery (buy) and to deliver (sell) a specified commodity or financial instrument at an agreed-upon price, settlement date, quantity, and location. The terms of this contract result from direct negotiations between the parties, and the parties accept the terms of the contract. Because these contracts are nonstandard ones, there is no organized exchange for trading forward contracts.

A futures contract is divided into two contracts—one to buy and one to sell—and it contains standardized features that cover the commodity in question. Because the terms are standardized, active secondary markets exist. Indeed, most futures contracts trade on an organized exchange that sets the terms of the contracts, provides the location for their trading, and monitors their settlements.

Futures contracts allow those who expect later to have or need that asset to establish a price and quantity ahead of time. Standardizing the contract's terms (grade, quantity, delivery location, and date) facilitates active trading. That is, a large number of interested parties can trade the same (standardized) contract. The market for futures contracts developed first in trading commodities because of the ability to specify a commodity's attributes.

Unlike forward contracts but like options, futures contracts are actually contracts between each contracting party and the exchange. Therefore, neither the person who is long nor the person who is short has to worry about the other party to the contract defaulting, since the exchange is obligated to honor the contract regardless of the actions of the party taking the opposite side of the contract. Thus, the two parties need only worry about the exchange defaulting, and it is the exchange that worries about any one party to a contract defaulting. As we will see shortly, significant safeguards are built into the trading process to minimize the risk of default.

Because of the standardized nature of futures contracts, transaction costs tend to be much lower than those of forward contracts. Forward contracts are private, customized agreements between two contracting parties. As such, there can be considerable transaction costs involved in the negotiation of a mutually acceptable agreement between the two parties.

Differences between Forward Contract and Futures Contract

- Forward contract: a nonstandardized (unique) contract between parties to accept delivery (buy) and deliver (sell) a specified commodity or financial instrument at an agreed-upon price, settlement date, quantity and location. There is no organized exchange for trading forward contracts.
- Futures contract: a standardized contract divided into two contracts—one to buy and one to sell—a specified commodity or financial instrument. Futures trade on an organized exchange that sets contract terms, which establish price, quantity, delivery location, and date.

The Commodity Exchanges

Just as we saw that there are multiple exchanges for the trading of stocks, so there are multiple exchanges for futures contracts. The oldest such exchange is the Chicago Board of Trade. In late 2003, the *Wall Street Journal* listed quotations from 19 different exchanges. It should be noted that these exchanges are from all over the world, and are not just domestic.

Different Types of Commodity Traders

A substantial number of commodity traders are professionals. For example, large firms in commodity-related industries (mining, baking, meatpacking, grain, and so on) often maintain representatives on the relevant exchanges. These particular professionals seek to provide a future supply or market for their companies' products. They make it their business to have access to, and a detailed understanding of, the latest information relevant to their particular commodities. For instance, they may be following the latest crop estimates, cost comparisons, weather reports, possible government policy changes, trade figures and the international economy, and a host of other useful data. Access to all of the relevant and available knowledge tends to give these professionals a decided advantage over less-informed traders.

Several additional classes of professional commodity traders bear mentioning. They include scalpers, day traders, position traders, and arbitrageurs. Like stock exchange floor traders and specialists, these traders usually have seats on the exchange and trade for their own accounts.

scalpers

Scalpers are people who hold positions for a few minutes at a time, at most. They stand at the hub of trading activity looking for temporary misalignments in prices. If one contract appears to become slightly overpriced due to a temporary surge in buy orders, scalpers will move in to sell this contract and bring the price into alignment with other contracts. They may make 50, 100, or more trades in a single day, trying to reap small gains of an eighth or a quarter of a point each. They thrive on action. Concentration, quick thinking,

---

Types of Professional Futures Market Traders

- Firm representatives: hedge needs or outputs of firms that deal with these commodities
- Scalpers: hold positions for a few minutes at most
- Day traders: short-run traders who close their positions each day
- Position traders: may hold positions for several days based on fundamental or technical factors
- Arbitrageurs: seek to exploit departures from expected relative price relationships

day traders
position traders

arbitrageurs

and reliable, high-speed access to the markets are essential. Timing is everything.

Day traders usually close their positions by the end of each day. They hope to profit from modest price moves. Unlike day traders, *position traders* seek to profit from fundamental or technical forces that may manifest themselves over several days. Finally, *arbitrageurs* try to exploit misalignments of relative prices by simultaneously taking long and short positions.

Different Types of Futures Contracts

As mentioned before, contracts are broadly grouped as agricultural, metal, and financial. Agricultural futures contracts include the following: cattle, hogs, chickens, wheat, oats, corn, soybeans, barley, sugar, potatoes, coffee, orange juice, and cocoa. Agricultural futures also include such items as lumber, plywood, cotton, and wool. The minerals traded on futures exchanges include crude oil, natural gas, gasoline, heating oil, copper, zinc, gold, silver, platinum, tin, palladium, and lead. Financial futures can be broken down into three sub-groups: interest rates, stock market indices, and foreign currencies. The primary interest rate contracts are for the federal funds rate, Treasury bills, and long-term government bonds. Stock market index contracts focus primarily on the S&P 500 and the DJIA indices. The currency contracts include the currencies of all of the major trading partners for the U.S.

Successful futures contracts possess most, if not all, of the following characteristics:

- a relatively competitive spot market
- a meaningful standardized contract (for example, a well-defined deliverable)
- storability or its equivalence (that is, ongoing production)
- sufficient price volatility to attract (or require) speculative and hedging interest
- a significant business use for the product

For example, no legal or theoretical barriers prevent futures trading in rhubarb or peppermint, but volume would probably be insufficient to justify these listings because there is not enough business need for these products. When the price of gold was fixed at $35 per ounce by the U.S. Treasury and it was illegal to own gold, there was no futures market in gold for two reasons: delivery could not occur (illegal to own) and there was no uncertainty as to price.

All of the commodity exchanges are constantly looking to establish new contracts for trading. For example, contracts for turkeys, shrimp, apples, and diamonds were tried and failed. Many other items such as steel reinforcing bars (re-bars), scrap aluminum, returnable drink bottles, uranium, milk, butter, coal, cement, cinder blocks, sulfur, and nails might or might not support futures trading. Even when all of the above conditions are met, a particular futures contract will not necessarily succeed.

Characteristics of Futures Contracts

Many Contracts per Commodity

For any commodity that is traded, there are actually multiple contracts. The most common distinction among contracts is the month of delivery. For example, at the start of December 2003, the Chicago Board of Trade traded seven different contracts of Corn. The nearest term contract was December 2003 (delivery can be made any time during the delivery month). The furthest out contract was March 2005. At the same time, wheat contracts were traded on three different exchanges: the Chicago Board of Trade, the Kansas City Board of Trade, and the Minneapolis Grain Exchange. Although each exchange traded six contracts that differed by delivery date, each exchange had the same delivery months as the other. Nonetheless, there were substantial differences in prices among the exchanges. This meant that either there was a substantial difference in the quality or type of wheat that could be delivered under each contract, or the delivery location designated by each contract was different. Anyone trading a commodity should be familiar with the technical features of the contract traded (that is, quantity of product to be delivered, quality of product to be delivered, time of delivery, location of delivery, penalties for failure to honor each specific term, and so on).

Delivery on a Contract

Although we have mentioned several times now that the person who goes long (that is, buys) a contract is committing to take delivery of the commodity and the person who goes short (that is, sells) a contract is committing to make delivery, deliveries rarely occur. The reason is that nobody actually wants to make or take delivery because that can be expensive. Instead, nearly everyone with a contract closes out his or her position by entering into an offsetting contract. Remember, although a contract is created when a buy and a sell order of two people without prior positions in that commodity are matched on the trading floor of the exchange, the contract of each party is actually with a clearing house. Thus, a futures holder who is long (owns) a September wheat futures contract can then liquidate his or her position by placing a sell order (taking a short position) on the same contract. On the records of the clearing house, being simultaneously long and short the same contract terminates one's position in that contract.

For someone who enters the contract on the short side (has promised to make delivery), he or she liquidates by placing a buy order for the same contract. Again, being simultaneously long and short a contract abolishes one's position.

Clearinghouses

Each futures exchange has its own clearinghouse. Membership in the clearinghouse is composed of well-capitalized members of the exchange. Exchange members who do not join the clearinghouse association must clear their trades through a member of the association. Each clearinghouse member must post and maintain margins, which in turn are posted by their customers (margins will be discussed shortly).[1]

Large Dollar Value

Although stocks and bonds normally trade in round lots of 100 shares or five bonds, the standard trading unit for each contract is unique. For example, each contract for corn is based on 5,000 bushels, and each contract for soybean oil is 100 tons. Prices are quoted on a per unit basis. Agricultural commodities are usually quoted on a pennies per unit basis. Thus, if corn were trading at 250.00, the trade price is $2.50 per bushel. As there are 5,000 bushels per contract, this means that this particular contract would be valued at $12,500.

Trading Futures Contracts

The individuals or firms that generate the majority of the trading in futures contracts do so for the following reasons: hedging, speculating, or spreading.

Hedging

Hedging is the practice of offsetting the price risk in the cash market by taking an equal-size but opposite position in the futures market. Let's consider a classic example of a hedge. Suppose Jack Lessard is a farmer who is planting some corn, and anticipates that he will harvest 50,000 bushels of corn in four months. The current price of corn in the local cash market (the spot market) is $3.00 per bushel. Suppose also that there is a futures contract that calls for deliver exactly four months from now, and that this contract is trading for $2.90 per bushel. Finally, let's assume that Jack would be perfectly happy to sell his corn at $3.00 per bushel. This would mean gross revenue for Jack of $150,000 for his corn.

At this point in time, Jack has two major risks. One is that something might destroy the crops (for example, fire or hail storm), and the other is that the cash price of corn may drop over the next four months. Although Jack might consider something like crop insurance for the first risk, that risk is not our concern here. Our concern is the second risk, known as price risk. Futures contracts may substantially reduce the price risk.

To do this, Jack takes a short position in 10 corn futures contracts that mature in four months (remember, each corn contract is for 5,000 bushels). Jack is committing to delivering 50,000 bushels of corn under the terms of the contract. We can now describe Jack's position as being long the crop (he has or will soon have the crop planted in his field), and short the futures contract, which is known as a *short hedge*. It is a short hedge because Jack is short the futures contract. In our next example, we will consider a long hedge in which the hedger is short the physical commodity and long the futures contracts.

short hedge

At the time Jack planted his crop, the cash market price is $3.00, but he had no corn to sell. When he sells the futures contract, the price is $2.90 per bushel. The difference between the cash price and the futures price is known as the *basis,* that is

basis

$$\text{basis} = \text{cash market price} - \text{futures market price.}$$

In Jack's case, his basis is $.10 per bushel. The key to the success of Jack's hedge is what happens to the basis between now and when the crop is harvested.

perfect hedge

In a *perfect hedge*, the basis would not change. The cash and futures prices might change, but they change in perfect tandem, leaving the basis unchanged. Suppose that four months from now, the cash price is $2.50 and the futures price is $2.40. Jack will then harvest his crop; sell it in the local cash market, and close out his futures position. By selling his crop in the cash market, Jack will receive $125,000 ($2.50/bushel x 50,000 bushels). When Jack closes out his futures contract, he will pocket a profit of $25,000 ($.50/bushel x 50,000 bushels). This is because he will have sold the contracts at $2.90 per bushel and bought them for $2.40 per bushel, thus providing a profit of $.50 per bushel. So, even though the cash market price declined by $.50 per bushel, Jack's gross revenue is the same as what he anticipated when he set up his hedge. It is exactly the same because the basis did not change.

One might ask why didn't Jack just deliver the corn under the terms of the futures contract. There could be several reasons. The most common is that it would likely involve substantive transportation expense to ship the corn to the location specified in the contract. It is much easier for Jack to sell in the local cash market.

Suppose the cash market price had gone up $.50 per bushel, and the basis had stayed the same. In this case, Jack would sell his corn for $3.50 per bushel, taking in gross revenue of $175,000 in the cash market. However, his futures contracts would be trading at $3.40 per bushel. He will incur a loss of

$.50 per bushel on these contracts, or a total loss of $25,000. So his net revenue will still be $150,000. Jack may be sad that he would have been wealthier by $25,000 if he had not set up the hedge, but this is the consequence of a hedge. Namely, one gives up the chance for a windfall gain in exchange for protection from an unanticipated loss.

Basis Risk

In practice, the basis does not necessarily stay the same. Let's revisit the first example above by assuming that the cash price falls to $2.50 per bushel, as before, but that the futures price falls only to $2.50 (same price as in the previous example). The basis is now zero. When Jack sells his corn in the cash market, he will still receive gross revenue of $125,000. When he buys back his future contracts, he will receive a profit of only $20,000, based on the fact that he sold the contracts at $2.90 each and bought them back for $2.50, or a gain of $.40 per bushel. So Jack's net revenue on the sale of the corn is now $145,000, not the $150,000 he had originally anticipated. Jack has been a victim of basis risk, or the risk that the basis will change.

The key point here is that if Jack had not set up the hedge at all, he would have been $25,000 worse off. Instead, he is only $5,000 worse off. So the hedge clearly accomplished something, just not everything Jack had hoped. *The goal in hedging is to substitute basis risk for price risk.* With any luck, basis risk will be less than price risk. So, as long as there is basis risk, a hedge will only reduce the risk, not eliminate it.

There is, obviously, the chance that one might gain from basis risk. Suppose in the above example the futures price drops to $2.30 per bushel. The basis has now widened to $.20. In this case, Jack will take in $125,000 from his sale in the cash market, and another $30,000 ($.60/bushel x 50,000 bushels) on the liquidation of the short positions. This totals $155,000. So Jack had the benefit of substituting basis risk for price risk, and a gain from the basis risk to boot!

Clearly, when one embarks on setting up a hedge, one needs to be sure that the futures contract chosen for the hedge has the smallest basis risk possible. If an ineffective contract is chosen, the basis risk might turn out to be greater than the price risk!

Long Hedge

Let's now consider the case of a heating company who is planning for the upcoming winter. The company wants to sign its customers to contracts for the season, but to compete it must guarantee the price per gallon for the heating season. If the company guesses too high, it may not take in much business. If it guesses too low, it could get a lot of business and lose money on all of it. Let's assume the company wants to make its profit on the delivery of oil, and not on price speculation. It can do so by going long the appropriate heating oil contracts. It will likely have to guess as to the number of contracts (each heating oil contract is for 42,000 gallons), but this is probably an easier guess than having to guess the price of the oil during the heating season. As winter arrives, the company then sells each contract as it buys the heating oil in the cash market. Again, buying in the cash market probably saves substantial transportation costs over taking delivery on the futures contract.

As in the short hedge, the major concern is whether the basis risk will be substantially less than the price risk. If that is the case, then the heating oil company can focus on delivering oil, confident that it has substantially reduced its price risk.

Speculating

Individuals who use speculating as an investment tactic anticipate that the price of a commodity or financial future will change during the duration of the contract, and they take a position in which they expect to benefit from the price movement. If a speculator expects the price to rise, he or she purchases futures contracts (goes long). If the market price of the commodity or financial instrument rises, the speculator can sell the contract for a profit.

A speculator who expects the price to fall sells (shorts) the futures contract and gains if the price does as expected. The loss from a rise in the price of the commodity or financial instrument can be virtually unlimited if the speculator is unable to close out the open position during the upward price movement and ultimately has to purchase the commodity in the spot market so that delivery can be made. As we will see in a later section, this can be a serious problem.

Spreading

Users of spreading as an investment tactic buy one futures contract (go long) and sell a second futures contract (go short) that has different terms. The objective in spreading is to look for misaligned prices. There are two types of spreads: intra-commodity and inter-commodity. Let's consider an example of each.

Example 1:	An intra-commodity spread might start with a December wheat contract trading for $4.50 per bushel, and the subsequent March contract trading for $4.70. A spreader might have reason to believe that this spread is too large. Hence, he or she expects the December wheat contract to rise relative to the March contract. Both may rise or fall in absolute terms, but the key is

whether the spread will narrow or not. In this case, the spreader would buy the December contract and sell the March contract. Let's suppose the spreader is correct, the December contract rises to $5.00 per bushel, and the March contract rises to $5.10 per bushel over the holding period. When the spreader closes out his or her positions, he or she will make $.50 per bushel (buy at $4.50/bushel and sell at $5.00/bushel) on the December contract, and lose $.40 per bushel on the March contract (sell at $4.70/bushel and buy at $5.10/bushel). Thus, the spreader makes $.10 per bushel.

Example 2:   An inter-commodity spread example might start with noting that the January heating oil no. 2 contract trades at $.85 per gallon, and the January gasoline NY unleaded contract trades at $.80 per gallon. If the spreader believes that this differential is too narrow, then he or she believes the price of the heating oil contract will fall *relative* to the price of the gasoline contract. Hence, the spreader would take a short position in the heating oil contract, and a long position in the gasoline contract. Let's suppose that the price of the heating oil rises to $.90 per gallon, and the price of the gasoline contract rises to $.89 per gallon. In this case, the spreader will lose $.05 per gallon on the heating oil (sell at $.85/gallon and buy at $.90/gallon), but will make $.09 per gallon on the gasoline contract (buy at $.80/gallon and sell at $.89/gallon). In this case, the spreader will make a profit of $.04 per gallon.

Spreading requires knowledge about the product, the contract, and the history of price differentials. It is really an activity only for professionals.

Commissions

As described earlier, investors in futures contracts typically close out their position without having to deliver or accept delivery of the underlying commodity or financial instrument. Delivery actually takes place in only a small percent of all futures contracts. Since the standard procedure is to close out the position by acquiring an offsetting contract, the transaction cost paid at the formation of a long or short futures contract position is a *round-trip fee* that covers the commission at both ends of the transaction. The size of the commission varies, depending on the commodity or financial futures contract and the number of contracts being traded.

round-trip fee

Margin Deposits

earnest money

Investors can purchase stocks and bonds by paying in full at the time of purchase or by using a margin transaction in which the investor places the initial margin requirement (percentage of purchase price) with the broker and borrows the remainder. In the futures market, the term margin has a slightly different meaning. Both the buyer and seller must make a margin deposit, which *is earnest money* (security) to guarantee the performance by *both* participants in the futures contract. The transaction does not involve any borrowing. The margin deposit stays with the broker through whom the order is placed until the contract is either completed or closed out.

mark to the market

Like margin accounts with stocks and bonds, these margin deposits have initial and maintenance requirements established for each commodity or financial instrument. In general the margin percentage for each type of contract is set just high enough to limit the risk of default by the buyer or seller, typically 5–15 percent of the contract's value. For example, a wheat futures contract with a market value of $25,000 might require an initial margin or deposit of $1,500 and a maintenance margin of $1,000.

To maintain the integrity of the margin, the futures market uses a procedure called *mark to the market*. In this process, the futures contract is valued at the close of business each day, and the investor's deposit is adjusted for the full change in the dollar value of the contract for that day. Under this procedure, losses in value reduce the investor's deposit, and a margin call is made if the deposit falls below the maintenance amount for that particular futures contract. If the investor fails to meet the margin call, the broker will close out the account by making an offsetting transaction, and the investor must then settle any loss on the account with the broker.

If the mark-to-the-market procedure results in a gain to the contract holder, the deposit is increased by the gain. The investor can use the gain, if sufficient in amount, as the initial deposit on additional futures contracts, thus pyramiding his or her holdings in exactly the same manner as used in margin accounts for stocks and bonds. The investor might also be able to remove cash from the account, as a kind of early distribution of the profit on the trade.

Example: A December wheat futures contract trades at a price of $3.00 per bushel. An investor takes a long position (buys one contract) and places the minimum initial margin of $1,500 in his brokerage account. The next day, the price of the contract falls by $.25 per bushel. The value of the contract has declined by $1,250 (5,000 bushels x $.25/bushel) from $15,000 to $13,750. The broker removes the $1,250 from the investor's account, leaving a balance of $250. If the minimum margin requirement is $1,000, the investor is now required to come up with at least $750 to get the account back up to the minimum requirement. Failure to do so will result in the broker's selling the contract; the remaining cash in the account ($250, assuming the price of the contract has not changed in the meantime) is returned to the investor.

Had the price of wheat risen by $.25 per bushel, the investor would have been able to remove the $1,250 gain from his account.

Price Limits

daily price limit (interday limit)

In the stock markets, there is no limit on the amount the price of a stock can change in a given trading day (other than it cannot fall below zero). Not so for futures contracts. The *daily price limit* rule (sometimes called the *interday limit*) prohibits any trades taking place outside a range defined by the prior day's closing price plus or minus the limit for that contract.

Example: Assume that the daily price limit for wheat is $0.25 and that September wheat futures closed at $5 yesterday. Today's opening price for September wheat futures can be neither lower than $4.75 nor higher than $5.25, no matter what new information might have come to the market between the closing and opening times. For instance, suppose that during the night, a severe storm ravaged the wheat-growing section of the Midwest and early reports describe widespread damage to wheat crops. This information would make many individuals and businesses seek to immediately acquire wheat futures contracts for September delivery in anticipation of sizable price increases. Without the daily price limit, the price of wheat would skyrocket—perhaps unnecessarily—to as high as $6, but the daily price limit means the opening trade cannot be at a price greater than $5.25. Although buyers at this price of September delivery wheat futures would be numerous, there may well not be any sellers. If there are no sellers, no contract will trade at $5.25 or less, and no trade takes place for the day. The closing price is set at $5.25 so that all investors can be marked to the market.

The following day, the upper limit of the opening price is $5.50 (lower limit $5). Again, if no contracts are traded, then no trading takes place, and the following day's opening price can be as high as $5.75. Following this procedure, the market will eventually find the price range in which trading will occur. The major benefit of the price limits is that if there are abrupt changes in the trading price of a contract, the limit means that the necessary marking to the market will be spread over several days. This gives people (in this case, those with short positions) more time to come up with the cash to cover their losses

Each different commodity has a different daily price limit, depending on the price per unit of the underlying commodity or financial instrument.

Open Outcry

The stock exchanges use specialists to maintain an orderly market in the securities, and the auction system is used to match buy and sell orders. By contrast, futures trading uses a system called *open outcry,* wherein traders shout out their desire to sell (or buy) a contract. In addition to shouting their preferences, traders use a system of hand and finger signals to indicate the number of contracts they wish to sell (or buy) and how much (in fractions of a cent) they are willing to accept or pay above or below the last-traded full-cent price. When someone acknowledges a willingness to trade at those terms, the contract is formed and recorded. Although this may sound chaotic (and usually looks chaotic to the observer), the success of the futures markets proves it to be a highly efficient method of trading.

Differences between Commodities and Securities Markets

The futures market has no specialist system. Commodity and option positions must be closed out with the brokerage firm that handled the initial transaction. Stocks and bonds may, in contrast, use different brokerage firms to buy and sell (unless the securities are held in street name).

In the previous pages, we have noted substantial differences in the markets and mechanics of futures contracts and stocks and bonds. A few more differences should be noted.

Hedge Trading Results

We indicated earlier that there are two basic motives for trading futures contracts: hedging and speculating. No market would exist if there were only

Differences between the Markets in Commodities Futures and Stocks

Commodities Futures	Stocks
• Limited term	• Unlimited term
• Maximum daily price moves	• No limit on daily price moves
• Margins of 5% to 15%	• Margins of 50% or more
• Long interest equal to short interest by definition	• Short interest usually small fraction of long interest
• No short selling restrictions	• Short sales not permitted on a downtick
• No interest charged on unpaid balance	• Interest incurred on monies borrowed to buy
• Market has no specialist system	• Market making by specialists
• Positions must be opened and closed with same brokerage firm	• No restriction on opening and closing positions with different firms

hedgers or only speculators participating. An active market requires both. So an interesting issue arises. If hedgers use the markets to substitute basis risk for price risk on the belief that the former is much smaller than the latter, and speculators are simply looking to profit from price changes, are the speculators successful? Put another way, hedging is akin to purchasing insurance. Thus, those who facilitate hedge trading (speculators) might well be expected to earn a risk premium.

Financial Planning Issue

A new client, Ted Casey, sits down with a financial planner and as a part of the process, the planner is reviewing Ted's portfolio for the last couple of years. Most of the holdings seem normal and appropriate, but the planner notices an occasional commodities trade. There are trades in pork bellies, soybean oil, gold, and natural gas futures contracts. The typical trade is for two to three weeks. What is an appropriate action for the planner?

The planner needs to ascertain first whether Ted is aware of the trades, and if so, whether he or the broker is the source of the trades. If Ted indicates he is speculating in futures based on "hot tips" he is getting from various sources, then the planner should make sure Ted is aware of the tremendous risk exposure he is taking on, and the poor track record of individual speculators such as himself. If Ted is aware of the trades but indicates the broker suggests them, then the planner needs to make sure the broker has fully explained the speculative nature of these contracts and the risk exposure to Ted. If Ted is unaware of the trades, then the broker has clearly been irresponsible and it would be appropriate to suggest that Ted find a new broker ASAP.

Testing this proposition requires identifying those who are seeking to hedge and separating them from those who are speculating. Discriminating between risk takers and hedgers from aggregated data, however, is relatively difficult. Nevertheless, several studies that have attempted such desegregation indicate that professionals (large speculators) may profit at the expense of small traders, and small speculators do not seem to receive a risk premium for their risk taking.[2]

FINANCIAL FUTURES MARKETS

So far, the discussion has focused only on agricultural futures, because the tangible nature of the examples makes them easier to understand. Individuals are more likely to have legitimate need to use financial futures for hedging purposes. So in this section, we will review the basic elements of some of these contracts. Transactions in financial futures deal with contracts for foreign currencies, debt securities (commonly called interest rate futures), and stock indexes (index futures). Many of the characteristics and trading concepts of financial futures are the same as for agricultural futures, but there are a few differences.

Futures on Indexes and Cash Settlement

Traditionally, futures contracts have specified delivery of some specific asset. Although most contracts may and usually are closed out with offsetting trades, those still in force at the time the contract expires must result in the long side's taking and the short side's making delivery. For some contracts, however, the underlying asset would be relatively difficult, expensive, or inconvenient to deliver. Specifically, futures contracts on various market indexes present a potential problem with delivery. Rather than settling by delivery of a physical asset, index contracts are settled with cash. That is, contracts still in existence at the close of trading on the contract's last day are treated as if both parties make the appropriate offsetting trade at the actual closing price of the index on that day. Because of the daily marking-to-the-market prices, this usually requires minimal cash payments. Both parties then have their margins (earnest money) returned to them.

Interest Rate Futures

Trading in interest rate futures began in the early 1970s with the Chicago Board of Trade's Government National Mortgage Association (GNMA) futures contracts and the Chicago Mercantile Exchange's (CME) T-bill contracts. The market subsequently expanded to include long-term Treasury bonds, one- and 5-year Treasury notes, municipal bonds, CDs, and

Eurodollars. Most of the recent trading has been in Eurodollars, T-bills, and Treasury bonds. GNMA futures are no longer actively traded.

Like all futures contracts, interest rate futures call for delivery of a specific amount of the relevant commodity at the contract's expiration. For example, the Treasury bond contract specifies the delivery of $100,000 face amount of Treasuries with an 8-percent coupon yield. The contract itself specifies the magnitude of the penalties for delivery of bonds with different coupon rates. If someone who is short a Treasury futures contract finds that it is cheaper to deliver bonds with a 7-percent coupon rate and pay the penalty, then that is what will be delivered. The actual price of the contract will be based on which bonds would most likely be delivered, not what bonds should be delivered. Price fluctuations in the contract reflect variations in the expected bond interest rate.

Individuals in either short hedges or long hedges can use interest rate futures. A short hedge (a short position in a futures contract) would be undertaken by someone concerned that interest rates will rise, and a long hedge (taking a long position in a futures contract) would be undertaken by someone concerned that interest rates would fall. Let's consider two examples.

Example 1:   Ralph Edwards is looking to buy a home sometime in the next three or four months. He could afford the home at today's interest rates. But if rates go up, he is concerned he would have to buy a smaller home than he desires, or be squeezed out of the home market altogether. What could Ralph do?

Answer: There is the possibility Ralph could set up a short hedge. One concern is the size of the mortgage Ralph would need, and a second concern is whether Ralph is sufficiently comfortable that a contract exists for which the basis risk is substantially less than the price risk. Let's suppose that Ralph (and the planner) are comfortable that local mortgage rates would move in tandem with the price on the Treasury Note Futures Contract. The contract calls for delivery of $100,000 worth of principal. So Ralph would need to be planning on a mortgage of at least $100,000. If interest rates rise, bond prices fall, and so the price of this contract would decline. Ralph could then take the profit from this short position and use it to increase the down payment on his house, thus reducing the size of the mortgage he would need. The smaller mortgage would then help offset the increase in the mortgage rate. The downside to the short hedge is that if interest rates fall,

Ralph would incur a loss on the futures contract. However, this loss would be compensated for by the lower mortgage payments Ralph would be making in the future. The worst-case scenario would be if Ralph does the short hedge, interest rates fall (giving him a loss), and then he changes his mind about buying a home!

Example 2:   Connie James has just learned that she will inherit $500,000 in 6 months. She is elated. However, she likes the interest rates she could invest the money at if she had it today, and she is afraid that rates will decline over the next 6 months. What should she do?

Answer: She can look for an interest rate futures contract that most closely represents the type of security she would be most likely to buy when she actually receives the money. She could then buy (go long) $500,000 worth of principal of this contract. Six months later, she can actually take delivery if she wants, or she can sell the contract and buy the appropriate investments in the spot market. If interest rates do go down over the next 6 months, as she fears, then the value of her futures contract will have risen. She will end up investing the money at a lower yield, but she will be able to offset that with the profit from her futures position. If interest rates instead go up, then she will lose money on her futures contract, but she will be able to invest her cash at a higher rate than she thought she would. Thus, she is hedged in the sense that the gain or loss on her futures contract will match up with an opportunity loss or gain in her cash position (when she actually receives the money). If the contract she buys is for delivery of the exact security she intends to buy when she receives the money, the hedge may be a perfect hedge. The worst case would be if she takes a loss on the future contract and then it turns out that there is no inheritance.

Stock Market Index Futures

The successful introduction of debt instrument futures spurred interest in equity futures. Today, the most popular stock market index futures are the Chicago Mercantile Exchange's S&P 500 Index and its Mini S&P 500 Index contracts. The Chicago Board of Trade (CBT) has a Dow Jones Industrial Average index, but it is not nearly as popular as the S&P contracts. Several

European indexes are traded on European futures markets, the most popular of which is the DJ Euro STOXX 50 Index.

The CME trades contracts based on the Russell 2000 and the NASDAQ 100. The Russell 2000 provides a vehicle for speculating or hedging in relatively small-capitalization stocks. Large and small technology stocks heavily influence the NASDAQ 100 index. These equity contracts offer a variety of ways to speculate or hedge on the stock market's movement. In particular, the contracts are an ideal way for portfolio managers to hedge either their anticipated funds needs or their portfolios against anticipated market reversals. One has to be very careful when working with stock index futures to choose the best contract and the number of contracts to hedge with so that the basis risk is minimal. Selection of an inappropriate index, and/or use of the wrong number of contracts could mean that the basis risk is greater than the price risk one is trying to obviate.

There are two techniques to selecting the best contract. One is to analyze the portfolio that is being hedged with regard to the nature of the companies, and then find the index that provides the best match. The second technique is to compute the rates of return from this index and the rates of return on the portfolio to be hedged, and then to compute the correlation coefficient for these two series of numbers. The higher the correlation coefficient, the more appropriate the index is for hedging.

The number of contracts to use in the hedge can be derived with the following formula:

$$\frac{\text{Number of contracts}}{\text{needed for hedge}} = \frac{\text{Portfolio value}}{\text{Contract value}} \text{ x } \frac{\text{Weighted average}}{\text{beta of portfolio}}$$

Note that this formula will simultaneously account for differences in the size of the portfolio and the index, as measured by market values, and in the volatility of the portfolios, as measured by the beta of the portfolio. Note that the beta in the above formula should be computed using the selected index as the market index. Let's consider an example.

Example: Suppose Anne Gleason, an older client, is concerned about a significant market retrenchment. She has an extremely large common stock portfolio, but does not want to liquidate the portfolio on either a permanent or temporary basis. To liquidate and later reinvest the portfolio would be costly (spreads, commissions, and so forth). How can you help Anne with her concern?

Answer: The financial planner might advise a short hedge. If the market declines, Anne will make money on the short position in the futures market, and if it is a good hedge, such profit should substantially offset the losses in her personal portfolio. The first issue is: which index should be used? Let's say you review Anne's portfolio and observe that it has a large number of companies in many industries, and most have recognizable names. This suggests the S&P futures index. You collect some rate of return data for both this index and Anne's portfolio, and find that the correlation coefficient is .90, a really good match. Next, you compute the beta coefficient for her portfolio using the same data, and obtain a portfolio beta of 1.14. Finally, you note that Anne's portfolio has a market value of $20 million. The S&P futures contract value is $2.50 multiplied by the S&P Index future value.[3] Assume the current S&P Index future is 146000. Thus, a single contract would be worth $365,000 ($2.50 x 146000).

Accordingly, the number of contracts needed to short is as follows:

$$\text{Number of contracts needed for hedge (short)} = \left(\frac{\$20,000,000}{\$365,000} \right) \times 1.14$$

$$= 62.465753 \text{ (rounded to 62, the nearest whole contract)}$$

Futures Options

A commodity option, or futures option, is an option on a futures contract. As such, it is an abstraction on an abstraction. The futures contract is itself a deferred-delivery agreement that trades and has a life of its own. An option on such an agreement represents the right, but not the obligation, to enter into such a contract. Thus, a call option on a futures contract is a right to buy such a contract at a prespecified price over a prespecified period. Similarly, a put is an option to sell such a futures contract. The unique feature of options on futures is that they give the investor the opportunity to make a small dollar investment that can control a sizable position in a particular futures commodities or financial instrument. Currently, futures options are listed on a number of agricultural, mineral, and especially financial assets.

It should be noted that in the various examples given above as to how a client might use futures contracts for hedging purposes, futures options provide an alternative approach. One of the earlier examples dealt with how Ralph Edwards could use a Treasury Note futures contract to alleviate his concern that mortgage interest rates might rise. Ralph could also consider buying a put option on the Treasury Note futures contract. If interest rates rise, Ralph would benefit from the decline in the value of this contract. If interest rates fall, Ralph's option would become worthless. Although he could lose 100 percent of the premium he paid for the option, at least Ralph would know in advance the magnitude of his loss. It should be noted, though, that it is much more difficult to make the gain on one position closely match the loss on the other when the premium on the futures contract is tossed into the equation.

Similarly, Connie James could have bought a call option on one of the interest rate futures contracts to protect against a decline in market interest rates. The one drawback here is that there is a limited number of contracts for which there is an active futures options market. Hence, it is not as clear that Connie could find a futures call option that would match well with her prospective investment.

Finally, Anne Gleason could have bought a put option on the S&P 500 futures contract. But as with Ralph, Anne could end up losing 100 percent of her premium, and not having this match up with the gain in her actual portfolio holdings.

Program Trading

The advent of stock index futures and options has facilitated the rise of a type of trading that generally uses the indexes: program trading. In a broad sense, program trading refers to any large-volume, mechanical trading system. This trading is usually based on some computerized model of theoretically appropriate price relationships. Normally, a program involves the simultaneous execution of trades in a number of stocks. The large-capitalization stocks that are members of one of the major indexes, such as the S&P 500, are particularly likely to be involved. These trades also often involve the use of stock index futures or options on these index futures. Program trades for stocks listed on the New York Stock Exchange are facilitated by their *designated order turnaround (DOT)* and *SuperDOT* systems that were discussed in chapter 2. These two systems allow the near simultaneous execution of large trades of a number of stocks. The orders are submitted directly to the system and then transmitted electronically to the specific stock trading posts of each of the securities.

designated order turnaround (DOT) SuperDOT

By far, the most popular types of program trading are portfolio insurance and index arbitrage. Both involve the use of index contracts (futures or options on futures), and large institutional investors and traders, including some brokerage firms trading for their own accounts, are the primary users of both.

Portfolio Insurance

The index futures example above (Anne Gleason) illustrates an increasingly popular strategy of portfolio managers. Portfolios, particularly

portfolio insurance

large portfolios, can be managed to limit their exposure to market downturns. The process of limiting a portfolio's market exposure is called *portfolio insurance*. This insurance can be structured to greatly reduce the possibility that losses will exceed some prespecified limit. At the same time, the portfolio will still retain an opportunity to profit from a rising market. The portfolio insurer can use various types of contracts, including index futures, options on index futures, and options on individual stocks.

Under one form of downside protection, the insurer closely monitors the market. When the stock market has a significant pullback, the client's portfolio is hedged. Usually, the insurer sells an appropriate number (for the portfolio's size and beta) of index futures contracts. Alternatively, the insurer may purchase an equivalent number of stock index put options. Either approach largely neutralizes the impact of further downward movement in the market. For example, a short position in index contracts would appreciate as the value of the portfolio declines. Similarly, index puts would place a floor on losses in the portfolio, while upside potential would remain.

Both of these approaches to portfolio insurance (futures or options hedges) generally protect the portfolio against a downturn. Protection, however, has a cost. In addition to the relatively modest direct costs (insurer's fee, commission, and forgone interest on margin deposits), the investor sacrifices some potential gains. Purchasing puts entails a premium paid for the option, while selling index futures contracts shifts any profits from a stock market rise to the purchaser of the contracts. Moreover, the implementation of the strategy requires the availability of sufficient potential supply of, or demand for (at reasonable prices), the hedging contracts. A substantial drop in stock prices may create a major imbalance in the supply-demand relationships for these contracts. Everyone cannot abandon ship at once. The supply of available lifeboats is limited.

In short, portfolio insurance can provide some protection against market downturns. It is not, however, always possible or cost effective to implement, and when it is possible to apply, a portfolio insurance strategy may reduce potential profits from subsequent upturns.

Index Arbitrage

The existence of stock index futures has facilitated and stimulated another relatively new type of trading. Index arbitrage is a strategy designed to take advantage of disparities between index futures prices and the spot market prices of the securities that make up the index.

Suppose, for example, the futures contract on the S&P Index is priced appreciably above the current value of the index itself. The final settlement price of an index futures contract is the closing value of the underlying index. Thus, at the expiration of the index future, the index and the futures contract on the index must have the same value. Accordingly, a long position in the stocks that make up the index, coupled with a short position in futures on that index, will produce a gain that is approximately equal to the difference between the values of the two positions. Some adjustments must be made for the impacts of commissions, bid-ask spreads, and dividends on the underlying stocks. The precise amount of dividends and the level of prices after deducting trading costs are not known at the outset. Moreover, the index programs must be initiated quickly when price disparities open up. Still, when the futures price exceeds the corresponding index, something close to a guaranteed trading profit is possible. If such a profit is attractive compared with alternative risk-free returns, an index arbitrage trade is indicated.

Similar index arbitrage opportunities are available when the futures contract is priced somewhat below the index. In this circumstance, the index arbitrageur shorts the underlying stocks while purchasing the futures contract. This type of program trade is profitable only if the difference in the two prices is sufficient to offset the trading costs (commissions and bid-ask spreads) and dividends on the shorted stocks.

Program Trading, the Brady Commission, and the Crash of 1987

Program trading—particularly index arbitrage—was subject to a substantial amount of criticism in the wake of the stock market's 1987 crash. The exchanges' regulators (and others) have studied the causes of the crash. The best known of these studies was sponsored by Congress and is referred to as the Brady Commission (named after the commission's chairman Nicholas Brady, later Secretary of the Treasury). Several other institutions also conducted studies. Many financial commentators and some of the committee reports blamed the crash, at least in part, on financial futures trading, and particularly blamed index arbitrage and portfolio insurance. More generally, trading in financial futures was blamed for the apparent increase in stock market volatility. The commissions, regulators, financial commentators, stock exchanges of New York, and the futures exchanges of Chicago argued vigorously over this and related issues. No one contends that financial futures have no impact on the markets for the underlying financial instruments. Whether the impact is relatively minor, short, and perhaps stabilizing or is more serious, longer, and destabilizing remains controversial.

circuit breaker

Most critics of the present system would like to restrict index arbitrage, program trading, and, in some instances, financial futures. One possibility is to impose larger margin requirements on financial futures. Another proposal seeks to stop any panic by the installation of so-called *circuit breakers,* whereby both stock and financial futures trading would stop briefly if the market moves more than some predetermined amount. In fact, circuit breakers were implemented in the late 1980s and then, more recently, scaled back. Other analysts assert that any attempt to restrict or ban financial futures or cash-market trading on U.S. exchanges will simply shift the markets overseas.

Hedge Funds

Some pooled investments called hedge funds (see chapter 10) use trading futures and options contracts as their main investment strategy. These funds—and some professionally managed portfolios—typically require minimum investments of $25,000, $100,000, or more. Therefore, they are not available to the investor with modest means. To this point, these funds are relatively unregulated because they are available only to investors who are qualified by virtue of both wealth and financial sophistication. An episode a few years ago with a hedge fund has caused some people to argue that more regulation is needed.

The Long Term Capital Management (LTCM) hedge fund near debacle in late September 1998 reveals both the power and risks of hedge fund performance and behavior. LTCM was funded by many of the largest investment firms and commercial banks on Wall Street and abroad. In summer 1998, fund managers and partners believed that abnormal interest rate spreads between U.S. government debt instruments and other debt securities, which were widening, would narrow sooner rather than later. They bet on this by buying options, futures, and other derivatives on the non-U.S. debt instruments.

The widening worsened dramatically, however, after the Russian government's default on its foreign debt and the spillover effect on Latin American financial markets. This led to a worldwide investor "flight to quality," which meant even more investors fleeing to U.S. government instruments. This, in turn, greatly exaggerated the spread and required the fund managers to cover their positions with even more capital. At the time, they had leveraged some $98 billion of exposure with $4.8 billion of capital. By the end of September, capital had dwindled to some $600 million.

The managers went to their lead lenders and asked for more capital. Enough of the lenders balked that it became necessary to force a bailout masterminded by the head of the New York Federal Reserve Bank. In the end, the lenders (under duress) invested $3.6 billion of new capital, and the original partners' share in the company dwindled to 10 percent.

moral hazard

Debate then raged as to whether the original investors' punishment fit the risks and losses they had caused. The major issue was *moral hazard*—the assumption of risks by one party that causes widespread costs that are not fully borne by that one party, thereby forcing other parties to bail them out. In general, a moral hazard is a situation in which people have incentives to behave in ways that can be detrimental to others or to society as a whole. Taking excessive risks because of the expectation that others will bail one out is a prime example of a moral hazard.

SUMMARY AND CONCLUSIONS

A large dollar volume of futures trading takes place on the various futures exchanges. Futures contracts that are standardized with respect to grade, size, location, and delivery date facilitate substantial hedge and speculative trading. The relatively low percentage margins required to trade futures allow investors to magnify greatly the profits and losses generated by a given price move in the underlying asset. Financial futures markets have grown rapidly because of the opportunities to hedge and speculate on the price changes of securities in other financial markets and because of the introduction of a variety of new types of contracts. An effective futures market requires a well-defined, deliverable commodity, a commodity with significant business use, and enough price volatility to make it interesting to speculators and appropriate for hedgers.

Financial futures differ from stock trades in a number of ways, including term, trading limits, margin percentages, short restrictions, interest on margin, specialists, commission structure, and opening and closing positions with the same broker. Because of their relatively independent (not related to the stock market) volatility, financial futures contracts may be useful in diversification, but their own volatility limits their appeal to amateurs.

Several different types of professional futures traders compete with the amateur speculator: Scalpers trade on the floor of the exchange, seeking very quick turns; day traders close their positions at the end of each day; position traders may hold for several days; arbitrageurs seek profits from disequilibrium price relations; firm representatives trade for the accounts of firms that deal in the underlying assets. Ultimately, all investors are either hedgers or speculators.

Probably the single most important feature of futures contracts is the relative small margin that must be posted by both those taking long positions and those taking short positions. Because gains and losses are based on the full market value of each contract, huge potential exists for substantial percentage gains and losses. Two other critical features of futures trading are the daily limits on price changes and the daily marking to the market.

Financial futures instruments include currency, interest rate, and stock market index futures. Financial planners may be able to use some of these financial futures to help clients deal with various forms of price risk. Hedging is not the elimination of price risk; it is the substitution of basis risk for price risk.

CHAPTER REVIEW

Answers to the review questions and the self-test questions start on page 733.

Key Terms

spot market	scalpers
forward contract	day traders
futures contract	position traders

arbitrageurs
hedging
short hedge
basis
perfect hedge
long hedge
speculating
spreading
round-trip fee
margin deposit
earnest money
mark to the market

daily price limit (interday limit)
open outcry
interest rate futures
stock market index futures
futures options
designated order turnaround
  (DOT)
SuperDOT
portfolio insurance
index arbitrage
circuit breaker
moral hazard

Review Questions

12-1.   Compare commodity futures trading with stock market trading.

12-2.   What factors have led to the recent growth of financial futures?

12-3.   A silver futures contract is based on 5,000 troy ounces, and is priced on a per ounce basis. Suppose you start with $5,000 that you invest in silver futures at $5 per ounce, putting down margin equal to 10 percent.
   a.   How many contracts can you buy initially?
   b.   A month later, silver rises to $6 per ounce. What is the dollar profit to the investor?
   c.   If this dollar profit is compared to the margin requirement to provide a rate of return measure, what is the rate of return?

12-4.   What characteristics are needed for a commodity contract to be traded actively on a futures exchange?

12-5.   A farmer has planted enough corn to produce 50,000 bushels. The spot price for corn is $3 per bushel. The corn will be ready to harvest in 4 months. The futures contract for that delivery date is $3.25.
   a.   What is the current basis?
   b.   What type of hedge might the farmer set up if he would like to lock in as well as possible the current spot price? What are the positions in this hedge?
   c.   Suppose that at the time of harvest the spot price is $2.50 per bushel, and the futures price is $2.60. What are the farmer's proceeds on the sale of the corn (net of the gain or loss on the futures contract)?

12-6.   Explain the motivations and advantages that firm representatives, position traders, and scalpers each possess.

12-7.   What is wrong with saying that people hedge in order to eliminate risk?

12-8. a. Compute the number of contracts needed to hedge a $50 million stock portfolio having a beta of 1.07. Assume the S&P Index future is at 145000.

b. A client has a $50 million portfolio with a beta of 1.07. The client is concerned the market is going to decline in the next few months, but does not want to cash out the portfolio. What sort of hedge could be set up, and what are the positions?

12-9. a. What is unique about stock index futures?

b. Some of the stock index futures include DJIA, S&P 500, S&P Midcap 400, NASDAQ 100, Russell 2000, Russell 1000, NYSE Composite, and the DJ STOXX 50. How does the financial planner decide which is the appropriate index in which to hedge a client's portfolio.

12-10. Define a futures option.

Self-Test Questions

T F 12-1. People rarely engage in spot market transactions.

T F 12-2. Forward contracts are highly standardized.

T F 12-3. In a forward contract, each party has to worry about the other honoring the terms of the contract. In a futures contract, there is an intervening third party.

T F 12-4. If the owner of a futures contract does not like the subsequent prices, he or she can always just walk away from the contract.

T F 12-5. Two of the most important characteristics for a futures contract to be successful are a significant business use for the product and price stability.

T F 12-6. Each exchange typically has one contract per commodity.

T F 12-7. Most contracts conclude with delivery of the commodity.

T F 12-8. Commissions are paid only when one buys a futures contract.

T F 12-9. A scalper will typically take a position for at least a day but no longer than a week.

T F 12-10. Position traders base their trading on fundamentals.

T F 12-11. The buyer of a futures contract is required, if the contract is held at its expiration, to take delivery of the item covered by the contract.

T F 12-12. Only the number of contracts and the price (per unit) are negotiable between buyers and sellers of commodity futures contracts for a specified commodity.

T F 12-13. In contrast with stocks and bonds, margin is hardly ever used in commodity futures contracts.

T F 12-14. Someone taking a short position on a futures contract will receive the margin posted by the buyer.

T F 12-15. The margin required for futures transactions is a specified dollar amount that varies according to the type of contract and is the amount an investor borrows when making margin transactions.

T F 12-16. Like investors in stocks and bonds, investors in futures contracts must meet two types of margin (or deposit) requirements.

T F 12-17. The buyer of a futures option has no additional obligation to the seller and is not subject to a margin call as occurs with a futures contract.

T F 12-18. Futures contracts are marked to the market on a daily basis.

T F 12-19. Recognizing the volatile nature of commodity contracts, the exchanges impose daily price limits for each of the futures contracts traded on the exchanges.

T F 12-20. An investor who expects interest rates to decline in the near future would profit by selling interest rate futures.

T F 12-21. If a speculator anticipates that interest rates will rise in the future, he or she might consider buying (going long) interest rate futures to make a profit if interest rates do rise.

T F 12-22. The oldest commodity exchange is the Chicago Mercantile Exchange.

T F 12-23. An investor who holds a portfolio of bonds and plans to sell the bonds within a 6-month period could now sell a futures contract against this portfolio as a short hedge.

T F 12-24. A short hedge that involves selling a stock index future while holding a portfolio of stocks enables the investor to offset a decline in the value of the portfolio should the market fall.

T F 12-25. The greater the volatility of the basis, the more successful an effort to hedge will be.

T F 12-26. A short hedge involves a short position in the futures contract, and a long position in the underlying commodity.

T F 12-27. Speculators always take the short position in a futures trade.

T F 12-28. Spreading involves simultaneous long and short positions in two different contracts.

T F 12-29. Index arbitrage seeks to profit by exploiting differences in the prices of stock index futures and the prices of the stocks in the index underlying the contract.

T   F   12-30.   The biggest difference between a futures option and a futures contract is that the option limits the investor's loss exposure to the price of the option.

NOTES

1. www.tfc-charts.w2d.com/tafm/tafm7.html, December 3, 2003.
2. E. Chang, "Returns to Speculators and the Theory of Normal Backwardation," *Journal of Finance* (March 1985), pp. 193–208; E. Fama and K. French, "Commodity Futures Prices: Some Evidence on Forecast Power, Premiums, and the Theory of Storage," *Journal of Business* (January 1987), pp. 55–73.
3. The S&P 500 contract is quoted in points, where one point equals $2.50. Thus, the prices that are published for this index are approximately equal to 100 times the actual index value. When the published prices are multiplied by $2.50, one obtains the actual value of the contract. One will obtain approximately the same number if one multiplies the current value of the S&P 500 Index by $250.

Tax Issues in Investing

Learning Objectives

An understanding of the material in this chapter should enable the student to

13-1. Explain the basic model of personal taxation.

13-2. Compute a tax liability.

13-3. Measure after-tax returns and determine a combined marginal tax rate.

13-4. Figure the tax consequences of capital transactions.

13-5. Discuss the pros and cons of tax-loss harvesting and tax-efficient investing.

13-6. Discuss the tax treatments of stock splits, stock dividends, warrants, rights, short sales, and liquidating dividends.

13-7. Discuss the tax treatment of bonds.

13-8. Compute a tax-equivalent yield.

13-9. Determine the impact of the wash-sale rule on various trades.

13-10. Determine the cost of mutual fund shares, options, and master and limited partnerships.

13-11. Explain the tax treatment of annuities.

13-12. Describe investment strategies for tax-advantaged accounts.

Chapter Outline

Although taxes play an extremely important role in the investment process, they have heretofore been ignored so that we can focus on the tax aspects of investment planning as a separate topic. The integration of taxes requires a basic knowledge of how our personal income tax system works. The most important concept to derive from this discussion is the concept of the marginal tax rate, or the rate at which incremental income is taxed. With the most recent change in the tax code, we have to be aware of a variety of marginal tax rates that apply to different forms of income. Unfortunately, the tax code also contains a substantial number of rules with which we should be familiar. The rules do not always make sense, but they are critical to making sound investment decisions.

TAXATION OF ORDINARY INCOME

Personal taxation is based on requiring each individual who meets certain criteria to file the tax return known as Form 1040.[1] The basic outline of this form has not significantly changed since the modern version of the income tax was introduced in 1913. The model for the determination of personal taxation has two steps. The first step is the determination of taxable income, which is derived as follows:

>   Total gross income
> – <u>Adjustments to gross income</u>
> = Adjusted gross income, or AGI
> – Standard deduction or itemized deductions (whichever is larger)
> – <u>Personal exemptions</u>
> = Taxable income

Based on taxable income, the taxpayer can determine his or her tax liability according to what is referred to as filing status. Then the following formula is applied:

>   Tax liability (based on taxable income and filing status)
> – Credits
> + <u>Other taxes owed</u>
> = Total taxes for the year
> – <u>Taxes paid to date</u>
> = Tax refund to be received or tax due

Let's consider each component of this model.

Computation of Taxable Income

The first step in filing a return is the declaration of filing status. Although there are five different statuses, the two most common ones are single and married filing a joint return. Our discussion will focus only on these two statuses. The treatment of material covered in this chapter for other filing statuses can be found in The American College's *Fundamentals of Income Taxation* or at the Internal Revenue Service web site (www.irs.gov).

gross income

ordinary income

The first section of Form 1040 determines the taxpayer's total income, which is frequently referred to as *gross income*. The first line of this section is the summation of all wages, salaries, tips, and any other income. Whenever any other income is classified as *ordinary income*, it simply means that income will be subject to the statutory marginal tax rates discussed below. Other income that is treated as ordinary income includes

- taxable interest
- dividends other than qualified dividends
- taxable refunds, credits, or offsets of state and local income taxes
- alimony received
- business income
- taxable portion of IRA distributions
- taxable portion of pensions and annuities
- net income from rental real estate, royalties, partnerships, S corporations, trusts, and so on
- farm income
- unemployment compensation
- taxable portion of Social Security benefits
- other income that is taxable and not listed elsewhere

In addition to the above, net capital gains are included as part of total income. However, the tax treatment of the capital gains depends on the time frame and the amount of the capital gains (or losses). Hence, capital gains must be distinguished from ordinary income. Thus, if the taxpayer has capital gains, he or she has to use a special form to determine tax liability.

Qualified dividends are not taxed at the same rates as ordinary income. Like capital gains, if the taxpayer has qualified dividend income, he or she has to use a special form to determine tax liability.

Because investment decisions affect the amount and type of dividend income; interest income; capital gains and losses; and IRA, pension, and annuity income, we will discuss each of these topics later in the chapter.

Adjustments to Gross Income

Total or gross income is then reduced by certain investment-related adjustments:

- IRA deduction
- self-employed SEP, SIMPLE, and qualified plans
- penalty on early withdrawal of savings

adjusted gross income (AGI)

Adjusted gross income (AGI) is derived by subtracting these adjustments from gross income.

Standard and Itemized Deductions

The next step is to determine which is larger, the standard deduction to which the taxpayer is entitled based on filing status, or the sum of itemized deductions. For 2004, the standard deduction is $9,700 for joint filers and $4,850 for single filers.

The more common itemized deductions are relatively straightforward with regard to definition and amounts. The seven categories of itemized deductions are

- medical and dental expenses (to the extent that they exceed 7.5 percent of AGI)
- taxes (state and local income taxes, real estate taxes, and personal property taxes)
- certain interest expenses
- gifts to charity (not to exceed 50 percent of AGI)
- casualty and theft losses (reduced by $100 per event, and only to the extent they exceed 10 percent of AGI)
- job-related expenses and most miscellaneous deductions (only to the extent they exceed 2 percent of AGI)
- miscellaneous deductions

Investment decisions can have a major impact on state and local taxes, interest expenses, and miscellaneous deductions subject to the 2 percent floor. Taxpayers who own homes (real estate taxes) and have a mortgage on that home (mortgage interest) will almost always find it beneficial to itemize. Those who do not own homes usually find that their standard deduction is larger than the sum of their itemized deductions.

Net Investment Income

When buying on margin, the interest expenses on the loans may qualify as an itemized deduction.[2] The rule is as follows:

> Interest payments on a nonbusiness loan incurred in the course of an investment activity are referred to an investment interest. Deductions for investment interest expenses are allowed but are limited to the taxpayer's "net investment income" for the year.

The rules as to what counts as "net investment income" were changed in 2003. Ordinary dividends clearly count as investment income; qualified dividends do not, unless the taxpayer elects to waive the special lower tax rates applicable to such dividends. Gains on property sold, other than capital gain, count as investment income. An example of a gain on property sold that

---

Financial Planning Issue

Your client, Hortense, has $10,000 in investment interest she paid during the year. She has $1,000 in investment expenses, $4,000 in qualified dividends, $3,000 in (ordinary) nonqualified dividends, and $8,000 in long-term capital gains. (Capital gains will be discussed in the next section.) The investment interest and investment expenses give her $11,000 ($10,000 + $1,000) of potential deductions. Because the qualified dividends do not count against investment interest, only the nonqualified dividends ($3,000) can be offset by the investment expenses, leaving Hortense with $8,000 of currently nondeductible investment interest expenses.

    Hortense suggests using the $8,000 in capital gains as investment income to take full benefit of this deduction. Although that strategy will work, it has a potentially costly side effect. The capital gains will be taxed at a much lower rate than Hortense's other income. If Hortense carries forward the unused investment interest, she might be able to shield more nonqualified dividends or other interest income next year that would otherwise be taxed as ordinary income. On the other hand, if Hortense expects her investment interest and investment expenses to exceed her net investment income for the foreseeable future, using the interest expenses this year to eliminate taxation on the capital gains may be a good idea. Simply put, getting some tax benefit from the investment interest is better than getting no tax benefit.

---

is not a capital gain is the recapture of depreciation associated with the sale of depreciable assets. Capital gains can be included as investment income, but the taxpayer has to treat those capital gains as subject to ordinary income tax rates, and not apply the lower capital gains tax rates to them.

net investment income

    Net investment income refers to investment income after the deduction of investment expenses. Investment expenses are generally all deductible expenses (other than interest expenses) that are connected with the production of the taxpayer's investment income. An example of an investment expense is a subscription to an investment publication the investor uses in the management of his or her investments.

    Note that if a taxpayer has more investment interest than can be deducted in the current year, he or she can carry the balance forward to the next year. Any amount not used that year can again be carried forward.

Personal Exemptions

    The last step to derive taxable income is to subtract personal exemptions. In 2004, the personal exemption is $3,100. Each taxpayer automatically receives a personal exemption, plus a personal exemption for the spouse if the return status is married filing jointly, plus an exemption for each dependent claimed.[3] The only exception to claiming a personal exemption is if the taxpayer is claimed as a dependent on someone else's tax return.

Computation of Taxes

The actual tax liability incurred depends on both the individual's taxable income and filing status. The computation uses a schedule similar to table 13-1, which shows the relevant figures for 2004 for married individuals filing jointly and for unmarried individuals. For each filing status, the table is **brackets** broken down into what are known as *brackets*, which are based on income ranges.

TABLE 13-1
Individual Tax Rate Schedules for 2004

Filing Status	Taxable Income	Tax
Married filing jointly	Not over $14,300	10% of taxable income
	Over $14,300 but not over $58,100	$1,430 plus 15% of the amount over $14,300
	Over $58,100 but not over $117,250	$8,000 plus 25% of the amount over $58,100
	Over $117,250 but not over $178,650	$22,787.50 plus 28% of the amount over $117,250
	Over $178,650 but not over $319,100	$39,979.50 plus 33% of the amount over $178,650
	Over $319,100	$86,328 plus 35% of the amount over $319,100
Single return	Not over $7,150	10% of taxable income
	Over $7,150 but not over $29,050	$715 plus 15% of the amount over $7,150
	Over $29,050 but not over $70,350	$4,000 plus 25% of the amount over $29,050
	Over $70,350 but not over $146,750	$14,325 plus 28% of the amount over $70,350
	Over $146,750 but not over $319,100	$35,717 plus 33% of the amount over $146,750
	Over $319,100	$92,592.50 plus 35% of the amount over $319,100

Suppose a married couple filing jointly has a taxable income (all ordinary income) of $60,000. According to the table, their taxable income falls in the range of over $58,100 but not over $117,250. Hence, their tax liability is $8,000 plus 25 percent of the amount over $58,100. Specifically, it is $8,000 plus 25 percent times the difference between $60,000 and $58,100, which works out to be $8,475 ($8,000 + $475).

Example: In 2004, Jan Q. Investor's $50,000-per-year income is the sole support for her family of four. The four personal exemptions (including one each for herself and her husband and two dependency exemptions for her children) total $12,400 (4 x $3,100). The standard deduction for married couples filing jointly is $9,700. This gives her and her husband a taxable income of $27,900 ($50,000 − $12,400 − $9,700). Table 13-1 shows that joint filers (Jan and her husband file jointly) with taxable incomes between $14,300 and $58,100 pay (2004 rates) $1,430 plus 15 percent of the amount over $14,300. This formula yields a tax liability of $3,470 ($1,430 + $2,040).

A crucial point to note about the tax rate schedule is that it changes every year. Congress has indexed the brackets to the inflation rate. Hence, unless there is no inflation or there is deflation, the bracket intervals will be increased each year. In addition, every few years Congress changes the tax rate associated with each bracket. Thus, a financial planner needs to be aware each year of what the brackets will be and what the tax rate for each bracket will be.

Average Tax Rate

There are two tax rate numbers with which every consumer (and financial planner) should be familiar. The first is the average tax rate. The average tax rate[4] is defined as

Average tax rate = Total taxes paid/Total income

In the case of Jan and her family, the average tax rate is 6.94 percent ($3,470/$50,000). This means that on average, 6.94 cents of every dollar Jan earned went to pay income taxes. This number is useful in preparing budgets. It is also useful in understanding the impact of federal income taxes on an individual's personal situation. It gives a sense of the relative burden of taxes that an individual is carrying. However, this number has no relevancy in financial decision making. Simply put, it is a descriptive number, not a financial planning number.

Marginal Tax Rate

The relevant number that the financial planner needs when analyzing the impact of taxation on investment decisions is the marginal tax rate. The most common definition is that this is the rate at which incremental income is taxed. The marginal tax rate is the tax rate associated with the income bracket into which an investor falls. In most cases, the marginal tax rate is relatively simple. For example, suppose in the previous example, Jan Q. Investor is considering buying a certificate of deposit that will generate an extra $100 in interest income, which will be taxed as ordinary income for the current year. We only have to look at table 13-1 to see that this $100 will be taxed at the 15 percent rate. Thus, Jan will owe an additional $15 in taxes ($100 x 15%) if she buys the certificate. Hence, 15 percent is the marginal tax rate.

Example: The Lyn Hayes family projects a taxable income for 2004 of $58,000. They will use the married filing jointly status. They are considering the purchase of a certificate of deposit that will generate $300 in interest that will be taxed as ordinary income. What is the marginal tax rate?

In this case, the income tax bracket changes at $58,100. Thus, the first $100 will be taxed at the 15 percent marginal tax rate, and the other $200 will be taxed at the 25 percent marginal tax rate. Therefore, the marginal tax rate for this particular investment is 21 2/3 percent, which is computed as ($100/$300) x 15% + ($200/$300) x 25% = 21 2/3%.

Marginal tax rates can also be relevant when considering reductions in income. Consider the following example.

Example: Hunter is a single person whose taxable income is $350,000. He is considering selling some bonds that had been generating $10,000 per year in interest income (which is taxed as ordinary income). He complains that he uses that $10,000 to pay for a nice vacation each year and really doesn't want to give up the income. The problem here is that Hunter fails to understand that by selling the bonds, he is not giving up $10,000 in cash inflow. The marginal tax rate on this income is 35 percent. Hence, along with the income is a tax liability of $3,500. In selling the bonds, he is giving up $6,500 in after-tax dollars, not $10,000.

The Alternative Minimum Tax

Individuals with large amounts of tax-sheltered income (accelerated depreciation, for example) or high itemized deductions may be subject to the alternative minimum tax (AMT). To determine whether the AMT applies, the tax liability is first computed in the regular way. Then all of the includible tax-sheltered items are added back to adjusted gross income, and certain allowable deductions are subtracted to obtain the income subject to the AMT. The AMT equals 26 percent (or 28 percent of the taxable amount exceeding $175,000 for married taxpayers filing jointly) of this sum. The individual's tax liabilities computed for the two different ways (regular and AMT) are then compared. The higher of the two tax figures is the one that must be paid. In other words, the AMT can raise but cannot lower an individual's tax liability. When an individual pays taxes based on the AMT, his or her marginal tax rate becomes the AMT tax rate.

The AMT came into existence years ago when enough people in Congress decided to make an issue out of the fact that a certain number of millionaires were paying zero income taxes each year. It was certainly possible for someone to get away with paying no income taxes if he or she emphasized avoidance of taxation as the foremost principle of investment planning. Such a strategy may not be a particularly good one for wealth accumulation, but it was one used at least by some people. Note that there was no accusation that these taxpayers were doing anything illegal. They were simply following the rules of the tax code that had been created by Congress. Thus, to attempt to ensure that everyone paid at least some taxes, Congress enacted the AMT.

When it was first created, the AMT affected few people. However, unlike the regular tax schedule (for example, table 13-1) where the income brackets are indexed each year, the AMT is not indexed. Hence, with the presence of inflation alone, more and more people each year are finding themselves subject to the AMT. It appears to be one of the least understood aspects of our tax system, and one that comes as a big shock to people who suddenly find for the first time that they have to pay additional taxes, even though they are obeying the tax code to the letter.

Determining the Final Tax Bill

Note that even after computation of the tax liability as represented in table 13-1, there are some additional calculations. The first adjustment is for tax credits. The two credits related to investment decisions are the following:

- foreign tax credit
- retirement savings contribution credit

Foreign Tax Credit

The foreign tax credit occurs whenever an investor owns stock in a corporation that is headquartered in a foreign country, and the foreign taxes are paid out of the dividends received by the investor. Note that if the foreign taxes paid are less than $300 for a single taxpayer or $600 for a married taxpayer filing a joint return, the taxpayer may take the full credit automatically.[5] If the foreign taxes paid exceed the $600 limit, the taxpayer must fill out Form 1116 to determine the percentage of the foreign taxes that qualify for a credit.

Retirement Savings Contribution Credit

The retirement savings contribution credit began in 2002 and is scheduled to run only through 2006. It helps to offset the cost of the first $2,000 contributed to IRAs; 401(k)s; 403(b)s; and 457, SEP, and SIMPLE plans. The credit applies only to individuals with incomes up to $25,000 and married couples with incomes up to $50,000.[6]

The credit is a percentage of the qualifying contribution amount, with the highest rate for taxpayers with the least income, as shown in table 13-2.

TABLE 13-2
Retirement Savings Contribution Credit Schedule

Credit Rate	Income for Married, Joint	Income for Single
50%	Up to $30,000	Up to $15,000
20%	$30,001–32,500	$15,000–16,250
10%	$32,501–50,000	$16,251–25,000

When figuring this credit, taxpayers must subtract the amount of distributions received from their retirement plans from the contributions they have made. This rule applies for distributions starting 2 years before the year the credit is claimed and ending with the filing deadline for that tax return.[7]

The retirement savings contributions credit is in addition to whatever other tax benefits may result from the retirement contributions. For example, most workers at these income levels may deduct all or part of their contributions to a traditional IRA.

Example: Consider the case of Betty (married filing jointly) with an annual wage income of $20,000. Because of the standard deduction and personal exemptions, her marginal tax rate is 10 percent. Suppose she actually has enough cash to make a $2,000 IRA contribution, and qualifies to use this as an adjustment to her total income. What is the net contribution Betty will be making?

Betty will receive two tax breaks. The first is the tax break from using the contribution as an adjustment to total income. Based on her 10 percent marginal tax rate, this saves her $200 in taxes ($2,000 x 10%). By also claiming the contribution as a tax credit, she saves another $1,000 in taxes ($2,000 x 50%). Thus, her total tax savings is $1,200. The contribution is therefore actually a net cash outflow of only $800 ($2,000 – $1,200).

Other Taxes

The final two categories to consider in determining the final tax bill are other taxes and payments. The primary other tax item related to investments is any tax that might be due in conjunction with qualified plans, including IRAs, and other tax-favored accounts. These would include taxes based on the following:

- any premature distribution from a tax-qualified account, which carries a tax penalty (generally 10 percent of the taxable amount withdrawn)
- any excess contribution that is made to an IRA, a Coverdell educational savings account (ESA), or an Archer medical savings account (MSA)
- any taxable distribution taken from a Coverdell ESA or qualified tuition program (which normally means a distribution that was not spent on tuition or other designated expenses)
- any shortfall in a minimum required distribution (MRD) from any IRA or other qualified retirement plan

Payments

Payments include the withholding taxes on payrolls, any estimated taxes paid during the year, any refund from the prior year that was carried forward, and any excess Social Security contribution made. An excess contribution can occur if a person holds more than one job during the year, and his or her combined income exceeds the maximum amount of income that is taxed by Social Security for its retirement program.

People with substantial investment income need to do one of the following:

Financial Planning Issue

Many taxpayers "enjoy" getting large tax refunds. In fact, the average tax refund is nearly $2,000. The easiest way for taxpayers to obtain a substantial tax refund is to authorize the maximum withholding of taxes from their paychecks. (This is achieved by declaring zero withholding allowances.) Some taxpayers do this because they believe (perhaps rightly so) that if they do not overwithhold, they will simply spend the money as they receive it and never achieve a chance to save. They can then save the large refund and use it to buy something that otherwise would not be affordable. The only problem with this strategy is that the taxpayer is lending his or her money to the U.S. Treasury at a zero percent interest rate.

When clients are overwithholding, a financial planner should find a way to authorize automatic payments from a client's paycheck into a savings program (such as a savings account at a bank or a mutual fund). This way, the money is out of the client's reach (the same effect as overwithholding), and the client is earning more than a zero percent rate of return.

- Make estimated payments during the year.
- Adjust the amounts withheld by employers on wage income.
- Elect to have 20 percent of their investment income withheld for taxes.

Naturally, a taxpayer may use more than just one of the above methods to assure taxes are paid during the year.

Measurement of After-tax Returns

Heretofore in this book we have discussed returns solely on a pre-tax basis. In some situations, that is appropriate. For example, some investors may not have enough taxable income so that their marginal tax rate is zero. Remember, a married couple filing jointly has at the minimum a standard deduction and two personal exemptions. This means that the first $15,900 ($9,700 standard deduction + $3,100 husband's personal exemption + $3,100 wife's personal exemption) of income is tax exempt. Furthermore, if this couple is retired and Social Security is a significant portion of their income, they may have substantially more income and still not owe any taxes. Another situation is when a taxpayer has a Roth IRA wherein the distributions are tax exempt, provided certain conditions are met.

Nonetheless, for most clients and investors, the tax consequences do matter, and decisions and analysis should be based on after-tax returns, not pre-tax returns. The appropriate adjustment depends on the nature of which marginal tax rate is applied and when any tax is due to be paid. We will discuss specific examples of tax treatments in conjunction with individual investment instruments.

Note that there is a general formula for relating pre-tax returns to post-tax returns:

$$r_{post\text{-}tax} = r_{pre\text{-}tax} \times (1 - \text{marginal tax rate})$$

In some cases, investors want to convert post-tax returns to pre-tax returns. In this case, the formula is

$$r_{pre\text{-}tax} = r_{post\text{-}tax} / (1 - \text{marginal tax rate})$$

State and Local Taxes

Most discussions of taxation focus only on income taxation at the federal level. This is somewhat appropriate because it is federal income taxation that accounts for the majority of income taxes paid. Some states have no income taxes, and others have minimal income taxation. A few tax only interest and dividend income. A few states, however, have really significant marginal tax rates for people in higher income brackets. For example, California's highest marginal tax rate is 9.3 percent, the District of Columbia's highest is 8.7 percent, and Montana's is 11 percent.

Combined Marginal Tax Rate

The impact of state income taxation on the marginal tax rate is complicated by the fact that state income taxes are an itemized deduction if the taxpayer itemizes. In general, the appropriate marginal tax rate to use (defined herein as $MTR_{combined}$) is computed as

$$MTR_{combined} = MTR_{federal} + MTR_{state}$$

if state income taxes are not taken as an itemization on the federal tax return. However, when state taxes are itemized on the federal return, the effective combined marginal tax rate is

$$MTR_{combined} = MTR_{federal} + MTR_{state} \times (1 - MTR_{federal})$$

Example: A wealthy client, George, has the good fortune to be in the highest marginal tax brackets for both federal and state taxation. He lives in New York, where the highest marginal rate is 7.7 percent. What is George's appropriate marginal tax rate if he does not itemize his deductions? What is it if he itemizes?

If George does not itemize his deductions (unlikely for people in the highest marginal tax brackets), for taxation of ordinary income the effective marginal tax rate is

$$\text{MTR}_{\text{combined}} = \text{MTR}_{\text{federal}} + \text{MTR}_{\text{state}}$$
$$= 35\% + 7.7\%$$
$$= 42.7\%$$

If he does itemize, his effective marginal tax rate is

$$\text{MTR}_{\text{combined}} = \text{MTR}_{\text{federal}} + \text{MTR}_{\text{state}} \times (1 - \text{MTR}_{\text{federal}})$$
$$= 35\% + 7.7\% \times (1 - .35)$$
$$= 40.01\%$$

TAX ISSUES FOR STOCK INVESTORS

When an investor buys, sells, or otherwise holds stock, the two major tax issues are the taxation of dividend income and the taxation of capital gains and losses.

Dividend Income

As mentioned above, in 2003 Congress changed the tax treatment of dividend income so that dividends are now classified as ordinary (or nonqualified) and qualified. Qualified dividends are taxed at a rate of 15 percent, except for taxpayers whose marginal tax bracket is 15 percent or less. For the taxpayers in the lowest two tax brackets (that is, 10 and 15 percent), the tax rate on qualified dividends is 5 percent.[8]

"Qualified" dividends for purposes of the 15 percent maximum tax rate include dividends from most domestic corporations, whether or not publicly traded. Dividends from certain foreign corporations also qualify, including those paid by companies traded publicly on an established U.S. exchange. Qualified dividends may include dividends paid directly to the taxpayer by individual corporations, as well as those passed through by mutual funds. Certain dividends are not qualified dividends, including those paid by credit unions or mutual insurance companies. Any dividend paid on stock purchased with borrowed funds, if the dividend was included in net investment income for purposes of claiming an investment interest expense deduction as discussed above, is also not qualified. To qualify for the reduced maximum rates, a shareholder must own the dividend-paying stock for a minimum period of 60 days during the 120-day period beginning on the date that is 60 days before the stock's ex-dividend date.

Capital Distribution

Sometimes companies will make what are known as capital distributions, or a return of capital. Such a distribution technically arises from any distribution with respect to stock at a time when the corporation does not have current or accumulated earnings and profits. The good news is returns of capital are not taxed as dividend income. The bad news is that, at the very least, an investor needs to reduce his or her cost basis (to be discussed in the next section), by the amount of the capital distribution. If the investor's cost basis is at zero or is less than the return of capital, the capital distribution or the differential must be treated as a capital gain.

Example: Zsa Zsa owns 10,000 shares of XYZ stock. The company has a capital distribution of $.10 per share. Zsa Zsa's cost basis in the stock is $400. Because her capital distribution is $1,000 (10,000 shares x $.10 per share), the distribution will reduce her cost basis to zero, and she will have to declare $600 in capital gains, meaning that the capital distribution is being treated as if she has sold some of her stock.

Capital Gains and Losses

Capital gains and losses arise whenever capital assets (essentially, any assets such as stocks or bonds that are held for investment purposes) are bought and sold for different amounts. Normally, the taxable gain equals the sale price (minus commission) less the purchase price (plus commission). The purchase price plus its associated commission is referred to as the *cost basis*. Any capital distributions must, however, be subtracted from the purchase price to determine the basis.

cost basis

Example: Suppose 100 shares of the BDC Company are purchased for $25 per share and sold for $35 per share. The commission for each trade is $29. The cost basis for the investment is $2,529, and the proceeds from selling the investment are $3,471 ($3,500 – $29). The capital gain on this transaction is $942 ($3,471 – $2,529).

Determination of Holding Period

The treatment of capital gains and losses starts with determining the time frame for the investment. All capital transactions are classified as either short-term or long-term. A *short-term capital transaction* is defined as one whose holding period is exactly one year or less. A *long-term capital transaction* is defined as any one with a holding period longer than one year.

short-term capital transaction
long-term capital transaction

Example:	Martha bought some stock on March 17, 2003, and sold it on March 17, 2004. Is this a short-term or long-term holding period?
	Trades 12 months apart but on the same day in both years are treated as being one year apart. Thus, this is a short-term holding period. Martha would have needed to wait until March 18, 2004, to sell the security and qualify for long-term status.

There is one exception to the above 12-month dividing line. Any property that is acquired as an inheritance is automatically treated as having a long-term holding period, regardless of how long the beneficiary holds the asset.

Carryover of Holding Period and Cost Basis

In certain situations, the holding period and cost basis of one taxpayer who previously owned an asset carries over to the cost basis and holding period of the subsequent owner. This typically occurs in donative transactions where a taxpayer gives property to another or surrenders one property in exchange for another in a transaction in which no gain is recognized under the Internal Revenue Code. It also applies to situations wherein gifts are made among family members.

Example:	Gail owns an antique ring that she gives to her daughter, Darla. Gail's cost for the ring was $1,000, and she had owned it for 5 years. Its value is now $2,000. Darla's basis in the ring for purposes of computing taxable gain is $1,000, and her holding period is 5 years.[9]

The reason this rule is important is that a taxpayer cannot avoid a capital gain by giving the property to a child. Hence, if a client has stock worth $100,000 that has a cost basis of $1,000, the client might like nothing more than to give the property to his or her child, hoping that the child will be able to establish the current market value as his or her cost basis. But because the cost basis transfers to the child, the $99,000 capital gain is still present. In fact, the client might actually be better off holding the stock because if he or she dies owning the stock, depending on the size of the estate, the stock may pass tax free to the child, who can then establish the current market value as his or her cost basis.

Treatment of a Capital Gain or a Capital Loss

Let's consider the treatment of a capital gain or loss in cases where a taxpayer has only one transaction for the year. There are four possible situations.

Short-term Capital Gain. A net short-term gain is taxed as ordinary income. Hence, the relevant marginal tax rate is the tax rate on ordinary income.

Long-term Capital Gain. The long-term capital gains tax rate is 5 percent if the marginal tax rate on ordinary income is 10 or 15 percent; otherwise it is 15 percent. Unrealized gains (appreciation on assets that have not yet been sold) are not subject to tax. Gains become taxable only if and when they are realized, which would normally occur only if the underlying asset is sold.

Financial Planning Issue

Your client, Ralph, bought 1,000 shares of GrowFast Co. one year ago for $10 per share, or $10,000 total (ignore commissions). The stock had been trading as high as $20 per share but has suddenly declined to $15 per share. Ralph calls you to indicate that he really thinks the stock should be sold before it falls further. Ralph is in the 28 percent marginal tax rate. You note that today is the first anniversary of the stock's purchase. What do you recommend to Ralph?

If Ralph sells the stock today, he will owe $1,400 in taxes ($5,000 capital gain x 28% marginal tax rate). If he waits one more day, he will owe $750 in taxes ($5,000 capital gain x 15% long-term capital gains tax rate) if he can sell for the same price. In other words, Ralph can save $650 in taxes. Selling the stock today nets Ralph the equivalent of $13,600. In fact, as long as Ralph can sell the stock for more than $14.24 per share, he will benefit from waiting one more day to sell it. If he sells at $14.24, he will have a long-term capital gain of $4,240, and he will owe taxes of $636, leaving him with $13,604 after taxes ($14,240 – $636).

Short-term and Long-term Capital Loss. The treatment of a capital loss is much simpler than the treatment of a capital gain. A net capital loss must be used to reduce ordinary income by an amount up to $3,000 per year.[10] It does not matter if the capital loss is short-term or long-term. A capital loss in excess of $3,000 must be carried forward to the next year. Note that the use of the $3,000 capital loss as a reduction of ordinary income is independent of whether or not the taxpayer has taxable income.

Example: You have an older client, John Century. The majority of his income is Social Security. All of John's income, as well as some of the principal of his portfolio each year, is spent on his nursing home bills. Many of John's bills are deductions that can be itemized as medical expenses. As a result, John has zero taxable income. To pay part of his nursing home expenses, John had to sell some stock, and the stock he sold this year caused him to recognize $5,000 in long-term capital loss. John must recognize $3,000 of this capital loss on his tax return, even though he has no taxable income to offset. The remaining $2,000 of long-term capital loss will be noted as a carry-forward to next year's tax return.

The Treatment of Multiple Gains and Losses

On a return, capital gains and losses are treated collectively, not separately. Thus, the first step in figuring the tax consequences of trades (which are reported on Schedule D of Form 1040) is to aggregate all of the short-term trades and all of the long-term trades. As a result, one of the following eight possible scenarios will apply:

1. net short-term capital gain, no long-term gains or losses
2. net short-term capital loss, no long-term gains or losses
3. net long-term capital gain, no short-term gains or losses
4. net long-term capital loss, no short-term gains or losses
5. net short-term capital gain and a net long-term gain
6. net short-term capital loss and a net long-term gain
7. net short-term capital gain and a net long-term loss
8. net short-term capital loss and a net long-term loss

In the first four scenarios, the tax treatment is the same as if the taxpayer had only one such transaction for that category. For example, suppose a taxpayer reports five trades for the year, all short-term gains or losses, and the sum of the gains and losses is a gain of $5,000. This $5,000 is then taxed as ordinary income, just as if there had been only one trade that resulted in a $5,000 short-term capital gain.

In the fifth scenario, the net short-term gain is taxed as ordinary income, and the net long-term gain is taxed at the long-term capital gains tax rate of either 5 or 15 percent.

In the sixth and seventh scenarios, the short-term capital gain and the long-term capital loss, or the short-term capital loss and the long-term capital gain, are combined. The resulting number may then be either short-term or long-term gain or loss, depending on which number is larger. Whatever the case, the new net gain or net loss is now treated as in one of the first four scenarios.

Example: Jaime Morales has the following four trades during the year:

- a short-term capital gain of $7,000
- a short-term capital loss of $1,000

- a long-term capital gain of $2,000
- a long-term capital loss of $4,500

When Jaime groups the short-term and long-term transactions, he will have a net short-term capital gain of $6,000 and a net long-term capital loss of $2,500. When these two numbers are combined, Jaime ends up with a net short-term capital gain of $3,500. This is taxed as ordinary income.

Although the eighth and final scenario is always a sad one for any taxpayer, the result is that the taxpayer will use the capital losses to reduce current income, up to a maximum of $3,000 ($1,500 if married filing separately), and carry the rest forward. Technically, it is the short-term capital losses that are used up first.

Example: Juanita Gonzalez has a $2,000 short-term capital loss and a $1,500 long-term capital loss. Juanita, who is filing as a single person, will reduce her ordinary income by $3,000, wherein $2,000 comes from her short-term capital loss and the other $1,000 from her long-term capital loss. The remaining long-term capital loss of $500 is carried forward to next year. In the following year, this carry-forward will be treated as a trade in that year in which Juanita loses $500.

Note that the law on the taxation of capital gains has been changed frequently in the past. At different times, long-term capital gains have been fully taxed, taxed at half the ordinary rate, and subject to a 6-month or 18-month (as opposed to 12-month) holding period. It is likely that the capital gains tax rules will change again in the future. However, it is unclear whether they will become more lenient (as some people want), or return to where everything is taxed as ordinary income (as other people want).

Tax-Loss Harvesting[11]

The preceding section should make it clear that taxpayers may want to recognize at least $3,000 per year in capital losses. The savings from a capital loss equal the taxpayer's marginal tax rate times the amount of the loss. Thus, a person in the 28 percent tax bracket who takes the full $3,000 capital loss will save $840 ($3,000 x 28%) in taxes. Naturally, it would be better to have no capital losses. Recognizing a capital loss for tax purposes is simply akin to the concept of making lemonade when the stock market gives you lemons.

One of the least enjoyable parts of being a financial advisor is the task of pointing out to clients that they have sustained losses. Nonetheless, when there are losses in a client's portfolio, an advisor should point out that there are several benefits to taking the losses, a concept referred to as tax-loss harvesting. The first benefit is the immediate savings in income taxes. The second benefit is that capital losses also allow a client to take capital gains without paying taxes. This is particularly valuable if the gains are short-term in nature. Thus, if a client has accrued a $5,000 long-term capital loss in one holding and a $5,000 short-term capital gain in another holding, the client can recognize both the loss and the gain and not have to pay any taxes.

Keep in mind, however, that capital losses provide the maximum benefit when they are used to offset ordinary income or short-term capital gains. Capital losses are least effective when they are used to offset long-term capital gains because these gains are taxed at a much lower tax rate.

A third benefit of tax-loss harvesting is that it provides the opportunity to rebalance a client's portfolio. As will be discussed in the next chapter, each client's portfolio should have an asset allocation standard associated with it. Over time, the actual weights of the categories will change as some of the categories do well and others poorly. Taking capital losses in those categories that have done poorly allows the taxpayer to take capital gains in the sectors that have done well and use the freed-up cash to rebalance the portfolio back toward the desired asset allocation weights.

Note that it is far easier to describe and promote the benefits of tax-loss harvesting than to do it in practice.[12] The reason is that when portfolios have been held for several years, and particularly if those years include a significant bull market, the taxpayer simply runs out of losses to take.

Tax-Efficient Investing

Tax-efficient investing is a topic related to tax-loss harvesting. Tax-efficient investing means the avoidance of taking of capital gains on which the taxpayer must pay a capital gains tax. There are two problems with tax-efficient investing.[13] First, when practiced to the extreme (which means no capital gains taken that offset any long-term capital losses, and making sure that any capital losses taken always exceed capital gains by at least $3,000 per year), a portfolio can become extremely concentrated. If an investor is lucky enough to hold a stock that does extremely well over a period of several years, it can grow from being a small percentage of the portfolio to constituting as much as 25 percent or more of the portfolio. When one security represents 25 percent or more of a portfolio, the portfolio is clearly losing its diversification. At some point, there will be a tough choice to make between paying taxes and retaining diversification.

The second problem with tax-efficient investing involves one of appearances. Again, truly tax-efficient investing means a minimal number of trades.

Financial Planning Issue

Your client, Warren Buffer, started with you 30 years ago. Early on, he put a few thousand dollars into Berkshire Hathaway (BH) and a few thousand more into Microsoft (M). Today, his portfolio is worth $10 million, but BH constitutes 50 percent of his holdings, and M is another 40 percent of the portfolio. To achieve an appropriate degree of diversification, he should sell nearly all of both of these holdings (which together are $9 million in market value). However, because the cost basis is negligible on both, virtually the full value would be taxed as long-term capital gains. At a 15 percent long-term capital tax rate, this would mean a tax liability of approximately $1,350,000 ($9M x .15). Because this would constitute 13.5 percent of Warren's portfolio, it would be a tough sale to promote the unknown benefits of diversification over the tangible tax bill of $1,350,000.

If a financial advisor recommends no trades for a portfolio during the year, and then presents the client with a bill for portfolio management services, the client is surely going to start wondering why he or she should be paying the financial advisor!

Wash-Sale Rule

There is one catch in the asset reallocation scenario. The IRS has what is known as a wash-sale rule. Under the wash-sale tax rules, a loss sustained on the sale of a security is not deductible for tax purposes if the investor purchases a "substantially identical" security within a period beginning 30 days before the sale and ending 30 days after the sale.

Although this rule sounds simple, there are two aspects to the wash-sale rule that create problems. First, what happens to the gain or loss if the investor does violate the wash-sale rule? For example, suppose an investor buys 100 shares of Bellcamp stock for $1,000 that is later sold for $750. Let's say the investor then buys another 100 Bellcamp shares 2 weeks after the sale for $800. By buying the stock within 30 days, the investor forgoes the $250 capital loss. The one compensation to the investor is that the capital loss sustained during the first holding period can be added to the cost basis of the second holding period. Hence, in this example the cost basis of the replacement Bellcamp stock will be $1,050 ($800 purchase price + $250 capital loss on the first sale).

The second aspect that creates a problem is what is meant by "substantially identical" securities. In the case of a company with one class of common stock, it is clear the investor cannot buy back the same common stock. However, if a company has more than one class of common stock, the rule is not as clear, because the purchase of a different class of common stock depends on the relationship between the class of stock sold and the class of stock bought. Similarly, the purchase of a contract, a call option, or rights to purchase essentially the same stock also creates a wash sale.

Another scenario that constitutes a wash sale is if the spouse or a corporation owned or controlled by the taxpayer or the taxpayer's spouse buys essentially the same stock. Naturally, the purchase of the stock in a different account is also subject to the wash-sale rule. So the sale of stock in a personal account coupled with the purchase of the same stock in an IRA account also falls under the wash-sale rules.

Convertible securities may or may not constitute a substantially identical holding. Equivalency depends on whether the convertible is indistinguishable from the common stock in terms of ownership and price changes. A convertible bond or convertible preferred stock is considered substantially identical if it meets the following five conditions:[14]

- It is convertible into common stock.
- It has the same voting rights as the common stock.
- It is subject to the same dividend restrictions.
- It trades at prices that do not vary significantly from the conversion ratio.
- It is unrestricted as to convertibility.

Stock Splits/Dividends

Companies occasionally declare stock splits and stock dividends. There is no taxable event associated with these, other than the treatment of cash in lieu of a fractional share. Thus, if an investor owns 100 shares of a company that declared a 2 x 1 stock split, he or she would end up with 200 shares. The investor needs only to adjust his or her per share cost basis. Thus, if the stock previously had a cost basis of $10 per share, the new cost basis is $5 per share. If all 200 shares are sold at the same time, this adjustment is immaterial, because the original purchase price for the 100 shares will be used as the cost basis. However, if only some of the shares are later sold, then the original cost basis has to be prorated based on the number of shares sold.

The treatment for a stock dividend is the same as a stock split in that the cost basis has to be prorated. Most corporations automatically pay the shareholder the cash equivalent value of the fractional share, based on the market value of the stock on the day of the dividend.

Example: Sally owns one share of common stock that she bought on January 3, 1996, for $100. The corporation declared a common stock dividend of 5 percent on June 30, 2004. The fair market value of the stock at the time the dividend was declared was $200. She was paid $10 for the fractional-share stock dividend. Her gain or loss is as follows:

Fair market value of old stock	$200.00
Fair market value of stock dividend (cash received)	+$10.00
Fair market value of old stock and stock dividend	$210.00
Basis (cost) of old stock after the stock dividend ([$200 ÷ $210] × $100)	$95.24
Basis (cost) of stock dividend ([$10 ÷ $210] × $100)	+$4.76
Total	$100.00
Cash received	$10.00
Basis (cost) of stock dividend	−$4.76
Gain	$5.24

Because Sally had held the share of stock for more than one year at the time the stock dividend was declared, her gain on the stock dividend is a long-term capital gain.[15]

Warrants

In the case of the wash-sale rule, the sale of common stock and the purchase of warrants to buy that stock within 30 days of the sale is the same as the purchase of an option, and it is clearly treated as a wash sale. However, the reverse is not necessarily the case. If the taxpayer sells the warrants first and then buys the underlying stock, the rule is violated only if the warrants qualify as substantially identical under the rules given earlier for convertibles.

If a warrant is exercised, the cost basis of the warrants is added to the exercise price for the stock to determine the new cost basis of the shares acquired. For example, if an investor buys 100 warrants for $500, and later exercises these warrants to buy 100 shares of stock at $20 each, the cost basis for the stock is $2,500 plus any commissions.

Rights

Although the distribution of stock rights may be taxable or nontaxable depending on the nature of the rights, in practice such distributions are almost always nontaxable. If the investor allows these nontaxable rights to expire without exercising them, the cost basis is zero and there is effectively no transaction. But if the investor exercises the rights, then some of the original cost basis of the stock must be allocated to the rights if the fair market value of the rights equals or exceeds 15 percent of the fair market value of the stock at the time of the distribution. If the fair market value of the rights is less than 15 percent, the investor has the choice of leaving the cost basis of the original stock unaltered, or dividing it between the rights and the old stock. If the cost basis is divided between the original stock and the rights, when the rights are exercised, the cost basis of the new stock equals the subscription price plus the allocated cost basis of rights.

Example: Thomas owns 100 shares of Wolf Company stock, which cost $22 per share. The Wolf Company gave him 10 nontaxable stock rights that would allow him to buy 10 more shares at $26 per share. At the time the stock rights were distributed, the stock had a market value of $30, not including the stock rights. Each stock right had a market value of $3. The market value of the stock rights was less than 15 percent of the market value of the stock, but Thomas chose to divide the basis of his stock between the stock and the rights. The basis of the rights and the basis of the old stock is computed as follows:

100 shares × $22 = $2,200, basis of old stock
100 shares × $30 = $3,000, market value of old stock
10 rights × $3 = $30, market value of rights
($3,000 / $3,030) x $2,200 = $2,178.22, new basis of
    old stock
($30 / $3,030) x $2,200 = $21.78, basis of rights

If Thomas sells the rights, the basis for figuring gain or loss is $2.18 ($21.78/10) per right. If he exercises the rights, the basis of the stock he acquires is the price he pays ($26) plus the basis of the right exercised ($2.18), or $28.18 per share. The remaining basis of the old stock is $21.78 per share.

Short Sales

What is different in the treatment of a short sale for tax purposes is that the selling date occurs before the purchase date. Despite this reversal, the distinction between a long-term and short-term classification depends on whether the sale and purchase are more than one year apart. The computation of the gain or loss is still the sale price less the purchase price.

Liquidations

Sometimes companies will sell off part or all of their assets. In the case of bankruptcy, the court may decide to sell all of the assets of the company. Usually when this happens, there is not enough cash after the creditors are paid to distribute to stockholders, but occasionally there is. A partial liquidation of a company is treated as a return of capital, which was discussed earlier. That is, the distribution is applied to cost basis. If the cost basis is greater than the distribution, the taxpayer can declare a capital loss. It is only when the distribution exceeds the cost basis that the taxpayer has to declare a capital gain based on the difference and the holding period of the stock.

A more interesting situation arises if the investor has bought the stock in multiple batches. Each batch will likely have a different cost basis. For complete liquidations, it is not uncommon for the liquidating dividends to be made in multiple payments. If this is the case, any payment received must be distributed among the batches based on the number of shares in each batch. Once a liquidating dividend exceeds the cost basis of any one batch, the difference becomes a capital gain, even though the cost basis on another batch is still greater than zero.

TAX ISSUES FOR FIXED-INCOME INVESTORS

All interest income is either taxed as ordinary income (that is, at the same rates as wages and salaries) at the federal level or is tax exempt. Thus, interest income on savings accounts, corporate bonds, and U.S. government bonds is taxed as ordinary income. Even accounts at credit unions where the interest payments are technically called dividends, are still taxed as interest income. The one exception to taxing interest as ordinary income is that interest income from most state and local bonds (known as municipals) is not taxed within the state that issues them. Hence, municipals are frequently

tax-exempts   known as *tax-exempts*. As a practical matter, not all municipals qualify for this tax-exempt treatment. Thus, the buyer of municipals needs to make sure that they are, in fact, tax exempt, although almost all are. Certain municipal bonds may produce income that is subject to the alternative minimum tax, but not to the regular income tax.

State taxation is somewhat different. Some states, including New Hampshire and Tennessee, tax only interest and dividend income. The interest income on municipal bonds issued by other jurisdictions is fully taxed in the owner's own state and local residence jurisdiction. However, the interest income on U.S. Treasury issues is exempt from state and local income taxes. It is obviously somewhat of a misnomer, therefore, to talk about municipals as being tax-exempts and governments as being taxables, when the former might be taxed, and the latter do enjoy some tax exemption. However, because it is the federal tax bite that people worry more about than the state tax bite, discussions of tax treatment are usually limited to the federal tax aspects.

The state income tax treatment becomes more ambiguous when it comes to securities issued by government agencies and government-sponsored corporations. As shown in table 13-3, whereas all securities issued by the U.S. Treasury are exempt from state and local income taxes, some of the

TABLE 13-3
Tax Status of Common U.S. Treasury and Federal Agency Issues

Type of Issue	Tax Status
U.S. Treasury Bills	Subject to federal income taxes, but exempt from state and local taxes
U.S. Treasury Notes	Subject to federal income taxes, but exempt from state and local taxes
U.S. Treasury Bonds	Subject to federal income taxes, but exempt from state and local taxes
Zero-Coupon Treasuries	Subject to federal income taxes, but exempt from state and local taxes
Federal Home Loan Bank (FHLB)	Subject to federal income taxes, but exempt from state and local taxes
Federal Farm Credit Bank (FFCB)	Subject to federal income taxes, but exempt from state and local taxes
Student Loan Mortgage Association (SLMA)	Subject to federal income taxes, but exempt from state and local taxes
Tennessee Valley Authority (TVA)	Subject to federal income taxes, but exempt from state and local taxes
Federal National Mortgage Association Debentures (FNMA)	Subject to federal, state, and local taxes
Federal Home Loan Mortgage Corporation Debentures (FHLMC)	Subject to federal, state, and local taxes
Government National Mortgage Association (GNMA)	Subject to federal, state, and local taxes
FNMA Mortgages	Subject to federal, state, and local taxes

agency bonds are also exempt from state and local taxes (including those issued by the FHLB, FFCB, SLMA, and TVA); others are not (including those issued by FNMA, FHLMC, and GNMA).

Determination of Cost Basis

Determination of the cost basis on a bond is more complex than for stock. When a bond is traded, the buyer pays and the seller receives accrued interest, provided the company has not announced that it is defaulting on the interest payment. The payment of interest is not part of the cost basis. Rather, it is incorporated into computing the taxpayer's net interest income for the year. The cost basis for a bond is the price paid for the bond, plus the associated commission and any other fees or taxes paid in conjunction with the trade.

Example: On July 1, Tyriq bought 10 Treasury bonds (that is, $10,000 worth of par value). They have a coupon rate of 5 percent, mature on October 1, 2024, and pay interest every April 1 and October 1. Tyriq paid $9,725 for the bonds, but the payment included $40 for commission and $125 in accrued interest. Hence, he actually paid $9,560 for the bonds. His cost basis for tax purposes is $9,600 ($9,560 + $40). The $125 interest paid will show on his tax return as an offset to any other interest income. If he still owns the bonds on October 1 (the next interest payment date), he will receive 6 months' worth of interest, which is $250 ($10,000 x 5% x ½ year). On his tax return, he will report his interest income from this holding as $125, based on his cash receipt of $250 in interest, less his cash payment of $125 when he bought the bond.

Taxable Equivalent Yield

Once an investor has decided to buy some bonds and has chosen the quality of the bonds (for example, AAA, BAA, and so on), he or she usually needs to determine whether or not to buy taxable or tax-exempt bonds. For investors whose marginal tax rate on ordinary income is 0, 10, or 15 percent, the decision should automatically be to buy taxable bonds. This is because investments that offer a tax-free or tax-sheltered return are always priced to offer a lower before-tax return than otherwise equivalent investments whose returns are fully taxed, and the return differential reflects the highest marginal tax rates. When an investor's marginal tax rate becomes 25 percent or higher, it behooves the investor or his advisor to consider whether the investor should be in taxable or tax-exempt bonds. The primary technique for this analysis is either to convert the yield on a tax-exempt bond to a pre-tax equivalent, or to convert the yield on a taxable bond to its after-tax equivalent.

tax-equivalent yield   The traditional formula for converting the yield on a tax-exempt bond to its pre-tax equivalent, also known as the *tax-equivalent yield*, can be expressed as follows:

$$Y_{TE} = \frac{Y}{1 - T} \qquad \text{(Equation 13-1)}$$

where Y_{TE} = tax-equivalent yield
 T = investor's marginal tax rate
 Y = tax-exempt municipal yield

Table 13-4 shows the fully taxable yield that is equivalent to a 6 percent after-tax return (2004 rates).

TABLE 13-4
Tax Equivalent Yields for a 6 Percent
Tax-Exempt Yield

Marginal Tax Rate	Tax-Equivalent Yield
10%	6.67%
15%	7.06%
25%	8.00%
28%	8.33%
33%	8.96%
35%	9.23%

It should be obvious from this table that the higher an individual's marginal tax rate, the more attractive a tax-exempt bond becomes.

In some applications, the analyst wants to go from a taxable yield to a tax-exempt yield. This is done by multiplying the pre-tax yield by $(1 - T)$, as shown in equation 13-1a:

$$Y_{pre\text{-}tax} \times (1 - T) = Y_{after\text{-}tax} \qquad \text{(Equation 13-1a)}$$

The only problem with equation 13-1 is that it is perfectly correct only for bonds that are trading at par. In this case, the yield numbers in the formula refer to the current yield (coupon rate divided by price). When a bond trades at par, there will be no price change over the life of the bond, assuming that the bond will pay par at maturity. If a bond trades at any price other than par and the investor holds the bond to maturity, there will be a capital gain or loss on the price of the bond. This is true even for municipal bonds where the interest income is tax exempt. When a bond trades at a price other than par, the yield number in equation 13-1 is the yield to maturity. Because the price change might be taxed at the capital gains rate (depending on the investor's other capital gains and losses), equation 13-1 becomes slightly misleading. Fortunately, if the bond at least trades near par, then the bias is not excessive. If the bond being analyzed as part of a taxable-tax exempt decision trades at a price substantially different from par, the

---

Ethical Issue in Financial Planning

Your client, Robert Ramig, is 75 years old. His portfolio is worth about $750,000 and has a reasonable mix of stocks and bonds. Robert's taxable income is low enough that he has a 15 percent marginal tax rate. Robert takes great pleasure in denying taxes to the federal government. He has asked you to make sure all of his bonds are municipals so that he can minimize his tax liability. Given Robert's marginal tax rate, it is clear that he should consider only taxable bonds. Should you structure the portfolio as Robert requests, or should you explain to Robert the inappropriateness of his proposal and risk losing him as a client?

---

computation of a tax-equivalent yield becomes more complex, and it is discussed in the next section.

Tax Implications of the Coupon Tax Effect

The relative amounts of coupon and price appreciation in the return on a bond can have significant tax implications. For bonds originally sold at par, capital gains are taxed or capital losses recognized only when they are realized as the bonds either mature or are sold in the secondary market. Thus, the capital gains income on such bonds is both tax deferred and taxed at a lower rate. The tax benefits of any capital loss are also deferred. An investor in a high tax bracket may therefore prefer to buy bonds that pay a below-market coupon rate of interest and are sold at a discount in the secondary market. The market generally contains many low-coupon bonds that were initially sold at par but are now priced at a deep discount.[16] These are known **deep discount bonds** as *deep discount bonds*.

Accordingly, private investors in high tax brackets often tend to prefer deep discount bonds to higher coupon issues. The before-tax yields to maturity on low-coupon, deep-discount issues are usually somewhat below yields on otherwise similar issues trading nearer to par. This relationship is **coupon tax effect** also called the *coupon tax effect*. When capital gains are taxed at a lower rate than ordinary income, as they are currently, the coupon effect has an even greater impact.

To figure the after-tax yield-to-maturity on a bond, we have to look only at after-tax cash flows and compute the yield to maturity (that is, the internal rate of return) on these numbers. In other words, the after-tax yield to maturity is the discount rate that makes the following equation true:

$$P = \left\{ \sum_{t=1}^{n} \left[(1 - T_{OI}) \times C_t / (1 + i)^t \right] \right\} + \left[PAR - T_{CG} \times (PAR - Cost) \right] / (1 + i)^n$$

(Equation 13-2)

where T_{OI} = marginal tax rate on ordinary income
C_t = the coupon payment in period t
PAR = the par or face value of the bond
T_{CG} = marginal tax rate on capital gains
Cost = price paid for the bond

Example: Mike buys a bond ($1,000 par value) with a 3-year maturity for $900. The bond has a 6 percent coupon rate. Assume the bond pays interest in annual installments starting one year from today. If Mike's marginal tax rates on ordinary income and capital gains are 28 and 15 percent, what is the after-tax yield to maturity?

We need to solve for the discount rate that makes the following equation true:

$$900 = \frac{(1-.28)\times 60}{(1+i)^1} + \frac{(1-.28)\times 60}{(1+i)^2} + \frac{(1-.28)\times 60}{(1+i)^3} + \frac{\left[1,000 - .15 \times (1,000 - 900)\right]}{(1+i)^3}$$

$$900 = \frac{43.20}{(1+i)^1} + \frac{43.20}{(1+i)^2} + \frac{43.20}{(1+i)^3} + \frac{\left[1,000 - 15\right]}{(1+i)^3}$$

SHIFT, C ALL
900, +/−, PV
43.2, PMT
985, FV
3, N
I/YR (display: 7.7172 or 7.72%)

Note that in this last example, if we had just solved for the pre-tax yield, the keystrokes would have been:

SHIFT, C ALL
900, +/−, PV
60, PMT
1000, FV
3, N
I/YR (display: 10.0228) or 10.02%

If we had just taken the pre-tax yield to maturity and multiplied this by 1 minus the marginal tax rate on ordinary income, we would get as an approximation of the after-tax yield 7.2164, or 7.22 percent. This is different from the correct answer by 50 basis points. The accuracy of the approximation formula improves as the price of the bond gets closer to par.

So far in our discussion of after-tax returns, we have focused only on discount bonds. There is an interesting complication that can arise in computing an after-tax yield when dealing with premium bonds. When an investor buys a premium bond and holds it to maturity, he or she has a guaranteed capital loss. For example, if the cost basis of the bond is $1,100, there will a $100 capital loss if the bond pays par value at maturity. The complication arises because we do not necessarily know in advance what the tax benefit of a future long-term capital loss will be. If it is used to offset long-term capital gains, the tax savings is based on the capital gains tax rate. If it is used to offset a net short-term capital gain or to reduce ordinary income, the tax savings is based on the ordinary income tax rate. There is no simple answer on how to project this tax savings.

Convertible Bonds

If a convertible bond is simply bought and later sold, there is no special tax treatment accorded to it over other bonds. If the investor converts the bonds, the conversion does not result in a taxable event that would generally occur with a sale. The IRS treats this as an exchange of like assets. The important points for convertibles are that the cost basis for the shares of stock so acquired are based on the cost basis of the convertible, and the holding period of the stocks starts with the purchase date of the convertibles.

Example:　　　Amy buys 10 convertible bonds for $900 each in January 2002 (ignore commissions). In 2004, she converts the 10 bonds into 500 shares of stock. The cost basis for the 500 shares is $9,000, the original purchase price of the bonds, or $18 per share ($9,000/500). The holding period for the stock is already on a long-term basis because the bonds have been held for more than 2 years at the time of conversion. Thus, there is no taxable event associated with the conversion itself.

Zero-Coupon Bonds

As discussed in an earlier chapter, zero-coupon bonds pay no interest. The return on these securities is derived from the difference between their purchase price and selling price or maturity value.

For tax purposes, the IRS imputes an annual tax liability for these zero-coupon bonds. Determining a zero-coupon bond's tax liability requires

imputed interest　　determining the relevant amount of *imputed interest,* which is the bond's yield to maturity at the time of issuance. The imputed interest rate does not change over the life of the bond, regardless of what happens to interest rates. Thus, a zero-coupon bond that was sold at an 8 percent yield to maturity would be treated for tax purposes as if it did, in fact, earn 8 percent each year. The issuer is allowed to deduct the imputed interest cost each year, while the owner incurs an equivalent tax liability. As a result, the issuer obtains a tax deduction, while the owner is obligated for the taxes on this income, even though no actual cash is received.

Example:	LH Corp. zero-coupon bonds, par value $1,000, due to mature in September 2022, were sold to the public for $240 in September 2002. Calculation of the imputed annual interest rate is a simple present value/future value problem that uses the following keystrokes:

> SHIFT, C ALL
> 1000, FV
> 240, +/–, PV
> 20, N
> I/YR   (display: 7.40)

Imputed interest in the first year is $240 x .0740 = $17.76. The investor must declare this as ordinary income. At the end of the year, the cost basis of the bond increases by $17.76 to $257.76. ($240 + $17.76). The imputed interest rate for the second year is $19.07 (.074 x $257.76). By the end of the 20th year, the imputed interest will bring the cost basis of the bond to $1,000.

Zero-coupon bonds can be quite attractive to issuers in that they can receive a tax deduction for the interest payment, even though they pay no interest in cash. Because many investors find it discouraging to have to declare taxable income when they in fact received no cash, zero-coupon bonds are much more attractive when purchased in a tax-qualified account (such as an IRA or Keogh) than in a regular account.

Original-Issue Discount Bonds

An original-issue discount bond is one whose coupon rate is set sufficiently below the current market rate for bonds of like quality and maturity that it will be issued at a discount. Like zero-coupon bonds, there will be imputed interest income, but the calculation requires an extra step. This is because once the imputed interest payment is calculated, the actual interest payment is deducted from the imputed number. The difference is then reported as the non-cash income, and it is this difference that is added to the price of the bond to adjust its cost basis.

Example:	The IJK Company issues a 5-year, original-issue discount bond. The coupon rate is 5 percent paid annually, and the yield to maturity at the time of issue is 8 percent. As a result, the issue price is $880.22. The imputed interest for the first year is $70.42 ($880.22 x .08). However, investors actually received $50 in coupon payments. Hence, the imputed interest for tax purposes is the difference, or $20.42 ($70.42 – $50). At the end of the year, the cost basis is adjusted to $900.64 ($880.22 + $20.42). The process then continues for each year.

Taxation of TIPS

TIPS work like original-issue discount bonds. Because TIPS are Treasury instruments, they are exempt from state and local tax, but the investor will owe federal tax on the interest earned as well as on the increase on the principal value, even though he or she will not receive the adjusted principal value until the bond's actual maturity. The investor will have reportable income; however, it cannot be used until maturity. Because of this adjustment process, an investor should attempt to purchase TIPS only in tax-deferred or tax-exempt accounts.

Taxation of Savings Bonds

Because they are Treasury securities, the interest income on savings bonds is exempt from state or local income taxes. When Series EE and Series I bonds are bought, the owner has the option of reporting the increase in the redemption value of the bonds each year as interest income and paying taxes thereon. (As with other zero-coupon bonds, this involves the payment of taxes without an accompanying cash inflow.) Most owners elect to defer the federal income tax until the bonds are redeemed or reach the end of their interest-bearing lives. Savings bond earnings are exempt from federal tax under certain conditions if their proceeds are used to pay the tuition and fees of higher education. As a result, savings bonds' tax-equivalent yields can be significantly higher than their nominal rates of return.

Wash-Sale Rule

The wash-sale rule is much easier to avoid in bond investments than in other types of investments. This is because each bond issue is different. Thus, if an investor buys some of a company's 10-year bonds and the bond prices fall, the investor can sell those bonds, and buy 10-year bonds of like quality rating and coupon rate for any other company, and be safe. In fact, the investor can even buy 20-year bonds issued by the same company. Thus, the wash-sale rule is avoided as long as there is at least one significant characteristic that is different, be it issuer, maturity, or coupon rate.

TAX ISSUES FOR INVESTMENT COMPANY INVESTORS

To qualify as a regulated investment company under chapter M of the Internal Revenue Code, the fund must distribute at least 90 percent of its gross income (dividends, interest, and capital gains). Accordingly, virtually all funds comply with the income distribution requirements. The investor is liable for income taxes on these distributions, regardless of whether they are accepted as cash payments or reinvested in the account. Because the content of the investment portfolios of most investment companies is regularly changing, the amounts of these distributions may not always be easy to predict, although the timing is fairly predictable. Dividends and interest are distributed as ordinary dividends, and they may be paid monthly, quarterly, semiannually, or annually. They are treated as any other dividend and interest income by the taxpayer and taxed accordingly.

Capital Gain Distributions

Capital gain distributions are usually paid in January of the year following the distribution and with few exceptions can be paid only once per year.[17] This is one of the few instances where income received after December 31 is taxed to the prior year. The short-term and long-term natures of any capital gains are also passed to the shareholder.

One of the drawbacks to an investment company holding is that capital losses are not passed through to the shareholders. Thus, in periods of extended down markets, such as 2000–2003, not only do most investment companies cease to make capital gain distributions because they have no net capital gains to distribute, but they also accrue capital losses that provide no immediate tax benefit to an investor. Once the markets turn up again and the investment companies start to generate capital gains on their trades, the initial capital gains are essentially tax free due to the capital loss carry forward on the books of the company.

Example:	As a financial advisor, you are looking at two mutual funds you are considering recommending to your clients. The Knockout Fund is an aggressive growth, no-load fund with a $10 NAV. The Also-Ran Fund is also an aggressive growth, no-load fund with a $20 NAV, whose expense ratios and turnover activity are virtually identical to those of the Knockout Fund. You also note, however, that the Also-Ran Fund has an accumulated capital loss carry forward equivalent to $2.00 per share, whereas the Knockout Fund has virtually no capital loss carry forward. Which fund should you recommend?
	The NAV is immaterial to the selection. You should probably recommend the Also-Ran Fund because the first $2.00 per share of capital gains will be completely shielded from taxes—unless you believe the capital loss carry forward is indicative of management's ability.

"Buying Taxes"

Because dividends generate taxation, buying shares in a taxable account shortly before distributions means that taxes will be payable almost immediately, thereby reducing the value of the investment. This is a particular problem for capital gain distributions because they are made only once per year for most funds. Even more worrisome is that the fund's portfolio likely includes many appreciated stocks that will generate a capital gain when sold. When this occurs, the fund allocates the gain proportionately to all shareholders, whether they have owned shares for many years or only a few weeks. Thus, recent purchasers must pay taxes on phantom gains.

An even more awkward situation that sometimes arises is when an investor buys some mutual funds shares, the shares decline in value, and then at the end of the year the fund declares a capital gain distribution. Therefore, even though the investor has lost money at that point on his or her investment, he or she must still pay taxes on the capital gain distribution. The only saving grace in this situation is that after the capital gain distribution, the fund's NAV will adjust downward by the size of the capital gain distribution. This increases the investor's capital loss, so that if the investor sells the holding, he or she will be able to declare a capital loss on those shares that is larger than otherwise would have been the case, and the step-up in the loss equals the capital gain distribution.

Tax-Friendly Funds

Some funds are more tax friendly than others. The tax friendliness of a fund can usually be measured by the magnitude of its portfolio turnover ratio.

The lower the turnover ratio, the more tax friendly the fund. This is because funds with low portfolio turnover ratios tend to generate fewer taxable capital gains on their portfolios, and thus will have smaller capital gain distributions. Furthermore, the lack of the fund's recognition of capital gains (that is, the lack of sales within the portfolio) means that the NAV can increase more rapidly, and the investor can control the timing of capital gains through the sale of the mutual fund shares.

By the nature of their objective, index funds are more tax friendly than traditional funds. They sell shares relatively infrequently, so there are fewer capital gain distributions. Also, unlike many traditional fund managers, index fund managers do not make end-of-quarter decisions to "dress up" their portfolios. Sometimes these decisions make no substantive change in the portfolio's risk-return characteristics but do trigger distributions that are taxable to the shareholder.

Another group of mutual funds that typically have a low turnover ratio are the sector funds. Sector funds are committed to staying invested in one sector. Hence, although they might want to adjust their investments among companies in that sector, there is little advantage for sector funds to gain through a large amount of trading.

The concept of a fund's making one of its objectives to minimize capital gain distributions is actually relatively new; the first such fund marketed to the public was the Schwab 1000 fund.[18] It was at about this same time that Morningstar began producing tax-adjusted return numbers for funds.

Determination of Basis[19]

Record keeping can get rather complicated for mutual funds. If the investor buys mutual fund shares in a single purchase, and neither reinvests any dividends or capital gain distributions nor buys any additional shares, determining the cost basis upon sale is like any other capital transaction. However, most investors end up acquiring mutual funds shares over time, from reinvestment of dividends or capital gain distributions, purchase of new shares, or both. The cost basis can be based on specific share identification, FIFO (first in, first out) or average costs.

Specific Share Identification

If the investor adequately identifies the shares sold, he or she can use the adjusted basis of those particular shares to figure gain or loss. The investor will adequately identify mutual fund shares, even if he or she bought the shares in different lots at various prices and times, by doing both of the following:

- specifying to the broker or other agent the particular shares to be sold or transferred at the time of the sale or transfer

- receiving confirmation in writing from the broker or other agent within a reasonable time of the specification of the particular shares sold or transferred

First-in First-out (FIFO)

If shares were acquired at different times or at different prices and the investor cannot identify which shares he or she sold, the investor should use the basis of the shares acquired first as the basis of the shares sold. In other words, the oldest shares owned are considered sold first. The investor should keep a separate record of each purchase and any dispositions of the shares until all shares purchased at the same time have been disposed of completely.

Average Basis

The investor can calculate gain or loss using an average basis only if he or she acquired the shares at various times and prices and left the shares on deposit in an account handled by a custodian or agent who acquires or redeems those shares. Once he or she elects to use an average basis, the investor must continue to use it for all accounts in the same fund. This does not preclude the use of a different cost basis for shares in other funds, even those within the same family of funds.

Example:	Eve owns two accounts that hold shares of the income fund issued by Fund A. She also owns 100 shares of the growth fund issued by Fund A. If Eve elects to use average basis for the first account of the income fund, she must use average basis for the second account. However, she may use cost basis for the growth fund.

The following two methods are used to calculate average basis:

- single-category method
- double-category method

Single-Category Method. Under the single-category method, the average basis of all shares owned at the time of each disposition is computed, regardless of how the investor acquired them. This includes shares acquired with reinvested dividends or capital gain distributions, as well as those bought outright.

Even though all unsold shares of a fund are included in a single category to compute average basis, the investor may have both short-term and long-term gains or losses when he or she sells these shares. To determine the holding period, the shares disposed of first are considered to be those acquired first.

Example:	Trevor bought 400 shares in the LJO Mutual Fund: 250 shares on May 15, 2003, at $10 per share, and 150 shares on May 15, 2004, at $15 per share. On November 11, 2004, he sold 300 shares. The basis of all 300 shares sold is the same—that is, Trevor paid $2,500 for the first batch and $2,250 for the second batch, and the aveage cost is $11.875 per share (($2,500 + $2,250)/400). With regard to the holding period, Trevor held 250 shares for more than one year, so the gain or loss on those shares is long-term. He held 50 shares for one year or less, so the gain or loss on those shares is short-term.

Note that the cost basis of the shares the investor still holds after a sale of some shares is the same as the average basis of the shares sold. The next time the investor makes a sale, the average basis will still be the same, unless he or she has acquired additional shares (or has made a subsequent adjustment to basis).

Double-Category Method. In the double-category method, all shares in an account at the time of each disposition are divided into two categories: short-term and long-term. Shares held one year or less are short-term. Shares held longer than one year are long-term. The basis of each share in a category is the average basis for that category. This is the total remaining basis of all shares in that category at the time of disposition, divided by the total shares in the category at that time. To use this method, the investor specifies, to the custodian or agent handling the account, from which category the shares are to be sold or transferred. The custodian or agent must confirm the specification in writing. If the investor does not specify or receive confirmation, he or she must first charge the shares sold against the long-term category and then charge any remaining shares sold against the short-term category.

After the investor has held a mutual fund share for more than one year, he or she must transfer that share from the short-term category to the long-term category. The basis of a transferred share is its actual cost or other basis unless some of the shares in the short-term category have been disposed of. In that case, the basis of a transferred share is the average basis of the undisposed shares at the time of the most recent disposition from this category.

An investor chooses to use the average basis of mutual fund shares by clearly showing on the income tax return, for each year the choice applies, that he or she used an average basis to report gain or loss from the sale or transfer of the shares. He or she must specify whether the single-category method or the double-category method was used to determine average basis. This choice is effective until the investor gets permission from the IRS to revoke it.

Taxation of Unit Investment Trusts

Unit investment trusts (UITs) hold fixed portfolios, which mature over time (if bonds are held) or are liquidated at a fixed point in time (if stocks are held). During the life of the UIT portfolio, the interest and dividend income are distributed to shareholders on a regular basis, as with any other investment company. As the bonds mature, the principal is distributed to the investors as a tax-free return of capital. The investors must adjust their cost basis for such returns. When a UIT equity portfolio is liquidated, investors usually have the choice of receiving the liquidating dividend, or rolling it over into the next such equity UIT that is being created. Regardless of which option is chosen, the investor must recognize the capital gain or loss for tax purposes at the time of the liquidation.

Wash-Sale Rule for Investment Companies

The wash-sale rule applies to investment companies the same way it applies to any other securities. However, there is one issue that confuses investors. Do the sale and purchase of two different index funds (or ETFs) within a 30-day window constitute a violation of the rule? The answer depends on which index is being tracked. If both index funds track the same index, such a trade will be considered a violation of this rule. As long as the two index funds track different indexes, the investor is not in violation of the rule.

TAX ISSUES FOR OTHER INVESTMENTS

Options

The first tax aspect of an option transaction is the tax treatment of the payment of the premium. The treatment of premium depends on the nature of an underlying security. For stocks, it is a capital transaction.

If both the buyer and the writer of the option are initiating a new position, there are no tax consequences for either party. If the option lapses (that is, expires as worthless), the writer must treat the premium as a capital gain, and the buyer can write off the option as a capital loss on the date of expiration. The lapse of a call or put option is treated as if it were sold for zero.

If the writer of a put closes out the option by purchasing an identical put, he or she recognizes a short-term capital gain or loss in the difference between the amount paid to purchase the put and the amount received as an option premium to write the put. Similarly, if the writer of a call closes the option by purchasing an identical call, he or she recognizes a short-term capital gain or loss in the amount of the difference between the amount received as an option premium on writing the call and the amount paid to purchase the call. These gains or losses are short-term because the maturities of these instruments are less than one year. LEAPS®, which are discussed in chapter 11, are an exception. The transactions could be long-term for these options.

If a call is exercised, the writer sells the underlying stock for the strike price. He or she recognizes a gain or loss as measured by the difference between the sum of the premium, the sales price, and the adjusted basis of the stock delivered to the purchaser. The holding period is measured from the date the stock was purchased to the date the stock was delivered under the terms of the option agreement. When a naked call is exercised, the writer, by definition, does not own the underlying stock required to cover the call at the time the call is written. Thus, the writer will have to simultaneously buy and sell the underlying stock. Hence, this is clearly a short-term transaction.

Example:	Suppose Jason writes a call for 100 shares at $40 per share; he also owns 100 shares purchased 6 months before writing the call at $30 per share and 100 shares purchased one month before writing the call at $35 per share. The writer receives a premium of $100 for the call. Nine months later, the holder of the call exercises the option. If Jason uses the first block of stock, he recognizes $1,100 of long-term capital gain ($4,000 exercise price + $100 option premium − $3,000 basis), because the call is exercised after the stock was held for 15 months. If he uses the second block of stock to cover the call, he recognizes a $600 short-term capital gain ($4,000 exercise price + $100 option premium − $3,500 basis), because the call is exercised after he held the stock for only 10 months.

If a put option is exercised, the writer purchases the underlying stock and has a basis equal to the net investment—that is, the strike price reduced by the option premium. The stock's holding period begins with the exercise of the option.

Annuities

The basic tax rule on the payments from either a fixed-period or fixed-amount annuity during the distribution phase is that a designated portion of each payment is excludible from gross income as a tax-free recovery of the purchaser's investment, and the balance, which is income earned on the contract, is taxable as ordinary income.

If the annuity is part of a qualified plan, the usual tax treatment applies in that all of the payments during the payout period are fully taxable as ordinary income. This is because the premiums were tax deductible and the taxation of the earnings in the account (that is, interest, dividends, and capital gains) was deferred.

If the annuity is a nonqualified account, a substantial portion of the annuity may be tax exempt. This is because the premium payments were made with after-tax dollars; because part of each benefit payment is considered a return of the principal, that portion is tax exempt.

Example: Suppose Fred had paid $13,500 in premiums for a policy. When he is ready to start drawing monthly benefit payments, let's assume his life expectancy is 15 years (or 180 months). Let's also assume that the monthly benefit payment is $150. Over the next 15 years, Fred can expect to receive $27,000 ($150/month x 180 months) in benefits. In this case, one-half of each payment will be tax exempt, and the other half will be taxed as ordinary income. This one-half tax exemption is based on the ratio of $13,500 in premiums paid to the $27,000 in expected benefits. The federal tax code now requires that if the annuitant lives longer than the 15 years in this example, the entire monthly benefit must be taxed as ordinary income.

Master and Limited Partnerships

Master and limited partnerships are taxed essentially the same as a general partnership. Specifically, any income or loss is computed and allocated among partners based on the partnership agreement. The allocation is reported on a form known as Schedule K-1. Note that the allocation of income or loss is independent of any net cash flow achieved by the partnership and independent of any cash distributions. Thus, if the partnership elects to keep all of the cash generated by the business, the partners still have to pay personal income taxes on their shares of the partnership income.

The major advantage to partnerships arises when the partnership generates a loss. For a normal corporation, a loss results in no direct tax benefit to the shareholders other than any potential tax refunds due the corporation or any operating tax loss carry forwards the corporation can use. For partnerships, the loss can be allocated to the partners according to the same formula used to allocate gains. The individuals can then report these losses on their tax returns for the current year and thus reduce their taxable income.

INVESTMENT STRATEGIES FOR TAX-ADVANTAGED ACCOUNTS

In tax-deferred accounts, such as IRAs and 401(k) and 403(b) plans, there is no taxation as long as there are no distributions from the plan, regardless of whether the invested funds generate capital gain distributions, dividends, and/or interest income. Taxes are assessed when funds are withdrawn from the account, which for most people is at retirement or during the retirement years.

The traditional investment strategy is to hold fixed-income investments in tax-deferred accounts and equity investments in ordinary accounts. The reasoning for this rule-of-thumb is simple. Fixed-income investments pay interest, which is taxed as ordinary income anyway. Holding these investments in a tax-deferred account, therefore, does not change the marginal tax rate at which this income is taxed.

Equity investments pay dividends and provide capital gains (assuming the investor is fortunate enough to own stocks that go up in value). As we have already seen, both dividend income and capital gains are taxed at lower marginal rates. Furthermore, capital gains are not taxed until the investments are sold. By placing equities in tax-deferred accounts, the dividend income and capital gains are eventually taxed as ordinary income (that is, a withdrawal from a tax-deferred account), rather than retaining their special tax status.

A second problem that arises if an investor buys equities in tax-deferred accounts is that most of these accounts have minimum required distributions (MRDs). Regardless of whether the investor wants to withdraw the MRD from a tax-deferred account each year, he or she must do so; the penalty for not doing so is rather severe. Hence, if the cash for an MRD that is not needed must be obtained by selling some of the holdings in the account, the capital gain effectively becomes taxed as ordinary income at that time. Had the securities been held in an ordinary account, there would be no MRD, and the investor could continue to defer the capital gains tax. Remember, depending on the size of the estate, and who the beneficiaries are, if the investor still holds the stock when he or she dies, the tax on the built-up capital gain might be completely avoided because the cost basis can still be stepped up to market value at the time of death for the beneficiaries under the tax law currently in effect. If the securities are still held in a tax-deferred account at the time of death, the decedent's beneficiaries will have to pay ordinary income taxes on the withdrawals they are required to take.

Net Unrealized Appreciation[20]

Withdrawals from qualified plans, such as ESOPs, 401(k)s, and qualified pensions, may be made in one of two ways. The more common way is to have the holdings in the account sold and the cash rolled into an IRA account. There, it is invested until the individual starts to take his or her withdrawals. At that time, it is taxed as ordinary income. An alternative strategy, which is available when the investment in the qualified plan consists of the employer's stock, is that the stock can be directly distributed to the individual.[21] At the time of the distribution, the value of the stock consists of two parts. The first is the cost or tax basis, and the second is the net unrealized appreciation (NUA). The NUA is the difference between the market value of the stock and the cost basis. At the time of the distribution, the individual must declare the cost basis as ordinary income. The net unrealized appreciation is taxed as a long-term capital gain, but only when the stock is sold. Note that this holding period is long-term, regardless of how long the shares of the stock were held in the qualified plan. When the individual eventually sells the stock, any subsequent gain or loss is treated as a long-term or short-term gain or loss, depending on how much time elapses between when the stock is distributed and when it is sold, and whether the price has gone up or down during that period. In cases where there has been substantial price appreciation on the stock, the tax savings in taking the NUA approach can be substantial.

Example:	Roger Dean is getting ready to retire. The current fair market value of his employer's stock in his retirement plan is $1.3 million. He had been planning to take the cash and roll the money into an IRA account from which he plans to withdraw the money in 10 years. He believes he can earn 8 percent on this money. If that is the case, the account will grow to $2,806,602. Finally, if we assume his combined marginal tax rate on ordinary income at that time is 35 percent, he will owe taxes of $982,311 ($2,806,602 x .35) upon withdrawal, leaving him with $1,824,291.
	Suppose, however, that the stock has a cost basis of $117,780, and that Roger takes the stock, uses the NUA treatment, holds the stock for 10 years, and receives an 8 percent rate of return on the stock. The following will occur: Roger will pay an immediate tax of $41,223 on the basis of $117,780 (35% x $117,780). The remaining value of the holding, $1,258,777 ($1,300,000 − $41,223), will then grow to $2,717,605. If the stock is sold at this time, there will be a capital gains tax of $389,974 (based on a 15 percent capital gains tax rate) based on the difference between the market value of $2,717,605 and the basis on which tax was already paid of $117,780. After payment of the taxes, Roger will be left with $2,327,631. This is $503,340 more then he would have at this time if he rolled the distribution into an IRA.

**income in respect of
a decedent**

If the NUA strategy in the above example is followed, we have to consider what will happen if Roger dies before the stock is sold. The bad news is that NUA is considered *income in respect of a decedent*. Thus, although assets passed to beneficiaries at the time of death normally have an automatic step-up in cost basis for the beneficiary to the current market value, this option is not available for NUA. The good news is that the beneficiary can still claim the NUA as unrealized appreciation and thus have it taxed as a long-term capital gain. In addition, the tax does not have to be paid until the stock is sold.

Tax Deduction for Losses in an IRA Account[22]

Some IRA accounts have a cost basis associated with them. This includes traditional IRAs in which at least some of the contributions were not deductible at the time they were made. It also includes Roth IRAs wherein none of the contributions are deductible. If the value of the IRA account is less than the cost basis, the account can be sold and some of the loss written off on the individual's tax return.

There are a couple of catches. First, all of the IRAs of the same type must be completely liquidated. Suppose an investor has two traditional IRA accounts; the value of one is $50,000 less than the cost basis, and the value of the other is $60,000 greater than the cost basis. No tax break is available. Both accounts have to be liquidated to obtain the tax break, and their combined market value actually exceeds the cost basis. Second, the loss is deducted as an itemized deduction subject to the 2 percent of AGI rule.

Most people are aware that there is a 10 percent penalty for premature withdrawals from an IRA account. In this case, the penalty does not apply because there is no income being generated, just a loss.

Example: Your client, Peter Vergin, has only one traditional IRA. His investment selection has been poor, and the market value is $10,000, despite a cost basis of $50,000. His adjusted gross income this year is expected to be $60,000. What is his tax saving if he liquidates this account, assuming his marginal tax rate is 28 percent?

Peter has a loss of $40,000. If he has no other deductions that qualify under the 2 percent rule, he can take a deduction of $38,800 as 2 percent (.02 x $60,000 = $1,200). In a 28 percent tax bracket, this will save him $10,864 in income taxes. If he has other deductions that qualify under the 2 percent AGI rule, his tax savings will be slightly greater.

Note that in the above example, it is not clear that Peter would want to take this deduction. There are several other factors to consider. For example, once the money has been withdrawn, if it is reinvested in other securities, the returns on those securities will be subject to current income taxes. The analysis can become quite complex, but it clearly starts with recognition of the tax savings that can be generated.

SUMMARY AND CONCLUSIONS

The taxation of the four basic types of investment income for federal tax purposes is provided in table 13-5.

TABLE 13-5
Tax Treatment of Investment Income

Capital distributions on stock Interest on state and local (municipal) bonds	Not subject to federal income tax
Unrealized capital gains	Tax deferred until realized
Interest income (other than municipal bond interest) Nonqualified dividend income Payments from deferred-income plans, 401(k) plans, IRAs, and so forth Rents, royalties, and any other investment income payments Short-term capital gains and short-term capital gain distributions (from mutual funds)	Taxed at ordinary income tax rate
Long-term capital gains and long-term capital gain distributions (from mutual funds) Qualified dividend income	Taxed at a 5% or 15% rate

For someone making investment decisions, the most important tax number is the combined marginal tax rate for that particular type of income. Rates of return should always be expressed in after-tax returns when they are being compared.

Generally, a financial planner wants to engage in tax-efficient investing, even when this may give the impression that he or she is not doing much. It may also create a problem with regard to diversification. Tax-loss harvesting is extremely important, even though some clients may think a loss is not real until the security is sold.

Stock splits and stock dividends have no immediate consequence other than adjustments to the investor's records. Warrants and rights are treated as capital assets if sold. If a warrant is exercised, its purchase price is added to the subscription price to determine the cost basis of the security bought. When bonds are bought, the accrued interest paid is offset against interest income, and does not become part of the cost basis. Determining imputed interest income and cost basis can be complicated for zero-coupon bonds and original issue discount bonds.

A tax-equivalent yield is equal to the taxable yield times the difference between the investor's marginal tax rate and 1. There are a variety of methods to determine the cost basis of mutual fund shares sold, but once a particular method is selected, the investor must stick to it.

Options, like warrants, can be treated as capital assets if bought and sold. If they are exercised, however, the premium is used as an adjustment to the purchase or sale price. Partnership income or losses are allocated based on the partnership agreement, and they may be independent of actual cash distributions. A significant portion of annuity income can be tax-exempt.

It may be beneficial to take the distribution from a qualified account in the form of employer's stock, especially when the cost basis of the stock is low relative to the current market value of that stock. Finally, there are times when a taxpayer can use the capital losses in an IRA account to reduce his or her taxes.

CHAPTER REVIEW

Answers to the review questions and the self-test questions start on page 733.

Key Terms

gross income	long-term capital transaction
ordinary income	tax-exempts
adjusted gross income (AGI)	tax-equivalent yield
net investment income	deep discount bonds
brackets	coupon tax effect
cost basis	imputed interest
short-term capital transaction	income in respect of a decedent

Review Questions

13-1. Define the basic model used for personal taxation, starting with total income and ending with the tax refund to be received or the tax due.

13-2. Identify the seven categories of itemized deductions and any AGI rules associated with each one.

13-3. Your client is single. For 2004, she has wage income of $60,000, interest income of $2,000, nonqualified dividend income of $3,000, mortgage interest of $5,000, property taxes of $4,000, interest expense on margin loans of $6,000, and has paid $10,000 in withholding taxes during the year. Using table 13-1, what does she owe in taxes, or what is her refund?

13-4. An investor has a federal marginal tax rate of 28 percent and a state marginal tax rate of 6 percent. What is his or her combined marginal tax rate if the investor
  a. does not itemize his state income taxes
  b. does itemize his state income taxes

13-5. Stephen buys some bonds for $1,050 on their coupon payment date. The bonds mature in 3 years, pay interest annually, and have a 10 percent coupon rate. If Stephen is in the 28 percent tax rate and any capital losses will be deducted from ordinary income, what will the after-tax rate of return be if he holds these bonds to maturity?

13-6. What is the net short-term (ST) or long-term (LT) capital gain (CG) and capital loss (CL) for each set of trades?

a.	STCG	$4,000	b.	STCG	$2,000
	STCG	$2,000		STCL	$1,000
	LTCG	$1,000		STCL	$3,000
	LTCL	$5,000		LTCG	$500
c.	STCL	$3,000	d.	STCG	$2,000
	LTCG	$7,000		STCL	$4,000
	LTCG	$2,000		LTCG	$1,000
	LTCL	$4,000		LTCL	$5,000

13-7. For each scenario in question 13-6, compute the incremental taxes owed or the tax savings for someone in the 28 percent marginal tax rate for ordinary income.

13-8. Explain the difference between tax-loss harvesting and tax-efficient investing.

13-9. Last year, Roy bought 100 shares of DEF stock for $2,000. Later, DEF declared a 5 percent stock dividend. If Roy sells 50 shares, what is their cost basis?

13-10. On July 1, James bought 10 bonds in EFG Company for $9,500 total. This included $50 in commissions and $125 in accrued interest. On September 30, the bonds paid their semiannual interest payment. They have a 5 percent coupon rate. If James sells the bonds on December 31, what is the impact on his interest income for the year?

13-11. a. How much would Mac pay for a $1,000 par value, zero-coupon bond that was sold with an 8 percent yield to maturity and had 30 years to maturity?

b. What is his imputed interest income the first year?

c. If Mac sells the bond for $200 after one year, what is his capital gain or loss?

13-12. Which of the following is considered substantially identical securities for purposes of the wash-sale rule if Harold sells 100 shares of Class A common stock of the CDE company and buys the following:

a. Class B stock, which is convertible into Class A, at a 2 for 1 ratio

b. Class A stock bought in his wife's Keogh account

c. a call option that is deep-in-the money and has 30 days to maturity

d. convertible preferred stock that trades for $80 when the conversion value is $40

e. common stock in the company's closest competitor, where the two stocks tend to move together

13-13. Explain how Joan would owe capital gains taxes on a mutual fund at the end of a year even if these shares declined in price.

13-14. Elizabeth buys 100 shares of the GHI fund for $1,200, and later buys another 50 shares for $700. If she uses the single-category method to determine her average cost, what is her capital gain or loss if she later sells 60 shares for $780?

13-15. Chad writes a naked called option (100 shares) on HIJ stock for a strike price of $50, and he receives a premium of $5 per share, the option is exercised, and he must pay $60 to buy the stock in the open market for delivery. What is Chad's capital gain or loss? Is it long-term or short term?

13-16. Your client, Rodney, has $200,000 worth of his employer's stock in his 401(K) plan. He is leaving the company but will not retire for another 14 years. Assume he believes the stock will appreciate at a rate of 8 percent per year, as would alternative investments. Assume a 28 percent tax rate on ordinary income, and a 15 percent rate on capital gains. How much cash will Rodney have in 14 years if he

a. sells the stock, rolls the proceeds into an IRA, and liquidates that in 14 years

b. withdraws the stock and sells it in 14 years (assume it has a $50,000 cost basis)

13-17. Your client, Richard, has two traditional IRA accounts. The first has a cost basis of $100,000 and a market value of $40,000. The second has a cost basis of $50,000 and a market value of $60,000. His AGI is $70,000, and he is in the 28 percent tax bracket. What is the least Richard can save on his taxes this year if he liquidates both IRA accounts?

Self-Test Questions

T   F   13-1. Interest expense on margin loans is always deductible.

T   F   13-2. When making financial decisions, investors always need to be aware of their average tax rate.

T   F   13-3. Individuals with large amounts of tax-sheltered income or high itemized deductions may be subject to the alternative minimum tax.

T   F   13-4. If the amount of foreign taxes paid is low enough, an investor may automatically take the full foreign taxes paid as a credit.

T   F   13-5. From now through 2006, everyone may take a 50 percent credit for the first $2,000 contributed to qualified accounts such as IRAs, 401(k)s, and 403(b)s.

T   F   13-6. Interest on Treasury bonds is taxable on federal returns but is exempt from state and local income taxation.

T   F   13-7. The general formula for relating pre-tax and post-tax returns is that the post-tax return equals the pre-tax return times the marginal tax rate.

T   F   13-8. If state income taxes are not an itemized deduction on a taxpayer's federal tax return, the combined marginal tax rate is simply the sum of his or her federal and state marginal tax rates.

T   F   13-9. A short-term capital gain or loss involves a holding period of exactly one year or less.

T   F   13-10. An investor may deduct from ordinary income up to $3,000 in short-term capital losses and $3,000 in long-term capital losses each year.

T   F   13-11. Capital gains on municipal bonds are tax exempt.

T   F   13-12. All other things being equal, investors in high tax brackets are likely to prefer to purchase bonds at a discount in the secondary market (even though they pay a lower coupon rate) and hold them to maturity, rather than purchase bonds at par.

T   F   13-13. Tax-efficient investing means making sure a client pays taxes only on long-term capital gains.

T   F   13-14. A tax-friendly mutual fund is characterized by a high portfolio turnover ratio.

T   F   13-15. To obtain the special lower marginal tax rate on dividend income, the taxpayer must own the stock for at least a 60-day period beginning anytime up to 60 days before the dividend is paid and ending anytime up to 60 days after it is paid.

T   F   13-16. Stock dividends are taxable income; stock splits are not.

T   F   13-17. Holding periods for short sales are measured from the date of sale to the date of purchase.

T   F   13-18. The cost basis of a bond, like stock, is the total price paid for the bond.

T   F   13-19. The conversion of convertible bonds is not a taxable event.

T   F   13-20. If a tax-exempt bond selling at par has a current yield of 4 percent, the tax-equivalent yield is 5.33 percent for an investor whose marginal tax rate is 25 percent.

T   F   13-21. A wash-sale rule violation occurs anytime an investor buys a substantially identical security within 30 days of the sale of another security.

T   F   13-22. If an investor buys any other bonds from the same issuer within 30 days of selling some bonds, he or she has violated the wash-sale rule.

T   F   13-23. An investor can suffer a price decline on mutual fund shares and still owe capital gains taxes.

T   F   13-24. One way to track the cost basis of any mutual fund shares sold is to use FIFO.

T   F   13-25. All distributions from an unit investment trust are taxable income.

T   F   13-26. The premium received when a call option is written is a capital gain at the time of the writing.

T   F   13-27. One-half of annuity payments are taxable.

T   F   13-28. In general, an investor should hold equities in tax-qualified accounts because they have higher expected returns.

T   F   13-29. Net unrealized appreciation is the difference between the market value and the cost basis of an employer's stock that is distributed from a tax-qualified account.

T   F   13-30. Capital losses in an IRA account can be deducted under certain conditions if they exceed 2 percent of AGI.

NOTES

1. There are alternative versions of Form 1040, namely Form 1040A and 1040EZ. These are much simpler forms that can be used when a taxpayer's tax situation is relatively simple. The same tax model applies; it is just that the form is much simpler.
2. The material in this section is summarized from *Fundamentals of Income Taxation, 5th edition*, by James F. Ivers, III, The American College, 2004, pp. 201–202.
3. There are several requirements to qualify as a dependent, but the two major ones are that there be a familial relationship and that the taxpayer has provided the majority of that person's living expenses. Thus, dependents usually means children, but it can include other people.
4. An alternative definition of the average tax rate is total taxes paid divided by taxable income. As there is no IRS-specified definition for this term, we can find both uses in practice.
5. Actually, the credit is not automatic because there are several conditions that have to be met. These conditions are listed on page 39 of the 2003 1040 Instructions book published by the Internal Revenue Service. In reality, almost all taxpayers easily meet the conditions.

6. The person claiming this credit must also be at least age 18, not a full-time student, and not claimed as a dependent on another person's return.

7. The subtraction rule does not apply to distributions that are rolled over into another plan or to withdrawals of excess contributions.

8. Prior to the 2003 rule changes, all dividend income was taxed as ordinary income. This special treatment of dividends is set to expire in 2009.

9. This example is from *Fundamentals of Income Taxation, 5th edition*, by James F. Ivers, III, The American College, 2004, pp. 313–314.

10. The only exception to the $3,000 per year reduction is for married taxpayers who are filing separately. In this case, the capital loss reduction is limited to $1,500 per year.

11. Some of the ideas in this section are based on "Turning Losses to Gains" by Donald Whalen, *Investment Advisor*, November 2003, pp. 107–108, 110.

12. For a fuller discussion of the issues raised in this section, see "Tax-Efficient Investing Is Easier Said Than Done" by Robert H. Jeffrey, *Journal of Wealth Management*, summer 2001, pp. 9–15.

13. Ibid.

14. IRS Publication 550, 2003, p. 55.

15. IRS Publication 550, 2003, p. 22.

16. The existence of a large number of deep discount bonds is clearly more common when interest rates have been through a long sustained upward trend, rather than a downward trend.

17. www.rrdfin.com/download/services/pub_pdf_html_files/Invest%20Co%20Act%20of% 201940/section19.html, March 16, 2004.

18. Robert H. Jeffrey, "Tax-Efficient Investing Is Easier Said Than Done," *Journal of Wealth Management*, summer 2001, p. 9.

19. The information in this section is based on IRS Publication 564 for 2003. www.irs.gov/ publications/p564ar02.html

20. Material in this section is based on "Revisiting Net Unrealized Appreciation: A Tax-Wise Strategy That May Realize More Benefits Than Ever," by John A. Nersesian and Frances L. Potter, *Journal of Financial Planning,* February 2004, p. 55.

21. Internal Revenue Code Sec. 402(e)4.

22. This section is based on "Evaluating the Tax Benefits of Deducting Stock Market Losses in IRAs," by Julia M. Brennan, and David S. Hulse, *Journal of Financial Service Professionals*, September 2003, pp. 45–55.

Managing Portfolios: The Practice

Learning Objectives

An understanding of the material in this chapter should enable the student to

---

14-1. Name and describe the seven steps in the model for advising on portfolios.

14-2. Distinguish between strategic and tactical asset allocation.

14-3. Describe how an investor's stage in the life cycles might affect his or her strategic asset allocation decision.

14-4. Describe the relationship between the number of securities in a portfolio, the types of securities in a portfolio, and the riskiness of that portfolio.

14-5. Discuss other aspects of investment selection including investment effort, minimum investment size, ethical and moral issues, and concentrated portfolios.

14-6. Demonstrate how a dollar cost averaging plan works and describe examples of these plans.

14-7. Understand some of the psychological issues of investing.

14-8. Understand the distinction between creating a good investment plan and selling the client on that plan.

Chapter Outline

In an earlier chapter we looked at the theory of portfolio management. The theory is crucial because without it, many of the applications may appear as "voodoo investments" rather than as reasonable efforts to apply a rather complex theory. With this theory as background, let us now turn to the practical side of managing a portfolio. We do not have to be an investment whiz to be good at managing a portfolio. Remember, the majority of investments do well the majority of the time, and consequently the markets themselves will provide a reasonable rate of return. It is up to the portfolio manager to—first, do no harm. Second, the portfolio manager needs to help the client understand what needs to be accomplished with these investments, and how to stick to that goal through thick and thin. There are some tricks of the trade of which all planners should be aware, and we will review those in this chapter. But let us start with the fundamental issues of how to deal with the client and how to define the portfolio objectives.

WHAT SHOULD INVESTMENT ADVISORS BE DOING? [1]

Regardless of performance, advisors have many opportunities to make themselves valuable to their clients. One obvious way to do this is to keep in touch with the client. Blending periodic phone calls with quarterly meetings gives the advisor an opportunity to stay abreast of the client's situation.

It is critical to identify a client's comfort zones. Each client has unique expectations with regard to both a professional relationship and investment. The advisor's ability to communicate with a client in a way that makes him or her receptive directly correlates with moving the client toward sound financial decisions. When the advisor understands the client's value systems, the advisor can propose alternatives that might be more effective.

There is a seven-step model for advising clients about portfolios. These seven steps are:

1. Set investment goals.
2. Gather and analyze client data.
3. Develop an investment policy.
4. Determine asset allocation.
5. Specify industry weightings.
6. Select companies.
7. Monitor the portfolio.

It should be noted that this seven-step process is not all that different from the six steps of personal financial planning. These steps are:

1. Define your current situation.
2. Define where you want to go.
3. Identify barriers to getting to where you want to go.
4. Develop a written plan.
5. Implement the plan.
6. Regularly review and revise the plan. [2]

Let's now look at the seven steps of portfolio management in detail.

Set Investment Goals

Although goal setting is critical to creating a successful portfolio, few people actually set clearly defined goals. Financial service professionals should query the client to learn what he or she is trying to accomplish with various investments. Usually the response is couched in general terms such as, "Well, we want to have a comfortable standard of living when we retire." This is not good enough. The financial planner needs to have the client develop a more precise goal such as, "We want to retire in 20 years with an after-tax income of $60,000 per year in current dollars, and we want the income to continue as long as we live without depleting the principal."

Many clients will have multiple goals and may well have multiple accounts. Some accounts will be linked to specific goals such as a Coverdell Educational Savings Account for financing a child's college education. Other accounts may be for general accumulation without being tied to a specific goal. Thus, multiple precise objectives may need to be defined.

Going through the next few steps may make it clear to the planner (and client) that modification of these goals may be necessary because usually they may turn out to be relatively unachievable.

Gather and Analyze Client Data

There are two components to this step. The first is the easy one. It involves ascertaining the client's current asset accumulations. That is, what are the accounts in which investment assets are held? What are the investments in each account? What are their current market values? Equally important to this process are the client's projected contributions.

The second component is to identify any potential constraints. Of primary concern is evaluating the client's risk tolerance. For example, an extremely risk-averse individual may not be willing to utilize enough equity investments to earn a high enough rate to reach his or her financial goals.

A critical component of any plan is whether the client intends to liquidate or "spend down" the portfolio over a specified number of retirement years or leave the principal untouched. Spending down the portfolio means that there will be a smaller estate at the client's death. It also involves the risk that if the client lives longer than expected he or she could run out of funds.

The client's tax situation is often a severe constraint on portfolio flexibility. For example, an older client may own a large block of stock with a large built-in capital gain. (Capital gains are discussed in chapter 13.) If the stock is sold the tax bill could be enormous. If it is inherited, it might pass to the beneficiaries free of any taxation.

Another constraint is the individual's phase in the life cycle. For an older client, attaining the accumulation goal may not be possible without devoting a higher percentage of the portfolio to riskier assets than is usually suggested. A closely related constraint is the client's relative inflexibility with regard to a retirement date. If the client is adamant about retiring at a particular time—age 65, for example—the management of the portfolio is less flexible because the stock market's cycle of peaks and valleys may not cooperate with the client's plan. Any portfolio decisions in the years immediately before the retirement year will be dominated by the proximity of the retirement year, usually making the decisions more conservative. A more flexible client might be willing to ride out a decline in the stock market. This could mean postponing retirement or simply postponing any massive liquidation of the portfolio.

Determining a Client's Tolerance for Risk

As mentioned earlier, it is critical that the financial advisor determine the client's tolerance for risk. In chapter 4, we defined the client's tolerance for risk with the concept of indifference curves in a graph whose axes were expected return (vertical axis) and risk (horizontal axis). It is the slope (and shape) of the indifference curves that determine the optimal portfolio for a client to hold.

Unfortunately, no one has figured out how to truly measure investment risk aversion in an individual and how to translate this into a portfolio prescription. However, the fact that the perfect method of measuring risk tolerance has not yet been developed does not excuse the financial advisor from trying to determine how much financial risk a client is willing to tolerate. It is absolutely critical that every financial advisor make some formal legitimate attempt to make as precise a determination as possible.

The obvious approach is to have the client complete a risk tolerance questionnaire. An advisor could develop his or her own questionnaire but, unless the advisor holds advanced degrees in statistics and psychology, this could be dangerous. The reason is that there is a good chance that eventually a disenchanted client will sue the financial planner for investing funds inappropriately. A planner who cannot statistically prove the validity of the risk tolerance questionnaire could be in serious trouble. Thus, planners should use risk tolerance questionnaires that are developed by reputable professionals.

A risk tolerance questionnaire will produce some sort of "score." Low scores usually indicate a high degree of risk aversion, and a high score indicates a high degree of risk tolerance. The developer of the questionnaire will then indicate how this score compares with those of others who have filled out this questionnaire or how this score relates to a suggested asset allocation model. Keep in mind that investors with low scores will be directed to highly conservative asset allocation strategies, and those with high scores will be directed to aggressive asset allocations.

As a general concept, relating these scores to asset allocations is perfectly consistent with financial theory and highly appropriate. Nonetheless, the financial planner must always remember that there is no precision to this process. If a client's score produced a recommendation to hold 50 percent of assets in common stocks, this is a *guideline* and not a scientifically based factual statement.

Develop an Investment Policy

Although creating a written investment policy appears to be cumbersome and a time-consuming overkill, it need not be so. A planner may have a few standard investment policy statements from which he or she chooses according to each client's situation. Having a policy clarifies the client's understanding of the plan and helps keep him or her on the right track. A good investment policy provides a framework for advising the client.

When performance is disappointing, having an investment policy statement encourages discipline and patience. Having a reasonable, client-approved policy—and following that policy—helps protect the advisor in the event of misunderstandings or legal action. In short, developing an investment policy is an integral part of a professional approach.

There is plenty of latitude in setting a policy statement. In general, a good statement should be brief and in writing. It should provide enough information to clearly delineate the policy but not enough information to be overly constraining. The portfolio objective, investment characteristics, risk-return objectives, and any other factors the advisor deems worthy of mention are points to include in the statement.

The portfolio objective differs from the client's accumulation goal, described earlier. One way to understand portfolio objectives is to review some mutual fund prospectuses. Every prospectus contains a statement of the fund's investment objective as indicated by such phrases as "seeks maximum capital gains," "seeks current income; capital growth is secondary," and "seeks above-average income and preservation of capital." Typical goals are to "obtain long-term growth of invested capital," to realize "significant income along with long-term growth," and to achieve "current income and capital appreciation."

A second worthwhile component of a policy statement concerns the investment characteristics of the major portfolio components. For example, common stocks and/or their underlying companies may be further defined by terms such as growth-oriented, medium- to large-sized, well-established, small-capitalization, emerging, and dividend paying. Bonds may be further defined by terms such as U.S. government, U.S. agency, high-grade corporate, investment grade, and intermediate maturity.

An indication of the risk-return trade-off sought for the portfolio is beneficial although it should not be quantified. Sometimes the description of the trade-off is very explicit, such as "maximum total return consistent with moderate portfolio volatility." Other descriptions imply the risk-return trade-off. For example, using the word "aggressive" suggests that the portfolio seeks a high rate of return and will incur a high degree of risk. Note that there is always an assumption that risk and return are positively related. It would be inappropriate to state an objective of "maximum return and minimum risk."

Many financial service professionals mention other factors in the policy statement, especially if there is a strong commitment to a particular investment philosophy or strategy such as those noted in the following section. For example, if the client is committed to a passive strategy—similar to an index mutual fund—or a strategy of investing only in mutual funds, it is reasonable to include information relevant to those strategies. Remember, however, that it is best not to provide too much information in the policy statement. The following is a typical example of a policy statement:

> This tax-deferred portfolio seeks long-term capital appreciation subject to moderate volatility primarily through investment in the common stock of stable but growth-oriented companies.

Managers of retirement portfolios for individuals have a multitude of approaches, strategies, and techniques available to them. These methods are apt to change more frequently than the investment policy statement, but because they reflect the philosophy adopted by the client, they are still somewhat stable.

Financial service professionals should determine which methods are appropriate for the client and present them to the client for approval. As with the policy statement, the list of methods should be in writing. Most practitioners, however, find it helpful to provide a bit of latitude by stating "the following methods may be used in the management of the portfolio." Possible methods include fundamental analysis, technical analysis, contrarian investing, special-situation analysis, market timing, mutual fund investing, passive investing, socially responsible investing, and dollar-cost averaging.

Determine Asset Allocation

Asset allocation is the process of setting the portfolio proportions for the major asset categories. For most portfolios, the categories are limited to stocks, bonds, and money market instruments, but other categories such as real estate can be included also.

Based on the investment goals agreed to with the client, the financial planner can establish the approximate rate of return needed to attain the objectives of each portfolio. Next, the planner considers the major asset categories (such as stocks, bonds, cash equivalents) and their associated expected rates of return and risk parameters. The planner then looks at various combinations of asset allocation weights that will achieve the desired rate of return. Finally, the planner considers the client's risk tolerance and other constraints to see which of the asset allocation combinations would appear to be optimal for that client. If this sounds more like an art than a science, that's because it is!

Let's consider an example. Suppose the projected rates of return for stocks, bonds, and cash equivalents are 10 percent, 6 percent, and 4 percent, and the associated standard deviations were 15 percent, 6 percent, and 1 percent, as shown in the table below.

Asset Category	Rate of Return	Standard Deviation
Stocks	10%	15%
Bonds	6%	6%
Cash equivalents	4%	1%

Suppose also that you have determined that based on current assets and financial goals, the client needs at least a 6 percent rate of return. There are several combinations that would do the trick (in the next section, we will further consider the process of defining the possible portfolios). Let's look at three of them:

> A: 100% bonds
> B: 33 1/3% stocks, 66 2/3% cash equivalents
> C: 25% stocks, 25% bonds, 50% cash equivalents

The next step would be to consider how these three portfolios would fit with the constraints of the client, particularly the risk tolerance constraint. If the time horizon is long, Portfolio A suffers from purchasing power risk. A sustained period of high rates of inflation would do great harm to Portfolio A, some harm to Portfolio C, but minimal harm to Portfolio B. A significant bear market would do most harm to Portfolio B, some harm to Portfolio C, and might actually enhance Portfolio A. As we saw in chapter 4, if one specifies the covariances between these three asset categories, then one could also compute the standard deviations of these three portfolios.

Irreconcilable Differences?

An interesting issue may easily arise at this point. Suppose that the only portfolios that could be constructed to provide the necessary expected rate of return all proved to be too risky. In other words, given the client's risk tolerance, the client cannot achieve the desired goals. One of several events must happen. These are:

1. The client can set a lower, more reasonable goal and consequently accept a lower-than-desired lifestyle during retirement.
2. The client can retain the goal but make a commitment to set aside more money for savings in the intervening period. For example, if the client had been planning to contribute $2,000 per year between

now and retirement, he or she may have to agree to set aside at least $5,000 each year.

3.   The client can retain the goal but accept more risk to achieve a higher return that meets the goal. For example, if the client's risk tolerance calls for a maximum of 50 percent in stocks, and a weight of at least 75 percent is necessary to achieve the desired goal, then the client may have to reconcile to living with the added risk.

4.   In the case of retirement planning, the client can make use of principal. Many clients adopt an income-only approach with no principal directed toward retirement income. Since they plan never to spend their principal, they must accumulate a larger portfolio to generate the necessary cash flow. Clients who are willing to spend down principal or to purchase a life annuity at retirement can lower their funding needs significantly.

5.   In the case of retirement planning, the client can delay the planned retirement date. A delayed retirement date not only allows personal assets to grow, there also is a good chance that pension income will be higher, reflecting more service, shorter life expectancy, and probably a higher average income. Also, Social Security income will probably be slightly higher.[3]

A few advisors suggest so-called asset allocation mutual funds, in which the funds' portfolio managers decide the proportions. These fund managers, however, make their decisions regardless of the individual investor's risk tolerance and life-cycle phase.

Specify Industry Weightings

After deciding the proportion of the portfolio to invest in stocks and before selecting individual stocks, portfolio managers evaluate data to decide how much of the stock portfolio to invest in various industries. In general nearly all industries move in the same direction as the market. After all, the market consists of the stocks—it goes up because they go up. Nonetheless, different industries perform differently in different economic conditions. For

---

Ethical Issue in Financial Planning

A widow has just received a life insurance settlement check of $500,000 from her husband's policy. She does not know how to use it most effectively and so she calls three financial planners. Planner A says he can get an 8 percent annual rate of return on her money. Planner B claims she will achieve a 10 percent rate of return. Planner C claims he will earn at least a 15 percent rate of return.[4] Which planner should the client use? The answer is none of them. Without learning more about the client, her risk tolerance, her resources, and her goals, a planner is not able to discuss what rates of return he or she can achieve.

Ethical Issue in Financial Planning

A financial planner has ascertained a client needs a 12 percent rate of return to achieve his goal. This exceeds the rates of return the planner truly expects to achieve on any of his asset categories. The planner believes the client is unlikely to employ him if he suggests one of the five alternatives suggested above. Rather, the client will likely seek another planner. There is an easy solution. The planner can just change the numbers used in his or her projections (for example, change the expected return on stocks from 10 percent to 15 percent). If after a year or two the planner is unable to achieve these returns, he might then be able to convince the client to try some alternative adjustments such as those described above.

---

example, profitability in some industries such as the utility industry is especially interest rate sensitive. Political, regulatory, and international factors also affect industries in varying degrees. For example, a presidential proposal for health-care reform has much greater implications for the pharmaceutical industry than for the automobile industry.

Portfolio managers are always conscious of what percentage of the market value of all companies is represented by companies in each industry. For example, perhaps the market value of all companies in the widget industry equals 3 percent of the total market value of all companies. When a manager is convinced that the widget industry will outperform the market, he or she will decide to invest relatively heavily in that industry—more than 3 percent of the portfolio.

Except for sector funds, which concentrate investments in specific industries, management of industry allocations is rather subtle. Even if a portfolio manager thinks that the widget industry will outperform the market by 50 percent, it is imprudent to invest too much of the portfolio in that one industry. If the forecast turns out to be wrong, the impact of overinvesting in that industry may be severe.

Individual investors have the advantage of being able to dictate industry allocations without answering to shareholders or boards of directors. Through judicious use of sector mutual funds as an adjunct to a fully diversified portfolio, advisors can help clients to weight some industries more heavily without concentrating too much in an individual company.

Select Companies

Typically, advisors of retail clients do not perform security analysis. Instead, they rely on the output of professional security analysts. Still, even the investment advisor who limits recommendations to mutual funds should be familiar with the portfolio analysis process to be able to evaluate the fund managers and answer clients' questions. The process of security analysis was discussed in chapter 8.

Monitor the Portfolio

Investment advisors must continually monitor the suitability and performance of the portfolio. Remember, the clients' situations may and do change. Clients age and as they do their risk tolerances change. Personal situations change as a result of marriage, divorce, and the birth and death of children. Dividends flow in constantly, and most clients make regular deposits into and withdrawals from their accounts, all of which create a continuous need for new investment decisions. In addition, changes in economic and market conditions will sometimes dictate that the portfolio be changed. For example, in recent years there has been a dramatic decline in yields on bonds and money market instruments. This means the expected rates of return on asset categories may no longer match the original assumptions. Finally, the portfolio itself will most likely have performed better or worse than expected. In either case, a major review is appropriate. Simply put, the advisor to an individual investor should repeat all six prior steps periodically, noting in particular any change in the client's risk tolerance or goals.

Evaluating the performance of the portfolio is another aspect of the monitoring process. The portfolio evaluation techniques discussed in chapter 5 are the appropriate ones to use. These include the Sharpe ratio, the Treynor ratio, and Jensen's alpha. For advisors with retail investment clients, calculating these values for each client portfolio is rather daunting. It is quite easy to use these methods to evaluate mutual fund performance, however, because investor services perform these calculations regularly. Although both the Sharpe ratio and Jensen's alpha implicitly consider portfolio risk, the prudent advisor will compare performance results with mutual funds in the same generic category. For example, if the client's situation calls for an aggressive growth fund, comparing performance—even on a risk-adjusted basis—with growth and income funds is not very productive.

With regard to performance of the total portfolio, advisors should practice benchmarking. Benchmarking involves creating a synthetic portfolio as a comparison for the actual portfolio. The benchmark portfolio consists of relevant market indexes combined in asset allocation proportions that reflect the actual portfolio. For example, if the actual portfolio is 70 percent large company growth stocks and 30 percent long-term corporate bonds, a benchmark portfolio may consist of 70 percent Standard & Poor's 500 and 30 percent Lehman Brothers long-term corporate bond index.

Advisors typically make several comparisons. If the actual portfolio outperformed the benchmark portfolio, the advisor's active portfolio management was successful. The advisor can extend the comparisons to each asset category to see if, for example, superior performance was due to the bond fund selection, the stock fund selection, or both. So-called decomposition analysis can reveal more information. Some models allow the analyst to attribute performance to both strategic allocation and tactical allocation.

Seven-Step Model for Managing a Portfolio

---

1. Set investment goals.
2. Gather and analyze client data.
3. Develop an investment policy.
4. Determine asset allocation.
5. Specify industry weighting.
6. Select companies.
7. Monitor the portfolio.

ASSET ALLOCATION

As noted in the seven steps for managing a portfolio, the fourth step is asset allocation. Asset allocation must not occur until the advisor has helped the client to set investment goals, gathered and analyzed client data, and developed an investment policy. There are two types of asset allocation processes—and woe to the financial advisor who confuses them or treats them as one and the same. The two are strategic and tactical.

Strategic Asset Allocation[5]

For institutional portfolios such as endowment funds and pension funds—and even mutual funds—the board of directors or board of trustees should make the strategic asset allocation decision. For an individual client, strategic asset allocation is the roadmap that should provide the constraints under which the portfolio will be managed. The purpose of strategic asset allocation is to determine the overall risk exposure of the portfolio and not to produce an allocation that will "beat the market."

A strategic asset allocation decision is normally made with only a few broad asset categories. Thus, the simplest asset allocation decision might involve only three assets categories: stocks, bonds, and cash equivalents. A common asset allocation strategy would be 60 percent stocks, 30 percent bonds, and 10 percent cash equivalents. The strategic asset allocation often involves a range of weights rather than a precise weight. Thus, an asset allocation strategy might read as 50 to 60 percent stocks, 40 to 50 percent bonds, and up to 10 percent cash equivalents. There are two ways to consider what strategic asset allocation is accomplishing: determining the desired portfolio beta or defining a simple efficient frontier.

Determining the Desired Portfolio Beta

In chapter 4, we noted that the beta of a portfolio is computed as the weighted average of the betas of the individual securities in that portfolio.

Thus, if the betas of the major asset categories are defined, then setting the asset allocation defines the target beta for the portfolio.

Example: A board of trustees is advised that the betas for major asset categories are as follows:

Stocks[6]	1.2
Bonds[7]	0.5
Cash Equivalents[8]	0.0

The board opts for a strategic asset allocation of 60 percent stocks, 30 percent bonds, and 10 percent cash equivalents. Hence, the board has effectively dictated a target portfolio beta of

$$beta_p = .6 \times 1.2 + .3 \times .5 + .1 \times 0 = .87$$

A Simplified Efficient Frontier

Also in chapter 4, we discussed the derivation of the efficient frontier. The efficient frontier in a world without a risk-free asset is a concave locus of points, an example of which is reproduced in figure 14-1.

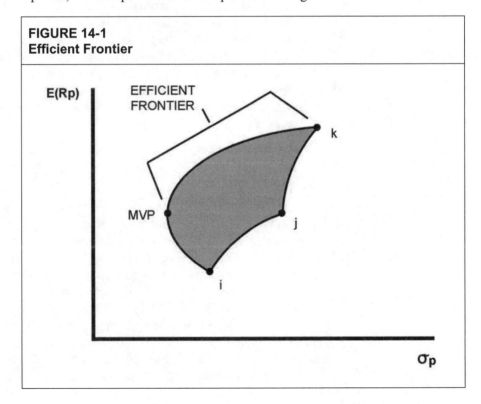

FIGURE 14-1
Efficient Frontier

When strategic asset allocation is being used, an efficient frontier is being defined u sing just the asset categories as inputs. For example, suppose we developed the following return statistics for our three assets:

Expected return:	Stocks	.10	Bonds .05	Cash Equiv.	.04
Standard dev.:	Stocks	.18	Bonds .08	Cash Equiv.	.02
Covariances:	Covariance (stocks, bonds)				.0072
	Covariance (stocks, cash equivalences)				.00018
	Covariance (bonds, cash equivalences)				.00032

Based on this information, we can use any of several software packages to produce an efficient frontier that would look similar to figure 14-1. The strategic asset allocation decision is then the decision of which portfolio on this efficient frontier one wants to hold. As discussed in chapter 4, it is simply a matter of imposing our indifference curves on this graph to find the portfolio that lies on the highest possible indifference curve.

When a client wants to strictly follow a strategic asset allocation approach, the ideal investments might well be index funds. Thus, the choice for stocks would be a stock index fund, the choice for bonds would be a bond index fund, and the choice for cash equivalents would be a broadly diversified money market mutual fund.

Strategic asset allocation decisions must be long-term decisions. It is acceptable to change a strategic asset allocation, but such a change should be associated with a significant discussion as to why the new allocation is better. The next section of this chapter discusses life-cycle issues regarding appropriate changes in strategic asset allocation. If the changes in one's strategic asset allocation are frequent, then decisions are tactical, not strategic.

Portfolio Rebalancing

One of the consequences of strategic asset allocation is that strictly adhering to it can cause the financial advisor to make recommendations that might seem foolish to the client. Remember, security prices fluctuate on a daily basis. Thus, although one's portfolio might start with a perfect asset allocation, such as 60 percent stocks, 30 percent bonds, and 10 percent cash equivalents, most likely the weights will have changed slightly at the end of one day of trading. Thus, implicit in strategic asset allocation is the frequency of verification. That is, at what frequency is the portfolio reexamined to check for adherence to the strategic weights? Weekly? Monthly? Quarterly? Annually?

A second issue is what ranges are tolerated. If the strategic allocation is 50 to 60 percent stocks, then as long as the stockholding is within this range, no trading is necessary. However, if during a bullish move, stocks increase to be 60.1 percent of the portfolio, then should some stocks be sold?

A third issue is that rebalancing the portfolio necessarily means selling what has done well and buying what has not done well. For example, if the client starts with the 60, 30, 10 mix, and over the course of the year one or two stocks have done spectacularly well, then the portfolio could suddenly have weights of 70, 22.5, 7.5. The decline in the bond and cash holdings is not because those market values have gone down but because the stocks have gone up as a percentage of the entire portfolio. The most likely way to rebalance the portfolio and to keep a diversified stockholding, is to sell a good percentage of the exact stocks that have done the best and put the money into bonds and cash equivalents. This creates the dual problem of having to pay capital gains taxes as a result of selling the strong performers (see chapter 13) and having to explain to the client why you are selling off the best performing stocks!

Tactical Asset Allocation

Tactical asset allocation decisions differ from strategic decisions in several ways:

- Decisions are made for the purpose of beating the market rather than setting the desired level of risk exposure.
- These decisions are made more frequently.
- Decisions may include many more asset categories.

pure market timer

With regard to beating the market, a *pure market timer* would be in the market when it is expected to rise and out of the market when it is expected to fall. There are few, if any, pure market timers. The more common approach to market timing is to shift asset allocations within the guidelines of any ranges specified in the strategic asset allocation.

Example: The strategic asset allocation for a portfolio might be specified as: 45 to 60 percent in stocks, 40 to 55 percent in bonds, and 0 to 10 percent in cash equivalents. A bullish market timer would then change the portfolio to 60 percent in stocks and 40 percent in bonds. A bearish market timer would put 45 percent in stocks, 45 percent in bonds, and 10 percent in cash equivalents. A neutral outlook might imply the following allocations: 55 percent in stocks, 50 percent in bonds, and 5 percent in cash equivalents.

Tactical asset allocations are usually more detailed in terms of asset categories. For example, a tactical asset proposal may divide a portfolio into several components such as the following:

- money funds for very low risk and high liquidity
- long-term, high-grade bonds for moderate risk
- junk bonds for speculative appeal in the debt market
- blue chip stocks for low-risk equity market participation
- growth and/or small-cap stocks for greater speculation in equities
- international equities for global diversification
- stock options for short-run speculation in equities

Tactical allocation decisions may be made monthly, quarterly, or annually or on an as-desired basis. Any changes in allocation weights that are not intended as long-term target objectives are by definition tactical allocation decisions.

LIFE-CYCLE ISSUES

As mentioned in the previous section, strategic asset allocations should rarely be changed. However, a traditional and good reason for changing these allocations is that as people age, their risk tolerances naturally change. Life-cycle investing (LCI) is the process of tailoring the investment portfolio to fit the client's phase in the life cycle. LCI also prescribes adjusting the investment portfolio to meet changes in objectives as the client passes through life's various phases.

Usually LCI involves reducing risk and emphasizing income as the individual grows older. However, LCI does not stress age differences to the exclusion of other factors, such as wealth and risk tolerance. Rather, LCI provides a framework within which the planner can integrate those factors.

Changes in Emphasis Over Time

Although the client's risk tolerance is always a critical factor, a financial advisor also needs to be concerned about the trade-off between current income and growth particularly when choosing among stocks. As investors age they typically reduce the emphasis on growth and increase the emphasis on current income. Figure 14-2 shows graphically this change in emphasis.

Older individuals typically recognize that they have a reduced opportunity to recover from investment setbacks, and their willingness to take the risk required for growth seems to decrease with age. They can achieve this change in the portfolio's characteristics by either (1) concentrating their annual

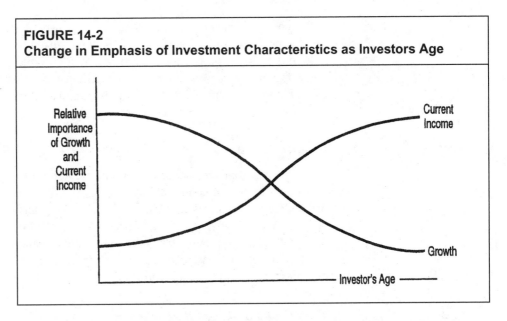

FIGURE 14-2
Change in Emphasis of Investment Characteristics as Investors Age

additions to the portfolio in some combination of higher current income and lower-risk investments or (2) shifting money realized from the maturing or sale of assets into these same types of securities.

Factors Other Than Age

As mentioned above, age is only one of the factors to consider in life-cycle investing. Personal characteristics and portfolio objectives weigh heavily in the LCI approach and will influence the shapes and relative positions of the portfolio growth and current income lines of figure 14-2. At least four types of personal characteristics or conditions affect the income-growth trade-off in life-cycle investing. These characteristics are

- stability, amount, and sources of income
- family situation
- the client's balance sheet
- the client's investment experience and knowledge

Each of these characteristics is discussed below.

Stability, Amount, and Sources of Income

A client with a fluctuating income, such as a commissioned salesperson, typically should not select a high-risk portfolio because of the possibility of a prolonged down period of employment income. If more than one spouse is employed, a higher-risk, lower-income portfolio can be selected. Higher income permits greater portfolio risk, since high-income individuals have the potential to save proportionately more than low-income individuals. If an individual has numerous sources of income, such as salary from a secure job (for example, a tenured professor), dividends, interest, and so on, greater portfolio risk can be taken due to the stability of the income flow.

Family Situation

A young, married investor with children should avoid aggressive, high-portfolio-risk investments until family obligations are met. Those with aged or handicapped dependents who might need long-term care and its attendant costs should likewise opt for a conservative portfolio. It is important also to note that marriage plans, plans involving career changes, and so on can affect risk tolerance, and that at any age, larger families may have a greater need for current income from the portfolio.

The Client's Balance Sheet

In looking at the client's balance sheet, the planner should be sure to take into account the client's debt relative to his or her net worth and attitudes toward debt. Also keep in mind the obvious fact that individuals with large net worth relative to assets are in a better position to own higher-risk portfolios.

The Client's Investment Experience and Knowledge

Recognize that novices are more likely to be sensitized by poor investment results so that a disastrous investment loss early on can seriously hinder implementing an effective, long-term investment program. Hence, the planner should initially place only a small portion of their investment money into any one high-risk instrument.

Life-Cycle Periods

There are five distinct periods of life in life-cycle investing. Although some clients will not experience all phases or will spend more or less time in a phase, the vast majority of clients go through all five, which are: (1) early career, (2) career development, (3) peak accumulation, (4) preretirement years, and (5) retirement.

The early career phase normally encompasses age 25 (or under) to 35. Often the individual is newly married and has young children, and one or both of the spouses are establishing employment patterns. The client is probably concerned about accumulating funds for a home purchase if he or she has not already done so. As the children grow older, the parents begin to think about saving for college, and many will accumulate funds to start a business. Job-related geographic relocation can put a strain on the family as well as the budget. This period, particularly the early years, generally affords little consideration of retirement planning.

The career development phase normally encompasses ages 35 to 50 and is often a time of career enhancement, upward mobility, and rapid growth in income from profession or business. This phase usually includes accumulation and expenditure of funds for children's college education. Clients make greater efforts to coordinate employee benefits with their spouses and to integrate employee benefits with investment strategies if both spouses are employed. Geographic relocation is still a possibility, and the client becomes increasingly concerned about financial independence and retirement income planning. The most successful clients will begin general wealth building beyond their basic objectives and may purchase a second home or travel extensively.

In the peak accumulation phase the client is usually moving toward maximum earnings and has the greatest opportunity for wealth accumulation. This phase may include accumulating funds for other objectives but is usually a continuation of retirement income planning, coordination of employee benefits with investment and retirement strategies, and saving for a vacation home or travel. Most clients begin reducing investment risk to emphasize income production for retirement (particularly near the end of this period) and become increasingly concerned about minimizing taxes.

Preretirement years are the 3 to 5 years prior to planned retirement age. This phase often includes winding down both the career and income potential. Clients begin restructuring the portfolio to reduce risk and enhance income. There is further emphasis on tax planning and the evaluation of retirement plan distribution options relative to income needs and tax consequences.

Retirement is the final phase in the cycle. For the successful client, it is a time of enjoyment with a comfortable income and sufficient assets to preserve purchasing power. It may involve a geographical relocation. Many clients become more active socially, take up new hobbies, and volunteer. Some seek a new career and many will look for a job (part-time or full-time) that is less stressful.

Portfolio Selection in the Phases of the Life Cycle

As already noted, a number of factors other than age influence decisions in life-cycle investing. However, many practitioners and clients find it helpful to see guidelines that relate investment choices to the phases in the life cycle.

Table 14-1 demonstrates a set of proportions that individuals in different phases of the life cycle might allocate to assets with specific risk-return characteristics.

TABLE 14-1 Investment Allocation Percentages			
Life-Cycle Stage	Investment Categories		
	Low Risk, Safe, Secure	Medium Risk, Moderate Growth	High Risk, High Growth
Early career	0% to 30%	60% to 80%	0% to 30%
Career development	10% to 40%	50% to 70%	0% to 20%
Peak accumulation	20% to 50%	40% to 60%	0% to 20%
Preretirement	30% to 80%	20% to 50%	0% to 20%
Retirement	40% to 90%	10% to 50%	0% to 10%

Where an individual's portfolio allocations should fall within the ranges depends on factors mentioned earlier. For example, consider a client who is single, wealthy, debt free, and risk tolerant and who has a high, stable income and extensive knowledge and experience in investments. This person can appropriately select asset categories that maximize growth and de-emphasize risk avoidance.

THE IMPACT OF PORTFOLIO SIZE ON RISK

A perennial question that financial planners must deal with is, What is the optimal number of securities for a portfolio? Unfortunately, there is no simple answer to this question—and it is important that the financial planner understand why there is no simple answer to this question.

Evans and Archer published the classic research on optimal portfolio size in 1968.[9] In their research they started with a large database of stocks and randomly selected 60 securities. For each of these 60 securities, they computed the standard deviation of returns over a fixed time period. They then computed the arithmetic average of the 60 standard deviations. They repeated the exercise by creating 60 portfolios each of which contained two randomly selected securities. The standard deviations of these 60 portfolios were computed and the arithmetic average again derived. This process was repeated for 60 portfolios of three randomly selected securities on up to 60 portfolios of 40 randomly selected securities. For each portfolio size, the average of the 60 standard deviations was computed. Finally these 40 average standard deviations were graphed with the vertical axis showing the standard deviation and the horizontal axis showing the portfolio size. Finally Evans and Archer computed the standard deviation for the portfolio consisting of every single security in their database. This was defined as the standard deviation of the market portfolio.

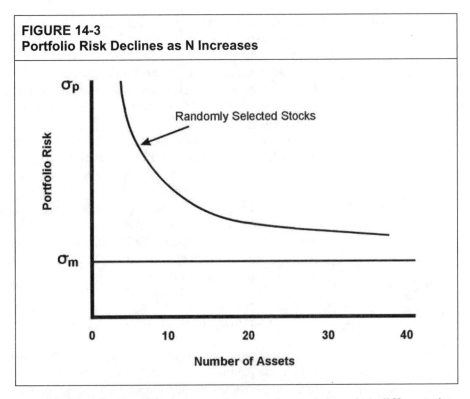

FIGURE 14-3
Portfolio Risk Declines as N Increases

This exercise has been repeated many times since using different data sets, different time periods, different time horizons, and so on. The actual numerical results differ with each application, but the general principles that emerge are always the same. The typical graph that is produced is shown in figure 14-3. The general conclusions from these studies form some of the most important principles of investments today. They include:

1. On average, the total risk of a portfolio declines as additional securities are added to the portfolio.
2. The total risk of a portfolio declines at a DECREASING rate as additional securities are added. Thus, the addition of a third security to a two-security portfolio will reduce total risk by a substantially greater amount than will the addition of a 40th security to a 39-security portfolio.
3. On average, the total risk of a portfolio converges downward toward the total risk of the market portfolio.
4. On average, no amount of diversification can reduce the total risk of a portfolio below that of the market portfolio.

That is, diversification does not eliminate all risk. It only eliminates nonmarket or nonsystematic risk. This means that systematic risk becomes an increasing portion of the portfolio's total risk.

The Evans-Archer graph brings us to the crux of the optimal portfolio size question. If we assume that there is some cost to adding a security to a portfolio, then at some point the cost of adding a security to a portfolio overwhelms the value of the reduction in risk from adding that security. Certainly for most investors the commission from buying 100 shares in each of two companies is more than the commission to buy 200 shares in one company. Some people would also argue that there is a monitoring cost. That is, a portfolio manager may have to spend more time monitoring stocks in a 50-stock portfolio than in a 10-stock portfolio. Hence, to the extent that each additional security necessitates additional time for monitoring, there is an implicit time cost when stocks are added to portfolios.

Let's ignore the monitoring cost issue by assuming that markets are efficient and therefore no monitoring is necessary. Let's also assume that the only transaction fee is the commission. If this were the case, then the optimal portfolio size is inversely related to the magnitude of the commission. This becomes our fifth principle:

5. The lower the commission one pays, the larger the number of securities that would be optimal.

If one paid no commission (for example, suppose one had a wrap account in which one paid an annual fee but did not pay any commissions per se), then in theory the optimal portfolio size becomes the market portfolio.

The Impact of Portfolio Composition on Optimal Portfolio Size

As one might suspect, the Evans-Archer graph can be quite sensitive to the composition of the portfolio. For example, suppose the securities that made up the portfolio were all mutual funds. Thus, each security would represent a portfolio of as many as several hundred or more securities. In other words, each security would already represent a highly diversified portfolio. In this case, the curve in figure 14-3 would converge much more quickly to the market portfolio than is the case when the securities represent individual stocks. This result can be easily seen as shown by the drop in the risk exposure curve in figure 14-4. Hence, the optimal number of holdings would likely be a much, much smaller number when one limits the holdings to only mutual funds.

Furthermore, if the mutual funds were load funds, then the optimal number of funds to hold would be limited. If they were no-loads, then once again the optimal number of securities to hold would be potentially unlimited even though there is negligible risk reduction as funds are added to the portfolio.

Over the years, various researchers have looked at the impact of other characteristics on the Evans-Archer curve. For example, Wagner and Lau[10] showed that far fewer stocks are necessary to achieve a specific level of diversification (that is, portfolio risk) when the portfolio consists of stocks

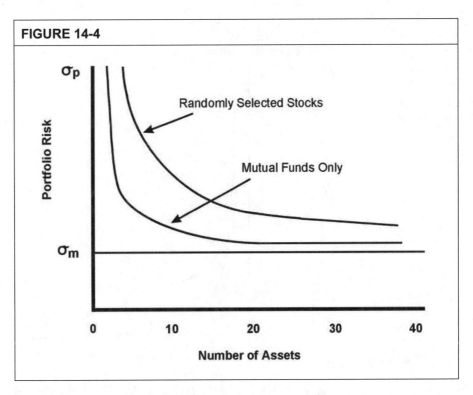

FIGURE 14-4

rated highly by the *Standard and Poor Stock Guide* than those rated poorly. Klemkosky and Martin[11] found that diversification could be more readily achieved with low-beta stocks than with high-beta stocks. Later, Martin and Klemkosky[12] showed that diversification could be more readily achieved when stock classifications are considered. Their stock classifications included growth stocks, cyclical stocks, stable stocks, and oil stocks.

International Diversification

Another famous research piece looked at the effect of including securities of foreign companies in one's portfolio.[13] The stock markets in different countries appear to have a large component of independent variability. That is, a large part of the variability in their returns is unrelated to fluctuations in any one other country's domestic market. Thus, a strategy of adding foreign securities to a portfolio of domestic securities can be used to reduce the impact of the home country's business cycle. In this case, the lower risk curve (figure 14-5) is marked as "international unhedged," which means that it is a portfolio created from both domestic and foreign securities and that there is no attempt to hedge foreign exchange rate risk. Investors can diversify internationally in a variety of ways. They can purchase shares in an international mutual fund, a U.S.-based multinational company, a foreign

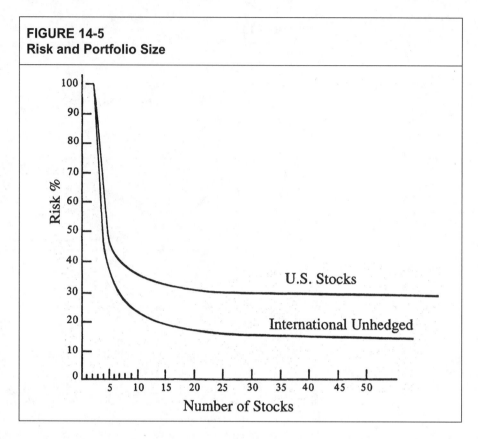

FIGURE 14-5
Risk and Portfolio Size

company's stock, or American depository receipts (ADRs) representing ownership of such securities.

The ownership expenses of both foreign and international funds tend to be somewhat higher than those of domestic funds because transaction costs abroad are higher, and it is more difficult to obtain information on the securities of foreign firms. Furthermore, offshore mutual funds are less closely regulated than U.S. funds. Finally, investing in foreign securities exposes the investor to exchange rate risk and political risk.

Most advisors believe that at least some degree of international diversification is appropriate even though many U.S. corporations already have extensive international involvement. Many investors view international investing as a source of returns that are higher than those available in this country and become disillusioned when international stocks underperform domestics. While it is true that there are excellent opportunities in other countries, the major benefit from international investing is diversification. The fact that foreign markets operate in cycles that do not coincide with the U.S. markets means that international investing reduces the variability—the risk—of the portfolio.

Market Volatility and Optimal Portfolio Size[14]

One of the major problems with all of the above research on risk and the number of securities in a portfolio is that the research is based on the assumption that all the securities in a portfolio have equal weights, and the portfolios are constantly rebalanced to maintain equal weights. For example, when Evans and Archer considered a portfolio of four securities, they assumed that 25 percent of the portfolio was invested in each security. Then, after one period (they used semiannual periods), the portfolio was rebalanced so that 25 percent was again invested in each security. This means that they were assuming that the shares of the stocks that went up were sold, and the money was used to purchase additional shares in those securities that went down.

The reality, of course, is that no one actually holds portfolios with equal weights. Even if on the day the portfolio is initially created the holdings are equally distributed, then the odds are overwhelming that after the first day of trading the weights will no longer all be equal. Hence, if one starts out with a four-security portfolio with equal weights, after a period of time it is likely that one or two securities will come to dominate the portfolio. This market reality that all securities do not change values at the same rate means that any rule of thumb about appropriate portfolio size is subject to distortion. Hence, although most investments textbooks and many financial advisors will indicate a minimum number of securities for an adequately diversified portfolio, that number can easily prove to be inadequate as soon as security prices start changing. It is interesting to note that if one looks at the number of securities actually recommended for an adequately diversified portfolio, the number will vary substantially. Some people go with as few as 10 securities, and others will be as high as 25 to 40 or more. The principle to remember is this:

6.   The minimum number of securities necessary to have an adequately diversified portfolio depends on the weights of those securities in the portfolio.

Example: Ted Kurtsy is a new client. Ted's portfolio has 20 securities in it. Normally 20 securities would be considered a well-diversified portfolio. However, upon a closer examination of Ted's portfolio, his financial advisor notes that the largest single holding represents 40 percent of the market value of the portfolio, and the largest three holdings combined constitute 75 percent of the market value. It is clear that although Ted's portfolio meets the numbers criteria for adequate diversification, it does not meet any market test as to adequate diversification.

OTHER ASPECTS OF INVESTMENT SELECTION

Investment Effort

The monitoring of stocks, bonds, and cash equivalents can be a fairly straightforward process requiring minimal effort. This is particularly true when one holds actively traded securities. There is little to do because the market is quite efficient for highly marketable assets. By the time the financial advisor hears any news about General Motors, the news is absolutely incorporated into the stock price. As soon as the advisor starts to invest in securities that have little marketability, or sets up hedged positions involving combinations of securities and options, or enters into futures contracts, then the need to monitor the portfolio goes up substantially. If a portfolio includes real assets such as apartment buildings, racehorses, and so forth, then managing the assets will take a substantial amount of time. The investment advisor has to decide up front in conjunction with the client how much investment effort will be put into monitoring the portfolio. Presumably the fees will match the effort.

Minimum Investment Size

Portfolios of some types of investments may be assembled with small sums whereas others require a much larger minimum commitment. Moreover, some investments have such low risk that a portfolio consisting of a single asset is an appropriate holding. For instance, a savings account can be opened for as little as $100 and some higher-yielding bank certificates are available in $500 denominations. Many mutual funds will accept initial deposits of $1,000. Indeed, mutual funds offer an attractive way for small investors to participate in the stock and bond market with relatively small sums of money. Many collectibles sell for a few hundred dollars or less. On the other hand, several thousand dollars are generally needed to purchase a single stock or bond position efficiently. If one believes that a minimum of 20 securities is needed for a well-diversified stock portfolio, and if an average investment of $3,000 is made in each holding, then the investor would need to commit at least $60,000 to create a diversified portfolio of 20 common stocks.

A single real estate purchase (to say nothing of a diversified real estate portfolio) is likely to require at least several thousand dollars (or more likely several tens of thousands of dollars) for just the down payment. Similarly, most brokers will not accept commodity accounts having less than $20,000 to $50,000 in investor capital.

Obviously the capital requirements of different types of investments differ appreciably. Those beginning with relatively small sums are restricted to investments that are available in modest size units. Over time, however, investors may be able to shift into investments that are traded only in larger increments.

Ethical and Moral Appeal

Investments may also differ substantially in their ethical and moral appeal particularly to certain groups of investors. Many investors take the attitude that if an activity is legal, it is a proper area in which to invest. Other investors, however, want their investment dollars associated only with activities of which they personally approve. What is socially unacceptable for some, however, is not socially unacceptable for others. Social responsibility is largely in the eye of the beholder. No doubt many investors would draw the line at pornography and prostitution even where these activities are legal. Others would refuse to become slumlords even if all health and safety codes are adhered to and the profit potential is substantial. Still others would object to investments in companies involved with one or more of the following types of products or activities: alcohol, tobacco, armaments, war toys, pollutants, nonunionized employees, unionized employees, child labor, misleading advertising, and poor safety records.

A decision not to invest in certain companies or industries always raises the question of whether this constraint on a portfolio means this portfolio is less likely to achieve an appropriate risk-adjusted rate of return. Most of the research in this field suggests that the answer is no. First, as noted above, there is no universal agreement as to what are inappropriate industries or companies in which to invest, so what one investor objects to may be perfectly reasonable to another. Hence, there are no industries or companies that are so objectionable that the few investors willing to invest in them are assured above-market rates of return. Second, most people have a relatively small list of industries or companies in which they would not invest. So this constraint typically has minimal impact on a portfolio recommendation list.

Splitting the Difference[15]

If a client has only one investment account, then the strategic asset allocation applies to this account. However, many clients have multiple accounts.

Ethical Issue in Financial Planning

As a financial planner, you are meeting with some new clients, Joe Bob and Sallie Mae Jenkins. They are in their mid-30s, are both employed, have young children, and have a high tolerance for risk. They agree on a portfolio that is 80 percent stocks, 15 percent bonds, and 5 percent cash equivalents. You then suggest 25 of your favorite stocks, headed by Philip Morris. Joe and Sallie immediately object because they believe smoking tobacco is a sin. This is a company you really feel has gotten terribly undervalued in recent years and represents an excellent investment opportunity. Unfortunately, good financial planning means you will have to remove this stock from your list as your objective is to help the clients achieve their goals in a manner satisfactory to them and not force on them what you think is in their best financial interest.

Furthermore, as discussed in chapter 13, the investment income and capital gains in some accounts are either tax exempt or tax deferred provided certain conditions are met. The standard recommendation is that one should hold assets with high current income (which usually means bonds) in one's tax-exempt or tax-deferred account, and investments with primarily capital gains (which usually means stocks) in one's regular accounts (that is, those without special tax treatment). This is fine, but only if the resulting allocation coincides with one's strategic asset allocation. The amount of assets in a tax-exempt or tax-deferred account is usually not something one has much control over.

Example:	James and Jennifer Watson are new clients. They have accumulated $50,000 in their company's 401(k) plan and hold $100,000 in personal assets. Their 401(k) is invested entirely in stock mutual funds, and their personal assets are 50 percent stocks, 50 percent bonds. You and the Watsons decide on a strategic asset allocation of 50 percent stocks, 40 percent bonds, and 10 percent cash equivalents. In dollars, this translates into $75,000 in stocks, $60,000 in bonds, and $15,000 in cash equivalents. The obvious first step in executing the plan is to sell the stock funds in the 401(k) and replace them with bond funds. This provides $50,000 of the desired $60,000 investment in bonds, which means that the regular stock account will hold $75,000 in stocks, $10,000 in bonds, and $15,000 in cash equivalents. Note that since the purpose of the cash equivalents is to provide cash reserves, they cannot be in the 401(k) plan because this would make them inaccessible unless a steep penalty is paid. Note that in the final plan the Watsons still end up with bonds in their taxable account!

Concentrated Portfolios

A particular problem arises when a client ends up with what is known as a concentrated portfolio, that is, a portfolio in which one or a few securities have disproportionate weights. There is no mathematical definition as to what constitutes a concentrated portfolio and no precise description, but when it exists a capable financial planner will recognize it. Recognition is one thing, action is another since most of the time there is a price to pay to reduce the concentration.

The problem with concentration is that it exposes the investor to non-market risk. Unless the investor has incredibly strong reason to believe that the security (or securities) creating the undue concentration is (are) expected to have excess return, there is no reward for the concentration to compensate for the risk exposure.

About the only time there is an easy solution is when the concentration occurs in a tax-deferred or tax-exempt account, and there is no restriction on selling the asset. In this case, the concentrated holding can be sold and replaced with a set of diversified holdings.

The more common case is that the concentrated position occurs in a taxable account. The concentration usually comes about because one security has strongly outperformed the rest. In this case, there will be a substantial capital gain associated with the position (capital gains are discussed in chapter 13). Selling the position creates a capital-gains tax, which will reduce the value of the account when the tax is paid. An alternative is to set up some sort of hedge with the position. Usually, options (discussed in chapter 11) would provide the best opportunity for hedging. The only problem is that when options are used for hedging, the expected return on the asset is then substantially reduced.

A financial planner will observe a concentrated position in one of three ways. A new client may walk in the door and the planner notes the concentrated position. The client is invested in something that does incredibly well. For example, the client may be put in something like Wal-mart, IBM, or Berkshire-Hathaway in the early days of each, or the client may be holding a dot-com type of company just as those got hot in the late 1990s. Finally, the position may arise as a result of the purchase of an employer's stock through a special program. It is nicer, of course, if the concentration arises as a result of a recommendation by the financial planner. Nonetheless, it is normally a painful problem to resolve that involves choosing between the lesser of two evils.

DOLLAR COST AVERAGING

One of the most common suggestions for investing is "buy low, sell high." The only problem with following this advice is that no one knows at the time whether the current price will later be viewed as a high price or a low price! Dollar cost averaging is a strategy that attempts to put this advice into practice. In simple terms, dollar cost averaging is the investment of a fixed amount of money at specified time intervals. For example, an investor might commit to buy $1,000 worth of a stock or mutual fund on the first day of each month for the period of one year. Investing a fixed dollar amount per period means that investors buy more shares when prices are low than when they are high. The benefit of such a strategy is that it frequently results in a lower average purchase price per share. It also helps some investors who are reluctant to invest a large sum of money in a single shot.

Unless a stock goes into a persistent decline, dollar cost averaging will accomplish its objective. It works best when the stock has an early decline and a later rise. It does not, however, protect the investor against losses in a steadily declining market.

Example: Hernando DeSoto,[16] a new client, has just found out that he has inherited $1,000,000 from a long lost uncle. After a consultation, the two of you agree that his strategic asset allocation should be 80 percent stocks, 15 percent bonds, and 5 percent cash equivalents. You then present a list of 40 stocks that would represent an appealing diversified portfolio of common stocks. He immediately blanches when he realizes you are proposing to take $800,000 of his newly acquired wealth to buy stocks the next day. He says, "But suppose the market starts going down?" In this case, he would surely be better off waiting. You then remember that many investors fear regret more than they desire success. That is, they are more concerned that they will regret rushing into an investment than they are concerned about paying more later. Of course, such an attitude could easily lead to perpetual postponement of the purchase of stock.

To overcome this fear of regret, you suggest dollar cost averaging because if stock prices fall, he can buy more shares later. You propose to invest $40,000 per month over the next 20 months until the portfolio reaches it strategic asset allocation. Hernando is quite pleased with this plan and agrees immediately to begin the investment program.

The only problem with the above scenario is that research has shown that in terms of expected future wealth, Hernando would do best if he agreed to plunk down all $800,000 immediately.[17] However, getting investors to do what is best for them sometimes requires the use of suboptimal tactics, but this may be the only way to get the job done.

Example: Many people have no other option but to engage in dollar cost averaging. They just aren't aware that this is what they are doing. For example, employees who contribute a certain percentage of their paycheck each month to a defined-contribution plan in which they have specified certain investments (usually mutual funds) for the account are engaging in dollar cost averaging. Employees probably think of this as a long-term savings program, and it is, but they are also using a strategy of dollar cost averaging.

Dividend Reinvestment Plans

One form of dollar cost averaging is a dividend reinvestment plan (DRIP)—a program in which stockholders can reinvest their dividends directly into the company's stock. These plans may acquire either existing or newly issued stock. The first plans to be established relied on existing stock purchases. Typically the corporation sends the dividends of participating stockholders to the managing bank's trust department. This bank maintains an account for each shareholder. Each participant is credited with his or her shares less brokerage fees and administrative costs. Many DRIPs also permit additional stock purchases for cash. Large round-lot purchases by the plan tend to reduce brokerage fees. Some companies give discounts on their dividend reinvestments. Firms selling newly issued shares charge no brokerage fees on the transactions.

Dividend reinvestment plans have a number of advantages. From the firm's standpoint, the plans add to stockholder goodwill, increase demand for the firm's stock, save some dividend-related expenses, and encourage small stockholders to increase ownership. In addition, plans involving new share purchases reduce the firm's debt-to-equity ratio, provide a regular source of equity capital, and permit new equity to be sold without incurring underwriting fees or other flotation costs.

There is one drawback to dividend reinvestment plans particularly for investors with larger portfolios. When investors have enough dividend income during the year, they can accumulate sufficient cash to purchase stocks in other companies. When one enrolls in a DRIP, one ends up buying more shares in the stocks held in the existing portfolio. Thus, DRIPs reduce one's ability to increase the diversification of one's portfolio by acquiring stock in other companies.

Direct Purchase Plans

Many companies now also offer a direct purchase plan (DPP). With a DPP the investor opens an account and arranges for a regular debit to a checking or savings account to purchase new shares. DPPs have the wonderful benefit of giving investors the opportunity to build a stock portfolio with what may be relatively small monthly purchases. They have the same drawback as DRIPs in that they limit diversification potential. However, DPPs are most attractive for new, younger investors who typically lack the resources to immediately build a diversified portfolio. In addition, after investors have accumulated a certain amount of shares in any one company, they can switch the DPP to other companies, thus building diversification over time.

An alternative to a DPP for one company is to set up an account with a firm such as Sharebuilder (www.sharebuilder.com), which allows the investor to create what is essentially a direct purchase plan for a variety of stocks, index funds, and even closed-end bond funds. Some brokerage firms have even set up similar programs for their clients and at times have also allowed for reinvestment of dividends in the stock paying the dividends. From the stockholder's perspective, this will end up creating fractional shares.

Employee Stock Purchase Plans

Corporate employees will sometimes have the opportunity to participate in an employee stock purchase plan (ESPP). These plans are defined in Internal Revenue Code Section 423. They allow a company to sell stock to employees at a discount from the fair market price. To be approved for special tax treatment, the option to buy the stock must be offered to employees on a nondiscriminatory basis. The option cannot be transferred, that is, only the employee can use the option during his or her lifetime.

If all of the conditions of the plan are met, then the purchase price of the stock can be as low as 85 percent of the fair market value either on the offer/grant date or on the sale date, whichever is less. Most plans allow employees to purchase stock every 6 months via payroll withholding.

The plans have good and bad features for both the company and the employee. They are a good deal for the company because it is able to raise equity capital without any transaction fee, other than the discount given to the employee. They are also good for the company because employees will presumably become more effective workers as an increasing amount of their wealth becomes tied up in the company. The drawback for the company is that if the discount given is substantial, then wealth is effectively being transferred from the existing shareholders to the employees.

ESPPs can be quite attractive for the employee if the discount is substantial. In addition, they can act as a forced savings plan. Remember, many folks will not save out of their paycheck; they will save only when the money is transferred elsewhere. (This is the same reason the vast majority of people overpay on their income taxes.) Hence, an ESPP provides an opportunity to save that they might not otherwise have.

The drawbacks for the employee are two-fold. First, if a company is struggling financially, then the employee is at risk of being laid off at the same time when the company's stock price may be hitting new lows. Hence, the employee has the double whammy of a significant drop in income occurring simultaneously with a significant drop in wealth. The other drawback is that if the employee accumulates a substantial amount of company stock through this plan, then he or she ends up with a concentrated holding. Concentrated holdings mean a lack of diversification so that even if the employee is not laid off, a decline in the company's stock price could still mean a substantial decline in the employee's wealth.

PSYCHOLOGICAL ASPECTS OF INVESTING

Investors need to take account of their own psychological tendencies. Otherwise, such factors may unduly influence their decisions. Investors are subject to all of the shortcomings and biases inherent in human judgment. Individuals who evaluate their own biases and tendencies may be better able to control and perhaps offset those that could lead them astray.

Example: A tendency to invest impulsively could cause the investor to trade too frequently. Overly active trading may be profitable to the broker (in commissions) but is usually rather costly for the investor. This tendency might be reduced if the investor could commit a day to thinking over each trade. That approach would allow for a cooling-off period to rethink the decision. Also, there is a tendency to believe that there must be active management of an account or the investor is not doing his or her duty. In truth, no research has ever shown a relationship between the volume of trading activity and account performance.

Paul Slovic and his coworkers at the Oregon Research Institute have studied human judgment biases and their impact on investor decisions. His classic work, "Psychological Study of Human Judgment: Implications for Investment Decision Making," synthesizes the investment implications of a number of psychological studies.[18] For example, Slovic observes that the human mind frequently makes random judgment errors. This trait may be dealt with by programming individual decision processes. The decision maker could use mathematical models of the considerations, weights, and estimates to check the logic of the decision. Random human error can cause the unprogrammed approach to yield different results from the programmed one. The programmed result may or may not be superior to the unprogrammed one, but knowledge of the differences is generally helpful.

Slovic also reports that people usually react to new information by revising their opinions in the correct direction but more conservatively than is warranted by the new information. On the other hand, people tend to extrapolate from a small nonrandom sample and expand what they have extrapolated to an unsupportable generalization. This is known as a "tidal wave of one observation."

Complex decisions may be divided into a series of smaller decisions, combining the judgments on each decision into a solution for the initial major problem. Systematic biases integrated into the smaller decisions, however, may lead to a biased decision on the larger question.

Note that systematic biases are different from random errors. For example, suppose that an investor can interpret new information in an overly optimistic, overly pessimistic, or accurate manner. An investor who makes random errors will be sometimes overly optimistic and sometimes overly pessimistic but on average will interpret new information accurately. An investor with systematic biases, however, will have either an overly optimistic or an overly pessimistic interpretation of events most of the time.

Selective recall is one typical human bias. People remember some events more easily than others. People also tend to see patterns where none exist (that is, charting) and to attribute a result to a particular cause even when there is no basis for causation, much less any real evidence of correlation. The claimed success of many investment chartists may be due to such tendencies. Another common fallacy is to attach undue importance to recent events relative to other events that occurred in the more distant past but are still relevant nonetheless.

Individuals also sometimes respond differently to the same question if it is asked in different ways. For example, an individual might simultaneously predict a 10 percent increase and a $5 price rise on a $40 stock (10 percent of $40 is $4, not $5). Questions, therefore, should be structured to elicit the most accurate approach to answering them. If available data are in percentages, for example, a question asked in terms of percentage may elicit a more reliable response.

The degree of risk aversion apparently is not a universally generalizable characteristic for a single individual. People may be quite risk averse in their investment decisions but much less so in their driving habits, or vice versa. Thus, even if a financial planner has a client who goes to Atlantic City to gamble every weekend, this does not necessarily mean the client wants an aggressive portfolio. Perhaps the client views gambling as entertainment and is willing to pay the price for such entertainment but wants a high degree of certainty with regard to retirement income.

Another factor in decision making is that decisions made by a group tend to be riskier than individual decisions.

Finally, many people tend to overrate the reliability of their own judgment. Others, however, tend to follow the herd and have little confidence in their own judgment.

SELLING A CLIENT ON A PLAN

We discussed earlier the issue whereby a planner may use the concept of dollar cost averaging to move a client into buying a substantial amount of stocks in order to overcome the fear of regret if he or she buys all of the stocks today. This is just one example of the fact that sometimes a financial planner has to create some type of story to give the client the confidence he or she needs to agree to setting up a particular plan. In other words, the financial planner has a good sense of what the client needs to do, but explaining this with facts using such terms as expected return, standard deviation, covariance, correlation, and strategic and tactical asset allocations, may leave a client too confused to act. Hence, sometimes the financial planner needs to give the client a "common sense" way to look at the portfolio and the investment process. In this section, we will consider three stories that a planner can tell a client.

Building a Bond Portfolio

The planner and the client agree to invest $200,000 in Treasury bonds. The client is super conservative and would like to put all of it in short-term bonds. However, the planner appreciates that the yield curve is currently upward sloping and, to meet the client's income needs, the portfolio needs to be at least 50 percent in long-term bonds. The planner could simply explain to the client that 50 percent in long-term bonds is necessary for income purposes, and 50 percent can be put in short-term bonds to reduce the standard deviation of the portfolio's return. A better story might be this: Put 50 percent of the portfolio into 10-year bonds, and 50 percent into one-year bonds. If rates fall, the prices of the 10-year bonds will rise, and the portfolio will have a strong rate of return. If rates rise, the investor can hold on to the long-term bonds and take one-tenth of the short-terms bonds (that is, 5 percent of the total portfolio) and use that to buy more 10-year bonds. If rates rise for each of 10 years, then the 10-year bonds will have matured by then and the client will still have his or her liquidity. Furthermore, the client will never have given up liquidity as he or she will always have a substantial portion of the portfolio in short-term securities.

Portfolio Liquidation: Scenario #1

You are discussing strategic asset allocation with a newly retired client. He has $1,000,000 in assets and wants to generate $50,000 in income per year from the portfolio. As a financial planner you know that what he actually wants is not $50,000 in income but $50,000 in cash. There is a big difference. A plan to generate $50,000 in income would mean a portfolio dominated by long-term, fixed income securities. A plan to generate $50,000 in cash would mean that the money could come from maturing assets or from the sale of securities. You know one of the greatest fears of retired clients is the concept of "liquidating the principal." You also know that, given the strong chance that this client may live for at least another 20 years or so, he must have a significant holding in equities or have substantial exposure to purchasing power risk.

You propose the following plan. Put $250,000 into cash equivalents and $750,000 into equities. If the stock market goes up, sell enough stocks to take out $50,000. For example, if the portfolio goes up 10 percent during the year, then at year end it will be worth $825,000 ($750,000 x (1 + .10)). Sell enough stocks to take out $50,000 in cash and start the next year with an equity portfolio worth $775,000. However, if the market goes down, take the $50,000 out of the cash equivalents. If the market goes up the second year, sell enough stock to take out the $50,000 cash and replenish the cash equivalents holding. If the market goes down the second year in a row, then again take the cash withdrawal from the cash equivalents and plan to replenish this account in the third year. The only way that the entire cash equivalents holdings would be eliminated is if the market went down 5 years in a row, an event that has never occurred in our modern era. This approach allows the planner to adopt a 75 percent stock, 25 percent cash portfolio strategy, which would most likely serve the client better than a portfolio that generates $50,000 in income each year.

It should be noted that the actual application of a strategy as suggested above would also require the financial advisor to incorporate the effect of dividends into the cash that will be produced at the end of the year. For example, if the average dividend yield for the portfolio was one percent, then the portfolio would generate about $7,500 in dividends during the year. Hence, the planner only needs to come up with an additional $42,500 at the end of the year. In addition, there would likely be some tinkering to the portfolio that would be necessary to stay on target with the strategic asset allocation of 75 percent stock and 25 percent cash.

Portfolio Liquidation: Scenario #2

A variation of the above scenario would allow a planner to put the client into a cash, bonds, and stocks portfolio. Let's assume again a $1,000,000 portfolio and a desire to generate an "income" of $50,000 per year. In this case, the planner could invest $50,000 in cash and $50,000 in each of four categories of bonds. The bonds range in annual maturities from 2 years to 5 years. The remaining assets are invested in stocks. The strategy for the generation of cash is then much the same as before. If the market goes up the first year, the investor can take the cash from the stock market gains. In addition, he or she would take the cash equivalents and buy a new set of 5-year bonds since each set of bonds would move up in maturity one year. If the market goes down, the investor can take the cash from the cash equivalents (less whatever dividends and interest income have been generated). Each set of bonds will have moved up in maturity by one year. At such time as the market goes up again, the bond holdings can be replenished.

SUMMARY AND CONCLUSIONS

There is a seven-step model for advising clients about portfolios. These seven steps are to set investment goals, gather and analyze client data, develop an investment policy, determine asset allocation, specify industry weightings, select companies, and monitor the portfolio.

There are two types of asset allocation: strategic and tactical. Strategic asset allocations should be set at the highest possible level in an organization, and for the individual client it is the most critical set of numbers. The purpose of strategic allocations is to set the overall risk exposure of the portfolio. These allocations would be changed only occasionally. Tactical asset allocations are made to try to outperform the market. They can be changed on a regular basis as long as they conform to the strategic weights. A financial planner needs to be keenly aware that as a client ages, his or her financial needs and risk tolerance change as well; that is, the need for income and conservatism increases.

The size of the portfolio as measured by the number of securities in the portfolio is a critical factor in establishing the total risk of a portfolio. The addition of a security on average reduces the total risk of the portfolio, but at a decreasing rate with the addition of each security. On average, the portfolio's total risk declines to equal the risk of the market portfolio. The determination of the optimal portfolio size involves a trade-off between the direct (commissions) and indirect (monitoring effort) costs of the added security and the amount of reduction in total risk. If direct costs are low and one follows a buy-and-hold strategy, then the optimal portfolio size may be almost unlimited.

Other aspects of investment selection a financial advisor should consider include the effort required to maintain an asset, minimum required purchase amounts, the ethical and moral appeal of various investments, reconciliation of the strategic asset allocation with the allocation of monies among various accounts with different tax treatments, and problems of a concentrated portfolio.

Dollar cost averaging is the process whereby a fixed dollar amount of purchases are made at preset intervals, usually monthly. Some investors engage in different types of dollar cost averaging because it is the only way they can accumulate the money to build a portfolio. Other investors engage in dollar cost averaging because it provides a way to overcome the fear of regret if the investor makes a huge purchase all at once. Investors may dollar cost average on their own, through a direct purchase program with a company, through an automatic debit program with a mutual fund, or through employee stock purchase plans.

An ongoing problem of investing is the issue of the psychology of investing. The psychology of investing means that financial planners often need to consider selling the client on a particular strategy that would give the appearance of greater safety of income than is actually the case.

Finally, a good financial planner will note that often it is important to have a "story" to tell a client about how the portfolio will work. Technical presentations involving such terms as expected returns, standard deviations, covariances, and efficient frontiers will often overwhelm a client. A story about how money will move into and out of a portfolio may be something that is much easier for a client to grasp and think about.

CHAPTER REVIEW

Answers to the review questions and the self-test questions start on page 733.

Key Term

pure market timer

Review Questions

14-1. Describe the seven-step model for advising clients about portfolios.

14-2. Describe the differences between strategic and tactical asset allocation.

14-3. a. What is meant by life-cycle investing?
        b. What are the normal characteristics of life-cycle investing?

14-4. Why is it difficult to specify the optimal number of securities in a portfolio?

14-5. Why would having multiple accounts with different tax treatments create a potential problem in matching an asset allocation scheme?

14-6. Explore the effect of dollar cost averaging by performing the following calculations.
        a. You purchase $100 worth of a $10 stock (ignore commissions). The stock's price declines to $5, whereupon you purchase another $100 worth. If the stock's price recovers to $10, what is the value of your portfolio?
        b. As before, begin with a $100 purchase of a $10 stock. When the stock price increases to $15, you purchase another $100 worth. If the stock price subsequently declines to $10, what is the value of your portfolio?
        c. List some examples of dollar cost averaging plans.

14-7. Why is the expected return on socially responsible portfolios not expected to differ from the expected return on other portfolios of equal riskiness?

14-8. Give an example of how a plan could be pitched to the client without using the terms asset allocation, expected return, and standard deviation of return.

Self-Test Questions

T   F   14-1. The first step of the seven-step model for advising on portfolios is to set investment goals.

T   F   14-2. Goals can be as general as wanting to leave children a decent inheritance.

T   F   14-3. The client's risk tolerance is always a critical constraint.

T   F   14-4. If the client's degree of risk aversion can be well measured, then it is clear what the asset allocation of the portfolio should be.

T   F   14-5. A written investment policy does not need to be expansive or detailed.

T   F   14-6. Asset allocation is the process of setting the portfolio proportions for the major asset categories.

T   F   14-7. The asset allocation is made independently of the desired rate of return.

T   F   14-8. If the asset allocation does not produce the necessary expected rate of return to achieve the client's goals, it is up to the financial planner to find a better asset allocation scheme.

T   F   14-9. A client should employ the financial planner who promises the highest rate of return.

T   F   14-10. Benchmarking involves creating a synthetic portfolio as a comparison for an actual portfolio.

T   F   14-11. For an endowment fund, the board of trustees should make both strategic and tactical asset allocation decisions.

T   F   14-12. Strategic asset allocation decisions always specify exact weights for each category, such as 60, 30, 10.

T   F   14-13. Portfolio rebalancing to return the desired asset allocation to its desired weights usually means selling what has done well and buying what has done poorly.

T   F   14-14. Strategic asset allocations are normally made to beat the market.

T   F   14-15. Tactical asset allocations are made more frequently than strategic ones.

T   F   14-16. A client's degree of risk aversion never changes.

T   F   14-17. Randomly adding securities to a portfolio will normally be expected to reduce its risk.

T   F   14-18. A truly diversified portfolio will have about the same amount of total risk as the market portfolio.

T F 14-19. There is a greater reduction in total risk when an 11th security is added to a portfolio of 10 securities than when a third stock is added to a portfolio of two securities.

T F 14-20. The major benefit of international diversification is that it usually allows one to create a portfolio with less total risk using fewer securities.

T F 14-21. The number of securities in a portfolio is always a good surrogate measure for the extent of diversification in the portfolio.

T F 14-22. Almost all socially responsible investors agree as to which stocks should not be held.

T F 14-23. Concentrated portfolios are more easily dealt with when they occur within tax-qualified accounts.

T F 14-24. Dollar cost averaging refers to any process whereby a one-time investment decision is made that commits the investor to a series of future purchases.

T F 14-25. From an investor's perspective, there are no drawbacks to a dividend reinvestment plan.

T F 14-26. In an employee stock purchase plan, the employee can only buy the stock at its current market value.

T F 14-27. The best way to eliminate impulse trading is to follow a self-imposed rule to wait one day on all trades.

T F 14-28. There is a natural human tendency to see patterns where none exist.

T F 14-29. One way for a financial planner to gauge a client's tolerance for risk is to look at such things as whether the client gambles or drives recklessly.

T F 14-30. A financial planner will sometimes sell the client an investment scheme rather than the technical details of strategic asset allocation, expected return, and standard deviation of return.

NOTES

1. Material in this section is based on the article "Investment Advising in Good Times and Bad" by David M. Cordell, *Journal of Financial Service Professionals*, Vol. 55, Iss. 4; July 2001, pp. 74–85.
2. See *Introducing Personal Finance* by Walt Woerheide, John Wiley & Sons, 2002, p. 3.
3. See, for example, "The Impact of the Pension Fund on the Decision to Work One More Year" by Walt Woerheide, *Financial Services Review*, vol. 9, no. 1 (1999), pp. 17–31.
4. This example is based on a true story told to one of the authors by someone who called The American College seeking advice about which planner to use.
5. Several of the ideas in this section are from "Strategic versus Tactical Asset Allocation: Beta versus Alpha Drivers" by Mark Anson, *The Journal of Portfolio Management*, Winter 2004, pp. 8–22.

6. Because the beta for the market portfolio is one, it is difficult to have large portfolios with betas significantly different from one. If the portfolio in this example was large, a beta value of 1.2 would be quite aggressive.

7. In the discussion of beta in chapter 4, all of the examples involved stocks. Nonetheless, one can compute a beta for any asset. Naturally, when betas are computed for any asset other than stocks, the values tend to be low and sometimes not significantly different than zero. Thus, a beta of .5 for bonds would be relatively high for that asset category.

8. Because of the short-term maturity and high degree of safety on cash equivalents, they function much the same as the risk-free asset. Hence, their beta would be zero because a security or portfolio with a beta of zero would be expected to have the same rate of return as the risk-free asset.

9. Evans, John, and Stephen Archer. "Diversification and the Reduction of Dispersion: An Empirical Analysis," *Journal of Finance*, 1968, XXIV: 761–769.

10. Wagner, W.H., and S.C. Lau. "The Effect of Diversification on Risk," *Financial Analysts Journal*, 1971, 27: 48–53.

11. Klemkosky, Robert C., and John D. Martin. "The Effect of Market Risk on Portfolio Diversification," *Journal of Finance*, 1975, XXX: 147–154.

12. Martin, John D., and Robert C. Klemkosky. "The Effect of Homogeneous Stock Groupings on Portfolio Risk," *Journal of Financial and Quantitative Analysis*, 1976, 12: 181–195.

13. Solnik, Bruno. "Why Not Diversify Internationally Rather Than Domestically?" *Financial Analysts Journal*, 1974, 30: 48–54.

14. Material in this section is based on "An Index of Portfolio Diversification" by Walt Woerheide and Don Persson, *Financial Services Review*, Vol. 2, Issue 2 (1993), pp. 73–85.

15. Material in this section is drawn from ideas expressed in an article that appeared on the Internet on March 15, 2004. Source: online.wsj.com/article/0,,SB107913655760354212,00. html?mod=home_inside_today_us, March 15, 2004

16. On April 1, 2004, Hernando de Soto, the Peruvian economist who has devoted his life to bringing real property rights to the world's poor, became the second winner of the Milton Friedman Prize for Advancing Liberty. Source: http://www.foxnews.com/story/ 0,2933, 117126,00.html, April 15, 2004.

17. Williams, Richard E., and Peter W. Bacon, DBA, CFP®, "Lump Sum Beats Dollar-Cost Averaging," *Journal of Financial Planning*, June 2004, pp. 92–95.

18. P. Slovic, "Psychological Study of Human Judgment: Implications for Investment Decision Making," *Journal of Finance*, September 1972, pp. 779–799.

Glossary

absolute-priority-of-claims principle • the principle in bankruptcy law that each class of liability claims is to be repaid in full before the succeeding category receives even partial payment

account maintenance fee • an annual fee charged by mutual funds, typically assessed to every account held by the investor

accumulation value • an annuity's value before any surrender charges

acid test ratio (quick ratio) • cash and accounts receivable divided by current liabilities; used to measure short-term liquidity

additional commitment risk • the degree to which an investment asset may require the buyer to put additional money into the investment

adjusted gross income (AGI) • the figure derived by subtracting certain adjustments from gross income

ADR • *See* American Depository Receipt.

advance-decline ratio • ratio of advancing stocks to declining stocks; high values are bullish if they persist

agency problem • the conflict of interests and disparity of goals between corporate managers and shareholders

agency security • a debt security issued by federal agencies such as the FNMA, GNMA, or Freddie Mac

AGI • *See* adjusted gross income.

all-or-nothing order • an order that must be executed in its entirety or not at all

alpha • the intercept term in the market model; in the arbitrage pricing model, the return that would be expected when all the independent variables equal their expected values

alternative minimum tax • tax that may be applicable to those with large amounts of otherwise sheltered income (preferences); applies when the tax liability computed by disallowing these preferences exceeds the liability when the tax is computed the normal way

American depository receipt (ADR) • a U.S.-traded security representing stock in a foreign corporation, priced in U.S. dollars

American option • an option that may be closed out or exercised at any time prior to or at its expiration date

American Stock Exchange (AMEX) • an organized stock exchange tending to deal in small- to mid-capitalization stocks; also known as the Curb Exchange

analyst neglect (neglected firm effect) • an alleged anomaly to the efficient market hypothesis that is characterized by the tendency of security analysts to overlook small or obscure firms in their security evaluations

annuity • a series of equal, consecutive, periodic payments. Also, an asset that usually promises to pay a fixed amount periodically for a predetermined period, although some pay a sum for an individual's lifetime.

annuity due • a series of equal, consecutive, periodic payments in which the first payment occurs immediately

anomaly • condition in the security markets that appears to allow for persistent abnormal returns after adjusting for risk

anxious trader effects • short-run price distortions caused by sales or purchases of impatient large traders

arbitrage • simultaneously buying in one market and selling equivalent assets in another for a certain riskless profit

arbitrage pricing model • a model used to explain stock pricing and expected return that introduces more than one factor in place of (or in addition to) the capital asset pricing model's market index

arbitrageur • a trader who attempts to exploit price differentials for equivalent investments or for the same investment in different markets

arithmetic mean return • the average return found by dividing the sum of the separate per-period returns by the number of periods over which they were earned

ask price (ask) • the price at which a dealer or market maker is willing to sell a particular security to an investor

asset allocation • the principal method of portfolio management by financial planners, based on the idea of dividing wealth among different types of assets

asset allocation fund • mutual fund that allows managers considerable flexibility in allocating the portfolio among the three major asset categories (stocks, bonds, and money market instruments) as market conditions change

asset turnover ratio • ratio of net sales to total assets

at-the-money option • an option whose strike price is equal to the current market price

average collection period (ACP) • net accounts receivable divided by daily sales

average tax rate • total amount of income tax paid divided by total income

back-end loads • fees assessed on a mutual fund account at redemption

balance of trade • the difference between a country's expenditures on imports and its proceeds from exports

balance sheet • a financial statement showing a firm's or individual's financial position that lists assets, liabilities, and net worth (equity) as of a particular point in time

banker's acceptance • a money market instrument usually arising from international trade and containing a bank's guarantee or acceptance

bankruptcy • a legal process for dealing formally with a defaulted obligation; may result in a liquidation or reorganization

bar chart • a type of graph that plots the price of the stock over time and typically contains data on the daily high and low prices, and volume

Barron's Confidence Index • a technical indicator based on the ratio of high-grade to average-grade bond yields, where a high value is bullish

basis • cash market price less price of a futures contract

basis point • one-hundredth of one percentage point; primarily used with interest rates

bear • one who expects a declining market

bear market • a declining market

bear raid • an attempt to drive prices down by massive short sales

bearish spread • an options strategy using two puts or two calls when a stock price decline is anticipated

benchmarks • standards of comparison used for portfolio performance goal setting and evaluation

Bermuda options • options that can be exercised on a multiple set of predetermined dates (the last being the expiration date)

best-effort basis • a securities offering in which the underwriter acts as an agent for the issuer and promises to use its best effort to sell the securities

beta • a parameter in the CAPM and APM models that relates stock or portfolio performance to market performance

bid-ask spread • the price difference between the bid price and the ask price for an asset

bid price • the price at which a dealer or market maker is willing to buy a particular security from an investor

Big Board • popular term for the New York Stock Exchange

binomial option-pricing model • a call option-pricing model that is an alternative to the Black-Scholes model

Black-Scholes model • the most commonly used call option-pricing formula

blind pool • a form of investment venture in which the precise purposes of the venture are not revealed to the pool of investors until later

block trade • a trade involving 10,000 shares or more, usually handled by a block trader

block trader • a member of the exchange who specializes in handling large trades in ways designed to minimize potential market disruptions

Blume-adjusted beta • a forecasted beta value that attempts to correct for the tendency for historically estimated betas to drift toward 1.0

bond • a debt obligation (usually long-term) in which the borrower promises to pay a set coupon rate until the issue matures, at which time the principal is repaid

bond equivalent yield • a historic formula used for quoting prices on Treasury bills; BEY = [(10,000 – price)/price] x (365/DTM)

bond fund • mutual fund that owns a portfolio of bonds

bond rating • a rating of a bond's investment quality and default risk, provided by a rating agency such as Standard & Poor's, Moody's, or Fitch

bond swap • a sale of one set of bonds and the purchase of another set to accomplish any one of several objectives

book value per share • the total assets of an enterprise minus its liabilities, minority interests, and preferred stock at par, divided by the number of common shares outstanding

brackets • the income ranges associated with different marginal tax rates

broker • an employee of a financial intermediary who acts as an agent (not a dealer) in buying and selling securities for customers

broker call-loan rate • the interest rate charged by banks to brokerage firms for loans that these firms use to support their margin loans to customers

brokerage firm • a firm that offers various financial services such as access to the securities markets, account management, margin loans, investment advice, and underwriting

bull • one who expects a rising market

bull market • a rising market

bullish call spread • an options strategy using two puts or two calls when a stock price increase is anticipated

business risk • the degree to which an enterprise's performance is subject to potential risk factors such as a change in consumer preference away from a particular good or service, ineffective management, law change, or foreign competition

buying on margin • the purchase of securities with borrowed monies

buying power • the dollar value of additional securities that can be purchased on margin with the current equity in a margin account

call feature • the provision that a bond is callable by the issuer. The call feature includes the call premium, the call price, and any timing constaints.

call-loan rate • *See* broker call-loan rate.

call option (call) • an option to buy stock or some other asset at a prespecified price over a prespecified time period

call premium • the additional amount above the face value that the issuer must pay to redeem a bond prior to its maturity date

call price • the price at which a bond, preferred stock, warrant, or other security may be redeemed prior to maturity. The call price is equal to the face value plus the call premium.

call provision • a provision in a bond indenture that gives the issuer the option of redeeming the bond prior to maturity

call risk • risk that a bond issuer may force redemption of its bonds prior to maturity

capital appreciation share • one of the two classes of shares in a dual purpose investment company. It promises no dividends during the life of the income shares.

capital asset pricing model (CAPM) • the theoretical model that seeks to explain returns as a function of the relationship between the risk-free rate, market risk premium, and beta

capital distribution • a dividend paid out of capital rather than from earnings. Such distributions are not taxed when received but do reduce the investment's cost basis.

capital gain (loss) • the difference between the market value of a holding and its cost basis, when the market value exceeds (is less than) the cost basis

capital market line • the line formed by combinations of the risk-free asset and the market portfolio

CAPM • *See* capital asset pricing model.

cash account • the most basic account for an investor, it is sometimes referred to as a Type 1 account. An investor must have sufficient cash already in the account to complete any purchases.

cash flow • sum of earnings plus depreciation

cash flow per share • the sum of after-tax profits and depreciation and other noncash expense divided by the number of shares of common stock outstanding

CD-type annuities • annuities that provide guaranteed rates over selected periods of time and a predetermined number of payments

Chapter VII • the chapter in the bankruptcy code that is used for the liquidation of businesses

Chapter XI • the chapter in the bankruptcy code that is used to allow firms the opportunity to reorganize under the protection of the bankruptcy court

characteristic line • the line defined by regressing the returns of a particular security against the return on a market index

charting • a graphical representation of stock price changes

chartist • technical analyst who uses price and volume charts to forecast prices

churning • trades that are made for the primary purpose of generating commission income for the broker

circuit breaker • a rule specifying conditions under which trading will be suspended

clearing firm • the firm that holds the customer's cash and securities and sends out statements describing the assets it holds as "on deposit" for the customer

closed-end investment company • a type of investment company whose shares are traded in the same markets as other stocks (the price varies from the fund's net asset value)

closing out a position • in options or futures trading, using an offsetting transaction to remove the investor from further exposure to the investment

CMO (collateralized mortgage obligation) • multiclass mortgage pass-through security that reduces uncertainty about prepayments by specifying time of repayment

coefficient of determination (R²) • a parameter that measures how much of the variance of a particular time series or sample of a dependent variable is accounted for (explained by) the movement of the independent variable(s) in a regression analysis. With respect to portfolios, it is a measure of diversification.

coefficient of variation • the standard deviation of return divided by the mean return

coincident indicators • an economic series published by the National Bureau of Economic Research that is believed to track concurrently with the status of the economy in the normal business cycle

collectibles • assets accumulated by collectors, includes such items as coins, stamps, art, and antiques

combination position • any position in which more than a single put, single call, or single position in the underlying stock is held

commercial paper • short-term, nearly riskless debt instrument issued by large corporations with strong credit ratings

commodity-backed bond • debt security whose potential redemption value is related to the market price of some physical commodity

common stock fund • mutual fund that holds a portfolio consisting primarily of common stocks

company analysis • an examination of a firm's relative strengths and weaknesses

compound interest • interest earned on interest as a result of reinvesting one period's income to earn additional income the following period

compounding • the accrual of interest on interest

concentrated portfolio • a portfolio in which a disproportionately large percentage of the value is in one or a few securities

constant growth model (Gordon growth model) • form of the dividend discount model in which dividends are assumed to grow at a constant rate forever

contingent deferred sales charge • a fee, calculated as a percentage of net asset value, that investors might pay to redeem their shares of a mutual fund depending on how long the shares are held

contrarian rationale • the concept that certain investors are wrong more often than they are right, so one should ascertain what these investors are doing and do the opposite

conversion premium • the difference between the market price and the conversion value of a convertible security

conversion price • the face value of a convertible bond divided by the number of shares into which the bond is convertible

conversion ratio • *See* exchange ratio.

conversion value • the market price of a stock multiplied by the conversion or exchange ratio

convertible bond • a bond that can be converted into a specified number of shares of common stock

convertible preferred stock • a preferred stock that may be exchanged for a specific number of shares of the issuing company's common stock

convex • the curvature of the relationship away from the horizontal axis

corporate bond • debt instrument issued by a corporation; its face value is usually $1,000

correlation coefficient • a measure of the comovement tendency of two variables, such as the returns on two securities

cost approach • a method of evaluating the value of a real estate investment in terms of the replacement costs of the property or the cost of equivalent land and construction

cost basis • the amount paid to purchase an asset

coupon effect • the lower a bond's coupon rate, the greater the percentage change in its price for a given change in interest rates

coupon rate • a bond's annual interest payments divided by its par value

coupon tax effect • before-tax yields-to-maturity on low-coupon, deep-discount issues are usually somewhat below yields on otherwise similar issues trading nearer to par

covariance • the correlation coefficient between two variables multiplied by each variable's standard deviation

covered call • a combination position of long the stock and short a call option

covered writer • an investor who owns the underlying stock at the time he or she writes a call option on that stock

credit balance • a positive cash balance in a brokerage account

cum-rights • the trading of common stock with rights attached

cumulative • a preferred stock for which any dividends in arrears must be paid before common dividends can be resumed

curb exchange • *See* American Stock Exchange (AMEX).

current assets • assets that are expected to be used up soon or quickly converted to cash (includes cash, accounts receivable, and inventory)

current liabilities • debts that will become due and payable in the next year (includes accounts payable, short-term bank loans, the current portion of long-term debt, and taxes payable)

current ratio • the ratio of current assets to current liabilities; a measure of short-term liquidity

current yield • a bond's coupon rate divided by its current market price

daily price limit (interday limit) • the rule established by the futures exchanges for the maximum range of price movement permitted between the closing price of the previous day and the opening price of the next day of trading for any given commodity

day order • an order that is canceled if it is not executed sometime during the day when it was entered

day trader • an investor who typically closes out his or her position daily, speculating on very short-term price movements

dealer • a security trader who acts as a principal rather than as an agent and who is considered a specialist or a market maker, not a broker

debenture • a bond that gives the lender no claim against any specific assets in the case of default

debit balance • a negative cash balance in a margin account—that is, a loan

debt capacity • a firm's ability to borrow money

debt-equity ratio • the ratio of total debt to total equity

debt management policy • the management of the maturity of the government's outstanding debt

debt ratio • total debt divided by total assets

decomposition analysis • the process of looking at combinations of other ratios that produce a particular ratio, such as the Du Pont analysis

deep-discount bond • a bond selling for substantially less than its par (face) value

default • a failure to pay principal and/or interest due on a debt obligation

default risk • the risk that a debt security's contractual interest or principal will not be paid when due

depletion allowance • a 15 percent deduction that may be taken against royalty income from the drilling of oil when computing taxable income

depository institution • an institution, such as a bank, that accepts deposits

derivative security • a security whose value is derived from the value of another security or combination of other securities—for example, options, futures, rights, and warrants

dilution • reduction in value of stock of existing shareholders resulting from issuance of additional shares, exercise of rights or warrants, or conversion of convertible bonds or preferred stock

direct purchase plan • a plan by which a specified amount of money is automatically applied toward the purchase of a company's stock at specified intervals (such as once a month); a form of dollar cost averaging

discount rate (for income stream) • the interest rate applied to an expected income stream to estimate its present value

discount rate (monetary policy) • the interest rate charged by the Federal Reserve System on loans to member banks

discounting • determining the present value of expected future cash flows based on the discount rate and the time until the cash flows are expected to be received

discretionary account • account over which a broker is authorized to exercise discretion with regard to purchases and sales

disinflation • a slowing of the inflation rate

dividend capture • a strategy in which an investor purchases securities in order to own them on the day of record and then quickly sells them to capture the dividend but avoid the risk of a lengthy hold

dividend discount model • a model to evaluate stocks on the basis of the present value of their expected stream of dividends

dividend payout ratio • the percentage of net income (after preferred dividends) paid out as dividends on common stock

dividend reinvestment plan (DRIP) • a company program that allows dividends to be reinvested in additional shares

dividend valuation model • *See* dividend discount model.

dividend yield • a stock's annual dividend divided by the stock price

dividends • payments derived from profits that companies make to their stockholders

dogs of the Dow • a strategy for beating the DJIA, based on the concept of selecting the 10 stocks in the index with the highest dividend yields at the start of each year and then recasting the portfolio each year

dollar cost averaging • an investment approach requiring periodic (such as monthly) fixed-dollar-amount investments

dollar-weighted rate of return • a portfolio's annual rate of returns based on its internal rate of return

DOT (designated order turnaround) • a system on the New York Stock Exchange in which orders are routed electronically to the trading posts where the securities are traded (often used by program traders)

downtick • a trade at a price lower than the price of the immediately preceding trade

Dow theory • a charting theory based on identifying major trends that was originated by Charles Dow

dual listing • a security listed for trading on more than one exchange

Du Pont formula • a formula that breaks return on equity into its component parts

duration • a statistic that serves as an index for bond price volatility, and is the basis for an immunization strategy

earnest money • the margin deposit that serves as a security to guarantee that the buyer and the seller of a contract honor the terms of that contract

earnings before interest and taxes (EBIT) • earnings computed as gross profit less cash and noncash operating expenses

earnings per share (EPS) • the net income of a company, minus any preferred dividend requirements, divided by the number of common shares outstanding

effective annual interest rate • the annual interest rate calculated when the frequency of compounding is considered

efficient frontier • a set of portfolios, each of which offers the highest expected return for a given risk and the smallest risk for a given expected return

efficient market hypothesis (EMH) • the theory that the market correctly prices securities in light of the known relevant information. It is comprised of the weak form, semistrong form, and strong form.

electronic communications network (ECN) • organizations that provide networks in which customers trade securities directly with each other. ECNs make up the fourth market.

equity • ownership interest in a firm; sometimes used interchangeably with common stock or net worth

equity multiplier • ratio of a firm's total assets to equity; a measure of financial leverage

equity note (mandatory convertible note) • debt security that is automatically converted into stock on a prespecified date at a specific price or one based on a formula that is prespecified

equity REIT • a real estate investment trust that invests in office buildings, apartments, hotels, shopping malls, and other real estate ventures

equity value • the market value of all the securities in an account less the loan balance

Eurobonds • bonds that may be denominated in dollars or some other currency and are traded internationally. They are denominated in a currency other than that of the country in which they are issued.

Eurodollar deposits • dollar-denominated deposits held in banks based outside the United States. Most are located in Europe, but some are in Asia and other areas.

European option • an option that may be exercised only on its expiration date

ex ante • before the fact. Ex ante data refers to possible future values.

ex-dividend date • the first day of trading on which buyers of stock will not receive a declared dividend

ex-post • after the fact. Ex post data is historical data.

ex-rights • without rights attached. Stock trades ex-rights after the date of record for a rights distribution.

excess reserves • actual reserves less required reserves

exchange fees • a fee charged by many no-load fund families whenever the investor moves money from one fund to another within the family

exchange rate risk • the risk of loss in value associated with movements in currency exchange rates

exchange ratio • the number of shares of stock received upon conversion of a convertible bond or stock

exchange-traded fund (ETF) • a closed-end investment company that duplicates the portfolio of a particular stock market index such as the Dow Jones Industrial Average or the Standard and Poor's 500 Index

exercise price • *See* strike price.

expected HPR • the expected return on an investment over the holding period

expiration date • the date on which an option expires; in standard stock option contracts, the Saturday following the third Friday of the stated month

face value • *See* par value.

fallen angel • a name given to poorly rated bonds

family of funds • a group of mutual funds owned and marketed by the same company

Fannie Mae • *See* Federal National Mortgage Association (FNMA).

Fed • short for either Federal Reserve Board or Federal Reserve System

Fed call • a margin call based on the account's violation of the minimum maintenance margin rate as defined by the Federal Reserve Board

Federal Deposit Insurance Corporation (FDIC) • agency that insures deposits at depository institutions up to $100,000 per depositor

federal funds market • the market where banks and other financial institutions borrow and lend money on deposit at a federal reserve bank

Federal Home Loan Mortgage Corporation (Freddie Mac) • a government agency that assembles pools of conventional mortgages and sells participations in a secondary market

Federal Housing Administration (FHA) • a federal government agency that insures home mortgages

Federal National Mortgage Association (FNMA) • a corporation, now privately owned, that operates a secondary market in mortgages and issues its own debt securities to finance its mortgage portfolio; also called Fannie Mae

Federal Open Market Committee (FOMC) • the Federal Reserve Board committee that decides on open market policy

Federal Reserve Board (Fed) • the governing body of the Federal Reserve System

Federal Reserve System (Fed) • the federal government agency that exercises monetary policy through its control over banking system reserves

fill-or-kill order • a type of security market order that must be canceled unless it can be filled immediately

filter rule • form of technical analysis that advocates buying stock when the price rises by a given percent or selling when the price falls by that same percentage

firm-commitment basis • a public offering in which the underwriter purchases the securities from the issuer and then sells them to the public

fiscal policy • government use of taxing and spending to stimulate or restrain the economy

fixed asset turnover ratio • net sales divided by net fixed assets

fixed-income security • any security that promises to pay a periodic nonvariable sum, such as a bond paying a fixed coupon amount per period

flat • the trading of bonds without compensation for accrued interest

flexible-premium deferred annuity (FPDA) • an annuity contract in which the payout period is deferred and the premium is flexible during the accumulation period

flight-to-quality • the tendency of investors to sell risky investments and buy less risky investments when disturbing news is disseminated

floating rate note • a type of debt security whose coupon rate varies with market interest rates

floor trader • one holding a seat on an exchange who trades for his or her own account. Also known as a registered competitive market maker (RCMM).

forced conversion • the calling of a convertible security to effectively force the holder to exercise the conversion option

foreign exchange risk • the degree to which an investment is affected by movements in currency exchange rates in the country where the investment is located

forward contract • a customized, nonstandard contractual agreement to accept delivery (buy) and to deliver (sell) a specified commodity or financial instrument at an agreed-upon price, settlement date, quantity, and location

fourth market • direct trading of listed securities between institutions without using a broker

Freddie Mac • *See* Federal Home Loan Mortgage Corporation.

front-end load • a load (commission) on a mutual fund assessed at the time of purchase

full employment • the employment rate that is thought to be the maximum level before inflationary pressures accelerate

fundamental analysis • the evaluation of firms and their investment attractiveness based on the firms' financial strength, competitiveness, earnings outlook, managerial strength, and sensitivity to the macroeconomy and to specific industry effects

future value • the value that a certain amount of money today is expected to have at a specified time in the future

futures contract • a standardized commodities or securities contract to deliver a certain quantity of a commodity or security at a specified price at a specified future date

futures market • any regulated exchange in which standardized futures contracts are bought and sold—for example, the Chicago Board of Trade, Chicago Mercantile Exchange, and Commodity Futures Exchange

futures option • a call or put option on a futures contract

general obligation bond • a municipal bond secured by the issuer's full faith and credit and taxing power

geometric mean return • the effective annual rate of return over multiple time periods, computed as $GMR = [(1 + PPR_1)(1 + PPR_2) \ldots (1 + PPR_n)]^{1/n} - 1$

Glass-Steagall Act • a 1933 federal act that required the separation of commercial and investment banking; prevented competition between financial institutions in the banking, insurance, and securities industries

global fund • mutual fund that invests in the United States and in foreign markets

going long • buying an asset

go public • the process in which a start-up or heretofore private firm sells its shares in a public offering

good-'til-canceled (GTC) order • type of order that remains in effect until executed or canceled

Gordon growth model • *See* constant growth model.

Government National Mortgage Association (GNMA) • a government agency that provides special assistance on selected types of home mortgages

governments • U.S. government bonds issued by the Treasury Department and backed by the full faith and credit of the federal government

Gramm-Leach-Bliley Act • passed in 1999, this act repealed the Glass-Steagall Act (the Bank Act of 1933)

greenmail • the practice of acquiring a large percentage of a firm's stock and attempting to be bought out at a premium by threatening to take over the firm

gross domestic product (GDP) • the sum of market values of all final goods and services produced annually in the economy of a country

gross income • the taxpayer's total income as determined in the first section of Form 1040

growth fund • a common stock mutual fund that seeks price appreciation by concentrating on growth stocks

growth investing • investing in stocks that have above-average P/E ratios and whose earnings are expected to grow rapidly

growth stock • the shares of a company that is expected to achieve rapid growth in earnings

head-and-shoulders formation • a pattern of stock price trends that looks like a head and shoulders and is believed by some technical analysts to forecast a price decline

hedge fund • a type of pooled portfolio instrument organized for maximum investment flexibility. Hedge funds typically invest in derivatives, sell short, use leverage, and invest internationally.

hedge ratio • in the Black-Scholes model, that ratio of the number of calls written that would exactly offset the stock price movement of a number of shares of the underlying stock held

hedging • taking opposite positions in related securities to reduce or eliminate an existing risk—for example, purchasing put options on a stock one owns

histogram • a discrete probability distribution display

Holding Company Depository Receipts (HOLDRs) • analogous to sector funds—that is, they are ETFs that, instead of mimicking an index, hold selected stocks in a particular industry

holding period return (HPR) • the rate of return over some specific time period

holding period return relative (HPRR) • the end-of-period value relative to the beginning-of-period value for a specific holding period; that is, the holding period return plus one (1)

house call • a margin call based on an account's violation of the maintenance margin rate as defined by the brokerage firm holding the account

hybrid convertible (exchangeable debenture) • a bond that is convertible into common stock of a company other than the company that issued the bond

hybrid REIT • a real estate investment trust that holds both equity and mortgage investments

immunization • the process of minimizing the interest rate risk on a bond portfolio by maintaining a portfolio with a duration equal to an investor's planning horizon

imputed interest • for a zero-coupon bond, the amount of interest income assigned to the bondholder each year

income annuity • *See* single-premium immediate annuity.

income approach • approach to valuing real estate as the discounted present value of its expected income stream

income bond • a bond on which interest is paid only if the issuer has sufficient earnings

income fund • a common stock mutual fund that concentrates on stocks that pay high dividends

income in respect of a decedent • if an investor takes a stock distribution from a qualified account and dies before selling the stock, the net unrealized appreciation would be treated as ordinary income on the investor's tax return for the year he or she died

income share • one of the two types of shares issued by a dual purpose investment company. An income share is like a preferred stock with a maturity date.

income statement • a financial statement that reports revenues and expenses over a specified period

indenture • the contract the company makes with its bondholders, including a commitment to pay a stated coupon amount periodically and return the face value (usually $1,000) at maturity

index arbitrage • a trading strategy involving offsetting positions in stock index futures contracts and the underlying cash market securities (stocks making up the index)

index fund • a mutual fund that owns a portfolio of either common stock or bonds that replicates a major market index such as the S&P 500 or the Lehman Brothers Aggregate Bond Index

index model • the model that expresses the return on a security as a function of the return on an index, that is $R_i = \alpha_i + \beta_i R_M + \varepsilon_i$

indifference curve • a locus of portfolios to which an investor is indifferent, on a graph that plots expected return on the vertical axis and risk on the horizontal axis

industry analysis • an assessment of the outlook for a particular industry

inflation • the rate of increase in the overall level of prices

inflation risk • the degree to which the purchasing power of an investment asset's future cash flows is affected by changes in the general level of prices in the economy

initial margin rate • the amount of equity that an investor must provide to purchase securities. If the initial margin rate is x, then the maximum amount that can be borrowed is 1 − x.

initial public offering (IPO) • the offering to the public of securities in a firm that previously was privately held. *See* go public.

insider trading • buying or selling by investors with access to material nonpublic information relating to the company being traded

interest rate futures • a futures contract calling for delivery of a debt security such as a Treasury bill or long-term government bond. Because the value of debt securities varies inversely with market interest rates, people can speculate on interest rate changes by trading futures contracts on debt securities.

interest rate option • an option to buy or sell debt securities

interest rate risk • for debt securities, the risk associated with changes in the interest rates; consists of price risk and reinvestment rate risk

interim cash flow • cash added to or removed from a portfolio during a specified holding period

internal rate of return (IRR) • the discount rate that causes the NPV of an investment to equal zero

international fund • mutual fund that specializes in investments outside of the United States and helps the investor to further diversify his or her portfolio

in the money • for calls, when the current stock price is higher than the strike price; for puts, when the current stock price is lower than the strike price

intraday dependencies • nonrandom price movements of transactions taking place over the course of a single day

intrinsic value (call, right, warrant) • the price of the associated stock less the strike price of the option, or zero if the difference is negative

intrinsic value (put) • the strike price of a put less the price of the associated stock, or zero if the difference is negative

intrinsic value (stock) • the value that a careful evaluation would produce; generally takes into account both the going-concern value and the liquidation or breakup value of the company

introducing firm • the firm that employs the individual broker who takes the customer's order and sees that the order gets executed

inventory turnover ratio • the ratio of the cost of goods sold to average yearly inventory

inverted yield curve • a yield curve showing short-term interest rates higher than long-term interest rates

investment advisory fee • a fee paid to the mutual fund's management for portfolio supervision and other managerial activities

investment banker • a firm that advises on new security offerings and/or underwrites the offering on either a firm commitment or best efforts basis. For larger offerings, the investment banker may form a syndicate.

investment company • a company that only invests in other companies. The company may be either a closed-end company or an open-end company.

investment-grade • relatively high-quality corporate bonds

investment style • a description of a mutual fund's characteristics that typically considers company size and price-earnings ratio for stocks and time to maturity and quality rating for bonds

January indicator (January effect) • an anomaly detected in past studies of stock market performance that indicates that buying in the small-cap stock market in January tends to produce above-normal returns

Jensen's alpha • a risk-adjusted measure of stock or portfolio performance; the difference between the actual return to a stock or portfolio and the return that would have been expected, based on the capital asset pricing model

junk bonds • bonds rated lower than BBB or Baa that have significant default risk

Keynesian • one who believes in the efficacy of fiscal policy (government spending and taxing) for correcting problems of unemployment and inflation

lagging indicators • an economic series published by the National Bureau of Economic Research that is believed to trail the economy in the normal business cycle

leading indicators • an economic series published by the National Bureau of Economic Research that is believed to precede turns in the overall economy

lettered stock • newly issued stock sold at a discount to large investors in a private placement prior to a public offering of the same issue

Level 3, 2, or 1 • different levels of subscriptions to NASDAQ quotations

leverage • using borrowed funds to increase the return on equity

leveraged buyout (LBO) • the process whereby a firm is bought, new debt is issued by the acquired firm, and the proceeds of the debt offering are used to reimburse the acquiring firm for part of the cost of the acquisition

LIBOR • the London Interbank Offered Rate, which is the rate at which London banks are willing to lend money to each other

lifeboat provisions • provisions offered by some closed-end funds specifying that the funds take some action to bolster their shares if they sell at a discount exceeding 10 percent for a specified period

life-cycle fund • a mutual fund designed to appeal to investors in specific phases of the life cycle by providing appropriate asset allocations

limit order • an order to buy or sell at a prespecified price

limited discretionary account • an account in which the investor gives the broker the authority to make only certain types of trades without the investor's prior consent

limited partnership • a form of business organization that has the advantage of being taxed as a partnership, rather than as a corporation; however, like a corporation, the liability of limited partners generally consists only of their initial investment

liquid assets • assets that can quickly be converted into cash such as marketable securities or receivables

liquidating dividend • *See* capital distribution.

liquidity • the ease with which an investment can be converted to cash with little or no change from the previous trade

liquidity preference hypothesis • the term structure hypothesis that asserts that most borrowers prefer to borrow long-term and most lenders prefer to lend short-term

liquidity premium • the premium demanded by bond investors for holding bonds with longer terms to maturity

liquidity ratio • a financial ratio (for example, current ratio or quick ratio) that is a measure of the firm's ability to meet short-term obligations

liquidity risk • the risk of an inability to convert an asset to cash quickly at any time and without any loss of principal

liquidity yield option note (LYON) • a zero coupon convertible debt security that is both callable and redeemable at prices that escalate through time

load • a commission applied to mutual fund trades

load fund • any mutual fund that charges a load

long hedge • a hedging position in which the investor is long the futures contract and short the physical commodity

long-term capital transactions • any trade in which the purchase and sale are more than one year apart

Long-term Equity Anticipation Securities (LEAPS®) • options with expiration dates of up to 3 years, as opposed to maximum expiration dates of 9 months or regulator options

low-price effect • an alleged anomaly to the efficient market hypothesis that is characterized by the tendency for low-priced stocks to earn above-normal returns

M1 • the basic money supply that includes checking deposits and cash held by the public

M2 • a broader-based money supply definition than Ml that includes everything in M1 plus most savings and money market deposit accounts

Macaulay's duration • the value of the duration statistic that is computed by (1) multiplying each cash flow by the time period in which it is received, (2) discounting these products to the present using the bond's yield to maturity, and (3) adding up these terms and dividing the total by the price of the bond

macroeconomic analysis • an analysis of the overall economy, often performed prior to evaluating the prospects for individual firms

maintenance margin percentage • the minimum percentage of equity that an ongoing margin account is required to maintain at all times

management expense ratio • a mutual fund's operating expenses divided by its total assets

manufactured (synthetic) call • a call-like position generated by a combination of a put and a long position in the underlying stock; position with a profit function similar to a call

manufactured (synthetic) put • a put-like position generated by a combination of a call and a short position in the underlying stock; position with a profit function similar to a put

margin account • brokerage account partially funded with money borrowed from the brokerage firm; regulated by the Fed

margin call • a request to pay down part of the margin loan by adding cash to the account, selling some securities from the account, or adding marketable securities to the account

margin deposit • earnest money required to enter a futures contract

margin rate • the percentage of a securities purchase that must come from the investor's funds rather than from borrowing

marginal tax rate • the percentage that must be paid in taxes on any incremental income

mark to the market • to recompute the value of the equity position on a daily basis

market approach • approach to real estate valuation that considers the listing and selling prices of comparable properties

market maker • one who creates a market for a security by quoting a bid and ask price

market model • a model that relates a security's return to the return of the market

market order • an order that requires immediate execution to buy or sell at the best price available

market portfolio • a hypothetical portfolio representing each investment asset in proportion to its relative weight in the universe of investment assets

market risk • the degree to which a specific asset's return is affected by political, economic, demographic, or social events and trends; also, the degree to which an asset's return is affected by the investment market as a whole; also called systematic risk

market segmentation hypothesis • the theory that there are separate markets for bonds of different maturities, so the interest rates on bonds of one maturity should not be affected by the interest rates on bonds of another maturity

market timer • an investor who attempts to make a profit by the timing of moves into and out of the market

marketable assets • assets that can be quickly converted to cash without loss of value

married put • a put option held by an investor who also owns the underlying security

master limited partnership (MLP) • a method of organizing a business that combines some of the advantages of a corporation with some of the advantages of a limited partnership. Shares of ownership trade much like corporate stock, but the MLP is taxed like a partnership.

maturity • the length of time until a debt security must be redeemed by its issuer

maturity effect • the fact that the price of a bond is more volatile for a given change in interest rates the longer the term to maturity

May Day • May 1, 1975, the day on which brokerage commission rates were fully deregulated and became established by competition among firms

mean return • the arithmetic average return in a distribution of returns

mixed portfolio fund • a mutual fund that owns a portfolio of bonds, stocks, and other investment instruments

modern portfolio theory (MPT) • *See* portfolio theory.

modified duration • the duration number divided by one plus the yield-to-maturity

momentum • tendency for movement to continue in the same direction, such as a rising trend in stock prices

monetarist • one who emphasizes the significance of monetary (as opposed to fiscal) policy

monetary policy • government policy that utilizes the money supply to affect the economy and that is implemented by the Fed through its control of required reserves

money market • the market for high-quality, short-term securities such as negotiable CDs, commercial paper, bankers' acceptances, and Treasury bills

money market deposit account (MMDA) • a type of bank or thrift institution account that offers unregulated money market rates, requires a minimum deposit, and limits withdrawals

money market mutual fund • a mutual fund that invests in short-term, highly liquid securities

money multiplier • the ratio of the change in the money supply to the purchase or sale of securities by the Federal Reserve Board

money supply • generally defined as the sum of all coin, currency (outside bank holdings), and deposits on which check-like instruments may be written. *See* M1.

Moody's Investors Service • a firm that rates bonds and publishes manuals containing extensive historical data on a large number of publicly traded firms

moral hazard • a situation that provides incentives to take inappropriate action, generally in the nature of unnecessary risks

mortgage • a loan collateralized by real estate

mortgage-backed security • a debt instrument representing a share of ownership in a pool of mortgages or backed by a pool of mortgages

mortgage bond • debt security for which real estate is pledged as collateral

mortgage REIT • a real estate investment trust that consists of a diversified portfolio of construction loans and/or mortgage loans

multi-class funds • mutual funds that have more than one class of shares. Usually the classes are A, B, and C.

multifactor asset pricing model • any asset pricing model with more than one factor or independent variable

municipal bond • a tax-exempt bond issued by a state or local government

municipal bond fund • a mutual fund that primarily holds municipal bonds

mutual fund • an open-end investment company

naked call • a call option written by an investor who does not own the underlying asset

naked writer • an investor who does not own the underlying stock at the time he or she writes a call option

National Association of Securities Dealers Automated Quotations (NASDAQ) • an automated information system that provides brokers and dealers with price quotations on securities that are traded over-the-counter

National Bureau of Economic Research (NBER) • a private nonprofit research foundation that tracks business cycles and sponsors economic research

national market issues (NMI) • selected NASDAQ securities that represent the largest firms listed on the quotation system

neckline • part of a bar chart pattern that resembles a person's head and shoulders

neglected-firm effect • *See* analyst neglect.

negotiable CD • a certificate of deposit that can be sold

net asset value (NAV) • the per-share market value of a mutual fund's portfolio; it equals the total net assets of the fund less any liabilities, divided by number of shares outstanding

net equity • with respect to a margin account, the total value of the account minus the amount of debt outstanding

net income • the number derived by subtracting net interest expense and taxes from earnings before interest and taxes (EBIT)

net investment income • investment income after the deduction of investment expenses

net profit margin (NPM) • net income divided by sales. This financial ratio is a measure of a firm's profitability.

net worth (equity) • the equity value of the balance sheet, computed as assets less liabilities

New York Stock Exchange (NYSE) • the largest organized stock exchange, based in New York City. Stocks listed tend to be large- to mid-capitalization stocks. *See also* Big Board.

no-load fund • a mutual fund for which no commission is required for purchase

nominal (interest) rate • the stated interest rate, not necessarily the effective interest rate

noncollectibles • unique, high price-tag items in which one might invest, including such items as a Broadway show, a movie, a racehorse, or a professional baseball team

nonmarket risk • risk not related to general market movements. This risk is diversifiable.

nonqualified annuity • an annuity that is purchased outside of any tax-sheltering program

normal distribution • a distribution corresponding to the shape of the normal (bell) curve

note • intermediate-term debt security issued with terms-to-maturity of one to 10 years

odd lot • a trade of fewer than 100 shares of stock

odd-lot activity • measure of the amount of odd-lot purchases or sales; said to reflect activity by less sophisticated investors

open-end investment company • a mutual fund; any pooled portfolio of investments that stands ready to redeem or sell its shares at their NAV (or NAV plus load if the fund has a load)

open market operations • Federal Reserve transactions (buying and selling) in the government bond market that are intended to influence the money supply, interest rates, and economic activity

open outcry • organization of futures trading on the futures exchanges in which traders shout their desire to buy or sell a contract, often using hand and finger signals

opportunity cost • implicit cost of an activity or course of conduct, based on forgone opportunities

option • a security giving the holder the choice to either purchase or sell a security at a set price for a specific period

option account • the account in which trades in puts and calls occur

Options Clearing Corporation (OCC) • the clearing house for listed options that facilitates options trading by guaranteeing execution of trades between options brokers and traders

ordinary income • income subject to the statutory marginal tax rates

out-of-the-money • for calls, when the current stock price is lower than the strike price; for puts, when the current stock price is higher than the strike price

over-the-counter (OTC) • the market in unlisted securities and off-board trading in listed securities

Pac Man defense • the process in which a company that is about to be acquired attempts to acquire the acquiring company

participating preferred stock • preferred stock that may pay an extra dividend in years in which the issuing firm pays unusually high dividends on its common stock

par value (bond) • the principal amount to be paid upon maturity of a bond or other debt instrument; sometimes referred to as the bond's face value

par value (preferred stock) • the value on which the security's dividend and liquidation value is based

pass-through • a share of a mortgage pool whose interest and principal payments flow through to the holders

payment date • the date on which dividend checks are mailed to investors

payment for order flow • the practice in which a dealer pays a firm or a particular broker for the number of orders that are sent to him or her

payout ratio • dividends per share as a percentage of earnings per share

P/E ratio • *See* price-earnings (P/E) ratio.

PEG ratio • the price-earnings ratio of a firm divided by the projected growth rate of its earnings

perfect hedge • a hedge in which there is a certainty that the basis will not change or a hedge in which the basis did not change

per-period return (PPR) • the return earned for a particular period (for example, an annual return)

perpetuity • an annuity that continues forever

pink sheets • quotation source for most publicly traded OTC issues

point-and-figure chart • a technical chart that has no time dimension. An x is used to designate an upward price movement of a certain magnitude, while an o denotes a comparable downward move.

political risk • the risk of losses on assets or investments located in foreign countries, where the losses are a result of such events as trade disputes, wars, political unrest, tariffs, corruption, or expropriation

portfolio insurance • a service in which the "insurer" endeavors to place a floor on the value of the "insured" portfolio. If the portfolio value falls to a prespecified level, the insurer neutralizes it against a further fall by purchasing an appropriate number of index puts or selling an appropriate number of index options.

portfolio theory • the combination of the capital asset pricing model (CAPM), efficient market hypothesis (EMH), and related theoretical models of security market pricing and performance

portfolio turnover ratio • the lesser of annual purchases or annual sales (excluding securities with less than one-year maturities) divided by the average monthly net assets

portfolio variance • a statistic that measures portfolio risk by quantifying the dispersion from the portfolio's average (mean) value

position trader • a commodity trader who takes and holds futures positions for several days or more

preferred habitat hypothesis • one of four hypotheses for explaining the term structure of interest rates, it is based on the idea of a tendency for borrowers and lenders to gravitate toward their preferred maturities

preferred stock • shares whose indicated dividends and liquidation values must be paid before common shareholders receive any dividends or liquidation payments

premium (option) • the market price of an option

premium over conversion value • the amount by which a convertible bond's price exceeds its conversion value

premium over straight-debt value • the amount by which a convertible bond's price exceeds its value as a nonconvertible debt security

present value • the value of an expected future sum or sums discounted by the appropriate interest rate or discount rate

price-book value ratio • the price of the stock divided by the book value per share

price-earnings (P/E) ratio • the share price of a stock divided by its actual or anticipated earnings per share. For trailing earnings, the P/E ratio is the stock price relative to the most recent 12-month earnings per share; for ex ante earnings, it is the stock price relative to the next 12-month expected earnings.

price risk • the risk of a bond's price changing in response to a change in interest rates

price stability • the absence of or low level of inflation or deflation. While the prices of specific goods would still fluctuate in response to market forces (supply and demand changes), the overall level of prices would be stable.

price-weighted index • an approach to calculating an investment index in which the relative effect of a security on the index is a function of the price of that security; larger prices have a larger effect

primary market • the market for the sale of new securities

prime rate • at one time, it was known as the borrowing rate that banks advertise as available to their least risky borrowers. Today, it is the rate banks use for pricing their loans.

principal • *See* par value.

private placement • a direct sale of securities to a small number of large buyers without the registration requirements of a public offering

probability distribution • a distribution of possible outcomes along with their associated probabilities

profitability ratio • a ratio, such as return on equity, that reflects the firm's profitability

program trading • a type of mechanical trading in large blocks by institutional investors that usually involves both stock and index futures contracts as in, for example, index arbitrage or portfolio insurance

promised yield • *See* yield-to-maturity.

prospectus • a document that all companies offering new securities for public sale must file with the SEC. It spells out in detail the financial position of the offering company, what the new funds will be used for, the qualifications of the corporate officers, risk factors, nature of competition, and any other material information.

proxy • a temporary transfer of one's right to vote

prudent investor • one who used the principles of modern portfolio theory to manage portfolios. A prudent investor focuses on the performance of the entire portfolio rather than the performance of individual securities.

prudent man rule • the selection of each security according to conservative investment standards. Thus a prudent man oversees each security separately rather than the entire portfolio.

purchasing power risk • the degree to which the purchasing power of an investment asset's future cash flows is affected by changes in the general level of prices

pure market timer • an investor who is in the market when it is expected to rise and out of the market when it is expected to fall

pure risk • risk that involves only the chance of loss or no loss

put-call parity • a theoretical relationship between the value of a put and a call on the same underlying security with the same strike price and expiration date

put option (put) • an option to sell a specified number of shares of stock at a specified price prior to a specified expiration date

qualified annuity • an annuity that is purchased through a tax-sheltered program

quick ratio • *See* acid test ratio.

R^2 • *See* coefficient of determination.

random walk • the random motion of stock prices that are as likely to move in one direction as another regardless of past price behavior

rating (bond) • a quality or risk evaluation assigned by a rating agency such as Standard & Poor's or Moody's

ratio analysis • balance sheet and income statement analysis that utilizes ratios of financial aggregates to assess a company's financial position, usually by looking for trends in financial ratios, by comparing a company's financial ratios with the industry average, or both

real estate investment trust (REIT) • closed-end investment company that buys and/or manages rental properties and/or real estate mortgages and pays out more than 95 percent of its income as dividends

real return • a return on an investment adjusted for changes in the price level. This amount equals the increase in purchasing power resulting from saving or investing money.

record date • the shareholder registration date that determines the recipients of that period's dividends

red herring • a copy of the registration statement that is filed with the SEC for a security offering. The front page of this statement contains a paragraph in red ink indicating that the company is not attempting to sell its shares before the SEC approves the registration.

regional exchange • any U.S. stock exchange other than NYSE or AMEX

registered competitive market maker (RCMM) • *See* floor trader.

registered representative • an employee of a registered brokerage firm who is qualified to serve as an account executive for the firm's customers. *See* broker.

registration statement • a statement that must be filed with the SEC before a security is offered for sale and that must contain all materially relevant information relating to the offering

regular annuity • a fixed number of equal, consecutive payments, with the first payment at the end of the first period

regular dividend • the distribution of dividend and/or interest income that a mutual fund has accrued

reinvestment load • a fee charged by some mutual funds for reinvestment of dividends

reinvestment rate risk • the risk associated with reinvesting coupon payments at unknown future interest rates

REIT • *See* real estate investment trust.

relative strength line • a line that plots the ratio of the stock's price to that of the S&P 500 Index or to some other appropriate average or index

RELP (real estate limited partnership) • a type of investment organized as a limited partnership that invests directly in real estate properties

replacement cost approach • *See* cost approach.

repurchase agreement (repo) • a type of investment in which a security is sold with a prearranged purchase price and the date is designed to produce a particular yield—in fact, an indirect form of borrowing

required rate of return • the rate of return on an investment required by investors to justify the degree of risk incurred; the risk-free rate plus the risk premium

reserve requirement • the percentage of reserves the Fed requires each bank to have on deposit for each increment of demand or time deposits

resistance level • a price or price range at which additional sellers enter the market, and thus would create the appearance of a barrier to additional price increases

return on assets (ROA) • net income after taxes divided by total assets

return on equity (ROE) • net income after taxes and preferred dividends divided by net worth

revenue bond • a municipal bond that is backed only by the revenues of the project that it finances

revenue sharing • the process whereby mutual funds pay brokers for promoting their funds' shares to investors

reward to variability ratio (RVAR) • *See* Sharpe ratio.

reward to volatility ratio (RVOL) • *See* Treynor ratio.

riding the yield curve • a bond portfolio management strategy that takes advantage of an upward-sloping yield curve by purchasing intermediate-term bonds and then selling them as they approach maturity

rights • securities allowing shareholders to acquire new stock at a prespecified price within a prespecified period, generally issued in proportion to the number of shares currently held and exercisable at a price that is usually below the current market price

rights offering • an offering of rights by a firm wishing to raise additional equity capital while avoiding dilution of existing shareholders' relative ownership

risk • the dispersion of possible returns from the expected return

risk-adjusted return • the return from an asset adjusted for the risk associated with the asset

risk averse • the degree of preference for less risky investments, even if they have somewhat lower expected returns

risk-free rate • the yield on a riskless investment, such as a Treasury bill

risk premium • the expected return in excess of the risk-free rate that is compensation for the investment's risk

round lot • the basic unit in which securities are traded, usually consisting of 100 shares

round-trip fee • the total commission costs of executing a transaction in the futures market paid at the time of the contract's formation

Rule 144 • an SEC rule restricting the resale of lettered stock

Rule 415 • an SEC rule allowing shelf registration of a security that may then be sold over a 2-year period without separate registrations of each part

run • an uninterrupted series of price increases or decreases

savings bond • a low-denomination Treasury issue designed to appeal to investors with minimal capital

scalpers • people who trade on the floor of the futures exchanges, seeking very quick turns in their holdings

seat • a membership in the New York Stock Exchange

secondary market • the market for already issued securities that takes place on the exchanges or OTC

secondary offering or distribution • a large public securities offering by existing investors made outside the usual exchange or OTC market

sector fund • a mutual fund that specializes in a particular segment of the market—for example, an industry (chemicals)

Securities Act of 1933 • securities law dealing with the issuance of securities and addressing the registration process, disclosure requirements, and related matters

Securities and Exchange Commission (SEC) • the federal agency with direct regulatory authority over the securities industry

Securities Exchange Act of 1934 • securities law dealing with existing securities, addressing the filing of periodic reports, regulating exchanges and brokerage firms, ongoing disclosure requirements, and prohibiting certain unethical practices such as market manipulation and insider trading

Securities Investor Protection Corporation (SIPC) • a federal agency that guarantees the safety of brokerage accounts up to $500,000, no more than $100,000 of which may be in cash

securitization • the process of turning an asset with poor marketability into a security with substantially greater acceptability—for example, a security that looks like a standard bond but is derived from real estate mortgage loans, auto loans, or credit card balances

security market line • the theoretical relationship between a security's market risk and its expected return under the capital asset pricing model. The equation form is as follows: $r_i = r_f + \beta_i (r_M - r_f)$ where r_i is security i's risk-adjusted expected return, r_f is the risk-free return, β_i is the beta measure for security i, and r_M is the return on the market portfolio.

self-regulatory organization • an organization regulated by the SEC under the authority of the Securities Act of 1934. SROs include the NYSE, the AMEX, and NASDAQ.

selling short • the act of borrowing and selling a security that belongs to someone else. The short seller covers by buying back equivalent securities and restoring them to the original owner.

semistrong form EMH • the hypothesis that current market prices fully reflect all publicly available information and react quickly to new information. An implication is that fundamental analysis of publicly available information and data cannot systematically yield superior returns.

semivariance • a measure of dispersion using only returns less than the mean

senior debt • debt that has priority over other (subordinate) debt

separation theorem • the idea that the decision of what portfolio of risky assets to invest in can be separated from the selection of an appropriate risk-return tradeoff. In this scenario, all investors would select the market portfolio.

serial bond • a bond issue in which portions mature at stated intervals rather than all at once

Series 6 • a license that qualifies the broker to sell open-end mutual funds, initial offerings of closed-end investment companies, and such variable products as variable annuities provided the individual also holds the appropriate insurance license

Series 7 • a general securities registered representative license, which qualifies the broker to solicit, purchase, and/or sell all securities products, including corporate securities, municipal securities, options, direct participation programs, investment company products, and variable contracts

Sharpe ratio (reward to variability ratio) • a measure of risk-adjusted performance of an asset, calculated as the ratio of the asset's rate of return minus the risk-free rate divided by the asset's standard deviation

shelf registration • an SEC provision allowing preregistration of an amount of a security to be sold over a 2-year period without specific registration of each sale

short hedge • a combination position in which the investor is short on the futures contract and long on the underlying commodity or asset

short interest (stocks) • the number of shares sold short; sometimes used as a technical market indicator

short selling • *See* selling short.

short-term capital transaction • any trade in which the purchase and sale are less than or equal to one year apart

short-term trading index • the ratio of two ratios. The first ratio is the *number of* advancing stocks divided by the *number of* declining stocks, and the second ratio is the *volume* of advancing stocks divided by the *volume* of declining stocks.

single-premium deferred annuity (SPDA) • an annuity that is purchased with one payment, but the payout period is deferred for a period of time

single-premium immediate annuity (SPIA) • similar to SPDAs, but the benefit payments begin upon receipt of the single premium; also referred to as income annuities

sinking fund • a fund to which a borrowing company makes periodic contributions to ensure that the principal amount of its bond indebtedness will be repaid when due

skewed distribution • a nonsymmetrical statistical distribution that is spread out more on one side of its mode than the other; a nonnormal distribution

small firm effect • a possible anomaly to the efficient market hypothesis characterized by the tendency for small firms to earn above-normal rates of return after risk is taken into account

socially responsible fund • a mutual fund that invests only in corporations or other entities that maintain social and/or ethical principles that are consistent with those specified by the fund

sophisticated investor rationale • the concept that some investors are more sophisticated or knowledgeable than other investors. Thus, one should figure out what these sophisticated investors are doing, and do the same.

special offering • a large block of stock offered for sale on an exchange with special incentive fees paid to purchasing brokers (also called spot secondary)

specialist • an exchange member who makes a market in listed securities

specialty fund • a mutual fund designed for investors who seek special investment opportunities

speculating • the act of committing funds for a short period at high risk in the hope of realizing a gain

speculative risk • risk associated with speculation in which there is some chance of a gain and some chance of a loss

speculative value • *See* time value.

speculator • one who engages in risky transactions in the hope of a large return

spot market • the cash market for immediate delivery of a commodity

spread (bid-ask) • the difference between the bid and the ask price

spread (options) • purchasing an option and writing an option on the same security with different expiration dates or exercise prices

spreading • creating a combination trade such as both a long and a short position in the futures market

Standard & Poor's (S&P) Corporation • an important firm in the investment area that rates bonds, collects and reports data, and computes market indexes

standard deviation • a measure of the degree of dispersion of a distribution. The standard deviation is the square root of the variance. *See also* variance.

Statement of Additional Information • a statement that the mutual fund investor may request from the mutual fund manager that provides additional information about the mutual fund that is not found in the prospectus

statement of cash flows • financial statement showing cash flows into and out of a firm during the reporting period

stock certificate • document showing ownership of a specified number of shares of a company's stock

stock index option • an option on the value of a stock index

stock market index futures • a futures contract on a stock index that does not require delivery of the underlying stock index but is instead settled in dollars according to the difference between the strike price and the actual price of the index

stock market overreaction • an analyst term used to describe the alleged tendency for the stock market to react more than is warranted to news, whether good or bad

stock split • the division of a company's existing stock into more shares (for example, 2 for 1 or 3 for 1)

stop-limit order • an order to implement a limit order when the market price reaches a certain level

stop-loss order • an order to sell or buy at market when a certain price is reached

straddle • a combination put and call option on the same stock at the same strike price and the same expiration date

straight bond • a bond that has no conversion feature

straight-debt value • the value of a convertible bond as a straight-debt (nonconvertible) bond, based on discounted present value of cash flows

strangle • similar to a straddle except that the options have different strike prices—that is, the strike price of the call option is above the strike price for the put option

street name • denotes a security held in a customer account at a brokerage house that is registered in the firm's name

strike price (exercise price) • the price at which the option holder can exercise the option to buy (call) or sell (put) shares

strip bond • a coupon bond (with its coupons removed) that returns only principal at maturity and thus is equivalent to a zero-coupon bond

strong form EMH • the view that market prices quickly and accurately reflect all public and nonpublic information (suggesting that even inside information will not consistently result in superior returns)

style drift • a portfolio that is drifting away from what had been an established style for a mutual fund

subordination • giving a bond issue a lower priority than other (senior) bond issues in bankruptcy

substitution swap • a type of bond swap in which an issue is sold to establish a loss and replaced with an equivalent issue, or a fairly priced bond is sold and replaced with an underpriced one

SuperDOT • advanced version of the DOT system

support level • a floor price that, according to technical analysis, tends to restrict downside price moves

surrender value • the value of an annuity contract after surrender charges have been deducted

switching • when an investor moves money from one fund in a family to another fund in the same family

synthetic call • *See* manufactured call.

synthetic put • *See* manufactured put.

systematic risk • *See* market risk.

taxable income • income on which an individual or corporation is taxed

tax-equivalent yield • the yield on state and local debt instruments after adjustment for the fact that the debt holder is not liable for federal income tax; calculated as $Y_{TE} = Y/(1-T)$ where Y_{TE} is tax-equivalent yield, Y is nominal yield on state and local debt, and T is the investor's marginal federal tax rate

tax exempts • municipal bonds that are not subject to federal taxation

tax-loss harvesting • selling a security at the end of the year to establish a capital loss for tax reporting purposes

tax risk • the extent to which investment returns would be affected by changes in tax laws

technical analysis • a method of evaluating securities and forecasting future price changes based only on past price and volume behavior

technical default • a technical violation of a bond indenture provision such as failure to maintain certain financial ratios

technical market indicator • a data series or combination of data series said to be helpful in forecasting the market's future direction

tender offer • an offer to purchase a large block of securities made outside the general market (exchanges, OTC) in which the securities are traded (often as part of an effort to take over a company)

term structure (of interest rates) • the relationship between yield-to-maturity and term-to-maturity for bonds of like quality

term-to-maturity • the length of time to maturity of a debt instrument

third market • the over-the-counter trading of exchange-listed securities

thrift institutions • institutions other than commercial banks that accept savings deposits, especially savings and loan associations, mutual savings banks, and credit unions

ticker tape • the display of securities transactions shortly after their occurrence, typically electronically

tight money • restrictive monetary policy

times-interest-earned ratio • earnings before interest and taxes divided by interest expense (a ratio used to detect possible risk of default)

time value (option) • the excess of an option's market price over its intrinsic value

time-weighted rate of return • an approach to calculating rates of return that excludes the effect of additions to or distributions from the portfolio, and is computed as the geometric mean return

total asset turnover ratio • sales divided by total assets

trading stations (posts) • the spot on the floor of an exchange where a stock is traded

trail commission (trailer) • a fee not to exceed an annual rate of 0.25 percent that can be paid to mutual fund salespeople, presumably for providing ongoing service and information

tranches • classes of collateral mortgage obligation securities that have varying characteristics

Treasury bill (T-bill) • a short-term debt security issued by the U.S. Treasury

Treasury bonds • debt instruments issued by the U.S. Treasury with an initial maturity of more than 10 years

Treasury notes • debt instruments issued by the U.S. Treasury with an initial maturity of anywhere from one to 10 years

Treynor ratio (reward to volatility ratio) • a measure of risk-adjusted performance of an asset calculated as the ratio of the asset's rate of return minus the risk-free rate divided by the asset's beta

trustee • a bank or other third party that administers the provisions of a bond indenture or that, in general, holds property for the benefit of others

turnover • the relative frequency of trading securities within a mutual fund or other portfolio

turnover ratio • *See* portfolio turnover ratio.

12b-1 fee • a charge against the net assets of a mutual fund that has the ostensible purpose of compensating the management company for marketing costs. It cannot exceed an annual rate of 0.75 percent of average net assets per year plus another 0.25 percent service fee (trail commission or "trailer") that can be paid to salespeople for providing ongoing service and information.

two-name paper • a debt instrument, such as a banker's acceptance, that is issued by one source (for example, a corporation) and guaranteed by another (generally a bank)

unbiased expectations hypothesis • a theory explaining the term structure of interest rates, which states that long-term rates are a function of current and expected future short-term rates

underwrite • to agree to buy all or part of a new security issue, with the intention to sell the securities to the public at a higher price

underwriter • an investment banker who agrees to buy all or part of a new security issue for resale to the public

unemployment rate • the percentage of the workforce that is actually out of work and actively seeking employment

Uniform Principal and Income Act • the key law affecting the management of trust assets. First established the prudent man rule; later this was replaced with the prudent investor rule.

unit investment trust • a self-liquidating unmanaged portfolio in which investors own shares; a concept similar to a closed-end fund but with a specified liquidation date

uptick • a trade at a price greater than the previous trading price

utility function • a function that indicates the value (or utility) of incremental wealth for a specific individual

VA (Veterans Administration) • government agency that provides a variety of services for veterans and their dependents, including the guarantee of repayment of certain home mortgages

valuation • determining the value of an investment as the discounted value of all expected future cash flows

value investing • assembling a portfolio of stocks that sell at low P/E ratios

value stocks • stocks with below-average PE ratios

value weighted • any index in which each company's contribution to the index is based on its total market value

variable annuity • an annuity whose payment is tied to a benchmark such as a stock market index

variance • a measure of uncertainty or risk based on squaring the difference between each return and the mean return

venture capital • risk capital extended to start-up companies or small going concerns that usually requires an ownership interest, as distinct from a pure loan

versus purchase • a selling order that specifies the purchase date of securities to be delivered

warrants • certificates offering the right to purchase stock in a company at a specified price over a specified period. Unlike options, warrants are issued by the same company that issues the underlying stock

weak form EMH • the hypothesis that stock price movements and trading volume cannot be used to predict future price changes; implies that technical analysis cannot provide superior rates of returns

weights • the percentage of the portfolio invested in each security, based on market values

white knight • an alternative buyer for a company when management is attempting to avoid being acquired by a primary buyer

white squire • a third party to whom management sells a significant minority ownership in the company to avoid being acquired by a primary buyer

World Equity Benchmark Shares (WEBS) • index funds that replicate the stock market of a particular foreign country

wrap account • an account in which a single annual fee known as a wrap fee is paid. It is also known as a separate account or managed account.

wrap fee • a management fee charged by investment advisers that includes any brokerage fees incurred

writer • one who sells a put or call option and is therefore obligated to make the agreed-upon purchase or sale if the holder chooses to exercise the option

yield curve • *See* term structure (of interest rates).

yield to earliest (first) call • the holding period return with the assumption that the bond will be called as soon as the no-call provision expires

yield-to-maturity (promised yield) • a measure of bond yield that takes into account capital gain or loss as well as coupon interest payments; the discount rate that would make the present value of the bond's cash flows (interest payments plus face value at maturity) equal the purchase price of the bond

yield-to-maturity effect • the effect that for a given change in interest rates, bonds with lower YTMs have greater percentage price changes than bonds with higher YTMs, all other things being equal

zero-coupon bond (zeros) • a bond issued at a discount that matures at its face value and makes no interest payments prior to maturity

zero-sum game • situation in which total gains equal total losses among the players

zeros • *See* zero coupon bond.

Answers to Review Questions and Self-Test Questions

Chapter 1

Answers to Review Questions

1-1. Liquidity is the ability to convert securities to cash at a price similar to the price of the previous trade in the security, assuming no significant new information has arrived since the previous trade. Equivalently, it is the ability to sell an asset quickly without having to make a substantial price concession.

1-2. a. BDY = [($10,000 − Price)/$10,000] x (360/DTM) = [($10,000 − $9,732)/$10,000] x (360/130) = .0742 or 7.42%.

    b. .0484 = [($10,000 − Price)/$10,000] x (360/88)

$$\text{Price} = \$10,000 − [.0484 \text{ x } (88/360) \text{ x } \$10,000] = \$9,881.69$$

    c. BEY = [(10,000 − Price)/Price] x (365/DTM) = [($10,000 − $9,855)/$9,855] x (365/120) = .0448 = 4.48%

    d. BEY = (365 x BDY)/[360 − (DTM x BDY)] = (365 x.0484)/[360 − (88 x .0484)] = .0497 or 4.97%

1-3. The five money market instruments are Treasury bills, commercial paper, negotiable CDs, bankers' acceptances, and Eurodollar deposits.

1-4. a. T-bill, because it is the safest of all of the securities

    b. Commercial paper, since companies issue commercial paper to get a better rate than prime

    c. Banker's acceptance, because it is two-name paper, versus one name on a CD

    d. Negotiable CD, because banks issuing Eurodollar deposits can pay higher rates due to less regulation

    e. Negotiable CD, because banks borrow money at the CD rate and lend it out at prime

1-5. Securitization is the pledging of illiquid assets as collateral on securities that can then be sold. By securitizing assets, banks can obtain more monies to lend out. More money to loan means a lower interest rate for borrowers.

1-6. The four types of annuities are single-premium deferred annuities (SPDAs), which are appropriate when one receives a large amount of money that one wishes to apply toward retirement; flexible-premium deferred annuities (FPDAs), which are retirement programs allowing monthly contributions; CD-type annuities, which are similar to SPDAs but have guaranteed rates over selected periods and a predetermined number of payments; and single-premium immediate annuities (SPIAs), which are similar to SPDAs but begin paying benefits immediately upon receipt of the single premium.

1-7. Few straight life annuities are sold because if the annuitant dies shortly after the purchase, his or her estate loses all values associated with the annuity. This could leave a bad taste in everyone's mouth, especially the beneficiaries.

1-8. Preferred stock can be thought of as a debt instrument because the dividend is nearly always a fixed dollar amount. Hence, the price of the security will fluctuate more with changes in interest rates than with changes in the fortunes of the company.

1-9. Call options are contracts created between any two investors. One investor gives the other the privilege of buying a fixed number of shares of the stock at a fixed price at any time up to an expiration date. Each option is usually for 100 shares. A warrant is usually issued in conjunction with bonds or a loan agreement for the primary purpose of obtaining a lower interest rate. Each warrant can be used to buy a fixed number of shares of stock (frequently one share per warrant) at a fixed price prior to an expiration date. A warrant allows a company to sell shares of stock later at a price that is usually higher than the current stock price. Warrants can have very long lives. Rights are given to each shareholder for the explicit purpose of the company's selling new shares of stock while allowing current investors to protect their pro rata ownership. Rights typically have a short life (usually a few months at most). The exercise price is usually well below the market price of the stock at the time of issuance.

1-10. Noncollectibles are not purchased by more investors because they come with incredibly high price tags (usually millions of dollars), and they frequently require special expertise to buy, manage, and even sell.

Answers to Self-Test Questions

1-1. True.

1-2. False. T-bills are pure discount instruments.

1-3. True.

1-4. False. Only a small portion of a negotiable CD is usually covered by deposit insurance.

1-5. True.

1-6. True.

1-7. True.

1-8. False. UITs always have an expiration date, and they are intended not to be managed.

1-9. False. Notes, not bonds, have maturities of 1 to 10 years.

1-10. False. Prices on notes and bonds are expressed in 32nds.

1-11. False. Treasury securities are exempt from state and local taxes, just as municipal bonds are exempt from federal taxation.

1-12. True.

1-13. True.

1-14. True.

1-15. False. Revenue bonds are backed by the revenue of a specific project.

1-16. True.

1-17. False. Common stockholders have the lowest priority. Preferred stockholders are the next to lowest.

1-18. False. There is no legal obligation to make dividend payments.

1-19. True.

1-20. True.

1-21. False. Mutual funds are open-end investment companies and continually issue and redeem shares.

1-22. True.

1-23. False. Rights always have much shorter lives.

1-24. False. The conversion value equals the exchange ratio (number of shares received upon conversion) times the current price of the company's common stock. (Par divided by the conversion price equals the conversion *ratio*.)

1-25. True.

1-26. True.

1-27. False. Commissions are usually a relatively trivial amount compared to the gains and losses on futures trades.

1-28. False. The income approach is relevant only for business properties. The market approach (or in some cases the cost approach) is best for owner-occupied, domestic residences.

1-29. True.

1-30. False. Many REITs hold mortgages and mortgage-based securities.

Chapter 2

Answers to Review Questions

2-1. The primary market is where companies raise new capital via the sale of new securities. Without the primary market, corporations would be greatly restricted in the amount of cash they could raise for new projects, and as such, economic growth would be stymied. Although corporations do not participate in the secondary market, except on the rare occasion when they buy back their own securities, the secondary market is crucial. Without the ability to resell securities in the secondary market, hardly anyone would be interested in investing in the primary market. So a well-functioning secondary market is critical for a healthy primary market.

2-2. The investment banker may choose to act as an agent for the issuing firm, in which case the job is taken on a best-efforts basis. Most underwriting, however, is done on a firm-commitment basis, which means the investment banker buys the securities from the issuer and then resells them to the public.

2-3. The two categories of brokers are full service and discount. In a full-service brokerage firm, a client works with a specific broker. Benefits like research are generously provided. Commissions are on the high side. In a discount brokerage firm, the account is with the firm, not a specific broker. Benefits like research may be minimal. Commissions, particularly for Internet-based brokers, may be extremely low.

2-4. The *third market* is the trading of listed stocks in the over-the-counter (OTC) market. It came about as a result of the former high fixed commissions of the NYSE. The *fourth market* refers to direct trading between institutions. The benefit of this method is that prices can be negotiated and commissions bypassed (although there may be a finder's fee for the party bringing the institutions together).

2-5. The specialist is an auctioneer who provides the best bid and ask prices during the trading day. The specialist is an agent, executing SuperDot orders and limit orders placed with him or her. The specialist is a catalyst who attempts to involve people in trading who have previously expressed interest. The specialist is a principal who trades for his or her own account when necessary and appropriate.

2-6. The NYSE generally has the highest listing requirements, followed by the NASDAQ's National Market Issues; the Amex has the lowest requirements of the three. Listing requirements are difficult to compare directly because each market has alternative combinations for listing.

2-7. A *market order* requires an immediate execution at the best available price. A *limit order* stipulates the minimum (sell) or maximum (buy) price acceptable for a trade to take place. A *stop-loss order* requires an immediate market trade if the specified price is reached. A *stop-limit order* activates a limit order if a specified price is reached.

2-8.   a. A market buy would probably have resulted in a purchase price of $15.20, the first in the sequence.
     b. A limit buy at $15 would have certainly been executed at $15.
     c. A short sale could have been executed at $15.15, the first uptick in the sequence.

2-9. The first guarantee is from the brokerage firm that borrows the stock. The second guarantee is from the short seller, who leaves the sale proceeds on deposit plus adds some additional cash to ensure there is sufficient money to repurchase the securities if necessary. The third guarantee is from the Security Investors Protection Corporation (SIPC).

2-10. Congress patterned the SIPC after the Federal Deposit Insurance Corporation (FDIC), which protects deposits in banks. SIPC protects brokerage customers against losses that would otherwise result from the failure of their brokerage firm. Of course, customers are not protected against losses due to market fluctuations. The SIPC liquidates troubled firms at the SEC's request. Customers are insured up to $500,000, not more than $100,000 of which may be in cash. Any claims above those sums are applied against the firm's available assets during liquidation. Most brokerage firms, however, have purchased additional insurance.

Answers to Self-Test Questions

2-1. False. Investment bankers generally agree to sell a new issue on a firm-commitment basis, which means that they buy the securities from the issuer and then sell them to the public.

2-2. True.

2-3. True.

2-4. True.

2-5. False. Churning is the practice of placing trades for the primary purpose of generating commission income for the broker.

2-6. True.

2-7. True.

2-8. True.

2-9. True.

2-10. False. The third market involves OTC trading of listed stocks. Informal arrangements for direct trading between institutions are referred to as the fourth market.

2-11. True.

2-12. False. Off-exchange member trading of listed securities is no longer prohibited *per se,* but restrictions still discourage such activity.

2-13. False. Since May 1975, each brokerage firm has set its own commission rate schedule.

2-14.   False. Spreads tend to represent a smaller percentage of the price for higher-priced and more actively traded stocks.

2-15.   False. A limit-order transaction must await an acceptable price because this type of order is executable only at the limit price or better. Some limit orders are never executed.

2-16.   True.

2-17.   False. The total commission on such a stretched-out trade would appreciably exceed that on a single transaction of the same number of shares.

2-18.   False. An all-or-nothing order can be executed only when sufficient volume is available because the order must trade as a unit. However, the order does not have to be executed immediately; it can wait until sufficient volume exists for a single transaction. The type of order that must be either executed immediately or canceled is a fill-or-kill order.

2-19.   False. The vast majority of trading is done with market and limit orders.

2-20.   True.

2-21.   False. Short sales may take place only in a margin account.

2-22.   False. Using short sales to drive a stock's price down is considered an illegal attempt to manipulate the market. If the last price change was a decline, a would-be short seller must wait until the price begins to rise again before implementing a short sale.

2-23.   True.

2-24.   False. The SIPC protects brokerage customers against losses that would otherwise result from the failure of their brokerage firm.

2-25.   False. The Securities Act of 1933 focuses on the primary market.

2-26.   False. The $100,000 insurance protection is by the accountholder's name, not by account type.

2-27.   True.

2-28.   True.

2-29.   True.

2-30.   True.

Chapter 3

Answers to Review Questions

3-1.   a.   HPRR = $7,000/$5,000 = 1.4
            HPR = 1.4 – 1 = .4 = 40%
       b.   HPRR = $3,000/$1,800 = 1.667
            HPR = 1.667 – 1 = .667 = 66.7%
       c.   HPRR = $228,500/$195,000 = 1.17
            HPR = 1.17 – 1 = .17 = 17%

3-2.   a.   Total value = $11.00 + $0.30 = $11.30
            HPRR = $11.30/$10 = 1.13
            HPR = 1.13 – 1 = .13 = 13%
       b.   HPR = ($70 + $940 – $950) / $950 = .0632 or 6.32%

3-3.   a.   The arithmetic mean return is computed as follows: (7.8% + 9.3% + 4.5% + 11.5%)/4 = 8.275%
       b.   If the amounts were in the proportions of .2, .3, .4, and .1, the mean return would be calculated as follows:
            .2(7.8%) + .3(9.3%) + .4(4.5%) + .1(11.5%) = 7.3%

3-4.   We must begin by determining the holding period return relative (HPRR):
            $GMR + 1 = (HPRR)^{1/n}$
            HPRR = (0.911)(1.056)(1.100)(1.077)(1.130) = 1.287861
            $GMR + 1 = 1.287861^{1/5} = 1.0519$
            GMR = .0519 or 5.19%
       HP-10BII keystrokes:
            SHIFT, C ALL
            .911, x, 1.056, x, 1.1, x, 1.077, x, 1.13, =
            SHIFT, y^x, .2, =, –, 1, =   (display: 0.0519)

3-5. a. Mean = (–5% + 0% + 5% + 10%)/4 = 2.5%
            Variance = $[(-5\% - 2.5\%)^2 + (0\% - 2.5\%)^2 + (5\% - 2.5\%)^2 + (10\% - 2.5\%)^2]/4 = 31.25\%$

            Standard deviation = $\sqrt{\text{Variance}}$ = 5.59%

      b. Mean = [.1(0%) + .15(5%) + .25(10%) + .25(15%) + .15(20%) + .1(25%)] = 12.50%
            Variance = $[.1(0\% - 12.5\%)^2 + .15(5\% - 12.5\%)^2 + \ldots + .1(25\% - 12.5\%)^2] = 51.25\%$
            Standard deviation = 7.16%

      c. Mean = 10%/1 = 10%
            Variance = $(10\% - 10\%)^2/1 = 0$
            Standard deviation = 0

3-6. a. Since there is only a single holding period, the overall return is simply the arithmetic mean (average) return:
            AMR = (80 – 25 – 15 + 12 + 10.5 – 80 + 350 – 100 + 0)/9 = 25.83%

      b. The geometric mean return (GMR) is calculated as follows:
            GMR = $(1.2583)^{1/5} - 1 = .047 = 4.7\%$
            HP-10BII keystrokes:
            SHIFT, C ALL
            1.80, +, .75, +, .85, +, 1.12, +, 1.105, +, .20, +, 4.50, +, 0, +, 1.0, =
            ÷, 9, =   (display: 1.2583)
                     SHIFT, y^x, .20, =, –, 1, =   (display: 0.0470)

3-7. Best guess = 15%(1 – 1/10) + 10%(1/10) = 13.5% + 1% = 14.5%

3-8. a. (1 + .05) x (1 + .04) –1 = .092 or 9.20%
      b. (1 + .15)/(1 + .10) –1 = .0455 or 4.55%

3-9. Expected return = (–15% + 10% + 35%)/3 = 10%
        Variance = $[(-15 - 10)^2 + (10 - 10)^2 + (35 - 10)^2]/(3 - 1) = [625 + 0 + 625]/2 = 625$ percent-squared
        Standard deviation = (625 percent-squared)$^{.5}$ = 25%
        Coefficient of variation = 25/10 = 2.5

3-10. a. $50 x 100 shares = $5,000
              $5,000 x .60 initial margin rate = $3,000 cash paid in
              $5,000 purchase price – $3,000 cash paid in = $2,000 loan

       b. Maximum cash withdrawal = [MV x (1 – IMR)] – L = [(100 shares x $80) x (1 – .60)] – $2,000 = [$8,000 x .40] – $2,000 = $3,200 – $2,000 = $1,200

       c. Buying power = (E/IMR) – MV = [(MV – L)/IMR] – MV = [($8,000 – $2,000)/.60] – $8,000 = $10,000 – $8,000 = $2,000. Number of new shares bought = buying power/price per share = $2,000/$80 = 25 new shares

       d. MV x (1 – MMR) ≥ Loan
              MV x (1 – .25) ≥ $2,000
              MV ≥ $2,000/.75 = $2,666.67
              MV/number of shares = $2,666.67/100 = $26.67

       e. Cash added = Loan – MV x (1 – MMR) = $2,000 – ($20 x 100) x (1 – .25) = $2,000 – $1,500 = $500

3-11. The $53,000 balance corresponds to the call rate plus 3/4 percent or 9 1/4 percent. This rate is equivalent to a monthly rate of 9.25/12 = 0.771%. The first month's charge is $53,000(0.771%) = $408.54. The second month's charge is ($53,000 + $408.54)(0.771%) = $411.69. Continuing with part a. and making the necessary adjustments for part b. with the relevant rates of 10 1/4 percent yields the following results:

a.	Month	Charge	b.	Month	Charge
	1	$ 408.54		1	$230.63
	2	411.69		2	232.59
	3	414.86		3	234.58
	4	418.06			$697.80
	5	421.28			
	6	424.53			
		$2,498.96			

Answers to Self-Test Questions

3-1. True.

3-2. False. An asset's PPR is defined as the sum of that period's income payments and price appreciation divided by its beginning-of-period price.

3-3. True.

3-4. False. This statement ignores the effect of compounding.

3-5. True.

3-6. True.

3-7. False. In the field of investments, risk is the chance that the actual outcome will *differ* from the expected outcome. It can be thought of as uncertainty, as the range of possible outcomes, or as the dispersion of possible outcomes from the expected outcome. Mathematical measures of risk include the standard deviation and the range (the highest possible outcome minus the lowest one).

3-8. False. Inflation risk is the risk of the loss of purchasing power. Disinflation is the phenomenon where the general level of prices grows at a slower rate.

3-9. True.

3-10. False. Interest rate risk has two components: price risk and reinvestment rate risk. The first is the change in value due to changes in interest rates, and the latter is the impact on the reinvestment of cash flows due to changes in interest rates. The rate on margin loans has nothing to do with this risk.

3-11. False. The inability to quickly sell an asset at its current market price is liquidity risk.

3-12. True.

3-13. False. Political risks are the risks from events that come from operating in a foreign country, such as expropriation. Exchange rate risk is the risk of loss in value due to fluctuations in the exchange rate.

3-14. False. Tax risk is the risk of loss due to changes in the tax code.

3-15. True.

3-16. False. All risk-averse investors would prefer B because it has a smaller standard deviation when the expected returns are equal.

3-17. False. Calculating the semivariance involves using only the prospective returns that are below the expected return.

3-18. False. The variance must be computed first. Then the standard deviation can be computed by taking the square root of the result.

3-19. True.

3-20. False. The calculation of the variance when all returns are equally weighted uses a denominator of n; when using historical data, the denominator is (n – 1).

3-21. False. The initial margin rate is the amount of cash the investor must put up.

3-22. False. The initial margin requirement on stocks is set at 50 percent.

3-23. False. Buying on margin *increases* the variability of an investor's returns.

3-24. False. The investor is charged the call-loan rate plus a mark-up that depends on the size of the loan balance.

3-25. True.

3-26. True.

3-27. True.

3-28. True.

3-29. True.

3-30. True.

Chapter 4

Answers to Review Questions

4-1. a. X (same expected return, less risk)
      b. Y (same risk, greater expected return)
      c. neither (Y has a greater expected return, but also has more risk)

4-2. a.

	(1)	(2)	(3)	(4)	(5)
t	R_{it}	R_{jt}	$R_{it} - \overline{R}_i$	$R_{jt} - \overline{R}_i$	(3) x (4)
1	.04	.05	.01	.04	.0004
2	.06	.03	.03	.02	.0006
3	−.01	−.05	−.04	−.06	.0024
$\sum R_{xt}$ $\div n$	.09 $\div 3$	.03 $\div 3$			.0034 $\div (n - 1)$ or 2
$\overline{R}_{xt}$	.03	.01			.0017

b.

	(1)	(2)	(3)	(4)	(5)	(6)
t	R_{it}	R_{jt}	P_{jt}	$R_{it} - \overline{R}_i$	$R_{jt} - \overline{R}_i$	(3) x (4) x (5)
1	.04	.05	.50	.01	.04	.00020
2	.06	.03	.30	.03	.02	.00018
3	−.01	−.05	.20	−.04	−.06	.00048
$\sum R_{xt}$ $\div n$	.09 $\div 3$	.03 $\div 3$				COV = .00086
$\overline{R}_{xt}$	.03	.01				

4-3. a. Correlation coefficient = covariance/product of the standard deviations = .0020/(.06 x .08) = .4167
   b. Covariance = product of the standard deviations x correlation coefficient = (.06 x .08) x (−.50) = −.0024
   c. Maximum value of correlation = 1, so if 1 = COV/(.06 x .08), then COV = .0048
      Minimum value of correlation = −1, so if −1 = COV/(.06 x .08), then COV = −.0048

4-4. Expected returns are the same, regardless of the correlation coefficient:

Portfolio	W_a	R_a	W_b	R_b	$(W_a \times R_a)$ $+ (W_b \times R_b)$
A	1	4	0	10	4.0
B	0.8	4	0.2	10	5.2
C	0.6	4	0.4	10	6.4
D	0.4	4	0.6	10	7.6
E	0.2	4	0.8	10	8.8
F	0	4	1	10	10.0

Portfolios when correlation coefficient equals .5:

Portfolio	W_a	W_b	Sigma a	Sigma b	Sigma p
A	1	0	5	16	5.00
B	0.8	0.2	5	16	6.25
C	0.6	0.4	5	16	8.32
D	0.4	0.6	5	16	10.74
E	0.2	0.8	5	16	13.33
F	0	1	5	16	16.00

Portfolios when correlation coefficient equals −.5:

Portfolio	W_a	W_b	Sigma a	Sigma b	Sigma p
A	1	0	5	16	5.00
B	0.8	0.2	5	16	3.67
C	0.6	0.4	5	16	5.55
D	0.4	0.6	5	16	8.77
E	0.2	0.8	5	16	12.33
F	0	1	5	16	16.00

4-5.   You should choose company D because it has the lowest correlation coefficient. This means that the efficient frontier will allow one to move to the highest possible indifference curve.

4-6.   The security market line shows the expected return for any holding, be it a single security, an inefficient portfolio, or an efficient portfolio (that is, one that lies on the capital market line). The capital market line is defined in terms of the risk-free asset and the market portfolio. Only the most efficient portfolios plot on the CML.

4-7.   a.   By varying the weights assigned to assets, we can draw a curve in risk-return space. At each point on the curve, no higher expected return can be achieved for a given risk level. Thus, the investment portfolios are efficient. When a risk-free asset is introduced, the efficient frontier becomes a straight line connecting the risk-free asset and the market portfolio (which consists of all assets in their exact value-weighted proportions). To hold a portfolio along this line is to hold both the risk-free asset and the market portfolio in varying proportions (points to the right of the market portfolio involve borrowing to purchase more of the market portfolio).

       b.   If only lending is possible, the efficient frontier consists of the line connecting the risk-free asset and the market portfolio. To the right, the frontier is once again the risky asset curve.

4-8.   a.   The total risk of a security can be broken down into two components: market risk, which is the product of the square of a security's beta and the variance of the returns on the market portfolio, and the nonmarket risk, which is the variance of its unique returns.

       b.   The beta coefficient determines the effect of market risk for an individual security.

4-9.   Because we know that the market portfolio always has a beta of 1.0, we can use the formula $r_i = r_f + \beta_i (r_M - r_f)$ to obtain the return for each of the portfolios.

Expected Returns for Efficient Portfolios					
		β_p			
Risk-free	Expected Market Return	0.7	1	1.3	1.6
0.07	0.14	0.119	0.14	0.161	0.182
0.09	0.16	0.139	0.16	0.181	0.202
0.05	0.1	0.085	0.1	0.115	0.13

Sample calculation for $r_f = 0.09$, $r_m = 0.16$, $\beta_p = 1.3$:

$$r_p = r_f + \beta_p(r_m - r_f)$$
$$= 0.09 + 1.3(0.16 - 0.09)$$
$$= 0.181$$

4.10. The prudent man investment objective says that each investment individually must be evaluated in light of what a prudent man who wanted to preserve his estate would do. A prudent investor is allowed to focus on the performance of the portfolio, rather than each security or holding separately.

Answers to Self-Test Questions

4-1. False. A portfolio of securities is less risky than its component securities. This is why diversification is an important investment strategy.

4-2. True.

4-3. False. A portfolio's return is the *weighted* average of the returns of its assets. The average assumes that each asset has an equal weight in the portfolio. As relative prices change, the relative impact of each asset on the portfolio return also changes. Therefore, using an unweighted average would result in an inaccurate measure of portfolio return.

4-4. False. A perfectly negative correlation (–1) of the returns between two assets would reduce the variability or risk of the portfolio. This would reduce the standard deviation of the returns to the portfolio. In fact, it would be possible to construct a risk-free portfolio by combining two assets whose returns have a correlation of –1. However, the weighted return of the portfolio would not change.

4-5. True.

4-6. True.

4-7. False. The covariance of a security's returns with itself is its variance.

4-8. False. When the correlation coefficient between two securities is +1, the minimum variance portfolio is 100 percent of whichever security has the less risk.

4-9. True.

4-10. False. When the correlation coefficient between two securities is –1, only those portfolios that lie on the line connecting the risk-free portfolio with the riskier asset constitute the efficient frontier.

4-11. False. When two assets are being combined into a portfolio, the most desirable combination is identified with indifference curves. Only the most risk-averse clients should hold the minimum variance portfolio.

4-12. False. The formulas are different.

4-13. False. No matter where one moves on the same indifference curve, one is indifferent among the portfolios.

4-14. True.

4-15. True.

4-16. True.

4-17. True.

4-18. False. If a portfolio is on the capital market line, it is a well-diversified portfolio.

4-19. False. Diversification only means a reduction in the riskiness of a portfolio, not necessarily a reduction in expected return.

4-20. True.

4-21. True.

4-22. False. Return by itself is insufficient to properly assess and compare the performance of different investments. Risk must also be considered.

4-23. False. Any dominated portfolios should automatically be removed from further consideration.

4-24. False. The highest possible expected return would require assets with the highest possible positive values of beta.

4-25. False. The required return for this investment is 10.6 percent. The market risk premium (10% – 4% = 6%) is multiplied by the stock's beta (1.1) and is then added to the risk-free rate (4 percent) for an expected rate of return of 10.6 percent (6.6% + 4%).

4-26. True.

4-27. True.

4-28. True.

4-29.   False. The prudent investor rule is more lenient because it looks at the entire portfolio, rather than each security separately.

4-30.   True.

Chapter 5

Answers to Review Questions

5-1.   a.   Because all of the deposits and withdrawals are made at the end of the period but the ending values incorporate these cash flows, the rates of return are

$R_1 = (65,000 - 50,000 - 10,000)/50,000 = .10$, or 10%

$R_2 = (60,000 - 65,000)/65,000 = -.0769$, or −7.69%

$R_3 = (55,000 - 60,000 - (-10,000)/\$60,000 = .0833$, or 8.33%

$R_4 = (55,000 - 55,000/55,000 = .00$, or 0%

b.   The time-weighted rate of return is the geometric mean of the rates of return computed in part a:

$[(1 + .10) \times (1 - .0769) \times (1 + .0833) \times (1 + 0)]^{1/4} - 1 = 1.099994^{1/4} - 1 = .0241 - 1 = .0241$ or 2.41%

The keystrokes are SHIFT, C ALL, 1.10, x, .9231, x, 1.0833, x, 1, =, SHIFT, y^x, .25, =, −, 1, = (display: .0241)

c.   The dollar-weighted rate of return is the internal rate of return, and it works out to be 2.1992 percent. The keystrokes are SHIFT, C ALL, 50000, +/−, CFj, 10000, +/−, CFj, 0, CFj, 10000, CFj, 55000, CFj, SHIFT, IRR/YR (display: 2.1992)

5-2.   a.   The dollar-weighted rate of return will give heavier weight to the performance of the portfolio when the portfolio is larger in dollar value, and lesser weight to the performance when it is smaller in dollar value. The greater the variation in the dollar value of the portfolio over time, the greater the chance for disparity between the two rates of return.

b.   If there are no interim cash flows, the two ways to measure the rate of return will be identical.

5-3.   For the price-weighted index, the values for the first 2 days would be 30 [(20 + 40)/2] and 30 [(19 + 41)/2]. Before figuring the third day, we have to adjust the denominator:

$$30 = (19 + 20.5)/\text{new divisor}$$
$$\text{new divisor} = 39.5/30 = 1.317$$

Therefore, the index for the third day would be 30.37 =[(20 + 20)/1.317].

For the value-weighted index, the base value is 20 x 100,000 + 40 x 10,000 = 2,400,000. The numerator for the second day is 19 x 100,000 + 41 x 10,000 = 2,310,000, and thus the index value is (2,310,000/2,400,000) x 100 = 96.25. For the third day, the numerator for the index is 20 x 100,000 + 20 x 20,000 = 2,400,000, so the index value is (2,400,000/2,400,000) x 100 = 100.

5-4.   a.   It is usually inappropriate to compare the rate of return on a client's portfolio directly to a market index because (1) indices do not pay transaction fees, advisory fees, or taxes, (2) indices are more diversified than individual portfolios and thus less volatile, (3) most portfolios hold cash and fixed income securities, and (4) the beta coefficients of indices will most likely be different from those of individual portfolios.

b.   The Russell 1000 is the 1000 largest stocks in the Russell 3000, and the Russell 2000 is the other 2000.

c.   It is the only index to provide equal weighting to all securities.

d.   MSCI EAFE

e.   Lehman Brothers

5-5.   Using the standard deviations and betas for each fund and the market index, the Treynor ratios and Sharpe ratios are as shown in the following:

	Beta	Arith. Mean	Standard Deviation	Treynor Ratio	Rank	Sharpe Ratio	Rank
Good Fund*	1.1	4.56	13.97	−.13	4	−.01	4
Bond Fund	0.6	6.93	7.31	3.71	2	.31	1
Go Fund	1.3	8.47	31.31	2.90	3	.12	3
Market	1	8.70	15.72	4.00	1	.25	2

HP-10BII keystrokes for Good Fund

To compute the arithmetic mean return:

SHIFT, C ALL, 10.5, +, 8.5, +/–, +, 15.7, +, 14.3, +, 21.3, +/–, +, 12.2, +, 9, /, 7, =   (display: 4.56)

To compute the standard deviation:

SHIFT, C ALL, 10.5, Σ+, 8.5, +/–, Σ+, 15.7, Σ+, 14.3, Σ+, 21.3, +/–, Σ+, 12.2, Σ+, 9, Σ+, SHIFT, $s_x s_y$

(display: 13.97)

Treynor ratio = (4.56 – 4.7)/1.1 = –.13

Sharpe ratio = (4.56 – 4.7)/13.97 = –.01

5-6. Jensen's alpha is $\alpha_P = \overline{R}_P - \left[R_F + \left(\overline{R}_M - R_F \right) \beta_P \right]$ = 12% – [3% + (10% – 3%) x 1.5] = -1.5%. Thus, this

company underperformed relative to the market.

5-7. There are several reasons why there might be a risk premium for nonmarket risk: (1) Investors may not be able to hold fully diversified portfolios, and hence demand a premium for the nonmarket risk they must assume, (2) estimates of beta may be correlated with nonmarket risk, (3) the fact that the borrowing and lending rate are not the same may limit the ability of the market to reward only market risk, (4) returns may be skewed and there may be a premium for positive skewness, and (5) returns may not be normal; they may be leptokurtic or platokurtic.

5-8. a. If a beta were estimated at 1.2, Blume's formula would suggest that an unbiased forecasted beta would be .35 + (.68 x beta estimate) = .35 + (.68 x 1.2) = 1.166.

   b. Sequential estimates of beta have a propensity to regress toward the mean (meaning 1). Thus, betas with values different from 1 are substantially more likely to move toward 1 than away from it.

   c. Portfolio betas are more stable than betas for individual securities. Hence, it is better to use beta in examples involving portfolios rather than individual securities. Thus, a problem such as 5-6 above, which analyzes the performance of a single stock, is a weak application of beta.

Answers to Self-Test Questions

5-1. False. This would be true only if there were no interim cash flows into or out of the portfolios.

5-2. False. When computing the geometric mean return, the sequence of returns does not matter if the actual returns are the same.

5-3. False. Interim cash flows are withdrawals from and deposits into a portfolio by the investor, not dividend or interest payments that accrue to securities held in a portfolio.

5-4. True.

5-5. False. All time periods are equally weighted, regardless of whether they are the most recent or the earliest observation.

5-6. False. The investor should use the dollar-weighted rate of return, as the investor presumably has some control over the movement of cash into and out of the portfolio.

5-7. True.

5-8. True.

5-9. True.

5-10. True.

5-11. False. The divisor is adjusted to reflect stock dividends, stock splits, and changes in the index. Its value is substantially less than 30.

5-12. False. The DJIA is price-weighted; the S & P 500 is value-weighted.

5-13. False. The Wilshire Index currently has more than 7,000 stocks in it.

5-14. False. Direct comparison with indices is incorrect for several reasons, and the DJIA would be the worst index to use for comparisons.

5-15. False. The oldest stock market index is the DJIA.

5-16. False. Some of the stocks in the S & P 500 are listed on the NASDAQ, and a few on the AMEX.

5-17. False. The FTSE 100 index represents the largest 100 on the London Stock Exchange.

5-18. True.

5-19. False. When there is a stock split for a stock in a price-weighted index, the divisor is adjusted.

5-20. False. The initial value is actually trivial. All subsequent values are relative to whatever the initial value is set at.

5-21. True.

5-22. True.

5-23. True.

5-24.　True.
5-25.　True.
5-26.　True.
5-27.　True.
5-28.　True.
5-29.　False. Investors have a strong preference for positive skewness (the chance of a large gain combined with limited downside potential) and a strong distaste for negative skewness (the chance of a large loss combined with limited upside potential).
5-30.　False. Estimates of portfolio betas are relative stable, but estimates for individual stocks are not.

Appendix 5A

Answers to Review Questions

5A-1.　a.　This is a future value of a lump-sum problem:
$$FV = PV \times (1 + i)^n = 50,000 \times (1 + .08)^{30} = \$503,132.84$$
Keystrokes: SHIFT, C ALL, 50000, PV, 8, I/YR, 30, N, FV (display: −503,132.84)

b.　This is a present value of annuity problem:
$$PV = \text{payment} \times \left(\frac{1 - \dfrac{1}{(1+i)^n}}{i} \right) = 50,000 \times [(1 - [1/(1 + .06)^{20})]/.06] = \$573,496.06$$

Keystrokes: SHIFT, C ALL, 50000, PMT, 6, I/YR, 20, N, PV (display: −573,496.06)
No, the $50,000 today is not quite enough to meet the client's goal.

c.　This is a future value of annuity problem:
$$FV = \text{payment} \times \left(\frac{(1+i)^n - 1}{i} \right) = 6,000 \times [(1 + .08)^{30} - 1]/.08 = \$679,699.27$$

Keystrokes: SHIFT, C ALL, 6000, PMT, 8, I/YR, 30, N, FV (display: −679,699.27)
The client will be substantially better off.

d.　This is a future value of annuity with compounding greater than once per year problem:
$$FV = \text{payment} \times \left(\frac{(1+i)^n - 1}{i} \right) = 500 \times [(1 + .08/12)^{360} - 1]/(.08/12) = \$745,179.72$$

Keystrokes: SHIFT, C ALL, 500, PMT, 8, / , 12, =, I/YR, 30, x, 12, =, N, FV
(display: −745,179.72)

e.　This is a future value of an annuity due with compounding greater than once per year problem:
Keystrokes: SHIFT, C ALL, SHIFT, BEG/END, 500, PMT, 8, ÷, 12, =, I/YR, 30, x, 12, =, N, FV (display: − 750,147.59)

5A-2.　a.　This is a present value of a lump-sum problem:
$$PV = FV \times 1/(1+i)^n = 1,000,000 \times 1/(1+.10)^{35} = \$35,584.10$$
Keystrokes: SHIFT, C ALL, 1000000, FV, 10, I/YR, 35, N, PV (display: −35,584.10)

b.　This is a future value of annuity problem:
$$PMT = FV/ \left(\frac{(1+i)^n - 1}{i} \right) = 1,000,000 / [(1 + .10)^{35} - 1]/(.10) = \$3,689.71$$

Keystrokes: SHIFT, C ALL, 1000000, FV, 10, I/YR, 35, N, PMT (display: −3,689.71)

5A-3.　This is a conversion of a nominal rate to an effective annual rate problem.
$$r_{ear} = \left(1 + \frac{r_{nom}}{m} \right)^m - 1$$

The best deal is c., 4.15% compounded quarterly, as shown below:

a. $r_{ear} = (1 + .04/365)^{365} - 1 = .0408$, or 4.08%

Keystrokes: SHIFT, C ALL, 4, SHIFT, NOM%, 365, SHIFT, P/YR, SHIFT, EFF%

(Then be sure to change the compounding frequency back to once per year.)

b. $r_{ear} = (1 + .041/12)^{12} - 1 = .0418$, or 4.18%

Keystrokes: SHIFT, C ALL, 4.1, SHIFT, NOM%, 12, SHIFT, P/YR, SHIFT, EFF% (display: 4.1779)

(Then be sure to change the compounding frequency back to once per year.)

c. $r_{ear} = (1 + .0415/4)^4 - 1 = .0422$, or 4.22%

Keystrokes: SHIFT, C ALL, 4.15, SHIFT, NOM%, 4, SHIFT, P/YR, SHIFT, EFF% (display: 4.2150)

(Then be sure to change the compounding frequency back to once per year.)

d. $r_{ear} = (1 + .042/1)^1 - 1 = .042$, or 4.2%

Keystrokes: None necessary; an annually compounded rate is the answer.

5A-4.i. a. The net present value for each project is as follows:

First project:

$NPV = -Cost + CF_1/(1 + i)^1 + CF_2/(1 + i)^2 + CF_3/(1 + i)^3$

$NPV = -100,000 + 30,000/(1 + .08)^1 + 40,000/(1 + .08)^2 + 50,000/(1 + .08)^3 = \$1,762.94$

Keystrokes: SHIFT, C ALL, 100000, +/–, CFj, 30000, CFj, 40000, CFj, 50000, CFj, 8, I/YR, SHIFT, NPV (display: 1,762.94)

b. Second project:

$NPV = -Cost + PMT \times [(1 - [1/(1 + i)^n])/i]$

$NPV = -150,000 + 30,000 \times [1 - [1/(1 + .10)^{10}]/.10 = \$34,337.01$

Keystrokes: SHIFT, C ALL, 150000, +/–, CFj, 30000, CFj, 10, SHIFT, Nj, 10, I/YR, SHIFT, NPV (display: 34337.01)

c. Third project:

$NPV = -COST + PMT/i = -75,000 + 10,000/.10 = 25,000$

ii. Based on NPVs, the second project is the most attractive, with an NPV of \$34,337.01.

iii. a. The IRR for the first project is 8.90%.

Keystrokes for IRR: SHIFT, C ALL, 100000, +/–, CFj, 30000, CFj, 40000, CFj, 50000, CFj, SHIFT, IRR/YR (display: 8.8963 or 8.90%)

b. The IRR for the second project is 15.10%.

Keystrokes for IRR: SHIFT, C ALL, 150000, +/–, CFj, 30000, CFj, 10, SHIFT, Nj, SHIFT, IRR/YR (display: 15.0984 or 15.10%)

c. The IRR for the third project is 13.33%.

IRR = PMT/cost = 10,000 / 75,000 = .1333 or 13.33%

Note: The rank order based on IRR is not always the same as rank order based on NPV. When this happens, ignore the IRR calculation and base the decision strictly on the NPV.

Answers to Self-Test Questions

5A-1. True.

5A-2. False. The intrinsic value equals the present value of payments expected to the owner of that security.

5A-3. True.

5A-4. True.

5A-5. False. The higher the interest rate, the lower the present value of a future cash flow, because you do not need to set aside as much money today to grow to that future value when the interest rate is higher.

5A-6. False. It only means you entered the present value as a positive number. Had you entered the present value as a negative number, the future value would have been a positive number.

5A-7. False. You have to remember to adjust both the interest rate and the number of time periods.

5A-8. True.

5A-9. True.

5A-10. False. An annuity requires consecutive and equal payments.

Chapter 6

Answers to Review Questions

6-1.　The weak form of EMH implies that historical price behavior cannot be used to predict future prices. If true, this view negates the efficacy of technical analysis. Research has indicated that this form of EMH holds, especially when transaction costs are taken into account. Under the semistrong form, all publicly available information is already incorporated into an asset's price; therefore, both technical and fundamental analyses are useless for price anticipation. Evidence supporting this version is mixed. The implication is that astute fundamental analysts may in some cases be able to anticipate price changes. Under the strong form of EMH, all information is incorporated into asset prices; therefore, it is not possible to predict price movement. Financial research has generally not found substantial evidence supporting the strong form of EMH.

6-2.　It is possible that the sheer magnitude of data may obscure relevant information. This may delay or prevent prudent investor action. Achieving efficient markets requires ease of access. In practice, investors may not have the resources or understanding to act upon information. They may lack the desire to undertake adequate investment research; in other words, other activities may take precedence. It is possible that the market is, for the most part, efficient, but efficiency may not extend to all securities. For example, the information of small firms may be difficult to obtain, thereby making valuation more fraught with error.

6-3.　The use of trading data on short sales is often motivated by the belief that short traders have superior market insight. Implementation of this doctrine requires that their actions be mimicked in anticipation of price declines. A spin-off is the belief that short pressure will likely lead to higher demand, thus driving up prices; investors should, therefore, buy when short volume increases. Studies have refuted both of these strategies. Other theorists focus on odd-lot traders and their perceived poor market timing. It is thought that contrary positions should produce profits. Research has found that some positive gains may have been achievable in the 1950s and 1960s; more recently, this is not the case.

6-4.　a.　Many assume that specialists have superior market insight. This belief dictates following specialists' short-selling.

　　　b.　A similar market timing method entails monitoring mutual funds' cash position. If the cash position becomes large, a significant market upswing is expected. The implication is that the fund is waiting for the right buying opportunity. Mutual funds have generally not been successful with their cash management timing strategies.

　　　c.　Some investors view the bond market as offering clues about future moves of the stock market. A low value of a statistic, such as the Barron's Confidence Index (BCI), indicates that the rate spread between high-grade and speculative bonds is wide, thus revealing that investment is shifting away from speculative bonds. This demonstrates pessimism and does not bode well for the stock market. Results using this method have not been encouraging.

6-5.　Barron's Confidence Index = high-grade rates/average-grade rates

$$\text{BCI} = \frac{5.67}{6.01} = .943 \qquad\qquad \text{BCI} = \frac{10.34}{13.89} = .744$$

6-6.　a.　The advance-decline ratio has been shown to have some persistence. In other words, advances (declines) tend to extend beyond one trading day (sometimes termed momentum).

　　　b.　The short-term trading index uses the ratio of average decline volume to average advance volume. Traders using this statistic have claimed positive results.

　　　c.　The January indicator suggests that if the market rises in January, there is a good chance that it will continue to do so for the rest of the year. The January effect is based on the observation that small stocks consistently outperform the market for the early part of January. This effect may be due to tax implications, and it has diminished in recent years.

　　　d.　Some studies have found that there is a disparity between price changes on Monday and Friday. Prices are apt to fall on Monday and rise on Friday. This is based on the idea that bad news is most likely to be revealed after the market closes on Friday.

6-7.　a.　Chartists' basic premise is that future prices can be predicted based on observation of past prices and volume. Supporters of the random walk hypothesis believe that this is not possible, that there is no link between past and future price patterns. From this perspective, price movements can be viewed as random.

　　　b.　The belief in the separation of past and future prices is a subcategory of the weak form of the efficient market hypothesis. This theory states that a stock's current price incorporates all previously available information. In other words, no abnormal profit can be consistently obtained by analyzing past price movements. Profit opportunities are precluded because price adjustments occur too quickly.

Answers to Self-Test Questions

6-1. False. The efficient market, as the term is used in investments, is one in which the prices of all securities fully reflect all known information quickly and, on average, accurately.

6-2. True.

6-3. True.

6-4. False. The semistrong form of the EMH holds that all publicly available information (including past market data) is reflected in stock prices. However, it does not hold that nonpublic information is also contained in stock prices.

6-5. True.

6-6. True.

6-7. False. The semistrong form of the EMH states that neither technical nor fundamental analysis will lead to excess profits.

6-8. False. One of every 1,024 people who tries to predict the market 10 years in a row would likely be correct, even if they were all just guessing. This one person could be the 1,024th person.

6-9. True.

6-10. False. The weak form of the EMH allows for random overreaction as a part of the noise in the data.

6-11. True.

6-12. False. Several studies of corporate insiders found that they earned abnormal returns on their stock transactions.

6-13. False. Money managers need to be concerned with diversification and risk of the securities; they must also consider transaction costs and taxes in the design and management of the portfolios.

6-14. True.

6-15. True.

6-16. True.

6-17. False. The Dow theory seeks to confirm if a primary trend, either upward or downward, has emerged. The theory relies on the secondary moves for this purpose.

6-18. True.

6-19. True.

6-20. True.

6-21. False. The ratio tends to be greater than 1 because people sometimes buy several odd lots over time and accumulate a round lot, which they later sell as a round lot.

6-22. True.

6-23. False. Chart reading is a type of technical analysis.

6-24. True.

6-25. True.

6-26. False. Time is completely omitted from point-and-figure charts.

6-27. False. It typically takes a $3 reversal to start a new column.

6-28. False. Volume numbers are occasionally shown at the bottom of bar charts. There is no volume shown on a point-and-figure chart.

6-29. False. It is the level at which a significant number of investors start *selling* their stock.

6-30. False. It is bullish. It is the right-side-up pattern that is bearish.

Chapter 7

Answers to Review Questions

7-1. a. Over the 5-year period, dividends will be paid out at the rate of $3.25, $3.50, $3.75, $4.00, and $4.25. At the end of 5 years, the stock will sell for 12 x $4.25 = $51. Thus, we need to compute the present value at 8 percent of the income stream: $3.25, $3.50, $3.75, $4.00, and $4.25 + $51. $PV = \$3.25/(1 + .08)^1 + \$3.50/(1 + .08)^2 + \$3.75/(1 + .08)^3 + \$4.00/(1 + .08)^4 + \$55.25/(1 + .08)^5 = \$49.53$

b. At a discount rate of 10 percent, the present value of the income stream is:
$$PV = \$3.25/(1+.10)^1 + \$3.50/(1+.10)^2 + \$3.75/(1+.10)^3 + \$4.00/(1+.10)^4 + \$55.25/(1+.10)^5 = \$45.70$$
c. At a discount rate of 12 percent, the present value of the income stream is:
$$PV = \$3.25/(1+.12)^1 + \$3.50/(1+.12)^2 + \$3.75/(1+.12)^3 + \$4.00/(1+.12)^4 + \$55.25/(1+.12)^5 = \$42.25$$
d. At a discount rate of 15 percent, the present value of the income stream is:
$$PV = \$3.25/(1+.15)^1 + \$3.50/(1+.15)^2 + \$3.75/(1+.15)^3 + \$4.00/(1+.15)^4 + \$55.25/(1+.15)^5 = \$37.69$$
e. At a discount rate of 18 percent, the present value of the income stream is:
$$PV = \$3.25/(1+.18)^1 + \$3.50/(1+.18)^2 + \$3.75/(1+.18)^3 + \$4.00/(1+.18)^4 + \$55.25/(1+.18)^5 = \$33.76$$
f. With a stable dividend of \$3.00 and a discount rate of 8 percent:
$$PV = \$3.00/(1+.08)^1 + \$3.00/(1+.08)^2 + \$3.00/(1+.08)^3 + \$3.00/(1+.08)^4 + \$39.00/(1+.08)^5 = \$36.48$$
HP-10BII keystrokes:
a. SHIFT, C ALL
    0, CFj, 3.25, CFj, 3.50, CFj, 3.75, CFj, 4.00, CFj, 4.25, x, 12, =, +, 4.25, =, CFj
    8, I/YR, SHIFT, NPV   (display: 49.53)
(b. through e. can be solved without reentering cash-flow data unless the memory is cleared)
b. 10, I/YR, SHIFT, NPV   (display: 45.70)
c. 12, I/YR, SHIFT, NPV   (display: 42.25)
d. 15, I/YR, SHIFT, NPV   (display: 37.69)
e. 18, I/YR, SHIFT, NPV   (display: 33.76)
f. SHIFT, C ALL
    0, CFj, 3, CFj, 4, SHIFT, Nj, 3, x, 12, =, +, 3, =, CFj
    8, I/YR, SHIFT, NPV (display: 36.48)
    Or alternatively:
    SHIFT, C ALL
    3, PMT, 5, N, 3, x, 12, =, FV, 8, I/YR, PV (display: –36.48)

7-2. Over the 5-year period, dividends will be paid out at the rate of \$1.10, \$1.20, \$1.30, \$1.40, and \$1.50. At the end of 5 years, the dividend will grow at a rate of 4 percent forever. Thus, we need to compute the present value of the income stream: \$1.10, \$1.20, \$1.30, \$1.40, and \$1.50 and the present value of the stock price at that time. At a discount rate of 16 percent, the present value of the dividends is
$$PV = (\$1.10/(1.16)^1) + (\$1.20/(1.16)^2) + (\$1.30/(1.16)^3) + (\$1.40/(1.16)^4) + (\$1.50/(1.16)^5) = \$4.16$$
$$V_5 = (1.50 \times 1.04)/(.16 - .04) = \$13$$
$$V_0 = \$13/1.16^5 = \$6.19$$
Price = PV of dividends + PV of stock price in 5 years = \$4.16 + \$6.19 = \$10.35
HP-10BII keystrokes:
    SHIFT, C ALL
    0, CFj, 1.10, CFj, 1.20, CFj, 1.30, CFj, 1.40, CFj, 1.50, CFj, 16, I/YR
    SHIFT, NPV   (display: 4.16)
    SHIFT, C ALL
    1.50, x, 1.04, = (display 1.56)
    ÷, .12, = (display 13.00)
    FV, 5, N, 16, I/YR, PV = (display 6.19)
    6.19, +, 4.16, = (display 10.35)

7-3. a. $$PV = (\$1.10/(1.10)^1) + (\$1.20/(1.10)^2) + (\$1.30/(1.10)^3) + (\$1.40/(1.10)^4) + (\$1.50/(1.10)^5) = \$4.86$$
      $$V_5 = (1.50 \times 1.04)/(.10 - .04) = \$26$$
      $$V_0 = \$26/1.10^5 = \$16.14$$
      Price = PV of dividends + PV of stock price in 5 years = \$4.86 + \$16.14 = \$21.00
      HP-10BII keystrokes:
      SHIFT, C ALL
      0, CFj, 1.10, CFj, 1.20, CFj, 1.30, CFj, 1.40, CFj, 1.50, CFj, 10, I/YR
      SHIFT, NPV (display: 4.86)
      SHIFT, C ALL
      1.50, x, 1.04, = (display 1.56)

÷, .06, = (display 26.00)

FV, 5, N, 10, I/YR, PV = (display −16.14)

4.86, +, 16.14, = (display 21.00)

b. PV = ($1.10/(1.20)^1) + ($1.20/(1.20)^2) + ($1.30/(1.20)^3) + ($1.40/(1.20)^4) + ($1.50/(1.20)^5) = \$3.78$

$V_5 = (1.50 \times 1.04)/(.20 − .04) = \$9.75$

$V_0 = \$9.75/1.20^5 = \$3.92$

Price = PV of dividends + PV of stock price in 5 years = $3.78 + $3.92 = $7.70

HP-10BII keystrokes:

SHIFT, C ALL

0, CFj, 1.10, CFj, 1.20, CFj, 1.30, CFj, 1.40, CFj, 1.50, CFj, 20, I/YR

SHIFT, NPV (display: 3.78)

SHIFT, C ALL

1.50, x, 1.04, = (display 1.56)

÷,.16, = (display 9.75)

FV, 5, N, 20, I/YR, PV (display −3.92)

3.78, +,3.92 , = (display 7.70)

7-4. a. This problem uses the constant growth case of the dividend discount model:

$P_0 = d_1/(r − g) = d_0(1 + g)/(r − g) = 1.1/(.12 − .1) = \$55$

b. $P_0 = \$2.22/(.12 − .11) = \$222$

c. $P_0 = \$1.62/(.12 − .08) = \$40.50$

7-5. A right is essentially an option, but it is issued by the same firm that issued the stock. The shareholder receives one right per share that entitles him or her to an additional fractional share. The stated price is frequently below market levels. Rights can be traded. Warrants can also be traded but are usually initially tied to bonds, rather than equity. Warrants are generally much longer term than rights and are way out-of-the-money when first issued.

7-6. a. Initial stock price = S_0 = $50

Subscription price = S = $47

Number of rights required to buy one new share = N = 20

Intrinsic value of one right $= \dfrac{S_0 - S}{N+1} = \dfrac{50 - 47}{20 + 1} = \$.14$

b. If the price falls by $.14, the new price of the stock is $49.86 (intrinsic value = [S0 −S]/N =[$49.86 − $47]/20 = $.14)

Answers to Self-Test Questions

7-1. False. The capital gain a shareholder can reasonably expect when selling a stock is based on the discounted present value of the stock's expected future cash flows.

7-2. True.

7-3. True.

7-4. True.

7-5. True.

7-6. False. When using the constant growth model, the price of a stock should equal *the next period's dividend* divided by (k − g).

7-7. True.

7-8. True.

7-9. False. The price-to-past earnings ratio is always a definitive number. The price-to-future earnings ratio is always speculative.

7-10. False. Historically, it is small company common stocks that have provided the highest rates of return.

7-11. False. Past earnings growth has not been found to be a very accurate predictor of future earnings growth.

7-12. True.

7-13. True.

7-14. True.

7-15.   False. Many businesses cannot raise prices or can raise them only in a limited manner for a variety of reasons, including contractual agreements, heavy competition, and foreign competition.

7-16.   True.

7-17.   False. Participating means only that the shareholders may be able to participate in extra dividends if the company pays a huge dividend to common stockholders.

7-18.   True.

7-19.   True.

7-20.   True.

7-21.   False. Historically, it is corporations that have had special tax breaks on dividend income.

7-22.   False. Companies issue rights primarily to raise new equity capital and to allow current investors to maintain their pro rata ownership of the company.

7-23.   True.

7-24.   True.

7-25.   False. When warrants are issued, the subscription price is almost always above the market price, so that the warrants have only speculative value.

7-26.   False. Dividend payments on stock tend to increase over time.

7-27.   False. The ex-dividend date is the only date not set directly by the board of directors.

7-28.   False. The ex-dividend date is the first date on which one can buy the stock and not receive an already declared dividend.

7-29.   False. The ex-dividend date is the trading date 2 business days before the record date.

7-30.   False. Firms are most likely to increase dividends in whichever quarter they have previously established as the one in which they tend to do so.

Chapter 8

Answers to Review Questions

8-1.   The government can act on the economy either through direct transfers (tax cuts or cash payments/vouchers) or indirectly through government programs or projects. Government expenditures are occasionally aimed at increasing production. The theory is that the fruits of increased spending and production flow through the economy, resulting in an overall increase in output. Offsetting this effect is the funding mechanism; taxes and borrowing decrease funds available privately for investment. The tools for spurring the economy are increased government spending and tax cuts. Tax increases and reduced government spending tend to restrain the economy. Keynesians believe that government spending is more effective than tax cuts for economic stimulation. Two caveats should be observed: (1) Spending and its funding work at cross-purposes, thereby partially nullifying each other, and (2) the effect of governmental action depends on the current state of the economy; if the economy is near capacity, inflation may result.

8-2.   a.   With lower interest rates comes easier credit, which—all other things being equal—should serve as a catalyst for the economy. The stock market should therefore rise.

       b.   A rise in stock prices should be expected.

       c.   The stock market is likely to react negatively to this major disruption in the international credit market, causing a decline in stock prices.

8-3.   The goals are price stability and full employment. This means that during contractions and at the trough of the business cycle, the policies should be expansionary, with increases in the money supply and deficits in government spending. During expansions and at the peak of the business cycle, the policies should be to restrain the economy from overheating. This means lower growth in the money supply and budget surpluses.

8-4.   The Federal Reserve influences the economy via the credit markets. Its primary tools are reserve requirements, open market operations, and the discount rate. Changing the reserve requirement is a powerful but seldom used tool. Open market operations alter total banking reserves that, in turn, affect the level of lending. For the most part, this has been the Fed's chosen economic tactic. Changes in the discount rate signal the Fed's intent with regard to monetary policy, but relatively little borrowing is actually obtained at the "discount window." When the Fed embarks on an economic policy shift, it signals its intention by announcing a target for the federal funds rate.

It then proceeds to alter aggregate reserves through open market transactions. The federal funds rate is determined by the supply of and demand for loanable funds, but these are, in turn, strongly influenced by Fed activity in its open market operations.

8-5. Reasons for following monetary policy include the following: It has a unique influence on the economy; its effects are easier to model and predict than those attributable to fiscal initiatives; influential economists tout the primacy of monetary policy; interest rate changes have effects throughout the economy. Monetary policy's effect on the stock market occurs through pricing models (via the federal funds rate); rate changes alter the relative attractiveness of various securities; margin costs modify the ability to support the market through borrowing. A sophisticated model of the stock market should include both fiscal and monetary drivers, but as with most models, the devil is in the details. The recent trend among market prognosticators has been to minimize the effect of fiscal policy on the economy. Research has shown that the stock market is relatively efficient in pricing (capitalizing) the effects of monetary action. Opportunity may arise from effective implementation of market expectations as opposed to mechanical rules.

Another factor to keep in mind is that monetary policy can be implemented much more quickly than fiscal policy. For example, the Fed can make a determination to increase the money supply through open market operations and purchase government securities through member banks, which then have money to loan. The impact on the economy is felt within days.

On the other hand, suppose Congress decides to use a tax cut to stimulate the economy. The tax bill will be debated in committees in both Houses of Congress, then debated by the entire House and Senate. A joint committee will negotiate a compromise between the two versions of the bill. The bill will finally be sent to the President, where there will be the risk of a veto. Even when the bill becomes law, it will take time to implement, and even more time for its effects to be felt in the economy. The total lag time might be as much as a couple of years, during which time the economy may have already recovered from the recession.

8-6. The *balance sheet* lists assets and liabilities; it provides a glimpse of how the assets were financed. The debt side of the ledger yields the debt-to-equity ratio that can be used to assess whether the firm is taking on too much financial risk. The *income statement* begins with total revenues, then details the expenses that are deducted to reach the final earnings figure. This statement reveals expenses and their relation to each other, and it puts them into a historical perspective. The *statement of cash flows* furnishes financial data that reveal cash flows. The firm's liquidity position can be determined from this information.

8-7. Current ratio = current assets/current liabilities

Jan. 2003 current ratio = 7,777/4,385 = 1.77

Quick (acid test) ratio = current assets other than inventories/current liabilities

Jan. 2003 quick ratio = 1,221/4,385 = 0.278

Inventory turnover ratio = cost of goods sold/average inventory

Average inventory = 1/2 x (beginning inventory + ending inventory)

Jan. 2003 average inventory = 1/2 x (6,556 + 5,489) = 6,022.5

2003 inventory turnover ratio = 32,057/6,022.5 = 5.32

Debt-equity ratio = debt/stockholders' equity

2003 debt-equity ratio = (21,385 – 15,004)/15,004 = 42.53%

Net profit margin = net income/sales

2003 net profit margin = 2,581/45,738 = 5.64%

Asset turnover ratio = sales/total assets

2003 asset turnover ratio = 45,738/21,385 = 2.14

Return on assets = net income/total assets

2003 return on assets = 2,581/21,385 = 12.07%

Equity multiplier = total assets /stockholders' equity

2003 equity multiplier = 21,385/15,004 = 1.43

Return on equity = net income/average stockholders' equity

2003 return on equity = 2,581/15,004 = 17.20%

8-8. a. These dramatic growth rates suggest that the company is growing its sales by lowering its credit standards. If there is a substantial increase in the default rate on its receivables, the company could be substantially worse off.

b. The decline in the inventory turnover ratio may indicate that the inventory is no longer selling the way it used to. The increase in the current ratio may reflect only the accumulation of inventory that is not selling.

c. An increase in the equity multiplier means that the company is increasing its risk of default and bankruptcy. There is a limit to the increases in the equity multiplier that can occur, because lenders will eventually stop lending. A decline in the profit margin is a fundamental weakness of a company.

Answers to Self-Test Questions

8-1. True.

8-2. False. There is no stability in the timing of the business cycle.

8-3. True.

8-4. True.

8-5. False. Increases in government spending stimulate the economy (spur growth); tax increases have a restraining effect on the level of economic activity.

8-6. False. Restrictive monetary policy raises interest rates and limits credit availability to stronger credit risks, thereby affecting the allocation of funds away from financially weaker borrowers.

8-7. True.

8-8. True.

8-9. True.

8-10. False. The Federal Reserve Board has primary authority over monetary policy.

8-11. True.

8-12. True.

8-13. True.

8-14. False. The federal funds rate is the rate that banks charge each other for the overnight use (loan) of funds.

8-15. False. The tools of fiscal policy are changes in tax rates and the level of government spending.

8-16. False. The primary goals of both monetary policy and fiscal policy are the same—full employment and price stability.

8-17. True.

8-18. False. Price stability is the absence of either a rising or falling trend in overall prices. It is desirable to have the price level (average) remain stable, while individual prices fluctuate to reflect changing supply and demand conditions for individual goods and services.

8-19. True.

8-20. False. During the consolidation, firms are merging or simply going out of existence due to an inability to compete. There is no less of a need to be careful about company selection at this point in time.

8-21. False. The basic balance sheet equation is as follows: Assets – liabilities = net worth.

8-22. False. The quick ratio of current assets minus inventories divided by current liabilities is used to assess the firm's liquidity.

8-23. False. Using the Du Pont formula (ROE = net profit margin x asset turnover x equity multiplier), it is clear that raising the debt ratio would raise return on equity, all other things being equal, unless the profit margin is negative. The firm's financial risk would be increased, however.

8-24. False. Fully diluted earnings per share are calculated after assuming convertible debt has been converted into shares of stock to establish a conservative estimate of earnings for P/E ratio calculation purposes.

8-25. True.

8-26. True.

8-27. False. Although the total asset turnover may be consistent with industry averages, some of the individual assets (inventory, accounts receivable, fixed assets) may by stronger or weaker than they should be, and these strengths may be masked when an overall average is computed.

8-28. True.

8-29. True.

8-30. True.

Chapter 9

Answers to Review Questions

9-1. Income bonds pay interest only if the issuer earns sufficient profits to do so. Floating rate bonds have the interest payment tied to some index number, zero-coupon are pure discount securities that only pay par at maturity, and consols are perpetual.

9-2. A cap is an upper limit on the interest rate on a floating rate bond. A third party pays any interest beyond this amount. A collar is a cap combined with a floor rate, so that the interest paid is always bounded on both the upper and lower side.

9-3.   a.   Coupon rate   = annual coupon ÷ par value
                  = 35 ÷ 1000 = 3.5%

      b.   Current yield = annual coupon ÷ price
                  = 35 ÷ 975 = 3.59%

      c.   HP-10BII keystrokes:
          SHIFT, C ALL,
          975, +/–, PV, 35, PMT, 1000, FV, 12, N, I/YR   (display: 3.76[%])

      d.   HP-10BII keystrokes:
          SHIFT, C ALL,
          975, +/–, PV, 35, PMT, 1035, FV, 3, N, I/YR   (display: 5.53[%])

      e.   HP-10BII keystrokes:
          SHIFT, C ALL,
          975, +/–, PV, 35, PMT, 990, FV, 5, N, I/YR   (display: 3.87[%])

9-4. As expected, both durations declined, but the $100 coupon bond declined .53 years as opposed to .47 for the $60 coupon bond (see tables that follow). In general, the higher the coupon rate, the greater the change in duration when market interest rates change.

Bond A			
Year	Cash Flow	Present Value at 20%	Year x Present Value (Column 1 x Column 3)
1	$ 60	$ 50.00	$ 50.00
2	60	41.67	83.34
3	60	34.72	104.16
4	60	28.94	115.76
5	60	24.11	120.55
6	60	20.09	120.54
7	1,060	295.83	2,070.81
Total	$1,420	$495.36	$2,665.16
Duration = $2,665.16/$495.36 = 5.38			

Bond B			
Year	Cash Flow	Present Value at 20%	Year x Present Value (Column 1 x Column 3)
1	$ 100	$83.33	$ 83.33
2	100	69.44	138.88
3	100	57.87	173.61
4	100	48.23	192.92
5	100	40.19	200.95
6	100	33.49	200.94
7	1,100	306.99	2,148.93
Total	$1,700	$639.54	$3,139.56
Duration = $3,139.56/$639.54 = 4.91			

Using the alternative formula:

Bond A: $(1 + .20)/.20 - [(1 + .20) + 7(.06 - .20)]/(.06 [(1 + .20)^7 - 1] + .20) = 5.38$

Bond B: $(1 + .20)/.20 - [(1 + .20) + 7(.10 - .20)]/(.10 [(1 + .20)^7 - 1] + .20) = 4.91$

9-5.   Immunization is the protection of bond portfolio value against interest rate changes. In practice, this might entail matching cash inflows with outflows or simply matching a zero coupon bond's maturity with the investor's horizon. More sophisticated methods involve constructing a portfolio with the desired duration.

9-6.   a.   Investors should evaluate their needs and preferences in relation to such factors as risk, expected return, maturity/duration, taxes, diversification, and liquidity. Decisions on these factors will determine the makeup and management of their portfolios.

     b.   Bond swaps are the selling and buying of components of a bond portfolio to accomplish specific objectives.

     c.   Three strategies to set up a bond portfolio are as follows: laddered portfolio, barbell portfolio, and riding the yield curve.

9-7.   According to the *market segmentation theory,* investors and borrowers have preferred time horizons; therefore, they each occupy a distinct segment along the yield curve. This theory, when it is applied to the normal, upward-sloping yield curve, means that there are fewer people interested in investing in longer time periods; higher yields must therefore be offered to entice investors to lend (as opposed to holding cash).

     The *preferred habitat theory* modifies market segmentation with the provision that investors can be induced to leave their preferred segment by the offer of higher yields. In this case, the upward-sloping curve is explained by premiums being offered to entice investors to move from short-term to long-term debt.

     Under the *liquidity preference theory*—all other things being equal—investors prefer their money sooner rather than later. To combat this tendency, borrowers must offer interest rates that increase with the length of the loan. This theory best explains a rising yield curve.

     The *unbiased expectations theory* explains that the yield curve is based on the market's expectations of short-term rates that will occur in the future. Each long-term rate is, in essence, an average of short-term rates. With a rising yield curve, the market must be expecting future short-term rates to be higher than current short-term rates.

9-8.   a.   *Marketable* issues have lower bid-ask spreads, thereby lowering trading costs and raising prices, reducing the yield.

     b.   *Seasoned* issues are priced higher than new issues because of greater confidence in the market acceptance of the bond and the presence of marketability, and therefore have lower yields.

     c.   *Call protection* protects future cash flows, which generally enhances a security's value, so the yield is lower.

     d.   *Sinking funds* reduce the probability of default, enhancing value and lowering the yield.

9-9.   a.   HP-10BII keystrokes:

       SHIFT, C ALL,

       1000, FV, 4, I/YR, 9, N, 1000, x, .08, =, PMT, PV   (display: –$1,297.41)

     b.   Step 1: Determine the future value of the coupon payments.

       SHIFT, C ALL,

       6, I/YR, 7, N, 1000, x, .08, =, PMT, FV   (display: –$671.51)

       Step 2: Determine the selling price of the bond.

       SHIFT, C ALL,

       6, I/YR, 2, N, 1000, x, .08, =, PMT, 1000, FV, PV   (display: –$1,036.67)

       Step 3: Add the two ending values together.

       $671.51 + $1,036.67 = $1,708.18

       Step 4: Determine the HPR for this 7-year period.

       SHIFT, C ALL,

       1708.18, FV, 1297.41, +/–, PV, 7, N, I/YR   (display: 4.00[%])

     c.   Step 1: Determine the future value of the coupon payments.

       SHIFT, C ALL,

       2, I/YR, 7, N, 1000, x, .08, =, PMT, FV   (display: –$594.74)

       Step 2: Determine the selling price of the bond.

       SHIFT, C ALL,

       2, I/YR, 2, N, 1000, x, .08, =, PMT, 1000, FV, PV   (display: –$1,116.49)

Step 3: Add the two ending values together.
$594.74 + $1,116.49 = $1,711.23
Step 4: Determine the HPR for this 7-year period.
SHIFT, C ALL,
1711.23, FV, 1297.41, +/−, PV, 7, N, I/YR   (display: 4.03[%])

9-10.   The most serious default is a firm's failure to make interest payments when due. However, a firm can also be in technical default if it has failed to fulfill any of its indenture provisions (in any of its issues). Most defaults are signals of minor financial difficulties and do not result in bankruptcy. However, the investor should actively monitor subsequent events because they may result in the indenture agreement's being altered and cash flows threatened. Default in some cases is just the first event in a worsening situation that subsequently leads to bankruptcy. Markets are therefore very sensitive to defaults. Their reactions can be severe and can exacerbate the company's problems.

9-11.   Once liquidation of a company's assets begins, claims are paid according to the absolute-priority-of-claims principle. This method assigns claims to classes, each of which is in a strict hierarchy. The firm's remaining assets are then paid out, beginning with the highest class. The process continues until funds are exhausted. The last class to be paid might receive only partial payment. If this is the case, all claimants within the class are treated equally, thereby receiving proportional payments. In most bankruptcies, some claimants and/or classes receive no payment.

Answers to Self-Test Questions

9-1.   True.

9-2.   False. An income bond means only that the issuer has to pay the promised interest if it has earned sufficient money to do so. The issuer does not owe any interest beyond the promised amount.

9-3.   True.

9-4.   False. A call provision gives the issuer the option of redeeming the bonds prior to maturity.

9-5.   True.

9-6.   True.

9-7.   True.

9-8.   False. The coupon rate is the contractually stated rate on a bond. The current yield is the coupon amount divided by the bond's price.

9-9.   False. The yield to maturity is based on the market price of the bond as well as the coupon rate. Therefore, it changes every time the price of the bond changes; the coupon rate never changes unless the bond is a variable rate bond.

9-10.   False. The YTM is higher than the current yield for discount bonds. They are equal when bonds trade at par, and the current yield is greater when bonds trade at a premium.

9-11.   True.

9-12.   False. The one exception to this statement is that some low coupon bonds may have less price sensitivity with longer terms to maturity than if they had slightly fewer years to maturity.

9-13.   False. Duration is a better measure than maturity of a bond's sensitivity to interest rate changes because it also includes the coupon effect and the yield-to-maturity effect.

9-14.   True.

9-15.   True.

9-16.   False. If rates were about to rise, one would want to shorten one's price risk. Therefore, one would move to shorter duration holdings, not longer.

9-17.   False. It is the reverse: A pure-yield pick-up has no expectation of rates changes, and an intermarket swap does.

9-18.   True.

9-19.   False. A barbell strategy involves heavy weights in short-term and long-term bond holdings. It has nothing to do with the asset allocation between bonds and stocks.

9-20.   False. Bond ladders have equal weights among all maturities covered.

9-21.   True.

9-22.   True.

9-23. False. Under the liquidity preference hypothesis, investors prefer to invest in short-term debt securities, while borrowers tend to prefer to borrow long term.

9-24. True.

9-25. False. Riding the yield curve can be done only when the curve is upward sloping. It involves buying bonds at the peak and holding them to a point where the curve is flat.

9-26. False. The market segmentation hypothesis says that each maturity segment of the yield curve has its own supply and demand functions, which are independent of those for other segments.

9-27. True.

9-28. False. Aside from general credit conditions, the most significant factor that influences the coupon rate of a bond is the risk of default.

9-29. True.

9-30. True.

Chapter 10

Answers to Review Questions

10-1. a. The initial NAV of the $$$ mutual fund is $21.67, calculated as follows:

$$\text{Initial NAV} = \frac{\$652,000,000 - \$2,000,000}{30,000,000} = \$21.67$$

b. The increase in the NAV is 15.37 percent, as shown below:

$$\text{New NAV} = \frac{\$802,000,000 - \$2,000,000}{32,000,000} = \$25.00$$

$$\text{Percentage increase} = \frac{\$25.00}{\$21.67} - 1 = 15.37\%$$

10-2. Suppose the investor purchases one share. The one-year return can be determined as follows:

$$\text{Cost} = \frac{\text{NAV}}{1-L} = \frac{\$21.67}{1-.03} = \$22.34$$

Final value = Final NAV + Distributions = $25.00 + $.70 = $25.70

$$\text{Return} = \frac{\$25.70}{\$22.34} - 1 = 15.04\%$$

10-3. Load fees can be either front end or back end. Front-end loads can be up to 8 1/2 percent, but they are usually 3 percent to 5 percent of NAV and deducted upon purchase. Back-end loads occur upon redemption. They are generally lower than front-end loads and frequently decrease as the ownership period lengthens. 12b-1 fees are annual fees, not in excess of 1 percent of NAV per year, to cover a fund's marketing and distribution expenses.

10-4. a. At $495,000, the load is 2.75 percent. Hence, the price paid per share is $54.2519 ($52.76/[1–.0275]). Therefore the investor can buy 9,124.104 shares ($495,000/$54.2519).

b. At $495,000, the load is $13,612.50 (.0275 x $495,000), so $481,387.50 goes toward the purchase of shares. At $500,000, the load is $10,000 (.02 x $500,000), so $490,000 goes toward the purchase of shares. This means an additional $8,612.50 goes toward the purchase of shares.

c. A $100,000 purchase has a load of 3.25 percent, or $3,250. Therefore, five separate purchases means a total commission of $16,250 (5 x $3,250). Under a letter of intent, these purchases would be treated as a $500,000 single purchase, for a load of $10,000 (2% x $500,000) and a savings of $6,250 ($16,250 – $10,000).

10-5. If the NAV goes up 10 percent per year, it will be $11 next year, and $12.10 in 2 years. The Class A shares will cost $.53 per share. The Class B shares will cost .25 percent of $11.00 at the end of the first year, .25 percent of $12.10 at the end of the second year, and the redemption fee of 3 percent of $12.10. This works out to fees of $.0275, $.0303, and $.3630 per share, for a total of $.4208. The Class C shares will cost 1 percent of $11.00 the first year and 1 percent of $12.10 the second year. This works out to fees of $.11 and $.121 per share, for a total of $.231 per share. Hence, the cheapest over the 2-year period is the Class C shares.

10-6. Mutual funds compete with other similarly equipped institutions such as banks. It is in comparison to individual investors that disparities become pronounced. For example, funds have lower trading costs, superior analytical means, and vast credit resources. An additional benefit is lowered risk through diversification. On the other hand, individuals are exempt from the costs associated with fund management and enjoy total freedom in asset choice.

10-7. a. Investors of modest means are probably the greatest beneficiaries of the existence of mutual funds. Funds can be found that allow small initial and/or continuing contributions. Participating in a large pool of investments lowers risk.

b. All mutual fund investors receive the benefits mentioned in 10-7a. Additional benefits include time savings, record keeping, and choice of risk level and fund specialization.

10-8. a. The stocks in a sector fund generally have a unifying theme. The number of sector funds is vast, as are the variety of themes. Examples of sectors include such themes as industry, geographical region, and investment philosophy.

b. A single investment company manages families of funds. By offering a variety of funds, the investment company hopes to appeal to as wide a market as possible. Exchanges between family funds generally have much lower transaction costs than exchanges outside the family. In this way, the investment company hopes to attract and retain customers.

10-9. There are several reasons. First, one normally has to pay a brokerage commission to buy a closed-end fund, which would make a closed-end money market fund unattractive. Second, most, if not all, investors in MMMFs use the check-writing feature to redeem their shares. A closed-end fund cannot allow check writing because it does not redeem shares. Therefore, an investor would have to sell shares (and pay a commission) every time he or she wanted cash.

10-10. Mutual funds are open-end investment companies. Open-end companies have a flexible number of shares that can expand or shrink with demand as the fund buys shares from and sells shares to investors. The price of open-end shares is determined by the value of the underlying shares—in other words, the NAV. Closed-end investment companies have a fixed number of shares that are determined at the inception of the fund. The share price of a closed-end fund is determined by supply and demand; it is therefore generally different from the NAV. Purchase of closed-end shares occurs in the open market, unlike the purchase of open-end shares, which ultimately come from the issuing company. Closed-end companies can decide to become or be forced into becoming open-end companies. The change from a closed-end to open-end company results in shares selling at the NAV. This usually involves a price increase.

Answers to Self-Test Questions

10-1. True.

10-2. False. No-load mutual funds are typically sold directly to the public without a sales force.

10-3. False. Few funds charge a front-end load of 8.5 percent of the purchase price of the shares. Most front-end-loaded funds charge less than 5 percent.

10-4. True.

10-5. False. A 12b-1 fee is an annual charge for marketing and distribution expenses, and it is different from a load. Only those funds with large 12b-1 fees must classify themselves as load funds.

10-6. False. At least 90 percent of gross income must be distributed to shareholders for the fund to qualify as a regulated investment company.

10-7. True.

10-8. False. Typically, institutional investors restrict their analysis to a small percentage of traded stocks.

10-9. False. Few mutual funds are able to consistently beat the returns on S&P 500 Index funds.

10-10. True.

10-11. False. Mixed portfolio funds hold a variety of securities, such as stocks and bonds.

10-12. True.

10-13. True.

10-14. True.

10-15. True.

10-16. False. A right of accumulation usually applies at the very least to all accounts owned by one investor at a fund.

10-17. True.

10-18. False. Class A shares usually have large front-end loads, but minimal 12b-1 fees.

10-19. True.

10-20. True.

10-21. False. A REIT is essentially a closed-end investment company whose shares trade on an exchange or OTC.

10-22. False. In addition to direct investments in property, hybrid REITs make construction and mortgage loans.

10-23. False. The shares of closed-end investment companies are sold in the open market at prices determined by supply and demand. They may sell at a premium or discount to their net asset value.

10-24. False. Closed-end funds may convert into open-end funds.

10-25. True.

10-26. False. Variable annuities allow funds to grow and accumulate tax deferred. During the distribution phase, however, all gain is taxed as ordinary income.

10-27. True.

10-28. True.

10-29. True.

10-30. False. Fees are far more critical because they can eat up a significant portion of an investor's returns.

Chapter 11

Answers to Review Questions

11-1. a. The buyer of the call breaks even when the intrinsic value of the option on the expiration date equals the premium paid. If the premium paid is $1.75, and the strike price is $35, then the stock price must be:

Intrinsic value = stock price – strike price

$1.75 = stock price – $35

Stock price = $36.75

   b. $HPR_{Stock} = (45/32) – 1 = 40.63\%$

   $HPR_{Call} = [(45 – 35)/1.75] – 1 = 471.43\%$

   c. The dividend must be added to the stock's price when calculating the stock's returns in b. above. This is not the case with the call's calculations; only the market price is used.

11-2. a. A call involves the right to buy (from the option's writer) at the strike price, whereas a put grants the right to sell (to the writer) at the strike price. Calls participate in the underlying security's price appreciation; puts participate in its depreciation.

   b. A call writer must deliver the promised asset at the specified (strike) price if the call is exercised prior to expiration. Similarly, the put writer must purchase the underlying asset upon exercise.

   c. The holder of a call has a choice whether or not to exercise the option. The writer of a put has no choice but must purchase the underlying asset if the option holder chooses to sell. A call derives its value gains from those of the underlying asset. The call owner's loss is capped by the call's price if the asset's value is unchanged or declines. A put writer's profit is capped at the put premium and not affected by increases in the price of the underlying asset. The put writer's loss increases as the underlying asset's price decreases. The lack of equivalency between purchasing calls and put writing is demonstrated by the differences in profit patterns.

11-3. a. The strike price is the price at which a transaction in the underlying asset will take place if an option is exercised.

   b. The intrinsic value for calls is the maximum of (1) the difference between the market price of the underlying asset and the strike price or (2) zero. In the case of puts, the intrinsic value is the strike price minus the market price, but not less than zero. Speculative value is the difference between the option's market price and its intrinsic value. The strike price determines whether an option is in or out of the money. If the price of the underlying asset is above the strike price, a call is in the money and a put is out of the money. If the underlying asset's price is below the strike price, the positions are reversed.

11-4. a. Purchase of a put will protect the investor from decreases in the stock's value and allow the investor to continue to receive dividends.

   b. Selling the stock protects the investor from price decreases, but the investor forgoes dividends and any profits from subsequent price increases.

   c. If the put were free, its ownership would clearly be the superior strategy. This strategy's value varies inversely with the put's price. The investor should also consider transaction costs and the time horizon (puts expire). On the other hand, the put still allows the investor the upside potential of holding the stock.

11-5. a. In exchange for the premium, the writer is obligated to turn over the stock (receiving payment at the strike price) if the call is exercised.

b. Covered call writers receive the premium and dividends but forgo any future gains from stock price appreciation above the strike price. Stock price gains are canceled out by losses on the call (assuming exercise). Writers retain the risk of price declines. As is evident, covered call writers desire that stock prices remain stable or rise; this optimal result allows retention of the premium and any dividends that were received.

11-6. a. A straddle is a simultaneous position in a put and a call on the same underlying asset, with the same strike price and the same expiration date.

b. Straddle buyers are anticipating price movement in the underlying asset. The straddle begins to pay off whether prices move up or down.

c. Investors who feel that the underlying asset's price is stable are likely to write straddles. If their predictions are realized, they will have little in the way of loss to offset the premium received.

11-7. a. The holder of a spread buys a call and writes a call on the same security. The calls have different strike prices.

b. A bullish spread holder expects the purchased call's value to rise faster than that of the written call. The two positions can be seen as a form of insurance that limits gains but also limits losses.

11-8. a. The five variables are the price of the underlying stock, the exercise price, the time to expiration, the variance of the underlying stock, and the risk-free interest rate.

b. Increases in the price of the underlying stock, time to expiration, variance of the underlying stock, and risk-free interest rate increase the value of the option. An increase in the strike price reduces the value of the option.

11-9. The value of the call option is $1.43, as follows:

$S_0 = S = 30, P_0 = 1, t = .25, r_f = .06$
$(1 + .06)^{.25} = 1.0147$
$C_0 = P_0 + S_0 - [S/(1 + r_f)^t] = 1 + 30 - (30/1.0147) = 1.43$

11-10. Rights have short lives (usually a few months) and warrants have long lives (several years to perpetual). Rights are in the money at the time of issuance, whereas warrants are nearly always out of the money at the time of issue. Rights are issued to raise new equity capital immediately, while at the same time protecting stockholders' pro rata ownership percentage of the stock. Warrants are usually issued to obtain a lower coupon rate on an associated debt issue and to sell stock at a higher stock price in the future.

11-11. a. Call risk is particularly relevant to convertibles because once the market price of the convertible bond exceeds the call price, the investor is at risk that the bond will be called and any conversion premium in the price will be immediately eliminated.

b. Convertibles are most likely to be called as soon as it becomes clear to the issuing company that the cost of dividend payments on the common stock that will be issued upon conversion will be cheaper than the interest paid on the bonds, and that the price of the bonds has risen to such a level that eventual conversion is a near certainty.

11-12. The owner of a convertible bond gains an option to exchange the bond for a predetermined number of shares of common stock. This option gives the bond some of the upside potential of common stock. Convertibles offer lower coupon rates than otherwise comparable straight bonds because of this feature. From the straight bondholder's perspective, convertibles offer more upside potential, but a call feature often limits this potential. From the stockholder's viewpoint, convertibles offer more downside protection because of the bond portion. Also, interest rates tend to be higher than dividend rates. Offsetting this are the interest rate risk and default risk.

11-13. Conversion premium = market price − (conversion ratio x price of underlying common stock) = $100 − (2 x $40) = $20.

11-14. a. The computations are as follows:
- Conversion price = $1,000/20 = $50
- Conversion value = $40 x 20 = $800
- Conversion premium = $1,050 − $800 = $250 and $250/$800 = .3125 or 31.25%
- Premium over straight-debt value = $1,050 − $900 = $150
- Current yield = $100/$1,050 = 9.52%

b. In this case, the minimum value is the conversion value because the option is in the money. The profit could be even greater because of the conversion premium. Conversion value = 55.5 x 20 = $1,110; profit = $1,110 − $1,000 = $110.

Answers to Self-Test Questions

11-1.   False. Options are written by investors and sold to other investors.

11-2.   True.

11-3.   False. The intrinsic value of an option can never be less than zero.

11-4.   True.

11-5.   False. The writer of a put expects the price either to stay steady or to rise so that the option holder will not exercise the right to sell the shares.

11-6.   True.

11-7.   False. If the market price is in excess of the strike price, the call is in the money and the put is out of the money. When the market price of a stock is below the strike price, a call option is out of the money but a put option is in the money.

11-8.   False. The maximum amount that can be lost is the premium, or price paid, for the option

11-9.   True.

11-10. True.

11-11. True.

11-12. True.

11-13. False. An investor anticipating a drop in the price of a stock might want to short the stock but would not use a put to hedge the position. If a hedge is desired, the investor might buy a call that would allow the purchase of stock to cover the short at a known price should the stock price not move as anticipated. An alternative is simply to buy a put.

11-14. True.

11-15. False. With a straddle, the stock, exercise price, and expiration date are identical. The investor does not care in which direction the stock moves, provided it moves by a sufficiently large amount. The investor who uses a straddle loses if the stock's price does not change by an amount that is enough to compensate the investor for the premiums paid for both the call and the put.

11-16. True.

11-17. True.

11-18. False. With the exercise of any index option, the settlement is made in dollars, not in actual delivery of the securities. This settlement is $100 for each point difference between the stock index close and the strike price of the option on the index.

11-19. True.

11-20. False. The maximum maturity is 3 years.

11-21. True.

11-22. True.

11-23. True.

11-24. True.

11-25. False. Conversion premium refers to the difference between the market price of the bond and its conversion value.

11-26. False. The conversion premium tends to be greater when the price of the stock is lower. As the price of the underlying stock rises above the conversion price, the conversion premium declines; the value of the convertible approaches the value of the underlying stock. In essence, the conversion premium represents the amount the investor is willing to pay to have downside protection (provided by the bond value) while retaining upside potential. As the conversion value further exceeds the bond value, the downside protection becomes less important. Therefore, the conversion premium declines.

11-27. False. The conversion option is a feature that is favorable to the bondholder. As such, it gives the issuing corporation the opportunity to sell the bonds for their face value, while at the same time paying a slightly lower interest rate than would be required for comparable bonds that lack the potential gain from convertibility.

11-28. True.

11-29. False. The performance of convertibles depends heavily on the price of the underlying stock.

11-30. True.

Answer to Appendix A Question

11A-1. The estimated value of the call option is $13.70, calculated as shown below:

$S_0 = 100$

$S = 95$

$S_0 / S = 100/95 = 1.0526$

$\ln(S_0/S) = .0513$

$\sigma = .5$

$.5 \times \sigma^2 = .5 \times .5 \times .5 = .125$

$r_f = .10$

$r_f + .5 \times \sigma^2 = .10 + .125 = .225$

$t = .25$

$(r_f + .5\sigma^2)t = .225 \times .25 = .0563$

$\sigma\sqrt{t} = .5 \times \sqrt{.25} = .25$

$d_1 = (.0513 + .0563)/.25 = .4302$

$N(d_1) = .6665$

$r_f - .5\sigma^2 = .10 - .5 \times .5 \times .5 = -.025$

$(r_f - .5\sigma^2)t = -0.25 \times .25 = -.0063$

$d_2 = (.0531 - .0063)/.25 = .18$

$N(d_2) = .5714$

$r_f t = .10 \times .25 = .025$

$e^{r_f t} = e^{.025} = 1.0253$

$C = 100 \times .6665 - (95 \times .5714)/1.0253 = 66.65 - 52.94 = \$13.71$

Chapter 12

Answers to Review Questions

12-1. Commodity exchanges restrict futures price movements. Commodity price changes can trigger a shutdown in trading, which is extremely rare in equity markets. Commodity futures have limited lives and much lower margin requirements than are permitted with stock transactions. There are an equal number of long and short futures trades, while short sales of stock constitute only a small fraction of stock transactions. There are no short-selling restrictions on futures trades. Futures positions must be opened and closed with the same brokerage firm.

12-2. Much of the recent growth in futures markets can be attributed to the creation of innumerable new types of financial futures. Interest rates have a direct effect on financial institutions and, to a lesser degree, on a vast number of other markets. An increase in interest rate volatility has increased demand for interest rate futures for both hedging and speculation. Rapid futures innovation has attempted to satisfy demand for hedging and speculation in this area. Global trade and corporate expansion have increased the need for currency futures. Booming investment in stocks and other financial assets has sparked demand for related instruments, such as index futures.

12-3. a. The full market value of a contract = 5,000 ounces per contract x $5 per ounce = $25,000.
        If the investor has to put down 10 percent as margin, this is $2,500 per contract.
        If the investor has $5,000 initial capital, he or she can buy two contracts ($5,000 capital/$2,500 per contract).
     b. Ending value = 2 contracts x 5,000 ounces per contract x $6 per ounce = $60,000
        $60,000 ending value – $50,000 beginning value = $10,000 profit
     c. $10,000 profit/$5,000 initial margin = 200% rate of return

12-4. An initial condition is an active and competitive spot market. Another good attribute is a standardized contract that reduces trading costs. Price volatility will attract participants who want price protection (hedging) and those who wish to speculate. These participants make for a deeper market. Some commodity futures are predicated on the existence of storage. In these cases, storage must be available at a reasonable cost.

12-5. a. Basis = cash market price – futures market price = $3.00 – $3.25 = –$.25
     b. The farmer may set up a short hedge, going short the futures contract and long the crop in the field.
     c. The farmer sells his crop in the cash market for $2.50/bushel x 50,000 bushels = $125,000. The profit on the short position is $32,500 ([$3.25–$2.60] x 50,000). So the farmer's net proceeds are $157,500 ($125,000 + $32,500).

12-6. Firm representatives are active traders who seek either to promote the market for their firm's output or to obtain good prices on inputs; they are generally knowledgeable and experienced. Day traders try to take advantage of short-term price movements in the futures market and close all positions at each day's end. Scalpers are minute-to-minute traders who focus on the action of the trade itself and the emotions of other buyers and sellers.

12-7. When someone hedges, that person is substituting basis risk for price risk. Unless a perfect hedge can be constructed (that is, one in which the basis is guaranteed not to change), there will still be risk. A hedge is successful only to the extent that the basis risk is smaller than the price risk.

12-8. a. The number of contracts needed to neutralize a $50 million stock portfolio with a beta of 1.07 is as follows:

$$\text{Number of contracts} = \frac{\text{Portfolio}}{\text{Contract value}} \times \text{Beta} = \frac{50,000,000}{\$2.50 \times 145,000} \times 1.07 = 148$$

b. A short hedge could be set up, whereby the client is long the portfolio and would sell (short) 148 contracts.

12-9. a. Stock index futures are comparable to other futures except that there is no delivery of the underlying commodity. There is only a cash settlement that is based on the value of the index on the last trading day of the delivery month.

b. The appropriate index is the index whose returns have the highest correlation coefficient with the returns on the client's portfolio.

12-10. A futures option is an option on a futures contract. The owner, therefore, possesses the right but not the obligation to buy (in the case of a call) or sell (in the case of a put) futures contracts at a specified price within a prescribed time limit. This instrument gives the owner a great deal of leverage and means that the owner risks only the premium. Prospective owners should be aware that determining whether the option's price is fair is difficult because a commodity option is a derivative of a derivative; any errors in the input estimates compound the error in the resulting price.

Answers to Self-Test Questions

12-1. False. Spot market transactions are the daily transactions of people's lives.

12-2. False. Each forward contract is unique.

12-3. True.

12-4. False. The owner can always walk away from an option but never from a futures contract. It is a contract.

12-5. False. A significant business use is critical, but so is price volatility, *not* stability.

12-6. False. Each exchange has multiple contracts per commodity, wherein the contracts differ in terms of expiration dates.

12-7. False. Few contracts result in delivery.

12-8. False. Commissions are paid on the first trade only, whether it is a long or short position.

12-9. False. A scalper will never take a position for more than a few minutes.

12-10. True.

12-11. True.

12-12. True.

12-13. False. In fact, all commodity futures are traded on margin.

12-14. False. Both parties post margin on futures trades. It is held by their brokerage firms.

12-15. False. The margin required on commodity futures transactions is defined on the basis of a specified dollar amount per contract, but this usually ranges from 5 percent to 10 percent of the value of the contract, depending on the underlying asset. However, the investor is not required to borrow the remaining balance to complete the transaction. Margin on futures transactions is actually a deposit (or earnest money), because the commodity is not actually bought or sold until the contract expires. (Most futures contracts are closed out before the contract expires. Therefore, most commodity futures contracts never involve the actual purchase or sale of the commodity.)

12-16. True.

12-17. True.

12-18. True.

12-19. True.

12-20. False. If the investor follows this tactic and interest rates fall as expected, the investor will need either to close out his or her position or deliver the securities. In either case, with the decline in interest rates, the prices of the bonds and the futures contracts will have risen, and there will be a loss on the transaction. If an investor expects interest rates to decline substantially in the near future, it might be advisable to purchase interest rate futures. Like the underlying bonds, interest rate futures increase in price when interest rates decline.

12-21. False. When interest rates rise, the price of bonds (or other fixed-return instruments) falls. If interest rates are expected to rise, the speculator should sell (go short) these futures contracts, because the actual instrument being contracted for is a bond whose price will decline if interest rates rise.

12-22. False. The oldest one is the Chicago Board of Trade.

12-23. True.

12-24. True.

12-25. False. A successful hedge depends on the basis being stable.

12-26. True.

12-27. False. Speculators may be either long or short.

12-28. True.

12-29. True.

12-30. True.

Chapter 13

Answers to Review Questions

13-1. The first part of the model is as follows:

Total income
–   <u>Adjustments to gross income</u>
=   Adjusted gross income, or AGI
–   Standard deduction or itemized deductions (whichever is larger)
–   <u>Personal exemptions</u>
=   Taxable income

The second part is   Tax liability (based on taxable income and filing status)
–   Credits
+   <u>Other taxes owed</u>
=   Total taxes for the year
–   <u>Taxes paid to date</u>
=   Tax refund to be received or tax due

13-2. The seven categories of itemized deductions are
- medical and dental expenses (to the extent they exceed 7.5 percent of AGI)
- taxes (state and local income taxes, real estate taxes, and personal property taxes)
- interest expenses
- gifts to charity (not to exceed 50 percent of AGI)
- casualty and theft losses (reduced by $100 per event, and only to the extent they exceed 10 percent of AGI)
- job-related expenses and most miscellaneous deductions (to the extent they exceed 2 percent of AGI)
- miscellaneous deductions

13-3.

Wages	$60,000		
Dividends	3,000		
Interest	<u>2,000</u>		
AGI	$65,000		
Deductions:	Mortgage interest	$5,000	
	Property taxes	4,000	
	Margin interest	<u>5,000</u>	
		$14,000	

Note that the margin interest deduction cannot exceed the investment income of $5,000.
Taxable income   = $65,000 – $14,000 = $51,000

Tax liability   = $4,000 + (25% x $21,950)
                      = $9,487.50
Refund due   = $10,000 − $9,487.50 = $512.50

13-4.   a. 28% + 6% = 34%

        b. 28% x 6% (1 − .28) = 32.32%

13-5. $$1{,}050 = \frac{100(1-.28)}{(1+i)^1} + \frac{100(1-.28)}{(1+i)^2} + \frac{100(1-.28)}{(1+i)^3} + \frac{1000+(1050-1000)\times.28}{(1+i)^3}$$

       $i = 5.78$

       Keystrokes:
          SHIFT, C ALL
          1050, +/−, PV
          72, PMT
          1014, FV
          3, N
          I/YR (display: 5.778) or 5.78%

13-6.   a. $2,000 STCG

        b. $1,500 STCL

        c. $2,000 LTCG

        d. $2,000 STCL and $4,000 LTCL

13-7.   a. $2,000 x .28 = $560 taxes owed

        b. $1,500 x .28 = $420 tax saving

        c. $2,000 x .15= $300 taxes owed

        d. $3,000 x .28 = $840 tax savings (remember, the maximum write-off is $3,000 per year)

13-8.   Tax loss harvesting involves recognizing losses through the sale of shares to generate tax savings and/or allow the sale of other holds with capital gains in order to rebalance a portfolio. Tax-efficient investing is minimizing the recognition of capital gains through a minimization of trading.

13-9.   5% x 100 = 5 new shares
       $2,000 cost basis/105 shares = $19.05 cost basis/share
       19.05 x 50 = $952.50

13-10. 5% x 10,000 x ½ = $250 interest on Sept. 30
       5% x 10,000 x ½ x ½ = $125 interest received upon sale of bonds
       $375 − $125 interest paid upon purchase = $250 interest income for the year

13-11. a. $PV = \dfrac{\$1{,}000}{(1+.08)^{30}} = \$99.38$

       Keystrokes:
          SHIFT, C ALL
          1000, FV
          30, N
          8, I/YR
          PV (display: −99.3773)

        b. 99.38 x .08 = $7.95

        c. Cost basis: $99.38 + $7.95 = $107.33
          Capital gains: $200 − $107.33 = $92.67

13-12. a. identical

        b. identical

        c. identical

        d. different

        e. different

13-13. Joan would owe capital gains taxes if either before or after she purchased the fund, the portfolio recognized more capital gains than losses, forcing the fund to make a capital gain distribution even if the NAV declined during the year.

13-14. $1,200 + $700 = $1,900 total costs
$1,000/150 shares = $12.67 cost/share
12.67 x 60 = $760 cost basis of shares sold
$780 – $760 = $20 capital gains

13-15. Selling price = $5 premium + $50 strike price = $55
$60 purchase price – $55 selling price = $5 loss/share
$5 loss/share x 100 shares = $500 capital loss
The purchase and sale are on the same day, so it is a short-term capital loss.

13-16. a. $200,000 x $(1 + .08)^{14}$ = $587,438.72 value in 14 years
$587,438.72 x (1 – .28) = $422,955.88 value after taxes

b. $50,000 x .28 = $14,000 in taxes due today
($200,000 – $14,000) x $(1 + .08)^{14}$ = $546,318.01 future value of stock
($546,318.01 future value – $50,000 cost basis) x .15 = $74,447.70 in capital gains taxes dues
$546,318.01 future value – $74,447.70 taxes due = $471,870.31 future value after taxes

13-17. Combined liquidation value = $40,000 + $60,000 = $100,000
Combined cost basis = $100,000 + $50,000 = $150,000
2% limitation = 2% x $70,000 = $1,400
$50,000 loss – $1,400 limitation = $48,600 deduction
$48,600 deduction x 28% tax rate = $13,608 tax savings

Answers to Self-Test Questions

13-1. False. Interest expense on margin loans is deductible only if it does not exceed net investment income.

13-2. False. The average tax rate is basically irrelevant except for planning purposes. It is the marginal tax rate that is critical.

13-3. True.

13-4. True.

13-5. False. Only single taxpayers with incomes up to $15,000 and married filing jointly taxpayers with income less than $30,000 may take this credit.

13-6. True.

13-7. False. Post-tax returns equal pre-tax returns times one minus the marginal tax rate.

13-8. True.

13-9. True.

13-10. False. A total of $3,000 may be deducted from ordinary income, regardless of whether it is short term or long term.

13-11. False. Capital gains on municipals are taxed exactly like any other capital gains.

13-12. True.

13-13. False. Tax efficient investing means the avoidance of taking capital gains on which one would have to pay a capital gains tax.

13-14. False. A tax-friendly fund is characterized by a *low* portfolio turnover ratio.

13-15. True.

13-16. False. Neither are taxable events.

13-17. True.

13-18. False. The cost basis for a bond does not include any accrued interest paid to the seller of the bond.

13-19. True.

13-20. True.

13-21. True.

13-22. False. As long as there is one significant difference, such as coupon rate or maturity, the wash-sale rule is not violated.

13-23. True.

13-24. True.

13-25. False. Some of the distributions will always qualify as return of principal and therefore be tax exempt.

13-26. False. It is a capital gain or loss when either the option is repurchased or exercised.
13-27. False. The proportion of annuity payments that is taxable depends on the interest rate and the life expectancy of the individual buying the annuity.
13-28. False. In general, one should hold fixed-return securities in tax-qualified accounts because the interest is taxed as ordinary income.
13-29. True.
13-30. True.

Chapter 14

Answers to Review Questions

14-1. The seven steps are (1) set investment goals, (2) gather and analyze client data, (3) develop an investment policy, (4) determine asset allocation, (5) specify industry weightings, (6) select companies, and (7) monitor the portfolio.

14-2. Strategic asset allocation decisions should be at the highest level of an organization, are rarely changed, may be in ranges rather than point estimates, and are made to set the overall risk exposure and liquidity desired. Tactical asset allocation decisions must be made at lower levels, may be changed frequently, are usually point estimates, and are made to attempt to beat the market.

14-3. a. Life cycle investing (LCI) is the process of tailoring the investment portfolio to fit the client's phase in the life cycle.
       b. Usually LCI involves reducing risk and emphasizing income as the individual grows older.

14-4. It is difficult to specify the optimal number of securities in a portfolio, because this number depends on the trade-off between the direct (commission) and indirect (monitoring) costs of adding a security to the portfolio and the perceived magnitude of the reduction in total risk. In addition, the optimal number depends on the distribution of market values among holdings.

14-5. The traditional rule is that debt instruments should be held in tax-exempt or tax-deferred accounts, and equities in taxable accounts. However, the amounts in these accounts may not match the asset allocation scheme. In addition, as market values change, if the investor wanted to buy more bonds, he or she might not be able to add the necessary cash to a tax-qualified account. Hence, the investor would end up holding bonds in a taxable account, or failing to meet his or her target asset allocation scheme.

14-6. a. The value of your portfolio is determined as follows:

       P = $10, buy 10 shares; total shares = 10   Portfolio = 10 ($10) = $100
       P = $5, buy 20 shares; total shares = 30   Portfolio = 30 ($5) = $150
       P = $10   Portfolio = 30 ($10) = $300

       b. The value of your portfolio is calculated as follows:

       P = $10, buy 10 shares; total shares = 10   Portfolio = 10 ($10) = $100
       P = $15, buy 6.67 shares; total shares = 16.67   Portfolio = 16.67 ($15) = $250
       P = $10   Portfolio = 16.67 ($10) = $166.67

       c. Dividend reinvestment plans (DRIPs), direct purchase plans (DPPs), and employee stock purchase plans (ESPPs) are examples of dollar cost averaging plans.

14-7. Because not everyone objects to the same types of stocks, as long as enough people are willing to hold any one stock, its expected return will be consistent with its risk.

14-8. Refer to any of the examples used in the text, wherein the client and planner determine the amount sufficient in cash and/or bonds to assure the client that the cash will be available to meet his or her needs for a specific number of years.

Answers to Self-Test Questions

14-1. True.
14-2. False. Goals should be as precise as possible, and they should include dollar objectives if possible.
14-3. True.
14-4. False. There is no theory or obvious scale for relating risk aversion to asset allocation.
14-5. True.

14-6. True.

14-7. False. The desired rate of return may be a critical factor in determining the asset allocation.

14-8. False. In some cases, the client may have to adjust his or her goals, or make other accommodations to achieve the desired goals.

14-9. False. The client should avoid any financial planner who promises a specific rate of return.

14-10. True.

14-11. False. The board of trustees should make only strategic asset allocation decisions.

14-12. False. Strategic asset allocation decisions frequently include ranges for each weight.

14-13. True.

14-14. False. Only tactical asset allocations are made to try to beat the market. Strategic allocations are to set the portfolio's level of risk.

14-15. True.

14-16. False. The degree of risk aversion will normally change over time as people tend to become more risk averse as they age.

14-17. True.

14-18. True.

14-19. False. The reverse is true.

14-20. True.

14-21. False. The number of securities in the portfolio may be meaningless if the weights are not evenly balanced.

14-22. False. Different socially responsible investors use different criteria as to what are appropriate investments.

14-23. True.

14-24. True.

14-25. False. One drawback is that it limits the investor's ability to increase the diversification potential of the account.

14-26. False. The stock can be sold to the employee at a discount from the fair market price.

14-27. True.

14-28. True.

14-29. False. Risk-taking behavior in one aspect of life does not automatically carry over to other aspects.

14-30. True.

Index